ISBN 978-1-331-54025-0
PIBN 10203255

1 MONTH OF
FREE
READING

at
www.ForgottenBooks.com

By purchasing this book you are eligible for one month membership to ForgottenBooks.com, giving you unlimited access to our entire collection of over 1,000,000 titles via our web site and mobile apps.

To claim your free month visit:
www.forgottenbooks.com/free203255

English
Français
Deutsche
Italiano
Español
Português

www.forgottenbooks.com

Mythology Photography **Fiction**
Fishing Christianity **Art** Cooking
Essays Buddhism Freemasonry
Medicine **Biology** Music **Ancient**
Egypt Evolution Carpentry Physics
Dance Geology **Mathematics** Fitness
Shakespeare **Folklore** Yoga Marketing
Confidence Immortality Biographies
Poetry **Psychology** Witchcraft
Electronics Chemistry History **Law**
Accounting **Philosophy** Anthropology
Alchemy Drama Quantum Mechanics
Atheism Sexual Health **Ancient History**
Entrepreneurship Languages Sport
Paleontology Needlework Islam
Metaphysics Investment Archaeology
Parenting Statistics Criminology
Motivational

RECIPROCITY WITH CANADA

HEARINGS

BEFORE THE

COMMITTEE ON WAYS AND MEANS OF THE HOUSE OF REPRESENTATIVES

61ST CONGRESS, 3D SESSION

ON

H. R. 32216

FEBRUARY 2, 4, 6, 7, 8, AND 9, 1911

WASHINGTON
GOVERNMENT PRINTING OFFICE
1911

COMMITTEE ON WAYS AND MEANS,

HOUSE OF REPRESENTATIVES,

SIXTY-FIRST CONGRESS, THIRD SESSION.

SERANO E. PAYNE, CHAIRMAN.

JOHN DALZELL,
SAMUEL W. McCALL,
EBENEZER J. HILL,
HENRY S. BOUTELL,
JAMES C. NEEDHAM,
WILLIAM A. CALDERHEAD,
JOSEPH W. FORDNEY,
JOSEPH H. GAINES,
NICHOLAS LONGWORTH,

JOHN W. DWIGHT,
WILLIAM R. ELLIS,
CHAMP CLARK,
OSCAR W. UNDERWOOD,
EDWARD W. POU,
CHOICE B. RANDELL,
ROBERT F. BROUSSARD,
FRANCIS BURTON HARRISON,
WILLIAM G. BRANTLEY.

ARTHUR E. BLAUVELT, CLERK.

2

RECIPROCITY WITH CANADA.

COMMITTEE ON WAYS AND MEANS,
HOUSE OF REPRESENTATIVES,
Washington, D. C., Thursday, February 2, 1911.

The committee met at 10.30 o'clock a. m., Hon. Sereno E. Payne (chairman) presiding.

Present: The chairman and Messrs. Dalzell, McCall, Hill, Boutell, Needham, Calderhead, Fordney, Gaines, Longworth, Dwight, Ellis, Clark, Underwood, Pou, Randell, Broussard, Harrison, and Brantley.

The committee thereupon proceeded to the consideration of the bill (H. R. 32216) to promote reciprocal trade relations with the Dominion of Canada, and for other purposes.

The CHAIRMAN. The committee will be in order. The hearing this morning is on the McCall bill, the purpose of which is to carry out and perfect the agreement made by the Executive with Canada. Is there any gentleman here who desires to be heard?

STATEMENT OF HON. AUGUSTUS P. GARDNER, A REPRESENTATIVE FROM MASSACHUSETTS.

Mr. GARDNER. Mr. Chairman, I want to make a very short statement, and then I would like to present these witnesses, who are business men and master mariners and practical fishermen. I would like to ask them questions myself, I can in that way save a great deal of time. Then I would like to turn them over to you to cross-examine them. They do not want to make speeches. It takes up time. For that reason I would like to ask them a number of questions, myself, and then turn them over for cross-examination. If you have authority to administer oaths I would ask that they be put under oath.

The CHAIRMAN. We have no authority to administer oaths.

Mr. GARDNER. Mr. Chairman and gentlemen of the committee, there are here from Gloucester men who represent every shade of opinion on this treaty. In the first place, there are the men who catch the fish, and they without exception are in favor of protection on both the raw material and the finished product. This treaty takes the duty off of both the raw fish and the manufactured fish. On the other hand, there are a number of gentlemen here who do not fish themselves, but who manufacture fish. They wish to retain the duty on the finished product, but are not in favor of the duty on the raw fish. Of that number one gentleman, Col. Charles F. Wonson, is, as I judge from his telegram to Mr. McCall and to me, in favor of free fish from first to last. So far as I know, judging by the tremendous shower of telegrams that I have received, Col. Wonson is not largely upheld in that view by the people who are engaged in the manufacture of fish; but at the same time he is a man of ability, and I think in fairness he ought to be heard after I have put on my witnesses.

Now, just a short statement. I want to put on the mayor of Gloucester, simply to present a petition. He will make no statement. If you choose, he can read the petition which was passed

3

by the mayor and municipal council, and which is signed unanimously by the municipal council. He will only take up a minute of your time. Then I wish to put on the president of the board of trade of Gloucester, who is here—Mr. Carroll. Mr. Carroll is familiar with the fish business from beginning to end. The firm which he represents (not as the president of the board of trade, but as an individual—the Gorton-Pew Co., which manufactures the Gorton codfish—"no bones"—you have probably seen the advertisement), is engaged both in fishing and in packing fish. It owns vessels. That firm is what some of you gentlemen would call a "trust." It consists of what were formerly five independent concerns in Gloucester, which were all bought up by one concern a number of years ago; and in the entire period of their existence in their best year they have never earned over 4 per cent. I blush for having such a "trust" in my district, Mr. Chairman. [Laughter.]

Of the other gentlemen, two are master mariners both of whom own their own vessels, one representing the cod-fishing industry and the other the mackerel and herring fishing industry. As a general rule, men who go mackereling in the summer eke it out by going for herring up to the middle of January, and after that, in disposing of their catch, we might say the middle of February will be reached before the finishing up of everything connected with the herring season.

Invariably the crews who go on cod-fishing trips are employed on shares of the catch. The same is true with regard to mackerel. At all events, that is true in the sailing fleets. In herring fishing the crews that take the vessels from Gloucester down to Newfoundland are on wages. I expect to show you by the Government expert— that is, the local agent and statistician of the United States Fish Commission—the figures that you want to know as to the scope. I should prefer to have you call him rather than to call him myself. He is here to give you those figures. He would not take a partisan view of the question. You can develop the facts, but I thought it would be more satisfactory to you if you had the Government expert here.

Mr. McCALL. 'What is his name?

Mr. GARDNER. His name is Arthur L. Millett. He represented the United States as one of our experts at The Hague Conference last summer. He is the agent for the Bureau of Fisheries in Gloucester.

Mr. BOUTELL. I would like to ask you one question before you call any witnesses, so that we may know at the outset just what we are to meet in the evidence. In this reciprocal arrangement are you opposed to any other item except the item of fish?

Mr. GARDNER. I personally? I am opposed to the whole treaty.

Mr. BOUTELL. You are opposed to the whole treaty?

Mr. GARDNER. Yes, sir.

Mr. BOUTELL. Will these witnesses that you call before us oppose any other item except the item of fish?

Mr. GARDNER. Not to my knowledge, except in so far as they will have to point out certain things in order to explain the scope. That is, for instance, the glue industry and the cordage and twine industry, and the sailmaking industry. All those things are closely allied. Practically speaking, the men here are interested in cod-packing and the shipping of cod, haddock, hake, and other fish of the cod family; and mackerel and herring. Incidentally some of them probably catch sword fish and halibut.

Mr. BOUTELL. What I wanted to know was whether you were advocating an amendment of one provision of the treaty?

Mr. GARDNER. I presume that is what these gentlemen are advocating, an amendment of one provision of the treaty. But you asked me how I stood on the treaty, and I say I am against the treaty.

The CHAIRMAN. Is not an amendment to this agreement equivalent to the defeat of it? What is the difference between the two?

Mr. GARDNER. I am not capable of discussing the constitutional question with you, nor the mechanical question of this thing. I really am not prepared to do it.

The CHAIRMAN. I just wanted your off-hand opinion. That is all.

Mr. GARDNER. I prefer not to give my offhand opinion until I have made a study of the matter.

Mr. HILL. I was going to ask a similar question to the question asked by Mr. Boutell. Had the mayor and the common council of the city of Gloucester at the time they passed the resolution which I understand you to say they passed, opposing the fish proposition, given any consideration to the treaty? Had they read and did they understand the general terms of the whole treaty, and in passing that resolution did they express their antagonism to the proposition as a whole?

Mr. GARDNER. I would answer that question by asking you whether you think the resolutions favorable to the treaty have been adopted by those who read the treaty from one end to the other?

Mr. HILL. I simply wanted to know the aspect in which they appear.

Mr. GARDNER. In my opinion they have not one of them read the treaty and the schedules from end to end.

Mr. CLARK. If this fish proposition were out of the treaty, would you be for it?

Mr. GARDNER. No, sir; I would be against the treaty.

Mr. CLARK. Why?

Mr. GARDNER. Because I am opposed to reciprocity in competitive articles.

Mr. CLARK. Let me ask you one other question. You say this fish trust——

Mr. GARDNER. I did not say that. I said "what you would call a trust."

Mr. CLARK. What I want to ask, then, is this: You said it never paid over 4 per cent dividend, as I understood it.

Mr. GARDNER. Yes, sir.

Mr. CLARK. You do not know how much water there was in the stock originally?

Mr. GARDNER. No, sir.

Mr. CLARK. That is all.

Mr. GARDNER. But I can tell you that they have never paid a salary of over $5,000 a year, if that is an indication.

Now, in addition, I am going to present a gentleman who was formerly president of the Fish Skinners' Union. There is no longer a fish skinners' union in Gloucester. This gentleman is now a practical fisherman.

Would the committee first like to hear the Government expert as to the scope of this business?

Mr. FORDNEY. I would be glad to hear him.

Mr. GAINES. I think so, Mr. Gardner.

The CHAIRMAN. Is he here?

Mr. GARDNER. He is here. He is Mr. Arthur L. Millett.

STATEMENT OF MR. ARTHUR L. MILLETT.

Mr. GARDNER. Mr. Millett, will you please give your full name?

Mr. MILLETT. Arthur L. Millett.

Mr. GARDNER. Mr. Millett was one of our experts at The Hague tribunal, and is probably as familiar with the question of these fisheries as any man alive. Mr. Millett, will you please tell the committee the scope of this industry?

Mr. MILLETT. As far as Gloucester is concerned, or all of it?

Mr. GARDNER. Would you gentlemen like to have the information concerning the fish industry only as far as Gloucester is concerned, or altogether?

Mr. McCALL. Altogether, I think.

The CHAIRMAN. Yes.

Mr. MILLETT. Speaking of Gloucester first, the total number of fishing vessels in Gloucester of over 5 tons register—and those are the only ones recognized by the customhouse—is 261. That is according to the official report of the collector of customs on the 31st of December, 1910. Those vessels have a tonnage of 21,107 tons. Estimating as carefully as may be the value of those fishing vessels, it would be about $2,175,000. That is, of course, fitted and ready for sea—ready for catching the fish.

Mr. McCALL. About $10 a ton, on the average?

Mr. MILLETT. No, sir; about $100 a ton.

Mr. McCALL. Yes; that is right—$100 a ton. I made a mistake in the decimal.

Mr. MILLETT. On sailing vessels, as to the number of fishermen in Gloucester, where they are constantly shifting about from one port to another, we have no statistics. The city has no figures and the Government has none. As nearly as we can figure, there are 4,500 men engaged in the vocation of fishermen in the port of Gloucester.

According to one of the recent reports of the Bureau of Fisheries, for 1908, I think—the last one we have had—the total number of persons employed in the fisheries of the United States that year was 143,881, and the value of the product in that year was $54,030,629.

Mr. McCALL. That was in 1908?

Mr. MILLETT. 1908, sir. In answer to your question about the $100 a ton, we figure the sailing vessels at about $100 a ton and the gasoline auxiliary vessels at about $175 a ton value. I would like to speak in regard to the fleets of other ports in New England, to correct a wrong impression that Gloucester is the only place having any vessels. Boston has a fleet of 115 fishing vessels. Provincetown has a fleet of 75 fishing vessels. Portland has a fleet of 65 fishing vessels, although those are mostly small vessels. Duxbury has a fleet of 8 fishing vessels. Buckport has a fleet of 6 fishing vessels. Orrs Island has 1 fishing vessel; Plymouth has 1. Kennebunk has a fleet of 12 fishing vessels. Salem has a fleet of 6 fishing vessels. Marblehead has a fleet of 12 fishing vessels; Portsmouth has 5; Rockport, Me., has 8; Boothbay Harbor has 12; Southwest Harbor has a fleet of 37; Eastport has 4; Newport, R. I., has a fleet of 48 fishing vessels; and Providence, R. I., has a fleet of 15 fishing vessels.

There are other ports of which I do not know the real number—ports like Chatham, and all along on the back side of Cape Cod—that have a large fleet of small boats. There are many along the Maine coast of which we have no late record, because most of them are under 5 tons.

Mr. DALZELL. Is the fishing industry confined to New England?

Mr. MILLETT. No, sir; it is not confined to any particular coast. You will find it on the Gulf, on the west coast, the east coast, and all along. There are different branches of it. New England has practically the cod and mackerel fishery and fish of that sort. As you go farther south, there is a difference. On the Pacific coast they catch salmon and halibut, and also salt cod to some extent, but the latter is not as large an industry as ours.

Mr. McCALL. There are great fisheries on the lakes, are there not?

Mr. MILLETT. Yes, sir; the lake fisheries are very large indeed—far larger than one has any idea.

Mr. DALZELL. Have you the figures there for the entire United States?

Mr. MILLETT. Yes, sir; I have the figures for 1908, the last we have. The total number of persons employed in the fisheries of the United States in 1908 was 143,881, and the value of the product was $54,030,629.

Mr. CLARK. Is that for the whole United States, or just New England?

Mr. MILLETT. That is for the whole United States. I can give you the figures for New England if you wish it. No; I can not. I can give you the figures for Massachusetts, Maine, Connecticut, and Rhode Island, which would practically be New England. I have the figures for those States for 1908, which is as late as I have been able to get.

Mr. McCALL. On the question of statistics in connection with fisheries, how far back can you get the statistics in regard to the product of our fisheries?

Mr. MILLETT. I have them in my pocket from 1899. I have kept the figures myself, taken from the books of the concerns. I have to do that for the Bureau of Fisheries.

Mr. McCALL. Have we not available statistics which show the growth of the industry? Have we not statistics which show what it was, for instance, 100 years ago; how many men were employed at that time, and so forth?

Mr. MILLETT. I suppose Lorenzo Sabine's report would give that information. It is a House document. I have forgotten the name of it. It was published in 1852.

Mr. McCALL. Just refer me to some authorities that will give statistics in regard to the fishing industry.

Mr. MILLETT. I think, without any trouble at all, Mr. McCall, the Bureau of Fisheries here would be able to give you everything that there is on the subject, on demand.

Mr. McCALL. I would be very much obliged if you would indicate the books or documents that we should ask for.

Mr. MILLETT. Ask for the report of the Commissioner of Fisheries for each year.

Mr. GARDNER. If you were to talk to Dr. Smith you could probably be able to indicate what reports would give the information these gentlemen seek. They want historical figures, to show the growth or the diminution of the industry over a period of time.

Mr. McCALL. I understand that the fishing industry in Gloucester started in 1623.

Mr. MILLETT. Yes, sir.

Mr. McCALL. Mr. Gardner corrected that by saying 1624. [Laughter.] That has been continuous from that time?

Mr. MILLETT. As far as we know. There are only two years that we can not account for, in a very early part of it.

Mr. McCALL. What I wanted was to get the history of it.

Mr. MILLETT. I will talk with Dr. Smith, and I will leave a note of it.

Mr. GARDNER. He is the Deputy United States Fish Commissioner.

Mr. MILLETT. He is the Deputy United States Fish Commissioner. I believe I was answering your question about the Massachusetts fleet, was I not?

Mr. LONGWORTH. Is this the number for Massachusetts, or for New England?

Mr. MILLETT. The number of fishermen employed in Massachusetts in 1908 was 11,577, and the value of the product was $7,095,229. That is the raw product, of course.

Mr. LONGWORTH. Then Massachusetts constitutes something over 10 per cent of the entire amount?

Mr. MILLETT. Yes, sir. Maine employed 6,861, and the value of their product was about $3,000,000—$3,256,581. Connecticut had 2,147 men employed, and the value of their product was $2,981,721.

Mr. HILL. I would like to ask you a question right there. Are the same character of fisheries contemplated in the statistics in regard to Connecticut that are considered in regard to Massachusetts? Are they not entirely different?

Mr. MILLETT. Yes, sir; entirely different.

Mr. HILL. What is the character of the fishing in Connecticut?

Mr. MILLETT. I suppose the porgy fishery would come in very extensively there.

Mr. HILL. And that in no way should be classified as a competitive industry. Is not that correct? They fish there for fish to get oil?

Mr. MILLETT. Oil and fertilizer, sir.

Mr. HILL. And lobsters, etc.?

Mr. MILLETT. Yes.

Mr. GAINES. Do they have lobsters in Connecticut? [Laughter.]

Mr. MILLETT. They have lobsters in Maine. The lobster industry in Maine is very large.

Mr. HILL. Do the statistics, so far as Connecticut is concerned, relate to an industry similar in character to that maintained at Gloucester?

Mr. MILLETT. I should think not, sir; but I gave those because he asked for the New England figures. That is all. That completes New England. I might give you the figures for New York. New York has 6,775 men, and the value of the product is $4,593,702.

(At this point Mr. Millett exhibited to Mr. McCall a paper containing the figures above stated by him.)

Mr. McCALL. I would suggest that these figures be given to the stenographer and be printed. They are very valuable for reference.

(The figures above referred to are as follows:)

GLOUCESTER FISH RECEIPTS.

	1899	1900	1901	1902	1903	1904
	Pounds.	Pounds.	Pounds.	Pounds.	Pounds.	Pounds.
Salt cod	} 62,030,620	{ 30,790,700	33,133,700	31,498,900	28,371,000	22,514,600
Fresh cod		{ 15,655,900	19,293,300	14,919,400	9,410,000	11,564,000
Halibut	6,949,800	5,733,700	4,305,500	4,080,200	3,205,000	1,970,000
Haddock	8,717,800	5,352,100	4,646,300	4,861,500	3,387,000	7,274,400
Hake	6,512,600	5,057,800	4,198,000	5,512,100	5,614,900	11,342,400
Cusk	2,638,500	1,282,000	1,339,000	987,000	1,593,000	4,128,200
Pollock	3,300,250	3,029,000	2,165,000	4,819,000	5,017,700	8,964,400
Flitched halibut	590,000	1,597,000	341,000	873,800	625,000	742,000
Fresh mackerel	361,400	1,239,000	1,086,400	634,400	634,800	648,000
Salt mackerel	3,476,800	14,896,400	12,518,600	6,872,600	8,032,200	5,010,600
Fresh herring	2,370,000	1,539,800	1,557,800	993,852	2,015,200	1,747,000
Salt herring	8,358,800	8,108,592	12,156,276	13,610,688	10,697,304	16,894,116
Frozen herring	9,022,400	4,803,048	3,961,728	5,465,616	3,988,000	4,565,000
Swordfish	305,000	18,900	177,000	12,200	22,325	121,100
Cured fish	834,400	1,260,000	1,452,640	2,741,700	2,553,600	3,436,608
Frozen squid		263,500	32,642		100,000	
Porgies			110,000	136,000		327,000
Fresh fish from small boats	5,000,000	5,000,000	3,350,000	3,500,000	1,750,000	600,000
Miscellaneous fresh fish from Boston	500,000	500,000	500,000	664,200	826,000	1,792,400
Total at Gloucester	120,967,570	106,133,040	106,374,886	102,183,156	87,843,029	103,528,924
By Gloucester vessels at other ports	6,000,000	30,250,000	40,000,000	40,000,000	36,900,000	31,776,000
Grand total	126,967,570	136,383,040	146,374,886	142,183,156	124,743,029	135,304,924

	1905	1906	1907	1908	1909
	Pounds.	Pounds.	Pounds.	Pounds.	Pounds.
Salt cod	18,139,000	18,387,800	15,712,700	23,115,705	33,116,200
Fresh cod	11,281,060	8,550,700	16,167,400	13,130,700	12,300,200
Halibut	2,324,700	3,442,400	3,081,765	2,816,050	2,368,582
Haddock	13,694,190	14,095,100	6,063,800	8,409,100	4,407,200
Hake	13,517,315	5,437,910	9,081,950	7,868,400	1,806,900
Cusk	6,895,830	4,021,900	4,805,300	3,405,800	1,363,800
Pollock	17,637,535	7,314,400	16,754,400	7,133,200	5,908,700
Flitched halibut	453,578	582,935	826,210	880,542	800,882
Fresh mackerel	456,800	383,800	613,400	873,000	669,600
Salt mackerel	5,210,000	2,199,800	5,945,000	3,490,000	2,961,000
Fresh herring	1,451,400	2,416,800	2,618,200	4,107,400	1,057,600
Salt herring	8,633,800	15,451,788	16,315,908	8,376,036	10,572,360
Frozen herring	5,550,400	5,077,800	4,313,000	6,612,500	4,408,750
Swordfish	23,240	3,001	8,250	11,954	6,184
Cured fish	4,754,370	3,496,950	2,004,800	3,404,800	4,121,100
Porgies	245,200	45,000			163,400
Fresh fish from small boats	900,000	1,000,000	750,000	600,000	300,000
Miscellaneous fresh fish from Boston	1,391,400	1,908,200	4,097,776	2,487,400	2,033,200
Total at Gloucester	112,459,818	93,816,284	109,879,859	96,722,587	88,365,658
By Gloucester vessels at other ports	44,650,000	34,271,000	39,100,000	32,601,850	36,359,800
Grand total	157,109,818	128,087,284	148,979,859	129,324,437	124,725,458

Total catches, Gloucester, January 1 to December 31.

	1910	1909	1908
Salt cod..pounds..	27,734,049	33,116,200	23,115,705
Fresh cod...do....	9,698,841	12,300,200	13,130,700
Halibut...do....	2,283,092	2,368,582	2,816,050
Haddock..do....	4,908,053	4,407,200	8,409,100
Hake...do....	3,548,979	1,806,900	7,868,400
Cusk...do....	2,404,518	1,363,800	3,405,800
Pollock..do....	9,437,224	5,908,700	7,133,200
Flitches...do....	950,636	800,882	880,542
Swordfish..do....	14,305	6,184	11,954
Total..do....	60,979,697	62,378,648	67,371,451
Fresh fish from small boats.........................do....	700,000	300,000	600,000
Miscellaneous......................................do....	1,011,000	1,743,800	1,285,200
Fresh mackerel....................................barrels..	490	3,348	4,365
Salt mackerel......................................do....	2,830	14,805	17,450
Fresh herring......................................do....	18,800	5,288	20,537
Frozen herring.....................................do....	18,325	17,635	26,450
Salt herring [1]...................................do....	59,867	46,420	36,737
Porgies..do....	....	817	....
Halibut fins.......................................do....	429	298	358
Whiting..do....	5,000	500	4,000
Shad...do....	368	749	1,653
Total..do....	106,109	89,860	111,550
Cured fish......................................quintals..	28,925	36,150	30,440

RECAPITULATION.

	1910	1909	1908
Grand total at Gloucester..........................pounds..	89,822,473	88,365,658	96,722,587
Total by Gloucester vessels at other ports direct (estimated), pounds..	32,250,000	36,359,800	32,601,850
Total at Gloucester and by Gloucester vessels at other ports...pounds..	122,072,473	124,725,458	129,324,437

[1] Includes pickled herring.

Mr. DALZELL. Have you the figures for the Pacific coast fishing industry?

Mr. MILLETT. I have not; no, sir.

Mr. DALZELL. And Alaska?

Mr. MILLETT. No, sir; I have not.

Mr. DALZELL. Where would we get those?

Mr. MILLETT. At the Bureau of Fisheries. You can get them very easily on demand.

Mr. DALZELL. Have you any idea what proportion of the whole the Pacific coast fisheries represent?

Mr. MILLETT. I should judge, speaking of salmon, it would be very large. If you take the salmon into account and the halibut, it would be q e large, especially in value.

Mr. DALZELL. Do you include the Alaska industry in that?

Mr. MILLETT. Yes, sir; that would be included, I am quite sure.

The CHAIRMAN. As I recollect, the advocates of a duty on fish have been chiefly from Massachusetts and Maine. I do not suppose you have any knowledge about that?

Mr. MILLETT. Only locally and personally, sir. That is all.

The CHAIRMAN. Your tables show the amount of the fishing indus-try in Gloucester and Massachusetts. I suppose Gloucester covers Massachusetts pretty well in the fishing industry; but your statistics show the fishing industry in Massachusetts in comparison with the whole country, do they not? I withdraw that about Gloucester, Mr. Gardner.

Mr. GARDNER. I was going to say that I have a telegram from the Provincetown Board of Trade, containing a unanimous protest against this treaty. As Provincetown is not represented in Congress I feel that there could be no objection, at all events, to my represent-ing the position of their board of trade.

Mr. MILLETT. I will try to answer any questions that may be asked. That is about all, I think, that I have to say.

The CHAIRMAN. Are there any further questions?

Mr. GARDNER. I should suggest, gentlemen, that Mr. Millett has a general knowledge of this whole question, and I think the members of the committee could get a great deal of information from him.

Mr. NEEDHAM. Have you any statistics showing whether the fishermen are native-born Americans or foreign-born citizens?

Mr. MILLETT. The great majority, sir, of the fishermen of Glouces-ter, in my opinion, are foreign born. Applying that to all New Eng-land, I can not answer your question.

Mr. HILL. Are they citizens of the United States? You have no statistics concerning that?

Mr. MILLETT. No, sir; I have nothing.

Mr. GARDNER. I will put on a witness to cover that matter.

Mr. HILL. Can you give us the information at your convenience as to the cod, mackerel, and herring fisheries, representatives of which can appear? What I want to do is to see if we can not sepa-rate it from the other classes of the fishing industry and let them speak for themselves.

Mr. MILLETT. You mean with reference to other places in the business?

Mr. HILL. Yes.

Mr. MILLETT. That is something that I would not have, because I only gather the Gloucester figures. Boston has a local agent that gathers the figures for that port, and the statistics at the other ports are only gathered about once every four years. The figures at Bos-ton and Gloucester are gathered every week, being the principal places.

Mr. HILL. There is one other question I would like to ask. I ask it because I happened to read an article in the paper during the week. Is the herring industry an industry of American labor, or is the product largely bought and brought in and sold? Is the fishing itself, the actual fishing, being done by others in Newfoundland and Canada?

Mr. MILLETT. The Newfoundland herring fishery is prosecuted by American vessels with American crews, "with the assistance of men and boats that are hired for the purpose." This latter part is the form of the Government oath.

Mr. HILL. The statement made by the board of appraisers this week, in making their decision, then, is not exactly correct, is it?

Mr. MILLETT. I should not care to pass any opinion on the opinion of the board of appraisers.

Mr. HILL. You saw that decision?

Mr. MILLETT. I did; yes, sir.

Mr. FORDNEY. I take it for granted that you do not think it would be wise to put this treaty into law, and leave this part in it that refers to fish, and put fish on the free list?

Mr. MILLETT. Are you asking me as an individual, or as a repre-sentative of the Bureau of Fisheries?

Mr. FORDNEY. I am asking you as a citizen of the United States, protected by the tariff law.

Mr. MILLETT. In answer to that, I will say that I believe in the theory of protection.

Mr. FORDNEY. I agree with you.

Mr. LONGWORTH. Can you give us in round numbers the relative per cent of the fish industry on the Atlantic Coast, in the Lake district, and on the Pacific coast?

Mr. MILLETT. I can not, because I did not come provided with those figures; but that can be very easily secured.

Mr. GARDNER. Will the committee allow me to ask a leading question such as has just been asked?

The CHAIRMAN. Yes.

Mr. GARDNER. Mr. Millett, in your opinion, could the Gloucester fishing industry survive if the treaty was passed?

Mr. MILLETT. Do you mean survive as it is at present?

Mr. GARDNER. I mean survive as a profitable occupation for fishermen? Could these gentlemen, these master mariners, and so on, here, get a livelihood at the port of Gloucester?

Mr. MILLETT. Not at the port of Gloucester, in the present mag-nitude of the business, in my opinion. I believe they would have to go elsewhere to do the business, if that is what you mean.

Mr. HARRISON. Is the business on its last legs at the port of Gloucester?

Mr. MILLETT. We do not think so. From the number of men employed there, and the increase in savings-bank deposits, and so on, it does not look that way.

Mr. FORDNEY. You think that it will be on its last legs if we put this into law?

Mr. MILLETT. Yes, sir; that is my personal opinion.

Mr. RANDELL. How do you think the enactment of the treaty into law would affect the question of providing food for the poorer people in that part of the country? Would it be beneficial or hurtful in that case?

Mr. MILLETT. I suppose I could explain it, but it might take me longer than you would want to listen.

Mr. RANDELL. I want to know how it would affect the poorer people.

Mr. MILLETT. Salt-fish duty is only three quarters of a cent a pound. The average family in the United States probably does not use over a pound or a pound and a half of salt fish a week.

Mr. RANDELL. You think the consumer of fish, then, is not inter-ested in the treaty?

Mr. MILLETT. I do not think so, so far as that part is concerned. Other parts I do not feel competent to speak about.

Mr. HILL. Have you statistics showing the prices of fish at the port of Gloucester for a number of years back?

Mr. MILLETT. Every bit of fish, the product of the American fisheries, is reported to the bureau once a week. They report the number of pounds each week and the value of each kind of fish. Then they make out monthly and also yearly statements.

Mr. HILL. Is that available?

Mr. MILLETT. Yes, sir; the bureau has an abundant fund of information.

Mr. LONGWORTH. Is the Gloucester fleet as large to-day as it was 10 years ago?

Mr. MILLETT. I should say it has decreased a little in numbers, perhaps. I do not think it has decreased in tonnage. If it has decreased in tonnage, it would be a very slight decrease; but there are fewer vessels than there were 10 years ago, in my opinion, sir.

Mr. GARDNER. I will now call Capt. Peoples.

STATEMENT OF CAPT. GEORGE H. PEOPLES.

Mr. GARDNER. Gentlemen, this is Capt. George H. Peoples, president of the Gloucester Master Mariners' Association. What kind of fishing are you engaged in, Capt. Peoples?

Capt. PEOPLES. I am engaged in mackerel and swordfishing in summer and in herring fishing in winter.

Mr. GARDNER. Do you own your own vessel?

Capt. PEOPLES. Yes, sir.

Mr. GARDNER. Does it represent the savings of a few years or the savings of a lifetime?

Capt. PEOPLES. The savings of 26 years.

Mr. GARDNER. Does your crew sail on shares?

Capt. PEOPLES. Yes, sir.

Mr. GARDNER. How many have you got in your crew?

Capt. PEOPLES. Ten.

Mr. GARDNER. How many of them are American citizens?

Capt. PEOPLES. Eight.

Mr. GARDNER. How many children have they?

Capt. PEOPLES. That is a question that I am not just prepared to answer [laughter], but, judging from the families of fishermen in general, I should say that they represent at least three or four each.

Mr. GARDNER. What will you do with your vessel if this treaty goes through?

Capt. PEOPLES. Well, there is only one thing, to my mind, and that would be to dispose of her.

Mr. GARDNER. Where would you dispose of her?

Capt. PEOPLES. That is a question that I can not answer. I might sell her in the provinces or I might sell her somewhere else.

Mr. GARDNER. What will you do yourself?

Capt. PEOPLES. I myself would go to Nova Scotia. In fact, I have had an offer already from parties in Nova Scotia to sail a vessel from one of their ports.

Mr. GARDNER. What will your crew do?

Capt. PEOPLES. They will have to do the same, as far as I can understand. I do not see anything else for them to do.

Mr. GARDNER. How many of them are married?

Capt. PEOPLES. Six.

Mr. GARDNER. Six out of ten?

Capt. PEOPLES. Six out of ten are married.

Mr. GARDNER. They would have to take their families away from Gloucester, would they not?

Capt. PEOPLES. Undoubtedly. There is not anything else for them.

Mr. GARDNER. You are one of the men who pay wages. Let me state for the benefit of the committee that Mr. Hill is perfectly right. That is a question that has been thrashed out before The Hague Tribunal—the question of the manner of conducting the herring fisheries. We send a sailing crew from Gloucester. That sailing crew gets on the fishing grounds on the coast of Newfoundland. We have a right to fish in Newfoundland's back yard under the treaty of 1818. There they hire natives to set the nets under their superintendence in catching the fish. Formerly, it is true, under the guise of having fish caught for them, they used to buy the fish, in order to meet a theoretical state of affairs by which Newfoundland compelled the fish to be sold.

Mr. HILL. You are perfectly familiar with this matter. I am seeking for information. I read in a paper yesterday, coming down on the car, that the board of appraisers had made this decision, that as to British vessels with British crews catching fish in British waters the fish, under this recent decision of last week, were admitted free to the United States if they were working with American capital.

Mr. GARDNER. That is not so. The new customs regulations, which were published about 10 days ago, in accordance with the decision of The Hague Tribunal, provides that an American vessel may go with a sailing crew—obviously you could not take a huge fishing crew and keep them idle—to Newfoundland. They go with a sailing crew. There they hire a crew to set the nets and cure the fish on scaffolding. These new Treasury decisions say that those men who are hired must perform every operation in the presence of the American vessel and under the supervision of her master or crew. The crew need not necessarily take the process of curing under their supervision, because the vessel might meanwhile have moved off to another fishing station, somewhere else. In fact, the State Department and the Treasury Department and the United States Fish Commission have a man on the spot now down there, Mr. Alexander, to see that, under the guise of curing fish, fish are not bought and slipped in onto the vessels.

Mr. HILL. Why does not that decision practically break down the present duty on fish, so far as herring is concerned?

Mr. GARDNER. On the contrary, this decision is more strenuous than the old Treasury regulations as to what constituted the product of American fisheries. This is a restriction instead of being an enlargement. It is brought about partly by The Hague Tribunal decision, and partly by the so-called Capt. Carter case, where the Board of General Appraisers decided in favor of Capt. Carter, whose vessel was not present at all. They decided in favor of Capt. Carter. That case has been appealed by the Government. I think the Government is right in appealing the case, though my constituents would probably not agree with me.

Captain, part of your crew, when you go after herring, are on wages, are they not?

Capt. PEOPLES. They are all on wages; all of them.

Mr. GARDNER. The men you hire are paid by the barrel, are they not?

Capt. PEOPLES. The men we hire down there are; but the crew that we sail the vessel with from Gloucester to the fishing grounds are all on wages.

Mr. GARDNER. What can you say as to the wages and the pay as compared with the wages at the port of Lunenburg?

Capt. PEOPLES. The wages paid at Lunenburg two years ago were $22 a month for men before the mast, $35 for cooks and mates, and $60 to $65 for captains. Against that we have a wage out of Gloucester of $30 to $35 for men before the mast, $60 to $70 for cooks and mates, and $100 to $125 for masters. Those are the wages out of Gloucester.

Mr. FORDNEY. In other words, the wages paid by you are about double the wages that are paid for the foreign fishermen?

Capt. PEOPLES. Practically double; yes, sir.

The CHAIRMAN. Does anybody desire to ask the witness any further questions?

Mr. GAINES. Of course those men get their pay and are found. What is the relative cost of victualing?

Capt. PEOPLES. The bill of fare, of course, of the Nova Scotia fishing fleet engaged in the business would be practically the same as to the particular items; but in the cost of those particular items there would be a material difference, to my mind. I am not prepared to say just how much the difference would be, but there is a material difference.

Mr. DWIGHT. Do you know what it costs you a week to board your men?

Capt. PEOPLES. To board our men it would cost about $2 or $2.50 a week.

Mr. DWIGHT. What does it cost the Newfoundland fishermen?

Capt. PEOPLES. I am not prepared to say that.

Mr. GARDNER. Can you tell what it costs to board men out of Lunenburg, Nova Scotia?

Capt. PEOPLES. No, sir; I can not tell exactly. I am not prepared to make a statement on that, because I do not know.

Mr. HILL. Can you fish anywhere now in Canadian waters?

Capt. PEOPLES. No, sir.

Mr. HILL. Can you fish at all within the 3-mile limit?

Capt. PEOPLES. No, sir; not in Canadian waters.

Mr. GARDNER. You can fish at the Magdalen Islands?

Capt. PEOPLES. Of course; that is included in our rights under the treaty of 1818.

Mr. HILL. Do you have permission from the Canadian Government now to fish?

Capt. PEOPLES. Not to fish. Only to buy bait, fishing supplies, and to ship crews.

Mr. HILL. How much do you have to pay for that privilege?

Capt. PEOPLES. $1.50 per ton.

Mr. HILL. You can sail down there and take your crew from the citizens of Canada, after you sail?

Capt. PEOPLES. Under the terms of the modus vivendi; yes, sir.

Mr. HILL. You can not fish under that license within the 3-mile limit?

Capt. PEOPLES. We can only fish on the coast of the Magdalen Islands.

Mr. HILL. You can not go into the large bays and harbors, etc, and fish?

Capt. PEOPLES. No, sir.

Mr. HILL. Does the new license that is proposed to be given you change that in any respect?

Capt. PEOPLES. I can not see that it does. It does not give us a chance to fish inside of the 3-mile limit.

Mr. HILL. Can you take your fish ashore now and ship them to the United States?

Capt. PEOPLES. We can by paying $1.50 a ton.

Mr. HILL. Do they pay duty when they come in here?

Capt. PEOPLES. No, sir; they come in free of duty.

Mr. GARDNER. They have to be certified by the consul.

Capt. PEOPLES. Yes; you have to have the consular certificate to that effect.

Mr. HILL. But you can now bring in free those caught by American ships?

Capt. PEOPLES. Yes; and transship them.

Mr. GARDNER. What have you to say about the law licensing auxiliary vessels?

Capt. PEOPLES. Of course they discriminate against our vessels in that respect. A vessel with auxiliary power is denied the privilege which they give to the sailing vessel. She is not allowed to purchase a license by paying $1.50 a ton.

Mr. GARDNER. In other words, this reduction in the cost of the license, which would amount on a 100-ton vessel to about $149 a year, is valueless so far as the auxiliary fleet is concerned?

Capt. PEOPLES. Yes, sir.

Mr. GARDNER. The license which the Canadian Government is in the habit of issuing to-day gives them a chance to buy ice and supplies and to ship crews, but not to fish anywhere except on the shores of the Magdalen Islands, where they have a right to fish. The new treaty does not alter that in any way, except that it saves a vessel of 100 tons about $149 a year. You were evidently a little bit misled. You asked about hiring crews down there. That is not the practice in Canadian waters. The practice is to hire the crew when they go to the herring fisheries in Newfoundland waters, because setting the nets to catch the herring takes a vast number of men. You hire as many as 50 now and then, do you not?

Capt. PEOPLES. Yes, sir; as many as 50; and sometimes more than 50.

Mr. GARDNER. These nets, you understand, are stretched across the mouths of the inlets in order to catch the herring as they approach the spawning beds.

Capt. PEOPLES. Yes, sir. And we furnish fishing gear for those fishermen and pay them $1.25 a barrel and higher for their product.

STATEMENT OF CAPT. WILLIAM H. THOMAS.

Mr. GARDNER. Capt. William Thomas has one of the largest vessels in the fishing business. He is engaged in deep-sea fishing. You catch cod and haddock, do you not?

Capt. THOMAS. Yes, sir.

Mr. GARDNER. Do you own your own vessel?

Capt. THOMAS. Yes, sir.

Mr. GARDNER. Not entirely?

Capt. THOMAS. Three-quarters.

Mr. GARDNER. How many years' savings does that vessel represent to you?

Capt. THOMAS. Thirty-seven years.

Mr. GARDNER. How many men have you in your crew?

Capt. THOMAS. Twenty-three of them.

Mr. GARDNER. How many of them are American citizens?

Capt. THOMAS. Somewheres around 21.

Mr. GARDNER. How many children have they?

Capt. THOMAS. I believe we count somewhere around 52.

Mr. GARDNER. Fifty-two to the schooner?

Capt. THOMAS. Fifty-two to the schooner; yes, sir.

Mr. GARDNER. Is your crew on shares?

Capt. THOMAS. They are all on shares; yes, sir.

Mr. GARDNER. What will you do with your vessel if this treaty goes through?

Capt. THOMAS. Well, I suppose I will dispose of it.

Mr. GARDNER. If you can?

Capt. THOMAS. If I can; yes, sir.

Mr. GARDNER. You can not tell us anything about the wages, because you do not pay wages?

Capt. THOMAS. I never was on a wage basis; no, sir.

Mr. GARDNER. But you do know something about the cost of feeding the men?

Capt. THOMAS. I do; yes, sir.

Mr. GARDNER. And the cost of fittings and outfittings, sails, cordage, paint, oil, supplies, and all that sort of thing?

Capt. THOMAS. Yes, sir.

Mr. GARDNER. How does it compare in Gloucester and in Lunenburg?

Capt. THOMAS. In the first place, take our sails. We have to pay 18 cents a yard to get a sail made in Gloucester.

Mr. GARDNER. That is the Gloucester Sail Makers' Union scale?

Capt. THOMAS. Yes, sir. In Nova Scotia, if I am not mistaken, it is 8 cents a yard. They can hire a carpenter in Nova Scotia for $1.75; and we have to pay from $2.50 to $2.75 and up to $3, in Gloucester. The cost of calking and painting is almost double. It is one-third more, anyhow. It is one-third larger in Gloucester than it would be in Nova Scotia; and everything else accordingly. The cost of our fishing supplies is higher. I judge that what costs us on a voyage $1,000 I could duplicate in Nova Scotia for about $800. Our fishing gear is higher—our hooks. We have to pay a duty of 40 cents on the fishhooks that we use. In Nova Scotia they cost 14 cents a gross.

Mr. GARDNER. What is the duty on hooks?

Capt. THOMAS. I think it is in the neighborhood of 40 cents—or 40 per cent.

Mr. GARDNER. You buy a great many imported hooks?

Capt. THOMAS. Yes, sir; we do.

Mr. GARDNER. Do you, in Gloucester, buy imported hooks?

Capt. THOMAS. Yes, sir; we do. That is all we can get. Everything, I should judge, is one-third higher.

Mr. GARDNER. So that you can not carry on a profitable business if this treaty goes through?

Capt. THOMAS. It is my belief that it would be impossible. With the vessels we have we could not do it. I do not believe I could hold a crew of men, anyhow. They would have to go to a foreign port somewhere—because we are all fishermen. That is all we are. We have no trade of any other kind.

Mr. GARDNER. That is all these crews are—fishermen, and nothing but fishermen?

Capt. THOMAS. Nothing but fishermen; no, sir. They mostly have their families in Gloucester.

Mr. McCALL. What time do you start out on your cod fishing? What time of the year?

Capt. THOMAS. We follow it the year round, 12 months, sir.

Mr. McCALL. You are not in the herring fishing business?

Capt. THOMAS. No, sir; I have never done it.

Mr. GARDNER. As a general thing, the boats engaged in herring fishing are faster boats than those that are engaged in cod fishing?

Capt. THOMAS. Yes, sir.

Mr. GARDNER. And the same vessel is not really suitable for both?

Capt. THOMAS. No; we have to have auxiliary power for seining.

Mr. HARRISON. What is the size of your vessel?

Capt. THOMAS. One hundred and forty tons gross, ninety-two tons net.

Mr. HARRISON. Is it an auxiliary vessel?

Capt. THOMAS. No, sir; it is a sailing vessel.

Mr. HARRISON. You get a license from the Canadian Government, then?

Capt. THOMAS. Well, we have to obtain a license once a year from the Canadian Government.

Mr. HARRISON. That is based on the tonnage of the vessel?

Capt. THOMAS. Yes, sir.

Mr. HARRISON. It amounts to about $225 a year for your vessel?

Capt. THOMAS. We pay on the net tonnage. It is about $138, if I am not mistaken, besides other dues that we have to pay.

Mr. HARRISON. If this agreement becomes a law in both countries, your vessel will only have to pay a nominal license of $1 a year.

Capt. THOMAS. Yes, sir.

Mr. HARRISON. Is there any guarantee, if the agreement does not become a law, that the present system of licensing by the Canadian Government will continue?

Capt. THOMAS. That is guaranteed for this year.

Mr. GARDNER. I can answer that

Mr. HARRISON. Wait a minute. Let me ask one more question. The exchange of letters between the officials of the two governments who negotiated this arrangement provides for the continuance of issuing licenses to American vessels, does it not?

Capt. THOMAS. I do not know.

Mr. HARRISON. It does, I will say as a fact.

Mr. GARDNER. I think, Mr. Harrison, that the Canadian Government did not consent to that. I think it is worded in this way: That the modus vivendi shall continue so long as they want it to, but we for our part do not pledge other things to continue any longer than they continue the modus vivendi. Substantially, the modus vivendi, in other words, under the exchange of notes, is in no danger of being broken. That change of the note was drawn up before the treaty. That was in consequence of the action of The Hague Tribunal.

Mr. HARRISON. I will read the paragraph. It is very brief:

The Government of Canada agree that, until otherwise determined by them, the licenses hitherto issued to United States fishing vessels under the provisions of section 3 of chapter 47 of the Revised Statutes of Canada, granting to such vessels certain privileges on the Atlantic coast of Canada shall continue to be issued and that the fee to be paid to the Government of Canada for such license by the owner or commander of any such United States vessel shall hereafter be $1 per annum.

Mr. GARDNER. That was the sentence we could not get out—"until otherwise determined." We could not get an absolute agreement, and therefore did not make an absolute agreement on our part.

Mr. HARRISON. But in good faith it is considered that that is one of the inducements for entering into this treaty?

Mr. GARDNER. I do not understand so. That arose in an entirely different way. Mr. Millett can explain that better than I can. Mr. Millett was the expert at The Hague Tribunal, and was also one of the American commissioners for drawing up those notes for the two Governments.

Mr. Millett, did you understand that there was any connection between the settlement of those regulations under this treaty of 1818, as provided by The Hague Tribunal for a mixed commission, and the question of a treaty with Canada on the reciprocity matter?

Mr. MILLETT. Not at all. The question of the Canadian license comes up in connection with the question of regulations. I think Mr. Ellsworth——

Mr. CLARK. Speak a little louder. We can not hear you.

Mr. MILLETT. I say the matter of the Canadian license for fishing vessels had no connection, so far as I know, with anything in this present treaty. It was brought up the first part of January, when Hon. Allen B. Ellsworth was here from Canada seeking to straighten out the regulation with Canada, and to make a business agreement rather than to bring it before a board of experts.

Mr. GARDNER. Let me explain it from the beginning. The question of regulations was before The Hague Tribunal on this point. We have certain rights under the treaty of 1818, in regard to fishing, both in Canadian and Newfoundland waters. They undertook by passing certain local regulations to control the situation, as we claimed, to the advantage of their own people as against ours. We denied their right to regulate the fishing by local regulation. The Hague Tribunal decided that they had the right to pass those local regulations, but that there must be a permanent mixed commission to pass on the reasonableness of the regulations. In other words, that Canada and Newfoundland should not be the sole judges of the reasonableness of any regulation. In response to that the permanent mixed commission turned it over to a committee of experts to pass on the reasonableness of the existing regulations; and what Mr. Harrison has been reading you is the report that was agreed upon by the representatives of the United States and the representatives of Canada as to the reasonableness of regulations passed in consequence of our treaty of 1818. It has no connection whatever, Mr. Harrison, and I think you will find the State Department would bear me out in the view that it never was allied in mind, thought, or word with the question of this reciprocity treaty. It has been going on for years.

Mr. HARRISON. Whatever may be this decision of the mixed commission, the gentleman from Massachusetts will agree with me that this clause, appearing where it does at this time in these negotiations, although it does not bind the Canadian Government (because these officials can not do so until Parliament acts or fails to act), nevertheless is a guaranty of good faith in the matter, that seems to secure for American fishermen the continuance of the license which now can only be obtained from year to year.

Mr. GARDNER. We all know the modus vivendi. This same talk has been going on for a generation, about that modus vivendi.

Mr. CLARK. Is this fishing industry in New England a flourishing industry, or is it a vanishing one?

Mr. GARDNER. I think it has been just about holding its own for a good many years past, so far as fishing is concerned. Unquestionably, so far as packing is concerned, I think I am safe in saying it has developed.

The CHAIRMAN. Turn around, please, so I can hear you.

Mr. GARDNER. I turned around to get the assent of my witnesses to the fact that the packing industry has developed.

Mr. CLARK. In the last 100 years the population of the United States has multiplied about 18 times, and there have been that many more people to eat fish. If this is a flourishing industry, why has not the size of the industry kept up with the population?

Mr. GARDNER. I do not think it is a flourishing industry, Mr. Clark.

Mr. CLARK. What is that?

Mr. GARDNER. I say, I do not think it is a flourishing industry.

Mr. CLARK. It is not a flourishing industry, no matter what you do with it?

Mr. GARDNER. Oh, you can ask these gentlemen. Ask Capt. Thomas's crew and they will tell you there is some difference. Because the industry is not flourishing is no reason why you should root it out.

Mr. CLARK. I am not trying to root it out.

Mr. GARDNER. Well, it would seem so.

Mr. CLARK. Well, you are wrong. I would like to ask Capt. Thomas a question or two. Captain, are the fish as plentiful as they used to be? How old a man are you?

Capt. THOMAS. I am 53 years old.

Mr. CLARK. How long have you been in the fishing business?

Capt. THOMAS. About 37 years.

Mr. CLARK. Are the fish as plentiful now as they were when you first began that business?

Capt. THOMAS. At times; yes, sir. Year before last—a year ago—the fish were more plentiful than I have ever seen them. Last year they went off.

Mr. CLARK. Are your crew in partnership with you or do you pay them salaries?

Capt. THOMAS. We all take shares. The vessel takes a part and the crew takes part, the same as I do.

Mr. CLARK. You have been at this business ever since you have been a grown man?

Capt. THOMAS. Yes, sir.

Mr. CLARK. Of course, I do not know much about the business and am inquiring for information. Would these men that constitute your crew be classed as skilled laborers or as common laborers?

Capt. Thomas. They are nothing but fishermen, the same as you would call them sailors. That is all.

Mr. Clark. They are nothing but fishermen?

Capt. Thomas. No, sir.

Mr. Clark. Do you mean that they could not do anything else?

Capt. Thomas. Well. I do not mean that they are blockheads entirely, but that is their branch of business.

Mr. Clark. If they were what are called ordinary common laborers, they could do almost anything.

Capt. Thomas. Well, they might take a pick and shovel, I suppose.

Mr. Clark. It is only skilled laborers who are confined to one branch of industry.

Capt. Thomas. Well, I suppose so.

Mr. Clark. You would not go out of business if this thing were passed, would you?

Capt. Thomas. I do not know that I am capable of anything else.

Mr. Clark. But you would go on and make money just as you do now, would you not?

Capt. Thomas. I do not know where I would go, unless I went to a foreign port. I would not expect to make any money at home.

Mr. Clark. Would your ship be good for anything else?

Capt. Thomas. For fishing? It would depend on what part of the world she would go to. I do not believe they would want her in the Provinces. A different type of vessel entirely is used there.

Mr. Fordney. Have you more than one vessel?

Capt. Thomas. I own a small part in another one—one-eighth.

Mr. Fordney. What I mean by the question is this, Captain. Mention has been made of the fact that the business is a flourishing industry. You have been 27 years in the business, and you own but one vessel. You have not made a great deal of profit; or else you have been a spendthrift.

Capt. Thomas. No; I have brought up a large family.

Mr. Gardner. He has been in the business 37 years?

Mr. Clark. How much is your interest in this vessel worth?

Capt. Thomas. She cost us $14,000.

Mr. Clark. And you own three-quarters of it?

Capt. Thomas. Yes, sir.

Mr. Clark. How much of this other boat do you own?

Capt. Thomas. I own one-eighth.

Mr. Clark. How much is that whole boat worth?

Capt. Thomas. Now, sir?

Mr. Clark. No; how much was it worth new?

Capt. Thomas. It was worth $13,000.

Mr. Clark. About $6,000?

Capt. Thomas. Yes, sir.

Mr. Clark. Do you own the house where you live?

Capt. Thomas. Yes, sir.

Mr. Clark. How much is it worth?

Capt. Thomas. It depends on how things are going to turn. If it is this way, I suppose it is worth $7,000. If it goes the other way, it would not be worth anything. [Laughter.]

Mr. Clark. Do you own any other real estate?

Capt. Thomas. Yes.

Mr. Clark. How much?

Capt. Thomas. Another house, $3,000.

Mr. Clark. How much are they worth?

Capt. Thomas. I can tell you what they cost me. I can not put a value on them now.

Mr. Clark. How much did they cost you?

Capt. Thomas. They cost me $10,000.

Mr. Clark. Apiece?

Capt. Thomas. No, sir; for both.

Mr. Clark. Do you own any land, unimproved?

Capt. Thomas. No, sir; just the little yard in front of each one.

Mr. Clark. Have you any bank stocks?

Capt. Thomas. No, sir.

Mr. Clark. How much are you worth altogether?

Capt. Thomas. At present?

Mr. Clark. Yes. $50,000?

Capt. Thomas. No, sir; far from it. About $18,000 would cover it.

Mr. Fordney. How long did it take you to accumulate that?

Capt. Thomas. Thirty-seven years.

Mr. Fordney. Any ordinary Congressman could do better than that. [Laughter.]

Mr. Hill. You are engaged in the deep-sea fishing, on the banks?

Capt. Thomas. Yes, sir.

Mr. Hill. Cod fishing?

Capt. Thomas. Yes, sir; cod fishing and halibut and haddock.

Mr. Hill. Would you say there is less money in the cod fisheries than there is, as a general rule, year after year, in inshore fishing?

Capt. Thomas. No, sir; it is hard for me to decide. It changes about. Some years the inshore fishing will offset the offshore fishing.

Mr. Hill. I do not want to be inquisitive, but are you an American citizen born in the United States?

Capt. Thomas. No, sir.

Mr. Hill. Where were you born?

Capt. Thomas. I was born in Nova Scotia.

Mr. Hill. Were you engaged in the fishing business in Nova Scotia before you came to the United States?

Capt. Thomas. No, sir.

Mr. Hill. What I wanted to get was a comparative statement as to the two classes of industry—the deep-sea fishing and the inshore fishing. Which of the two is generally considered to be the more profitable?

Capt. Thomas. Well, it changes. Some years the inshore fishing will beat the offshore fishing, and then it goes back the other way.

Mr. Hill. You have been engaged all the time in deep-sea fishing?

Capt. Thomas. Yes, sir.

Mr. Gardner. You do some inshore fishing, do you not?

Capt. Thomas. We do some haddock fishing; yes, sir. In the summer time we run to Gloucester with our fish and in the winter time we run to Boston to market the fish.

Mr. Hill. I suppose there is no standard price for fish; it varies from year to year?

Capt. Thomas. Yes.

Mr. Hill. What affects the price? What makes the variation?

Capt. Thomas. It depends upon the quantity, the same as other things.

Mr. HILL. According to the supply and demand?

Capt. THOMAS. Yes, sir.

Mr. HILL. What are the general variations from year to year in the price?

Capt. THOMAS. About 50 cents is as much as we generally have.

Mr. HILL. Fifty cents a hundred pounds?

Capt. THOMAS. On salt fish; yes, sir.

Mr. HILL. What is the price this year?

Capt. THOMAS. This year it is $5.50, I think.

Mr. HILL. $5.50 a hundred pounds?

Capt. THOMAS. $5.50 a hundredweight; yes, sir.

Mr. HILL. What was it last year?

Capt. THOMAS. It was somewhere around $3.75, if I am not mistaken.

Mr. HILL. $1.75 difference between this year and last?

Capt. THOMAS. Yes, sir.

Mr. HILL. What is the highest you have ever known it to be?

Capt. THOMAS. This year.

Mr. HILL. $5.50?

Capt. THOMAS. Yes, sir.

Mr. HILL. That is the highest you have ever known it to be since you have been fishing?

Capt. THOMAS. Yes, sir.

Mr. HILL. What is the lowest you have ever known it to be?

Capt. THOMAS. $1.50.

Mr. HILL. When was that?

Capt. THOMAS. If I am not mistaken it was at the time of the treaty with Canada.

Mr. HILL. During the reciprocity treaty with Canada?

Capt. THOMAS. I am not positive; but I think so.

Mr. HILL. It was then $1.50, and it is now $5.50?

Capt. THOMAS. Yes, sir.

Mr. HILL. Was that effected, in your judgment, by the supply and demand, or was it effected by the reciprocity treaty?

Capt. THOMAS. I should judge that it was effected by the quantity—the overproduction.

Mr. HARRISON. You are a native of the Province of Nova Scotia?

Capt. THOMAS. Yes, sir.

Mr. HARRISON. How does the price of fish in the Nova Scotia markets compare with the price of fish in the Boston markets?

Capt. THOMAS. I do not know that I could give you very much of an idea about that. In Nova Scotia they have different ways of weighing the fish. They weigh it by the quintal, 112 pounds, dry, as they call it. I am told that this fall they got as high as $6.25 for 112 pounds.

Mr. HARRISON. How does that compare with the price of fish in the Boston market?

Capt. THOMAS. We almost doubled that this year.

Mr. HARRISON. It is almost twice as expensive here?

Capt. THOMAS. Yes; we get $5.50 for a hundredweight at the port of Boston.

Mr. GARDNER. I want to get that evidence correctly, because it is misstated in its present form. You do not mean that a dry quintal in the Boston market sells for $5.50?

Capt. THOMAS. $5.50 a hundredweight, sir, green.

Mr. GARDNER. What does a dry quintal sell for in Nova Scotia?

Capt. THOMAS. Somewhere around $6—$6.25. I am not positive. That is 112 pounds, dry.

Mr. FORDNEY. You have stated that the lowest price that you could remember was caused by overproduction?

Capt. THOMAS. Yes, sir.

Mr. FORDNEY. Was that overproduction not caused or partly caused by importations from Nova Scotia?

Capt. THOMAS. I could not say positively.

Mr. FORDNEY. You say it was during the time of the treaty with Canada?

Capt. THOMAS. I am not positive. It was in that neighborhood. But I know the lowest we got was $1.50.

Mr. McCALL. Do you remember the year? Can you give the year of that price?

Capt. THOMAS. I think it was somewhere around 1882—somewhere in that neighborhood. I am not positive of that, either.

Mr. GARDNER. I can put on witnesses later who can tell you those things positively—some of the older men.

Capt. THOMAS. Yes, sir. I have not got those things down very well.

Mr. LONGWORTH. In what shape are those fish when they are sold in the Boston market?

Capt. THOMAS. They are what we call market fish. They have to be first class, on ice.

Mr. LONGWORTH. Are they packed?

Capt. THOMAS. They are on ice.

Mr. LONGWORTH. They are not salted?

Capt. THOMAS. They are not salted for the Boston market; no, sir.

Mr. LONGWORTH. Is that the condition of all the codfish in the Boston market?

Capt. THOMAS. Yes, sir.

Mr. LONGWORTH. They are sold packed in ice?

Capt. THOMAS. They are sold packed in ice; yes, sir.

Mr. GARDNER. Is that right?

Capt. THOMAS. That is called "Boston market."

Mr. GARDNER. Of course on the T wharf, they are fresh fish; but there is a good deal of salt fish in Boston.

Capt. THOMAS. I thought he was asking about my fish.

Mr. GARDNER. I think he was asking about the business.

Capt. THOMAS. Some of the fish are brought to Boston in salt.

Mr. HARRISON. What is the price in Boston?

Capt. THOMAS. It goes up and down. It varies.

Mr. HARRISON. Do you know what it is now?

Capt. THOMAS. No, sir.

Mr. HARRISON. It was 5½ cents a pound on Saturday, and 7½ cents a pound on Tuesday of this week. How do those prices compare with the prices that are paid back in the provincial markets?

Capt. THOMAS. I can not say.

Mr. HARRISON. You have been in and out of the provinces all your life?

Capt. THOMAS. But I can not say what the prices are in the fish markets.

Mr. LONGWORTH. Do all of your fish go to the fresh fish markets?

Capt. THOMAS. No, sir; not all. In the summer season we take a salt trip. We have a fresh trip and a salt trip. We have different voyages.

Mr. LONGWORTH. Where do you salt the fish?

Capt. THOMAS. We salt in one part of the vessel and ice in another. That is the reason we have to have such large vessels.

Mr. LONGWORTH. But in the main, your business is the fresh, iced business?

Capt. THOMAS. I have been carrying on the fresh and salt fish business almost all my life.

Mr. HARRISON. Is there any agreement between the fishermen of Gloucester to regulate the distribution of fish along the Atlantic seaboard or to regulate the prices at which they shall be sold?

Capt. THOMAS. No, sir; not that I know of.

Mr. GARDNER. That would be a pretty hard agreement to make.

The CHAIRMAN. A man comes in with a cargo of fish and sells it to the packer for the best price he can get?

Capt. THOMAS. Yes, sir.

The CHAIRMAN. And the packer attends to the rest—including the price.

Capt. THOMAS. Yes, sir.

Mr. BROUSSARD. You said that you operated the vessel on shares.

Capt. THOMAS. Yes, sir.

Mr. BROUSSARD. Explain what you mean by that. What proportion of it goes to the crew?

Capt. THOMAS. That is arranged in different ways. Sometimes it goes on halves. The vessel takes one-half and the crew one-half. Sometimes it goes on fifths. The vessel takes one-fifth and the crew takes four-fifths. I get one-quarter. I take one-quarter and the crew takes three-quarters and pays all expenses.

Mr. BROUSSARD. The crew pays the expenses?

Capt. THOMAS. The crew pays all expenses, and the vessel takes one-quarter. We have to pay the Nova Scotian license and all those things.

Mr. BROUSSARD. Does the crew contribute to the license, too?

Capt. THOMAS. They pay three-quarters of the license.

Mr. BROUSSARD. So that any law that would affect your business as a boat owner would affect the entire crew?

Capt. THOMAS. Yes, sir.

Mr. BROUSSARD. Under the system under which you operate?

Capt. THOMAS. Yes, sir.

Mr. GARDNER. I have here the agreement on quarters, which I will submit to the commmitte. I will leave this printed agreement on quarters with the committee, to show how the thing is done according to proportion. The lay[1] has not been changed for a great many years?

[Fishing Shipping Paper.]

UNITED STATES OF AMERICA.

DISTRICT OF GLOUCESTER.

It is agreed between ———— ————, agent or owner of the schooner ————, qualified by law for carrying on the bank and other fisheries of the United States, and ———— ————, master or skipper of the said schooner, and the fishermen whose

---

[1] The lay indicates the proportional share of the profits of the voyage.

names are to this agreement subscribed, that the said ——— ——— will at —— own expense equip the said schooner ——— with all the necessary tackle and apparel for a fishing voyage or voyages, the provisions, salt, and craft shall be provided and paid for by ——— ———, and that said ——— ———, master or skipper, with the said fishermen, will pursue the cod or other fisheries, in the schooner ———, and will use their best endeavors for the success of the voyage or voyages they may go until this agreement is terminated; and will be ready at all times, and will not leave the said schooner without permission of the master or owner thereof. And it is agreed that in consideration of the share hereinafter mentioned the seamen and fishermen shall do all the labor necessary to the fitting of said vessel for the voyage or voyages, and shall also at the expiration of said voyage and voyages clean up said vessel and stow away her *sails, gear,* and all *tackle* and *apparel,* to the satisfaction of the owner or agent of said vessel. And the cook shall clean up all the dishes and cooking utensils and also the forecastle, to the satisfaction of the owner or agent of said vessel. And it is agreed that the entire product of said voyage or voyages shall be delivered to the owner or agent of said vessel. And that said owner or agent shall sell or dispose of the same, and immediately account to the master, cook, and crew as follows, viz: The price of said product shall be the price ———, and the owner or agent shall adjust, divide, and distribute the proceeds of said voyage or voyages as follows, viz: To the owner or owners of said vessel one half, to the master, cook, and crew the other half in proportion to the quantity or number of fish caught by each, respectively, unless otherwise agreed to as below.

And it is agreed that one-half of the following charges shall be deducted from the master, cook, and crew's shares in proportion to the quantity or number of fish caught by each, respectively, viz: The entire expense of shipping fish home or to a market, commission for selling, barrels and packages, and packing mackerel.

And there shall also be deducted from each share an equal portion of one-half of the entire expense incurred for bait, ice nippers, towing, chronometer hire, license fees paid for commercial privileges in foreign ports and all other foreign port charges, and all commissions and exchange on drafts drawn to pay said charges.

And also an equal portion of the whole of the following charges, viz: Sawing wood, medicine, water, hoisting, scraping and slushing mast, tarring rigging, scrubbing vessel and preparing her for painting, tarring, mending and hanging seines, hire of patent purser, teaming or lightering salt and barrels, and also all condensed milk, canned goods, preserves, and similar luxuries not included in the regular outfit.

And it is also agreed that there shall be deducted from the shares of the master and each of the crew an equal portion of the whole of the cook's wages or extra compensation for cooking, but in no case shall the owner or owners of said vessel be liable to pay such wages or compensation to the cook unless the same shall have been deducted from the shares of the master and crew.

And it is also agreed that an equal portion of all money paid for labor for fitting said vessel for the voyage or voyages, watching and cleaning up said vessel at the expiration of said voyage or voyages, shall be deducted from each of the shares of each of the crew.

And it is also agreed that if, for any cause, the fish are neither counted nor kept separate the master and each of the crew are to share and share alike. And if the fish are caught in dories or with trawls or seines the master is to receive an average share unless otherwise specified and agreed to.

And it is further agreed between the parties that the master or skipper, together with the fishermen, are entitled to all the benefits and privileges and subject to all the duties and penalties provided by the laws of the United States. Said fishermen expressly agree and promise and oblige themselves to do their duty on board said vessel, and to obey all lawful commands of said master or the officers of said vessel whoever they may be, and at all times and places, until this agreement is fully performed.

Time of entry	Men's names.	Quality.	Witness to their signing.	Time for which they engage.

Countersigned.

——— ———, *Agent or Owner.*

[Fishing Shipping Paper.]

UNITED STATES OF AMERICA.

DISTRICT OF GLOUCESTER.

This agreement, made this —— day of ——, 190—, by and between ——
——, the owners of the fishing schooner ——, now lying in the harbor of ——,
of the first part, and the persons whose names are below subscribed intending to gó
as fishermen on said schooner under the command of —— ——, as master, of
the second part, witnesseth as follows:

1. The said parties of the first part hereby charter and let to the said parties of
the second part, in consideration of the agreements herein made by them, the whole
of said vessel, with the sails, rigging, and appurtenances, to be used by them under
their sole control for and during ——, unless this agreement is sooner terminated,
as below provided, in the prosecution of the fishing business.

2. The said parties of the second part hereby agree in consideration of the agreements herein made by the parties of the first part to provide and furnish all necessary
fishing gear, including dories and all outfits and provisions for the prosecution of
said fishing enterprise, including salt, ice, bait, etc., at their own expense—to use
their best efforts during all the time this agreement remains in force for the success
of said fishing enterprise—and to pay said parties of the first part, as compensation
for the use of said vessel, —— of the gross proceeds of the fish which may be
caught on said schooner or in the prosecution of said fishing enterprise during said
time, all expenses of towing, wharfage, and weighing being first deducted from said
gross proceeds.

3. It is expressly agreed that neither the parties of the first part nor said vessel
shall be liable for any debts or liabilities incurred by said parties of the second part
for fishing gear, outfits, provisions, or other expenses in the prosecution of said fishing enterprise, but for all such debts and liabilties said parties of the second part
shall be solely responsible.

4. It is also agreed that each fishing trip made during the continuance of this
agreement shall be settled up and payment made to said parties of the first part of all
sums due to them under this agreement, to the close of said trip, before the vessel
leaves port for another trip.

5. It is also agreed that the parties of the first part may at any time cancel and
terminate this charter party by taking possession of said vessel, and that they may
take possession for that purpose wherever said vessel may be found.

. 6. For the due performance of all their agreements herein expressed the parties
of the second part agree to be jointly and severally liable to the parties of the first
part.

7. It is also agreed that all fish taken during the continuance of this agreement
shall be delivered to and sold by —— —— as agent of both parties thereto, and
that the accounts of each trip shall be settled and adjusted by him as such agent.

8. In case the said vessel shall be employed by the parties of the second part in
towing or assisting vessels in distress, it is agreed that for such use the parties of the
first part shall be paid one-half of all the salvage compensation received or collected
by said parties of the second part.

—— ——, *Agent for Owners.*

Time of entry.	Men's names.	Quality.	Witness to their sign-ing.	Time for which they engage.

Countersigned.

—— ——, *Agent or owner.*

Capt. THOMAS. No, sir; not to my knowledge.

Mr. GARDNER. I will leave this with the committee. It is very
interesting. It will show you how it is done.

The CHAIRMAN. Are there any further questions?

Mr. GARDNER. I think I will call now a working fisherman, a fish skinner, and then I will call the president of the board of trade, and he will be perhaps the most expert witness.

STATEMENT OF MR. FREEMAN BROWN.

Mr. GARDNER. Mr. Brown, you used to be the president of the Fish Skinners' Union when the union was in existence?

Mr. BROWN. Yes, sir.

Mr. GARDNER. And you were the former president of the Gloucester Central Labor Union?

Mr. BROWN. I was at that time; yes, sir. I was president of the Central Labor Union at that time.

Mr. GARDNER. You were the champion fish skinner of Massachusetts, also, on test, were you not?

Mr. BROWN. Yes, sir.

Mr. GARDNER. Fish skinners are the men who prepare the fish for packing, for manufacture, and so on. Will you tell the attitude toward this treaty of the men who skin the fish after they come ashore and prepare them for the market?

Mr. BROWN. Well, gentlemen, I have not the true sentiments of the people as a body; but I can speak for myself, and can tell you what I think it would mean to every man who works in the shop if this treaty were to take effect. I know that if the shop people had been consulted on this question they would certainly have taken action; but there is no organized body in Gloucester to-day of fish skinners. The union has gone out of existence. I came down here to represent the fishermen, and also the wage earners in the shop, where I have earned my livelihood for nearly 35 years.

Mr. GARDNER. You are both a fisherman and a skinner; but your profession is that of a fisherman, is it not?

Mr. BROWN. Yes, sir; I am both.

Mr. GARDNER. What can you tell about the wages and hours in fish-skinning establishments in Nova Scotia as compared to the wages and hours in fish-skinning establishments in Gloucester?

Mr. BROWN. In Gloucester we have wages on a scale. Every man receives the same amount. In Nova Scotia one man working at a bench may be receiving 20 cents for a box of fish, and another fellow alongside of him may receive 15 cents. In Gloucester every man working at the bench receives very fine wages. The work is done on a piecework basis. The smarter a man is the more money he makes. In Nova Scotia, along Cape Shore places where I have been, the wage earner there receives anything. One will be working by the week, and another one will be working by the hour, and probably another will be working by the piece. Of course they do not have any faculties such as we have in Gloucester for that business.

Mr. GARDNER. How much in wages would the average smart man knock out in a week's time up in Nova Scotia, along Cape Shore?

Mr. BROWN. I have been in shops where men were working, at Cape Shore, and I have told them the amount of fish that I have taken the skins off of in one day, and they have said: "If you had been here you would have made a fortune"—and they are receiving about half as much for a box as I was receiving in Gloucester.

Mr. GARDNER. That is, you got twice as much for skinning a box of fish as they did?

Mr. BROWN. Yes, sir.

Mr. GARDNER. How about the hours of labor down there?

Mr. BROWN. There are practically no hours of labor. They work any old time.

Mr. GARDNER. Whereas in Gloucester the hours of labor are what?

Mr. BROWN. In Gloucester nine hours constitutes a day.

Mr. GARDNER. You have no personal knowledge on the question of women fish cleaners in the provinces, have you?

Mr. BROWN. No, sir; I have not.

Mr. GARDNER. Does the committee wish to ask Mr. Brown any questions?

Mr. HILL. Do none of the men work by the day in Gloucester? Is it all piecework?

Mr. BROWN. A few work by the day.

Mr. HILL. There can really be no actual comparison of the difference in wages, can there, between piecework and day's work?

Mr. BROWN. Yes, sir; there is. The smart pieceworker certainly makes more than a man who is hired by the day or week; but the average man probably would compare equally with the day worker.

Mr. HILL. How long have you been working on piecework?

Mr. BROWN. I have been working on piecework——

Mr. HILL. I do not mean you, personally; but how long have skinners been working on piecework?

Mr. BROWN. Always.

Mr. HILL. Always?

Mr. BROWN. Yes, sir.

Mr. RANDELL. You say you were the head of the labor union that was there?

Mr. BROWN. I was.

Mr. RANDELL. How did it come to break up?

Mr. BROWN. We secured satisfactory conditions and prices.

Mr. RANDELL. You dissolved the union because you had won everything you wanted? Was not the union practically broken up by the parties engaged in the manufacturing business there?

Mr. BROWN. No, sir; it was not practically broken up by that. The union went out on a strike, but it gained all it wanted.

Mr. RANDELL. The strike broke the union?

Mr. BROWN. Well, practically so. I could not say just that, either.

Mr. GARDNER. Was not this the way it came about: The union went out on strike, making certain demands, and part of the settlement of that strike was the granting of the demands and the dissolution of the union. Was not that it?

Mr. BROWN. It was something similar to that. The union did not go out of existence until a year after the strike was over. It practically dwindled away.

Mr. RANDELL. It languished for a year, and then died?

Mr. BROWN. Yes, sir.

Mr. GARDNER. The men did not pay their dues after they got what they were after. I think that was it.

Mr. BROWN. Yes; that was it.

Mr. RANDELL. You were a good deal like the man who went out after a lion, and the lion died.

Mr. BROWN. No, sir; we received 15 per cent increase in wages and shorter hours.

Mr. RANDELL. And the laboring men have never had the courage to organize the union since. How long ago was that?

Mr. BROWN. That was six years ago.

Mr. GARDNER. That is not a proper statement of the situation, I take it. The laboring men have all the courage in the world, but when they found they could make a satisfactory arrangement they did not care to go ahead paying dues to the union; but they would form the union to-morrow if there was any attempt to lower wages. Is not that the fact?

Mr. BROWN. Yes, sir.

Mr. HARRISON. Do you work for the "trust" up there?

Mr. BROWN. I have been working for the Gorton-Pew Co.

The CHAIRMAN. I would suggest that we now take a recess until 2 o'clock this afternoon. Without objection, a recess will be taken until 2 o'clock.

(The committee thereupon took a recess until 2 o'clock p. m.)

AFTER RECESS.

(At the expiration of the recess the committee resumed its session.)

The CHAIRMAN. You may proceed, Mr. Gardner, whenever you are ready.

Mr. GARDNER. Mr. Chairman, your committee has received this telegram:

A very strong feeling in favor of the reciprocal agreement with Canada exists among citizens of Gloucester. Neither the board of trade, as an organization, nor the citizens generally have authorized any committee to protest against it. From careful inquiry I am convinced the board of trade would favor it.

CHARLES F. WONSON.

Mr. Wonson is president of a fish company.

As that will go into the record, I want to read this telegram, and have it in the record side by side with the other. It is from the vice president of the Gloucester Board of Trade, the president being present here to-day:

GLOUCESTER, *February 1.*

Of the 174 resident members of the board of trade, 140 have declared themselves as against the proposed trade arrangement. Only 3 are for it; 6 noncommittal. Not time to see the remaining 24 members.

FRED. A. EARCE, *Vice President.*

I have another telegram, from the chairman——

The CHAIRMAN. I suppose you are reading those to show that the people of Gloucester are not an exception to the people of the United States, in that there is always a difference of opinion?

Mr. GARDNER. I am showing that there is always a small minority trying to hold itself out as representing public opinion.

Before I go on with the hearing I should like to introduce Mayor Patch, of Gloucester.

The CHAIRMAN. After all, Mr. Gardner, the facts in the case are the best criterion.

Mr. GARDNER. Certainly.

I wish to simply have Mayor Patch, representing the city of Glouces-ter and its citizens, march up to your desk and present you with the petition signed by himself and every member of the municipal council. I shall not ask him to give any evidence.

Mr. ISAAC PATCH. Mr. Chairman and gentlemen, I have not the petition here, but I understand a copy of it was sent to you.

Mr. McCALL. We have copies of it, and will regard it as having been introduced by Mayor Patch.

Mr. GARDNER. Now I want to call on Mr. Orlando Merchant, of the firm of Orlando Merchant & Co., who has nothing to do with the Gorton-Pew Co., but represents one of the outside concerns. All the outside concerns have agreed to have their case presented by the general manager of the Gorton-Pew Co., which concern Mr. Clark and Mr. Harrison characterized as the "fish trust." Meanwhile, I want to present one particular item of evidence from Mr. Orlando Merchant, and then I will go on with the other gentlemen.

This is Mr. Orlando Merchant, of the firm of Orlando Merchant & Co.

STATEMENT OF MR. ORLANDO MERCHANT.

Mr. GARDNER. Mr. Merchant, in 1907, as I understand it, your firm built two vessels, both called *Clintonia*. One was built in Lunen-berg, Nova Scotia, the other was built in Gloucester, Mass. Those two vessels, as I understand it, were built on precisely the same models, with precisely the same molds, the same spars and the same rig, and were identically sister ships in every respect, even to the extent of having the same name.

I wish you would tell the committee what the *Clintonia*, of Lunen-berg, Nova Scotia, cost when ready for sea, and what the *Clintonia*, of Gloucester, Mass., cost when ready for sea?

Mr. MERCHANT. The *Clintonia*, of Gloucester, Mass., cost ready for sea about $15,500. Of course I did not build the other *Clintonia*; she was built down there. She cost $9,400 ready for sea.

Mr. GARDNER. That is the only piece of evidence I wish to bring out from Mr. Merchant. Thank you, Mr. Merchant.

Gentlemen, as I said to you, there are a number of gentlemen here who represent those firms who have no fishing vessels, but are simply packers. Of course they would like to have their green fish brought in free, provided the duty can be retained on their finished product. With one exception they are all against the treaty. That exception I shall not introduce as one of my witnesses, but I think you ought to hear him.

Now, I am going to introduce to you a representative of the wicked Fish Trust.

Mr. CLARK. Mr. Gardner, if you will permit me, I want to correct you about one thing. Neither Mr. Harrison nor myself ever men-tioned the Fish Trust; and so far as I am concerned I never heard of one until you said something or other about a Fish Trust.

Mr. GARDNER. It is always a well-known form of endeavoring to prejudice public opinion, to speak of the largest concern in any locality as the Fish Trust, or some other form of trust.

Mr. CLARK. That may be.

Mr. GARDNER. Now I am going to introduce Mr. Carroll, who is general manager of the Gorton-Pew Co. and also president of the Gloucester Board of Trade. He is a man that you gentlemen can riddle full of holes, because he is a wicked "trust magnate," on a salary of $5,000 a year. He will come before you and answer almost any questions that can be put, because he is thoroughly familiar with the entire Gloucester business. In one thing he will differ from the captains who have testified before you, like Capt. William H. Thomas. He will testify, if you ask him, that fresh fish might come in free without injuring his business. On the other hand, Capt. William H. Thomas would have testified, if I had asked him the question, that to have fresh fish coming in free would be just as bad for him as salt fish.

Mr. LONGWORTH. Let me ask you a question right there.

Mr. GARDNER. Do you wish me to recall Capt. William H. Thomas?

Mr. LONGWORTH. No; all I want to ask you is this: Is it your contention that under this treaty the price of codfish packed in ice would be less on the Boston market than it is now?

Mr. GARDNER. You mean to say, am I trying to ride both horses, and saying that it would be no cheaper to the consumer, and yet would put the fresh-fish men out of business?

Mr. LONGWORTH. No; I am not asking about the consumer at all. I am asking whether the price of codfish packed in ice on the Boston market would be less if this treaty were passed than it is now?

Mr. GARDNER. The price of codfish varies so much from time to time that it will require averages, which have been prepared by Mr. Carroll, to answer that question. I will answer it now by reading you what the New England Fish Exchange says. That is an exchange at T Wharf in Boston, dealing, I think, exclusively in fresh fish. It says:

At a meeting of the directors of the New England Exchange, held this day, on motion, duly seconded, it was voted:

That the New England Fish Exchange will work with Gloucester in its effort to continue the present duty on fish. We, the undersigned fish dealers of Boston, protest against the free entry of fish into the United States, believing it will seriously affect, if not wholly destroy, the fishing industry of the New England States.

That, coupled with the evidence which I forgot to bring out from the captains this morning, shows that the fresh-fish people are just as much involved in a desire to defeat this treaty as the salt-fish people.

Mr. LONGWORTH. Then, I want to ask why that is?

Mr. GARDNER. Suppose we ask Mr. Carroll.

Mr. LONGWORTH. I am asking for my own information. As I read this trade agreement, the duty in this country on fresh fish packed in ice is three-quarters of a cent a pound.

Mr. GARDNER. Exactly.

Mr. LONGWORTH. And in Canada it is 1 cent a pound.

Mr. GARDNER. Exactly.

Mr. LONGWORTH. Then why would putting it on the free list reduce the price?

Mr. GARDNER. Because the profit is less than three-quarters of a cent a pound.

Mr. LONGWORTH. But Canada has a higher duty by a quarter of a cent.

Mr. GARDNER. But we do not ship any fish of the kind we are discussing into Canada, and their 1-cent duty on fish is about as much protection to them as if we put a thousand cents duty on cotton in this country. In other words, we could not ship into Canada under any circumstances.

Mr. RANDELL. Let me ask you a question, please, for my own information. You say the difference between these two gentlemen is that one would say that as applied to fresh fish this would be all right?

Mr. GARDNER. So far as his business is concerned.

Mr. RANDELL. The other would say differently. The difference is, as I understand it—and I want to be put straight if I am wrong— that this gentleman is a fish packer, and the bringing in of fish——

Mr. GARDNER. No; I beg your pardon. His firm has a fleet of vessels to catch fish, and also packing houses in which to pack them. Do you see?

Mr. RANDELL. One is interested in the packing and the other is not interested in the packing?

Mr. GARDNER. This man is interested in both.

Mr. RANDELL. And the other?

Mr. GARDNER. The other man takes the fish into Boston for the fresh-fish market, as well as into Gloucester for the packing. The fresh-fish business is entirely, or practically entirely, conducted in Boston.

Mr. RANDELL. Is it not to the interest of the fish packer to get the fresh fish as cheaply as he can?

Mr. GARDNER. If the fish packer can get his raw material free and can have a duty on his finished product, undoubtedly it is to his interest, provided the taking off of the duty does not drive the fleet to some other port. But if you admit manufactured fish free, it is obvious (though Col. Wonson does not agree with me) that——

Mr. RANDELL. What I am getting at is this: Would not this, as applied to fresh fish, make fresh fish cheaper to the consumer?

Mr. GARDNER. I realize that you are trying to make me ride both horses.

Mr. RANDELL. No, indeed; I am simply inquiring of you in the interest of the man who eats; that is all.

Mr. GARDNER. You are inquiring in the interest of the retailer?

Mr. RANDELL. No; in the interest of the man who eats.

Mr. GARDNER. The retailer will reap that intermediate profit. Without question the retailer can make more money under this plan. I will admit that.

Mr. RANDELL. The consumer will get more fish, will he not, for his money?

Mr. GARDNER. I do not believe the consumer will ever get the difference.

Mr. RANDELL. It is not a question of whether he gets the difference; the question is whether he gets more fish for the same money.

Mr. GARDNER. Just wait a moment. We have some figures here on that point, although it is a little digression.

Mr. RANDELL. I do not want to argue with you about it. I simply ask you the question.

Mr. GARDNER. I have a telegram here from a man who has calculated the consumer's interest, the secretary of the board of trade.

Mr. McCALL. Let us hear from Mr. Carroll, Mr. Gardner, and put that in afterwards.

Mr. GARDNER. This will only take a moment. I have to ask Mr. Carroll some questions, and it will only take a second to find that. Here it is :

We have figured that if the American public will consume 72,000,000 pounds of boneless codfish a year, the reduction in the cost of living by the wiping out of the duty, and the destruction of the fishing industry, will be an average of 1 cent a year saving to each inhabitant.

[STATEMENT OF MR. THOMAS J. CARROLL.

Mr. GARDNER. Mr. Carroll, you are general manager of the Gorton-Pew Co.?

Mr. CARROLL. Yes, sir.

Mr. GARDNER. And you are president of the board of trade?

Mr. CARROLL. Yes, sir.

Mr. GARDNER. Mr. Carroll, you have known all about the fish business in Boston since your boyhood?

Mr. CARROLL. Yes, sir.

Mr. GARDNER. And your father before you?

Mr. CARROLL. Yes, sir.

Mr. GARDNER. Was your father a fisherman?

Mr. CARROLL. Yes.

Mr. GARDNER. How did he meet his death?

Mr. CARROLL. He was drowned on Georges.

Mr. GARDNER. Fishing?

Mr. CARROLL. When I was a baby; yes, sir.

Mr. GARDNER. How did your brother meet his death?

Mr. CARROLL. The same way.

Mr. GARDNER. He was drowned on Georges?

Mr. CARROLL. Yes, sir.

Mr. GARDNER. At what point in your history does your knowledge of fishing begin? At what age did you go to work?

Mr. CARROLL. When I came out of school I was 11 years of age, and I went to work on a fish wharf in Gloucester. That was the time when my brother was drowned, and we had no one else to support the family, and I had to come out and do what I could.

Mr. GARDNER. And you have been all this time in Gloucester?

Mr. CARROLL. Ever since; yes, sir.

Mr. GARDNER. You are one of the most successful men in Gloucester?

Mr. CARROLL. Well——

Mr. GARDNER. You are held to be—one of the ablest men. What salary are you getting now?

Mr. CARROLL. Five thousand dollars a year.

Mr. GARDNER. And that after an entire lifetime spent in the business. You are the man who is brought forward by the men who are your competitors, the independents, and the wicked "fish trust," to present this matter?

Mr. CARROLL. Yes, sir.

Mr. GARDNER. Mr. Carroll, I want you to tell this committee as to the profits in the fishing business.

Mr. CARROLL. May I say just one word myself?

Mr. GARDNER. Yes. I should like to have Mr. Carroll make his own statement before I ask him any questions.

Mr. CARROLL. I wanted to correct a wrong impression. I wish to say to the committee that I stand squarely with Capt. William Thomas in everything he said, absolutely. What I told Mr. Gardner was this: That the introduction of fresh fish into this country would do me personally very little harm. But I do say that it will do the industry as a whole lots of harm; and for that reason I am against it, absolutely.

Mr. LONGWORTH. Will you please explain that to me? I do not understand that?

Mr. CARROLL. As best I can, Mr. Longworth. (Pardon me for calling you by name.) It means that the T wharf fresh-fish industry will be thrown open to the Canadian vessels, with their cheaper labor, cheaper cost of production, and lower standard of living. Neither Capt. Thomas nor any other man who goes out of Gloucester can compete with them. They are going to come in, and they are going to bring in more fish—there is no question about it—when the duty is taken off. They are going to come to our markets. We can not go to theirs under any consideration, duty or no duty. That is going to mean that under certain conditions, when there is what we call a "glut" of fish—that is, a big catch in one day—the price will go down. Fresh fish, being a perishable article, sells in accordance with the supply more than the demand. Of course the demand comes in, too, but there will be so many more fish that the price paid to men like Mr. Thomas is going down. You understand, gentlemen, that if it goes down a quarter or a half cent a pound, it is a serious matter to this man, because he might have in a week's catch 100,000 pounds. Let us say it goes down to him half a cent a pound. That cuts down the earnings of his vessel, his percentage, and his share of the profits of the voyage.

The CHAIRMAN. The duty is a quarter of a cent?

Mr. GARDNER. Three-quarters of a cent a pound.

The CHAIRMAN. Three-quarters of a cent a pound?

Mr. CARROLL. Three-quarters of a cent a pound now. But as I look at it, regardless of what the duty is now, the fact that it will be on the free list, and the additional number of pounds of fish coming in are going to put it down a certain amount. That is the idea. There is duty enough now to keep them out. If you take it off, they come in, and down goes the price.

Mr. LONGWORTH. You say that the market is now protected against Canadian fishermen?

Mr. CARROLL. Yes, sir.

Mr. LONGWORTH. By three-quarters of a cent a pound duty?

Mr. CARROLL. Yes, sir.

Mr. LONGWORTH. And you say they would try to get possession of the Boston market?

Mr. CARROLL. Yes, sir; they will come in with our fishermen.

Mr. LONGWORTH. You say, also, that our fishermen will never attempt to capture the Canadian market?

Mr. CARROLL. Oh, no, no; absolutely not.

Mr. LONGWORTH. Why not?

Mr. CARROLL. Because ours is the big market, and theirs is the small market. Ours is a market, we will say, of 90,000,000 people; and theirs is a market of eight or nine million people. They can produce more than their market can take. They are nearer the fishing grounds, and they can run right in home and land their fish.

Under no circumstances would our men ever go in to compete for their market.

Mr. LONGWORTH. How big is the Canadian fishing fleet as compared with ours?

Mr. CARROLL. The Canadian fishing fleet is not as large when you come to take into consideration the big vessels. I can not give the statistics, gentlemen, because I left all of that with Mr. Miller. But the Lunenburg fleet—the "bankers," so called—is quite large. It is composed of something over 100 vessels, I think. They are all what they call 99-ton vessels; that is to say, about 100 tons.

Mr. McCALL. Do the Canadians have any surplus of fresh fish to dump on our market when they happen to make a big catch?

Mr. CARROLL. Fresh fish? No, sir; because they do not follow the fresh-fish industry very much. But I contend that they will when they take the duty off, because to-day the duty on fresh fish is a great deal higher than it is on salt fish, in this respect: It is the same actual duty, three-quarters of a cent a pound, but the salt fish have shrunk. In other words, a thousand pounds of fresh fish, as caught, would be practically 500 pounds of the salted fish. So, you see, there is a saving for the Canadian. He goes and salts his fish. If he did not, he would be paying on the same basis, we will say, a cent and a half duty on the fresh fish. Do you catch the point I wish to make?

Mr. McCALL. I do. It seems to me, then, that the Canadian could not afford to bring in fresh fish, even if we took off the three-quarters of a cent a pound duty, because what you have said just now shows that he could manufacture that fish into salt fish and practically save a cent and a half a pound.

Mr. CARROLL. No; pardon me. There are times when the fresh-fish market is high. The fresh-fish market varies from day to day. It is up to-day and perhaps down to-morrow. The salt-fish market is more steady. Sometimes Capt. Thomas will come in and get $4 a hundred for his haddock; sometimes more. At other times he might come in and get a dollar a hundred, according to the catch. There is no stated price for fresh fish. They have to take what is given to them on T wharf by the dealers; and they have got to sell them or else take them back home or come down and sell them to us in Gloucester, to be split and salted.

The great danger of taking off the duty on fresh fish is something that has not been brought out at all. What we fear down in Gloucester on that point is that they will get a fleet of beam trawlers from the other side of the water—from England. That is a new way of fishing. There are a lot of beam trawlers over in England that can be brought into Canada cheaply, and operated from there, and take possession of the T-Wharf market, because they bring in lots of fish. They do not need any bait at all. They will come in and take this market. We can not do that, because we would have to go over and pay an enormous duty—I do not know just what, but I think about 30 per cent ad valorem—on those same vessels.

Mr. LONGWORTH. I see that the figures we have here show that of fresh fish of all kinds we exported into Canada last year more than 13,000,000 pounds.

Mr. CARROLL. I think a great deal of that was up on the lakes.

Mr. LONGWORTH. That is what I want to ask you. How much of that is cod?

Mr. CARROLL. Very, very little. I should say less than 1 per cent; a great deal less than that.

Mr. LONGWORTH. That includes fresh-water fish?

Mr. CARROLL. Yes, sir. Of the deep-sea fish, nothing goes into Canada.

Mr. LONGWORTH. You say there is practically nothing of that exported into Canada?

Mr. CARROLL. Practically nothing.

Mr. HARRISON. Does that include shellfish of all kinds?

Mr. LONGWORTH. No. It includes fresh-water fish, mackerel, halibut, salmon, eels, smelts, and all other fish.

Mr. GARDNER. Oysters?

Mr. LONGWORTH. Not according to this list.

Mr. CARROLL. If you will let me make another statement, gentlemen, I should like to explain the situation here. There seems to be a little difference of opinion as to the conditions in Gloucester—not only in Gloucester, but in the whole New England fisheries. We have them all back of us. This is not a Gloucester measure by any means, gentlemen. Mr. Gardner has told you about the Providence Board of Trade and the New England Fish Exchange, who are the real fish dealers in Gloucester. You will be told by-and-by that the Boston Fish Bureau has voted against us. The Boston Fish Bureau are not fish dealers.

Mr. GARDNER. "Of Boston," you mean. You said "Gloucester."

Mr. CARROLL. The Boston Fish Bureau, I say, are not fish dealers.

Mr. GARDNER. But you said, "the New England Fish Exchange, of Gloucester."

Mr. CARROLL. Of Boston; yes. They are the two that you read. In addition to that, we have the whole State of Maine, with one exception. We have Capt. Nicholson, of Bucksport, here—the largest dealer in the State of Maine—who will tell you the same thing. We have got Vinalhaven—we have got every dealer there is.

What I want to say is that there are four distinct propositions here in the way of people interested in fish.

First, there are the fishermen, represented by these captains. These men are unalterably opposed to a reduction in the duty on any kind of fish at all, because the raw material of these other gentlemen who want free fish is their finished product, and they can not compete with Canadians on account of the high cost of their vessels, such as has been shown you.

Then there come the men on shore—what we call the packers, fish-cleaners, and all—as stated by Mr. Brown. I think they are divided on this question, though not at all on the main question. I think they are unanimously against the treaty; but they are divided, because they think that if they could get free green fish in here, and a duty on the manufactured product, Canada would send her fish in here to be manufactured down in our town of Gloucester. That is where they stand.

Then there comes another class, some of whom are represented here to-day by what we call shippers. That is, they are manufacturers who do not own vessels. They are not interested, of course, in the price of fish to the fisherman, except to buy it at a reasonable price. They are all honorable gentlemen, good friends of mine. They differ with me in this respect; but they are entitled to their opinion.

Then comes the vessel owners, of whom I am a representative. I have telegrams here from every vessel owner in the city of Gloucester, every man who owns one vessel or a dozen, or a part of a vessel, saying: "Save me from this?" Some of the most pathetic telegrams I ever saw, gentlemen, are right there—they came to me yesterday—from men who realize that it means their destruction.

We are against the reduction of the duty on any part of the industry because we are interested in the whole of it. I hope I have made that point clear. The vessel owners are unanimously against the the treaty in any form. The shippers would like to have free green fish, but a duty on their manufactured product. The fishermen are opposed to any change, because their finished product is the other man's raw material.

Mr. HARRISON. Do any of the vessels in which you are interested engage in bringing herring to the market?

Mr. CARROLL. Yes, sir.

Mr. HARRISON. Do they catch them or buy them?

Mr. CARROLL. They go down there, as Mr. Gardner explained this morning, with crews from Gloucester. Under the treaty of 1818 they have the right to employ Newfoundlanders to assist them in securing the fish. The rate of wage that they have to pay is regulated by the Government, which says that it must not be less than $1.25 per barrel. There is an industry, gentlemen, of which there will be nothing left.

Mr. HARRISON. Do I understand that they catch herring or buy them?

Mr. CARROLL. They go down there with a crew from Gloucester, and they have the right to ship Newfoundlanders as their crew. They sign articles, and they become members of the crew. That is authorized by the United States Government, and by the Newfoundland Government as well. Instead of taking these men, say, at the rate of $25 or $30 a month, their compensation is $1.25 a barrel and their food. They keep them on board the vessel while the vessel is there.

Mr. HARRISON. I suppose I fail to understand you. I ask you whether they catch herring or whether they buy them and then bring them back here?

Mr. CARROLL. I will try to explain that again, sir. They go down there all fitted out with nets for catching herring. It takes a large crew to catch a cargo of herring with nets. All the crew that they take from Gloucester is crew enough to work the vessel—to manage the vessel. Down there they ship a crew of Newfoundlanders on their articles; and they ship them in this way—that they will bring herring to that vessel on which they are shipped as crew, and their compensation is to be $1.25 per barrel. Now, you can call it buying or hiring, whichever it is.

Mr. McCALL. That is, they hire them to catch the fish?

Mr. CARROLL. Yes, sir.

Mr. McCALL. Paying them certain wages.

Mr. GARDNER. The transaction is a perfectly clear one. It has been the subject of international dispute for years. It is perfectly obvious that if you need a crew of 50 men to set a lot of nets all over the mouths of arms of the bay, you can not support 50 men on board of your ship and take them from Gloucester to the banks and keep them there until the fishing is good. You have got to go down with a small crew; and then, when the fishing is good, you employ a large number of men to set out those nets for you. The thing has been gone over a thousand times, and it has been decided by the United States Government and confirmed by the International Tribunal at The Hague. It is perfectly clear. It is the catch of Gloucester fisheries. You can not look into the question of the credentials and the nativity and the naturalization papers of each man of your crew.

Mr. CARROLL. I made a statement a moment ago which I should like to back up, if I can. I said a minute ago that the industry would be wiped out; and I will tell you why. If these Canadian vessels have the right to go to Newfoundland, and get herring and bring them in free of duty, as we feel they will under this treaty, they can go down there and beat us to death.

For instance, we chartered a Nova Scotia vessel to bring some fish up for us awhile ago; and we paid $475 a month for the vessel, crew, provisions, and all. On one of our own vessels, under the same conditions, the cost of the labor alone would be a trifle over $400, according to the statement made by Capt. Peoples this morning, which is absolutely true. How long can we do that?

Again, that is a very important industry, because we have a large class of men who do not do as Capt. Thomas does—go the year round. They fish in the summer. There is nothing doing in their line in the winter except to go to Newfoundland for herring. And in the case of a good, smart man like Capt. Peoples, who gets $100 to $125 a month, it is up to him to go down to Lunenburg and get $50 or $60 a month, or walk the streets at Gloucester.

Mr. HILL. You represent the firm of Gorton-Pew & Co.?

Mr. CARROLL. The Gorton-Pew Fish Co.; yes, sir.

Mr. HILL. What is your total output? You need not state it exactly; just in round figures.

Mr. CARROLL. We do about a three-million-dollar business. I can not tell you the number of pounds.

Mr. HILL. How much of that is American fish? Do you import any?

Mr. CARROLL. This year we imported a lot; but in a normal year——

Mr. HILL. About how much have you imported this year?

Mr. CARROLL. We imported about 2,000,000 pounds of fish this year.

Mr. HILL. Was that fresh or salted?

Mr. CARROLL. Salted.

Mr. HILL. Salted?

Mr. CARROLL. Yes, sir.

Mr. HILL. Salted in Canada?

Mr. CARROLL. Yes, sir; in Newfoundland.

Mr. GARDNER. That was herring, was it not?

Mr. CARROLL. No; codfish.

Mr. HILL. Will you tell me why Canada charges a higher rate of duty on fish imported into Canada than the United States charges on the same fish imported into the United States?

Mr. CARROLL. No, sir; I can not answer that question. I have often wondered why it was.

Mr. HILL. Do you not suppose it is to protect them against American fishermen?

Mr. CARROLL. It would appear so on the face of it; but I have often wondered why it was.

Mr. HILL. Why should they do it? Why should there be a higher duty—a cent a pound?

Mr. LONGWORTH. A quarter of a cent.

Mr. HILL. It is three-quarters of a cent higher.

Mr. CARROLL. I could not tell you, sir.

Mr. HILL. They know their business up there, do they not, about as well as we know ours?

Mr. CARROLL. I do not doubt that.

Mr. GARDNER. May I interrupt you and answer that question?

Mr. HILL. I shall be glad to have anybody answer it.

Mr. GARDNER. It has always been supposed that they did it in order to give them a basis for trading on in a reciprocal agreement.

Mr. HILL. But their regular duty is a cent a pound on fish imported into Canada; and our regular duty, which these people say they are satisfied with, is three-quarters of a cent. Why is the difference?

Mr. CARROLL. I can not answer you that, except in this way: If our claim is right that we can not compete with them in our own country, we certainly can not go up into Canada and compete with them in theirs.

Mr. LONGWORTH. I understood you to say that even if Canada had free fish, we would not have a market there.

Mr. CARROLL. We could have their market if we could get it; but if we can not compete with Canada in our own country, how can we compete with them up in their country?

Mr. LONGWORTH. I understood you to say that the Canadian market was so trifling in comparison with ours that if they took off their duty, if Canada had free fish, we would not attempt to take their market away?

Mr. CARROLL. We might do a little salt fish business, perhaps, up in the Canadian Northwest.

Mr. LONGWORTH. I am only speaking of fresh fish.

Mr. CARROLL. I do not believe we would do any even then. Perhaps up along Montreal we might do a little. I do not doubt that there might be a little done there.

Mr. HILL. May I ask you one more question, Mr. Carroll?

Mr. CARROLL. Yes, sir.

Mr. HILL. With the Canadian duty at a cent a pound, and our duty at three-quarters of a cent a pound, would it make any difference whatever with the trade relations of the two countries if we took off three-quarters of a cent, or the whole of ours, and they took off three-quarters of a cent from theirs, and left the same difference?

Mr. CARROLL. We would then be in just the same position we are in now.

Mr. HILL. Exactly. Then if we made fish free and Canada reduced her duty to a quarter of a cent a pound, we would both be in the same position that we are now?

Mr. CARROLL. When I say we would be in the same position we are now, I mean to say that we would be in the same position we will be if this treaty is passed in its present form. That is what I mean to say.

Mr. GARDNER. It does not make any difference to you what the duty on fish is in Canada—you can not ship fish into Canada anyway?

Mr. CARROLL. Not at all.

Mr. HILL. Do you not export any of your finished product to Canada?

Mr. CARROLL. No, sir. In all my time I never remember sending over 25 boxes of fish into Canada. They were little bundles of what we call smoked bloaters that we sent up into Montreal.

Mr. FORDNEY. If you could tell why Canada has a higher rate of duty on fish than we have you would be competent to tell why Russia and Germany have a higher rate of duty on goods going into those countries than we have here; would you not?

Mr. CARROLL. I think so, sir.

• Mr. FORDNEY. That is an impossibility.

Mr. GARDNER. Anyone who has read the Canadian agreement with France will see that the Canadian tariff is exceedingly ingeniously devised for the express purpose of making concessions.

Mr. HILL. I should like to ask you another question, Mr. Carroll: You say that in case fish came into this country free, you would expect that British trawlers now operating in the English Channel would come over here and engage in the fisheries?

Mr. CARROLL. Yes, sir.

Mr. HILL. Why do they not come now?

Mr. CARROLL. Because of the duty—three-quarters of a cent a pound. That keeps them out. That is a big amount, gentlemen.

Mr. HILL. But on the same basis they would get a price to correspond, would they not?

Mr. CARROLL. No.

Mr. HILL. Do they not now get a price to correspond?

Mr. CARROLL. Here is what I say, gentlemen: There is a fleet of beam trawlers over in Grimsby, England, lying idle—lots of them—that could be bought by Canadian fish dealers and operated along the Banks, and come into Boston free of duty. Their fish could come in free of duty. You ask why they do not come in now: The reason is that there is a duty of three-quarters of a cent a pound, which is a tremendous profit in our business.

Mr. HILL. If the duty of three-quarters of a cent a pound were added now, they would get three-quarters of a cent a pound more for their fish, would they not?

Mr. CARROLL. No, sir. They will not get any more. In fact, they will not get any more whether there is a duty or not. They might get a little more, but the three-quarters of a cent would not be the basis. They have got to deduct that three-quarters of a cent a pound from whatever they get for their fish; and what they get will depend on how many fish there are at T Wharf in Boston the day they land there.

Mr. HILL. As a matter of fact, is not the price of fresh fish, iced fish, in the Boston market, absolutely controlled by supply and demand, without any reference to the tariff?

Mr. CARROLL. I should say yes, sir—not without reference to the tariff, but it is controlled by the law of supply and demand.

Mr. FORDNEY. Then, if you get an overproduction of fish from Canada, of, course the price goes down?

Mr. CARROLL. That is it.

Mr. FORDNEY. That is as plain as A, B, C to the man who could not hear.

Mr. GARDNER. The gentleman from Connecticut was asking why they can not come in and pay their three-quarters of a cent a pound. It is very obvious that they can not pay three-quarters of a cent a pound duty and still have a profit, if on our vessels the profit is less than three-quarters of a cent a pound.

Now, Mr. Carroll, I should like to ask you what the average profit was during the last year—which, mind you, gentlemen, is one of the best we have ever had in our history. What was the average profit per pound on codfish brought into the United States?

Mr. LONGWORTH. You should ask him first what the average price was during the last year. He said it went as high as $5.50. I want to know what the average price was.

Mr. CARROLL. The average price? They started in, in the spring, at three dollars and a quarter, as I remember, and they stayed along there until away into the fall, when, on account of bad weather on the Banks—and these captains know that in the month of October they only had three fishing days—the supply fell off, so that the price went up accordingly.

Now, gentlemen, I am going to make another statement to you.

Mr. LONGWORTH. That is, $3.25 per hundred pounds?

Mr. CARROLL. Yes, sir.

In a year like last year free fish would not have done us one bit of harm. I am speaking now of 1910, not 1909, the year Mr. Gardner spoke about, because in that year on account of bad weather there was a shortage in the catch. But in 1909, when we had more codfish than we have had for many, many years, free fish would have demoralized us so that our vessels would not have come out anywhere near whole.

I have a statement here, which is absolutely true, that I should like to refer to in reply to Mr. Gardner's question. In 1909 (a banner year for us in the catch of fish) our own vessels landed about 27,000,000 pounds of fish. Their net earnings were $33,578. If they had sold that catch at a quarter of a cent a pound less they would have lost $2,964. That is to say, our profits on our vessels were less than a quarter of a cent a pound in that year.

Mr. ELLIS. And what was your aggregate profit?

Mr. CARROLL. $33,578. When I say "27,000,000 pounds of fish," I mean codfish. There is a lot more herring than that, which I included in the whole——

Mr. LONGWORTH. Is that fresh fish?

Mr. CARROLL. That is salt fish.

Mr. LONGWORTH. It is all salt fish?

Mr. CARROLL. That is fish, some of which we took in fresh and salted, as Capt. Thomas explained this morning. He goes out and brings in some fish fresh, and some salted. If the market is good for fresh fish, he lands them in Boston. If it is not good, we get them to salt.

Mr. FORDNEY. My friend, may I ask you another question?

Mr. CARROLL. Yes, sir.

Mr. FORDNEY. When your profit was but $33,000 in the whole year, or less than a quarter of a cent a pound, if the Canadian catch had been in proportion to your catch, and there had been no duty upon that fish, they would have driven you out of the market; would they not?

Mr. CARROLL. Yes, sir; absolutely.

Mr. FORDNEY. You simply would have had to go out of business?

Mr. CARROLL. Yes, sir.

Mr. FORDNEY. And Canada would have supplied us with fish during the time when the catch was very plentiful?

Mr. CARROLL. That is true, sir. That is absolutely true.

Mr. McCALL. Do you say, Mr. Carroll, that that was one of your best years?

Mr. CARROLL. Yes, sir; in the number of pounds of fish landed.

Mr. GARDNER. Which year?

Mr. CARROLL. 1909.

Mr. McCALL. And how was it as to price?

Mr. CARROLL. The price averaged about three to three and a quarter dollars a hundred pounds for salt fish—salt codfish.

Mr. McCALL. Was that price abnormally high or low?

Mr. CARROLL. That was a good price for the quantity, but it was abnormally low. It was lower than it had been for—well, the year before it was only a trifle higher than that; but a few years back it went a little higher—half a cent, perhaps, or three-quarters of a cent a pound higher.

Mr. McCALL. Was the price that year unusually low?

Mr. CARROLL. Compared with the year before my recollection is that it was about the same; perhaps an eighth, as we call it, less. But it was lower than the average years; yes, sir.

Mr. GARDNER. How much did that figure out a pound—three and a half a quintal?

Mr. CARROLL. I was giving it by the pound.

Mr. GARDNER. Three cents and a half?

Mr. CARROLL. Three to three and a quarter cents; yes.

Mr. GARDNER. What would the retailer charge for that?

Mr. CARROLL. It depends upon what style it is put up in. There are a great many styles. We have what we call the absolutely boneless fish, in which——

Mr. GARDNER. How about the cheapest?

Mr. CARROLL. The cheapest codfish?

Mr. GARDNER. The cheapest retailer. What did he charge?

Mr. CARROLL. Per pound? About 10 cents.

Mr. GARDNER. And what did the most expensive one charge?

Mr. CARROLL. Fifteen cents. No; there are some that are a little higher; but for that grade of fish that I was speaking about, 15 cents.

Mr. CLARK. How much fish does it take to make a pound of this boneless stuff?

Mr. CARROLL. Twelve hundred pounds of fresh fish, caught right out of the water, makes 311 pounds of boneless fish, put up salt

Mr. CLARK. You get from $3 to $3.25 for the fresh fish?

Mr. CARROLL. No, sir; salted fish. I thought you asked me how much it would shrink.

Mr. CLARK. No. What I want to find out is, if a pound of bone-less fish sells for 10 cents how much raw material in volume do they put into that pound?

Mr. CARROLL. I would have to think that over for a minute. What do you mean by "raw material"?

Mr. GARDNER. May I interrupt for a moment?

Mr. CLARK. Yes, sir. I will be obliged to you if you will tell me that.

Mr. GARDNER. In the first place, when the fresh fish comes in it is full of water. Very often that is sold as it is; the whole fish is sold, dried, and salted by the retailer. In the case of the specialty which he puts up, the heads are cut off and all sorts of things are cut off that fish and the scrapings are used for an inferior quality and the bones are extracted. The real comparison which you wish to get at, and which I was trying to get at, was between a fish that comes in fresh and the same fish without any special fancy packing that is sold simply as a whole fish. You are undoubtedly familiar with what it looks like in the grocery shop. That is the real basis of comparison. Then, by taking the difference in weight and the loss in water you get at the true basis of comparison.

Mr. CLARK. Now, just finish that up; go on. You bring that fresh fish in there full of water, as you say, and you fix it up and sell it whole in the store. How much difference is there between what it costs originally and the sum that this fellow gets for it who sells it at retail?

Mr. GARDNER. I should say it was about twice as much.

Mr. CLARK. How much will it shrink?

Mr. GARDNER. I may be wrong. I do not put the shrinkage at 2 to 1, as he does. I think the Canadian measurements are 157, as against 112, are they not?

Mr. CARROLL. Yes. But you are on a different tack entirely. You said "fresh fish." I never said salt fish was in the proportion of 2 to 1. I only want to know what he wishes me to answer.

Mr. CLARK. What I want to find out is, what is the profit that the groceryman or retailer makes off of these fish?

Mr. CARROLL. I can answer that right off the reel.

Mr. CLARK. How much is it?

Mr. CARROLL. Twenty per cent; from 20 to 25 per cent.

Mr. CLARK. That is not an exorbitant profit, is it?

Mr. CARROLL. A package that retails for 15 cents sells to the retail grocer for 12, and the jobber gets 10 per cent off of that. There is the way it stands. There may be some retailer who will buy cheaper fish and get the price of the good fish; but I am talking about our best standard package, which we sell for 12 cents a pound to the jobber, less 10 per cent, which is his profit. The retailer gets 15 cents for that.

Mr. CLARK. The wholesaler and the jobber and the retailer among them get 20 per cent, do they?

Mr. CARROLL. No; they get more. They get 20 and 10.

Mr. CLARK. Thirty?

Mr. CARROLL. Well, you can call it "thirty," if you wish.

Mr. CLARK. There are three of them to divide it among, are there not?

Mr. CARROLL. No, sir; no, sir; only two. The jobber gets his 10 per cent and the retailer gets 20. There are only two.

Mr. CLARK. The way you left it a while ago it sounded as though the retailer and the wholesaler between them got about 300 per cent profit.

Mr. CARROLL. I noticed that, but I did not mean to say that. I was talking about salt fish and he thought I was talking of fresh fish.

Mr. GARDNER. Now, let me ask the questions in my own way.

Mr. CLARK. All right. You know more about it than I do.

Mr. GARDNER. I want to get at the facts.

Mr. RANDELL. Right at that point there is one thing that I should like to have explained. You say the jobber pays 12 cents for that 15-cent package and he gets 10 per cent of that, and the other 3 cents out of the 15 cents goes to the retailer?

Mr. CARROLL. Yes, sir.

Mr. RANDELL. You say he sells it for 15 cents. Do all of them sell it for 15 cents?

Mr. CARROLL. Yes, sir.

Mr. RANDELL. Do not some of them sell it for 16 and some of them for 14?

Mr. CARROLL. As a rule, they sell it for 15.

Mr. RANDELL. Do they have to sell it for 15 cents?

Mr. CARROLL. They do not have to; no, sir.

Mr. CLARK. They have a "gentlemen's agreement" that they will do it?

Mr. CARROLL. I do not think there is any "gentlemen's agreement" among retail grocers.

Mr. CLARK. I will state, just for your information, that it is claimed here in Washington that one of the worst trusts in America is this very same, identical Retail Grocers' Association. That is what the people of this town have been claiming for 12 months; and I should like to find out about it, if you know.

Mr. CARROLL. I do not know about it, sir.

Mr. CLARK. How do they happen to sell this package for 15 cents?

Mr. CARROLL. They do not, necessarily.

Mr. CLARK. I thought you said they did.

Mr. CARROLL. A great many manufacturers have a list price—a selling price. We have a selling price, according to which we think a man ought to get 15 cents for that package; but he does not have to get 15 cents. If he can get 20, he can, as far as we are concerned, or he can sell it for 12, and we have no right to say one word to him.

Mr. CLARK. You have not gotten as far along as the Tobacco Trust have, then?

Mr. CARROLL. No, sir.

Mr. GARDNER. In my experience, the most cutthroat business in the world——

Mr. BOUTELL. What does Capt. Thomas get for the fish that sells finally to me for 15 cents a pound?

Mr. CARROLL. If he brought it in salted last year?

Mr. BOUTELL. No; if he brings it in fresh.

Mr. CARROLL. And sends it to us to split and salt it? That is the way it would come about.

Mr. BOUTELL. I do not care how it comes about, or what happens. I pay 15 cents for a pound of salt fish.   What does Capt. Thomas get for that salt fish?

Mr. CARROLL. In an average year about 2 cents a pound, fresh.

Mr. GARDNER. The gentleman will understand that if people bring fresh fish into the Boston market, that is, for consumption, fresh.   If it is that kind of fish which is half way between fresh and something that is not fresh, it probably will not have any sale as fresh fish in the Boston market.   Let me ask the gentleman a question here, in a way that I think will clear up the situation.

When a cargo of salt fish comes in, the fish is already split?

Mr. CARROLL. Yes, sir; split and salted.

Mr. GARDNER. It is split and salted and the entrails are taken out?

Mr. CARROLL. Yes, sir.

Mr. GARDNER. Is the head taken off?

Mr. CARROLL. Yes, sir.

Mr. GARDNER. And the fish is in the same shape as we see it on the flakes to dry, later, after it has been in pickle?

Mr. CARROLL. Exactly the same shape.

Mr. GARDNER. All right.   We will leave out the manufacturing of the boneless fish.   But that same fish, after it has been dried on the flakes, and after it has been pickled, is sold throughout this country without any special manufacture, is it not?

Mr. CARROLL. Yes, sir.   That is the whole fish.

Mr. GARDNER. In other words, you have exactly the same article that came in, except that it has been pickled and prepared for the market?

Mr. CARROLL. And dried.

Mr. GARDNER. What price is paid for that salted fish as it comes in off the vessel

Mr. CARROLL. That is what I said a minute ago.   Last year it averaged from 3 to 3¼ cents a pound.   That was in 1909.

Mr. GARDNER. All right.   Now we will take that very same fish that is not boneless and not subjected to any manufacturing process at all, but is in its original shape, after being pickled and cured and dried in the sun and steamed in the pile and put in the loft there, or whatever it is.   At what price does the retailer sell that identical fish?

Mr. CARROLL. That is a good question.   There is no standard price on that at all.   That is nobody's brand.   That is just the whole fish, like they used to have it years ago.

Mr. GARDNER. Just as they sell apples?

Mr. CARROLL. Yes, sir.   An average price on that would be 10 cents a pound.

Mr. GARDNER. That is what you want to get at.

Mr. CLARK. How is it that Brother Boutell, here, pays 15 cents a pound for his fish?

Mr. GARDNER. But he does not buy that kind of fish.   He buys a package of boneless codfish which has gone through a process of manufacture.

Mr. CARROLL. Yes, sir.

Mr. LONGWORTH. Just like wool tops, for instance.

Mr. CLARK. I know; but he says he buys ordinary salt fish, and pays 15 cents a pound for it.

Mr. GARDNER. That is because he is a Member of Congress, and they always overcharge us; that is all.

Mr. LONGWORTH. He is the original "ultimate consumer," you know. [Laughter.]

Mr. CLARK. But surely he could tell whether it is boneless fish or not.

Mr. GARDNER. You said "package fish," did you not?

Mr. CARROLL. Have you gentlemen got clearly in your minds the process of the thing? I ask that because I want to have it perfectly clear.

Mr. CLARK. We have got the process plainly enough, but I have not got the profit plainly.

Mr. BOUTELL. It looks to me as though Capt. Thomas did not get his fair share of this.

Mr. HILL. I can see a reason why he does not; and I am going to ask a question about it in a moment.

Mr. GARDNER. He brings in fresh fish, salt fish, and fish that are in between the two. Here is a man who can tell you the price of a "critter" which looks like this (exhibiting sketch to committee). It looks like an inverted triangle when it comes in. It is without a head; it has no insides; the only waste on it, I think, is the tail, is it not? I mean as it comes in salted.

Mr. CARROLL. There is no waste.

Mr. GARDNER. That is spread out on flakes and put into pickle, and one process and another of curing is gone through. That is sold at wholesale off the vessel, we will say, for 3 cents. Am I correct?

Mr. CARROLL. From 3 to 3¼ cents in 1909.

Mr. GARDNER. After this process of curing, and so on, has been gone through, what is the loss in weight from it as it comes off the ship?

Mr. CARROLL. In which condition—after it is put up in the package, as this gentleman buys it?

Mr. GARDNER. No; not in the package, but as it is sold—the whole fish, as you get it at the corner grocery store, hanging by the tail from the beams?

Mr. CARROLL. It would take 1.4 or 1.3 pounds to make 1 pound, approximately.

Mr. GARDNER. In other words, the shrinkage is about 33 per cent?

Mr. CARROLL. Yes, sir.

Mr. CLARK. Thirty-three per cent of 3.25 would be 1.08, which, added to 3.25, would make 4.33 cents; and Mr. Boutell pays $15 a hundred for that fish. Who gets the difference?

Mr. GARDNER. No, he does not; he pays about 10 cents for that particular fish.

Mr. CLARK. He said he paid 15.

Mr. GARDNER. But he pays 15 for boneless codfish, or package codfish.

Mr. CARROLL. Which is an entirely different proposition.

Mr. CLARK. Suppose he pays 10, who gets the difference?

Mr. GARDNER. In the first place, there is all the cost of curing, pickling, handling, and shipment, and all the other profit comes in in the middlemen—the jobber and the wholesaler and the retailer.

Mr. CARROLL. There is the box, and the labor, and the salt, and the shrinkage. The retailer does not get any too much in that proposition. If we got half a cent a pound on it—and I am speaking in the presence of some gentlemen who do not feel too kindly to me——

Mr. CLARK. I want to find out this: Senator Reed Smoot stated over here, when they had the tariff bill up and kept hammering on the proposition, that the average retail profit in the United States was between three and four hundred per cent on merchandise generally. I did not believe it then and I do not believe it now, and I want some evidence to back up my opinion.

Mr. CARROLL. It is not so down our way, sir, because the retail grocers are not prospering with us, and they would if they got anywhere near that. We figure that if a retail grocer gets 20 per cent profit on our goods he is doing pretty well. You would think he would get more than that on this whole fish that we are talking about; but he has more or less shrinkage.

Mr. GARDNER. I should like to ask you a question. Do you not ship a great deal of fish to Porto Rico?

Mr. CARROLL. Yes, sir.

Mr. GARDNER. It is one of your most profitable markets, is it not?

Mr. CARROLL. Well, at times, yes, when there are not too many down there. You see, we do some consignment business down there, and sometimes we get a pretty good market.

Mr. GARDNER. Under this treaty, Canadian fish would be taken over to Porto Rico, would it not?

Mr. CARROLL. Yes, sir.

Mr. GARDNER. And what would happen to your trade?

Mr. CARROLL. It would be in the same condition that it would be in this country.

Mr. GARDNER. You would not expect to sell another pound of fish in Porto Rico, would you?

Mr. CARROLL. We could still do some consignment business there. We would send them down there on consignment for awhile. When the returns we got were the same as the Nova Scotia man got for his, we would stop selling to Porto Rico, because of the old story that I told you awhile ago—in the first place, the extra cost, and all that sort of thing.

The CHAIRMAN. Mr. Hill has been waiting for some time to ask you a question.

Mr. CARROLL. All right, sir.

Mr. HILL. Mr. Carroll, your people are fish buyers and fish carriers, are they not?

Mr. CARROLL. Yes, sir.

Mr. HILL. You own vessels which you send down and secure fish with, and bring them to Boston?

Mr. CARROLL. Yes, sir.

Mr. HILL. And you manufacture?

Mr. CARROLL. We bring them to Gloucester, mostly.

Mr. HILL. You have the advantage of a protected market in your manufactured product?

Mr. CARROLL. Yes, sir.

Mr. HILL. Mr. Chairman, I am going to ask that there be made a part of the record this Treasury decision, which has just been handed to me. I will ask that it be printed as a part of the record. I should like to have you explain this:

One Capt. Carter, owner and master of the vessel *Sarah C. Wharf*, duly documented under the laws of the United States, had maintained her in the waters about the treaty coast of Newfoundland for a number of years previous to the fall of 1909. During the time when these fish were caught the vessel had on board a crew of five men, of whom the temporary captain and one other man were citizens of the United States. The vessel was used as a base of supplies, and for the use of the master in the conduct of his operations while catching the fish. The fish, however, were not caught from this vessel; in fact, they were not ever on board the vessel. They were caught by citizens of Newfoundland, or of the provinces, by means of tackle and appliances which were in some cases supplied by the men themselves, etc.

The appraisers decided that if that business was paid for by American capital, even if all the labor was performed by citziens of Newfoundland, the fish so caught must be admitted free. Why does not that, therefore, give your cencern (Gorton-Pew & Co.) free fish from the fisheries of Canada and Newfoundland, and give you the benefit of a protected market on the manufactured product?

Mr. CARROLL. If that decision would stand, gentlemen, it would mean——

Mr. HILL. It has just been made.

Mr. CARROLL. Yes, sir; it would mean this: That we could go down on the treaty coasts of Newfoundland (not all over Newfoundland, but on the treaty coast, where Captain Carter was) and do as he did, and get in; and it would be a great help to us in a year like last fall.

(The Treasury decision referred to by Mr. Hill will be found printed in full at the end of to-day's proceedings.)

Mr. GARDNER. That was solely with regard to herring; was it not?

Mr. CARROLL. No; codfish.

Mr. HILL. Would it not be absolutely impossible for the captain who has testified here to take his vessel from Gloucester and go and personally conduct his own operations with an American crew, if you had the privilege of doing what it is decided here you can do?

Mr. CARROLL. It would take that privilege from him, I think, because his crews would cost him a great deal more. But I am not asking for that privilege, gentlemen—not at all.

Mr. HILL. But you have it, under the decision.

The CHAIRMAN. I want to say to the witness, in fairness to him, that this decision of the Board of General Appraisers was recently made; the Treasury Department caused it to be appealed to the customs court; and probably it has not been actually carried into effect except in this particular instance.

Mr. HILL. Your interest, therefore, is in having the duty kept up so as to give you a protected market for your product, when if this decision is sustained you have a free raw material?

Mr. CARROLL. No, sir—absolutely not. I said in the beginning, gentlemen, that I believed the industry needed protection from beginning to end.

Mr. HILL. It has not got it, under this decision.

Mr. CARROLL. That is a very small proposition, gentlemen. That is the treaty coast. Capt. Thomas could do it if he wished; but he never would think of doing it, because he makes a lot more money out of what he is doing than what he would be doing then. I stand with Capt. Thomas on everything he said. His interests are identical with mine, excepting on this point—that I am a manufacturer in addition to being a producer; that is the idea. Capt. Thomas would never do it, gentlemen—never. No live man in Gloucester would do it. He will make more money the other way. Capt. Thomas does well. He makes good money. You gentlemen this morning thought this industry was not profitable. These men make a lot of money. That man has nine children living, and two dead. He has brought them up so that they are a credit to him and the city, and he is fairly well off. But he does not get any bounty. We do not ask for it, either. I want to put myself on record there. We do not want any bounty. We do not ask for it.

Mr. GARDNER. What is the Canadian bounty?

Mr. CARROLL. The Canadian bounty is the interest on what they call the Halifax award—$5,156,000.

Mr. GARDNER. I will put in the figures on the subject of the bounty.

Mr. CARROLL. In addition to that they get subsidized cold-storage plants, so that they can buy their bait cheaper than any Gloucester man can go down there and buy it, and the license——

Mr. CLARK. 1909 was a year when you made an extraordinary catch, was it not?

Mr. CARROLL. A good catch of codfish; yes, sir.

Mr. CLARK. You made $33,000 that year?

Mr. CARROLL. On the vessels?

Mr. CLARK. Yes.

Mr. CARROLL. I do not want to leave any wrong impression.

Mr. CLARK. That is what I asked. In 1910 you had a small catch?

Mr. CARROLL. Yes, sir.

Mr. CLARK. How much did you make that year?

Mr. CARROLL. We do not know. We will not know until April.

Mr. CLARK. Why do you not figure it out?

Mr. CARROLL. I did not know the question would be asked. Our year is not up.

Mr. CLARK. Did you make more in 1910 than you did in 1909?

Mr. CARROLL. Yes, sir.

Mr. CLARK. Then, although the catch was smaller, you made more money

Mr. CARROLL. I did not understand you. 1909 was our good year. I do not know just what the profit in 1910 was, because our year ends the first of April; but I know it was not as good as the other, possibly, because our vessels did not catch the fish.

Mr. GARDNER. May I have the attention of the gentleman from Connecticut (Mr. Hill)? This Treasury decision refers only to herring.

Mr. CARROLL. Pardon me—codfish.

Mr. GARDNER. Well, I mean, practically speaking, it refers only to the treaty coast of Newfoundland, which is a very small part of it. That operation of Capt. Carter's was not performed by a Gloucester vessel, but by a Boston vessel. Everybody knows that the decision was very questionable in Capt. Carter's case. The Government has appealed it to the courts; and in addition the Treasury has issued instructions which will prevent it in the future, which have been accepted by my constituents.

Mr. HILL. I think, Mr. Gardner, that you will concede that if that decision stands, the situation to-day is far worse than it would be if the market were entirely free and open.

Mr. GARDNER. As far as herring coming from the Bay of Islands is concerned, that does not effect anything.

Mr. CARROLL. Not at all; not at all.

Mr. GARDNER. Now I should like to ask Mr. Carroll two or three questions. For instance, let me ask you what duties you will pay on your supplies, your raw material, if what you produce is to be free? Tell us about the sails and cordage and hooks and paint and oil, and so on—the duty on those things.

The CHAIRMAN. I do not think that is worth while. He can tell us what he uses, but he need not go into the duties themselves.

Mr. GARDNER. You can look up the figures yourselves, of course.

Mr. CARROLL. Yes, sir.

Mr. GARDNER. You use dutiable articles, many of which you import. Tell us some of them.

Mr. CARROLL. Hooks, sails, nets——

Mr. GARDNER. Seines, especially. A mackerel seine is worth a thousand dollars, or somewhere around there, is it not?

Mr. CARROLL. Yes; yes.

Mr. GARDNER. Those are very expensive things.

Mr. LONGWORTH. I want to know why you can not buy hooks in this country?

Mr. CARROLL. I do not know, but I do know that they send them right through in bond.

Mr. CARROLL. We have to pay a duty on them.

Mr. LONGWORTH. Why are they not made in this country?

Mr. CARROLL. The hooks that the fishermen like are made in England. Capt. Thomas, where are those hooks made, mostly?

Capt. THOMAS. They are made in Grimsby.

Mr. CARROLL. They are made in Grimsby, England. They have to have a certain kind of hook, or they will not get the fish.

Mr. GARDNER. What can you tell us about the preparations being made by Nova Scotia——

Mr. CLARK. Mr. Gardner, let me ask this witness one question. Can they not make that kind of fishhook in the United States?

Mr. CARROLL. I think they could, sir.

Mr. CLARK. Why do they not do it?

Mr. CARROLL. I do not see why not; but they do not. They do not do it; and we are not in the fishhook business.

Mr. CLARK. I thought perhaps you had investigated the matter and found out the reason.

Mr. LONGWORTH. Are they patented? Do you know that?

Mr. CARROLL. Yes; they are patented, sir. I did not think to answer that.

Mr. GARDNER. Now I should like to know about the information you have derived from the Maritime Fish Company, at Lunenberg, as to the preparations they are making for increasing their catch in Canadian waters; and also about the vessels that are now on the stocks in Lunenberg in anticipation of this treaty, of which there seems to have been knowledge on the part of the Canadian fisherman prior to what there was in our own country. Incidentally, I have here the figures that Mr. Longworth asked for, about the value of the Canadian fisheries at present.

(The figures above referred to are as follows):

Value of Canadian fisheries for 1909		$25, 451, 085
Vessels of all kinds	number..	1, 414
Boats	do....	39, 965
Fishermen	do....	71, 070
Nova Scotia:		
Value, 1908		$8, 009, 838
Cod	number..	40, 237, 500
Dried	do....	4, 105, 500
Fish vessels (20,503 tons; value, $1,599,588)	number..	679
Fish boats (value, outfits, $1,149,994)	do....	15, 442

The CHAIRMAN. I do not suppose they have put any vessels on the stocks since this treaty has been proposed.

Mr. GARDNER. I think, sir, they had an intimation from their own Government last summer, at the time when the question of the threatened tariff war was raised; and they took their chances, just as you remember our shipbuilding companies took a chance on the ship subsidy and started in with the Fore River Shipbuilding Co. Now, let us hear what they are doing in Lunenberg.

Mr. CARROLL. I will simply say, in a general way, that there has been a great boom down there in the fishing business. They have started to build a number of new vessels. I have it on the best of authority that they started early last fall to build a fleet of 20 in anticipation of our markets. They have been figuring on our markets for a long time. Whether or not they knew anything about this, I do not know. But I do know that they are making great preparations to invade our markets with their fish; and I do know that every dollar's worth of fish they sell in this country means $1 less than we sell.

I should like to make one statement about the condition of the industry. There seemed to be a feeling here this morning that it had gone back; that it was dwindling; that it was on its last legs. There is one part of the industry that has gone back, and that is the mackerel catch. There has been a failure of the mackerel catch, for which no one is responsible. Some years ago, about 1883-84, in one year there were 454,000 barrels of salted mackerel caught by the New England mackerel fleet. Last year there were 3,000 barrels caught. There is the part of the industry that has dwindled. The other has not. The fresh-fish industry has gone ahead tremendously, and will keep going along.

Mr. CLARK. What made the mackerel industry dwindle?

Mr. CARROLL. The catch fell off.

Mr. CLARK. Did they catch all the fish out of the sea?

Mr. CARROLL. Opinions differ on that point. I do not think they caught them all. I think they simply went over across to Ireland, or Norway, or somewhere else, where they have been getting tremendous catches all the time—especially last year

Mr. CLARK. What went over there—the fish?

Mr. CARROLL. Yes, sir. The mackerel left our shores. We have a captain here who is an expert on that point; but that is what I should say. They left our shores, and that is what has resulted in the dwindling of that industry. During those years we had a great fleet of vessels that did nothing but go after mackerel. As the mackerel disappeared the fleet went with them. But in exchange for that there has come up the tremendous demand for fresh fish. That market is mostly in Boston. Many of our vessels supply it.

The CHAIRMAN. What is the principal fish market in Canada, corresponding to Gloucester?

Mr. CARROLL. Lunenberg is what they call the Gloucester of Nova Scotia.

Mr. GARDNER. What information can you give the committee as to the Maritime Fish Co., which has stations in various parts of Canada?

Mr. CARROLL. Recently there has been a merger of several concerns down in Nova Scotia, backed by the Bank of Montreal. They are large concerns. They are building up a business through Canada. The manager of that concern told me and some other dealers within a month that as soon as this thing went through he would have his agency in every large city of the United States, after our business—which he will get, absolutely.

Mr. HARRISON. Mr. Carroll, right in line with that statement, let me ask you this question: Have you ever heard of Gen. William Stopford, of Beverly?

Mr. CARROLL. Yes, sir.

Mr. HARRISON. It is stated that he has been for more than 40 years one of the most prominent men in the fish trade in that part of Massachusetts. I should like to read you just a few sentences from an interview with Gen. Stopford in the Boston Herald of yesterday, and ask your opinion about it.

Mr. CARROLL. Yes, sir.

Mr. HARRISON. He is reported as saying:

With free fish Gloucester has a chance to boom its business as a distributing point, and to make it the biggest salt-fish port in the coun ry, if not in the world. It will mean that firms who engage in business in that city can secure the green fish, cured, handled, and put into shape for distribution. It will mean that more firms will engage in business there; and instead of a few combinations, the city will have many independent firms. Since 1882 the fleet from Gloucester has gradually dwindled, until to-day it is not more than a third as large as during the years of free trade. There will be no Gloucester firms going to Nova Scotia to do business. The business will come to Gloucester; and Gloucester is in a position to take advantage of it.

That is only a part of the interview.

Mr. CARROLL. Do you want me to speak of the interview or of the gentleman giving it?

Mr. HARRISON. I should like to have you express your opinion as to that statement.

Mr. CARROLL. This gentleman has kept a retail fish market in Salem and Beverly all his life, since I have known him. If that man is more competent to give an opinion as to what is best for us than we men of Gloucester—I am not talking now for the Gorton Pew Fish Co. alone, but for every man engaged in that industry, with two exceptions—if he knows more than we do about what is good for us, it is folly for me to come down here and talk to you gentlemen.

Mr. HARRISON. It is stated here that he has been in the business of sending out his own fleet as well as preparing the fish.

Mr. CARROLL. That is absolutely not true—absolutely not true. He is a retail fish dealer, who would sell you a fish if you went down and wanted a haddock for your dinner. That is his standing.

Mr. GARDNER. Gen. William Stopford, who was the major of the battalion in which I served in the Eighth Massachusetts, is a very old friend of mine. I bought fish from him at retail, or my family did, all through my boyhood. He was the adjutant general that Douglas chose when he was elected governor of Massachusetts. So far as I know, he has always been a fish dealer—and a very delightful and charming fish dealer at that. But I have never heard that he was a fish producer. He can make the best clam chowder that you could possibly ask for, and he is one of the most delightful men I know.

Mr. HARRISON. Do you mean to discredit his statement on that account?

Mr. GARDNER. Oh, no, no, no! I know him.

Mr. McCALL. Mr. Carroll, I had a letter this morning from a gentleman in Bradford, Mass., named Charles J. Roberts. Mr. Gardner may know him.

Mr. GARDNER. I do not. He is a constituent of mine; but I do not think I place him.

Mr. McCALL. He says he is very strongly in favor of this treaty; but he makes a statement here that I should like to ask you about. You can tell me whether it is true or not. He says:

The fish, I think, is one of the most important items that is in the treaty; and I do not think a few people down in Gloucester that are packing pollock and putting it on the market and selling it for codfish ought to be considered when it comes to a question of benefit to nine-tenths of the people of the United States.

How about that statement?

Mr. CARROLL. I will refer you to Dr. Wiley on that point, sir. He was down there about two years ago.

Mr. McCALL. He adds this:

All I say about the pollock is true, as I have a package of it here that my wife purchased yesterday to use in a New England fish dinner, and it was so hard, tough, and stringy that we could not use it.

Mr. CARROLL. Pollock is a very dark fish that looks nothing at all like codfish. But I will say, in answer to that, that two years ago I wrote to Dr. Wiley and asked him if he would not send Dr. Bitting (his very best man in that department) down to Gloucester to investigate our industry. Dr. Bitting camped in the office of our main factory all last summer, and all the summer before. He had access to the entire works; he was out and around all the time; and he gives us a clean bill of health, sir. He knows whether we pack codfish, pollock, or anything else.

Mr. McCALL. After writing further upon that subject, and recurring to another subject, he puts on a sort of postscript in which he says:

The price of packed pollock was 15 cents for 15 ounces.

How about the weight?

Mr. CARROLL. That may be possible, sir, because fish shrinks. We pack 16 ounces to the pound, but it will shrink more or less. That is one of our great troubles, and it is something that we shall have to face some day when you gentlemen say that the weight must be stamped on every package, because we can not tell absolutely how much it will shrink. If it has been in the retail grocery store a long while, it will be apt to contain about 15 ounces. But you understand that you have just as much fish in there as you had when it first came in and weighed 16 ounces.

Mr. GARDNER. The only further point that I wish to bring out is as to the state of affairs under the old treaty—the last time we had free fish with Canada. I should like to put on the stand Capt. Sylvanus Smith. He is 82 years old, and it is a good deal to ask of him. But I thought perhaps a few words from Mr. Carroll or somebody else that he might suggest would cover that point. Then my end of the hearing will be closed, except that I should like the privilege of cross-examining some of the witnesses that will come before you on the other side. Whom have you settled on to present the state of affairs existing under the old treaty?

Mr. CARROLL. Capt. Sylvanus Smith himself is here. I should think he would be the best one, because he is the only man who has personal knowledge of that matter. That was before my time, gentlemen. I know what happened, but I would rather have some-body tell about it who knows of it personally.

Mr. GARDNER. These men here all know by hearsay what happened. Capt. Smith is 82 years old, but I think you will find he is perfectly able to testify if you desire to hear him.

STATEMENT OF CAPT. SYLVANUS SMITH.

Capt. SMITH. Mr. Chairman, I did not expect to be called on. I came here two years ago, and I have been in this business for a great many years—for the last 40 years.

Mr. McCALL. Captain, you were a member of the Massachusetts Legislature. I think I had the honor of serving with you.

Capt. SMITH. We had a reciprocity resolution then, on which I took the floor twice. I have had a little experience in the business. I was brought up in it from the time I was a boy. I think it was in 1837 when I first went to work on a small boat. I have been through all the stages of the fish business. I retired some years ago, in 1864, and went into business. For the last 15 years or so I have not been actively employed in the business. The boys carry on the business, but I still take an interest in it, as I have in the past.

As I say, I have been in the fight for all these years. I have been on here a good many times on all of your reciprocity treaties. I recollect well the old treaty of 1855, as we called it. Perhaps some of you have heard that we had good times in the fishing business in 1855, during the continuance of that treaty. Our business then was altogether different. The provinces sent in very few codfish, and the codfish were hard-cured; and their mackerel did not amount to very much in the American market. Then there were large quantities of mackerel caught in the Bay of Chaleur. We had a large fleet of vessels there fishing all those years, and we had a number of smaller vessels than we have now fishing in those waters; and we did not feel the effect of that treaty any.

As I say, it has been said by a good many that we had good times during that treaty. The war came on and all business was boomed, and in 1867 the treaty was abrogated. Then, by the way, since 1792 there was a bounty that was given the fishermen. That was taken off about 1867. Then there was an effort made on the part of the

Canadians for the continuance of the old treaty of 1855. Many vessels were seized, a great many of them illegally, and there was a great deal of irritation between the two sections. Perhaps some of you recollect that the President had power given by Congress to declare nonintercourse with Canada. When the Washington treaty was fixed up——

Mr. GARDNER. What you call the Washington treaty is the treaty of 1871?

Capt. SMITH. Yes, sir. When that treaty was fixed up, there was a committee appointed to come on to Washington and tell them how we stood. I happened to be one of that committee, but for some reason or other I did not come. Hamilton Fish was Secretary of State at the time, and he did not get proper information, and it was provided that we should reinstate the old reciprocity treaty. That provided for free fishing and that a commission should sit in Halifax to see how much we should pay them, if anything. That commission met. Mr. Delfox was the third man; and I was down there some two weeks before that commission. They decided that five millions and a quarter should be paid them as indemnities. It was understood that that money was taken by the Canadians, and they received their bounties from it to-day. That treaty was abrogated as soon as it could be done, at the end of the 10 years.

The next treaty was the Chamberlain-Bayard treaty, which is practically the same treaty we have now. We were very much wrought up over that. We felt that our interests were being sacrificed, and we made great efforts, and we sent a committee on here, and the result was that the Senate committee investigated the whole question. The whole fishery industry of New England was arrayed against it, and the treaty was set aside. Then, there have been two others since that have not become a law.

We earnestly feel that if this treaty should go into effect it would mean the wiping out of the Gloucester fishing industry. I take a great interest in the business. I should like to see it left prosperous. Of course, the business has changed from time to time. The old methods of putting up fish have given place to new ones. The old method, when they were dried and shipped off to market in the original state, has been changed. There have been great factories erected. Take my plant, where I do business: That plant itself stands me probably $50,000. We employ lots of men, boys, and girls—a great many of them. If the business goes I do not know what will become of them. I have not got long to stay; I can get along; but what will become of them?

I feel confident, gentlemen, that if this treaty goes into effect it will result in practically the annihilation of the business with us. It will not be this year; it will not be next year; but it will gradually come about. They started out up there to do the distributing business, and there is where the matter of labor comes in. The men that can do the labor the cheapest will be the ones to do it. The Canadians can do the labor cheaper than we can.

Mr. GARDNER. Captain, the last treaty—the Chamberlain-Bayard treaty—was, of course, as you said, rejected; and so was the Hay-Bond treaty. The last treaty that was in effect——

Capt. SMITH. The Blaine-Bond and Hay-Bond treaties?

Mr. GARDNER. The Blaine-Bond treaty and then the Hay-Bond treaty. The last treaty that was in effect was the Washington treaty, which, if I recollect rightly, provided not only for free fish but provided for the settlement of the Alabama claims award and a number of other things, and gave us the right to the inshore fisheries of Canada and Newfoundland. Is not that so?

Capt. SMITH. Unrestrictedly; yes.

Mr. GARDNER. That does not appear in this treaty. Now, let me ask you this question: During the continuance of that treaty (the last one), between 1871 and the time it was denounced, the time when we got rid of it (it was a 10-year treaty), what was the condition of the cod fisheries of Gloucester? I will ask you about the mackerel fisheries later.

Capt. SMITH. The cod fisheries? In the beginning of that treaty the codfish business was good. The vessels that came up there sold their argoes at about $4 or $4.12½ to $4.25 per 100 pounds in the vessels.

They went up that year into what we call the Cape towns, around the western shore of Nova Scotia, and built some 60 or 70 vessels. By the time they got them going there was an overproduction of fish or something and the price of fish went down. I took in fish on my premises for $1.45 per 100 pounds. We sold fish for $1.75 a quintal—that is, 114 pounds—dried. We shipped cargoes of fish to Surinam that we did not get enough out of to pay the freight and the other expenses—the commission, etc.

That was the condition of things during that treaty, the Washington treaty. We had one thing that saved us. The mackerel fishery has since been annihilated, but we then had a good catch of mackerel that helped us out. During that treaty quite a large number of firms sold their vessels or went out of business. The mackerel business has always been a great help to the fishing business.

Let me say one thing about what was spoken of in regard to the herring business and the Newfoundland business on the treaty coast. It has always been the custom, since away back in the days of the treaty of 1818, that we would go there and hire men. Our men have a certain percentage of the catch—one-half. These vessels go down there and their owners hire the men to navigate the vessel. That began away back in the time of the treaty of 1818. Under the Washington treaty we had a right to go into any of their coasts to fish. Probably you gentlemen are aware that when we undertook to fish in Fortune Bay there was a lot of trouble. They destroyed our seines, and their Government had to pay some $90,000 damages. In any part of the Newfoundland Provinces where we had a right, we had to make a bargain with the fishermen or hire them to fish for us. That is the way these men are employed.

We had the right to fish on what we call the treaty coast, and we could not exercise that right by setting our seines and setting trawls, or anything else; that is their natural right. But then they said to us "What are we going to do if you take the fish away? Our families will starve. We will fish for you." So that the consequence was that we had to employ their men to fish for us. They live aboard the vessels, and if they do not catch any fish they do not get any pay. If they do catch fish, they get big pay. We find the nets for them, and everything else. So far as boats are concerned, they use their own boats.

Any questions that you gentlemen would like to ask, I will try to answer.

Mr. GARDNER. Substantially speaking, during the continuance of that treaty, what saved Gloucester was the mackerel fleet?

Mr. SMITH. Yes.

Mr. GARDNER. And that has very largely gone to pieces, has it not?

Mr. SMITH. Yes. I would say, in my own experience of that treaty, in regard to the vessels, the captain of one, in particular, got so many fish that I turned him out of the vessel, and I took one of my large vessels, the captain of which is here now, and sent her mackerel fishing, and I took all my vessels out of the banks fishing. When it came to the end of my season, my bookkeeper asked about taking stock and I said: "Oh, everything that is there is mine," and I did not like to take any stock. I know we have lost a good deal of money, a great many seasons, doing that, and had to give it up.

Mr. GARDNER. What Capt. Smith refers to is those Fortune Bay riots. We had the treaty right of the in-shore fisheries, and when we came to exercise the treaty right the natives came out with guns and said that treaty or no treaty they did not propose to have us fishing in their back yard. I think the only skipper who got away with a trip at that time was Capt. Solomon Jacobs. After a great deal of diplomatic correspondence, Great Britain settled those claims for damages for the Fortune Bay riots, but since that time, in fishing for herring on the treaty coast, we have found it expedient to keep the peace with the natives.

I close my side, gentlemen, with the request that I may be permitted, later on, to ask questions of those who wish to be heard in support of the treaty.

The CHAIRMAN. Are there any gentlemen here who desire to present opposing views on the fish subject.

SEVERAL GENTLEMEN. Yes.

The CHAIRMAN. Let one of you come forward. I do not know the names of any of you.

STATEMENT OF CHARLES F. WONSON, OF GLOUCESTER, MASS.

Mr. WONSON. Mr. Chairman and gentlemen of the committee, I had very little time to prepare myself for this hearing, but coming down on the train last night I attempted to scribble what I wanted to say, and if you will permit me I will proceed in that way. It will not take me ten minutes, and then I will be open to questions, or you may interrupt me at any time if you wish. But few of us can prophesy accurately what effect this legislation, if enacted, will have on the fisheries of Gloucester, but we can tell to a certainty the present condition of these fisheries, and make a comparison between conditions now and in 1885, when the treaty of 1872 was abrogated. Permit me to say, first, that I had hoped that an agreement acceptable to both countries could have been made by admitting free green fish only, but I consider the necessity for free green fish so great that, as a business man, I am forced to accept this whole agreement rather than sacrifice the opportunity of securing green fish, which I sincerely believe spells prosperity for Gloucester.

In 1880 my brother and I purchased the only piece of wharf property available for the fishing business that was for sale in Gloucester. Yes, we had the temerity, after reciprocity had been in force seven years, to go into the fish business for a life vocation. At that time there were between 40 and 50 concerns, large and small, engaged in the fish business in Gloucester. The report says 58. I did not have time to verify it, and I want to be conservative, and so I put it between 40 and 50. To-day there are not over 25, large and small, and this number includes all the fresh fish concerns. The number of vessels operated in Gloucester in 1880, when I went into business, was over 400, and to-day, according to the latest report of the Gloucester customhouse, they number 183. The gross tonnage in 1900 was 30,208. In 1910 it was 19,908, and this is also verified by the customs records in Gloucester.

The total catch of salted fish and fish to salt landed in Gloucester in 1893 was 111,000,000 pounds. The average price paid the vessel for these fish was a little over 3 cents per pound. In 1909, which has been called the banner year in the fisheries, the total product, according to the figures collected by the statistician of the Government, who is also the marine reporter for the Gloucester Times, was 88,000,000 pounds. My figures say 90,000,000 pounds, and his say, I think, 88,000,000 pounds. This was in 1909. The average price in 1909 was a little under 3 cents per pound. Such a record does not appeal to me as showing general prosperity. To-day water-front property in Gloucester is lying idle, expensively constructed wharves and buildings are unoccupied and decaying. Our young men to-day find no incentive to engage in the business, and as soon as they are educated, depart for other cities.

I have been represented as a small dealer. I admit it; but yet I do a business of $125,000 a year, and have done so since 1902. I pay out to labor from $12,000 to $15,000 yearly.

I gave up the business in 1898 and served in Cuba and the Philippines until May, 1901, and resumed business in 1902 with nothing but credit, energy, and a determination to make good. I have made good. I refer you to my banker.

I am a small dealer in comparison with the big dealers who are represented in this delegation, but what I have done I have done alone, while the largest company among these big companies is a consolidation of four other big companies, two of which inherited prestige and wealth from their ancestors. I inherited nothing but a good business education and the disposition and energy to work. If you will take the amount of business in dollars that this company does yearly, and divide it by the number of original members of the concern, nine, you will see that my business is quite a respectable item in regard to the welfare of Gloucester; and I want to say here, gentlemen, right now, that there are at the present time eight men, if I am informed correctly, members of that corporation, who are drawing $5,000 per year each.

May I proceed a little further, gentlemen?

The CHAIRMAN. Yes. Does the committee desire to ask any questions?

Mr. GARDNER. I should like to ask a few questions.

Mr. WONSON. I have not finished yet. I have taken notes since this hearing began, and I wish to controvert some statements that have been made here.

The CHAIRMAN. Proceed.

Mr. WONSON. The question was asked here if very many of the men manning our vessels were native citizens, and if I understood the answer correctly; the answer was that a large proportion of them were American citizens. As a matter of fact, gentlemen, the men and the captains of our vessels are pretty nearly, if not quite, 90 per cent foreign born, and to-day 75 per cent of the men who are manning our fleet are foreign born and are not naturalized citizens. I prove that statement by a statement made to me yesterday by a deputy collector of the city of Gloucester, who has been in office for 20 years. He is now the tax collector. He said that 20 years ago he collected from the fishermen of Gloucester $15,000 to $20,000 each year in poll taxes. Last year he did not collect $5,000. Does that show that the men manning our fleet are American citizens?

Of this delegation who are present, there are three who have told me personally that they thoroughly believe in the admission of free green fish. They do not want me to go so far as to say that they will accept the other part rather than lose the free green-fish provision.

Capt. Peoples has told you he owned his schooner, but he did not tell you that this schooner is a small one, worth about $2,500 to $3,000; that he goes in her in the summer time, and then takes a vessel from one of the firms and goes down to Newfoundland in the winter time.

The part of Capt. Thomas's vessel which he does not own is owned, I think, by members of the Gordon-Pew Co.

One of the delegates who was presented here as representing a labor union is employed by the Gordon-Pew Co. He, I am informed, is not a member of any union, and does not represent them here.

In speaking about our inability to ship fish into Canada, I think the next witness will show that there has been a considerable quantity of fish shipped from the United States into Canada, and particularly in the years of reciprocity.

Coming down on the train last night I struck this gentleman, Mr. H. H. Brauligam, who is secretary and manager of the Bridgeport Motor Co. (Inc.), of Bridgeport, Conn. He tells me that his trade in Canada is considerable, and he also informed me that the duty was 27 or 27½ per cent. In spite of that the Canadian manufacturers maintain the price; they do not cut the price, but let him come in with his product and meet him. If a motor manufacturer can, in competition with the cheap labor of Canada, send his motors into Canada and sell them at a profit and pay a duty of 27½ per cent and do a profitable business, I should think we might do something in the way of fish.

Just a moment and I will be through. I want to read you the following newspaper clipping:

GONE TO NOVA SCOTIA HOMES.

Capts. Newman Wharton, Alden Geel, Walter Doucette, and William Morrissey, who returned a few days ago from Newfoundland herring trips, left to-day by steamer from Boston for their homes in Nova Scotia. They will return here the latter part of February, when they will fit out schooners *Arkona*, *Tattler*, *Arcadia*, and *Premier* for salt cod hook fishing trips. They are among the best known cod fishers of the New England fishing fleet.

The gentleman in Gloucester who sold them the tickets to go home told me that they told him that they were to stop on the way home and order a set of dories for their vessels in Shelburn, Nova Scotia, and they would pick up these dories as they went down. Those boats are supposed not to be landed in the United States. As a matter of fact they are landed, and no duty is paid on them.

One thousand nets in one consignment last fall went from Scotland for Gorton-Pew and Cunningham and Thompson, consigned to Ingram at Sydney, Cape Breton, were landed at Montreal by Allen Line steamer, and forwarded by the Intercolonial Railway to Sydney, where they dumped them off without notifying consignees, and the claim was made that they spoiled in bundles. and a claim was presented to the Canadian Government.

This gentleman says, "How about getting dories made at Shelburn to supply these Gloucester fish-trust magnates?"

That, Mr. Chairman, is all that I have prepared. I will be glad to answer anything that I can.

Mr. GARDNER. Mr. Chairman, the gentleman said that Freeman Brown, who gave evidence here, is an employee of the Gorton-Pew Co. Did I understand you correctly?

Mr. WONSON. I understood that he was.

Mr. GARDNER. Mr. Freeman Brown, will you stand up and tell the committee whether that is a true statement?

Mr. BROWN. No, sir.

Mr. WONSON. Mr. Chairman, I do not admit the right of Mr. Gardner to examine me unless the committee demand it. I am not going to submit to his cross-examination unless the committee demand it; but I will very cheerfully answer any questions that the committee or he ask.

Mr. FORDNEY. If it will give the committee any information that they have not got I would like to hear it.

Mr. WONSON. All right, sir.

Mr. FORDNEY. Mr. Chairman, it seems to me that that question is important. I would like to have the committee give permission to Mr. Gardner to ask that question, so that the committee might be better informed.

The CHAIRMAN. I understand that Mr. Gardner is to be allowed to cross-examine the witnesses. Is there any objection on the part of any member of the committee to Mr. Gardner being allowed to cross-examine?

Mr. CLARK. Oh, let him go on and examine him. He knows more about it than we do.

Mr. GARDNER. Now, Mr. Brown, are you an employee of the Gorton-Pew Co.?

Mr. BROWN. I am not, at present.

Mr. WONSON. Whom is he an employee of?

Mr. GARDNER. Now, Mr. Wonson, you stated that the part of the vessel not owned by Capt. Thomas was owned by the Gorton-Pew Co.

Mr. WONSON. I beg your pardon, I did not make that statement.

Mr. GARDNER. Well, we will have the reporter's notes.

Mr. RANDELL. It seems to me this is in the nature of testimony in rebuttal, and this is not cross-examination.

The CHAIRMAN. I was going to suggest to Mr. Gardner that as long as the witness objects, he ought to confine himself strictly to a cross-examination. This is rather liberal for a cross-examination.

Mr. WONSON. Mr. Chairman, if you will permit me, I would say that I have come down here backed by no Congressman. I come down here alone.

The CHAIRMAN. Oh, you are just as well off as if you had a Congressman.

Mr. WONSON. I know, but I have a right to expect fair treatment; that is all I ask, and I will tell you anything I know.

Mr. CLARK. You will get that.

The CHAIRMAN. All you have got to do is to tell the truth and you will be just as well off as if you had a Congressman.

Mr. GARDNER. In regard to this statement that a part of Capt. Thomas's ship was owned by the Gorton-Pew Co., did you say that Capt. Thomas had not told them that a part of his ship was owned by the Gorton-Pew Co., clearly leaving the implication that they did own it?

Mr. WONSON. No, sir; I did not.

Mr. GARDNER. May I have the stenographer's notes read on that point?

Mr. WONSON. I was informed that the other part of it was owned by the Gorton-Pew Co.

Mr. FORDNEY. Then you do not know whether that statement is correct or not?

Mr. WONSON. No, sir.

Mr. FORDNEY. Then you ought not to make it.

Mr. GARDNER. Mr. Wonson, there are here certain gentlemen engaged in substantially the same business as yourself. Take Mr. Gale, Mr. Moore, Mr. Smith, and Mr. Bradley, four of them that I can count with my eye; now, do they, any of them, agree with you in this advocacy of the treaty?

Mr. WONSON. That is not a fair question.

Mr. GARDNER. Oh, I submit, Mr. Chairman——

Mr. WONSON. I refuse to answer the question put in that way.

Mr. GARDNER. All right, sir; you are not under oath and I can not compel you to. Are the Crown Packing Co., Mr. Smith, and Henry E. Pinkham in the same business with you?

Mr. WONSON. No, sir.

Mr. GARDNER. In what respect does it differ?

Mr. WONSON. The Crown Packing Co. are what we call an express-order company.

Mr. GARDNER. It is substantially the same, is it not?

Mr. WONSON. No, sir; it is altogether different. Henry E. Pinkham is in a very much smaller way.

Mr. GARDNER. Now you were talking about the fact that you had started in 1880, and that you had no backing, and that you had fought everybody, which of course would be very creditable. Who are W. H. Wonson & Son?

Mr. WONSON. Oh, they are people there, very well known. I did not make the statement that I started in 1880 with no backing. I did not start without any backing in 1880. I said that I had no backing in 1902 when I came back from the Philippine Islands. Your memory is not good, sir.

Mr. GARDNER. W. H. Wonson & Son are in substantially the same business as you are?

Mr. WONSON. No, sir.

Mr. GARDNER. In what does their business differ from yours?

Mr. WONSON. They are smoked-halibut people, altogether, and have been.

Mr. GARDNER. They do not own any vessels; they are manufacturers of salt fish?

Mr. WONSON. Their business is confined entirely to smoked halibut and herring, and has been, so far as I know, always.

Mr. GARDNER. There may be some difference, but they are substantially in the same business; they are fish shippers in Gloucester?

Mr. WONSON. No, sir; you will have to permit me to differ from you. You show that you have not an intimate knowledge of the situation.

Mr. GARDNER. Well, at all events, they are generally supposed to be in the same business. Now, have you a letter there which you wish to read to the committee from P. J. O'Brien?

Mr. WONSON. Yes; I have a number of letters, if the committee wants to listen to them.

Mr. GARDNER. I would like to hear that P. J. O'Brien letter.

Mr. WONSON. This letter is as follows:

GLOUCESTER BOARD OF TRADE,
Gloucester, Mass., February 1, 1911.

Mr. CHARLES F. WONSON.

DEAR SIR: Replying to your inquiry as to how I stand on the question of the reciprocal agreement with Canada, I beg to say that I believe if the agreement is ratified my business will be materially benefited. I am a strong advocate of the entry of free green fish, believing that part of the agreement will greatly benefit Gloucester as a whole. While the entry of free manufactured fish will benefit me personally in a business way, I am not sure but that feature of the agreement would take away the employment of labor in Gloucester, and I would advocate no legislation which would have that effect.

Yours, truly,

P. J. O'BRIEN & Co.,
By P. J. O'BRIEN.

Mr. CLARK. I would like to ask Mr. Gardner how he knew that the witness had that letter?

Mr. GARDNER. I will read a telegram, which will explain that, saying that Mr. Wonson has with him a letter from P. J. O'Brien.

(Mr. Gardner here read the telegram referred to.)

Mr. GARDNER. I am through with the witness.

Mr. WONSON. Mr. Chairman, if you will allow me just a minute; I had supposed from a telegram that was read here that nearly all of the 140 members of the board of trade had been seen; but I want it understood that it was not at a regular meeting of the board, because there was none called last night when I left Gloucester at 4 o'clock, and Article No. 7 of the by-laws of that organization reads this way:

Meetings may be called at any time by the president of the board of trade or upon the written application of 10 members to the secretary, notice thereof to be published in one or more Gloucester daily papers, and by notice mailed to each member 24 hours in advance of each meeting.

I happen to have been elected a member of the board of directors of that board of trade, and I have not been notified of any public meeting.

Mr. CLARK. Mr. Witness, that does not make a bit of difference. What you state you believe. If Mr. Gardner has got a lot of people who want to contradict you, let him bring them in.

Mr. WONSON. All right, sir.

Mr. CLARK. If you have anybody to back you up, bring him in.

Mr. GARDNER. I am ready to ask Mr. Treat, of Boston, to address you.

Mr. HILL. I would like to ask just one question. I am looking for information. I would like to ask your opinion as to why Canada charges a cent a pound duty on fish, one-quarter of a cent a pound more than we do? Have you any opinion on that?

Mr. WONSON. No, sir.

Mr. HILL. All right.

Mr. CLARK. If we do not ship fish up there, it does not do any good to anybody, does it, that cent a pound?

Mr. WONSON. We do ship fish up there.

Mr. CLARK. How much do you ship?

Mr. WONSON. I do not know. I ship none.

Mr. CLARK. Who does ship any?

Mr. WONSON. This gentleman who will follow me is a shipper, I think, and has been.

Mr. CLARK. One of these witnesses testified that they never sent but 25 pounds.

The CHAIRMAN. It was stated in the statistics of that company that they sent as much as that. They shipped more pounds than that.

Mr. GARDNER. He says his firm has never shipped above 25 pounds.

A BYSTANDER. Twenty-five boxes.

Mr. GARDNER. Twenty-five boxes; I beg your pardon.

Mr. McCALL. Is that all you desire to say?

Mr. WONSON. Yes, sir.

Mr. CLARK. Mr. Chairman, before the next witness begins I would like to ask you a question. How long are these hearings going to last?

The CHAIRMAN. I do not know.

Mr. CLARK. About how long do you think they will last?

The CHAIRMAN. It is pretty hard to guess.

Mr. CLARK. You are not going to try to report this bill before Monday, are you, or Tuesday?

The CHAIRMAN. I am not going to try to report it before Monday.

Mr. CLARK. What do you say about Tuesday?

Mr. FORDNEY. A lot of people from my State wanted to be heard, and they could not get here before Monday.

The CHAIRMAN. It will take, necessarily, as long as that.

Mr. CLARK. You will not do it before Tuesday? That is, you will not try to do it. You do not know whether you can do it at all or not.

Mr. LONGWORTH. This hearing to-day, Mr. Chairman, is not a precedent for hearing people interested from all over the country?

The CHAIRMAN. What is that?

Mr. LONGWORTH. I say I hope this hearing is not to furnish a precedent for persons from all over the country who are interested to be heard.

The CHAIRMAN. I do not think it is a precedent for anything. Of course, the committee can shut off hearings at any time.

Mr. LONGWORTH. I mean, I think it ought to be understood that it is not such a precedent.

The CHAIRMAN. Some gentlemen wanted to be heard on some subjects on which we had hearings during the tariff discussion in

1909, and I thought the committee would be unwilling to go over that discussion again, but we would hear them on facts that have occurred subsequently to those hearings, but would not be in favor of going over the hearings generally. For instance, the maltsters up in the West desired to be heard during the hearings on the tariff bill, and we heard the maltsters of Buffalo and Rochester, but we did not hear those in the West, in Milwaukee and elsewhere, who desire to retain the duty. Then, one of my colleagues from New York desired some people to be heard, and I told them to appear here to-morrow, in regard to agricultural products and products up in his district, in his part of the State.

Mr. ELLIS. My colleague informs me that some of the paper manufacturers and the lumbermen of the Pacific coast want to be heard.

The CHAIRMAN. No paper manufacturer, so far as I recollect, has asked to be heard. I have two or three letters from paper manufacturers in which they state their case fully, and I was going to put them in the record.

Mr. DAVIDSON. Mr. Chairman, just in that connection; I did not mean to interrupt this hearing, but when Mr. Clark asked you a question about the hearings, I was present in the room for the purpose of asking for a hearing. I have this telegram just received from Wisconsin:

In view of disastrous effect ratification of Canadian treaty will have on paper and pulp industry in this country, regard it of utmost importance that the representatives of the industry be given an opportunity to be heard before Ways and Means Committee.

Now, I just got that dispatch, and I want to reply to it.

The CHAIRMAN. Is that from Kimberly Clark?

Mr. DAVIDSON. Yes.

The CHAIRMAN. I will have to amend my statement. I did receive a similar telegram to that, and I answered that the committee were now having hearings, and people were to appear here on paper schedule, but that what they said would have to be confined to something which has taken place since the investigation made in 1909, and I said, "If you desire to be heard, come on at once." I telegraphed that this afternoon.

Mr. DAVIDSON. Then I will telegraph them practically the same thing—to come at once if they want to be heard. This is on the assumption that they will have opportunity to be heard.

The CHAIRMAN. I have here a long letter in the shape of a brief, from a paper manufacturer, which they ask to have printed in the record, but these parties do not ask to be heard, either one of them. I had forgotten about that telegram.

Mr. LONGWORTH. I think it ought to be understood that we are not going to hold general hearings on this bill, and that we will only have a hearing in a very exceptional case and at the special request of a Member of the House.

The CHAIRMAN. Yes; I do not think we will. Of course we had very full hearings during the tariff discussion, and we do not want to open up any question again except on something that has occurred since. For instance, that would apply to paper and pulp. It was pretty thoroughly investigated by the Mann committee, and I would not be in favor of going into anything on that subject except something that had occurred since that investigation was made.

Mr. FORDNEY. Mr. Chairman, in the treaty there is a provision relating to wood pulp which provides that news print paper shall be admitted from Canada free of duty, provided Canada permits the pulp wood to come into this country unrestricted. The lumbermen are very much interested in having a proviso of that same kind relating to lumber. It is proposed to put lumber on the free list. There is an embargo against logs. Is there any reason why we should not receive information on the subject? Is there any good reason why lumber should not be admitted free as well as paper pulp, when they are both forest products?

The CHAIRMAN. The question whether lumber should be treated in that way is a question independent, by itself, in my judgment. We will cross that bridge when we come to it.

Mr. FORDNEY. The point is, I say these lumbermen want to be heard on that subject. Are we going to permit a hearing on that subject. Mr. Longworth suggests that we do not have general hearings. Now, here are these lumbermen who want to be heard on that point, and some of them want to come from Seattle. I have a telegram from them in my office.

The CHAIRMAN. Those people out there can not have exclusive knowledge on that subject.

Mr. FORDNEY. Mr. Chairman, I am frank to say that the lumber industry of the country is of more importance than the fish industry, and while I am very friendly to the suggestion that the fishmen be heard in full, why should we choke off any important industry?

Mr. McCALL. We had these gentlemen come here at once. Mr. Gardner had his men come on immediately, but you are now proposing to have men come on here from Seattle.

The CHAIRMAN. Wait a moment, if you please. I think we will defer this discussion until we are in executive session.

Mr. FORDNEY. Very well.

STATEMENT OF LEONARD A. TREAT, OF BOSTON, MASS.

Mr. TREAT. My credentials are from the Boston Fish Bureau. The question that I wish to present to your committee, Mr. Chairman and gentlemen, is the question of the salt fish industry. I am not interested in the fresh fish industry. I have no particular knowledge of it. But we have heard a great deal of what is going to happen, and largely on the line of prophecy. I hold that the best lamp for most of us is the lamp of experience, and the only way we can know, it seems to me, what would happen is by referring to what has happened. Fortunately, we have had one reciprocity treaty, and we know that when we had that reciprocity treaty the same fish business was conducted as is being conducted now, but in larger volume and in a more profitable manner. There are three kinds of fish that largely compose the fish industry of New England, the codfish, the mackerel, and the herring. You have been told that the mackerel, for some reason or other, as soon as the treaty was enacted, disappeared from our coast. As to the herring, they, too, are slowly disappearing. There seem to be less and less of them caught each year. But there remains the codfish industry, and about that I would like to speak to you for a moment. Under that treaty we had reciprocity from 1872 to 1886, and that was an era of prosperity in the fish business, and with your permission I will take the last five years of reciprocity and compare them with the first five years after the abrogation of the treaty. During the years 1880, 1881, 1882, 1883, and 1884, the last five years of reciprocity, there were engaged in the New England codfish industry from 579 vessels to 765 vessels. Now taking the five years that followed the abrogation of the treaty, in the first year, 1885, there were 730 vessels in the fleet, in 1886 there weer 589, in 1887, 560, in 1888, 495, and in 1889 it had dwindled away, during that fifth year, to 295 vessels.

Taking, now, the product of the last five years of reciprocity, we have the following figures:

Total catch in hundredweight or quintals.

1880	647, 426
1881	775, 027
1882	898, 094
1883	1, 061, 699
1884	1, 001, 303
Total	4, 383, 548
Average catch	876, 709

In the following five years, the first five years after the abrogation of the treaty, we have the following figures in regard to the catch:

Total catch in hundredweight or quintals.

1885	902, 455
1886	828, 572
1887	676, 723
1888	585, 581
1889	498, 989
Total	3, 492, 320
Average catch	698, 464

Not only had the number of vessels shrunk, but the output had shrunk. Now, not only was this true of the vessels and not only was it true of the product, but it was also true of the price.

The average price during the last five years was $4.63 per 100 pounds of salted fish as they came from the vessel, going onto the railroad coming from these curers, while after the abrogation of the treaty the average price was $3.70.

Now, I contend that with these figures before us, which are more eloquent than any man can possibly be, there is nothing left for us to say but that reciprocity, as we have it presented to us under this bill, would cause all these bugaboos our friends from Gloucester presented to you to-day to disappear like mists before a rising sun. It certainly seems to me that with this industry, which they all admit, in the 25 years that it has existed since 1886, has been continually shrinking from year to year, it is about time that they changed doctors. If any of us had been sick for 25 years with a doctor of one school, I think we would have listened to somebody else, even though we might think he was a charlatan. In 1885 and 1886 there were more than 50 concerns in the salt-fish industry in Boston. The years have rolled by, and there are less than 15 of these concerns now. I am now speaking of nothing but the salt-fish industry. These vessels that I am talking about were wholly engaged in the salt-fish business, salt codfish and other ground fish.

That is all I have to say, and I am now open to any questions.

Mr. LONGWORTH. I would like to ask you, in the first place, about that reciprocity treaty. In what respect does it differ from the one we have here now?

Mr. TREAT. I am not familiar with the details of it, but it is practically the same. There were some inshore fisheries that were granted to us under the old reciprocity treaty that are not granted us now.

Mr. LONGWORTH. Your last figures there were for 1886, were they not?

Mr. TREAT. Yes.

Mr. LONGWORTH. Can you give us the figures since 1900?

Mr. TREAT. Yes. I just wanted to give you the catch.

Mr. LONGWORTH. Only the catch?

Mr. TREAT. Yes; that is all I can give you.

Mr. LONGWORTH. Can you give the number of vessels?

Mr. TREAT. No, sir; I have not those figures.

Mr. HILL. I understand you represented the Boston Fish Association.

Mr. TREAT. Yes; the Boston Bureau of Salt Fish.

Mr. HILL. Do you live in Gloucester?

Mr. TREAT. No, sir; in Boston.

Mr. GARDNER. Now, gentlemen, I would like to ask a few questions.

The CHAIRMAN. Very well.

Mr. GARDNER. Mr. Treat, you entirely differ from the position taken by the New England Fish Exchange?

Mr. TREAT. That is a fresh-fish organization.

Mr. GARDNER. Yes.

Mr. TREAT. I know nothing about their position, except as stated here to-day.

Mr. GARDNER. Are you a producer of fish?

Mr. TREAT. No, sir; I am a curer of fish.

Mr. GARDNER. What were those figures you just read, as to the amount; was that the amount of the catch landed in Boston?

Mr. TREAT. In New England.

Mr. GARDNER. In New England?

Mr. TREAT. Yes.

Mr. GARDNER. And during the existence of the reciprocity treaty; and just what did you wish to convey to the committee by pointing out that after the treaty was abolished and a duty was imposed on Canada, they could not send fish here? Would it not be natural to expect that the amount of fish would very much fall off in the next five years?

Mr. TREAT. No, sir; because the fish landed from these vessels were fish caught by American fishermen in American vessels.

Mr. GARDNER. In the first five years?

Mr. TREAT. Yes, in the first five years.

Mr. GARDNER. Mr. Chairman, I think we will have to get the figures from the Fish Commission on that. Now, on what do you base your figures as to the price in the last five years of reciprocity and the first five years of dutiable fish?

Mr. TREAT. Do you mean where did I get those figures?

Mr. GARDNER. Yes.

Mr. TREAT. All those figures that I have here, I would like to say to the committee, I got from this Boston Fish Bureau. This Boston Fish Bureau is a statistical organization that has existed for a great many years, just simply gathering figures and facts with reference to the production of salt fish in New England. All these figures I have here are from the books and files of the Boston Fish Bureau, and are now open to any member of the committee, or anybody else, I suppose.

Mr. FORDNEY. Then, as a fish dealer, it does not make any difference to you whether the fish come from American or Canadian fishermen, or Novo Scotian fishermen?

Mr. TREAT. No, sir.

Mr. FORDNEY. You do not care where they come from, as long as you get your profit?

Mr. TREAT. No, sir; that is the principal thing. I am not interested in fishing men or fishing vessels.

Mr. FORDNEY. That is the general attitude of an importer, is it not?

Mr. TREAT. No, sir.

Mr. FORDNEY. I think it is. I never found one that did not have that attitude.

Mr. GARDNER. As I understood you, under reciprocity you had to pay a higher price for fish than you had to pay after the reciprocity treaty was abrogated. Why are you in favor of a reciprocity treaty, if that is the case?

Mr. TREAT. I am in favor of the reciprocity treaty because the experience of the last five years of the reciprocity treaty showed that that was a period of very great prosperity to the whole business. It was not true of the fishing vessels only. While I have not any figures, my memory goes back. I went into the business in 1867 and as a young man of 20 to 30, the years from 1872 to 1886 covered that period of my life. I know that the business was prosperous and I know that the number of firms engaged in that business was large. I know that the amount of business was greater both in the number of those employed and in point of fish cured and shipped.

Mr. GARDNER. I fear you did not catch my question. You are a purchaser of fish which come into the Boston market from Canada and from the vessels that come in at the wharf, of the various kinds of fish, and you tell us that under reciprocity the prices were higher and you had to pay more for your raw material than you did after the reciprocity treaty was abolished. Now, I never saw any manufacturer who desired to pay more for his raw material, and if reciprocity raises the price of fish, why are you, a purchaser of fish, in favor of reciprocity?

Mr. TREAT. Because it is one of those peculiar things that you may think strange. Here was where we were fair with our neighbors. Our neighbors prospered with us.

Mr. GARDNER. Oh, it was because your neighbors were prosperous?

Mr. TREAT. No, sir; not at all. That is not my answer to that question.

Mr. GARDNER. Mr. Chairman, I wish this committee would call for the figures from the United States Fish Commission as to the prices of fish in those years.

Mr. TREAT. I think the United States Fish Commission, if I may be allowed to say so, was not in existence in those years.

Mr. GARDNER. Mr. Millett can probably inform us as to that fact.

Mr. MILLETT. I think Stephen J. Martin was agent in those years.

The CHAIRMAN. You can get those figures at the bureau of statistics.

Mr. GARDNER. I would like to have all those figures. I think that Mr. Millett, who understands the thing pretty well, would undertake to secure those figures and have them sent to the committee, as well as the statistics that were referred to while he was testifying.

Mr. MILLETT. If you will have your clerk give me the years you want figures upon, I will undertake to get them for you and send them to you from the department.

The CHAIRMAN. Find out just what period you want, Mr. Gardner.

Mr. GARDNER. Substantially, we want all the figures during the reciprocity period and the figures since. That is what you want, is it not? That will tell the whole story.

Mr. HILL. Yes.

The CHAIRMAN. Leave that information with the clerk of the committee, and I think we can get it.

Mr. GARDNER. That would be my idea. Mr. Treat, did you ever hear of Wilcox's report?

Mr. TREAT. Yes.

Mr. GARDNER. He was the special agent of the Bureau of Fisheries, was he not?

Mr. TREAT. I never knew exactly what his relation was with the United States Government.

Mr. GARDNER. Did he not go to Gloucester in the year 1885, the last year of the old treaty, and did not his report say that Gloucester was suffering very greatly from the treaty, and did he not say that they were looking forward with great anticipation to the revocation of the treaty?

Mr. TREAT. Quite likely.

Mr. GARDNER. Do you know of any other official report on that situation except Wilcox's?

Mr. TREAT. Yes.

Mr. GARDNER. What is that?

Mr. TREAT. From Provincetown.

Mr. GARDNER. And you think the Board of Trade of Provincetown is in favor of reciprocity?

Mr. TREAT. No, sir.

Mr. GARDNER. To-day?

Mr. TREAT. No, sir, or was not then.

Mr. GARDNER. I call your attention to the unanimous vote——

Mr. TREAT. It was not then. It was unanimous in favor of abrogation of the treaty.

Mr. GARDNER. That is all I have to ask the gentleman.

Mr. McCALL. Can you furnish the committee with the population of Gloucester at that time?

Mr. TREAT. Twenty thousand and odd, is it not?

Mr. McCALL. But in 1870, in the five-year periods when the treaty was in force, and afterwards?

Mr. GARDNER. Gloucester and the surrounding towns would be the fairest way to take it; Rockport and Gloucester; and then of course there is Marblehead.

Mr. McCALL. Yes.

Mr. TREAT. I have one paper here which gives the catch in New-foundland and in Canada in all these years, which shows that their fishery has practically been prosperous all this time.

Mr. FORDNEY. Will the gentleman permit me to ask one or two questions?

Mr. TREAT. Yes, sir.

Mr. FORDNEY. Have you studied the effect of this proposed meas-ure, other than that which relates to fish?

Mr. TREAT. No, sir.

Mr. FORDNEY. Now, let me ask you this: It is shown here that our exports to Canada, amounting to $47,327,000, and our imports from Canada, $47,127,000, worth of goods are affected by this treaty, and a very small proportion of it is fish. The duty collected by Canada on our goods going into that country under the present law is $7,767,000, and they propose to reduce that duty $2,560,000, while the collection of duty by us on a like amount of goods coming from Canada is $5,649,000, and we reduce that duty $4,849,000, which will leave the duty collected by Canada on our goods going into that country almost equal to the amount that we collect on their goods coming from the country now. Do you not believe it would be a pretty good bill for other people than those interested in the fish business?

Mr. TREAT. I should have to plead ignorance in regard to the other industries.

Mr. FORDNEY. Are you in favor of the adoption of this treaty as it has been written or prepared?

Mr. TREAT. I am in favor of the treaty because of the opportunity it gives the fish business to revive.

Mr. FORDNEY. Then, whatever the sacrifice, if it was a sacrifice, of all the other industries mentioned in there except the fish industry, you would still be in favor of it?

Mr. TREAT. No, sir; I would not. I plead ignorance on the other. I presume that that has been prepared in the same careful manner in which this has been prepared—the fish part of it.

Mr. FORDNEY. If Canada is getting the best of the deal according to the treaty, would you still be in favor of adopting it?

Mr. TREAT. It would make no difference to me whether Canada was getting the best of the deal or not, if I was getting a fair thing out of it myself.

Mr. FORDNEY. There is every evidence of that, because you said you did not care what became of the American fishermen.

Mr. TREAT. I beg your pardon.

Mr. FORDNEY. Well, I beg your pardon. I asked you if it made any difference to you, as a packer or dealer, whether you got your fish from an American or a Nova Scotian or a Canadian fisherman, and you said it did not.

Mr. TREAT. That is right.

Mr. FORDNEY. Then you do not care a snap about the American fisherman?

Mr. TREAT. Oh, yes, I do. It is because I care so much for the American fisherman that I want to see this go through. I am perhaps contradicting myself about being a prophet, but, judging from the past, it is fair for me to assume, if you please, that prosperity would dawn from the very start and would increasingly come to us as the years roll by.

Mr. FORDNEY. Pardon me, let me ask you this: A certain amount of fish is prepared in this country for the market. It is supplied by the American fishermen and if, by the removal of the duty on fish, a large influx of fish would come from Canada and Newfoundland it would naturally injure the man that catches the fish in American waters, would it not?

Mr. TREAT. No, sir.

Mr. FORDNEY. How can you figure that out?

Mr. TREAT. Because it might open up more markets.

Mr. FORDNEY. Do you mean it might make us eat more fish?

Mr. TREAT. No, sir; open up other markets.

Mr. FORDNEY. What other market in that case can it open up?

Mr. TREAT. In Canada.

Mr. FORDNEY. For fish?

Mr. TREAT. Yes.

Mr. FORDNEY. Would you give away the market of 90,000,000 people for the market of 9,000,000 people in Canada?

Mr. TREAT. Is it not apparent that the 90,000,000 people are not salt fish eating people?

Mr. FORDNEY. What are you going to assume, that those 90,000,000 people——

Mr. TREAT. My dear man, excuse me, but we have grown from 30,000,000 people at the time this old reciprocity treaty was in effect to 90,000,000 people now, and they are producing one-sixth as much, in proportion. The fact is that the people of this country are not eating salt fish. Salt fish are consumed in warm countries.

Mr. FORDNEY. Do you propose to make them eat more fish?

Mr. TREAT. No, sir; I wish I could.

Mr. FORDNEY. Then what is your object in getting the fish of Canada?

Mr. TREAT. So that we may have a larger supply and have a larger market.

Mr. FORDNEY. Is it not because you want a larger market in which to buy fish?

Mr. TREAT. No, sir; it would do me no good if I could not open a larger market to sell them in.

Mr. FORDNEY. Is it not true that it would open up a larger market for you to buy fresh fish, and is not that what you want?

Mr. TREAT. No, sir; I am not for lower prices; I am for a larger trade.

Mr. FORDNEY. Do you not believe foreign competition would give you a larger market for salt fish?

Mr. TREAT. No, sir; there is this 13 years' experience that shows we had better prices and greater prosperity for fishermen, producers and manufacturers and dealers.

Mr. FORDNEY. Then you think it would increase the price, do you, if we put fish on the free list from Canada?

Mr. TREAT. Not increase the price over this year, because the testimony from the other side—if I may so refer to them—shows that the prices were exorbitant.

Mr. FORDNEY. I must say, my friend, I can not understand why you favor free trade between this country and Canada in fish.

Mr. TREAT. I am sorry.

Mr. HILL. As representing the Boston Fish Bureau, can you give me any information as to why the rate of duty on fish into Canada is higher than it is in the United States?

Mr. TREAT. I think if you would make your inquiries of the Great Lakes and the Pacific coast, you would get an answer that was satisfactory.

Mr. HILL. What I want to get at is why that is.

Mr. TREAT. You will have to get that from the other gentleman.

Mr. HILL. You have no opinion to express?

Mr. TREAT. No, sir.

Mr. McCALL. Did you mean that it was not possible to prevent fishermen coming across at the lakes?

Mr. TREAT. Yes.

Mr. HILL. I would like to ask Mr. Patch a question or two.

STATEMENT OF ISAAC PATCH.

Mr. HILL. You are the present mayor of Gloucester?

Mr. PATCH. Yes.

Mr. HILL. When were you elected?

Mr. PATCH. Last December.

Mr. HILL. What is the population of Gloucester?

Mr. PATCH. 24,398.

Mr. HILL. What is the voting population?

Mr. PATCH. Last fall there were about 5,000 votes cast.

Mr. HILL. About 5,000?

Mr. PATCH. If I remember correctly.

Mr. HILL. What proportion of the voting population are engaged in the fish industry, in your judgment?

Mr. PATCH. That would be a very hard question for me to answer.

Mr. HILL. Half of them; three-quarters; one-quarter? Well, never mind that.

Mr. PATCH. I can not say.

Mr. HILL. Was this subject of the duty on fish a subject of discussion in the campaign of 1910?

Mr. PATCH. Not in the municipal campaign.

Mr. HILL. No; I do not mean in the municipal campaign; I mean in the gubernatorial campaign.

Mr. PATCH. Yes.

Mr. HILL. It was a matter of discussion?

Mr. PATCH. Yes.

Mr. HILL. Was it a matter of interest, the duties shown in the Payne bill, and the position taken by other parties in opposition to it?

Mr. PATCH. Yes.

Mr. HILL. And if so, what was the verdict of the collector?

Mr. PATCH. That is rather a hard question to answer.

Mr. GARDNER. Did the fish question have anything to do with the election of Mr. Foss?

Mr. PATCH. I think not.

Mr. GARDNER. Did he favor free fish?

Mr. PATCH. He was in favor of free green fish.

Mr. GARDNER. Did he say so in Gloucester?

Mr. PATCH. Yes.

Mr. GARDNER. And did he have a majority there?

Mr. PATCH. No, sir; he did not.

Mr. McCALL. Did he not carry the town?

Mr. PATCH. No, sir; he did not carry the town of Gloucester.

Mr. McCALL. About what was the vote?

Mr. PATCH. If I remember correctly, although I would not want to state it positively, there was a majority of several hundred for Mr. Draper.

Mr. HILL. In Gloucester?

Mr. PATCH. There may have been reasons why Mr. Draper did not get more.

Mr. HILL. I wanted to know whether the people of Gloucester, with the matter before them, had fairly given a verdict on that matter.

Mr. PATCH. I do not think that the State elections had anything to do with the fish question, although it was discussed.

Mr. HILL. Did Mr. Foss favor a duty on salt fish?

Mr. PATCH. I do not know, anything except free green fish.

Mr. RANDELL. What percentage of the population there is adult males?

Mr. PATCH. That is rather a hard question for me to answer.

Mr. RANDELL. You seem to be very well posted about things in general, there.

Mr. PATCH. Of course it would have been very easy for me to get the information if it had occurred to me. I think there are between 7,000 and 8,000. I would not want to state that positively.

Mr. RANDELL. There might be a very great difference between the number of adults and those who voted.

Mr. PATCH. Yes. Of course there are a considerable number who are not naturalized.

Mr. RANDELL. That is the reason I asked what percentage of the 24,000 are adult males.

Mr. PATCH. It would only be a guess on my part. I think the other sex predominates.

Mr. HILL. Then you think no inference could be drawn from the result of the election as to the views of the people of Gloucester on this question?

Mr. PATCH. No, sir; not at that election; but of course I think the people as a whole are against the treaty as it stands.

Mr. HILL. You think the people of Gloucester are against the treaty?

Mr. PATCH. Yes; but there is a bona fide opinion, and a very strong one, in favor of free raw material.

Mr. FORDNEY. Pardon me, my friend. for asking the question; I would not ask it except for the fact that it is being tried to be made to appear here that the anticipation of this treaty had something to do with the result of the election last fall in Massachusetts. The State of New York gave an overwhelming democratic majority. Do you think free trade had anything to do with it?

Mr. PATCH. No, sir; I think not.

Mr. FORDNEY. Pardon me for asking.

Mr. GARDNER. If I might say a word as to that question. this proposition has never been put squarely before the people of Gloucester. Of course, Gloucester is a great fish-packing point, and if you put the question, "Will you have free green fish and protected finished products," obviously a lot of people will say yes; and of course we all know here that producers of raw material in the United States outnumber the manufacturers, and therefore we can not expect the manufacturers to be protected if the producers of raw material are not to be. That is not understood in a municipality like

Gloucester. That is the issue Mr. Foss has been presenting for a number of years.

Mr. HILL. Did he simply take the position of favoring free green fish or free fish all the way through?

Mr. GARDNER. Free green fish, and he said nothing about the rest. Is that correct?

Mr. PATCH. That is correct.

Mr. FORDNEY. Are you speaking of Mr. Foss?

Mr. GARDNER. Yes.

Mr. FORDNEY. Why, he has been published through the newspapers as being in favor of reciprocity with Canada on everything that grew on Canadian soil, or was imported in there.

Mr. GARDNER. Well, but there is not everybody that reads those things carefully; and we have often noticed that a man's position has local shades of difference.

Mr. FORDNEY. He has fought and labored for reciprocity with Canada.

Mr. GARDNER. I had a joint debate with him before the Massachusetts Club on that question eight years ago.

Mr. FORDNEY. You know him better than I do.

The CHAIRMAN. If you have an expert opinion on that gentleman's election there, perhaps you had better let it drop. Does any other gentleman desire to be heard on the fish question? Is there any other gentleman here who desires now to be heard on any part of this reciprocity question?

Mr. GARDNER. By the way, so far as political evidences are concerned, I had a very, very large majority in Gloucester, and my position has never been one on which there was any misapprehension whatever.

The CHAIRMAN. The committee will be in executive session for a few minutes.

At 5.30 o'clock p. m. the committee went into executive session.

(The following letters and papers submitted by Mr. Wonson are here printed in full in the record.)

GLOUCESTER, MASS., *February 1, 1911.*

Col. CHARLES F. WONSON, *Washington, D. C.*

DEAR SIR: Regarding matters which are now transpiring in Washington in which Gloucester is much interested, and in reply to your request for my views in writing regarding same, I will try and give you as fair a statement as I can of the actual conditions as I see them, endeavoring to throw aside any personal business interest in the matter.

The recommendations to Congress so far as fish is concerned are so sweeping that I believe that there is no one in Gloucester who, if he had the privilege of making the law, would have reciprocity to go through under the recommendations as presented to Congress, the reason being that our Canadian neighbors get too much and ourselves too little by this proposition.

While I believe the above statement to be fully true, it is nevertheless a fact that there is and has been for some time past a very decided opinion prevailing in Gloucester that there should be some arrangement whereby Gloucester's merchants and packers might obtain more liberal supplies of stock with which to conduct their business. Shortages in the supplies and very high prices have prevailed to a greater extent than the business interests of the city would warrant, and the packers have been obliged either to pay very fancy prices or go without, thus throwing male and female employees out of work at times when they could be employed quite steadily were proper supplies of stock obtainable with which to do business.

While the State campaign was in progress last fall, a mass meeting of Gloucester's citizens was held at the City Hall to discuss the reciprocity issue, and both sides of the question were heard. For a good many years past, or until the last few years, the preponderance of opinion in Gloucester regarding the entrance of Canadian fish to our ports free of duty had decidedly opposed such a proposition in any form.

At the mass meeting in the city hall the proposition was advanced that the admission of green or "raw product" salt fish might be a distinct benefit to Gloucester, and the question was gone into quite thoroughly, and the doings of the meeting were well reported in the public press.

Our present governor, Foss, during last fall's campaign, in his speech at Gloucester came out squarely for "free green fish," and told the people of Gloucester that such an arrangement would be a distinct benefit to Gloucester's business men and laborers, as well as to real estate values and wharf property in general.

I think it is a fair statement that the free green fish question was paramount in the minds of the Gloucester voters during the campaign, and the opinion prevailed that a vote for Gov. Foss was a vote in the direction of free green fish.

While the meeting at the city hall was not held with the idea of getting votes for one candidate or another, but simply for an open public discussion of the reciprocity question, it was openly stated after the meeting and during the rest of the campaign that the meeting at the city hall had changed several hundred votes to Gov. Foss which were normally Republican. I can personally testify to quite a number of voters who said that they had usually voted a Republican ticket who stated openly that they would vote for Mr. Foss on election day. The result, as well known, was that Mr. Draper, the Republican candidate, carried the city by only 253 votes, in a city which ordinarily was strongly Republican, often casting about 2 to 1 for the Republican candidates. The people seemed to have done a good deal of thinking during the campaign and the result was not unexpected, if one could judge by expressions about the streets, shops, and wharves previous to election day.

The term "free green fish"[1] refers, of course, to the salt fish in the state as landed by our New England vessels, and a very much larger supply of this kind of salt fish is to my mind what Gloucester has stood seriously in need of for quite a number of years. Shortages in the salt-fish supply have been entirely too frequent during the last decade to allow Gloucester's retail merchants and laborers to longer submit quietly to present conditions, if some more beneficial arrangement to Gloucester can be obtained. That Gloucester needs something different from present conditions I believe is quite generally conceded by Gloucester's citizens, and I hope that the present discussion may result in some arrangement more beneficial to our fish trade without conceding altogether too much to our Canadian neighbors.

I honestly believe that free green salt fish from Canada with a duty retained on the manufactured fish would give Gloucester, as a whole, a lift ahead and would not drive out Gloucester's fishing fleet, as seems to be anticipated by vessel owners and master mariners. A large country and a growing population will take care of a very large amount of salt fish, and an oversupply of the raw product seems entirely out of the question for the years that are to come.

I am aware that this letter considers the question almost entirely from Gloucester's standpoint; but whatever is done by Congress, Gloucester should have an opportunity to live and to do business in her old fish industry, and I trust that the Members of Congress will try to give us as fair a chance as possible to build up our fish manufacturing business, which seems to offer an opportunity of enlargement, provided good supplies of the raw product are obtainable at all times.

I trust there may be some other way for Gloucester to obtain the free green fish than as proposed in the reciprocity recommendations as they now exist.

Trusting the best results may be obtained, I remain,

Yours, respectfully,   W. O. ANDREWS.

GLOUCESTER, *February 1, 1911.*

Mr. CHARLES F. WONSON,
    Gloucester, Mass.

DEAR SIR: In reply to your inquiry as to my views on the fishing situation, I would say that in my opinion while dutiable fish may benefit a few it is injuring the many as far as the fishing industry as a whole is concerned. But five firms here, as far as I know, are in favor of a duty on all grades of fish. These parties are in control of the financial situation here, being practically in control of the banks, and in this way have quite a following. Since the merger of several firms some years ago this city has gone behind rapidly. About two-thirds of the wharves are unoccupied and going to decay. The population is decreasing rapidly.

---

[1] Green fish: Fish as they come from the ocean, simply dressed, split open, and preserved in salt.

Under the years of reciprocity business was booming here. Fish came here direct from the Banks. All wharves were full of fish and many people occupied in curing and preparing for market. While I am not so sure that free dried fish would help us, it would be an improvement on the present system, which is practically a monopoly of a very few people. Under reciprocity before I had four wharves occupied where now have not business for one. The present system is making a back number of Gloucester and any change, in my opinion, will be an improvement.

Yours, very truly,

STANWOOD & CO.,
JOHN J. STANWOOD.

GLOUCESTER, MASS., *February 1, 1911.*

Mr. CHARLES F. WONSON,
    Gloucester, Mass.

DEAR SIR: I have been intimately connected with the fishing business of Gloucester for 40 years, both as an operative fisherman, captain and owner of vessels, and handling the fish in all its different ways, and since this reciprocity question has come up I have talked with fishermen, men on the wharves and people whom I have met on the street, and I am firmly convinced that among these people there is a strong feeling in favor of the treaty.

Very truly, yours,

Capt. ROBERT N. MILLER.

The records in the Gloucester customhouse show that the fishing tonnage of Gloucester, on the 30th day of September in each year from 1872 to 1910, both inclusive, was as follows:

Years.	Vessels.	Total gross tonnage.	Fishing tonnage.	Net tonnage.
1872		22,962		
1873		21,517		
1874		21,638		
1875		21,997		
1876		23,078		
1877		24,114		
1878		21,457		
1879		19,187		
1880		18,528		
1881		18,330		
1882		20,026		
1883		23,468		
1884		24,051		
1885		24,339		
1886		27,152		
1887		27,380		
1888		26,852		
1889		26,641		
1890		26,799		
1891		29,366		
1892		30,620		
1893		36,164		
1894		35,739		
1895		35,127		
1896		34,751		
1897		31,699		
1898		31,395		
1899		29,117		
1900	354		30,208	23,452
1901	351		27,914	21,287
1902	372		31,304	22,107
1903	382		31,285	23,844
1904	377		30,223	22,086
1905	372		28,932	21,650
1906	344		26,902	19,953
1907	322		22,965	19,253
1908	293		23,189	17,152
1909	283		22,274	16,166
1910	[1] 181 / [2] 76		18,877 / 1,031	12,063

[1] Over 20 tons.   [2] Under 20 tons.

(Exhibits submitted by Mr. Treat:)

NEWFOUNDLAND CODFISH CATCH.

Years.	Catch in quintals of 112 pounds each.	Years.	Catch in quintals of 112 pounds each.
1880	1,383,131	1891	947,575
1881	1,462,439	1892	795,549
1882	1,231,607	1893	1,175,836
1883	1,624,037	1894	1,107,696
1884	1,397,637	1895	1,436,093
1885	1,284,710	1896	1,150,297
1886	1,344,180	1897	1,145,540
1887	1,080,024	1898	1,226,336
1888	1,175,720	1899	1,300,622
1889	1,075,567	1900	1,233,107
1890	1,040,916	1901	1,238,955

CANADIAN CODFISH CATCH.

Years.	Catch	Years.	Catch
1880	1,092,514	1891	849,838
1881	1,075,582	1892	880,184
1882	903,030	1893	892,978
1883	1,075,121	1894	938,027
1884	1,022,329	1895	806,415
1885	1,077,393	1896	809,608
1886	1,061,416	1897	974,656
1887	1,078,355	1898	714,683
1888	1,050,877	1899	932,577
1889	904,560	1900	897,765
1890	857,734	1901	1,004,586

UNDER RECIPROCITY.

Years.	Number of vessels engaged in New England in the cod-fishery.	Total catch figured in quintals of 112 pounds each.
1880	579	647,426
1881	604	775,027
1882	692	898,094
1883	746	1,061,699
1884	765	1,001,303

UNDER PROTECTION.

Years.	Number of vessels	Total catch
1885	730	902,455
1886	589	828,572
1887	560	676,723
1888	495	585,581
1889	295	498,989

(At the request of Mr. Hill, the following Treasury Decision is made part of the record of the hearing. It is from No. 45, volume 19, of "Treasury Decisions under the customs, internal revenue, and other laws," published Thursday, November 10, 1910.)

(T. D. 31028—G. A. 7121.)

AMERICAN FISHERIES.

(Fish imported from the shores of the "treaty waters" of Newfoundland admitted to free entry as products of American fisheries. The term "American fisheries" defined. United States General Appraisers, New York, November 7, 1910. In the matter of protests 411276, etc., of W. B. Redding et al. against the assessment of duty by the collector of customs at the port of Boston. Before Board 3, Waite, Somerville, and Hay, general appraisers.)

WAITE, General Appraiser: These protests arise over the importation of fish which were caught in what is known as the "treaty waters" off the island of Newfoundland, pursuant to the provisions of the treaty of 1818 between Great Britain and the United States. The fish were imported into the United States after the tariff act of August 5, 1909, went into effect. They were assessed under paragraph 273 of said law, which reads as follows:

"273. Fish, fresh, smoked, dried, salted, pickled, frozen, packed in ice, or otherwise prepared for preservation, not specially provided for in this section, three-fourths of one cent per pound; fish, skinned or boned, one and one-fourth cents per pound; mackerel, halibut, or salmon, fresh, pickled, or salted, one cent per pound."

It is claimed by the importer that they should be admitted free under the provisions of either paragraph 567 or 639 of said law. Paragraph 567 grants free entry to—

"Fish, fresh, frozen, or packed in ice, caught in the Great Lakes or other fresh waters by citizens of the United States, and all other fish, the products of American fisheries."

Paragraph 639, in so far as pertinent hereto, reads as follows:

"639. * * * spermaceti, whale, and other fish oils of American fisheries, and all fish and other products of such fisheries; * * *"

From the above quotations it will be seen that the last-named paragraphs provide for the free entry of fish caught where these were caught in case they are the product of American fisheries. The only question for us to decide here is whether they come within that category. Evidence was introduced at the hearing which shows the following to be the circumstances under which these fish were caught:

One Capt. Carter, owner and master of the vessel *Sarah C. Wharf*, duly documented under the laws of the United States, had maintained her in the waters about the treaty coast of Newfoundland for a number of years previous to the fall of 1909. During the time when these fish were caught the vessel had on board a crew of five men, of whom the temporary captain and one other man were citizens of the United States. The vessel was used as a base of supplies and for the use of the master in the conduct of his operations while catching the fish. The fish, however, were not caught from this vessel; in fact, they were not ever on board the vessel. They were caught by citizens of Newfoundland, or of the provinces, by means of tackle and appliances which were in some cases supplied by the men themselves and in some cases by the master of the vessel, who was responsible for and conducted these fishing operations. He says that from $800 to $1,000 was invested by him in such tackle and appliances for catching the fish. The men who caught the fish were employed on different bases. Some of them were paid by the pound, according to weight after the fish had been dressed or split. Some of them, however, were employed on a time basis at so much per day for catching the fish. Payment was also made on the same bases for their services in curing the fish. These fish were cured at various places along the shore, which were provided by the witness Carter, the master and owner of the vessel. The evidence does not disclose how complete these curing stations were; it is fair to assume, however, that they consisted of necessary appliances, such as sheds, racks, receptacles for receiving the fish and offal, and places for drying the fish. We have not had our attention called to any definition of a fishery which has been recognized by the courts. The ordinary definition as given by the dictionaries is:

"Fishery. 1. The business of catching fish or any aquatic animals; the fishing industry; * * * 2. A place where fish or other aquatic animals are or may be taken regularly; fishing grounds. 3. The buildings and equipment generally required in any particular fishing business; a fishing establishment. Standard Dictionary.

"Fishery. 1. The business of catching fish; the fishing industry. 2. In law, a right of fishing in certain waters. 3. A place where fish are regularly caught, or other products of the sea or rivers are taken from the waters by fishing, diving, dredging, etc. Century Dictionary."

In our judgment three things are necessary to constitute a fishery within the meaning of the statute: The fishing grounds; a place for curing the fish or preparing them for the market, if they are not marketed as taken from the water; and the necessary tackle and appliances for catching the fish, such as lines, hooks, nets, boats, etc. We think the testimony shows that a fishery was maintained by Capt. Carter on the treaty coast at this time. It appears he had been engaged in this business on these grounds for several years.

Having arrived at this conclusion, the next step is to determine whether it was an American fishery. It has been held by the Treasury Department under similar laws that it was not absolutely necessary that the fish should all be caught, handled, and cured by Americans. Note T. D. 7933 and T. D. 10588, where it was stated that fish caught by the crew of an American vessel licensed for the fisheries, with the assistance of men and nets hired in Newfoundland for that purpose, would be free of duty as the product of American fisheries. To the same effect, see also T. D. 28768. And in G. A. 5453 (T. D. 24738) it was held that fish taken at the Bay of Islands, Newfoundland, by an American vessel, under a license from the Canadian Government, with the assistance of men, boats, and gear hired for the purpose, are entitled to free entry under paragraph 626, tariff act of 1897, as the "product of an American fishery." We note, in passing, that the arbitration court at The Hague has recently decided that inhabitants of the United States, while exercising the liberty to take fish on the treaty coasts, may employ as members of their fishing crews persons not inhabitants of the United States.

While none of these fish were actually caught by the manual labor of Americans, still the opportunity, funds, place, and appliances necessary for the operation to be carried on were furnished by an American with American money. The whole enterprise was conducted and carried on by an American who was responsible for the operations. The law was intended, in our judgment, to favor operations carried on by Americans in this way and to encourage the taking of fish in the treaty waters. We are of the opinion, therefore, that this plant, carried on, fostered, and maintained as it was, should be held to be an American fishery, the products of which should be admitted to the United States free of duty under the existing law. The protests are therefore sustained.

RECIPROCITY WITH CANADA.

COMMITTEE ON WAYS AND MEANS,
HOUSE OF REPRESENTATIVES,
Saturday, February 4, 1911.

The committee met at 10.30 o'clock a. m., Hon. Sereno E. Payne (chairman) presiding.

Present: The chairman, and Messrs. Dalzell, McCall, Hill, Boutell, Calderhead, Fordney, Gaines, Longworth, Dwight, Ellis, Clark, Pou, Randell, Broussard, and Brantley.

The CHAIRMAN. Is there any gentleman here who desires to address the committee at this time?

STATEMENT OF HON. L. B. HANNA, A REPRESENTATIVE IN CONGRESS FROM THE STATE OF NORTH DAKOTA.

Mr. HANNA. Mr. Chairman, I would like to say just a word or two, if I might.

The CHAIRMAN. If it is simply to fill in the time, we do not care to hear you. If you have any argument to present, we will hear you.

Mr. HANNA. I do not know that I have any special argument to make.

The CHAIRMAN. I was going to have read this letter which was presented by your friend, and which he wants read, and if you no not want to say anything in particular we will have the letter read.

Mr. HANNA. I simply wanted, in a general way, to protest against the enactment of this reciprocity treaty.

The CHAIRMAN. Then proceed, if you think it is more important than to have this communication read.

Mr. HANNA. I desire to protest, for the reason that there is not a solitary thing that the State which I have the honor to represent produces but under this proposed treaty will be put on the free list— wheat, barley, oats, flax, horses, cattle, everything—while on the other hand as soon as a product is manufactured there is a duty placed upon it. Now, it hardly seems right to me and to the farmers of the Northwest, throughout the country up there, that everything they produce should be put upon the free list and that they should be obliged to sell everything they produce in an open market, while on the other hand they must buy manufactured articles with the duty upon them. There is nothing that will come down from the Canadian northwest, from that side of the line, that will help the farmers in this country, either in the production of butter and eggs or in the raising of wheat, flax, or whatever it may be; and I do believe that the enactment of this reciprocity agreement between this country and Canada will be a bad thing for the country generally. For years I have stood for a protective policy in this country, because I believed in it and do now, but it would seem to me as though this proposed reciprocity agreement was the beginning of the end of the protective policy. If one class of people in this country are to have their products put upon the free list, it can only result in one thing, and that is that the free list will go all along down the line.

Our State Legislature, North Dakota, in the last few days has passed a very strong resolution against the enactment of this proposed reciprocity treaty. I have here a copy of the Fargo Forum, a daily paper published in my home city, Fargo, N. Dak., which shows the price of wheat in Winnipeg, on the other side of the line from us, and the price in Minneapolis, on this side, and upon the day this paper was gotten out, which was February 1, wheat was worth 12 cents more a bushel on this side of the line than it was on the other side; flax was worth 25 cents a bushel more on this side than on the other; and barley and oats were worth more on this side of the line in the same proportion.

I want to emphatically protest, so far as it lies within my power to do so, against this proposed treaty. The backbone of the Republican party for 50 years has been the farmers out upon the farms, and if what protection the farmers have for what they raise shall be taken from them, the farmers must naturally swing to the other side and will insist that the tariff upon manufactured products shall be removed.

The CHAIRMAN. Would you like to have this gentleman's letter read?

Mr. HANNA. All right; I am very willing.

The CHAIRMAN. What the committee want to hear is something new on the subject. This is a matter that has been thrashed over for the last 50 years, and especially for the last 20 or 30 years, the duty on agricultural products, and you have introduced your friend here and he is very desirous of having this letter which he has presented read to the committee, and if you will give way the letter will now be read by the clerk of the committee.

Mr. HANNA. Very well; I am quite willing.

(The clerk of the committee here read the letter referred to, as follows:)

WASHINGTON, D. C., *January 30, 1911.*

To the honorable George T. Oliver, United States Senate, Washington, D. C., and James J. Hill, esq., St. Paul, Minn., part owner and full controller of the two northern transcontinental railway lines leading from Minnesota to the Pacific Ocean and the many "feeders" or branch lines of said railroads running into northwestern Canada.

GENTLEMEN: I read in yesterday's Sunday papers both of your views or statements in regard to the new tariff treaty with Canada now pending in Congress.

As I understand the situation, Senator Oliver is opposed to granting "free trade" for the products of the farmers and Mr. Hill wants all duties removed, so far as they relate to the products of the farm.

In other words, Senator Oliver is opposed to and Mr. Hill is in favor of the new treaty with Canada.

Senator Oliver, on Saturday night at Pittsburg, is reported to have said, while addressing "seven hundred or more members of the Young Men's Republican Tariff Club," as follows:

FARMERS WILL BE LOSERS.

"As a result of this, therefore, our manufacturers, merchants, and industrial laborers will profit at the expense of the farmers. The farming interest always has been one of the great bulwarks of the Republican Party, and while I naturally hesitate about antagonizing any important measure favored by the administration of President Taft, I will have to experience a change of heart before I vote to deprive one class of our industries of that protection to which they are justly entitled under all the theories and practices of the Republican Party for the benefit of others."

As a resident of North Dakota, and quite extensively engaged in farming, I write to thank Senator Oliver for having uttered the foregoing sentiments. Your position shows that you not only correctly represent the great State of Pennsylvania, but of the whole country.

The farmers, and more especially those residing in the Northwest, are entitled to the same degree of tariff protection for the results of the 14 hours "a day's work" on the farm as those who raise cotton, tobacco, sugar, and rice, south of us; also the same as the producer of oil, coal, minerals, and materials of all kinds, including manufactured articles used by the people.

I believe that all unbiased people not controlled or influenced by selfish personal interests will applaud and thank you for the efforts that you are making for all the people.

While the duty of 25 cents a bushel on wheat does not make that difference in the price realized between the grain growers of the two countries when they ship from their own ports direct to Europe, yet at all times in the Northwest the farmer on our side of the dividing line realizes from 10 cents to 15 cents per bushel more than his neighbor on the other side of the line. And this applies not only to wheat, but more especially to barley suitable for brewing purposes. Remember that nearly all our barley used in the United States is produced mostly in the west and northwest of our country, and comes in more direct competition than any other kind of grain with the "short crop season" of northwestern Canada.

Barley matures from 20 to 30 days earlier than wheat and quite often the early frosts of northwestern Canada affects the wheat crop, but never catches the barley crop. If you remove the 30 cents per bushel tariff from barley, then northwestern Canada will flood the United States with cheap barley, mostly for our brewers. Of course it may reduce the price of beer, etc., then you will have the temperance people after you.

The public must remember that while the United States has many million acres of ublic lands left, yet only a small amount of it is arable or suitable for "homesteads" without expensive irrigation. About all the choicest arable public land has been "taken up" by actual settlement during the last 30 years.

Consequently land seekers who go to the northwest looking for lands must purchase it a good price from those who have acquired title or cross the line into the great northwest territory of Canada and take up free or purchase the cheaper lands and pay our tariff.

Many of our good American citizens have crossed over the line. Fifteen thousand of them last year became dissatisfied with farming conditions in northwestern Canada, principally because of their home market for the products of the farm and being shut out of our market by reason of (tariff) our tax, and have returned by way of Minnesota, North Dakota, Montana, and Washington to the United States. This tax or tariff on all products of the Canadian farmers helps or causes the return of our own good citizens and their wealth, amounting to millions of dollars.

I am a farmer and have resided in North Dakota for more than 30 years. The choicest available lands suitable for farming without being irrigated are about taken up and occupied.

Thus you will understand with 25 cents per bushel tax on wheat to start with the land seeker or purchaser will hesitate a long time before locating or purchasing land in northwestern Canada. The market facilities of eastern Canada for export shipments are more like or nearly equal with our own. Yet that does not help the northwestern part of Canada. You must also remember that the arable quantity of lands for wheat-farming purposes in Canada are about equal to the remaining wheat-raising land in our own country.

Only a few years ago land in North Dakota was selling from $15 to $20 per acre, but now land sells very readily at a price from $40 to $75 per acre in nearly all parts of our State, and this increase in price is caused principally from the fact that our choice public land suitable for farming without irrigation is occupied and when the land purchaser comes, rather than go over the line into Canada and take free public land or purchase cheap land with a fixed incumbrance in the shape of tariff on everything produced, they not only hesitate but refuse to go, therefore we get a good price for our land and keep both the citizen and his money in our own country.

When you remove all incumbrance, tax, or tariff, on imported farm products, then you will reduce the price of land in the United States and more especially in the northwestern part, in the aggregate—many, yes, very many millions of dollars—and you will lose hundreds of thousands of our good American citizens with the vast amount of money and personal property they take with them, going to the cheap lands of that vast territory in northwestern Canada. Are you willing and ready for this?

Woe to the office seeker, so far as the farmers of our country, and more especially those residing in that chain or line of States bordering on or near Canada and the Northwest—running from Massachusetts on the Atlantic to California on the Pacific Ocean—are concerned, if he supports this treaty.

Do you see? If you do not, you may realize it at the next election.

JAMES J. HILL, ESQ.

I clip the following from the Washington Sunday Star:

"PHILADELPHIA, PA., *January 28.*—The North American wired James J. Hill, asking for an expression of opinion on the proposed reciprocity treaty with Canada. Mr. Hill replied as follows:

" 'The proposed reciprocity agreement between Canada and the United States is a measure of true statesmanship. Intelligent citizens and public men approve it. It is mainly opposed by the demagogue.' "

The people of that part of the Northwest through which the transportation lines that Mr. Hill in part owns and wholly, either directly or indirectly, controls have a high regard for his sagacity, energy, and great ability from a business standpoint. The results of his work in building one (the Great Northern) of the great transcontinental lines of railroads on the northern (Dominion of Canada) boundary line of our country, with its many branches as "feeders" running up into northwestern Canada, has been of vast benefit, both financially and for personal comfort. And I know, as one of them, that we all fully realize and appreciate what Mr. Hill has done for us, and we are more than pleased—in fact, we rejoice to learn that while Mr. Hill has done a vast amount of good in aiding in developing the country for the people of Minnesota, North Dakota, South Dakota, Montana, and the adjoining States to the Pacific Ocean, that he has been personally rewarded, having accumulated many millions of dollars for himself and also for those directly associated with him. His wealth is only a just reward for his foresight, intelligent work, and untiring energy. Whenever he induced or caused a man or family to locate and cultivate the land within a certain radius of the many railroads that he has caused to be built in that region of the country he realized that the only outlet for that product to market was over his roads, and of course Mr. Hill was developing the country by helping the farmer to take his grain to market over his line of railroads.

The extent of the land suitable for farming in the great northwestern part of Canada is not fully realized by many of our people.

They have in northwestern Canada, including British Columbia, as many acres of land suitable for raising wheat, barley, flax, and oats, that has not been in part exhausted by continuous farming as we have.

They now raise about 200,000,000 bushels of grain, and in the very near future will raise many hundred million more bushels each year. They have but one local market—Winnipeg—with only the eastern Atlantic coast outlet very many hundreds of miles away for the large part of northwestern Canada, and as long as the fence or tariff wall built along several thousand miles of the border is kept up the price of both land and grain will be higher in our country than it is in Canada.

Duluth, the great shipping point at the "head of the Lakes," to the East, and then to European markets—and Minneapolis, the greatest milling center in the world for making flour—both in Minnesota—are the most profitable markets for northwestern Canada, provided this new treaty is ratified.

MR. HILL'S BUSINESS PROPOSITION.

Pull down this wall—this fence—by taking off the tariff, and then all of the many million bushels of grain and all other (surplus) of the products of the Canadian farm will seek the best (Duluth and Minneapolis) markets in the western part of our country.

Of course, the man or set of men, or corporation who owns or controls about all the transportation (railroads) routes from Northwestern Canada to Duluth and Minneapolis, will no doubt favor taking off the tariff—to induce the shipping over these railroads.

Even with my limited knowledge—being a farmer—of the present aggregate amount in dollars of the freight charges or money received by the carriers of the commodities between Canada and our own country, I can imagine and fully realize that when you remove the fence—the "stone wall"—now existing and adopt reciprocity as provided in the pending treaty between the two countries, that you will then enhance, yes, double the income, and greatly increase the value of all the stock and bonds issued by such railroad companies doing a traffic business between Canada and the United States.

The people who invest their money in such transportation enterprises have a right to, and ought to, receive a good and fair income. Such improvements are not only valuable, but most of them are absolutely necessary to the prosperity of our country. Yet we farmers—among ourselves—talk the matter over something like this: Why should our law makers remove our tariff protection, thus lower our (farmers') income and thereby, both indirectly and directly, increase the income of all the stock and bondholders of these transportation companies, when in fact the most of them—the owners—reside in Europe, and to whom our good, hard-earned, mostly American farmers' money is sent. If the American people as a whole were in any way benefited by this extra amount of income received by our corporations instead of its being spent in Europe, it would at least be some, although quite remote, consolation.

I will take the chance of being classed by Mr. Hill as a farmer "demagogue," by being something like himself, to wit, shouting for the tariff, because it will not only help the country as a whole, but will at the same time help me financially, as farmer and landowner. I will not, however, designate Mr. Hill as a "demagogue" because he, as owner and controller of the transportation lines, may want to remove the tax or tariff so that his lines can handle the goods. That is his business affair.

I am quite anxious to learn what course the "calamity howlers" in the good (half century) old Republican Party who want "lower" tariff will say, now that President Taft has put it up to them. Will they take the medicine or will they again come back, join the good, the true, the faithful believers to the final end. It may be a bitter pill. If they will be brave and take it we might "kill the fatted calf."

Very respectfully,

C. W. BUTTZ, *Buttzville, N. Dak.*

The CHAIRMAN. Are there gentlemen who desire to be heard on the barley or malt question this morning? I am informed that Mr. Stafford's people were to be here on the 10.30 train, and they will get up here as soon as they can. Is there anyone else to be heard on this subject?

Mr. FORDNEY. Mr. Chairman, if you please, I have here a letter from the National Association of Lumber Manufacturers, asking for a hearing, and stating that Thursday would be the earliest possible day they could get their people here, and earnestly requesting an opportunity to be heard before this committee acts upon this bill, and if they are going to be given a hearing they must know it now, in order to get their people here by that time.

The CHAIRMAN. Mr. Fordney, are there any new facts that have occurred since the very full hearing of two years ago?

Mr. FORDNEY. They claim that the conditions in the lumber market have so changed that they feel they ought to have a hearing in this very important matter.

Mr. HILL. Why can we not hear Mr. Hines? He is the largest lumber man in the United States, and he is here now.

Mr. FORDNEY. Mr. Hines is the gentleman who sent me this communication, and I would be very glad to have you hear what he has to say about this.

Mr. HILL. I have known Mr. Hines for a great many years, and I think he possesses all the information that the association can give us.

Mr. FORDNEY. Mr. Hines has a great deal of information on this subject, but I think there are others in the lumber business who have some information that he has not, and I think they ought to be heard also.

STATEMENT OF EDWARD HINES, OF CHICAGO, ILL., PRESIDENT OF THE NATIONAL LUMBER MANUFACTURERS' ASSOCIATION.

Mr. HINES. I just want five minutes; and I would like to answer the gentleman's questions.

In the first place, gentlemen, the experience we have had in suffering the reduction of $37\frac{1}{2}$ per cent within the past year in our lumber duties is such that I would not attempt, from the actual practical experience, to place the proper information before this body. The Pacific coast should be represented here. It will take four days for the representatives to come here from the Pacific coast. They are now on the way. Hence, Thursday is the earliest possible date on which we could have them here.

You say, "any new facts," Mr. Chairman. A great many statements that were made before the Ways and Means Committee by our various members were seriously questioned by the opposition. Since that date we have had the actual experience of the results of this cut of 37½ per cent in the duty. They are not supposition or theory; they are facts. We wish an opportunity to place before you a statement of the facts, and the results that have occurred under which we have suffered, from that reduction of 37½ per cent. We do not feel that this so-called "snap judgment" is a fair way to treat this great industry represented by more than 40,000 manufacturers in the United States.

The CHAIRMAN. You know what those facts are?

Mr. HINES. No, Mr. Chairman; I do not.

The CHAIRMAN. We will hear from you now as to what you know about those facts.

Mr. HINES. In the first place——

The CHAIRMAN. The matter of the other hearing will be taken up before we adjourn, at 12 o'clock, in executive session; but we would like to hear from you now. I do not think we could have a better opportunity.

Mr. HINES. I wish to call attention to one very peculiar and significant fact, which has a strong bearing on this question, in the case of pulp wood. A provision is made that pulp wood in the raw state can be imported from Canada free of duty. In the case of lumber it is left out. Now, I want to call your attention to this one important fact. North of Minnesota, in the Rainy Lake district of Canada, there are billions of feet of pine timber; the last pine forest left in this country. All of that timber can be taken and manufactured better in Minnesota than in Canada. The Rainy Lake River runs into the northern part of Minnesota and drains that great tract of timber land.

The provision in the reciprocity treaty makes it necessary for that timber to be manufactured in Canada. Why not open the same door that the pulp people have, and have that timber taken across into Minnesota, across the so-called imaginary line, down the Rainy River, and manufactured in northern Minnesota, manufactured by American laborers, fed by American farm products? We say there is no reason, if you are legislating for American labor and American farm products, why, therefore, the raw material should not be allowed to come over into the United States and be manufactured here. If you want cheaper lumber—and you say you can get it in Canada cheaper than in the United States, and the consumer will be benefited—why not travel the straight channel and let that timber come across in the raw state and be manufactured in the mills now existing on the American side of the line by American labor, fed by the products of American farms, at a lower price? One of the companies of which I am president, the St. Croix Manufacturing Co., has a large mill, and it has expended a half a million dollars in its mill plant in Winton, Minn. Winton, Minn., is located just a few miles across the line from Canada. Naturally, along natural lines, along waterways, several billion feet of that great body of pine timber, the last body of timber left in the country, should come to Minnesota. That timber will come to Minnesota at the cheapest possible cost and it can be manufactured by the American mills and the laborers employed can be fed by the farm products taken right from the State of Min_ nesota. On the contrary, under the provisions of this reciprocity treaty, if it goes into effect, that timber can not be manufactured in that State. It is not a question of cost. It can not be taken from Canada and brought here until after it is manufactured—manufac_ tured by Canadians, who will be fed by Canadian farm products. Now, that is just one important practical question that I want to place before you gentlemen.

Mr. CLARK. Mr. Hines, if that thing was changed would you be in favor of that treaty then?

Mr. HINES. Mr. Clark, answering that question, I would say yes. If, in the judgment of you gentlemen, who are the judges in this case, it would appear that the American consumer can get cheaper lumber, then I would say I would be in favor of that proposition, coupled with this proposition, allowing the timber to be brought to the United States and manufactured here.

Mr. CLARK. I know, but you do not answer yes or no.

Mr. HINES. Some questions are pretty hard to answer directly, yes or no. I think my answer is, though, practically, yes.

Mr. CLARK. You do not claim that you suffer by reason of this duty of 37½ per cent on lumber, do you?

Mr. HINES. We have suffered very seriously from it.

Mr. CLARK. Is it not absolutely true that you put up the price of lumber before we got out of town?

Mr. HINES. Absolutely the contrary is true, Mr. Clark. Lumber has been going down for three years. At the present time it is the lowest, in my judgment, in comparison with the cost of labor and farm products, that it has been in 25 years. That fact can be substantiated. Any statement that I make here I make based on facts.

Mr. CLARK. I will tell you what I know. I know that these standpatters claimed the utter folly of cutting the tariff down to get lower prices, and last summer, fall, and winter they gave as an illustration of it that we cut the tariff on lumber 75 cents per thousand, and it went up before we got out of town.

Mr. HINES. That is simply like a great many rumors. We will give you the statement of the prices in a thousand places in the United States, showing that the cost of manufacture at the mills is less than it has been for many years. What the retailer gets we do not know. We are representing the manufacturers.

Mr. BOUTELL. I was going to suggest that you and he are talking about different things.

Mr. GAINES. You probably heard them talking about shoes.

Mr. CLARK. No; I am talking about lumber. They also came down here and said if we put hides on the free list, they would lower the price of shoes 50 cents a pair, and they did not do anything of the sort.

Mr. HINES. Now, Mr. Chairman, this particular thing I am familiar with. If what you are trying to accomplish is to get Canadian timber into the United States in order to hold down prices of timber by timber owners in the United States, then I am willing to go along with you and say, bring in the timber from Canada free; but do not debar the manufacture in the United States. Leave open the door where the raw material can come in.

Mr. CLARK. What do you suppose made that difference in the price of timber?

Mr. HINES. I do not know.

Mr. CLARK. What do you think?

Mr. HINES. I do not know. We are here looking for information. All that we demand is the same treatment on the part of our forests as you have given others. We have pulp wood on our lands and timber on our lands; and why take a part of a tree that grows 6 or 7 inches and allow it to come in free, if you are going to take a tree right alongside of it 20 inches in diameter and say that it must be manufactured in Canada, by labor fed with Canadian farm products?

Mr. CLARK. Now it must be assumed by you and me and every man who has any sense that everybody wants as much labor done in the United States as possible. We will agree about that. Then, if this shuts out labor, how do you account for it?

Mr. HINES. I am here seeking information from you gentlemen.

Mr. CLARK. You are not going to get much here.

Mr. HINES. I do not know what caused that to be written in the bill, but it is there. I am asking for information.

Mr. DALZELL. What do you refer to in the bill?

Mr. HINES. I am referring to the clause in which wood pulp is allowed to be imported into the United States free.

Mr. GAINES. Pulp timber, and not logs, as logs publish no newspapers.

Mr. CLARK. That the logs you make pulp out of come in free, but the timber you make lumber out of does not come in free?

Mr. HINES. It does not come in at all. It not only does not come in free, but it does not come in at all.

The CHAIRMAN. Of course they are on the free list, both of them?

Mr. HINES. No, Mr. Chairman.

Mr. FORDNEY. There is an embargo on logs. They can not come in at all.

The CHAIRMAN. So far as our tariff is concerned, they come in free. Now, what you want is a retaliatory clause similar to that in regard to pulp?

Mr. HINES. Absolutely.

The CHAIRMAN. How long has this embargo been on logs?

Mr. HINES. It has been in effect since the duty on lumber was put in effect, under the old Dingley law.

Mr. FORDNEY. It has been in effect since the Dingley law.

The CHAIRMAN. Since the Dingley law was put into effect?

Mr. HINES. Yes; they at that time put an embargo on it all.

Mr. McCALL. Has it not been longer ago than when the Dingley law went into effect that the tariff was put on lumber?

Mr. HINES. No, sir.

The CHAIRMAN. This is not a new condition that has arisen since the passage of the last tariff law, but it has been in existence since the Dingley Act was passed?

Mr. HINES. Yes, sir; but the condition, owing to the 37½ per cent reduction, has become more acute for us. We are suffering from a double hardship now.

Mr. FORDNEY. There never was an export duty on Canadian logs?

Mr. HINES. No, sir.

Mr. FORDNEY. There never was an embargo on Canadian timber coming in until the Canadians did it after the Dingley law went into effect?

Mr. HINES. No, sir. Take Vancouver Island, covered with virgin timber, and take on this side of it, covered with virgin timber. The mills on the Pacific coast do not own any timber. The timber is alleged to be owned by certain landowners. Now, if the actual manufacturers on the Pacific coast, the men who have millions of dollars invested in mill plants and in towns, could get this timber of Canada and bring the logs over, they would be in position to furnish the cheaper lumber in this country that you want for the consumer. There is every argument in favor of that proposition. We feel that lumber has suffered enough in taking a cut of 37½ per cent. We can show you by actual facts that the industry is in a terribly demoralized condition. We can show you that more plants in the lumber business have failed in the last five years than in any similar time, and we can demonstrate these things; but we have to have an opportunity of bringing the men here from the various parts of the country who know about these things. I know about them in a general way, but the operators on the Pacific coast want to be heard, and we feel that Thursday is the earliest day on which it would be possible for them to get here.

Mr. CLARK. I want to ask you that question over again. Do you say that the wholesale price of lumber has never increased any since this Payne bill was passed?

Mr. HINES. Mr. Clark, I will go further and say that the wholesale price has decreased in your own territory—in the South. I will bring men here from your own State whose testimony you will not question and prove that; and I will further say that on the Pacific coast common lumber is selling to-day at $6.50 to $8 a thousand, and that is lower than it was sold at in 1892. I will say further that the price of ordinary box lumber—and the box manufacturers use a larger amount of lumber than anybody else—is the lowest it has been in five years.

Mr. CLARK. You say lumber is selling cheaper now than in 1892?

Mr. HINES. Yes; I say in one section of the country. Then I will go further. I will say that lumber is selling at less than it was in 1892, considering the cost of wages and farm supplies.

Mr. CLARK. Well, now——

Mr. HINES. And what makes the cost is labor and farm supplies— 75 per cent of the finished cost: and adding the cost of transportation, 80 per cent.

Mr. CLARK. Now, you must concede that lumber jumped up a dollar a thousand in less than two weeks after President Taft signed this Payne bill, because it did do it.

Mr. HINES. You are making that statement, and you will pardon me if I say, representing the lumber industry, that I contradict the statement. I will furnish you the facts.

Mr. CLARK. Do you mean to say that the retailers did not sell lumber at a dollar a thousand higher?

Mr. HINES. I do not know anything about the retail business. I do not know what price lumber was selling at in Missouri. I do not know what price it was selling at in California or New Mexico.

Mr. CLARK. Do you mean to say that the papers all over the United States did not say that lumber had gone up a dollar a thousand immediately after the signing of the Payne bill?

Mr. HINES. What the newspapers have said in the last six months would fill a bucket full of falsehoods. That does not prove anything.

Mr. CLARK. What made these Republicans go around, then, claiming that we were a lot of fools when we claimed that if we cut the tariff it would put the price down, and the price of lumber they cited as a case that gave the lie to our contention, because we cut the tariff 75 cents a thousand, and the price immediately went up a dollar a thousand, and there was not any answer to it?

Mr. FORDNEY. You are talking about the price lists of the retailers, and Mr. Hines is speaking from the manufacturer's standpoint.

Mr. HINES. I am speaking in the broad terms——

The CHAIRMAN. Mr. Hines, I had a talk soon after that bill passed with one of the largest lumber dealers in the United States—a wholesaler, and not a retailer—and he assured me that the price was higher, and I saw him again this winter, and he made the same assurance—that the price was higher—and he assured me that the price of laths and shingles, on which we raised the duty, had been lowered. He is a reputable gentleman, and he knew what he was talking about, and he had no reason to lie about it, and I believed him, and I believe yet that his statement was true.

Mr. CLARK. Is there any connection between what you say about the manufacturer of lumber and about the wholesale prices—but I believe you do not know about the retailer. Now, is there any connection between the wholesaler and the retailer, except the fact that you sell the retailer the lumber?

Mr. HINES. Absolutely none whatever.

Mr. CLARK. Do you not fix particular prices?

Mr. HINES. Absolutely none. There are 40,000 manufacturers in the United States. Take, for instance, Springfield, Ill.; they buy spruce from five distinct groups of territory, from Florida to Washington, from Georgian Bay in Canada to West Virginia.

Mr. GAINES. I was about to say a moment ago that I can bring here from my own district—not from the whole State of West Virginia but from my own district—250 men who will swear that the price of lumber has been very much lowered in the last year and a half; very much.

Mr. CLARK. Are you talking about retailers or wholesalers?

Mr. GAINES. I am talking about the manufacturer's prices at his mill.

The CHAIRMAN. I will ask Mr. Hines if he knows what the price of Canadian lumber has been since the tariff bill went into effect and whether any reduction was made in the price?

Mr. HINES. In some cases where they were located at favorable points for transportation, as in the Georgian Bay, where they own the market, or on our Great Lakes, on account of the cheaper transportation, in such cases there was no material reduction made. They simply pocketed the difference. For instance, take Cleveland, Erie, or Buffalo, the rate from Canada is $1.75 on lumber. The nearest manufacturing market to those great consuming markets is the South, and the rate on lumber from those places is $8 a thousand.

The CHAIRMAN. Now you have spoken in answer to my question about the great lumber markets of the country where the bulk of the consumption is.

Mr. HINES. No, not the greatest consumption; the greatest manufacturing proposition. On the Pacific coast prices have gone down; in the interior prices have gone down. In the South prices have gone down.

The CHAIRMAN. I was speaking about the importing price. You say that has gone down west of the Rockies?

Mr. HINES. Yes.

The CHAIRMAN. At what particular points?

Mr. HINES. In the States of Washington, Oregon, Idaho, and Montana, absolutely.

The CHAIRMAN. Lumber is selling at less than it did before the tariff?

Mr. HINES. Absolutely, less.

The CHAIRMAN. Those are the points you refer to when you say that the price of imported lumber has gone down?

Mr. HINES. I will say further that at the Great Lake points box lumber has gone down a dollar to a dollar and a half a thousand, and that is the greatest part of the lumber we import from Canada. The best lumber goes to Europe, and the refuse comes to us.

Mr. FORDNEY. Box lumber is 50 per cent of the product of the log?

Mr. HINES. Fully 50 per cent of the product of the log. As to the South, I will say this, that 75 per cent of the mills in the South are suffering to-day and can hardly pay interest on their bonds. Their interest to-day is in default.

Mr. CLARK. Does not that grow out of the fact that a lot of lumber speculators, or rather speculators in lumber or timber, have been wildcatting the timber market until it got out of all reason?

Mr. HINES. No. Let me give you reasons why. For instance, take horses. We now have to pay $600 apiece for horses and we used to buy them for $125 apiece.

Mr. CLARK. Yes; I know that.

Mr. HINES. I am paying $18 a ton for hay, and I used to pay $9 and $10 a ton. I am paying $50 and $60 a month for men. We used to pay them from $12 to $20 a month. When you talk of the price of lumber, you must take into account that 75 to 80 per cent of that price is labor and farm products and transportation. Every one of those things has advanced, even including railroad freights; they have advanced.

Mr. CLARK. Now, you do not mean to say that the price of hay ordinarily is anything like $18 a ton?

Mr. HINES. The word "ordinarily" means what you are paying now as compared with what you were paying two or three years ago.

Mr. CLARK. No; there may be a local hay famine.

Mr. HINES. No, but local farm products are higher to-day. Look at prunes, for instance. We used to buy them for 4½ cents a pound, and we are now paying nearly double that. I can give you a hundred articles for which we are paying more.

Mr. CLARK. You take the bulk of the farm products in this country; do you say they are higher than they were a year ago?

Mr. HINES. Everything compared to two years ago is higher. Some things are, of course, only 5 or 10 per cent higher. But take prunes; I suppose they are a little lower than they were a year ago, but they are 100 per cent higher than they were two years ago.

Mr. CLARK. I am not talking about those things, but corn and wheat.

Mr. HINES. Everything is higher.

Mr. CLARK. You do not claim that corn is higher than it was two years ago?

Mr. HINES. Well, take wheat.

Mr. CLARK. Why, two years ago I sold my corn crop, over the telephone, at 55 cents a bushel on the stalk in the field, the day before I left home, and this year you can buy all the corn you want for 45 cents a bushel.

Mr. HINES. Yes; but compare that with 10 years ago, when we had 15-cent corn.

Mr. CLARK. Oh, 10 or 15 years ago everything went to pieces.

Mr. FORDNEY. Here is a quotation on hay last week in Buffalo, $18.

Mr. CLARK. That is because they did not raise any hay up there last year.

Mr. FORDNEY. Then here are other quotations, for instance, at Boston, $22. That was the price on hay last week.

Mr. CLARK. What was it in St. Louis and Kansas City?

Mr. FORDNEY. You come from that district. You tell me.

Mr. CLARK. I think it would be about $9 or $10 a ton.

Mr. FORDNEY. What is the freight from there to Buffalo? Tell me that and then you will get the price in Missouri.

The CHAIRMAN. I have a letter on my desk from a hay dealer in the State of New York, which tells all about the prices.

Mr. FORDNEY. I say——

The CHAIRMAN. Now, wait a minute. It may be that what I say will confirm you. Do not get so excited. You do not know it all.

Mr. FORDNEY. You say you know it all. I do not know it all.

The CHAIRMAN. This man says that hay of the very best quality is worth $22 a thousand, and he says there is a great deal of second-quality hay.

Mr. FORDNEY. Yes.

The CHAIRMAN. And that is very low; that is worth $16 and less. Now that confirms partially what the gentleman from Missouri says.

Mr. FORDNEY. Yes, partially.

The CHAIRMAN. The best quality of timothy he says sells for $22, and wheat is 85 cents a bushel, and so he goes on through the list. He is a very intelligent man and knows what he is talking about. He is complaining about the low prices of farm products as compared with the prices in the last two years.

Mr. FORDNEY. Let me say to the gentleman, if you please, that lumbermen do not and can not use refuse hay. It is not a marketable article. It is not quoted on the market.

The CHAIRMAN. I have not heard anything about refuse hay.

Mr. FORDNEY. You are talking about second-quality hay; that is refuse.

The CHAIRMAN. Oh, no.

Mr. FORDNEY. It is damaged by storm before it is cut. I am a farmer and I know what I am talking about, now.

Mr. HILL. Now, let us go back to the reciprocity treaty. I understand, Mr. Hines, that you are in favor of this legislation, provided the word "logs" is inserted in the proviso, so that all restrictions on the free exportation of logs are taken away, just the same as they are taken away on pulp wood?

Mr. HINES. I would answer that this way, Mr. Hill. If in your judgment you feel that after the lumber industry has suffered a cut of 37½ per cent, you want to make it absolutely free——

Mr. HILL. I do not want you to put it way to me, because I would not quite agree with you on it that way. I think there has been an actual reduction in the wholesale prices of lumber—a good deal more than the difference in the tariff, and not affected by the tariff.

Mr. HINES. Then I will answer you personally. What our association would say I do not know, as we have not had a meeting. I will answer you individually. Being an American and a Republican, and advocating here the protection of American industries, I can not see any reason why, with the logs on the other side of this imaginary line, with merely a stream separating us from them, the logs should not be taken and brought over on this side of the line and manufactured by American labor fed by American farm products, and everything that goes into the manufacture of lumber like steel and saws and chains come from this side, so that we may get the benefit of that, when we can manufacture the lumber on this side as well as it can be done on the Canadian side.

Mr. HILL. What is the language you would suggest to put in this paragraph?

Mr. HINES. As to just the legal verbiage, I do not know that I am capable of suggesting that, but I would say substantially the same clause as applies to pulp wood; namely, when Canada and the Provinces abrogate their duty——

Mr. HILL. It would only need the insertion of the items. That is all provided for, so far as pulp wood is concerned.

Mr. HINES. I will have this inserted in red ink after this hearing is over, and put it in proper shape, if you would like to have me.

Mr. HILL. With that done you would not appear here in opposition to the reciprocity treaty?

Mr. HINES. I could not say that, being president of this association.

Mr. HILL. I mean speaking for yourself, personally.

Mr. HINES. But I would say this, that that would go a long way toward satisfying our members. With this clause changed we should not be in nearly as strong a position to combat your argument about free lumber as we are to-day.

Mr. HILL. Let me ask you one question: Is there any restriction now on your logs from land which you own, which is not Crown land? If you own 100 acres of land in Canada, absolutely own the land in fee, you can cut your logs and do what you please with them?

Mr. HINES. Mr. Hill, there is no such land on which timber is located in Canada.

Mr. HILL. If there was, you could do it?

Mr. HINES. I do not know of any such land. It is all leased land.

Mr. HILL. Now, is not the restriction solely on timber from so-called Crown land, and is not that applied alike to Canadians and Americans and everybody?

Mr. HINES. No; as I understand it, no logs from any lands can be imported into this country from Canada.

Mr. HILL. If you own lands, you can import the logs from Canada into this country?

Mr. HINES. But the trouble is, you are putting a case that is not true. There are no such lands.

Mr. HILL. If there was such land there, you could cut off the timber, and there would be no duty on that timber imported into the United States?

Mr. HINES. The trouble is you are putting a supposititious case. There is no such case in Canada.

Mr. HILL. There might be a case where a man owns a farm and the timber has grown on it, and he can cut it and bring it in.

Now, you would favor this reciprocity treaty, or you would not object to it, if the restrictions which the Canadian Government puts on Americans and Canadians and everybody alike that logs cut from public lands in Canada shall be manufactured in Canada was removed? If that was removed and the timber and logs were treated precisely the same as the pulp wood which comes from the same lands——

Mr. HINES. Absolutely, yes.

Mr. HILL (continuing). I will admit that—then, there would be no objection to this? Now, I agree with you, and I think they ought to come in the same as the pulp wood, or the pulp wood ought to be restricted the same as the timber is restricted; but I wanted to get the precise position you occupy on this proposition.

The CHAIRMAN. You have it.

Mr. HILL. Now I understand it. I am much obliged to you.

Mr. FORDNEY. Mr. Hill's proposition to you is that with that provision put in you would not object to this?

Mr. HINES. No; I thought he said——

Mr. FORDNEY. No; he said you would agree to it if that was put in the bill.

Mr. HINES. No; I would not put it that way. I said I would not have nearly the same objection to the treaty; I would not feel that our particular industry was picked out to be sandbagged.

Mr. FORDNEY. In other words, if that was in there you could take the pill with a little less discomfort?

Mr. HINES. Yes.

Mr. FORDNEY. Mr. Chairman, I have an amendment to the bill, which has just been suggested by the chairman or Mr. Hill, that I would like to have the clerk read.

The CHAIRMAN. We are not considering the bill just now. That will be printed in the record. Of course the committee all under-stand that this bill, the material parts of it, must be adopted or rejected and that any amendment is equivalent to a rejection of it.

Mr. FORDNEY. I do not understand that. Where do you get that understanding?

The CHAIRMAN. I understand so.

Mr. FORDNEY. Where did you get your information?

The CHAIRMAN. I got a little previous information that I acquired a great many years ago.

Mr. FORDNEY. I do not understand it that way.

Mr. POU. If you are going to begin the great work of tariff reform, itt seems to me you have got to swallow the thing whole or not take it a all.

The CHAIRMAN. The gentleman knows that this is a treaty with another nation.

Mr. POU. Yes.

The CHAIRMAN. If there is any amendment of it, the thing will practically be at an end.

Mr. POU. That does not change my position.

The CHAIRMAN. Now, Mr. Fordney, I have this letter I referred to a few moments ago—a little bit on the prices of hay. This letter reads:

I am reading with much interest the dispatches regarding President Taft's recommendations to Congress in regard to the reciprocity arrangement with Canada.

I can not help feeling very deeply regarding the serious effect this will have upon the producers of farm products throughout all our Northern States should his recommendations to admit free all the farm products from Canada be adopted.

At the present time the markets for our hay are in about as bad condition as they have ever been known to be. Though Canada is paying $4 per gross ton duty, yet she is simply flooding all New England with her hay, and also a large percentage of the New York State markets, and while they have no practically No. 1 hay in Canada this year, and we are able to get around $21 per ton for what No. 1 hay we have in the States, yet for No. 2 hay we have to cut under from $3 to $5 per ton and mixed hay from $6 to $7 and $8 per ton. Clover hay was sold in New York last week as low as $9.50 per ton, delivered there. There were around 100 carloads of mixed hay standing there which could hardly be disposed of at any reasonable prices.

Our States are aflood with potatoes, we are buying from the farmers to-day at 30 to 35 cents per bushel, and there are probably more potatoes in the States than the market will be able to take care of in the spring, and I will not be surprised to see the price of potatoes to the farmers this spring down to 20 cents per bushel.

Oats are being bought at around 35 cents to the farmer and wheat has to be bought at around 85 to 90 cents per bushel to the farmer to permit of shipping it.

I mention these things to show you that this country is able to-day to produce all that its markets can take care of and have a large surplus to ship to other countries, and we believe that by careful handling our production can be tripled and quadrupled. During the last two or three years our farm lands have advanced quite materially and our farmers have commenced to feel a pleasure in their work, but this certainly can have no other effect than to depress them.

I believe the time is at hand when the people who voted against you and your ideas at our last election are realizing that the medicine they are now about to have administered to them is of a very bitter nature, and that they will regret the action at that election, and I believe that this protest I am uttering voices the sentiment of the great majority of the people at the present time, and that you will be commended for taking very strong and decisive steps to try to overcome the carrying out of the recommendations of our President in this matter.

Mr. HINES. Mr. Chairman, I want to say two more words on this question.

The CHAIRMAN. I just wanted you to hear that whole letter and to see if you did not agree with it.

Mr. FORDNEY. Will the chairman permit me to read a letter which I have just received?

The CHAIRMAN. Why, yes.

Mr. FORDNEY. This letter is as follows:

FREELAND, MICH., *February 1, 1911.*

Congressman J. W. FORDNEY.

DEAR SIR: Please do what you can to defeat the Canadian reciprocity treaty in so far as it would cheapen American agricultural products. I have talked with a good many farmers, and they all would like to see the bill defeated. If we want free trade we will vote for Bryan.

Respectfully,   C. E. LUDORCI.

Mr. CLARK. Does that man live in your district?

Mr FORDNEY. Yes.

Mr. CLARK. What was the use of his wasting his stamp to write to you, then?

Mr. FORDNEY. Why, he knew that he was writing to a man that would heed what he said.

Mr. CLARK. Yes; but did he not know that just as well before he wrote?

Mr. LONGWORTH. I want to ask Mr. Hines a question on a different branch of this subject. I read a sentence from the President's Message, as follows:

Free lumber we ought to have. By giving our people access to Canadian forests we shall reduce the consumption of our own.

Do you agree with that?

Mr. HINES. I would like the whole sentence read. It goes on to state other particulars.

Mr. LONGWORTH. I will read this again:

Free lumber we ought to have. By giving our people access to Canadian forests we shall reduce the consumption of our own, which, in the hands of comparatively few owners, now have a value that requires the enlargement of our available timber resources.

Now, leaving out that question as to whether or not it is in the hands of a few owners, I simply ask you this question, do you agree with this conclusion of the President's:

By giving our people access to Canadian forests we shall reduce the consumption of our own?

Mr. HINES. That question can be answered both ways. I call your attention to a statement made by Mr. Pinchot a year and a half ago in which he absolutely took the contrary view to that. At that time he was in charge of our conservation, and he is supposed to know as much about our forests as anybody else, or more than anybody else, and about what was the proper thing to conserve our forests, and he took absolutely the opposite view. It is something that takes an argument to demonstrate it. I differ with the President partly on that proposition.

Mr. LONGWORTH. Do you agree with Mr. Pinchot?

Mr. HINES. Not entirely. I take a middle ground.

Mr. LONGWORTH. What is that ground?

Mr. HINES. It is quite a story. I would be very glad to give you my views, but I would prefer to do it in writing, because I do not think I would have time this morning to give them. I will do that if you wish.

Mr. LONGWORTH. I would very much like to have that, because that was a question that was very much debated——

Mr. HINES. It is quite a debatable subject.

Mr. LONGWORTH (continuing). During the tariff hearings.

Mr. HINES. Yes.

Mr. LONGWORTH. And I think you are the first person I have heard advance the proposition that the higher the price of lumber was, the less tendency there would be to cut down trees.

Mr. HINES. Absolutely; absolutely.

Mr. LONGWORTH. Now of course the philosophical result of that is that the higher you place your duty, the more you are tending in the direction of forest conservation, so that if you had a duty so high as to absolutely prohibit importation from any country, that would be the best thing for forest conservation.

Mr. HINES. Not entirely. You can not answer that by a yes or no proposition.

Mr. LONGWORTH. Yes, but I wanted to know what ground you took.

Mr. HINES. There is a middle ground to take, which is better than either of the more radical courses.

Mr. LONGWORTH. Now, you will remember that former President Roosevelt recommended to Congress that lumber should be put on the free list.

Mr. HINES. Yes.

Mr. LONGWORTH. For the sake of forest conservation?

Mr. HINES. Yes.

Mr. LONGWORTH. And he sent to Congress quite an elaborate message, with illustrations printed by the Forestry Bureau.

Mr. HINES. Yes.

Mr. LONGWORTH. Of which Mr. Pinchot was then the head?

Mr. HINES. Yes; that is right. I read it.

Mr. LONGWORTH. That was some three years ago.

Mr. HINES. Yes, between three and four years ago.

Mr. LONGWORTH. And you will remember that Mr. Pinchot never made his views public on the question, so far as I know, until he came before this committee and presented an argument against the reduction of the $2 duty on lumber on the ground that it would not be in the direction of forest conservation?

Mr. HINES. He had made several arguments before that. We had met him half a dozen times here in Washington and had considerable discussion.

Mr. LONGWORTH. But that was within a month or so?

Mr. HINES. It was within six months.

Mr. LONGWORTH. It was after this question came up?

Mr. HINES. Yes. I simply wished to put this matter forward as a direct illustration. For instance, at Winton, Minn., there is a large town supported by sawmills, in which goes out in direct pay rolls every month about $30,000. Under the provisions of this reciprocity proposition just as soon as that small body of timber which is on the American side tributary to Minnesota is exhausted that whole town will go out of existence. There is nothing else to keep it there. The lands around there are not farm lands; the country is all rocks. Right across, within a distance of a few miles, is the largest body of pine timber left in the country, billions of feet of pine timber. The waters there run into the United States. The Rainy River runs down into Minnesota 200 or 300 miles and then turns and goes up into Hudson Bay. That tremendous tract of timber lies above and the waterway goes right down past our doors for a couple of hundred miles. There is enough timber there to furnish the great States of Minnesota and Iowa and Illinois with pine timber for 50 or 75 or 100 years. Now you can imagine the amount of money we will transfer from the United States to Canada if that timber is manufactured in Canada. If we are honest here and want to preserve our forests and want to cheapen the cost of lumber to the consumers in this country and give them the benefit of everything that is reasonable, what object is there in leaving a proviso there that makes it impossible to manufacture that lumber in the United States? Now, no matter whether a man is a Republican or a Democrat, if he is an American citizen that argument will appeal to him.

Mr. DWIGHT. Is not the price of lumber to the consumer fixed by a retail dealers' association?

Mr. HINES. There are practically 50 retail dealers' associations in the United States.

Mr. DWIGHT. Do they not work in harmony?

Mr. HINES. No, sir; they are local propositions. There is one in Baltimore and one in Philadelphia and one in Boston; each one of them local. They are local propositions.

Mr. DWIGHT. But is there not a short circuit between them all?

Mr. HINES. They do have general meetings, I think, or something to that effect.

Mr. HILL. You have more retail yards yourselves than any one association in the United States?

Mr. HINES. No, sir; we have no retail yards.

Mr. HILL. Do you not sell at retail?

Mr. HINES. None whatever. We are strictly in the manufacturing business.

Mr. HILL. You used to have, did you not?

Mr. HINES. No, sir.

Mr. HILL. I thought you had 400 or 500 retail yards.

Mr. HINES. No, sir; we are strictly manufacturing.

Mr. HILL. Are not you yourself interested——

Mr. HINES. No, sir; I am not interested individually in any company.

Mr. HILL. When did you get out of the retail business?

Mr. HINES. I never have been in the retail yard business; strictly manufacturing. We have a large distributing yard in Chicago that we ship to, and we ship through that yard to different country dealers.

Mr. CLARK. You own the stumpage?

Mr. HINES. Yes.

Mr. CLARK. Do you think putting lumber on the free list would reduce the price of stumpage?

Mr. HINES. On this side?

Mr. CLARK. Yes.

Mr. HINES. No, sir.

Mr. HILL. It is bound to go up anyway, is it not?

Mr. HINES. Stumpage naturally goes up. Why? You are paying interest and taxes every year, and the county assessor comes around and says that your stumpage is worth more every year, and he assesses accordingly.

Mr. RANDELL. Is not a stump worth more when the tree has grown more?

Mr. HINES. Certainly; timber grows.

Mr. RANDELL. Then why should stumpage go up merely because you hold the land if the timber is growing and you get the benefit of the growth?

Mr. HINES. It does not grow in proportion to pay interest and taxes. It does not begin to.

Mr. RANDELL. Then timber land is a bad investment?

Mr. HINES. No; it has not proved a bad investment in this country. No; it has not.

Mr. RANDELL. Is not the fact that the stumpage is held by so few parties practically the reason that lumber can be so high in the United States as it is?

Mr. HINES. That is an entirely mistaken view. The President's message just referred to is not based on fact. We do not know where he got the information from. Herbert Knox Smith has been investigating it for three years. We have not got a verdict yet.

Mr. RANDELL. I want to know about your opinion as to the effect of allowing lumber to be manufactured from Canadian timber on this side. If it is so arranged that you get a bountiful supply of logs on this side of the line, how far would that affect the market and be a benefit to the people in the Mississippi Valley, for instance?

Mr. HINES. It ought to affect directly on a line drawn, say, from Pittsburg to Kansas City, from there north.

Mr. RANDELL. It would be a direct benefit north of that line. Indirectly, how would it affect below that line?

Mr. HINES. It would affect a little bit, indirectly, naturally.

Mr. RANDELL. In what way?

Mr. HINES. When you bring a larger supply of anything it affects, of course, the nearer markets first, and sympathetically affects other markets.

Mr. RANDELL. Would it crowd the southern trade back further?

Mr. HINES. Yes; naturally it would.

Mr. RANDELL. Would that have a tendency to reduce prices?

Mr. HINES. Unless you could curtail the output.

Mr. RANDELL. Then if we had free lumber entirely from Canada, it would materially affect the price of lumber in the United States?

Mr. HINES. It would not affect it materially, because the duty at the present time is only $1.25 per thousand, which is only 5 to 6 per cent. Taking that all off would not make any material reduction. One dollar and twenty-five cents a thousand is a small sum. It would not amount, in building a house, to more than $10 or $15, on the ordinary house. But what I wish to impress on your mind is this particular proposition. Here is a place where there are several hundred billion feet of timber, north of Minnesota and Wisconsin. Now, you go further west and you have the great virgin forests of Canada, in British Columbia.

Mr. RANDELL. You say there is a tremendous lot of pine. How far is the southern pine sold up in there?

Mr. HINES. The southern timber is sold clear up into Michigan, to-day. It is the timber that is used for ordinary building purposes in Minnesota, and some in Wisconsin.

Mr. RANDELL. How far is the southern pine sold in the North; how far does it go where it comes in competition with northern pine?

Mr. HINES. It comes right in competition with it. Over half of the pine timber sold in Chicago to-day, 60 per cent of it, comes from the South.

Mr. RANDELL. Would the Louisiana mills and the Texas mills be affected if we had free importation of lumber from Canada?

Mr. HINES. Yes.

Mr. RANDELL. To what extent?

Mr. HINES. To at least the extent of present duties. At the present time they are in a very demoralized condition, and one of the reasons is the cost of transportation. The cost of transportation from Canada is $1.75, and from Texas it is between $8 and $10. That is the cost of transportation alone, not any other factor.

Mr. RANDELL. That is fixed by the railroads?

Mr. HINES. No; the transportation from Canada is by water.

Mr. McCALL. Do you understand that any export duties are levied by the Government of the Dominion of Canada on logs?

Mr. HINES. They are prohibited.

Mr. McCALL. But are any export duties levied by the Dominion Government itself?

Mr. HINES. No, sir; they are simply prohibited, as I understand it.

Mr. McCALL. I know; but whatever export duties are imposed are imposed by the Provinces?

Mr. HINES. Yes.

Mr. McCALL. And is there not a difference of practice among those Provinces?

Mr. HINES. There is.

Mr. McCALL. Is there any uniform policy about it?

Mr. HINES. As I understand it, there is not. In the Province of Ontario they are absolutely prohibited. In the Province of British Columbia it is left to the discretion of the officials, considering the market. If the Canadian market is dead, and they can not sell their logs, they are allowed to export them into the United States, at times.

Mr. FORDNEY. May I ask a question?

Mr. HINES. Let me answer that point.

The CHAIRMAN. Wait a minute, Mr. Fordney; he does not desire to be interrupted.

Mr. FORDNEY. All right.

Mr. McCALL. Very well; go ahead.

Mr. FORDNEY. You have asked whether the export duty is imposed by the Provinces. If it is imposed, it is imposed by the Dominion Government, but the restriction is imposed by the Province.

Mr. McCALL. I have here a pamphlet entitled "Export Tariffs of Foreign Countries," tariff series, No. 20, printed by this Government in 1909. On page 16 I find this quotation from the law of June 29, 1897, which was about coincident with the passage of the Dingley law, but still prior to the passage of the Dingley law. That did not pass until some time in July, so that the Canadian law was passed before it. This reads:

(1) If any country now or hereafter imposes a duty upon the articles enumerated in item 611 in schedule B to the customs tariff, 1897, or upon any of such articles when imported into such country from Canada, the governor in council may, by proclamation published in the Canada Gazette, declare the following export duties, or any of them, chargeable upon logs and pulp wood exported from Canada to such country, that is to say: On pine, Douglas fir * * *

Then in a note at the head, preceding that, there is this statement:

NOTE.—No export duties are levied by the Dominion Government.

That is directly upon the point of that suggestion.

Mr. FORDNEY. I agree with you.

Mr. McCALL. I understood you to say there was one.

Mr. FORDNEY. No; I said there never had been.

Mr. McCALL. This note continues:

Some of the Canadian provinces levy such duties enumerated below.

That is precisely the point that I was trying to bring out by Mr. Hines.

Mr. LONGWORTH. I would like to supplement what you say by reading from Mr. Fielding's letter on the subject. Speaking of this question of pulp wood and print paper, he says:

It is necessary that we should point out that this is a matter in which we are not in a position to make any agreement. The restrictions at present existing in Canada are of a provincial character. They have been adopted by several of the provinces with regard to what are believed to be provincial interests.

Mr. McCALL. Yes.

Mr. LONGWORTH. That is, the Dominion Government has nothing whatever to do with the imposition of export taxes or duties or restrictions.

Mr. FORDNEY. There is a misunderstanding. Each province controls its own timber. It has the right to put on a license fee or stumpage due or rebate, but the Dominion Government alone has the right to make their tariff laws, and not the provinces.

Mr. McCALL. The Dominion Government has, according to this statement, never imposed any of these export duties.

Mr. FORNDEY. None whatever.

Mr. McCALL. That is the point. Then, further, after the provision that the governor in council may declare these duties, it is provided further as follows:

Provided, That the governor in council may, by proclamation published in like manner, from time to time remove and reimpose such export duty.

So that it is left entirely, apparently, in his discretion.

Mr. HINES. Yes. My point is this. You have a range of country there, along the border, in fact almost the entire border from the Georgian Bay to the Pacific coast, and along that border the streams naturally run from the United States to Canada, and the timber can be manufactured just as well on this side as on the other side. Take the Rainy River. It runs over 300 miles in the United States, all along the border, and the mills can be located on this side just as well as on the other side. Now, if the lumber is to come on this side, if the Canadian subsidy owners are to get the benefit of our great market, why is it not fair to keep alive our towns on our side and create new ones, as compared with building towns on the other side?

Now, if you are going to do this on the Canadian side, what are you supposed to do? You have to buy your saws and your steel rails and everything you use over here. On the contrary, if you operate on this side you have the advantage of getting all those things over here, and you employ American labor, and you take advantage of all our farm products, and you find a greater market for your farm products, which have got to be eaten; you have to have somebody to eat them. If you go across into Canada they will not come across from Canada and buy our farm products. It is a question whether you want to hold down your stumpage in the United States, as Mr. Longworth argues, or whether——

Mr. RANDELL. Does it cost more to build your mill, to build your plant, in Canada than in the United States?

Mr. HINES. Yes.

Mr. RANDELL. Are log chains, and saws, and materials that are made of iron and steel higher—do they cost you more—in Canada than in the United States? Are they not cheaper in Canada?

Mr. HINES. No, sir.

Mr. RANDELL. Then they are the same?

Mr. HINES. But do you not see——

Mr. RANDELL. Do you say they cost the same?

Mr. HINES. Generally speaking, they are practically the same; but my contention is this: Here are the logs coming down the river. If you manufacture them on this side, the whole of that money remains in the United States. If you manufacture on the other side, it all goes to Canada. This question is a very important one, and I feel that our industry is scattered so widely throughout the United States that we should be given time for our representatives to come here from the Pacific coast, and Thursday is the earliest day that we could possibly have them here.

Mr. HILL. Do I understand that the exportation of logs is absolutely and entirely from the Crown lands in Canada?

Mr. HINES. Yes; absolutely.

Mr. HILL. I have here the Canadian statistical report for 1910, in which there is a statement that for 1910 there were 113,000,000 feet, board measure, of logs exported. What were those?

Mr. HINES. Mr. Hill, I did not answer your question exactly. I thought you were talking about the Province of Ontario. In the Province of Ontario the logs can not be exported. There is where the great body of pine timber is which is left. But on the Pacific coast and in British Columbia it is left to the discretion of the officials there. If the market gets dull, they are allowed to export. If the market justifies the removal of the restriction, it is removed.

Mr. HILL. Then, it is a come-and-go restriction?

Mr. HINES. Yes. For instance, if our market on this side is reasonably high they take the restriction off and dump the stuff over here.

Mr. HILL. But the greatest body of pine timber is in Ontario?

Mr. HINES. Yes; where it will go to our friends of the Middle West.

Mr. HILL. Then; this statement is not a statement of the difference between private lands and Crown lands?

Mr. HINES. No, sir.

Mr. HILL. It is the difference between localities and East and West?

Mr. HINES. Yes.

The CHAIRMAN. I want to ask you one question. Have we held our own since the passage of the tariff law? In the export trade and with foreign countries, have we held our own with the British possessions?

Mr. HINES. I could not answer that question intelligently. I have not kept track of the local conditions. How soon could we know about this hearing, Mr. Chairman? I would like to send some wires.

The CHAIRMAN. At 2 o'clock.

Mr. HINES. I am sorry to have taken so much of your time.

Mr. McCALL. It has been very interesting.

Mr. HINES. Thank you, Mr. McCall.

Mr. STAFFORD. Mr. Chairman, the delegation of maltsters from the Northwest have just arrived, their train having been delayed. Otherwise they would have been here sooner. I would like to know whether they can appear this afternoon?

The CHAIRMAN. Yes; soon after 2 o'clock, and I would suggest to you that one gentleman should present the facts to us. It is not the multitude of people who come before us; we want the facts.

Mr. STAFFORD. I believe one gentleman is prepared to present the facts.

The CHAIRMAN. I hope the members of the committee will be here promptly at 2 o'clock so that we can have a short executive session before we begin the hearing, and I hope also that all of the gentlemen who are to appear will be here at 2 o'clock.

(At 12 o'clock noon the committee took a recess until 2 o'clock p. m.)

AFTER RECESS.

The committee reassembled at 2.15 p. m. pursuant to the taking of recess.

The CHAIRMAN. The committee have decided to close the hearings on this bill at 5 o'clock on Thursday next. No one will be heard after that, and the hearings up to that time will be confined to new conditions that have arisen since the hearings on the general tariff bill two years ago. It is not the purpose of the committee to go into a second edition of the hearings on the general tariff.

I had said to my colleague, Mr. Malby, that he could be heard this afternoon, but I am going to ask him to wait until some gentlemen from a distance have been heard first.

Mr. MALBY. In relation to that, I have no particular objection to accommodating myself to the convenience of the committee, except I desire to call attention to the fact that I am a member of the committee having in charge the sundry civil appropriation bill, and we are having constant hearings and are now engaged in hearings there, and I would not want to wait around here, but if you will name a time when you will hear me, that will suit very well.

The CHAIRMAN. How much time do you desire, Mr. Malby?

Mr. MALBY. I should imagine about half an hour—perhaps 40 minutes.

The CHAIRMAN. Is there objection to hearing him now?

Mr. FORDNEY. None on my part.

The CHAIRMAN. There seems to be no objection. Mr. Malby had agreed to be here at half past 10 this morning, but was called away by a hearing before a Senate committee at that hour and for that reason could not appear. When the engagement was made I was very glad to get some one to fill in this afternoon and relied upon Mr. Malby for that purpose.

Mr. BOUTELL. Before Mr. Malby proceeds I would like to ask if there are any gentlemen of the press associations here; and if so, I suggest that this announcement in regard to the closing of the hearing on Thursday next might be made in this afternoon's papers. If the news were sent off now it could get into the western afternoon papers.

STATEMENT OF HON. GEORGE R. MALBY, A REPRESENTATIVE IN CONGRESS FROM THE STATE OF NEW YORK.

Mr. Chairman and gentlemen of the committee, inasmuch as the subject to which I shall call attention was not one which was debated or thought necessary to debate at the extended hearings held by this committee in the framing of the tariff bill, I assume that what I have to say will not transgress the rule which has been laid down by the chairman of the committee.

I may say in appearing before the committee that I appear more particularly of course for the constituency which I represent, which is composed very largely of those engaged in agricultural pursuits, those engaged in handling the products of the forest, of the mine, and particularly are they engaged in the manufacture of paper in various forms. It appears from the reading of the proposed treaty that in Schedule A thereof substantially all the products of the industries of at least the district which I have the honor to represent are proposed to be placed upon the free list. However, I apprehend that I only in a very small degree represent the opposition to that particular schedule, for there can be no material difference in the situation existing as between my constituents and those who are engaged in similar occupations throughout the length and breadth of our land.

I appear in opposition to H. R. 32216, introduced by Congressman McCall, of Massachusetts, which apparently is designed to make effective the so-called reciprocity treaty entered into by the Canadian Government and the United States. I will not attempt, for it will be impossible, to point out all of the objections which might be urged to its favorable consideration, for time sufficient has not been given for such examination of all of the interests affected to properly accomplish that end.

The President, in his message to Congress recommending its favorable consideration, seeks to accomplish, among other things, a reduction in the cost of living to the American laborer, as well as to that other and larger class who neither labor nor produce.

This is to be accomplished mainly as provided in Schedule A, which substantially places all farm products produced in the northern portion of the United States upon the free list, and includes cattle, horses, mules, swine, sheep, lambs, and all other live animals; poultry, dead or alive; wheat, rye, oats, barley, buckwheat, dried peas and beans, edible sweet corn, maize, hay, straw, and cow peas; potatoes, sweet potatoes, yams, turnips, onions, cabbages, and all other vegetables in their natural state; apples, pears, peaches, apricots, dried fruits, viz, apples, pears, peaches, apricots, etc.; dairy products, butter, cheese, and fresh milk and cream, eggs, honey, grass seed, clover seed, garden and field seed; timber hewn, sided or squared otherwise than by sawing, and round timber used for spars or in building wharves; sawed boards, planks, deals, and other lumber not further manufactured than sawed; paving posts, railroad ties, and telephone, trolley, electric light, and telegraph poles of cedar and other woods. In fact, substantially all of the products of the forest not manufactured; and, second, pulp of wood and manufactured paper valued at 4 cents per pound or less, to which subject I will hereafter more fully refer.

It may be stated in passing that these articles are also admitted free into Canada from the United States, but inasmuch as it is the intent and purpose of those who are advocating the passage of this bill to provide for the entry of such articles into the United States, and further because these articles are selling at a higher price in the United States than in Canada, as a matter of fact, it is quite a use-less provision so far as forming any consideration for the privilege granted by the United States.

It is attempted, however, to justify the placing of all of these articles upon the free list by certain concessions, so-called concessions, made by Canada for the admission of certain manufactured articles, the product of the United States, into Canada. In other words, the American farmer is called upon to compete with the Canadian farmer for the purpose of lowering the value of his product to the consumer and also to aid the manufacturer and his employees still further in securing a market for his product. This arrangement and demand upon the American farmer, in my judgment, can not be justified by reason of any of the benefits conferred upon any of our citizens in the proposed treaty and is contrary, at least, to pre-cedents established for over half a century by both of the great political parties in framing a tariff bill, as no tariff bill has been framed by either party during that period of time which did not recognize the fact that the farmer is as equally entitled to pro-tection as the manufacturer, and in particular it is opposed to all of the platforms of the Republican Party since its organization, which provide for a tariff which shall represent the difference in the cost of production here and abroad, together with a fair measure of profit to the producer. Even the tariff of 1789 provided for a duty of 4 cents per pound on cheese.

Not only has this theory of protection been uniformly followed, but it rests in sound judgment. There can be no possible reason or justice in the proposal that the farmer is less entitled to protection than the manufacturer, and in fact I think a careful examination of the subject will lead to the inevitable conclusion that the farmer is more entitled to additional protection than the manufacturer, be-cause he needs it more and his net profits are less, so far as we are able to judge from the statistics which we have at hand.

According to the United States census of 1900, that for 1910 not yet having been compiled, the value of farm lands with improve-ments, but without buildings, was $13,058,007,995; the value of the buildings was $3,556,639,496; farm implements, machinery, etc., $749,775,970; live stock, $3,075,477,703; making a total value of all farm property of $20,439,901,164.

Owing to the well-known fact that farm lands have been greatly improved, it may fairly be estimated that the value of all of the aforementioned properties at the present time will not be less than $30,000,000,000. The number of farms, by the same census, 1900, is stated to be 5,737,372; the total acreage in farms, 838,591,774; and the average acreage to the farm, 146.2. The number of farms mort-gaged at that time was 1,093,235, and the encumbrances, as nearly as we can judge from the best statistics obtainable, represented about 30 per cent of the entire values, or about $9,000,000,000.

Mr. McCall. That is what date?

Mr. MALBY. That is brought down as near to the present date as possible. The figures for the amount of the mortgages are not absolutely a matter that is obtainable. I did obtain them for several different States, including Pennsylvania and others, and striking an average, they would amount to about 30 per cent. They are as correct as it is possible to obtain. The number of persons engaged in agricultural pursuits, according to the census of 1900, was 10,381,765. The value of agricultural products, according to the report of the Secretary of Agriculture for 1909, was as follows:

Total value of all farm products	$8,700,000,000
Animal products	3,000,000,000
Crops	5,700,000,000

The capital invested in manufacturing industries in the United States, according to the census of 1900, was $8,978,825,200. This has probably increased, and it is estimated at the present time to be between $12,000,000,000 and $13,000,000,000.

The number of farms, as we have heretofore noted, was 5,737,372, by the census of 1900, and the number of manufacturing institutions was about 207,562. So that we have, according to the best obtainable statistics for the year 1909, farm products of the value of $8,700,000,000, and of manufactured goods about $15,000,000,000. The number of persons engaged in agriculture, according to the census of 1900, was 10,381,765, while those engaged in manufacture was about 5,079,225.

It will thus be seen that there is nearly twice as much property invested by the farmer as by the manufacturer, and twice as many people engaged in farming as in manufacturing, while we also perceive that the value of all the farm products is about one-half of the value of the manufactured articles, and undoubtedly represents a much smaller percentage of net profits.

Let us pursue the inquiry a little further. We find by the census of 1900 that there was a total of 29,073,233 persons over 10 years of age engaged in all of the gainful occupations in the United States at that time. Of this total, 10,381,765 were engaged in agricultural pursuits, of persons over 10 years of age, and 7,085,309 in manufacturing and mechanical pursuits. It will thus be seen that those engaged in agricultural pursuits exceeded those engaged both in manufacturing and mechanical pursuits by about 3,300,000 persons, and it will also be noticed that of the 29,000,000 (plus) engaged in all of the occupations more than 10,000,000 were farmers.

We find by the census of 1905 (manufactures) that the salaries of laboring men, 16 years of age or over, was $533.92, while those of salaried officials and clerks was $1,105.84, those engaged in the professions receiving much greater compensation, and while the average income of those engaged in agriculture is not given, it is undoubtedly much less.

From the foregoing statements, gathered from the best obtainable statistics, it is made to appear that it is proposed by the present law to affect injuriously more than 35 per cent of all of the people of the United States who toil for their daily bread. It appears from the same authority that they represent an invested capital which is nearly twice as much as that invested in manufacturing in the whole United States, and substantially 30 per cent of our entire national wealth.

Neither can it be claimed by anyone that the farmer has at any time during the history of the whole country ever received a real profit for his labor except during the past two or three years. In connection with this I desire to call your attention to the report of the Select Committee of the Senate of the United States, of which Senator Lodge, of Massachusetts, was a member, on "Wages and Prices of Commodities" in the United States, which says, at page 13 thereof, as follows:

Witnesses agree that farming operations were conducted at a loss, or at best with only a slight margin of profit for several years, and that only during the past two or three years have farmers been able to secure a fair return on their labor and investments. The wealth of the farmers has increased largely through the increase in the value of their land.

The State University of Minnesota has since 1902 kept in the greatest detail record of a number of farms in that State. Allowing the farmer, his wife, and children pay at current rates for all labor performed, the net profits during the three years, 1905 to 1907, was only 4.09 per cent, and this profit advanced to about 6 per cent during the years 1908 to 1909. The profit during the past two years approximates the average interest on farm mortgages in the State.

It is undoubtedly true that the above record, kept by the State of Minnesota, represents a much greater percentage of profits to the farmers of that State than the average throughout the United States, which doubtless ranges not higher than from 2½ to 3 per cent.

I desire also to call your attention to the minority report of the same committee. On page 6 thereof, referring to the report of conditions in Minnesota, I quote the following:

So it will be seen that notwithstanding the large increase in the price of farm products, the farmer has realized a small net return on his labor and investment, by reason of the increased cost of the articles necessary for him to purchase to carry on the business.

Continuing, the minority report says:

We should like to discover one single farmer in all the United States who was ever asked by the buyer the cost of production of his wheat, corn, hogs, or cotton when he was bargaining for them. The manufacturer may consider this question when he offers his product for sale, and he may limit his production to meet receding prices, but no such opportunity comes to the farmer; usually he must sell one crop before he commences raising another, and he can never consider shutting down his plant.

It may be important as well as instructive to inquire what are the material causes which have necessarily led to the increased price in farm production, and, again, I take pleasure in calling your attention to the select committee's report on wages and prices of commodities. At page 13 thereof I quote as follows:

Mr. BROUSSARD. When was that report made?
Mr. MALBY. 1910, I think.
Mr. CLARK. Is that the Lodge report?
Mr. MALBY. That is the Lodge report; yes.
Mr. BROUSSARD. And you quote from the minority report as well as the majority report?
Mr. MALBY. I did, sir. They both agree.
Mr. CLARK. They both agree on what?
Mr. MALBY. Well, on the fact that the farmer is securing just a bare living.
Mr. CLARK. That is Senator Lodge's opinion, is it?
Mr. MALBY. That is the minority's opinion also. I have just read that. The report is dated June 23, 1910. I will say again, it may be important as well as instructive to inquire what are the material causes which have necessarily led to the increased price of farm production, and again I take pleasure in calling

your attention to the select committee's report on wages and prices of commodities, at page 13, which is as follows:

" The testimony of practically all witnesses who have been familiar with farm conditions is to the effect that the cost of production of farm products has risen very rapidly during the past 10 years, wages of farm hands have increased on an average of about 60 per cent, and the original investment necessary to secure land has practically doubled during that period. The richness of the virgin soil is disappearing, and in many localities the crop averages can be maintained only by the use of expensive fertilizers, by rotation of crops, or by allowing the ground to lie fallow.

" The cost of producing live stock has materially increased with the disappearance of the range, which necessitates producing cattle on tame pasture and high-priced land. Witnesses agree that farming operations were conducted at a loss or, at the best, with only a very slight margin of profit for several years, and that only during the past two or three years have farmers been able to secure a fair return on their labor and investment."

Quoting again from the same report, at page 87, as follows:

Wages of regular farm hands have increased from 45 per cent to 75 per cent during the period from 1900 to 1910. Wages of harvest hands have increased in about the same proportion.

Then follows a table of wages paid in different portions of the Union, showing an increase from 45.8 per cent to 100 per cent from 1900 to 1910. After this table, they say as follows:

Another cause of the increased cost of production is the great increase in the value of farm land. This necessitates a much greater investment.

To substantiate this statement, a table follows showing that the price of farm lands in different portions of our Nation increased from 65 to 257 per cent from 1900 to 1910, and added:

It will be thus seen that the average farm land seems to have doubled during that time.

It then adds:

The cost of producing live stock has increased with the rapid disappearance of the range. Live stock is now largely produced on expensive lands instead of on the range, at a merely nominal rent. The expense of fattening cattle has also materially increased by reason of the advance in labor cost and in the advance of the cost of feed.

On page 90 of the same report it also appears that there has been an increase in the cost of farm implements of perhaps 10 to 30 per cent.

There can be no question, therefore, from an examination of these authorities and others of similar character that the increased cost of our food products has been fully accounted for by the increased cost of production, and that the farmer has benefited but little if any by reason thereof, and is illy prepared to stand any further losses in profit.

If he is expected to do the work on the farm and furnish our people with the necessaries of life, the farmer of to-day is not receiving too large a price for his products, or even a large price. It may be, and probably is, true that the consumer is paying a larger price than formerly, but the answer to this is twofold. In the first place, the consumer is being paid a much higher rate of wages than formerly, and lives more expensively and purchases more select articles for consumption; his income is more than keeping pace with the increased cost of living. I desire here to call your attention to some other items which enter into the cost of living of the consumer and to point out the reasons for the same. I quote from the report of the Secretary of Agriculture for the year 1909, at page 17, as follows:

In the North Atlantic States the retail price of beef is 31.4 per cent higher than the wholesale prices. In Allentown, Pa., 50 per cent; at Cortland, N. Y., 50 per cent; at Holyoke, Mass., 36 per cent; Boston, Mass., 36 per cent. In the South Atlantic States, Washington, D. C., 42 per cent; Augusta, Ga., 61 per cent. The average in the South Atlantic States being 38 per cent. In Chicago retail prices are 46 per cent; Kansas City, Kans., 50 per cent; Milwaukee, 40 per cent; St. Louis, 39 per cent. In the South Central States the average is about 50 per cent, as follows: Fort Smith, Ark., 57 per cent; Mobile, Ala., 64 per cent; Nashville, Tenn., 63 per cent; Natchez, Miss., 56 per cent; Shreveport, La., 68 per cent; Louisville, Ky., 52 per cent. A mean gross profit of 39.4 per cent is reported from the Western States. The highest is 62 per cent at Lewiston, Idaho, and the lowest 16 per cent at Tacoma, Wash. These figures were taken from 50 cities throughout the Union, and show an aggregate profit of 38 per cent to the retailer. This will indicate in some degree at least why the consumer is paying high prices for what he purchases.

The same report adds as follows:

There are some services connected with the retail meat or grocery business in the States that customers desire for their accommodation, which are costly to them. They want delivery of goods purchased by special delivery, and this necessitates at least one man and a horse and wagon. They want the market man to send a man to their dwellings to take their orders. The multiplicity of small shops is also a burden to the consumer and no source of richness to the small shopkeeper, when 20 of these small shops are devoted to the retail grocery business where one large shop could do the whole work and cover the trade of that community. What might be said of the meat market is true of all others. The milkmen, the grocery keepers, are more responsible for the prevalent high prices than anyone else.

Again, quoting from the report of the selected committee of the United States Senate on the wages and prices of commodities, on page 123, as follows:

The expense of distributing food products by wholesalers and retailers has increased by reason of the increase in rents, taxes, wages, and cost of horses and horse feed. The method usually followed by the housewife in buying in very small quantities adds materially to the cost, but no particular change has taken place in this respect during the past 10 years. In the cities orders for delivery often consist of a single article, such as "half dozen of eggs," a "quarter peck of potatoes," "2 pounds of sugar," etc. The cost of delivering a small order is practically the same as the cost of delivering a much larger one; in fact, in some cases the cost is larger by reason of the fact that many of the small orders are "rush" and delivery is made by a boy or man who takes with him only one single order.

Other reasons for the increase of cost to the consumer is attributable to cold-storage, sanitary, and other regulations, freight rates, with all of which the farmer has certainly nothing to do.

In conclusion I desire to call your attention to the report of the Secretary of Agriculture for the year 1909, as to the farmer's condition at the present time, as follows:

Advantageously situated as he is in most respects the farmer is less and less generally compelled to dump his crops on the market at the time of harvest. He does not need to work for his board and clothes, as he did in former times when prices were so low as to be unprofitable. He has paid off his mortgages, has made some profit from his labor and land investment, and has so cultivated his land as to make it more productive. Year by year the farmer is better and better able to provide the necessary capital and make the expenditures needed to improve his agricultural land and provide a living for his children.

Substantially all farm land throughout the United States which is worthy of cultivation is under cultivation to-day. The National Government, as well as the State governments, have been striving to scientifically educate the farmer for the purpose of improving his condition and enabling him to produce more crops on the same quality of land, and this he has succeeded in doing. The National Government is spending about $17,000,000 a year for the benefit of the farmer. The State of New York is spending about $1,600,000 a year. How much more is being spent throughout the United States by the various States I am unable to say at the present time, but I know that the sum is very large. Every effort is being made by the National and State Governments to keep the farmer on the farm by making his labors profitable and his home attractive.

Is the passage of this bill a step in the right direction or not? Are all of the efforts which have been made in the past and all the moneys expended to go for nothing.? Just at a time when the farmers are beginning to realize a fair income from their efforts and investments are they to be deprived of it? Are they to be told that they must compete with all others, and from whatever land—for I apprehend the trouble to be that the treaty passed with Canada is simply an entering wedge and that the United States will be compelled to make a similar treaty with all civilized nations.

It has been suggested that the present production of Canada is not sufficient to wholly destroy our markets. Such a suggestion in my judgment is not worthy of serious consideration. Suppose it is not to be destroyed; why is it diminished? What facts present themselves for our calm deliberation to show that the farmer is getting too much for his labor or that his business is too attractive. or will be made more attractive by the passage of this bill? On the other hand, what are the conditions of a manufacturer by which he comes to Congress and insists that the agricultural interests should be destroyed in order that he may make still more profit? Has not the manufacturer of this country found in the sturdy agriculturist from time immemorial the warmest and the best friend he ever had? Have not his representatives at all times appeared in the halls of Congress and insisted that there should be a tariff on what he produced which gave him a fair wage and his manufacturer a fair profit? Has indeed the time come when a manufacturer can say to the farmer, "I no longer need your assistance, I can get along without you"? The manufacturing industry which makes that statement will find ere many suns have set on future Congresses that he has counted without his host.

Again, is it good policy, is it prudent or wise, to place all of the products of the farmer upon the free list, thereby making free traders of them all? Does any one pretent or expect that when all that the farmer produced is placed upon the free list he will not demand a like reduction or a like competition for all that he purchases, and if he does, where does this lead us? What of the future? From where is our income for the support of the Government to come, and what becomes of our theory of protecting American labor and American industries?

Who wrote or who has been authorized to write into our national platform that the laborer is worthy of his hire, and that the same should be protected by a tariff representing the difference in the cost of production here and abroad with a fair profit to the producer? Who wrote that into that document, or who has been authorized to write it into it *"except those engaged in agricultural pursuits"*? Is it not so plain that all can see that the policy of protection must be national and applied to all our people, in whatever form of industry they may be engaged, who earn their daily bread by the sweat of their faces, or not at all? Is it possible that our friends from the Southland should have, for instance, a tariff on their tobacco, rice, sugar, and other things which they produce; that our New England friends should have a tariff on cotton and woolen goods and boots and shoes; that the Pacific slope should have a tariff on their fruits and wines which they produce, and that the farmers of the country should have no tariff at all upon anything which they produce, and in particular when no provision is made for a reduction in the tariff upon anything which they consume? In other words, are they to pay a tariff upon everything which they consume for protection's sake to all others, and be absolutely denied protection for themselves? Where do they come in, and how are they to profit?

Neither can this discrimination be justified by any single chapter in the history of our country. The first tariff act, passed in 1789, provides for a tariff of 4 cents per pound upon cheese, which is one of the chief products of the farmer in the United States. This was increased in 1816 to 9 cents per pound, where it remained for many years. Butter became dutiable at 5 cents per pound in 1842, and under the revision made at that time the farm products were placed upon the dutiable list, where they have remained ever since, except during the reciprocity period between 1854 and 1866, and no party has ever thought to remove the tariff from farm products from that time until this. It has withstood the assaults of free traders and theorists for more than a century of time, and is to-day, and has been for all time in the past, the very foundation of national prosperity. It has been the unbroken history of this country that when the farmers were prosperous the Nation was prosperous, and when the farmers were not the whole Nation suffered. Their prosperity has been the national barometer by which the prosperity of all other industries has been determined. It is entirely safe to say that the future history of our country will continue to repeat this truth.

We are informed by the advocates of this bill that the amount of farm products coming from Canada will not be a menace and wholly destroy our industries. The avowed object and purpose of this bill, however, is to lower the price. When we furnish a market for the Canadian producer, millions of acres of land in their country now uncultivated will be put under cultivation and will grow crops for the consumers in the United States. They have not as yet extensively cultivated these fields, because they have had no markets into which they could send the products of their soil; but when you open up to the farmers of Canada, which country has a tract of land nearly equal to that of the United States all told, all that vast area which is now uncultivated you will find it to be cultivated to just such an extent as they can find a profitable market for their production. It is not what they have done; it is what they are capable of accomplishing.

Mr. BROUSSARD. Will it interrupt you if I should ask a question?

Mr. MALBY. Not at all.

Mr. BROUSSARD. You asked a question, whether it was fair that southern farmers should have protection on sugar and the northern farmer not have protection on the agricultural products of his farm. Is it not a fact that in so far as sugar is concerned for many years we have been compelled to labor under the disadvantages which you complain are written in this agreement between Canada and the United States?

Mr. MALBY. You mean that you have not had sufficient protection?

Mr. BROUSSARD. We have had Cuban reciprocity for many years.

Mr. MALBY. I understand there is a tariff on your sugar.

Mr. BROUSSARD. There is a tariff, but there is reciprocity on it also.

Mr. MALBY. Reciprocity where?

Mr. BROUSSARD. With Cuba.

Mr. MALBY. Well, to a limited extent.

Mr. CLARK. What do you mean by to a limited extent?

Mr. BROUSSARD. Twenty per cent, is it not?

Mr. MALBY. Well, there is—you probably recall how much it is.

Mr. CLARK. But reciprocity does not necessarily mean that articles come in free or go into the other country free.

Mr. MALBY. I understand that. It does not make any difference to me, so far as my presentation of this case is concerned, if you call it reciprocity or free trade.

Mr. CLARK. I am not calling it anything. I was just simply trying to help you out——

Mr. MALBY. I am much obliged to the gentleman.

Mr. CLARK (continuing). Or correct you about a statement, if they had a limited reciprocity or partial reciprocity.

Mr. MALBY. Well, I did not mean that.

Mr. CLARK. That is exactly what you said.

Mr. MALBY. No; what I mean to say is that there is a difference in the tariff rates between the United States and Cuba and between the United States and somebody else.

Mr. FORDNEY. As between this country and Cuba the reciprocity treaty reduced our duty 20 per cent below the rate from any other country. But this puts those articles on the free list. It is limited as between this country and Cuba, but there is no limit as between this country and Canada.

Mr. MALBY. There is quite a difference. There is another provision in the bill to which I desire to call your attention, and that is that the products of the forest are also placed on the free list, or practically so; not only in the raw and unmanufactured condition, but also manufactured, etc., in particular with reference to lumber, wood pulp, and paper. I have heard a great deal said about conservation by those people who want me to conserve my property. My constituents and I have received a great deal of gratuitous advice from conservators of the forests who have no investments therein. I do not know of any good reason why I should not manage my forest land just as much as they manage their own business.

Mr. CLARK. Will you allow me to interrupt you there?

Mr. MALBY. Certainly.

Mr. CLARK. Do you not recognize the fact that you and the manufacturer both—that is, you speak of yourself as owner of the forest— do you not hold your property subject to the public good?

Mr. MALBY. Subject to the public good?

Mr. CLARK. Yes.

Mr. MALBY. We hold it just in the same manner as any other property.

Mr. CLARK. I know. But does not every man hold his property subject to the public good?

Mr. MALBY. In the same sense—I don't like to be singled out.

Mr. CLARK. If we people in the Mississippi Valley do not want our valley to dry up like Spain and Mesopotamia did, and therefore insist upon conservation of forests, I do not see that you have much room to growl.

Mr. MALBY. So far as the national domain is concerned, do with it as you will; but I have yet to find anyone who can successfully point out any obligation on my part to own property, pay taxes on it, and be without income from it, for the benefit of the policy of conservation.

Mr. CLARK. That is all we are trying to do—to conserve the forests that belong to the United States. It is a great pity we did not begin 40 or 50 years ago.

Mr. MALBY. I beg your pardon; I do not agree with that. This is one of the objects of this bill——

Mr. CLARK. I am not talking about this bill; I am talking about the doctrine of conserving the forests.

Mr. MALBY. I am trying to discuss this too, in connection with this bill.

Mr. CLARK. Go on, then.

Mr. MALBY. I am saying that by putting forests upon the free list that the conservators are trying to create a situation where it becomes unprofitable for me to longer engage in forestry. That is what I am saying—and that is what will be accomplished by this bill.

Mr. LONGWORTH. It would be unprofitable to destroy it.

Mr. MALBY. Well, they are not destroying it. I mean to say, it would be unprofitable to cut, to use. If they have a profit in their natural growth, few can afford to keep it that way.

Mr. RANDELL. Does not that rather mean that forests purchased at from $2 to $5 an acre would no longer be worth $25 an acre to the speculator?

Mr. MALBY. I am free to confess that I know of no forest lands purchased in recent years for the price that you mention.

Mr. RANDELL. You probably know of none in the East. There have been forest lands purchased in Texas and the West for that price.

Mr. MALBY. If they purchased it for that price I guarantee it is not worth much more to-day.

Mr. FORDNEY. What part of the country can forests be purchased for from $3 to $5 an acre now?

Mr. MALBY. Nowhere that I know of.

Mr. RANDELL. Not now, perhaps; but not long ago in Texas forest lands could be purchased for that price. They consolidated the mills and then raised the price of the land from $3 an acre to about $25 an acre.

Mr. FORDNEY. Do you know of any consolidation of mills anywhere? If so, furnish the proof of it.

Mr. RANDELL. It occurred in that part of the United States in 1903.

Mr. FORDNEY. It does not exist, and you know it.

Mr. RANDELL. Mr. Chairman, it did occur in Texas in 1903, and the gentleman is certainly very rude. His statement is without any truth in it.

The CHAIRMAN. The committee will be in order.

Mr. MALBY. I am not going to attempt to discuss at any particular length the forestry question beyond calling the attention of this committee to certain provisions in the proposed bill which admits into the United States from Canada all rough lumber free of duty and reduces the tariff on all kinds of planed lumber $1.25 per 1,000 feet.

The CHAIRMAN. It is the same as it is under the present law.

Mr. MALBY. I think you are mistaken about that.

The CHAIRMAN. I may be mistaken about that. Let me ask you this: The present tariff is 75 cents on rough lumber?

Mr. FORDNEY. No; $1.25.

Mr. MALBY. Yes; $1.25 per thousand on rough lumber.

The CHAIRMAN. It is the same as the present law.

Mr. MALBY. You are mistaken about this. All rough lumber under the provisions of the present bill comes in free of duty, and the tariff on planed lumber under the Payne tariff bill is determined by adding to the $1.25 on rough lumber the duty now proposed on planed lumber. In other words, by wiping out the duty on rough lumber the duty on planed lumber under this bill would be reduced $1.25 per 1,000 feet, and will be dutiable as follows:

Sawed boards, etc., planed or finished, 50 cents per 1,000; planed or finished on one side and tongued and grooved or planed or finished on two sides, 75 cents per 1,000; planed or finished on two sides and tongued and grooved, $1.12½ per 1,000 feet: planed or finished on four sides, $1.50 per 1,000 feet. It will thus be seen that upon all grades of lumber above enumerated that the reduction of the present tariff will be $1.25 per 1,000 feet.

The object of a protective tariff on manufactured lumber has been to induce its importation from Canada into the United States in the rough and to be planed and manufactured here by our own workmen, and this has built up a great industry in the United States. At my own home there are employed in the planing mills seven or eight hundred men who have built up a large industry by planing lumber which comes chiefly from Canada. In my judgment, the heavy reduction proposed upon planed lumber will ruin this great industry wherever located. Hereafter it will undoubtedly be found to be more profitable to plane and manufacture the lumber at the place where it is cut and send it direct to the markets from there. It can be done very much cheaper at the place of production, for the cost of living is much less, and, besides, they save the freight charges on that which goes to waste by planing. This at least is the judgment of those who are in a position best to know what the effect of this proposed legislation will be, and thus, most unnecessarily, as I claim, one of the greatest industries of our country is going to be destroyed without the slightest adequate return to those who are engaged in it, and substantially, I believe, without benefit to a single consumer. If there be a temporary decrease in the price of lumber by reason of this proposed change, it must of necessity operate disadvantageously to all of the lumber dealers in our own country who own high-priced lands and pay the highest wages in the world as compared with others engaged in the same industry. But, as I stated in the beginning, it is not my purpose to discuss at length this very important subject, for there are others to follow who are more intimately acquainted with the subject than I am.

I may say that I observe, in passing, that iron ore is reduced to 10 cents per ton, and perhaps that is so because it is another industry in which our people are engaged.

The CHAIRMAN. But you are aware that the tariff on iron ore is no menace to our industry owing to the low grade of the ore?

Mr. MALBY. I have not gone into the question of grade. I am simply stating what I find here, and our Canadian brethren evidently thought it was an advantage to have the tariff lowered to 10 cents per ton.

Now, there is one thing more of very great importance to which I desire to call your attention.

I have read with great care the provisions of the proposed treaty with reference to the admission of wood pulp and paper into the United States, and I must admit that its provisions are by no means clear, and, in fact, I think will be found not to carry into effect the views of the high-contracting parties. It is really bad enough as it is, but to have any mistake made about it would be worse. It must be borne in mind that the various Provinces of Canada own what is called "Crown lands," and each Province has the absolute right to determine what shall be done with its own products. The Province of Ontario about 12 years ago prohibited the exportation of any of the products of the forests in rough state to the United States. This policy was followed by the Province of Quebec just recently. The question now arises under the treaty, just what are we getting? It does not say in expressed terms, as it should, that the benefits of the American markets shall not be open to the Canadian manufacturers of paper until all restrictions of whatsoever kind are removed by the various Provinces. On the contrary, it is quite possible, and it is my construction that paper manufactured from wood cut on lands owned by individuals would be admissible into the United States whether the restrictions now maintained by the various provisions are removed or not. If I am correct in this construction the outrage of such legislation would simply be increased. The bill should at least be amended so as to leave no error in it upon this very important question, for unless the American manufacturer of paper secures a free and unlimited supply from Canada, then there is absolutely no excuse whatsoever for the terms of this treaty so far as this industry is concerned.

There was an exhaustive inquiry made into the question of the duty on print paper by a committee of which our friend from Illinois, Mr. Mann, was chairman two years ago, and while I did not agree with his deductions and conclusions, he reported at that time that there ought to be a duty of $2 per ton on white print paper. After a very careful investigation, Mr. Chairman, you and the members of this committee concluded to agree with him on a $2 tariff a ton, and I think that in good conscience you felt that that was very low. The bill went to the Senate and they concluded that $4 per ton more correctly represented the required tariff, and Congress finally compromised on $3.75 per ton.

Further, I have been informed upon the best of authority that the President of the United States at that time stated that the paper makers had made a better case than anyone else who had appeared before him for a protective tariff upon their industries. This subject has since that time been referred to the Tariff Board, which, during the past year, has made an exhaustive inquiry into this subject and nearly completed their investigations, and I am authoritatively advised that notwithstanding this fact that this Tariff Board has never been asked by the President of the United States or anyone else as to the results of their labors, although a quarter of a million dollars was appropriated for their use, and the avowed purpose of creating the board was to advise the President of the United States in enforcing the provisions of the Payne tariff law, and also to enable him to more correctly advise Congress as to any revision of the various schedules which, in his judgment, was necessary.

The CHAIRMAN. This committee has reported a resolution calling upon the Tariff Board for information on that subject, and I think it may be passed when the House sees fit to consider it.

Mr. MALBY. I hope so. But of what good will it be to me to have that Tariff Board report after this committee has acted? There isn't much fun in that.

Mr. FORDNEY. There is no use to lock the barn after the horse is stolen.

Mr. MALBY. Not much. I am informed that that information is already at hand.

Mr. CLARK. If that is true, then as soon as we pass this resolution we will get the information, won't we?

Mr. MALBY. I know, but——

Mr. CLARK. And these hearings are not going to close until 5 o'clock next Thursday.

Mr. MALBY. If I get even an intimation from this committee that the report of that commission is to receive consideration I have nothing more to say.

The CHAIRMAN. What is that?

Mr. MALBY. If the Tariff Board's report is going to receive consideration.

The CHAIRMAN. Well, this committee will bring the resolution before the House, and if the House adopts it, as I presume they will——

Mr. MALBY. I understand, Mr. Chairman, but why do we try to deceive ourselves? There is no use in that. I am aware of the fact that unless the high contracting parties between the United States and Canada get together again that this treaty must stand or fall as it is. If they get together and resume the negotiations and eliminate paper or establish a different schedule for paper then we would be permitted as a Congress to act upon it; but we must either accept the recommendations as a whole or not at all, if this treaty is to go into effect.

This is one of the greatest industries, in fact the second greatest single industry in the United States of America. Its capital is represented by tens of millions of dollars. The amount paid yearly to the laborers is represented in millions of dollars. Its toilers are numbered by the tens of thousands. What has it done that it should be singled out from all of the industries which concededly should be protected, for public execution—and in behalf of our Canadian brethren and a few newspapers?

Is it not possible for the Congress of the United States to do justice by its industries? And if we do, this treaty would fail, if for no other reason than that a tariff board, which has spent the entire summer investigating the affairs of every paper maker in the United States and which has got the information now, is never even called upon by anybody in authority, so far as I am advised, as to what their views are or what their conclusions in reference to the matter are.

The CHAIRMAN. Now, please except this committee from that statement after what has been said.

Mr. MALBY. I am not criticising the committee; I am stating the facts.

Mr. HILL. The committee passed a motion the other day calling on the Tariff Board for all the information they have upon the paper pulp schedule.

Mr. MALBY. I am grateful for that; I appreciate that. I was informed that was a fact. I think that was a good thing to do. I am simply wondering whether, under the conditions, if it comes in, this committee, no matter how they may feel about it, have any power to act.

Mr. CLARK. Any power to act on what?

Mr. MALBY. Any power to amend this McCall bill.

Mr. CLARK. The committee has unlimited power to recommend changes in this thing, if they want to do it.

Mr. MALBY. What will become of the treaty?

Mr. CLARK. I am not saying they are going to recommend any. They can change every single item of it if they want to.

Mr. MALBY. I appreciate that fact, sir.

Mr. CLARK. I don't know how many they will change.

Mr. MALBY. I appreciate that; but I think you understand very well what I mean.

Mr. CLARK. I understand that you are dead against the whole thing.

Mr. MALBY. I certainly have made you understand exactly where I stand.

Mr. CLARK. You did that. As a matter of fact, you need not have said a word anyhow; we knew it in the beginning.

Mr. MALBY. While some things we know intuitively, some things we have to have explained. But I am grateful to the chairman and the members of this committee for this opportunity of making a statement. We cherished the hope and have had some expectation that when I laid bare the situation, as I see it, a different view would be taken of this proposed negotiation, which is not new in the history of our country at all.

Reciprocity has been tried in this country several times but has failed for good reasons. In particular has this been so, and always will continue to be so, where there exists competition between two countries in the raising or production of the same articles which are affected by reciprocity. Of necessity it is intended that when articles are placed upon the free list, or tariff greatly reduced, it must place the producer of these articles upon both sides at a disadvantage with reference to such production. Take the present proposed treaty as an example. The farmer's products of all kinds are placed upon the free list, while the Canadian manufacturer is supposed in consideration thereof and of benefits accruing to reduce the tariff which is his protection upon the articles which he produces. Nothing is placed upon the free list for the benefit of either, yet they are .compelled to bear the whole burden for the alleged benefit of others. For instance, what return does the American farmer receive in consideration for the placing of all of his products upon the free list and which at the same time places him in competition with the producers of other lands? I submit that he receives nothing in return for this sacrifice on his part. He still continues to work his farm, which has cost him much more than his competitor; pays more for the wages of his farm hands and purchases all of the necessaries of life for himself and family in the highest markets of the world. No tariff is reduced on anything which he purchases but only on that which he produces. He pays just as high prices as before on the necessaries of life. Where, then, does he come in? He simply doesn't come in. He is left to shift for himself as best he can, bearing the additional burdens of state for the benefit of others.

At the same time how fares it with the Canadian manufacturer? Under the provisions of this bill he is also called upon to make sacrifice. He finds that everything that he and his employees purchase has gone up in price, and at the same time he is forced into competition with a strong neighbor with reference to all that he produces. Clearly, these two classes of citizens, to wit, the American farmer and the Canadian manufacturer, are being discriminated against for a more favored class. In this case the American farmer is discriminated against in favor of the American manufacturer, and on the other hand the Canadian manufacturer is discriminated against in favor of the Canadian farmer. In other words, one class of our citizens are made to suffer a loss for the proposed benefit of another, which policy no party can stand and endure, for the reason that it is grossly unfair as well as unequal treatment of our citizens who are being discriminated against. There should and must be equality of opportunity, or the principal of protection must perish. For myself, I am a protectionist. I believe in the principal of universal protection, but it must apply equally to all. It must apply to all parts of our common country, equally to the tillers of the soil and to those engaged in manufacture. Then the principal is safe; otherwise it must perish, for the people will no more endure half protection and half free trade than our forefathers would suffer our Nation to remain half free and half slave. It must be one or the other, and now is the time when that question is to be determined.

The human race is like a man lost in the forests—it moves in circles, but we come back to the starting point in time. So it is with reference to the Canadian reciprocity, for in 1854 a treaty was concluded between the United States and Great Britain, Great Britain acting in behalf of Canada, which placed substantially all the products of the farm upon the free list in consideration of certain alleged concessions in favor of our manufacturing industries. This treaty was to continue for a period of 10 years and as much longer as the contracting parties should mutually agree. It is interesting to note the workings of the treaty and the results. It is sufficient to say that the imports into the United States during the time the treaty continued in force, to wit, from 1854 to 1866, increased 261 per cent. I quote the following from a report of the committee of the Canadian Privy Council, dated February 19, 1864, viz:

It would be impossible to express in figures with any approach to accuracy the extent to which the facilities of commercial intercourse created by the reciprocity treaty have contributed to the wealth and prosperity of this province; and it would be difficult to exaggerate the importance which the people of Canada attach to the continued enjoyment of these facilities.

While it will thus be seen that the treaty was in great favor, on account of the benefits conferred, with Canada, how is it looked upon by the people of the United States? I find that on January 18, 1865, notice was given by this country to Great Britain of its intention to abrogate the treaty on the grounds " *that it was no longer for the interests of the United States to continue the same in force."*

This tells the whole story so far as the United States is concerned. The treaty lasted 12 years, and came to an ignominious end on March 17, 1866, and no statesman worthy of the name has sought to revive it up to the present day.

The efforts of Blaine and McKinley for reciprocity with the Central and South American States have been as fruitless as the Canadian treaty. They were wiped out unceremoniously by the passage of the Wilson tariff bill (August 28, 1894) and nothing has been heard of them since. The difficulty of such arrangements I have attempted to point out, to wit: It is impossible to deal fairly and without discrimination with our people, but on the other hand it favors one interest to the dertiment of another, for which no party can be responsible.

Mr. STAFFORD. Mr. Chairman, there are representatives here from the malting interests in Illinois, Minnesota, and Wisconsin. Mr. Bruno E. Fink, of Milwaukee, is here on behalf of the malting associations, and I am told there is an accredited representative here from the Society of Equity who would like to be heard on the subject of admitting barley free of duty.

The CHAIRMAN. How many appear for your interests?

Mr. STAFFORD. Only one appearing for the malting interests.

The CHAIRMAN. Whom do the others represent?

Mr. STAFFORD. One is from the Society of Equity.

Mr. LONGWORTH. What is that?

Mr. STAFFORD. An organization of the farmers of the West that looks to the betterment of the welfare of the farmer. It is a very extensive organization throughout the Middle West.

STATEMENT OF MR. BRUNO E. FINK.

Mr. Chairman and gentlemen of the committee, we have come here as manufacturers of malt and as the duly accredited representatives of all the other manufacturers of malt in the Middle Western States.

We have come to register their unanimous protest against the ratification of that part of the proposed reciprocity agreement which would place barley and barley malt on the free list.

We have hitherto never appeared before you and therefore now beg leave to lay before your honorable body some of the facts that underlie our reasons for opposing the duty-free admission of barley and barley malt. They are:

First. The production of malting barley is not general throughout the United States and Canada, but in both countries is limited to those sections where climatic and agricultural conditions are favorable to its growth. In the United States the States of Wisconsin, Iowa, Minnesota, and the two Dakotas produce the good malting barley, which is the source of supply of all the malting plants in the United States east of the Rocky Mountains.

Second. Practically 80 per cent of the malting plants in the United States are located in close proximity to the aforementioned five States, namely, in Illinois, Wisconsin, Iowa, Minnesota, South Dakota, and Nebraska. They were erected during the past 15 to 20 years under protective laws.

Third. About 20 per cent of the malting plants in the United States are located in the East, with Buffalo as the center, which district will be greatly favored by the proposed reciprocity agreement to the great disadvantage of the 80 per cent in the Middle West.

Mr. CLARK. Why would Buffalo be favored by this bill any more than you would be?

Mr. FINK. That will appear in the course of the argument.

Mr. CLARK. Very well, then.

Mr. LONGWORTH. Just a moment there. You say barley and barley malt?

Mr. FINK. Yes.

Mr. LONGWORTH. Where do you get barley malt?

Mr. FINK. Barley malt being the direct product of barley naturally would enter into consideration because of the great probability that, directly there will be free barley, there will be a period of erection of malt houses in Canada, which could send the barley malt over instead of the barley, and that would make the situation worse, if it were contemplated to place barley malt upon the free list alongside of barley itself.

Mr. LONGWORTH. But this bill does not provide that barley malt shall be placed there; it only provides that barley shall be placed there.

Mr. FINK. Then I shall be very glad to eliminate the words "barley malt" wherever they are used conjointly with barley.

Mr. CLARK. That would change your whole position then, would it not?

Mr. FINK. No, sir; not a particle.

Mr. CLARK. It seems to me if you were to cut out the thing you were complaining about you would quit complaining.

Mr. FINK. No; I beg your pardon——

Mr. CLARK. I don't want to interrupt you. Go on.

Mr. LONGWORTH. What is barley malt?

Mr. FINK. It is an article manufactured from barley.

Mr. LONGWORTH. But its position remains exactly as it is under the present law.

Mr. FINK. What I have to say in my argument will apply to barley, because the arguments are applicable in both cases.

Mr. DALZELL. Barley is 30 and barley malt is 45.

Mr. LONGWORTH. Then barley malt will remain at 45.

The CHAIRMAN. This is the same differential exactly, is it not?

Mr. LONGWORTH. No; barley malt is not touched in this bill.

Mr. HILL. Barley malt is left at 45 cents under Schedule B.

Mr. LONGWORTH. So there is a greater protection on barley malt, if this should pass, than there would be without it.

Mr. FINK. Then I will be glad to eliminate the words "barley malt," and continue the argument as if it was not there.

Mr. CLARK. Before you go to that, I would like to know how it happens—because you say it is a fact— that the only States that can grow the proper kind of barley for making malt are those five—Wisconsin, Iowa, Minnesota, and the two Dakotas? Why would it not be just as good grown in Kansas or Missouri?

Mr. FINK. Barley from Kansas and Missouri has been used, but the farmers there have quit raising it from the fact that for malting purposes those barleys are not desirable, as compared with barleys raised in more favorably located agricultural districts.

Mr. CLARK. You do not mean to say that those northern States are more favorably located for agriculture than the central Mississippi Valley States?

Mr. FINK. For the production of barley: yes.

Mr. CLARK. Oh—for the production of barley Go on.

Mr. FINK. The manufacturing plants which we represent in the Middle West were built close to their natural base of supplies, as aforesaid, and under the protection of favorable tariff laws the production of barley in this section of the country has grown to enormous proportions. Our investment in malting plants may be conservatively stated at $30,000,000. Our plants are useless for any purpose other than malting. They can not be moved at will. They will be a dead loss to us, and we, literally speaking, will be legislated out of business if the free admission of barley and barley malt under the proposed reciprocity agreement becomes the law of the land. Not only that, but the cultivation of barley here would practically become obsolete, for the duty-free Canadian barley would drive our American cereal out of the field, for the simple reason that, land and labor being cheaper in Canada, the Canadian cereal could be brought into our country at a price so low that our American barley farmers could not hope to compete with it.

Mr. HILL. How do you make that out? We are now exporting 4,000,000 bushels of barley a year and Canada is exporting 2,000,000, and they meet in the same market. How are they going to beat us?

Mr. FINK. There is a great difference, and I should state that the only American barley that is exported is the barley that is raised on the Pacific coast.

Mr. HILL. It is another product entirely.

Mr. FINK. And that is not used in this part of the United States.

Mr. HILL. But it is exported and goes into a common market with **Canada?**

Mr. FINK. It goes to England alongside Canadian barley, but only moves from the Pacific coast; none of the barley raised here is exported.

Mr. HILL. Can the Northwest barley compete in the United States with California barley?

Mr. FINK. Will you repeat that?

Mr. HILL. I say, can the Northwest barley compete in the United States, entirely amongst ourselves, with the California barley?

Mr. FINK. Yes, sir.

Mr. HILL. Then why can not you compete with the Canadian barley—if things equal to the same thing are equal to each other?

Mr. FINK. As the argument proceeds, I will reach that point.

Mr. HILL. All right.

Mr. CLARK. Now, I want to ask you another question. Is it not true that you people up there in the Dakotas and Minnesota and Wisconsin and Nebraska raise barley because you can not raise corn?

Mr. FINK. Hardly that. We could easily turn to other cereals on account of the modern ideas as to crop rotation, and they are taking firm hold of the people.

Mr. CLARK. Who said that the barley raised in those five States is superior to the barley raised in Missouri and Kansas and Kentucky and that belt; did the farmers say so or the maltsters say it?

Mr. FINK. Because the elemental qualities of barley have long been tested by practical use.

Mr. CLARK. Where did they get barley before they settled those States?

Mr. FINK. Barley was imported at one time from Canada. I recall when there was a duty of 15 cents a bushel, there were imported into this country over 11,000,000 bushels of barley from Canada.

The CHAIRMAN. That was prior to 1890——

Mr. FINK. That was at a time when the production of beer was less than one-half of the volume that marks the business at the present time.

The CHAIRMAN. Is not this a fact—without spending too much time on it: That under those conditions there was a low duty on barley, and a great deal of barley was imported from lower Canada into New York, into Rochester, and Oswego, and other places where there were malt houses on the border, and when the brewers required light malt for a light-colored beer, which is a kind of beer they made then to a large extent, that that 10,000,000 bushels or 11,000,000 bushels came in almost exclusively from Canada prior to the enactment of the McKinley bill? Have your researches gone back as far as that?

Mr. FINK. Yes.

The CHAIRMAN. And then the McKinley bill came along with this 30-cent duty demanded by you people in the West, and it was put on barley, and immediately almost by magic not only stopped the importation of barley from Canada, but stopped the raising of barley in New York and transferred the business to a poorer barley in the Dakotas?

Mr. CALDERHEAD. Because the land was cheaper.

The CHAIRMAN. I will leave out the poorer; but transferred it to the Dakotas and Wisconsin and Minnesota and those States?

Mr. FINK. Let me inform the gentleman that the quality of the barley raised in the Middle Western States is of such fine quality that the other day a prize bushel of that barley sold at $74. That was for seeding purposes—1 bushel.

The CHAIRMAN. Well, our people have stopped raising barley; but when they did raise barley they got a better price for their malt than you did up there in Wisconsin: It was lighter, it was not stained.

It did not make the dark beer, and people wanted the light beer those days. Now they have got weaned from the light beer, largely I suppose, on account of necessity. Now you are demanding a prohibitive duty on barley from Canada——

Mr. FINK. You are not quite exactly informed, Mr. Chairman.

The CHAIRMAN. What is that?

Mr. FINK. I take it you are not quite correctly informed on the subject of the quality of the barley.

The CHAIRMAN. Do you admit the rest of the statement? Do you admit that 50 cents a bushel is prohibitory?

Mr. FINK. It is prohibitory; yes, sir, as to the importation of Canadian barley, and with the view of affording protection to the American barley raiser.

The CHAIRMAN. And you admit that 15 cents a bushel would be practically prohibitory? Will you admit that?

Mr. FINK. No, sir; it will not be prohibitory, because they brought over 11,000,000 bushels into the United States from Canada alone at the time when the duty was 15 cents.

Mr. CLARK. How much do they bring in now?

Mr. FINK. Nothing at this time.

Mr. CLARK. It is prohibitive, then.

Mr. FINK. For the protection of the American farmer.

Mr. CLARK. No; you must not say it is protection if it is prohibitory.

The CHAIRMAN. It protects Dakota barley and Dakota malt against New York barley and New York malt. It has driven our people out of business entirely.

Mr. FINK. If you will kindly permit me to continue I shall reach that point.

The CHAIRMAN. Go on, then.

Mr. DALZELL. He seems to have tramped on the toes of New York.

The CHAIRMAN. Not at all; but I like gentlemen to come up here and state things just as they are, and claim the brutal privilege of keeping people out of the business entirely and keeping it for themselves.

Mr. FORDNEY. I think the gentleman is trying to state it as he understands it. Maybe other people do not understand it as he does.

Mr. FINK. Certainly; there are two sides to every question, and I am trying to present my side.

The CHAIRMAN. If there was nothing else in the treaty but that, I would be for it on all fours.

Mr. FINK. Our plants are useless for any other purpose than malting. They can not be moved at will. They will be a dead loss to us, and we, literally speaking, will be legislated out of business if the free admission of barley under the proposed reciprocity treaty agreement becomes a law of the land. Not only that, but the cultivation of barley here would practically become obsolete, for duty-free Canadian barley would drive our American cereal out of the field, for the simple reason that land and labor being cheaper in Canada, the Canadian cereal could be brought in at a price so low that our American farmers could not hope to compete with it.

Fourth. Eastern Canada supplies the only really good malting barley raised in Canada.

Mr. CLARK. Now, Mr. Witness, why is that? There is just an imaginary line between North Dakota and Minnesota and Canada, and if this excellent barley is raised in North Dakota and Minnesota, why is it not just as good over the line?

Mr. FINK. I have said eastern Canada.

Mr. CLARK. I know you said eastern Canada produced all that was fit to use in Canada.

Mr. FINK. Eastern Canada supplies—and when I say that I mean chiefly the product of Ontario and in that section.

Mr. CLARK. If that is true, how does it happen that they can raise such good malting barley in North Dakota and Minnesota, right on the Canadian line, and what is the reason they do not raise as good barley on the Canadian side of that imaginary line as they do on this side of the line?

The CHAIRMAN. I understand that lower Canada is where they raise their Canadian barley.

Mr. CLARK. Yes; he claims in one breath the best barley is raised in northern Minnesota, Wisconsin, and in the Dakotas, and yet when it comes to Canada he says the best barley is not raised on the other side of that imaginary line in that region, but in eastern Canada, much farther south.

The CHAIRMAN. He is right on the last proposition, but not on the first.

Mr. CLARK. Then, if your statement be true, the farther south you go the better barley you ought to raise.

The CHAIRMAN. Oh, no.

Mr. FINK. The climatic conditions, gentlemen, in respect to the Province of Ontario and up in the Winnipeg country are not the same. Likewise, the conditions of the soil are different, as you will be a e to easily ascertain from a reference to statistics in the brewing fieldbl

As I said before, eastern Canada supplies the only really good malting barley raised in Canada. The supply is adjacent to Buffalo. Buffalo and other eastern malting points now obtain their supply of American barley from the aforementioned five barley-growing States of the United States, via the Great Lakes, at a freight cost which enables these eastern malting plants to compete on an equal basis with the great malting plants of Illinois, Wisconsin, Minnesota, South Dakota, and Nebraska. Free barley, however, would give Buffalo an unfair and insurmountable advantage over the latter. Insurmountable, because the largest consumers of barley malt—that is to say, the brewing industry of the eastern States—are not far distant from Buffalo.

Mr. CLARK. The whole thing then resolves itself into this: That after practicing this high tariff system on all of us for a century you fall out among yourselves now and are fighting each other as to who shall get the best of it.

Mr. FINK. We have always had that little difference of argument with Buffalo, have always had that controversy, and I am here to adduce a reason why that plea of Buffalo should never be entertained.

Mr. CLARK. This thing resolves itself into a fight, then, between New York makers of malt and the western fellows, and the rest of us have nothing on earth to do with it.

Mr. FINK. Not quite as sectional as you seem to think or at first blush would, perhaps, appear. Let me repeat this sentence. Free barley would give Buffalo an unfair and insurmountable advantage over the great barley plants of Ilinois, Wisconsin, Iowa, Minnesota, South Dakota, and Nebraska. Insurmountable because the largest consumers of barley malt—that is, the brewing industry of the Eastern States—are not far distant from Buffalo. Buffalo would thus enjoy a double advantage as compared with middle western maltsters, because the latter would have to draw the Canadian barley a long distance to their respective plants, to begin with——

The CHAIRMAN. That is what Buffalo has to do anyhow.

Mr. FINK. I have stated the points right here. Buffalo and other eastern malting points obtain their supply of barley by way of the Great Lakes at a freight cost which enables these eastern malting plants to compete on an equal basis with the great malting plants in those Western States.

The CHAIRMAN. That is an assertion denied most emphatically by the Buffalo people when they presented the figures to this committee a few years ago.

Mr. FINK. We can controvert any statement to the contrary by equally strong official figures.

The CHAIRMAN. I agree with you on that. I think you can; between you I am not saying which is right.

Mr. CLARK. To help you and the chairman both out, would not the maltsters at' Milwaukee and other points in those western States get eastern Canada barley nearly as cheap as Buffalo maltsters can get it, taking into consideration the water transportation?

Mr. FINK. I would like to have the gentleman not lose sight of one important fact. Malt houses in Buffalo are all located right near a point where transfer from boat to malt-house elevator is immediately and easily possible, whereas the malt houses in the West are located in the interior, far removed from any point where a vessel bringing barley from Canada could with facility and cheaply transfer its cargo to the malting elevators.

Mr. CLARK. Why did not the men in the Northwest locate their malting plants as convenient to getting out the raw material as the Buffalo fellows did?

Mr. FINK. I have stated at the outset that the malting plants of the West were built close to their natural base of supplies.

Mr. CLARK. That is, if Congress will rig up a law that drives them into using this northwest barley; but suppose all the time that these New York people would have an equal chance with you, would you locate your malting establishments then where they are located now?

Mr. FINK. The fact that the eastern maltsters have an equal chance with us is proven by the additional fact that within the past few years there have been erected in Buffalo the largest plants practically in the United States.

The CHAIRMAN. Right there——

Mr. FINK. Right in Buffalo.

The CHAIRMAN. No; right at that point, in your argument. The barley is first loaded into the elevators along the railroads, in the West?

Mr. FINK. Yes.

The CHAIRMAN. It has to be transferred from those elevators to the cars, and from the cars to the Lakes, and from the Lakes to Buffalo.

Mr. FINK. Yes, sir.

The CHAIRMAN. So you would be at no more disadvantage if you got the barley loaded on the Lakes from Canada and brought to the railroad in the West—not Milwaukee, particularly, but the other points where you have your malt houses—and then had it transported by lake, you would have as much advantage as Buffalo, would you not, in the case of barley grown in Canada?

Mr. FINK. The malting plants in the East, Buffalo and New York City, where there is one, are so equipped with elevator machinery and so located at the water's edge that cargoes can easily be brought right into the plant, whereas the malt house in the West——

The CHAIRMAN. Then you have got to eliminate the point of elevator machinery for your malt house——

Mr. FINK. Oh, no; the location of the house is different. Our malt houses in the West are not located at the water's edge. Our malt houses in the Middle West are located at interior points where they have good railroad facilities but not water facilities.

Mr. CLARK. Why would it not have been easy to have located them in Chicago and Milwaukee at the water's edge as for somebody in Buffalo to locate theirs at the water's edge?

Mr. FINK. I can only assure the gentleman that if we had had any intimation or divination that it would be proposed to enact a reciprocity agreement such as the one under consideration, we would never have built our houses anywhere except Buffalo.

Mr. HILL. I want to get at the merits of the general proposition. I am disturbed about this California situation. Is it not true, then, that California barley does not come east; that aside from the amount they consume on the Pacific coast they have no benefit from this duty that now exists on barley?

Mr. FINK. That is true.

Mr. HILL. Then they are practically on free-trade terms on the Pacific coast now with Canada except for the surplus, only their surplus shipment. How much do they raise on the Pacific Coast?

Mr. FINK. I have not the statistics with me at the present time, but I think it is somewhere around 30,000,000.

A VOICE. 30,000,000 bushels; yes.

Mr. HILL. Then one-fifth of the entire crop of the United States now is on a free-trade basis?

Mr. FINK. But will you please bear in mind one other thing, and that is purely technical, that the brewers of the United States prefer not to use the character of barley that is raised on the Pacific coast?

Mr. HILL. That is all right; but they raise it in competition with Canada and sell it in the same market.

Mr. FINK. They raise it for home consumption and for export, because the character of the barley raised on the Pacific coast is somewhat similar to the character of the barley that is brewed in the breweries and the ale factories of Europe.

Mr. HILL. What are they going to do for beer when this great exposition comes off at San Francisco?

Mr. FINK. I might say that when it comes to employing barley for bottle-beer purposes, even the brewers of the Pacific coast resort to the barley grown in our section of the country and do not use their own barley for that purpose.

Mr. CLARK. Do you suppose that Congress is going to enter into a squabble about this tariff business between the interests at Buffalo and the interests out in your part of the country? That is all there is about this thing that you are fighting over.

Mr. FINK. But, gentlemen, our plea is simply to let well enough alone. We are all getting along nicely at Buffalo, as well as in the West. The business at Buffalo is increasing beautifully. They have advantages there that place them on a parity with us from the West all along the line.

The CHAIRMAN. How many millions of dollars were destroyed in New York State, money invested in malting property, by the increase of the duty to 30 cents a bushel—property at Oswego and other towns along the lake?

Mr. FINK. I am not prepared to state the value, but I will say this in opposition to your question: That the art of malting since that time has undergone most radical changes, and that old-time houses, such as you refer to, would no longer be in the running, no matter where they located.

The CHAIRMAN. They were wiped out completely; they had no chance to put in new houses or a new style of malting.

Mr. FINK. It was a case of the survival of the fittest, and that drove them to the barley fields of the Middle West, where they properly belong, unless you intend to legislate for Canada, and if that is so I agree with the proposition that the place to locate is Buffalo.

Mr. CLARK. What are you going to do if we annex Canada?

Mr. FINK. That is something I had not thought of——

Mr. CLARK. You had better think of it, because that is what we are all fixing to do.

Mr. FINK. Will the gentleman allow me to continue, just one more point. As I have said, this supply is adjacent to Buffalo. Buffalo and other eastern malting points now obtain their supply of barley from the aforementioned five barley-growing States of the United States via the Great Lakes at a freight cost which enables these eastern malting plants to compete on an equal basis with the great malting plants of Illinois, Wisconsin, Minnesota, South Dakota, and Nebraska. Free barley, however, would give Buffalo an unfair and insurmountable advantage over the latter. Insurmountable because the largest consumers of barley malt are not far distant from Buffalo. Buffalo would thus enjoy a double advantage as compared with the middle western maltsters, because the latter would have to draw the Canadian barley a long distance to their respective plants, to begin with, and would then have to send it back again over the same rails, as it were, and right through Buffalo, for that matter, to the consumer in the far East in the form of malt. Buffalo maltsters, therefore, if they favor this reciprocity agreement, do so not for the purpose of relieving themselves of any existing burden, but in order to secure this very advantage over their western competitors.

Mr. HILL. I would like to ask a question. I am seeking information and am not asking these questions to bother you at all. You can not compete with Canada in making barley malt if barley is free, can you?

Mr. FINK. Farmers can not afford to raise it in our country.

Mr. HILL. I see by the statistics, which I have before me, that the United States exported to Canada last year 2,184,000 pounds of barley. Will you explain that?

Mr. FINK. There may be some person in this room—the very gentleman who sold the goods that went into Canada may be here.

Mr. HILL. Where did that go from, do you suppose?

Mr. FINK. Is there anybody here familiar with that?

Mr. BULLEN. That came from Winona, Minn.

Mr. HILL. Then they could raise barley there and make malt?

Mr. BULLEN. It was sold to a gentleman in Seattle and he requested that part of it be delivered in Vancouver.

Mr. HILL. Then they could compete?

Mr. BULLEN. I don't know what the duty is; I sold that delivered at Portland and Seattle.

Mr. HILL. You not only sold it there, but it paid the duty.

Mr. BULLEN. I had nothing to do with the duty. The brewer at Portland had to stand that.

Mr. HILL. That is not the point. What I want to find out is whether it can be done or not.

Mr. BULLEN. I don't know the duty.

Mr. HILL. Forty-five cents a hundred pounds, going into Canada, and it paid that duty and there were 2,184,463 pounds that went into Canada.

Mr. BULLEN. I sold that cheap to Canada.

Mr. HILL. Did you sell this whole lot?

Mr. BULLEN. No; not the whole lot. I believe there were about 10,000 bushels——

Mr. HILL. What does it weigh?

Mr. BULLEN. Thirty-four pounds to the bushel.

Mr. CLARK. There is about as much going to Canada as coming from Canada here, then?

Mr. FINK. Will you let me state that the points in western Canada where some of this barley went, are in direct competition with American beers, and it is but natural therefore that those brewers near the American boundary in far western Canada, where they raise no barley to speak of anyhow, should seek to employ in the manufacture of their beer the same barley that the competing beers from the United States were made from.

Mr. CLARK. That comes right back to that same question that I have asked you a half a dozen times. Now, if the barley in North Dakota and Minnesota is so good that the Canadian brewers want it, what is the reason that they do not get the barley and the barley malt from Canada right over the line from Minnesota, Wisconsin, and the Dakotas?

Mr. FINK. Mr. Chairman, will you pardon me for saying to the speaker that there are reasons which actuate a business man, reasons that are perhaps not easily understood, except from the case I have just mentioned. If I am right on the Canadian line and I am trying to sell a beer that I make there and my strongest competition comes right from the States in the form of beers that have a reputation, it is but natural that I should seek to employ the same raw material for the manufacture of my beer, in order that I may say to my trade, "Now, please, there can not be any difference; I am also getting my malt from over there."

Mr. CLARK. What perceivable difference is there in the barley raised on the northern border of North Dakota and Minnesota and the barley raised on the south end of the Canadian possessions along there? That is an imaginary line.

Mr. FINK. There is always a difference in the quality of the barley raised on virgin soil and barley that comes from soil that has long been subject to rotation of crops, because of certain inherent elements in the soil that will be removed only after a rotation of crops.

Mr. CLARK. Well, is there any difference in the rotation of crops on the north edge of Minnesota and Dakota and the south edge of the British possessions, right along there; has not one been settled as long as the other, and don't they employ the same processes of farming; will not the soil change under the agricultural processes as quick in Canada as in our country, and vice versa?

Mr. FINK. We have not yet seen the day when brewers here would like to draw the quality of barley that is being raised just north of the Dakotas and Minnesota in Canada.

Mr. CLARK. Is not the whole thing this: That it pays to ship it from the United States to Canada and it pays to ship it from Canada to the United States, that while they were shipping some in here we shipped some over there; is not that the truth about it—owing to the geographical location?

Mr. FINK. The million pounds that we sent into Canada are hardly worth sneezing at, compared with the volume of business done.

Mr. CLARK. Did that fellow lose money on that shipment, do you suppose, or make money; what was his reason for sending it into Canada?

Mr. FINK. I don't know what his reason was. The people in Canada may have had some reason for wanting American barley.

Mr. CLARK. I am not talking about the Canadians; I am talking about our people. Did our people that shipped that stuff over there do it for love of the Canadians or for the love of the almighty dollar?

Mr. FINK. From my acquaintance with the people that shipped it over there, I think that they probably sent it over there for the love of the almighty dollar.

Mr. HALES. I would like to explain a little further the situation in reference to the barley malt that was sent to Canada. I myself was the exporter of the malt. It came about, not by reason of profits to the manufacturer of the malt, but by reason of the profits to the man who had made a contract for the malt at a very low price, and the market had advanced so materially that it was profitable—he was operating a factory or brewery in Canada and also in the United States. He simply transferred some of his products which he had purchased at a very low price in the United States to his factory in Canada, and that explains the reason for this importation.

Mr. CLARK. Did he make money or lose it?

Mr. HALES. I do not know anything about what he did. I merely state the facts.

Mr. CLARK. Your explanation does not explain, then.

Mr. FORDNEY. Permit me to ask one question for information.

The duty under existing law on barley malt coming into the United States is 45 cents a bushel. I see that this treaty provides that barley malt coming from Canada into this country after this treaty shall be 45 cents a hundred pounds. What is the difference between a bushel and a hundred pounds?

Mr. FINK. Thirty-four pounds constitutes an American bushel of malt

Mr. FORDNEY. Then this treaty proposes to reduce the duty very materially below that now collected by the United States on barley malt.

Mr. HILL. Fifty per cent.

Mr. FINK. The present schedule in force in Canada on barley coming into Canada from other countries is not our basis.

Mr. FORDNEY. Pardon me again, so I will understand clearly. Now, we collect 45 cents a bushel on barley malt under our law, the Payne tariff law?

Mr. FINK. Yes, sir.

Mr. FORDNEY. Canada collects 45 cents per hundred pounds.

Mr. FINK. There are 3 bushels in 100 pounds.

Mr. FORDNEY. And when this goes into effect it is proposed we shall collect 45 cents a hundred on Canadian barley malt coming into this country. Will that change our rate of duty from existing law?

Mr. FINK. Certainly; 45 cents per hundred is about 15 cents a bushel.

Mr. FORDNEY. That is the point I want to make.

Mr. FINK. And the present basis is 45 cents a bushel.

The CHAIRMAN. Now, let us get the whole of that.

Mr. FORDNEY. When it was stated that there was no change——

The CHAIRMAN. I said that there was no change in the differential. The duty on barley coming into the United States is 30 cents a bushel.

Mr. FINK. Yes.

The CHAIRMAN. And the duty on barley malt is 45 cents?

Mr. FINK. Yes.

The CHAIRMAN. So the differential is 15 cents a bushel?

Mr. FINK. Yes.

The CHAIRMAN. And the barley coming in here free and barley malt at 45 cents a hundred is 15 cents a bushel differential duty, is it not?

Mr. FINK. Yes, sir.

The CHAIRMAN. So the differential duty is the same under this proposed treaty or under the law?

Mr. FORDNEY. The differential between something and nothing makes a pile of difference.

The CHAIRMAN. But that does not answer the inquiry you were trying to make.

Mr. FORDNEY. I had reference to the remark made by Mr. Longworth and not the chairman. He made that statement.

Mr. FINK. Now, I would like to come to what I call the principal part of the argument, and I will be as brief as possible.

We do not know the reasons which prompted His Excellency the President of the United States to formulate or negotiate the proposed reciprocity agreement, but if we are to understand it as an effort on his part to secure for the people of the United States a reduction in the cost of living by lifting the import duty from necessities of life, then, so far as barley and barley malt are concerned, the effort fails utterly of accomplishing the purpose intended, because the price of a glass of beer will remain at 5 cents, as heretofore, whether the materials out of which it is made, namely, barley and barley malt, pay an import duty or not.

The CHAIRMAN. Right there, you remember, when we had the Spanish War tax we added a dollar of tariff on beer, and you gentlemen—I do not know whether you yourself, but some gentlemen representing the brewing interests—came here and desired to have that tax taken off; and when we asked them if it made any difference to the consumer, they said yes, because they were employing a glass that held less beer under the extra dollar a barrel, but that if we took that dollar off they would go back to the old-sized glass [laughter], possibly out of their generosity, and possibly because competition brought them to it. We asked them if we had free beer would they not get still a little larger glass; and then they said, in addition to that, that most of the beer was sold by measure, tin pails and pitchers, and all that sort of thing, and the extra tariff made a difference in the price per quart. That is what they said; I am not saying it is true. They said it made a difference, so that they made up the extra tax that way. There was no truth in all that?

Mr. FINK. No, sir.

The CHAIRMAN. What are we going to believe, gentlemen, what they said at the time of the Spanish War tax, when they were trying to have the tax taken off, or what they say now, when they are trying to keep this duty on? That is what puzzles me. You will have me between the devil and the deep sea. I do not know where I am.

Mr. FINK. It is easy to see that in the case of free wheat the consumer would be benefited.

Mr. CLARK. Before you start in on that, did you reduce the size of the beer glass on account of that $1 tax during the Spanish War?

Mr. FINK. I do not manufacture beer, but I do know from my own observation—and perhaps all of the gentlemen will bear me out [laughter]—that the size of the bottle in which beer is sold has been constantly growing smaller and the size of the glass has always been growing a little bit smaller.

Mr. CLARK. I know that. I made them sell 5 quarts of beer, so called, when I was prosecuting attorney, for a gallon, because there was not a quart bottle in the State of Missouri, except an exceedingly old one. There was not a quart bottle in the State of Missouri, or anywhere else, that held a quart, and there was not a pint bottle that held a pint, and the so-called quart bottle lacked just about a good, stiff drink of having a quart in it. They had a right to sell a gallon for so much. I did not care what they charged for the beer. But I was determined they should have 4 quarts in it. I doubt whether there is a quart bottle in the city of Washington that will hold a quart. If there is, it is a very old one and one that has been imported from Texas, called the " Hogg bottle," because when Hogg was circuit attorney down there he made them have a quart bottle and a pint bottle. What I was trying to get at was this: I think they did cut down the size of the glass during the Spanish War, and I do not know whether they have ever increased it to its old size again or not.

The CHAIRMAN. It never was increased, was it?

Mr. FINK. The same little glasses are doing business at the old stand to-day.

Mr. CLARK. You say they would not increase the size of the glass. How do you know they would not? Suppose one set of saloon keepers in Chicago or St. Louis should advertise they were selling a larger amount of beer in a glass than the other fellows, do you not know the other fellows would have to come to their sized glass?

Mr. FINK. Certainly; if they want to give a little more.

Mr. CLARK. Certainly; if they want to keep the trade.

Mr. FINK. But the price of the glass of beer will remain at 5 cents. Those are the conditions. You step into a barroom anywhere in the United States and ask for a glass of beer, and it will be handed to you at 5 cents, whether there is a duty of 30 or a duty of 15 cents, or whether there is no duty at all.

Mr. CLARK. Of course, they will have a 5-cent glass of beer, just the same as they have a 5-cent piece of pie, but now that pie is cut in five pieces. It used to be cut in four pieces. That is the way they do with this beer business. The same principle applies exactly.

Mr. FINK. It is easy to see that in the case of free.wheat, for instance, the consumer would be benefited by a corresponding reduction in the price of flour, but where, in the name of common sense, is any benefit to accrue to the masses from free barley and free barley malt, when it is absolutely certain that the chief product thereof, namely, beer, will continue to sell at 5 cents a glass?

Mr. CLARK. I know, and that is where you fall down about that. A glass is a glass, in one view of it; but a glass of beer is not a glass of beer in another view of it. They used to have what they called a "schooner." I do not know whether they have them yet or not. A schooner held about twice as much beer as one of these glasses you get at the Shoreham, or some of these other fine hotels.

Mr. FINK. Let me assure the speaker that the schooner was there before the Spanish War, was there during the Spanish War, and is there to-day, and is handed out for a nickel to whomsoever may call for it.

Mr. CLARK. Is it the same size?

Mr. FINK. The same size—the schooner remains a schooner.

The CHAIRMAN. If they use the same sized glass, they will put 20 per cent more foam on the beer.

Mr. FINK. That is getting down pretty fine if we have to count the bubbles you get on the foam.

Mr. CLARK. You put a piece of soap in the faucet so you can get more beer out of the keg. I know how it goes. [Laughter.]

Mr. FINK. Not more than 2 per cent of the barley grown in this country is used for human food in its unmalted state, all the rest of it, except that part which is used for feed and for seeding purposes, being converted into malt and this in turn into either fermented or distilled liquor.

In other words, we respectfully submit to your honorable committee that, by putting barley and barley malt upon the free list, you will not only fail of reducing the cost of living, but, on the contrary, will inflict incalculable injury and loss upon the barley-raising farmers of this country and will utterly and hopelessly ruin the great malting industry of the Middle Western States.

Mr. HILL. What was the average price of barley last year, the price that you were paying?

Mr. FINK. That I am not prepared to state offhand.

Mr. HILL. What is the present price?

Mr. FINK. The present price is about 93 cents for good barley.

Mr. HILL. And was it about the same last year?

Mr. FINK. It was cheaper.

Mr. HILL. About how low?

Mr. FINK. It was between the sixties and seventies. It ran 64 or 65 cents.

Mr. HILL. Not lower than 60?

Mr. FINK. The average, I think, did not run below that. Of course, I would have to consult statistics on the subject, which are very easily obtainable. But I should say it was about 65 cents.

Mr. HILL. The average for the year?

Mr. FINK. Yes, sir, last year; as near as my memory serves me. On account of these things we say that barley and barley malt should be eliminated from the proposed free list, and that the present import duties on these articles be undisturbed.

The CHAIRMAN. It is not a question of elimination; we can not eliminate barley and let the treaty stand. You are opposed to the treaty because of the change on barley?

Mr. FINK. Yes, sir.

The CHAIRMAN. I am glad the price of barley has come up. I have grown lots of it for market at 30 and 35 cents.

Mr. FINK. I do not suppose you made much money doing it.

The CHAIRMAN. And I am not a " kid " myself.

Mr. FINK. You did not make much money at it at that price.

The CHAIRMAN. That was New York State barley.

Mr. CALDERHEAD. What was land worth then?

The CHAIRMAN. As much as it is to-day.

Mr. CALDERHEAD. Do you mean it sold for the same price?

The CHAIRMAN. It was worth as much as it is to-day in the market; yes.

Mr. BRANTLEY. Why, Mr. Chairman, did you not take care of Buffalo in framing the present tariff law, and have free barley?

The CHAIRMAN. The committee lowered the duty 15 cents a bushel. I told them there was no use; it made no difference whether they made it 15 or 30. We got into the House, and it was enlarged there to 24 cents; it got over to the Senate, and they put it back to 30. I had nothing to offer between 24 and 30; either one was prohibitive. Fifteen cents is prohibitive; I do not care whether it is one or the other, as far as barley coming into the United States is concerned; as long as they would not get it down where the people could raise barley elsewhere than in the Dakotas and Wisconsin, and a few of the surrounding States, I was not very much interested in it myself.

Mr. FINK. In closing, Mr. Chairman and gentlemen, permit me to state that among the gentlemen who came with us to-day there is one who intended, and intends now, unless this reciprocity agreement becomes law, to build a malthouse in Milwaukee with a capacity of over 2,000,000 bushels per annum and with an investment of over $600,000. The gentleman is here.

The CHAIRMAN. If you think that makes any difference, I think the committee will admit that this gentleman desires to do so unless the treaty becomes a law.

Mr. FINK. In which case building operations already begun will promptly cease.

Mr. FORDNEY. Does he want to be heard?

Mr. FINK. The gentleman is here if he wishes to confirm what I have said—Mr. Carl Hansen.

Mr. HANSEN. I do not think there is anything that I want to add on the subject except to state that it is the fact.

The CHAIRMAN. I do not see what bearing it has one way or the other.

Mr. CALDERHEAD. I understood Mr. Longworth to say that barley malt was not mentioned in this treaty.

The CHAIRMAN. Malt?

Mr. CALDERHEAD. Yes.

The CHAIRMAN. It is; 45 cents a hundred pounds.

Mr. CALDERHEAD. That amounts to about 15 cents a bushel.

The CHAIRMAN. Yes; just the differential that there is on barley now.

Mr. CALDERHEAD. The speaker was allowed to go through his entire speech without referring to barley malt because Mr. Longworth said it was not mentioned in the treaty.

The CHAIRMAN. Did you desire to say anything about barley malt?

Mr. FINK. If any allusion is made to the duty necessary to protect the industry, I would like to have it kept upon barley as well as upon barley malt, where they now stand.

The CHAIRMAN. Certainly; I supposed that was your attitude.

Mr. FINK. I purposely omitted using the words "barley malt" upon the suggestion of one of the gentlemen, who said that that matter was not touched in the proposition.

In order that you may know, gentlemen, how thoroughly the maltsters of the Middle West are alarmed over the situation, I beg leave to read to you two telegrams which I have just received:

MILWAUKEE, WIS., *February 4, 1911.*

BRUNO E. FINK, *Washington, D. C.:*

The undersigned malt manufacturers of Wisconsin most emphatically protest against the proposed reciprocity treaty with Canada removing the duty on barley. The result would mean not only an enormous loss to the farmers of this country, but it would practically ruin the malting industry of the Northwest employing thousands of men and representing investments aggregating thirty to forty million dollars and at present manufacturing two-thirds of the entire requirements of the United States. The consumers of beer will not be benefited.

CHILTON MALTING Co., Chilton, Wis.
THE KURTH Co., Columbus, Wis.
KONRAD BROS. & WERNER, Hartford, Wis.
A. G. LAUBENSTEIN, Hartford, Wis.
MANITOWOC MALTING Co., Manitowoc, Wis.
M. H. PETTIT MALTING Co., Kenosha, Wis.
PORTZ BROS. MALT & GRAIN Co., Hartford, Wis.
RUBICON MALT & GRAIN Co., Rubicon, Wis.
L. ROSENHEIMER MALT & GRAIN Co., Kewaskum, Wis.
WM. RAHR SONS Co., Manitowoc, Wis.
KONRAD SCHREIER Co., Sheboygan, Wis.
WEST BEND BREWING & MALTING Co., West Bend, Wis.
WISCONSIN MALT & GRAIN Co., Appleton, Wis.
BADGER STATE MALT Co., Waterloo, Wis.
LYTLE-STOPPENBACH Co., Jefferson, Wis.
BORCHERT MALTING Co., Milwaukee, Wis.
DANIEL D. WESCHLER & SONS, Milwaukee, Wis.
MILWAUKEE MALTING Co., Milwaukee, Wis.
MILWAUKEE-WESTERN MALT Co., Milwaukee, Wis.
FROEDERDT BROS. MALT & GRAIN Co., Milwaukee, Wis.

DAVENPORT, IOWA, *February 3, 1911.*

BRUNO FINK, Esq.,
Care New Willard Hotel, Washington, D. C.:

Are sending Hon. A. F. Dawson night letter, as follows:

In the interest of western farmers growing barley and western maltsters using western barley, we protest against removal of present duty on Canadian barley or malt until such time as Middle Western States raise a surplus enabling us to export barley. Removal of duty will be inimical to best interest of barley-growing States, the only beneficiaries being the brewers and distillers. Kindly present this to committee considering Canadian reciprocity agreement and ask cooperation of all Iowa delegation.

D. ROTHSCHILD GRAIN Co.

The CHAIRMAN. I did not understand that statement or I should have corrected it at the time; I knew better than that myself.

Mr. FINK. I have endeavored in these few words, gentlemen, to present to you the case of the malsters. There is present in the room a gentleman who, better than I, can present to you the case of the farmers. I thank you.

STATEMENT OF MR. J. R. MAUFF, OF EVANSTON, ILL., REPRESENTING THE AMERICAN SOCIETY OF EQUITY.

Mr. MAUFF. Mr. Chairman, the American Society of Equity suggests through its name the character, purpose, and principles for which it was organized. It is composed of 30,000 farmers, 10,000 of whom are located in the State of Wisconsin. Equity granted and demanded in all relations of life briefly defines the position of the society. Agriculture is the foundation upon which rest all industrial and commercial structures. When crops fail all suffer. Those who attack this interest wound themselves.

The farmers of our society, understand that the proposed reciprocity agreement with the Dominion of Canada contemplates removing the tariff protection on our products, not only those to be raised in the future, but the products of this crop, much of which is unmarketed, without offering us any adequate compensation, desire to protest strongly against the consummation of this agreement by our legislative bodies, and respectfully offer for your consideration the following reasons:

Because the agreement does not contemplate any reduction in the duty on the necessities. The industry is greatly burdened by the enormous increase in the cost of labor, which alone has been made possible by a corresponding increase in the values of our products. Since the Hon. James Wilson became Secretary of Agriculture harvest-hand wages have increased 60 per cent and ordinary day labor 65 per cent. Also since that time the prices of necessities purchased by us have greatly increased.

I am going to quote the relative prices, based on the average wholesale prices, compared with the base price, which is represented by 100, taken from the records of the Department of Commerce and Labor. These prices are on the necessities the farmers are obliged to purchase at the store. Since the advent of Secretary Wilson in the Cabinet clothing has increased from 96 to 126; fuel and lighting, from 95 to 130; metals and implements, from 86 to 128; lumber and building material, from 95 to 151; house furnishing goods, from 92 to 109; miscellaneous, from 92 to 132; boots and shoes, from 96 to 128; crude petroleum, from 100 to 153; refined petroleum, from 99 to 127; cotton prints, from 72 to 145; cotton sheetings, from 86 to 134; cotton shirt-ings, from 83 to 126; cotton ticking, from 84 to 132; wool blankets, from 107 to 131; wool carpets, from 100 to 117; wool flannels, from 97 to 124; wool horse blankets, from 99 to 135; wool dress goods, from 88 to 140; cotton flannels, from 81 to 128; cotton thread, from 98 to 126; cotton yarns, from 90 to 131; cotton hosiery, from 83 to 93; cotton ginghams, from 83 to 124; cotton 2-bushel bags, from 95 to 143.

Another reason is because Canada has 3,000 miles of land contigu-ous to ours, but in value only one-quarter to one-third that of the good farm lands of the Mississippi Valley. That the farmers tilling that soil would enjoy a cheaper cost of living because of the greatly reduced cost of necessities through the free-trade relations between the Dominion of Canada and England. That in order to compete with these conditions our lands, farm labor, and value of our prod-ucts would necessarily have to decline.

Again, that an overproduction in our own country is already in evidence, according to all reports of the trade, and as shown by the fact that present prices of our leading farm products, with one. ex-ception, are the lowest in years.

Mr. HILL. What exception is that?

Mr. MAUFF. Barley.

That although the wheat crop for 1910 as reported by the Depart-ment of Agriculture was only 695,443,000 bushels, or 42,000,000 less than the crop of 1909, the average farm value on December 1, as compared with 1909, shows a decline of 10 cents per bushel.

Mr. HILL. What was the farm value of barley in Wisconsin last year, as shown by the same reports?

Mr. MAUFF. I have the reports here, but it will take up my valu-able half hour if I refer to them. I would be very glad to if I had time allowed. The average farm value of oats on January 1, 1910, was 10 cents per bushel more than the price on January 1, 1911, and the price on January 1, 1909, was 15 cents per bushel more than on January 1, 1911. Corn was 14 cents per bushel more on January 1, 1910, than on January 1, 1911. Barley was 2 cents per bushel less. That is the exception.

Mr. HILL. You have not got the actual farm value; you simply have the difference?

Mr. MAUFF. I have the difference, and the farm values are all in these papers; that, of course, I will not have time to refer to. The wheat crop of Canada usually averages about 150,000,000 bushels; oats, 350,000,000 bushels; barley, 50,000,000 bushels; that these crops would largely increase because of the further development of the vast areas in northwest Canada to our detriment and serious financial injury; that since January 27, the day this reciprocity agreement was given publicity, wheat has declined 3 cents, oats 2 cents, and barley 5 cents per bushel.

On the mere announcement of this agreement, and the details, wheat advanced in Winnipeg and declined in every market in the United States. That much of the Canadian crop is still to find a market. The visible supply alone in that country contains almost 15,000,000 bushels of wheat and 7,000,000 of oats. Congressman Malby gave the statistics of farm values, etc., so I will omit that.

The Crop Reporter, published by authority of the Secretary of Agriculture, for January, 1911, shows the following farm values per acre, December 1, 1909, being the latest statistics available: Corn, $15.20; wheat, $15.64; oats, $12.27; barley, $13.41; rye, $11.90.

These figures would have to be very much reduced to correspond with the very much lower prices, as compared with December 1, 1909.

Taking the figures of the Bureau of Plant Industry, being the 10-year average value per acre of crops in the six principal grain-growing States of the Mississippi Valley, we find the following: Corn, $12.71; wheat, $10.55; oats, $9.68; barley, $11.25.

It is difficult indeed to figure out how the farmers are receiving an equitable share when we consider that the cost of production per acre, not including fertilizer, wear and tear of property, or insurance, amounts to from $12 to $13, considering the land worth only $5 per acre to the renter. We are taking the renter who can not afford to own a farm.

Mr. HILL. Then, you say that the barley costs $13 an acre production?

Mr. MAUFF. Those are the figures for December 1, 1910, from the Crop Reporter.

Mr. HILL. You gave just about the number of bushels per acre yielded.

Mr. MAUFF. The number of bushels?

Mr. HILL. Yes.

Mr. MAUFF. This is dollars.

Mr. HILL. Thirteen dollars; but the number of bushels. You gave wheat, corn, barley, and so on, just a moment ago.

Mr. MAUFF. I did not refer to the number of bushels per acre, but the number is somewhere between 20 and 25.

Mr. HILL. Is it 20 or 25?

Mr. MAUFF. I would have to refer to the statistics; I have not got that. I am told it is 22.

Mr. HILL. Twenty-two?

Mr. MAUFF. Yes.

Mr. HILL. And $13 per acre was the net profit?

Mr. MAUFF. Thirteen dollars per acre are the figures in this crop report. To resume, it is difficult to figure how the farmers are receiving an equitable share, also figuring the planting and seed, $3 per acre; plowing, cutting, and shocking, $2 per acre; thrashing, $1 per acre; and hauling to market, from $1 to $2 per acre, depending on the distance. In the case of corn, the stalks sell for $1 per acre, and both the oats straw and the barley straw have a small feeding value. On the date these farm values were calculated, corn was worth 60 cents; wheat, 99 cents; oats, 40 cents; barley, 55 cents.

(The chairman retired and Mr. Hill took the chair.)

Mr. HILL. Is that 55 cents on the farm a fair average price throughout the United States, or is it just simply your locality?

Mr. MAUFF. Absolutely not; that is the average price given by the Department of Agriculture.

Mr. HILL. Fifty-five cents?

Mr. MAUFF. Fifty-five cents. These figures are actual figures, taken from the statistics of the department, all official statistics. It would appear as though the farmers of this country at the present time were carrying the entire burden of the effort to reduce the cost of living, and that an overproduction was responsible for this.

In 1910, 7,257,000 acres of land were devoted to the culture of barley against 7,011,000 acres in 1909. The production in 1910 amounted to 162,227,000 bushels against 170,284,000 bushels in 1909. The area in 1910 exceeded the area of 1909 by 246,000 acres, but the crop fell off 8,057,000 bushels. Using the figures of the Agricultural Department relative to the two years' crops for computation, we find that the returns in 1910 were about $12.15 per acre, figured at an average. The crop of 1910, on December 1, 1910, was valued at $93,785,000; the crop of 1909, on December 1, 1909, was valued at $93,971,000. The men, clamoring for a reduction of the duty on barley, point out that the price of barley is exorbitant, but a glance at the figures just quoted will convince any man that the farmers of the United States, notwithstanding the fact that they walked over 246,000 acres more land, spending their efforts and capital while doing so, received just $186,000 less than in 1909, when less work was performed, less barley put into the ground, and less taxes were paid on land devoted to the culture of barley.

I will go on and give that same comparison on the other cereals. As to wheat, the farmers in 1910 sold 2,482,000 acres more, but produced in value $110,918,100 less revenue. In corn they sewed 5,231,000 acres more, and produced 353,000,000 bushels more, producing, however, $121,000,000 less revenue. In oats they sewed 2,084,000 acres more, produced 120,000,000 bushels more, but produced in revenue $25,000,000 less.

To show the overproduction existing at the present time, with the prices the lowest in four years, there are 42,000,000 bushels of wheat in the visible supply in the United States; 8,000,000 bushels of corn, 16,000,000 bushels of oats, and 1,500,000 bushels of barley. We just take, in this overproduction, the wheat, corn, and oats. In addition to that there are 15,000,000 bushels of wheat in Canada and 7,000,000 bushels of oats. The invisible supply in this country, which we are unable to compute, is enormous. Never before in the history of the grain trade has so much grain been piled up in the farmers' granaries and the country elevators, to say nothing about the private elevators in the terminal markets, figures on which we are unable to obtain.

Mr. MAUFF. Since 1897 the farmers have increased the acreage of corn from 80,000,000 to 114,000,000, and the crop from 1,900,000,000 bushels to 3,125,000,000, and the wheat from 39,465,000 acres to 49,205,000 acres, and the yield from 530,150,000 bushels to 695,443,000 bushels; and oats from 25,730,000 acres to 35,288,000 acres, and the yield from 699,000,000 to 1,126,765,000 bushels.

In regard to barley, that is a pet hobby with the brewer. The Agricultural Department appropriated money for years and had a representative of the brewers in the Agricultural Department for one purpose, to increase, enlarge, and improve the barley crop. The work started in the year 1900, and if I had the opportunity I would quote you letters from the brewers acknowledging the fact. The farmers are growing barley for one purpose only, and that is for the brewing of beer. They have increased their crop three times since the Department of Agriculture encouraged the work for the benefit of the brewers, and appropriated money for that purpose. It was not done for the propagation or improvement of any other cereal grain by the farmer. At that time the barley crop was in the neighborhood of 55,000,000 bushels; to-day it is between 160,000,000 and 170,000,000 bushels.

I would like to show in what respect the farmers responded to this appeal of the brewers. In Minnesota at that time, 1900, there were 325,000 acres devoted to barley, to-day Minnesota devotes 1,285,000 acres, has increased almost 1,000,000 acres. Wisconsin has increased from 245,000 acres to 866,000 acres, South Dakota from 108,000 acres to 1,025,000 acres, North Dakota from 244,000 acres to 987,000 acres, and Iowa from 444,000 to 510,000 acres. Iowa is retrograding in the cultivation of barley, because the soil has exhausted its nitrogen. That is what the barley growers have done for the brewers, at the solicitation of the brewers, through the Department of Agriculture, and through the experimental stations, and now they ask for the removal of the duty on barley, when barley is grown but for one purpose, and that is for the brewing of beer. That is the point we are particularly strong on, because of the encouragement and the inducement to increase the crop, and in October, in the city of Chicago, they have an international barley show, and offer prizes, cups, and money to the farmers to further increase their barley crops. The brewers now ask for the removal of the duty, which will compel our Mississippi Valley farmer, with his land worth $100 an acre, with all the necessities carrying a high protective tariff, to compete with Canada.

Mr. HILL. Does not the California man have to compete with Canada?

Mr. MAUFF. The California man raises a bay-brewing barley. The Bass Ale house of England has a representative in California all the time to purchase that. It is suitable for the brewing of ale and it is not suitable for the brewing of lager beer. It contains a high percentage of starch and a low percentage of nitrogen. It has not the diastasic quality that the brewers in our community use as a substitute for barley malt. The Bass people use it because they manufacture a barley beverage. That is the thing in a nutshell, and 6,000,000 bushels of that barley have been exported from the Pacific coast, two and a half times as much at this particular price as a year ago, and if the brewers would stop using substitutes for barley they would find they could use Pacific coast barley very nicely. That is the explanation of that. I have the technical authorities, if I had the opportunity to present them.

The value of farm lands depend on the yield in money per acre, and in the Mississippi Valley averages three to four times the value in that section of Canada that has extensive areas and is rapidly increasing in population and production. In addition to that, because of the free-trade relations between Canada and England, these farmers can obtain the necessities of life at greatly reduced prices as compared with our farmers of the Mississippi Valley. The total area of Canada lands is 3,619,000 square miles as compared with 3,000,000 square miles in the United States.

Mr. HILL. You do not think that is a fair illustration as a comparison of the farming lands?

Mr. MAUFF. Those figures are taken from the statistics. Whether they are farming lands, mountainous lands, or stock lands the comparison is there.

Mr. McCALL. There is a great deal of uninhabitable coal land. The habitable rim of Canada, being so far north, is very narrow.

Mr. MAUFF. It stops, I should think, at Alberta; at the extreme western portion of it.

Mr. McCALL. I mean going north and south. The northern part of Canada is uninhabitable, practically, I think, is it not?

Mr. MAUFF. At the present time.

Mr. McCALL. I mean on account of the climate.

Mr. MAUFF. Of course, my time is limited to 30 minutes.

Mr. HILL. You can have all the time you want, if you will talk on the subject.

Mr. MAUFF. I would not want to get into an argument as to the condition of the climate in northern Canada. I am not here for that purpose. I am trying to show you gentlemen the injustice to the American farmer of reducing the protection he has, and not reducing and making equitable the necessities of life he has to purchase at the country store.

Mr. HILL. You have referred to a large number of other articles in which there has been a enormous advance during the past few years. Are you not aware that there has been a much greater advance in farm products, in percentages?

Mr. MAUFF. I have tried to give the statistics for the past 10 years, the average per acre for each cereal on the farm, the cost of production, and everything; I am not concealing anything. We will get into the Canada part of it again, and I can only get into Canada with statistics, because I have not been up there personally. The gentleman asked why is Canada barley raised in western Canada not as suitable for malt purposes as is Dakota barley? The most of the Canada barley is fed. I will read a letter from a malster in Winnipeg, who left Chicago to go to Winnipeg:

It will be years before they get the alkali out of the soil in this country. Then we may expect better barley. I have started a campaign already to educate the farmer to allow his barley to get thoroughly ripe before cutting it; also to stack it and change the seed.

And he asked me to engage them 20,000 bushels of barley similar to what is raised in the Mississippi Valley to be taken to Canada.

Mr. HILL. Then, why do you fear Canadian barley, if that is true?

Mr. MAUFF. Because of the fact that the farmers have trebled their crop.

Mr. HILL. If the Canadian barley will not answer the purpose, why do you fear it?

Mr. MAUFF. The Canadian barley answers the purpose in eastern Canada. Half of the barley of Canada is raised in the province of Ontario. There they have always raised a superior article; that is, the barley that went over and built up the brewing and malting business. It was not Saskatchewan and Alberta: they were not heard of. It is because this barley that is raised by the farmers to the extent of 160,000,000 bushels is sold to the malsters in the West, expecting that they will find an outlet for it in the East; that they will be sold out of their eastern markets because of the barley from Ontario, and thus curtail the consumption of barley for brewing purposes, leaving the surplus. There is a surplus at the present time.

Mr. HILL. Right there, and right on that point, I would like to ask you a question. Suppose the entire crop in Canada was wholly consumed in Canada; you would not object to its being free, because there would be none to come, if the entire crop of Canada was consumed there?

Mr. MAUFF. Exactly so.

Mr. HILL. As a matter of fact, there are only 2,000,000 bushels exported to the whole world from Canada out of 45,000,000 bushels that are raised. They do consume 43,000,000 out of 45,000,000 in Canada, and if the whole of it that is exported to England and everywhere else came to the United States it would only be one-eightieth of our consumption.

Mr. MAUFF. That I understand very well. But from the time this duty of 30 cents per bushel was put on the tariff barley raising for brewing purposes declined in Canada, and the bulk of the barley raised in Canada to-day, I venture to say, is fed to the animal and not brewed.

Mr. HILL. Was there not more barley raised in Canada last year than ever before?

Mr. MAUFF. I would not say so.

Mr. HILL. There could have been more raised. But I think you are mistaken about that.

Mr. MAUFF. I am referring to brewing barley.

Mr. MCCALL. I suppose the brewing industry is a great industry in Canada, is it not?

Mr. MAUFF. The brewing industry I would not say is great.

Mr. MCCALL. It is pretty large compared with the population?

Mr. MAUFF. If you compare the population with our country, it is very small; I mean per capita consumption.

Mr. MCCALL. Compared with their population is it not very large?

Mr. MAUFF. The per capita consumption of beer is small as compared with our country and as compared with Great Britain and Germany.

Mr. MCCALL. Are they a more temperate people, or do they use stronger drinks?

Mr. MAUFF. They use stronger drinks. This gentleman from Winnipeg, whom I quoted, said you could get a drink of their beer, a drink of ale, or a drink of whisky at the same price, and they handed out the same sized glass. Consequently, the consumption of strong drink is exceedingly large. I have not looked up the statistics, but that is the statement he made to me. They use, according to the Canada laws. nothing but barley malt in the manufacture of beer. They use about 2 bushels of barley. for which our brewers are substituting things like glucose and starch.

In the city of Washington there is a brewer who uses 50 per cent of substitutes for barley malt. Not only have they increased acreage and trebled the crop, but they are using as little of that crop as possible in the brewing of beer, substituting corn products and coarse ryes, which are cheaper. In Canada that is not allowed under the law. Any beer manufactured that way must be labeled "imitation beer."

The wheat crop of Canada of 1903 was no more than the wheat crop of Saskatchewan in 1909. This Province increased during those years from 15,600,000 bushels to 85,200,000 bushels, and the Province of Alberta from 1,200,000 bushels to 9,600,000 bushels.

Canada oats, during the same period of time, showed the following increases, respectively: 9,500,000 bushels to 97,500,000 bushels, and 5,400,000 bushels to 41,000,000 bushels; and in Manitoba, from 34,000,000 bushels to 59,000,000 bushels. and barley, during that period of time, from 39,000,000 bushels to about 55,000,000 bushels.

The point I make is that that vast area has not started to develop; it has not begun to grow, and it is for the immediate future, if this thing grows there. And our farmers have gone into Alberta and Saskatchewan. The population of Iowa has decreased in 10 years, as is shown by the census, and they have gone to sunny Alberta and Saskatchewan, with all the disadvantages of the tariff against them. Remove them, and there will be an exodus of farmers, who will go there.

Mr. McCall. You say "with all the disadvantages of this tariff against them." Is not the price of wheat for a third of the year greater than the Chicago price of wheat?

Mr. Mauff. Absolutely not.

Mr. McCall. And is there not a parity in the price of wheat in Winnipeg and Chicago and the Argentine, having reference to the freight rate to Liverpool?

Mr. Mauff. I am unable to answer that all in one breath.

Mr. McCall. That is just one question. Is there not a parity in the price of wheat, and is not the tariff at present inoperative in that respect?

Mr. Mauff. Necessarily, there must be.

Mr. Hill. Did you not give the farm price of wheat a few moments ago?

Mr. Mauff. I believe it was 88 cents the 1st of December and 99 cents a year ago, which is a decrease of 11 cents a bushel.

Mr. Hill. Was that farm price, or the market price?

Mr. Mauff. That is the farm price. Since that time there has been a further decline. I am taking the figures available from the statistics of the Department of Agriculture in regard to that question. Winnipeg wheat is 7 cents less to-day than Duluth wheat. Those are the two nearest markets. It is 7 cents in favor of the Winnipeg market; and, as I say, from the morning of the 27th, the day when this agreement was made public, Winnipeg wheat advanced, while every market in the United States went down. In the Province of Alberta the wheat crop increased from 1,000,000 bushels to 9,000,000 in that period of time, and they have not commenced to touch the soil in either Saskatchewan or Alberta. They have only 9,000,000 in all Canada against our 90,000,000. Canada oats during the same period of time showed the following increases: In Alberta from 5,400,000 to 41,000,000, and in Manitoba from 34,000,000 to 54,000,000. Barley during that time increased from 39,000,000 to 55,000,000, those increases being largely in northwest Canada.

Mr. Hill. When was that?

Mr. Mauff. In that period of time.

Mr. Hill. 55,000,000?

Mr. Mauff. From 39,000,000 to 55,000,000.

Mr. Hill. The Canadian Year Book gives the production as only 45,000,000 bushels in all Canada.

Mr. Mauff. I am referring to all Canada.

Mr. Hill. You say 55,000,000.

Mr. Mauff. Those are the statistics that I have. What is the crop date—the last crop?

Mr. Hill. This year, 45,000,000, just published by the Canadian Government.

Mr. Mauff. I will accept the correction. As I say, I took the figures from these papers, and I have not the time to go into it.

Mr. CALDERHEAD. Where did you get your figures?

Mr. MAUFF. From the Red Book, which is the book of statistics, or the Daily News Almanac, or the figures of the Department of Agriculture.

Mr. HILL. The figures are 45,147,600 bushels, of which they exported 2,044,901. The value on the farm was 47.4 cents per bushel.

Mr. MAUFF. I think my figures are pretty nearly correct on all I quote; I am not trying to exaggerate.

Mr. HILL. Of course; I understand you are not.

Mr. MAUFF. The present price of cereals, and the overproduction visible all over the United States, will quite satisfy anybody that the farmers are getting the short end of the stick.

Remove the tariff and allow the cereals from these vast areas to compete with the products of our farm lands, and you would produce a situation that would amount almost to a crisis so far as farm mortgages are concerned—and there are some—and it is well worth your serious consideration. All statistics would seem to indicate that the farmers are absolutely the last ones in a position to stand, alone and unaided, the burden of the reduced cost of living.

Congressman Malby did not refer to the cold-storage warehouses that are now collapsing and going under because they can not find a market for their stuff, and are sending it to Europe—their butter and their eggs.

Mr. HILL. You represent a very large and important society, and I want to submit this proposition to you, on the very question you are speaking of, as to eggs. Canada exported 160,650 dozens to the whole world, which amounts to 1,927,800 eggs. That would give 1 egg to 3 men once a year in the city of New York. Do you honestly believe that would affect the price of eggs in the United States, 1 egg to 3 men in the city of New York alone?

Mr. MAUFF. I am not arguing on the egg question at all.

Mr. HILL. But you just spoke of it.

Mr. MAUFF. That was a point that Congressman Malby overlooked. He was bringing in the middleman's promise, and he overlooked the other.

Mr. HILL. You have to take this question as a whole, one whole proposition. You cited eggs and Mr. Malby cited eggs, and the entire importation of eggs from Canada was only 29,000 dozen.

Mr. MAUFF. I rather think there would be an opportunity to increase the production of eggs in Canada if there was no duty.

Mr. HILL. You think the hens would respond to the tariff?

Mr. MAUFF. I suppose the owners of the hens would respond to the tariff.

Mr. HILL. You cited the egg question. The entire importation from Canada would only have given one egg to 13 people once a year in the city of New York alone.

Mr. CALDERHEAD. The question is, what would the entire production be?

Mr. HILL. You can not take the entire production; you have to take the entire exportation.

Mr. CALDERHEAD. Oh, no; the exportation is limited by our tariff.

Mr. HILL. We can not eat the eggs they consume in Canada.

Mr. CALDERHEAD. But the imports of eggs from Canada are limited by our tariff.

Mr. RANDELL. They might raise more eggs in Canada to respond to this market.

Mr. HILL. Do you claim there is any danger to the American far-mer, so far as eggs and those products are concerned, from making them free from Canada?

Mr. MAUFF. It would be very presumptuous for me to talk about eggs.

Mr. HILL. I thought you represented the Society of Equity on the whole line of farm products.

Mr. MAUFF. I am representing them here entirely and alone on the question of cereals.

Mr. HILL. Very well, then; let us take the largest one.

Mr. MAUFF. I came here yesterday morning, and I am here without any preparation except such as I got together on the train. I men-tioned that on the announcement of this agreement the prices in Win-nipeg had advanced, and prices had dropped all over the United States. Let me call your attention to figures relating to savings-bank deposits in 10 eastern States, amounting to $3,000,000,000, whereas in the 10 largest, you might say most important, grain-growing, agricultural States in the Mississippi Valley, the savings-bank deposits will amount to not over $500,000,000.

Mr. RANDELL. What 10 States do you mean?

Mr. MAUFF. I would be very glad if you would allow me to refer to the original manuscript, if I can find it here. Here are part of the figures, and I have taken these in an effort to get a fair comparison. I have taken the savings-bank deposits on June 30, 1909, in Con-necticut, Massachusetts, New Hampshire, New Jersey, New York, Pennsylvania, Rhode Island, Vermont, Maine, and Maryland—$3,018,000,000. Then I take Illinois, Indiana, Iowa, Kansas, Michi-gan, Minnesota, Ohio, South Dakota, Wisconsin, and Nebraka, less than $500,000,000.

Mr. HILL. That is not worth a cent as statistics, as those deposits have been only 10 years accumulating, while the others, perhaps, have been accumulating for 50.

Mr. MAUFF. It is a barometer as to the prosperity of the sections.

Mr. HILL. You ought to take the statistics of the States of the same age.

Mr. MAUFF. You can do that. I say the farmer is not the sharer of the luxuries of the present day.

Mr. RANDELL. Is it not a fact that under the protective system that has been established so long the eastern States have been getting the advantage of the western States, and that farmer in the West really has not gotten anything out of the protective tariff?

Mr. MAUFF. I do not know whether or not you were here when I cited the case of the barley industry. The barley industry is a special industry. We can use that as a special illustration, because it is raised for the brewers, for the production of beer.

Mr. RANDELL. In the case of barley you have an absolutely pro-hibitive tariff.

Mr. MAUFF. An absolutely prohibitive tariff.

Mr. RANDELL. You do not mean to say everything in this country ought to be run on a prohibitive tariff basis?

Mr. MAUFF. I am not sanctioning anything of that kind.

Mr. RANDELL. You have submitted figures stating that the bank account of the Eastern States has been larger than that of certain Western States which you say are the most important. Is it not a fact that they have not been getting out of this protective system the same amount of profit that those in the eastern States have?

Mr. MAUFF. That is our position exactly. All the American Society of Equity requests is that the purchasing power of a bushel of grain remain to-morrow as it is to-day.

Mr. HILL. That is a question of supply and demand, is it not?

Mr. RANDELL. Would it not be better for you to stand for a natural situation where you get your natural rights instead of coming in for a prohibitive tariff to help you build up your industries?

Mr. MAUFF. The lands are seeded and the crops are raised with the understanding that these farmers are to feed the ninety-odd million people of the United States and export the surplus. You are going to open up a territory which I have been talking about. In Saskatchewan the increase has been immense. You will bring that land and the cheaper labor in competition with Americans, and the labor is cheaper because of the cheaper prices for the necessities of life, because of Canada's free-trade relations with England. Give our farmers a free-trade relation on their necessities and they will give you the right hand on this whole proposition. They do not want anything but what is fair and equitable.

Mr. RANDELL. Why not do that, then, instead of standing for protection?

Mr. MAUFF. We have to protest; there is no question of removing the duty on manufactured articles.

Mr. RANDELL. You are asking for a prohibitive tariff.

Mr. MAUFF. I ask for nothing, excepting that the purchasing power of the bushel of grain shall not be depreciated 50 per cent, or 25 per cent. The farmer takes his bushel of grain, figuratively speaking, to the storekeeper to buy his family cotton goods, or flannels, or a handsaw, or harness; he is going to take two bushels, we will say to illustrate, to buy those identical things, as this agreement proposes.

Mr. RANDELL. Why do you stand for prohibitive tariff on cotton goods, a prohibitive tariff on your farm products, and pay this extra high cost of living; why not have it natural and get what you would naturally be entitled to?

Mr. MAUFF. We are absolutely willing to stand on that ground. If this tariff is revised from A to Z, my voice will not be heard here protesting.

Mr. RANDELL. Why have you not been voting for it, then?

Mr. MAUFF. I do not bring the vote question into the case at all; I do not know the politics of you gentlemen. But if you would undertake to go with me to the West and hear the expressions of the farmers, you would have your eyes opened. With this curtailment of time, and various other things, I am only able to give you this in the way I have.

Mr. HILL. You will have an opportunity to revise your figures and your paper, and I do not think there would be any objection on the part of the committee, if you choose to put your whole paper in, to your doing so. Is there any objection?

Mr. RANDELL. I should think not. Let him fix up the statement as he wishes.

Mr. MAUFF. My statement is a reproduction of the statistics of what Congressman Malby gave on various things.

Mr. HILL. You can give to the reporter your entire paper.

Mr. MAUFF. Here is a telegram I have just received from Wabasha, Minn.

[Telegram.]

WABASHA, MINN., *February 4, 1911.*

JOHN R. MAUFF,
　Care Ways and Means Committee, Washington, D. C.:

Enthusiastic mass meeting farmers assembled to-day. Free barley under reciprocity is of no possible good but to brewers only, and ultimately not to them. It will ruin barley industry in Northwest, without reciprocal return to the industry or consumer. We protest vigorously.

JOS. WELP, *Chairman.*

They make a point of that, because barley is raised for brewing purposes, and we have increased and trebled the crop at the solicitation of the brewers, acting through the Department of Agriculture, with an appropriation from the Department of Agriculture; and the brewers are not using barley malt as they used to in the manufacture of beer, but they are using over 50 per cent of substitutes for barley malt and disguising it as barley malt. There is to come up soon before the Board of Food and Drug Inspection the question of what is beer, and we have been trying for three years to get a decision on that subject. The brewers have not been treating the farmers right, and it is an outrage that an industry that has been fostered for one particular purpose should be brought into competition with the barley of Canada. They can raise a tremendous crop of barley there, after they have taken the seed over.

That telegram says it will ruin the barley industry. Then where will the brewers be? They will have to depend on Canada, and eventually they will ask you to let Russia come in with her barley, and she has 400,000,000 bushels. That is all the farmers ask. The Society of Equity stands for equity for what they sell and equity for what they buy, and it is an infant organization, with only 30,000 members. It is hard to cope with the older organizations that are opposed to this thing—and we have an idea where the older organizations are, where they live, and where they thrive. And what will become of the farmers when their lands have depreciated because of the depreciation in the earning power per acre? And who has the mortgages? The life insurance companies, the trust companies, estates? It is a serious question.

Mr. CALDERHEAD. You speak about the quantity of wheat produced in Saskatchewan and that Manitoba country up there; where is that wheat marketed?

Mr. MAUFF. I believe that goes largely to Winnipeg; probably some of it might go to the Pacific coast.

Mr. CALDERHEAD. The wheat that goes to Winnipeg goes where?

Mr. MAUFF. That eventually finds an outlet with the mills of Canada and the foreign countries. The mills of Canada, of course, have quite a lucrative business, too. The land that will not grow good barley grows the most excellent wheat.

Mr. CALDERHEAD. The reason I am asking is, for a long time there has been a demand on the part of the flouring mills, Pillsbury and others up in Minnesota, for a lower tariff on wheat, in order that they might get the Canadian wheat.

Mr. MAUFF. I understand the sentiment.

Mr. CALDERHEAD. The hard wheat. There is a constant protest on the part of our millers against lowering the tariff, because, if the Canadian wheat comes in, and that flour pushes down into our country, it drives our people to hunt a market in some other country for their flour.

Mr. HILL. I will call your attention to the fact that there were exported from Canada to the United States last year 152,383 bushels of wheat, and exported from the United States to Canada 2,111,370 bushels, or about 15 or 20 times as much.

Mr. CALDERHEAD. I will admit all that; but sometimes that sort of an argument makes me think of the mathematician's wife. She was sick and could not cook the breakfast, so she told her husband to cook the eggs three minutes. When the lady came to eat the eggs she found them solid. When she asked him how long he boiled the eggs, he said " Twelve minutes." She said " I told you to boil them three minutes." He said " Yes, but there were four eggs, so I boiled them twelve minutes." [Laughter.]

Mr. MAUFF. I would like to answer that question, and explain one of the features of that desire of the Minneapolis and Duluth millers to get that wheat from northwestern Canada. It is because of its very superior quality. It allows the use of inferior grades to make the blend that will come up to standard. With a little of that very superior wheat it is possible to use inferior wheat. That is the real reason; just the same reason that the brewers want this barley that is raised in Minnesota, and they have protested to the Department of Agriculture against the introduction of any other variety, California especially mentioned. It is because of that diastasic barley, because the surplus, excessive diastase in this barley has the power of converting the starch in the low grain, and the glucose. In California that barley has a minimum amount of diastase, and it has a maximum amount of starch, and they get their starch from the barley. Our brewers get their starch from the Corn Products Co., and only use barley for converting that into alcohol. That is the reason the Bass man is buying that and shipping it to England for ale, because they use no substitutes for barley.

The gentleman asked about Kansas and Missouri barley. When Adolphus Busch was first establishing his brewery, Missouri raised the best barley. But when the nitrogen leaves the soil you can not raise barley. In Kansas and Nebraska they have introduced the bay brewing seed from the Pacific coast, and the seed and the soil have not an affinity, and what have you raised? A bastard barley, that is used for one purpose only, and that is for animal feed.

Mr. RANDELL. Talking about the soil depreciating, what method have they or what method can they use for keeping up a soil where they raised this best barley?

Mr. MAUFF. You will find that the line is moving northward all the time. As I said, the best barley was grown in Missouri. It moved into Iowa. Iowa has lost it, largely, and it has moved into Minnesota. It has been getting farther and farther north all the time. Of course, the farmers have increased their crops by taking out to a large extent the acreage of wheat.

Mr. RANDELL. How about the loss in nitrogen?

Mr. MAUFF. The loss in nitrogen is the thing that puts the soil in condition for other cereals and not for barley. You put manure, for instance, on the soil and put the nitrogen into that soil, and there is too much nitrogen and your barley becomes nitrogen in its character. But the fact remains that at the brewers' solicitation the Department of Agriculture appropriated money and the farmers increased their crop of barley, and the records of the Department of Agriculture will show it, and if the gentlemen would allow me I would read from the Brewers' Journal the history of that iniquity, where the Department of Agriculture appropriated money and had a representative in there and encouraged and bamboozled the farmer to increase his barley crop three times over, and now they are only using one-third of it and converting raw substances to go into beer. The brewer has to have the diastase. That is the difference between the Mississippi Valley barley and the Pacific coast barley. We could not produce the Pacific coast barley there if we wanted to, because the brewers have protested to the Department of Agriculture. That industry has been discouraged by the Department of Agriculture. I could produce you gentlemen in the Department of Agriculture who would corroborate everything I say in this respect. That is why I lay special emphasis on this barley industry, and now that we have it in this condition and with the exposition that is to come off in October, the farmers to be given gold cups and money for further increasing the crop, along comes this demand from Saskatchewan and Alberta. It is only a matter of time when they will get the alkali out of the soil, etc., as that letter says.

Mr. HILL. But at present you do not fear that competition?

Mr. MAUFF. Not to-day.

Mr. HILL. The competition you fear is the eastern province?

Mr. MAUFF. Ontario has the soil to raise barley that will compete with our barley anywhere. But it is only a question of a short time when Saskatchewan and Alberta, that are now raising barley, will get their soil in condition where they can increase their crop of barley and produce a good crop of barley.

Mr. RANDELL. Why has not the land in Canada depreciated?

Mr. MAUFF. The barley land?

Mr. RANDELL. Yes.

Mr. MAUFF. In Ontario, as I think I mentioned, when this tariff was put on, the raising of barley shifted. They went to raising peas and things of that kind very largely. Peas and things of that kind are leguminous; they return something to the soil that restores the soil.

Mr. HILL. You say that you appear here not only on the question of barley, but as to cereals?

Mr. MAUFF. Not on the question of barley at all; it is cereals in general.

Mr. HILL. Does your society fear in any respect whatever the competition of Canada on a free basis, or a reciprocal basis, so far as corn is concerned?

Mr. MAUFF. Absolutely not. I believe at the present time corn can be shipped into 'Canada without any duty. I do not believe there is any duty on it now.

Mr. HILL. You do not care anything about that, so far as that is concerned. They are not raisers of corn. Then it is a question of wheat, oats, and barley?

Mr. MAUFF. Wheat, oats, and barley. I have shown the large increase in Saskatchewan. An investigation will show they have just commenced to touch the soil, and the men engaged in farming in Alberta and Saskatchewan have come largely from Iowa and from our other States, and Iowa shows a decrease in population, in the last census, and the men who have left there are in Saskatchewan. If you want to depopulate the country, put this through.

Mr. HILL. You are aware that this demand, so far as the Canadian side of it is concerned, comes largely from American citizens who have gone to Canada, are you not?

Mr. MAUFF. I dare say. I have a friend who has three houses in sunny Alberta and who has business in Minnesota, and yet to-day he stands against this agreement, simply on the ground of equity.

Mr. RANDELL. If that country happened to be in the United States, like Minnesota, this business would be ruined on account of the extent of the territory?

Mr. MAUFF. I do not think so. I think the extension would be gradual, and in this respect that the people settling the country would be large consumers of our products in their country, and our barley would increase to that extent. But you are going to depopulate your farms and send your farmers to Canada if you put this through. It looks as if there were an immigration agency here to depopulate the United States and increase the consumption of grain.

Mr. HILL. Is there any other subject on which you desire to be heard?

Mr. MAUFF. I should like to be heard Monday. I think I have a lot more to say.

Mr. HILL. I think if you have anything more we will have to hear you now, because the time will be taken up. The paper people have a right to be heard Monday.

Mr. MAUFF. It seems presumptuous to ask it, but there were so many of the members who were not here, and they asked so many questions and were not informed that it seemed to me I was doing them a favor to present my facts to them.

Mr. RANDELL. They will examine the record if you put your arguments in.

Mr. MAUFF. That does not allow me to answer the worthy gentleman of the committee who asked so many questions bearing on barley and other things. That touches us, and we would like to have an opportunity to explain it.

Mr. HILL. There is no objection to your submitting a supplemental statement if you wish. If any other gentleman wants to be heard, now is the opportunity.

Mr. HALES. I think we have presented our case as thoroughly as we can.

(Thereupon, at 5.20 o'clock p. m., the committee adjourned until Monday, February 6, 1911, at 10.30 o'clock a. m.)

The following telegrams were submitted by **Mr. Mauff**:

[Telegram.]

INDIANAPOLIS, IND., *February 3, 1911.*

J. R. MAUFF,
   New Willard Hotel, Washington, D. C.:

Kindly answer protest in behalf of our society against proposed reciprocity with Canada, and keep me informed on situation. Senator McCumber has copy resolutions of protest passed by American Society of Equity at its national convention.

THEO. G. NELSON,
President Grain Growers.

[Telegram.]

J. R. MAUFF,
   Hotel Willard, Washington, D. C.:

Represent the organized farmers of Wisconsin, especially the barley growers, before all hearings and strongly protest against proposed Canadian reciprocity agreement, which would reduce the import duty on barley and other farm products and work great hardship and ruin among our people.

WISCONSIN STATE UNION, AMERICAN SOCIETY OF EQUITY,
M. WES LUBBS, *Secretary.*

STATEMENT FILED BY THE MALT MANUFACTURERS' ASSOCIATION OF BUFFALO, N. Y.

NEW YORK, *February 6, 1911.*

COMMITTEE ON WAYS AND MEANS, HOUSE OF REPRESENTATIVES.

GENTLEMEN: The agreement recently negotiated between Canada and the United States, and now before Congress for ratification, among other things provides for the free admission of barley into either country from the other. The Malt Manufacturers' Association of Buffalo submit for your consideration the following statement, by reason of the statements made before your honorable committee by representatives of western maltsters. This statement is submitted, not for the purpose of creating an argument, but to refute assertions that are misleading and unjust.

The Malt Manufacturers' Asssociation of Buffalo has for many years past advocated freer trade relations with Canada, including a free interchange of natural products, and a revision of the schedules relating to manufactured products, believing that such an arrangement would be highly beneficial for both countries for their development and expansion. It is true that by such an arrangement the malting industry in the East would receive benefits; we do not believe or agree with the western maltster, however, that the free admission of barley will seriously injure, much less destroy, the malting industry of the Middle West, nor seriously affect the agricultural sections which are now the leading barley-productive States.

When the agreement now before you was negotiated, the eastern maltsters heartily joined with others to arouse public sentiment in favor of its ratification; it was not actuated, however, by the motive that this industry would be a recipient of favorable conditions to secure its raw material, but upon the broader ground that its ratification would promote our mutual trade, open up a market for products now denied, and firmly establish our share to the enormous business that is to be obtained by the opening up of Canada's vast areas yet undeveloped and rich in natural resources.

AS TO THE EFFECT OF THE PROPOSED AGREEMENT UPON WESTERN MALTING INDUSTRY.

The provisions of the agreement, relating to the free interchange of natural products, has been attacked by the western malsters, and they claim that it will destroy their industry. Their fear of direful effects to their industry and to the farmer in either section is more imaginary than real; they are actuated by a selfish motive only to restrict competition and to seriously cripple the malting industry in the East by continuing to control the supply of malting barley, which they are able to do by reason of the present prohibitive tax of 30 cents a bushel.

Since 1890 the malting industry in the East has constantly declined. Under the treaty of 1855 barley was admitted free, and after its abrogation a duty of 15 cents per bushel was imposed. This rate continued until 1883, when the duty was reduced to 10 cents per bushel, and it has continued until 1890, when the duty was increased to 30 cents per bushel. This has been the tariff upon barley ever since, except during the brief operation of the Wilson bill, under which a tax was imposed of 30 per cent ad valorem.

The malting industry in New York, in 1880, comprised 51 per cent of the whole, and manufactured 54 per cent of the entire malt produced. Under the favorable tax of 10 cents per bushel, the number of malt houses increased to 82 per cent in 1890, and manufacturing 42 per cent of the malt. Since 1890 the malt industry has declined until at present there is only about 25 per cent of the plants and manufacturing 20 per cent of the malt. As the malting industry declined, so did the production of barley in the eastern States, the agricultural sections being deprived of their market.

While the eastern malting industry has severely declined as above indicated, the consumption of malt in the States tributary to it still exceeds 50 per cent of the total consumed.

The malt manufacturers who have continued to operate their plants have done so under most adverse conditions by reason of the source of their supply of raw material becoming more distant, and were therefore compelled to pay excessive costs of transportation for their raw material and the shipment of their manufactured products at local rates to eastern consumers in competition with the western maltsters, having their source of raw material at their door and shipping their manufactured product on through rates to destination.

The free admission of barley has not been advocated to destroy the malting industry of the West, nor to injure the agricultural sections of the West and Northwest. On the contrary, it has submitted that the malting industry of the East is entitled to equal recognition and protection and facilities to secure its barley for malting purposes from territories tributary to its plants as the western, and that the farmer in the Eastern States should be offered as ready and profitable a market for his barley as the western; and it is further submitted that the ratification of the proposed agreement will tend to prevent and largely eliminate the domination of western elevating and other interests to arbitrarily fix and maintain fictitious prices of foodstuffs.

AS TO THE EFFECT OF THE PROPOSED AGREEMENT UPON PRICES OF GRAIN.

Western maltsters and representatives of agricultural sections also urge that the advocation of the proposed agreement would seriously affect prices, particularly of barley; that grains were cheaper in Canada than in the United States because of cheaper lands and labor.

On Friday last (Feb. 3) May wheat was quoted on the Chicago Board of Trade at 96¾ cents, and July 93¾ cents; while on the Winnipeg Board of Trade May wheat was quoted 96¼ and July at 97¼ cents; for May oats Chicago quoted 33 cents and for July 32¼ cents; while at Winnipeg 35¼ was quoted for May oats and 36 cents for July. These quotations alone are and should be sufficient to refute the argument that the prices of grains in Canada are lower than in the United States and that the free admission of such grains will in any way affect the prices in this country; rather, they indicate that the admission of Canadian grains would largely stimulate our markets.

In 1890 the barley crop of the United States aggregated 59,000,000 bushels, with the average farmer price of 40 cents per bushel, and of this total crop about 66 per cent was used for malting purposes. The crop of 1910 aggregated 162,000,000 bushels of barley, with an average farmer price of about 48 cents per bushel, and of the total crop only 38 per cent was used for malting purposes. The western maltster, therefore, has not been the benefactor to the western farmer, as he pretends to have been, as he apparently has not influenced the price of barley to the farmer. It is also to be noted that the tremendous increase in the production of barley has not seriously affected the price, nor has the farmer in Wisconsin and Minnesota been injured by the production of barley in the adjacent States of North and South Dakota and Iowa. In fact, they have been benefited, and the farmers of the West and Northwest will likewise be benefited by the admission of Canadian grains, including barley.

Upon the solicitation of this Government that concessions would be made, Canada admitted our corn free. Its importations of corn in recent years has aggregated annually upwards of twelve or fifteen million bushels. The States which are now the largest producers of barley are also the better corn-producing States, so that they should be interested to retain the Canadian market for their surplus corn.

The price of grain largely depends upon the law of supply and demand. While the producer of grain may properly claim that he is entitled to receive for his products a profitable sum, still there is the mass of consumers who far exceeds the producer in numbers, who are also entitled to equal consideration. We therefore submit that the adoption of the measure having great possibilities for the expansion of our foreign trade and the increased employment of labor at home should not be jeopardized by personal and sectional prejudices. It is to be hoped, therefore, that the proposed agreement will be promptly acted upon by our Congress, and to this end your favorable consideration is respectfully urged.

All of which is respectfully submitted.

C. H. McLaughlin.

COMMITTEE ON WAYS AND MEANS,
HOUSE OF REPRESENTATIVES,
Monday, February 6, 1911.

The committee met at 10.30 o'clock a. m., Hon. Samuel W. McCall (acting chairman) presiding.

Present: The acting chairman and Messrs. Hill, Boutell, Needham, Calderhead, Fordney, Gaines, Longworth, Ellis, Clark, Randell, Broussard, and Brantley.

Mr. McCALL. The committee will be in order. The clerk will note the presence of Members as they come in. What gentlemen are here this morning who desire to be heard?

Mr. HASTINGS. The American paper and pulp manufacturers are represented by myself and by Mr. Sensenbreener, from Wisconsin, and Mr. Hugo, from New York.

Mr. CLARK. What does the second man named want to be heard about, wood pulp?

Mr. HASTINGS. The effect upon his particular business, in the West, of this treaty.

Mr. CLARK. Is that wood pulp?

Mr. HASTINGS. Wood pulp and paper.

Mr. CLARK. I did not know but what there were two subjects you wanted to be heard about.

Mr. HASTINGS. We want to be heard on both. That is, we consider them one, practically. Mr. Hugo is from Watertown, N. Y.

Mr. HILL. I understand there are good reasons why this paper and pulp hearing should go over until to-morrow morning, and then the subject should be considered all at the same time and completed to-morrow, and I would suggest that so far as the hearing this morning is concerned, if there are any gentlemen who want to be heard on any other subject, we hear them and take the paper business up all at once.

Mr. McCALL. All right; if there are no objections.

Mr. CLARK. What are the reasons why this should be postponed?

Mr. McCALL. We can finish this all up to-morrow.

Mr. CLARK. Well, go on, then.

Mr. McCALL. Are there any gentlemen here who desire to be heard upon any feature of the bill other than that relating to paper and pulp?

Mr. HASTINGS. Mr. Chairman, it would not take, so far as the paper men who are here this morning are concerned, more than an hour to hear all we have to say, and two of these gentlemen tell me they must go home to-night.

Mr. HILL. If there is nobody else who wants to be heard we might hear them.

Mr. LONGWORTH. We might hear what they have to say.

Mr. McCALL. Those gentlemen who must go away may appear now.

Mr. HASTINGS. Thank you. I will call on Mr. Hugo first.

STATEMENT OF FRANCIS M. HUGO, OF WATERTOWN, N. Y.

Mr. HUGO. I regret, Mr. Chairman and gentlemen, that I am not able to remain over until to-morrow, but my engagements demand that I go home to-day, so that for that reason I will beg your indulgence to hear me this morning.

I come from northern New York, which is the locality where there is more paper produced than in any other section of the United States. We have there 42 paper mills—pulp mills—which represent an investment of from thirty to thirty-five millions of dollars.

Mr. LONGWORTH. In whose congressional district is that?

Mr. HUGO. In Mr. Knapp's district and Mr. Malby's district. Watertown is in Mr. Knapp's district and our mills are in Mr. Malby's district, in St. Lawrence County.

The paper industry of that section opposes the adoption of this measure for the following reasons: In the first place, it is unfair, in our judgment, to select one industry and take away its protection and make it pay the price of good fellowship between this country and Canada, especially when almost every article except the ground wood or pulp wood is most highly protected. Now, if this were a matter where all the protection was taken off, where all the duty was taken off of all the commodities that go into the manufacture of paper, all the commodities that go to make what we call machine clothing, there might be some justification for it, but as a matter of fact, for example, take woolens; the duty on woolens coming into the United States is 100 per cent. The duty on woolens into Canada is 36 per cent, and there is a preferential duty or reduction of 12 per cent of duty on the woolens going into Canada from Great Britain. In other words, we have a duty in this country of 100 per cent on woolens, and in Canada the duty is 24 per cent. There is also a duty of 45 per cent on machinery used.

Mr. CLARK. Wait a minute.

Mr. HUGO. I beg pardon.

Mr. CLARK. You did not know that the duty on some woolens was 182½ per cent?

Mr. HUGO. No; I thought it was bad enough to put it at 100 per cent.

Mr. CLARK. Some of it runs as high as 182½ per cent.

Mr. HUGO. The duty on machinery used in the manufacture is 45 per cent, and the duty on clay is $2.50 a ton. Roughly speaking, the duty on everything that goes into the manufacture of paper, outside of ground wood and pulp wood, is most highly protected, and we feel that it is an injustice, for that reason, in the first place, that this duty should be taken off paper and sulphite, when everything that goes into those commodities is most highly protected.

In the second place, we object to this measure because it does not give the industry any consideration for the protection which the bill proposes to take off. Now, as a matter of fact, the duty on pulp wood, on ground wood, is practically nothing; the duty on pulp wood is practically none; the duty on sulphite is $3.35 a ton. The average duty on print paper coming into this country from Canada is $4.75 a ton. It is proposed in this measure to take off the duty on sulphite of $3.35 and the duty on print paper of $4.75; and what do we get in return? We simply get a continuance of the conditions that exist to-day. In other words, we get no return for what we give up, and there is no consideration for putting print paper on the free list.

Mr. BOUTELL. What was that figure of $4.75 a ton?

Mr. HUGO. I beg your pardon?

Mr. BOUTELL. I thought the duty on print paper was $3.75 a ton.

Mr. HUGO. Yes; the duty on print paper coming into this country is $3.75, but plus any restrictions that may exist on pulp wood or ground wood coming into this country; so that the average duty on print paper, the actual duty on print paper, on the average, is $4.75 per ton. I am talking about the average duty. The duty under the Payne bill is $3.75, and to that is added the amount of any restriction that is put upon the importation of print paper, so that I say, taking the actual figures of the Treasury Department, the average duty on print paper is $4.75 a ton.

Mr. BOUTELL. What was the duty under the Dingley law?

Mr. HUGO. $6 a ton.

Mr. BOUTELL. And did that same restriction of $1 a ton prevail under the Dingley law?

Mr. HUGO. No, sir; I do not think it did.

Mr. BOUTELL. So that the comparison you have to make to-day between the duty under the Dingley law and the duty under the Payne law is the difference between $6 and $4.75 a ton?

Mr. HUGO. Yes.

Mr. BOUTELL. Now, right here, I would like to ask this question. That is the thing about the tariff that interests me more than anything else. There is a certain school of tariff philosophers who argue that immediately you reduce the duty you reduce the price to the ultimate consumer; automatically that it is reduced. Now, if that is the case, when we changed the duty from $6 a ton to $4.75 a ton, taking your figures, we made a reduction of $1.25 a ton. If you have the figures convenient, or remember them, I would like to ask if print paper is now selling at just $1.25 a ton cheaper than it sold, say, in February, 1908?

Mr. HUGO. I do not think that is the fact, for the reason that we all know that when there is tariff agitation——

Mr. CLARK. I know; but, Mr. Witness, Mr. Boutell asked you a definite question there, at last.

Mr. BOUTELL. If you have the figures, can you give the price of print paper in February, 1908, 1909, 1910, and 1911?

Mr. HUGO. I think the price of print paper is practically the same to-day as it was then.

Mr. BOUTELL. I may say that Dun's Review, which is the most convenient table of prices that I am able to find, with parallel columns for the week's wholesale prices of paper with the prices of the corresponding time in the previous year, shows, if my recollection is correct, that the price of paper is not only not less, but is more.

Mr. HUGO. Well, I think I can explain that, if you will give me just a moment.

Mr. BOUTELL. I wanted to get at the facts first.

Mr. HUGO. Yes.

Mr. BOUTELL. The first fact, then, which so many people forget, is that a reduction of the tariff does not automatically reduce the price by that amount to the ultimate consumer.

Mr. Hugo. I think in a matter of that kind you have got to take in lots of other considerations. For example, I was down here before when this matter was being agitated. The price of paper was depressed; because, as we all know, tariff agitation has a bear effect on the market. Prices were reduced at that time.

Mr. Boutell. As Bourke Cockran says, we can not put a tariff on apprehension.

Mr. Hugo. Certainly; there is the whole situation. During the past two years we have felt that there was a certain amount of stability in the paper market, and for that reason the prices have become stronger; there is no doubt about that. But I do not think it is directly due to the effect of the reduction of 6 cents a hundred on paper, but it is due to the fact that we know to-day something that we did not know two years ago, and that is what the tariff would be for a short time. Now, we will have the same effect to-day and as long as this agitation continues. The purchasers of paper do not know just exactly how this matter is coming out, and the result is that they may withhold the purchase of paper, and it all has a bear effect on the market.

Mr. Boutell. Now, that being so, as soon as the nervous condition produced by uncertainty in the market disappeared paper went up to what we call a normal price, a steady price, which was equal to what it was before the tariff reduction, which shows, of course, that in this instance the reduction of the tariff by $1.25, according to your figures, or $2.50 a ton, did not automatically press down the price of paper to the ultimate consumer when the market became normal, which brings me to this question: What ground is there for believing that under this reciprocity arrangement paper would not sell just as high as it is selling now; and if so, you would not have any objection to it, would you?

Mr. Hugo. Why; I most strenuously object to any change in the present tariff on paper, because I think it would have a most disastrous effect on the price of paper. Take an extreme case, if you please. The duty to-day on what we call craft paper is 35 per cent. That paper is worth 4 cents a pound, $8 a ton. If you take off the duty of $8 a ton on that commodity what is going to be the result? The market will be paralyzed. Now, the duties taken off by this measure will amount to all the way from $3.75 to $28 a ton. What will be the result? Our whole market is going to become chaotic. That is the trouble about this thing.

Mr. Boutell. It is going to become chaotic, as it did before, through apprehension; as soon as there is certainty the market becomes normal, and when the market for paper became normal it went back to the price it was under the Dingley law.

Mr. Hugo. I hardly think you can argue that, for this reason. In the first place, the duty was taken off print paper; it was reduced to $4.75 from $6. Now, it is proposed to take the duty off entirely, and if that is done it will bring the Canadian market into complete competition with the American market, which did not exist before.

Mr. Boutell. You know better than I do what the price of paper is, but if paper did not go down when $1.25 was taken off the tariff, what ground is there for saying that it would go down if you took off $6?

Mr. Hugo. That is the proposition I want to argue here.

Mr. BOUTELL. In other words, coming back to the old law of supply and demand, which is older than the tariff, there is only a certain amount of print paper available for the world's demand.

Mr. HUGO. Yes.

Mr. BOUTELL. And if paper comes in here from Canada it makes a kind of a vacuum, so to speak—if there is any such term in commercial parlance—which has got to be supplied in some way.

Mr. HUGO. Yes.

Mr. BOUTELL. If Canada is making just enough paper for its present market, and we take down the tariff, and paper comes in here from Canada, then there will be a vacuum in the Canadian market, and either more paper has got to be manufactured, or paper has got to come into Canada from some other place to take the place of the paper that comes here from Canada.

Mr. HUGO. But the trouble with that proposition is right here. It is not so much the amount of paper that comes in from Canada as it is the fact that some paper comes in from Canada into the United States. I know one case where an American concern that had 500 tons of paper gave options on that paper to three different purchasers. That is the trouble. It is the small amount coming in from Canada that regulates and fixes the price of the American product.

Mr. BOUTELL. If it comes in at a lower price, that would benefit the consumer?

Mr. HUGO. Well, it certainly must come in at a lower price, because we do not have to pay any more duty on print paper than the difference between the cost of production in Canada and in the United States.

Mr. HILL. One moment. How do you account for the fact that last year we sold 10,000 pounds of print paper to Canada?

Mr. HUGO. I presume that may be on account of the fact of accessibility to markets and all that kind of thing. I presume there are manufacturers in the Canadian northwest who can get their paper from our northwestern section on a cheaper freight rate than we can ship it for from here.

Mr. HILL. I say we sent from the United States, of print paper alone, to Canada, 9,613,000 pounds. Do you know what part of Canada that went to?

Mr. HUGO. I could not tell you, sir.

Mr. LONGWORTH. Do I understand your contention to be that the duty ought to be so high that no print paper could be imported?

Mr. HUGO. I do not take that position at all.

Mr. LONGWORTH. I thought that was your contention.

Mr. HUGO. No, sir; my position is this, that we ought to have the duty on print paper which was enunciated in the Republican platform, and that is the difference in cost of paper in Canada and in the United States plus a reasonable return to the manufacturer.

Mr. LONGWORTH. Yes; but a moment ago you said the trouble was that if there was any importation whatever from Canada it would make the market here. I thought you used that as an argument that the duty should be so high that no paper whatever under any circumstances could come here.

Mr. HUGO. I do not take that position. I feel we are entitled to a duty that is equal to the difference in the cost of production in

Canada and in the United States, and that will give us a reasonable return on our investment.

Mr. LONGWORTH. That does not answer my question.

Mr. RANDELL. I understood it like Mr. Longworth says.

Mr. LONGWORTH. I understood you to say that the trouble was that any importation whatever from Canada so disturbed the print-paper market here as to unsettle things and make bad conditions.

Mr. HUGO. That is right.

Mr. LONGWORTH. Any importation whatever.

Mr. HUGO. That is right.

Mr. LONGWORTH. So that you advocate a duty which will be so high that no print paper can be under any circumstances imported from Canada?

Mr. HUGO. No, I would not follow that out to that conclusion.

Mr. LONGWORTH. I do not see where you make you distinction.

Mr. HUGO. Because I feel that we ought to have a duty, as I say, that will protect us. I am not asking for any prohibitory duty. One would be prohibitory, the other would be protective.

Mr. LONGWORTH. I understand you to say that you wanted a duty under which no print paper could be imported under any circumstances.

Mr. HUGO. No: I brought up that matter in answer to the gentleman there in regard to print paper coming in from Canada, and he raised the question about the amount you can bring from there, and I said it is not altogether a question of the amount, but it is the question of the way that the amount that does come in is handled by the commission merchants in this country.

Mr. LONGWORTH. I did not understand you to say that.

Mr. HUGO. Yes.

Mr. LONGWORTH. Now, another question. Are you sure there were no restrictions on Canadian exports under the Dingley bill? In reply to Mr. Boutell you said that when the $6 duty was on there were no restrictions whatever. Are you sure of that?

Mr. HUGO. Mr. Hastings informed me there were not any.

Mr. HASTINGS. There were no penalties.

Mr. LONGWORTH. Then whatever restrictions have been imposed have been in the last two years?

Mr. HASTINGS. So far as Canada is concerned.

Mr. LONGWORTH. Mr. Hugo has been making an argument that the duty, while nominally it is $3.75, is in effect $4.75 on account of the Canadian restrictions. In reply to a question, Mr. Boutell asked as to whether, when the $6 duty was in force, there were not also restrictions, you answered no. In other words, you said that when the Dingley Law was in force, the duty was only $6, and when the Payne law came into force, the duty went to $4.75.

Mr. HASTINGS. If I may say just a word, under the Dingley law Ontario prohibited the importation of wood, but the duty on paper was $6.

Mr. LONGWORTH. Yes.

Mr. HASTINGS. In Quebec, where they had an excess stumpage on the wood exported, there was no opposition to its exportation into the United States from Canada, and the duty was still $6. When the Payne bill went into effect, the duty was made $3.75, if it was made from wood cut from private lands. If it was from wood which was cut on Crown lands, there was a $2 penalty, which made it $5.75. Now under the present conditions the actual facts are that half of the paper comes in here which is said to be made from private-land wood, and half of it is said to be made from Crown-land wood, and the Treasury Department, interpreting that, fixed a duty which amounts to from $4.77 to $4.99, and about half of that wood comes from lands in private ownership and half of it from Crown land, so that what Mr. Hugo says is that the Government collects about $4.75 on the paper that is now coming in.

Mr. LONGWORTH. That is it.

Mr. HASTINGS. Yes.

Mr. CLARK. Mr. Hugo, when we had the hearings here before, you and Mr. Hastings and other wood-pulp men came down here and tried to make the committee believe that if the tariff was cut down on wood pulp and print paper the whole business would go to smash. Well, we cut the tariff down on it, and you now come in and state that it did not put down the price of print paper at all, but that, on the contrary, the price of print paper is higher now than before we cut the tariff down. If that is so, what are you objecting to these changes for? If taking the tariff does not put down the price of your product, what do you care about it?

Mr. HUGO. It certainly will effect the price of paper.

Mr. CLARK. But how will it effect it this time, if it did not effect it before?

Mr. HUGO. Let me answer that indirectly. The argument of the gentlemen who wanted the duty taken off print paper was, "If you do not do it, you are not going to get any pulp wood from Canada." You made a reduction in the duty on print paper, and what has been the result? The duty has been continued at $4.75.

Mr. CLARK. But it was cut from $6, was it not?

Mr. HUGO. Yes, it was; it has been reduced some.

Mr. CLARK. Well, I know. Then why did not the price come down; or if it did not, how do you fellows account for it?

Mr. HUGO. Because the price was arbitrarily fixed; because of the tariff agitation at that time it was not a normal price.

Mr. CLARK. As a matter of fact, was not the price artifically fixed by you gentlemen after that tariff bill was passed?

Mr. HUGO. No, sir; not in the last. Now, as I was saying, in regard to the importation of pulp wood, it was talked about here, and it has been talked about through the newspapers all during this time, that unless we held out the olive branch to Canada there would not be any importation of pulp wood from Canada. The result is that we are buying pulp wood at $3 a cord, cheaper than when we were here before, the northern market is glutted, and the manufacturers are more anxious to sell us pulp wood to-day than we are to buy it.

Mr. CLARK. Then what are you kicking about?

Mr. HUGO. Because you are taking off all the duty and giving us nothing in return.

Mr. CLARK. If the price goes up if we take off the duty, you ought to be satisfied.

Mr. HUGO. That is not the point. The point is that you are talking about taking the duty off of print paper and sulphite, and you are not giving us anything in return, which is not reciprocity.

Mr. CLARK. If it automatically goes up, I do not see what complaint you have got if this bill passes this way.

Mr. HUGO. How do you mean, "goes up"?

Mr. CLARK. According to your own story, in answer to Mr. Boutell, you said that when we cut the tariff down 18 months ago, instead of going down it went up.

Mr. HUGO. Yes; it has gone up, but the rise has been very small.

Mr. CLARK. Suppose it has been small.

Mr. HUGO. It simply has gone back to the normal price. The other price is artificially low. That is the trouble with this question. You take any stable market and create disturbance all through the country and let people believe that the tariff is going to be taken off, and prices will go down.

Mr. CLARK. Do you think there was anybody fool enough in this country, when we passed the Payne bill, to believe that they were going to take the tariff off of print paper and pulp, except some Democrats? It was beaten in the House, was it not?

Mr. HUGO. No; it was beaten in the Senate.

Mr. CLARK. They all voted?

Mr. HUGO. No; but the majority of them voted, and it was put at $4 in the Senate, and it was adjusted in the committee between the two Houses on a basis of $3.75.

Mr. CLARK. If you had come to me and asked for information, you would have got it in advance that they were not going to change anything much in that bill.

Mr. FORDNEY. Mr. Boutell asked you if print paper had gone down in price since the passage of the Payne bill?

Mr. HUGO. Yes.

Mr. FORDNEY. You have explained it now, that on account of the additions added to the $3.75 on account of rebates or other restrictions over there the duty is $4.75, or, as Mr. Hastings said, $4.70 to $4.90.

Mr. HUGO. Yes.

Mr. FORDNEY. And that only reduced the duty on print paper $1.25?

Mr. HUGO. Practically.

Mr. FORDNEY. To answer Mr. Boutell's statement, is it not true that, generally, supply and demand cut a great figure in fixing the price of any commodity in this country or any other country in the world?

Mr. HUGO. Certainly.

Mr. FORDNEY. So that the supply and demand may have had much to do with the fixing of this rate?

Mr. HUGO. Yes.

Mr. FORDNEY. But is it not generally understood by everybody, both Democrats and Republicans—you must agree to that—that a reduction of the duty means a lowering of the article to the consumer in this country?

Mr. HUGO. Yes, sir.

Mr. FORDNEY. That is generally conceded, is it not?

Mr. HUGO. Yes.

Mr. FORDNEY. Then their argument does not hold good for a minute, that a reduction of the duty will not lower the price to the consumer. It will do it, all must concede, except when supply and demand regulate the price.

Mr. HUGO. As I said, there are so many conditions that have got to be taken into account.

Mr. FORDNEY. Yes.

Mr. HUGO. So that you can not lay that down as an absolute fundamental principle.

Mr. FORDNEY. Certainly; if not, when we reduced the duty on rawhides, why did not the price of leather go down? It went up.

Mr. CLARK. I can answer that.

Mr. FORDNEY. You can answer it?

Mr. CLARK. It was the Leather Trust.

Mr. FORDNEY. That may be true. But there are a great many thousand independent tanners in the country. I am just as much opposed to a trust that will fix prices and fleece the people as any other man, but there is a great deal of cry about those things, about trusts, a great deal of talk.

Mr. HUGO. If there was nothing else but the reduction of the duty of 10 or 12 cents a hundred, probably the result would be that it would work out as has been suggested; but I say that the price of paper at the time this tariff was agitated before was depressed on account of the fact that it was in the public imnd that paper might be put on the free list. In addition to that, the law of supply and demand enters into it, and a thousand other things.

Mr. FORDNEY. Now, the duty was reduced, we will say, $1.25 a ton. That might not have been sufficient, if there was any other reason, to reduce the price of imported paper from Canada at all. But now to take $4.75 more off of it before conditions have become settled, or many of the people know what the law is except those directly interested in the business, would most likely reduce the price of print paper in this country, would it not?

Mr. HUGO. There is no doubt about it.

Mr. FORDNEY. Especially when the supply of pulp wood for this country is in Canada largely?

Mr. HUGO. As I have stated, the duty that is to be taken off will range from $3 to $28 if this bill becomes a law. We can all take for granted what is going to be the result. Was that craft paper where the amount of importation was increased from 50,000 to 200,000 tons?

Mr. HASTINGS. No.

Mr. HUGO. What was that on?

Mr. HASTINGS. We do not know. It is not kept track of.

Mr. BOUTELL. There is no exchange that acts as a regulating medium for the price of paper?

Mr. HUGO. Absolutely nothing but the law of supply and demand, that I know of.

Mr. BOUTELL. So that there is nothing to give a uniformity of price?

Mr. HUGO. Nothing at all. The price of print paper will run to-day anywhere from $2.15 to $2.25, delivered. Now, there is a difference of 10 cents a ton right there. There are hundreds of things that go into the question of the price of paper.

Mr. BOUTELL. That $22.50 is to the wholesaler from the factory, or to the newspaper?

Mr. HUGO. We sell to the newspaper. Ordinarily, paper is sold sometimes direct to the newspaper and sometimes through a commission house, and we pay the commission house from 3 to 5 per cent commission for the sale; but the price is fixed to the ultimate consumer, the newspaper.

Mr. BOUTELL. What, for example, are Chicago newspapers paying for their paper?

Mr. HUGO. I should think the average price would be $2.25 per hundred.

Mr. BOUTELL. That is $45 a ton?

Mr. HUGO. I should say on an 18-cent freight rate. We have to pay the 18 cents out of that.

Mr. BOUTELL. Do you know what it was selling for in the early part of 1908?

Mr. HUGO. I would think that there was not over $1 or $1.50 a ton difference.

Mr. BOUTELL. More or less than it is?

Mr. HUGO. I should say, on account of the facts I have stated, the price may have been a little less. I am not going to take any other position here than this, that on account of the fact that the tariff has been settled there has been some increase in the price of paper.

Mr. BOUTELL. I was trying to get back to a point before it was unsettled. I took January, 1908; that was before any conventions had declared for tariff revision. I am willing to go further back.

Mr. HUGO. Yes.

Mr. BOUTELL. What was the price of paper in 1907?

Mr. HUGO. Do you remember that, Mr. Hastings?

Mr. HASTINGS. It was higher.

Mr. BOUTELL. Can you give it?

Mr. HASTINGS. There is no set price. There is no set price for 30 days, and in years it will vary 10 per cent in the price.

Mr. BOUTELL. That is the reason that I fixed the price then. I fixed it in Chicago. Dun's Review tables are given for New York City.

Mr. HASTINGS. They are not correct any more than the quotations given in the Journal of Commerce of New York City are correct. They pretend to give the price of paper, but there is no record of actual charges for pa er.

Mr. RANDELL. You say that the agitation at the time the tariff bill was enacted lowered the price of paper?

Mr. HUGO. Yes.

Mr. RANDELL. I was going to ask you how much it had been lowered by the agitation.

Mr. HUGO. You were going to ask me that?

Mr. RANDELL. Yes, that is what I was going to ask you.

Mr. HUGO. I think that on account of the tariff agitation the price of print paper on the whole was reduced at least $2 a ton.

Mr. RANDELL. Then it resumes its normal position afterwards?

Mr. HUGO. The price is better to-day than it was at the time the other measure was agitated, but it is on account of the more settled condition in the market.

Mr. RANDELL. Is it higher than it was two years ago?

Mr. HUGO. Would that be prior to this other bill?

Mr. RANDELL. Yes; the bill was enacted on the 5th of August, 1909.

Mr. HUGO. I think the price is about the same as it was then, and then when this tariff agitation came up before the people, the price was reduced somewhat on that account.

Mr. RANDELL. The 25 per cent reduction on the tariff made no perceptible change? It was the disturbance in the country? Is not the reason for that that both the $6 and the $4.75 average rate, or $4.50, or whatever it is——

Mr. HUGO. Yes.

Mr. RANDELL (continuing). The average rates are both practically prohibitive?

Mr. HUGO. No, sir.

Mr. RANDELL. And therefore one will keep the price up just as much as the other?

Mr. HUGO. No, sir.

Mr. RANDELL. Since the reduction in the tariff, what has been the increase in importation from Canada to this country?

Mr. HASTINGS. The increase there is from nothing to 6,500,000 pounds, an average of about 500,000 pounds of news paper a month.

I beg to call the attention of the committee to a misstatement made by Mr. Hill as to the imports into this country from Canada. There was only 2,300 pounds went into Canada, and 10,000,000 pounds came into this country.

Mr. RANDELL. Are you aware what have been the importations since this bill went into effect?

Mr. HASTINGS. About an average of 5,000 tons per month from nothing.

Mr. RANDELL. That would be 60,000 tons a year?

Mr. HASTINGS. Yes.

Mr. RANDELL. You say that has not lowered the price in this country?

Mr. HASTINGS. No, sir; it is through the law of supply and demand.

Mr. HUGO. Through the law of supply and demand.

Mr. RANDELL. Even with that, the price has not gone down. Why do you think the price would go down if it was lowered still more?

Mr. HUGO. If it was all taken off?

Mr. RANDELL. Yes.

Mr. HUGO. Because Canada can produce news paper cheaper than we could possibly produce it. The average cost of pulp wood at a Canadian mill is $4 a cord cheaper than it is in this country—that is, the wood laid down at the mill. It takes a cord and a half of wood to make a ton of paper, which means that the Canadians have an advantage over us of $6 a ton. In addition to that, it was demonstrated in the hearings before the Mann committee that the average price of unskilled labor is lower in Canada than it is in this country, although the price of skilled labor is practically the same in both countries. Now, suppose you take a cord and a half of pulp wood at Mr. Booth's mill in Canada. He can make that up and ship it to the United States on practically the same freight rate that we do. Now, if you ship that into Watertown, we have to pay $4 a cord freight on that wood, and when it is in our mill yard there is an advantage to Canada of $6 a ton on the wood going into a ton of print paper. We make it into paper and ship it to the market on the same freight as Mr. Booth ships his on.

Mr. RANDELL. How much reduction can you stand of the present tariff and still not reduce the price?

Mr. Hugo. We can not stand any reduction in the duty on print paper if the paper industry is to continue in this country.

Mr. Randell. Did you not say, when you were before the committee a year and a half ago, that if it was reduced any it would ruin the industry?

Mr. Hugo. Yes.

Mr. Randell. And that prophecy has not been fulfilled?

Mr. Hugo. Yes; but there is a difference between taking off $1.25 and taking off $4.75.

Mr. Randell. But did you not say the same thing then—that if we reduced it any——

Mr. Hugo. We argued the same thing then as we argue now in regard to taking off the whole duty. We were never asked to fix the duty at any particular spot.

Mr. Randell. Did you not say if the duty was reduced any at all it would practically ruin the paper industry?

Mr. Hugo. The argument I made was that if the $6 duty was taken off it would ruin the paper business.

Mr. Randell. Did you not say that if it was reduced at all it would ruin the paper business; that you could not any more than get along with the $6 rate?

Mr. Hugo. I did not say it. It may have been stated here by somebody. I argue here now against the taking off of any of the duty.

Mr. Randell. Then if we take off any of the duty, you think it will reduce the rate of paper in this country?

Mr. Hugo. What is that, again?

Mr. Randell. If any of the duty is taken off, you think that will reduce the price of paper in this country; if any of the duty is taken off?

Mr. Hugo. If the duty is reduced materially, of course it will.

Mr. Randell. So that if $1 is taken off it will reduce the price?

Mr. Hugo. No, I would not say that, because I can not tell you how much the law of supply and demand is going to enter into this thing.

Mr. Randell. The law of supply and demand will enter whether there is a tariff or not, unless the tariff is prohibitive.

Mr. Hugo. As we have stated, the present duty is not prohibitive, because under the $4.75 duty the importations have increased from nothing per month to 5,000 tons per month.

Mr. Randell. What is the amount consumed in this country?

Mr. Hugo. In this country, to-day?

Mr. Randell. Yes.

Mr. Hugo. The average production per day of print paper is 4,000 tons.

Mr. Randell. Then the amount that has come in not coming from Canada is a little more than one-thirtieth of the amount consumed in the country?

Mr. Hugo. I should think about that.

Mr. Randell. Or about 3 per cent?

Mr. Hugo. I have not figured it.

Mr. Randell. The importations are about 3 per cent, or something like that?

Mr. Hugo. Yes.

Mr. RANDELL. Are not those importations, as you stated awhile ago, in localities where really the tariff would cut no figure, because it is a question of freight rates?

Mr. HUGO. No, sir.

Mr. RANDELL. What made you say that, then?

Mr. HUGO. I will explain it. Mr. Booth in Ottawa to-day is supplying contracts in the American market that we had. He was able to take those contracts because he could sell paper cheaper than we could.

Mr. FORDNEY. Can you assign any reason whatever—of course you can not, because you are a protectionist, as I am—can you assign any reason at all by the advocates of this measure for reducing the duty unless it will lower the price of the product in this country; and if not, why rob the Treasury of the revenue? Ask them to explain that. They can not explain that to your satisfaction or mine or the satisfaction of the people of this country.

Mr. GAINES. You have been talking about a reduction of price by reason of the reduction of the duty?

Mr. HUGO. Yes.

Mr. GAINES. All this discussion with reference to the price of print paper is with reference to the reduction of the price at the paper mill?

Mr. HUGO. Yes.

Mr. GAINES. And the price that is paid by the large daily newspapers of the country, is it not?

Mr. HUGO. Yes.

Mr. GAINES. There is no question of price as it ordinarily goes to the ultimate consumer, the small purchaser, involved in all this discussion, is there?

Mr. HUGO. I do not think so.

Mr. GAINES. You said that the price would be lowered $2 a ton?

Mr. HUGO. Yes.

Mr. GAINES. The man who runs a small country newspaper, we will say a thousand copies a week, 52 times a year, does not use a ton of paper in a year, does he?

Mr. HUGO. I think it would be quite an establishment that did use that amount of that kind of paper you are describing.

Mr. GAINES. Therefore, if there was a reduction of $2 by reason of reducing the tariff, and the whole amount of that reduction inured to the consumer, the man who ran a small country newspaper would not probably get as much as $2 in a year?

Mr. HUGO. He is not the one who gets in on the ground floor; it is the big fellow.

Mr. GAINES. He does not?

Mr. HUGO. No, sir.

Mr. GAINES. In my opinion the small consumer is never affected.

Mr. HUGO. That is correct.

Mr. GAINES. Unless perhaps adversely.

Mr. HUGO. Yes.

Mr. GAINES. Do you know what the freight rate per ton on paper is from the Norway Mills to New York?

Mr. HUGO. I do not.

Mr. GAINES. Are you able to compare that? What I want to get at is a comparison of that rate with the freight rate, say, from Covington, Va., to New York.

Mr. Hastings. It is about the same. I do not know what the Covington rate is. I think it is about 15 cents from Norway, and I think it is about the same.

Mr. Gaines. Fifteen cents per hundred?

Mr. Hastings. Per hundred pounds; about $3 a ton.

Mr. Gaines. Does anyone know the rate from Covington to New York?

Mr. Hastings. It is 14 cents; so that it is $2.80. That is 20 cents a ton.

Mr. Gaines. Twenty cents in favor of the American producer?

Mr. Hastings. Yes.

Mr. Boutell. What are the largest consumers of print paper—the three or four largest newspapers?

Mr. Hastings. The biggest consumers are the Hearst set of newspapers.

Mr. Boutell. Hearst is the largest consumer?

Mr. Hastings. I think he is the largest individual buyer of print paper.

Mr. Fordney. He is in favor of free trade on news print paper.

Mr. Hugo. I think so, if he is logical. If I was a big consumer it might affect me somewhat.

Mr. Boutell. Of course that includes a chain of papers.

Mr. Hugo. Yes; one in New York, and one in Chicago, and he had another one in San Francisco. I do not know how much truth there is in it, but I was told that Mr. Hearst's chain of newspapers consumed a thousand tons of paper in getting out an Easter edition one year. I can give you my authority for that if you want it.

Mr. Boutell. What are the next largest consumers?

Mr. Hugo. The New York papers, I presume, are the next largest consumers. The New York World is a large consumer, and the New York Herald and New York Times; and in Chicago, the large papers there. What are the largest papers in Chicago?

Mr. Hastings. The Tribune and the Record. The Tribune is the largest.

Mr. Hill. I have just been consulting the statistical reports of the Treasury for last year, and I find this to be the situation, that we exported to Great Britain 27,000,000 pounds of print paper, to Australia 9,000,000 pounds, to Japan 5,000,000 pounds, to Canada 6,000,000 pounds, to Cuba 7,000,000 pounds, to Argentina 4,500,000 pounds, and to Chile 4,500,000 pounds.

That which went to Canada paid a duty of 15 per cent to get into Canada. I suppose it went in free to Great Britain. Those are the largest consumers, making up a total of shipment of about 72,000,000 pounds of print paper to these various countries, some of them free trade and some of them with a duty; Canada with 15 per cent, amongst others. That paper went from these ports in the following amounts:

	Pounds.
Boston	20,000,000
New York	36,000,000
Portland	5,000,000
Willamette	2,500,000
Memphremagog	1,500,000
Niagara	1,000,000
Oswegatchie	1,000,000
Vermont, Vt	1,000,000
	72,000,000

Now, I assume you accept that statement?

Mr. HUGO. What is the aggregate of that?

Mr. HILL. About 72,000,000 pounds, going and coming. Was that paper sold at a less price, if you know anything about it, than it is sold for within the United States?

Mr. HUGO. I would like Mr. Hastings to answer that.

Mr. HILL. That is paper shipped all over the world, and shipped mainly from Boston and New York.

Mr. HASTINGS. I heard what you said.

Mr. HILL. Was it sold at a lower price than paper was sold for here?

Mr. HASTINGS. No. In the first place, that shipment which went to Canada, which excites your interest, was made for the first time from this country by a little mill in Minnesota at International Falls, which is on the border.

Mr. HILL. The records here show that this is continuous in every year and that it has increased this last year.

Mr. HASTINGS. Not going into Canada. I beg your pardon, not going into Canada, because they only put in 2,300 pounds there a few months ago.

Mr. HILL. The record shows that there was exported from the United States to Canada, of print paper, in 1906, 6,900,000 pounds; in 1907, 6,700,000 pounds; in 1908, 5,200,000; in 1909, 6,100,000 pounds; and in 1910, since the Payne tariff bill was passe , it has increased 50 per cent, and gone up to 9,600,000 pounds.   d

Mr. HASTINGS. That increase was paper that was made for the first time this year at International Falls, Minn., and on account of the freight rate as compared with the freight rate from the eastern mills and Quebec, they could afford to pay that 15 per cent duty and get into Canada at that particular point.

Mr. HILL. There is no record in the Government reports of any paper being exported through the port that you speak of over the northwest boundary. There is no record of any paper going out of that port.

Mr. HASTINGS. I do not know where the entries are made.

Mr. HILL. These shipments were made from Boston, New York, and Portland; from Willamette 2,500,000 pounds——

Mr. HUGO. From Willamette it might come into Canada; that is, into British Columbia.

Mr. RANDELL. There is one port there in Vermont, is there not?

Mr. HILL. How is it that we can sell 27,000,000 pounds of print paper in 1909 to Great Britain in competition with Sweden and Norway, and in competition with Canada, if we can not ship it to Canada on the same basis, right here, within a day's travel?

Mr. HASTINGS. I do not see how you can say on the same basis, because England is free.

Mr. HILL. Exactly.

Mr. HASTINGS. The duty in Canada is 15 per cent.

Mr. HILL. Yes; but this proposed plan is free.

Mr. HASTINGS. I will not go into the question of that.

Mr. GAINES. Do you mean sell it to England, proper, or to Canada?

Mr. HILL. Sell it to England, proper. How can we do it?

Mr. HASTINGS. The way we have been treated as manufacturers of paper in this country, any market we have we propose to hold onto.

If Congress does not propose to protect us in our home trade, we will hold onto what markets we have and can get.

Mr. HILL. I say the same thing.

Mr. HASTINGS. And we want to hold onto as much of that trade as we can, because they have stuck to us.

Mr. HILL. And you would, anyway?

Mr. HASTINGS. We would under the resen conditions, the way we are treated before the Legislature ofpthis dountry. That is the plain answer to it. As manufacturers we propose to hold any market we have, because you are trying to take away all our protection, and we are attacked upon every quarter in every way.

Mr. HILL. This exported paper is sold like most other such exports, at a less price than the same is sold for in the United States?

Mr. HASTINGS. Very little less.

Mr. HILL. But it is sold for somewhat less?

Mr. HASTINGS. In order to get the trade and keep it we might have to sell at less, and we would do it under the conditions to-day.

Mr. RANDELL. The situation is that unless the Congress of the United States allows you to have the American market so that you have a prohibitive tariff, you are going to sell to other people abroad at a lower price so as to hold that market?

Mr. HASTINGS. We propose to keep our plants running as long as we can, and then if we can not run them any longer we will pack up and get out of the business.

Mr. GAINES. Do you know anything about such conditions abroad, whether other nations have a smaller export price than their domestic price?

Mr. HASTINGS. They certainly do. The Germans have a regular arrangement by which they sell, by the sanction of the Government, at a less price in foreign countries.

Mr. GAINES. I know it has been proved here half a dozen times that in the steel industry the difference between the domestic and export prices in the United States is less than the difference between the domestic and export prices in every other country in the world.

Mr. HASTINGS. Yes; we know it is on paper. That is so in many other countries; notably, Germany through her Government railroads and other devices favor the plan of assaulting foreign markets by the German manufacturers.

Mr. LONGWORTH. Can you state approximately what that difference is in the case of Germany?

Mr. HASTINGS. No; I would not attempt to state, because I do not know, but it is a matter of record there that they are allowed to do it.

Mr. GAINES. Germany does not manufacture paper?

Mr. HASTINGS. Yes; she does. She is one of the largest exporters into the English market to-day on certain grades.

Mr. FORD. Is it true that the labor in the manufacturing of paper in this country receives more pay than that class of labor receives in any other country you know of, unless it might be Canada?

Mr. HASTINGS. Yes. The average in Canada is less than it is here.

Mr. FORDNEY. Well, take that for granted that that is true. Now, the price of your wood is higher here, by $4, as Mr. Hugo says, than in Canada. It seems that you must have a reasonable amount of protection, or else you will be at a great disadvantage with your neighbors, in the industry?

Mr. HASTINGS. Yes; and I want to state further, in answer to questions asked here by Mr. Clark and others as to why it was that there was an apparent rise in the price of paper since the duty was reduced, and then going on and saying further "What would it hurt you if we took all the duty off; it would still go up." The facts are that if you take the duty off you will find mills building in Canada; and they are to-day building in Canada, and there are mills which are being proposed, and financed in England, to the extent of as high as a thousand tons, to-day. Those mills are not in the market to-day, and they will not be next year, probably, to any extent, but at the end of five years you will find very little newspaper made in the United States, and it will all be made in Canada. That is not going to affect the price of the commodity. You take it all off and the price would not go down. We have $300,000,000 invested in our business, and all that we want is a fair chance to get our money back, and we want to run a legitimate business and get a profit out of it, and under this bill you propose to turn this business over to Canada, and we have got to get out of the business, and that is just as certain as you gentlemen are sitting in your seats.

Mr. FORDNEY. Do you know how much money is invested in the manufacture of paper and pulp in this country?

Mr. HASTINGS. Probably nearly $300,000,000.

Mr. FORDNEY. Yes.

Mr. HILL. Did not a very large paper manufacturer in the State of New York advocate before the country, this fall, a great reduction in the tariff, a gentleman by the name of Dix, for instance?

Mr. HASTINGS. I hardly think that the whole industry should be changed by the ambitions of a man to be elected to a high office in the State. He makes wall paper in one mill and print paper in another, and it makes no difference to him; he charges on the wall paper any price he pleases, and if he can come down here and argue you gentlemen into increasing the duty on wall paper he can even up on the other end.

Mr. HUGO. He can play both ends against the middle.

Mr. GAINES. I hope that a leading Democrat is not engaged in a trust. [Laughter.]

Mr. HASTINGS. I do not know. I do not know what is a Democrat and what is a Republican, to-day. I do not know where you draw the line. I have always been considered as a Republican, but I am getting over it pretty bravely.

Mr. HUGO. Well, I have not lost heart, so far as I am concerned. Now, in the first place, my first argument was that it is unfair to select one industry and ask us to take this reduction, particularly when every article that goes into the manufacture of that commodity is highly protected; and, in the second place, because the paper manufacturer gets no reciprocity, gets no consideration whatever, for the large amount of consideration that we give up.

In the third place, this whole question was fully debated in Congress and before this committee two years ago, and after the most careful consideration Congress gave us a duty of $3.75 a ton. Now, I would like to ask, if it is a fair question, why Congress should not tell us what has happened in the meantime, why we should not be treated in the same way now as we were treated two years ago? What has happened in the last 18 months that the duty on print paper should be taken off entirely, of $3.75 a ton?

Mr. ELLIS. The reciprocity treaty has been promulgated.

Mr. FORDNEY. They have changed the Republican platform adopted in Chicago.

Mr. RANDELL. The people are going to have some say instead of the Republican party, I would say, if suggestions are being made.

Mr. HUGO. Yes. We have been asked to state any new arguments here on this proposition. I say, what right have they to ask us to inform them of any new arguments any more than we have to ask to be informed what has happened in the meantime, if anything has happened, to justify the curtailing of this duty and putting us in any less favorable condition for competing with Canada that did not exist 15 months ago? I think we have just as much right to ask that as the other fellow has to ask what new arguments we have to advance why we should protect our own bread and butter.

In the next place, in regard to the question brought up here in regard to the importation of pulp wood from Canada, it was argued at that time, and it has been the fundamental argument of Mr. Mann from the start in this matter, that unless we held out the olive branch to Canada in the way of free trade and lower duties on print paper we would have no pulp wood from Canada. I have stated to you that there is more pulp wood coming in than there was three years ago, and that the price is $2 a cord less than it was three years ago, and that the price in the United States is simply limited by the demand of the United States, and if we give up this duty of $3.75 a ton on sulphite and $4.75 a ton on print paper we get absolutely no consideration as an industry for giving up those considerations.

Now, in the next place, this measure will defeat one of the strongest arguments that has been advanced in favor of it. It has been argued here, and has been argued through the press, that the great reason for this is that it will conserve the timber lands in the United States if this duty is taken off under the provisions of the bill; and there is the question in regard to whether the duty is taken off paper made from wood simply grown on lands in private ownership or grown on Crown lands. Now, suppose it is taken off of paper made out of wood grown in private ownership, what will be the result? That duty of $4.75 will be an object to the Canadian manufacturer, and he will come into the market as a competitor against us for wood grown in private ownership, and the amount coming into the United States will be lessened and the price will go up, and the American manufacturer will be obliged, instead of conserving, to devastate our forests, because our supply from Canada will be lessened, and we will be obliged to cut wood where we can get it better and cheaper. We are trying to conserve our forests. We spend thousands of dollars every year planting seedlings, and we have foresters. There is going to be no incentive now for us to do that, because we can go up into our woods and cut a cord of wood and get it cheaper than we can from Canada. We are trying to conserve the wood by getting it from Canada, and this taking off of all the duty will mean a greater demand for wood grown in private ownership, because it comes in free, whereas the wood from Crown lands will not be free. The result will be that our wood coming from Canada will be curtailed to that extent.

As I have stated, we have asked that a duty be fixed at an amount equal to the difference of the cost of production in Canada and in the United States, and I have stated what that duty is. I have not changed my figures at all from what we gave here two years ago, and that is that Canadian wood can be put down at the mills over there at $4 a cord less than we can get it for in this country. It takes a cord and a half of wood to make a ton of paper, which gives them an advantage, right there, of $6 a ton on the wood going into a ton of print paper. In addition to that, the labor is cheaper than it is in this country, and we simply ask that the duty be retained. We do not ask a prohibitive duty. I go on record now, so far as we are concerned, that we do not want a prohibitive duty. We want a duty that will give us a square deal, that will put us on the same basis as to cost of production as they are on in Canada, so as to equalize the difference, which is at least $6 a ton.

Now, we had confidence in this matter, that this would be argued and discussed by the Tariff Board, and members of the Tariff Board have been up through our section and we have opened our books to them and given them all the confidential information we had, and we have done everything we could to enlighten the Tariff Board and Congress and the President in this matter, and it seems to me that at this time we should not bring this matter up before those boards have reported on it.

If they have made any report it has not been a complete report, because the mills have not been examined completely through the West, and there has been little or no investigation made in Canada, and it seems to me it is only fair that this matter should remain dormant until you get a report from the Tariff Board that will state in dollars and cents whether we are telling the truth or not.

Mr. GAINES. About when did the Tariff Board begin this investigation of print paper?

Mr. HUGO. I do not think it has been over three months ago. They were up in our district, and we opened the books, and we are only too glad to give all the information we have got; and I want to tell you right now, if we can not demonstrate through the Tariff Board that all we want is a fair deal, I will say, take the duty off; because I can demonstrate that we can not compete with the manufacturers of paper in Canada, and when we get $6 duty it is not any more than we are entitled to. That seems to me to be a fair and square statement.

Mr. HILL. Mr. Chairman, it is time for us to adjourn, is it not?

Mr. HUGO. I thank you, Mr. Chairman and gentlemen, for this hearing, and I presume you will hear others to-morrow.

STATEMENT OF MR. F. J. SENSENBRENNER, OF NEENAH, WIS.

Mr. SENSENBRENNER. Mr. Chairman and gentlemen of the committee, this treaty goes a good deal further in its effect upon the paper industry than the Payne tariff bill did, not merely because of its effect upon news print paper, the quality of paper used by the daily newspapers, altogether, but in its effect upon book paper and wrapping paper.

Upon book papers which come within the range of price from $2\frac{3}{4}$, say, to 4 cents per pound, there is at present a duty of $10 per ton, and upon wrapping paper there is a duty of 35 per cent ad valorem, making it from $17.50 per ton to $28 per ton. But right upon that point I want to answer a point raised by Mr. Hill. The exportations of paper from this country to Canada include all gra es of paper—book papers, wrapping papers, writing papers, wall paper, and news paper. In Schedule A of the commodities to be put upon the free list, or rather the articles to be put upon the free list, those articles exported to Canada, it is stated that only 2,300 pounds of news print paper was exported from the United States into Canada in the year ending March 31, 1910.

Mr. HILL. On page 19 of this pamphlet you will find that 2,300 pounds of print paper, valued at not more than 2¼ cents per pound. Then, right below that, in the next item, of print paper valued above 2¼ cents per pound and not above 2½ cents a pound, the amount exported from the United States into Canada was 3,615,881 pounds. That went at a duty of 24 per cent.

Mr. SENSENBRENNER. I assumed that that tonnage included everything above 2½ cents.

Mr. HILL. No; there are three items in that table, of print paper. The first is print paper valued at not more than 2¼ cents per pound, of which there were 2,300 pounds exported into Canada. That was at 15 per cent. Then of print paper valued above 2¼ cents and not above 2½ cents per pound, there were 3,615,881 pounds exported into Canada, and that went in paying a duty of 24 per cent. Then of the third class of paper, above 2¼ cents and not above 4 cents, there was none that went into Canada.

Mr. SENSENBRENNER. We know of our own knowledge that considerable paper within that range of prices went into Canada.

Mr. McCALL. What page have you?

Mr. SENSENBRENNER. This is on page 19, the same as Mr. Hill has.

Mr. HILL. Then if you look on page 63 of this same pamphlet you will find there all classes of paper, and you will find that of print paper last year there were 9,613,000 pounds; but it does not classify it as it is classified on page 19.

Mr. SENSENBRENNER. Anything that is used for daily newspapers, or printing books, and everything else, including all paper, I assume from this classification, is in there.

Mr. HILL. Here was a factor in that tonnage of paper hangings not classified separately.

Mr. HASTINGS. Not the raw material.

Mr. HILL. This refers to print paper below 2½ cents a pound.

Mr. SENSENBRENNER. That is, this item of 9,613,000 pounds?

Mr. HILL. No; that includes everything.

Mr. SENSENBRENNER. That is what I assumed.

Mr. HILL. It does not include writing paper or wall paper.

Mr. SENSENBRENNER. No; but printing paper.

Mr. HILL. And it does not include other classes of paper. It simply includes print paper. If you will look on page 63, you will see paper hangings, so much; printing paper, so much; writing paper and envelopes, so much; and all other paper, so much; and the item of printing paper is 9,613,685 pounds; and in the classification which I read you of 72,000,000 pounds, it is classified purely as print paper, sent to these foreign countries.

Mr. Hastings. May I suggest that print paper as known in the trade is solely news print paper, the paper that is used for the printing of daily newspapers, and writing paper is anything from a slab up to fine writing paper. That is where the delusion comes in. Since July, 1908, they have been separated into printing paper valued at not above $2\frac{1}{2}$ cents, and so on.

Mr. Hill. Let me ask you a question. Can you not compete better on the class of news print paper below $2\frac{1}{2}$ cents a pound than you can on the higher classes of paper, and writing and envelope paper, where fine labor is required?

Mr. Sensenbrenner. Not so far as Canada is concerned.

Mr. Hill. I should imagine you could.

Mr. Sensenbrenner. So far as the world is concerned.

Mr. Hill. The more labor there is in it the less able we are to compete?

Mr. Sensenbrenner. Yes.

Mr. Gaines. That is, provided they make it at all. Canada, perhaps, does not make the higher grades of paper.

Mr. Hill. I do not know about that.

Mr. Sensenbrenner. Now, on the question of the reduction of the tariff upon the price of paper: In the early part of 1907 we had a period of extreme demand. The price, according to my recollection, was higher in 1908 than in 1909, and higher than it is to-day.

Mr. McCall. The time has come for the committee to take a recess. The members desire to go to the House. Is there anyone who desires to be heard on any other subject than print paper this afternoon? If not, I think we had better take a recess until to-morrow morning.

Mr. Gaines. It might suit the convenience of these gentlemen if we could meet this afternoon.

Mr. McCall. It was arranged so that we were to let the print-paper matter go over until to-morrow and finish it up then. These two gentlemen were put in this morning to suit their personal convenience.

Mr. Fordney. Will it be as convenient for you gentlemen to come before the committee to-morrow instead of this afternoon?

Mr. Sensenbrenner. If I may be given just a few minutes more I can finish.

Mr. Hastings. If you are not able to hear Mr. Sensenbrenner further now, would you receive his statement in printed form?

Mr. McCall. Yes.

Mr. Hastings. The other gentleman here would stay until to-morrow.

Mr. McCall. It is impossible for the committee to remain longer now.

Mr. Longworth. If we are going to adjourn until to-morrow, let this gentleman put his statement in writing.

Mr. Sensenbrenner. I will remain over, Mr. Chairman, until to-morrow.

(At 12 m. the committee adjourned until to-morrow, Tuesday, February 7, 1911, at 10.30 o'clock a. m.)

RECIPROCITY WITH CANADA.

COMMITTEE ON WAYS AND MEANS,
HOUSE OF REPRESENTATIVES,
Tuesday, February 7, 1911.

The committee met at 10.30 o'clock a. m., Hon. Samuel W. McCall (acting chairman) presiding.

Present: The acting chairman and Messrs. Hill, Boutell, Needham, Fordney, Gaines, Longworth, Ellis, Underwood, Pou, Randell, Broussard, and Harrison.

Mr. McCALL. The committee will be in order. Without objection, the clerk will note the presence of a quorum. There is a gentleman here, Mr. McCullough, who was introduced to me by Mr. Cooper, who desires to leave town at once, and who has a brief statement to make which I am informed will only take a very few minutes. Mr. McCullough, the committee will hear you.

STATEMENT OF E. W. McCULLOUGH, OF CHICAGO, ILL.

Mr. McCULLOUGH. Mr. Chairman and members of the Ways and Means Committee, I speak for the National Implement and Vehicle Association of the United States of America, representing the manufacturers and wholesalers, large and small, in all lines of agricultural implements and vehicles used in the tillage, harvesting, and transportation of crops. The capital employed in these lines approximates to $500,000,000. The employees number over 250,000. A careful canvass recently made of our membership shows that all who are interested in the development of trade with Canada favor reciprocity. We therefore desire to express our satisfaction with the reciprocal agreement submitted to Congress, believing it to be a most important first step toward more satisfactory trade relations with our northern neighbors. That is all, gentlemen.

Mr. McCALL. Are there any questions? That is all, then, Mr. McCullough.

Now, the gentlemen who were being heard upon the paper and pulp and wood schedule or provisions of the bill may proceed.

STATEMENT OF ALFRED S. HALL, ESQ., OF BOSTON, MASS.

Mr. HILL. Mr. Hall, will you not, before you start, give to the committee your understanding of the provisions of this bill, so that we may listen intelligently; I mean, so far as it relates to your particular industry?

Mr. HALL. Yes, sir.

Mr. BOUTELL. I did not hear your statement as to your occupation, and so on.

Mr. HALL. I practice law in Boston, and I hold quite a good many securities of the International Paper Co. as a trustee for others. I

175

am not a regular attorney of the International or any other paper organization; but having such interests, I have for some years had quite a familiarity with the paper-making industry in its relation to the newspapers and other interests—publishers and their companies.

Mr. HILL. I referred in my question to the provisions on pages 19, 20, and 24, as to the effect of this bill introduced by Mr. McCall upon your industry, as you understand it.

Mr. HALL. Yes, sir. I am very much obliged for that inquiry, and I do not intend to speak at length, but will just take up that matter, then.

Now, of course, if the paper makers in the United States get anything reciprocal from the passage of this act, it would be free wood into the United States. It is giving to Canada, right out, the opportunity to avail of the market for the manufactured paper; no hindrance, no duty whatever, remaining. Now, if we do not get that wood with entire freedom, we get nothing at all, and the title is misleading. I understand the correspondence that makes the interpretation, so far as the President's message goes, to mean that the Canadian Commissioners understood that the exclusion duty—that is, the export charge—that is set up by some of the Provinces of Canada on pulp wood coming into the United States, must be abolished before print paper should come into this country free. That correspondence would seem to me to have that interpretation—that the expectation of the Canadian representatives was that, not only from private lands but from Crown lands, pulp wood should come in here free.

Now, Mr. Chairman and gentlemen, I do not feel sure that the language that has been referred to by Mr. Hill here would accomplish that, and if it should fail of that, it would be a great misfortune and a matter of inadvertence, I think. I do not understand why there should have been in the bill any possibility of ambiguity. I do not understand now that there ought to be left by this committee any possible ambiguity about it. I do not suppose it matters what my own construction is, or even what any lawyer upon the committee may be satisfied is the true construction, or even what may be the construction of the whole committee, but the question is to have such language as a court of final resort will surely interpret according to the intention of the two Governments, and have that distinct. Now, having under consideration just about the same language that is in this draft of the bill that is before us, the Treasury Department has made an interpretation, which appears in Treasury Decisions (vol. 18, p. 207) and is numbered Treasury decision 30045, dated October 16, 1909, and in reviewing a decision previously made, No. 29968. The language is just about the same in the tariff act of August 5, 1909, as in this bill here, and in construing and making application of paragraphs 406 and 409 of the Payne Tariff Act of August 5, 1909, the Treasury Department says this:

As the records on file in the department do not show that any Provinces in the Dominion except Quebec and Ontario impose an extra duty, or prohibit exportation of pulp or paper or wood, all ground pulp from other Provinces comes in free. Mechanically ground wood pulp produced from pulp wood produced on private lands in the Provinces of Quebec and Ontario should be admitted free of duty.

Now, that langugage applied here would, as I understand the meaning of the bill, let in print paper absolutely free the instant this bill is passed—right away.

Mr. LONGWORTH. From where?

Mr. HALL. From private lands anywhere in Canada, in any Province.

Mr. LONGWORTH. Absolutely free?

Mr. HALL. Yes.

Mr. LONGWORTH. Then when would print paper from this country go into Canada free?

Mr. HALL. The very last paragraph of the bill says that it would not go in until from every part of Canada their print paper and pulp would come into this country free.

Mr. HILL. That is not the bill.

Mr. HALL. Well, no.

Mr. HILL. That is the message to Congress.

Mr. HALL. Yes; but the bill is to the same effect.

Mr. HILL. I do not care two straws what the Treasury Department has construed. They always construe to fit the case.

Mr. HALL. Well——

Mr. HILL. And a precedent, in my judgment, is not worth a cent, because another precedent will be established when the case arises. What I would like to know is—I do not know whether the other members of the committee want to know it or not—what, in your opinion, is the meaning of this language?

Mr. LONGWORTH. I think it is very important to know what the opinions of these gentlemen are, and how they construe this bill, who are opposing it.

Mr. HILL. That is exactly it; not how the Treasury Department would construe it, but how you construe it.

Mr. HALL. Very good; I will come to that in a minute. Now, the second proviso in the message was as has been stated, and I construe this last section of the bill as accomplishing just what that second proviso states in express words—that is, that until from every part of Canada pulp and paper can come into this country absolutely free—from every Province, that is, we have no benefits of the bill at all. Well, now, this Treasury decision would make plain what I say, if that be law, which I do not contend or concede it to be. Nevertheless, it shows the danger. I understand some court has adopted that same construction, holding that that construction is the law, and the correct interpretation of the tariff act of 1909, although I can not give such citation. That is a communication to me that I am not sure of from verification of my own. But it is of very great importance whether the United States is going to be able to get only wood from private lands or to get the Crown land wood.

As was stated here yesterday, there is a great abundance of pulp wood right at our doors now from Canada, and with the mills being located in Canada, as this act would bring about, as we believe, the consumption of that wood on private lands would be so great in this country and in Canada, too, that soon the resort must necessarily be to the Crown land wood; this market here, and the Canadian market, too, would put up the price of the private land wood, so that there must be a resort to the Crown land wood soon.

Mr. FORDNEY. Have you any idea how much private land there is in Canada, compared with the Crown lands?

Mr. HALL. Well, I have made that inquiry, and I understand that the wood on private lands, as compared with that on the Crown lands, would not be more than about one-fiftieth, and perhaps not more than one one-hundredth.

Mr. FORDNEY. Not more than one one-hundredth part?

Mr. HALL. That is what I understand.

Mr. LONGWORTH. I do not think you have answered Mr. Hill's question.

Mr. HALL. I am going to, right away.

Mr. LONGWORTH. I think we want to know that, first of all.

Mr. McCALL. I think Mr. Hall is coming to it. He is saying that there will be an ambiguity anyway, regardless of his opinion, and he bases that on the Treasury decision, which, as he understands, is upheld by some court, and now I think he is coming to the po n .

Mr. HALL. I am assuming to give my own opinion, as I understand about it.

Mr. LONGWORTH. I will ask you just what your view would be on the passage of this bill as it is written, not viewed in the light of any negotiations?

Mr. HALL. Yes.

Mr. LONGWORTH. Or any other agreement; as this bill stands, what is your opinion? Is not that it, Mr. Hill?

Mr. HILL. Yes; just give us your own opinion.

Mr. McCALL. Of what the courts would hold to be the law.

Mr. LONGWORTH. In other words, we want to know on what basis, exactly, these gentlemen are basing their opinion about this bill.

Mr. HILL. That is right.

Mr. BOUTELL. Just preliminary to that, I would like to have you give your opinion on this question. If this bill in its exact language should be enacted into law, and should by any method of appeal come before the Supreme Court of the United States for construction, do you apprehend that that tribunal in forming its opinion would feel authorized under the precedents to take into consideration any of this preliminary correspondence between the United States and the Dominion of Canada?

Mr. HALL. I think, Mr. Boutell, that the Supreme Court would give a great deal of weight to that correspondence, as interpreting it. I think any court does that.

Mr. McCALL. That would be in a question of doubt.

Mr. HALL. In a question of doubt.

Mr. McCALL. In a question of doubt as to the meaning of Congress.

Mr. HALL. Yes. Then the court always goes, as I understand it, into the circumstances that attend at the enactment of the law, and that would take into review that correspondence, I believe. Now, apart from that correspondence, gentlemen. I should say as a lawyer that print paper could come in here right away without the Provinces being obliged to let in any Crown land wood.

Mr. HILL. Now, may I ask you a question right there?

Mr. HALL. Yes.

Mr. HILL. On page 24 of the bill it provides: ' Pulp of wood mechanically ground; pulp of wood, chemical, bleached or unbleached; news print paper and other paper, and paper board;'' and this specifies all these things, but does not say anything about the land.

Mr. HALL. Yes.

Mr. HILL. Now, if you turn right back on page 20, is not the language clear and explicit that these things on page 24 must have been provided for in Canada to be admitted there, all of them, free of duty, before the provisions on pages 19 and 20 go into effect at all?

Mr. HALL. I should say not.

Mr. HILL. Let me read the language.

Mr. HALL. Yes; I read it.

Mr. HILL. It reads:

Provided, That the articles above enumerated, the growth, product, or manufacture of the Dominion of Canada, shall be exempt from duty when the President of the United States shall have satisfactory evidence and shall make proclamation that the following articles, the growth, product, or manufacture of the United States or any of its possessions (except the Philippine Islands and the islands of Guam and Tutuila), are admitted into the Dominion of Canada free of duty.

And then on page 24 it specifies what those articles are.

Mr. HALL. Yes.

Mr. HILL. Now, why has not the President got to find that Canada has acted and admitted all these things free before our legislation goes into effect at all?

Mr. HALL. Because in the correspondence it is recognized, and the fact is, that it is not Canada which imposes these export charges.

Mr. HILL. I will get to that by and by.

Mr. HALL. That comes in right now.

Mr. GAINES. That is a part of the bill I would like to follow.

Mr. HALL. Yes.

Mr. GAINES. What is your reason for saying that?

Mr. HALL. I say the reason is that it is not the Canadian Government which imposes these export charges and stands in the way of our getting free wood from Crown lands, but it is the provincial laws. And now, the change that I want here is, on the twentieth page, after the words "shall have been imposed," to interline this——

Mr. GAINES. Whereabouts?

Mr. HALL. In the sixth line on the twentieth page. We could fix this bill and have it right, I think, so that there would not be any ambiguity or misleading construction possible. In the sixth line on the twentieth page I would insert after the word "imposed" the words, "by Canada or any Province thereof," and I think just that would accomplish it pretty much, but I would put in the seventh line, after the word "used," the words "in the United States." In the ninth line, again, I would insert the words "in the United States" after the word "used," and then I would have a proviso in the twelfth line, and I think this should be in not only for the paper schedules, but in regard to all these provisos that are in the bill. I would insert after the word "duty" in the twelfth line on the twentieth page the words "subject to the several foregoing provisos." There are quite a lot of provisos in this bill.

Mr. LONGWORTH. After what word?

Mr. HALL. After the word "duty."

Mr. LONGWORTH. Then you would put in what words?

Mr. HALL. "Subject to the several foregoing provisos."

Mr. LONGWORTH. May I ask you a question at that point?

Mr. HALL. Yes.

Mr. LONGWORTH. If you will turn to the treaty agreement, page 6, and look at the proviso on page 6, what, in your opinion, would be the effect of incorporating that proviso in this bill?

Mr. HALL. I think to incorporate it would help to make plain that the real intent was that on both sides there should be absolute freedom, and that there should not be let in here free paper until we had free wood. I think that would help us, because it would make it apparently more reciprocal than it is now. It would make it much plainer; because then the court would say, "Why Canada has seen to it that this language is not ambiguous nor equivocal as to them, and it is fair that the United States should have just as good a construction as they have secured."

Mr. HILL. Now, as far as we have got with the agreement, do you agree that the language on page 24 gives to the United States the freedom of the market of Canada for everything up to 4 cents a pound, wood pulp, paper and everything, up to 4 cents a pound?

Mr. McCALL. Mr. Hill, if you will permit me to interrupt there, before the hearings began I received a letter from Mr. Pepper, the commissioner, asking that that be stricken from the bill.

Mr. HILL. That is all right; but Mr. Pepper is not going to vote on this bill.

Mr. McCALL. Yes; but I wanted you to understand that Mr. Pepper asked that that be stricken from the bill.

Mr. HILL. Mr. Pepper has not got to vote on this.

Mr. LONGWORTH. He referred to the last clause of the bill?

Mr. McCALL. Yes; the last clause of the bill.

Mr. FORDNEY. The chairman said the other day that no amendment to this bill could be offered or made in this committee.

Mr. HILL. That is the reason I want to know what the witness understands about this.

Mr. McCALL. I doubt, Mr. Fordney, whether the chairman meant it in that sense.

Mr. FORDNEY. That is what he said.

Mr. McCALL. He meant if the amendment contradicted the terms of the agreement. Now, the chairman received a letter from Mr. Mr. Knox to the effect that there is no tentative agreement between this country and Canada in regard to pulp and print paper, and his letter must be accepted as authoritative upon that point; so that it is open to the committee entirely.

Mr. LONGWORTH. In other words, the amendment of one of these provisos would not affect the agreement. In other words, these are not an agreement; but these are the contingencies upon which the agreement might be arrived at.

Mr. McCALL. Yes. Secretary Knox says this is a subject on which there is no agreement between the commissioners of the two Governments.

Mr. GAINES. The chairman of the committee certainly did not mean that we could not adopt an amendment to the bill.

Mr. FORDNEY. He said that; but I do not believe him and do not now.

Mr. McCALL. I say I think he meant that in a certain sense; that he meant taking the agreement so far as it was an agreement between the two countries, if we made an amendment in the bill that was not in line with that agreement, it would destroy that agreement and throw the matter back into negotiation. That is entirely serious, that part of it; but on this point I understand from the State Department that the commissioners of the two countries were not in agreement.

Mr. LONGWORTH. On page 2 of the letter of Mr. Fielding and Mr. Paterson, near the bottom of the page, there is this language:

It is necessary that we should point out that this is a matter in which we are not in a position to make any agreement.

Mr. McCALL. Yes.

Mr. HILL. May I ask further: On page 24 the language covers everything from the wood up to a finished product not exceeding 4 cents a pound in value, going from the United States into Canada?

Mr. HALL. I think that was intended so, and it would rather seem that it should be so.

Mr. HILL. It should include the wood as well as pulp?

Mr. HALL. Yes.

Mr. HILL. In both cases?

Mr. HALL. Yes.

Mr. HILL. Now, the provisions on pages 19 and 20 do not take effect until that is done. What is it your understanding, under the provisions on pages 19 and 20, that we are to grant to Canada?

Mr. HALL. Well, that we grant them everything; that is, we grant them free entrance of pulp of every kind, and free paper up to the 4-cent limit, without any qualifications or terms whatever. And now, I do not consider these suggestions of my own as being really amendments to the bill. I consider them corrections of language, to make it clear and free from ambiguity; and as I said before, how I would guess the court would construe it, or how any member of the committee would guess, is not so very material, anyway, but it is material to have it so that a court must construe it in accordance with the intention of the Congress. This is before this committee now; that is, you are the Congress now; it has got away from the President, as I understand it, and is here, and the responsibility is on this committee to make this language unmistakable and clear.

Mr. HILL. Do you understand that the language on pages 19 and 20 differentiates between private-land pulp and Provinces where there are no restrictions and Crown lands where there are restrictions?

Mr. HALL. Well, I am afraid that that distinction exists.

Mr. HILL. What is your opinion about this language? In your opinion, does it exists?

Mr. HALL. Well, if I have to go before the court I do not want to be held, nor to have the interests I represent held, to any position here, because I want free scope to contend——

Mr. HILL. Either way?

Mr. HALL. Either way; but I should, guess, honestly, that whereas the Canadian commissioners, and probably the American parties who got this up, too, did think that paper should not come in here free until the Provinces took off those charges, nevertheless, that was not assured. Mr. Mann, of the House, has given great study to this, and he says that it lets in paper free right away, without taking off any of those exclusion duties of the Provinces, and the newspaper publishers, I understand, say so, and they are scattering circulars around the country.

Mr. HILL. Do you think so?

Mr. HALL. I should myself prefer to be on the other side of the case, and contend that, in view of all the correspondence, it did not mean that.

Mr. HILL. That it treats Canada as a whole on pages 19 and 20?

Mr. HALL. Yes.

Mr. HILL. And that there is no distinction between one Province and another, no distinction between privately owned lands and public lands.

Mr. HALL. Well, I know that is the way it ought to be, that is the way it was intended to be, and I would fight for that construction; but I should not feel at all sure that I could carry it. [Laughter.]

Mr. POU. If these amendments that you suggest are incorporated in the bill and one of the Provinces, we will assume, should decline to agree that the Crown land wood should be admitted into this country free, would not the whole treaty fail, then?

Mr. HALL. It would not fail; it would delay the admission of free paper until that was taken off, and it would not delay the operation of the bill.

Mr. POU. The language you have put in here, does it not put it up to the several Provinces?

Mr. HALL. It does put it up to the several Provinces, yes; and that is where it belongs, too: but it would not delay the general operation of the bill a minute. It would delay the importation of paper free until the Provinces took off these charges.

Mr. HILL. As a whole, off all the items? Not only paper, but these two clauses would not go into operation at all until that was done, would they, under your construction of the language?

Mr. HALL. That is so, and that is what the Canadian commissioners expected the effect to be.

Mr. McCALL. What do I understand you to say?

Mr. HALL. The Canadian commissioners contemplated that there would not be any free paper brought in here until the export charges were taken off in all the Provinces.

Mr. HILL. How do you know that?

Mr. HALL. Because the correspondence indicates it; that is, that they supposed that the American Government was smart enough to see to it that that was made the act, too. I do not know whether or not you have seen the Canadian bill. They do not have any doubt in theirs. They fix it so that they do not have any of these conditions offered at all, you know. Why, they are going to have free importation—exportation here—of paper. We are going to receive that with open arms. They contemplate that, and they do not allude to any of these things that belong to us to take care of—that is, these export duties from the Provinces.

Mr. HILL. Have you a copy of that bill there?

Mr. HALL. I have. Here it is. And now what is the reason gentlemen, we should not put in just these little verbal corrections? They are not amendments; they are the corrections that I should think any committee would insist upon making in order to have language plain, and to have it carry a meaning so that we will not have to go to the courts and will not have a row and fuss and contention and litigation over what ought to be plain; and just a few words inserted there would make this plain, and would accomplish fair play, if we are going to have a reciprocity agreement.

Mr. LONGWORTH. What do you want to insert?

Mr. HALL. I want to put in, in the twentieth line——

Mr. LONGWORTH. I mean, what is your object?

Mr. HALL. My object is to accomplish that there shall not be free paper here until we have free wool, not only from private lands but from the Crown lands of Canada. That is what I want to get, and to have that assured, too.

Mr. LONGWORTH. In other words, do you want the present duties against print paper imported from Canada to remain until every Province of Canada has removed all restrictions on the importation of wood?

Mr. HALL. Yes; I do.

Mr. LONGWORTH. Against the export of pulp wood into this country?

Mr. HALL. Yes.

Mr. LONGWORTH. That is it.

Mr. HALL. Yes.

Mr. LONGWORTH. Now, you fear that under this bill as it stands, immediately upon its taking effect, print paper could be imported into this country free of duty from any Province which imposes no restriction, is that it?

Mr. HALL. Yes; or from those which do.

Mr. LONGWORTH. Or from those which do impose restriction, if that print paper is made from wood cut from private lands?

Mr. HALL. Yes.

Mr. LONGWORTH. And, on the contrary, the Canadian duties on print paper imported into Canada from this country should all remain until the last Province of Canada had removed those restrictions?

Mr. HALL. Yes.

Mr. LONGWORTH. That is it?

Mr. HALL. Yes; it is.

Mr. LONGWORTH. You would not object to this treaty if it was made clear that the print paper should not go onto the free list in this country until Canada had removed all restrictions?

Mr. HALL. Well, yes; I should be obliged to object still; and I do. All the paper manufacturers in the country—we have sort of put our heads together, you know—we all feel obliged to oppose it after it is made clear, and just as good as it can be, because this great industry we think can not stand an equal chance as against Canada after the duties are taken off, and it is not a great duty that we have now, and we think that it ought to stand.

Mr. FORDNEY. If it should become a law, you would like to see it amended so that some of the sting might be taken out?

Mr. HALL. Yes. Well, now, I do not intend to talk on the general proposition, because it was thrashed out in 1909, and the paper manufacturers stand just as they did then, and I think that they are sincere in their feeling that these lines would be hard. It would make it ambiguous and throw it right over so that they could send in free paper here and not have those export charges on Crown land wood removed. That is not a fair game, anyway, and it would be too bad, and it would be too bad for this committee, I think. I do not know what a committee is for unless it is to get the measure correct, anyway, when it is sent along. What is the reference to the committee for unless they have that liberty and obligation?

Now, I am just going to state again, if I may, what I think is the practicable thing, as some members of the committee may have come in since I stated it before. My suggestion would be that on the twentieth page you should interline on the sixth line, after the word "imposed," the words "by Canada or any Province thereof." Then in the seventh line, after the word "used," put in the words "in the United States," and insert after the word "used" in the ninth line, also the words "in the United States;" and then in the twelfth line, on page 20, after the word "duty," put in the words "subject to the several foregoing provisos."

Mr. McCALL. Mr. Hall, if you put in after the word "impos d" the language you have suggested, "by Canada or any Province thereof," where you are describing wood used in the United States, might it not be held that you were putting a restriction on the exportation of wood, and that it would have to be shown that it was to be used in the United States?

Mr. HALL. Your suggestion there I think is very good, and may be of value. If after the word "imposed" we put "by Canada or any Province thereof," and then put in the twelfth line "subject to these provisos," I think that is important in order to have the act go into effect.

Mr. Pou. Where do you want these provisions put, in line 12?

Mr. HALL. After the word "duty" in the twelfth line.

Mr. Pou. What do you want put there?

Mr. HALL. "Subject to the foregoing provisos." There are others relating not to paper matters.

Mr. McCALL. There is something about seal, herring, whale, and fish oil?

Mr. HALL. Yes; I think so.

Mr. HILL. Do you think the language of this Canadian bill absolutely contemplates complete reciprocity on paper and wood?

Mr. HALL. Yes.

Mr. HILL. Then why not use the same language as they use, so that it would read, after stating the articles:

Provided, That such wood pulp, paper, or board, being the products of the United States, shall only be admitted free of duty into Canada from the United States when such wood pulp, paper, or board, being the products of Canada, are admitted from all parts of Canada free of duty into the United States.

Mr. HALL. Because the correspondence does show, and they say right out in the correspondence, "Why, Canada has nothing to do with this export charge at all. That is a matter for the several Provinces." And having given us that warning, we have got to put that in.

Mr. GAINES. Mr. McCall, there is no reciprocity in that feature. Was there intended to be? [Laughter.]

Mr. McCALL. I would not like to express an opinion upon that point, and you have a very acute mind, and you have read the correspondence, and you can form your own opinion.

Mr. GAINES. I have such a profound regard for the capacity as well as the personal acumen of the author of the bill, that I would substitute his judgment even for my own.

Mr. McCALL. It may be that the putative author is not entitled to the credit for all that is in the bill.

Mr. LONGWORTH. Mr. Hall says that in the correspondence it is evident that it was not the intention of the Canadian Government to delay the operation of the free list, here. What was your statement there?

Mr. HALL. That the Canadian commissioners did not expect that we would let in paper free until they had made the wood free.

Mr. LONGWORTH. From every Province?

Mr. HALL. Yes; and Mr. Fielding in his address, since he went back to the House of Commons up at Ottawa, said that just as plainly as he could, as I read the report of his utterance. And if we do not come up to what they thought we would surely insist on and what they granted, really it seems as if we are really giving them even more than they dreamed of asking or contemplating at all.

Mr. LONGWORTH. In Mr. Fielding's letter it seems to me that this language is misinterpreted. He says:

The provisions you are proposing to make respecting the conditions upon which these classes of pulp and paper may be imported into the United States free of duty must necessarily be for the present inoperative.

Mr. HALL. Well, they would be, of course, if we make this as I say it ought to be. They would have to wait until the Provinces took off that export charge. I do not think that would be a great while, but they would have to wait until that was done; no doubt about it.

Mr. GAINES. Under the provisions of this bill it seems to me we do not make it incumbent on them to reduce anything at all, because we go on to provide that when certain articles are admitted into Canada free of duty, and the President makes proclamation of the fact, then those things, including print paper, shall be admitted here free of duty, and although there has been a lot of talk about requiring the Canadian Provinces to remove their restrictions on the introduction of logs and pulp wood, and so forth, as a consideration for it, when it comes to drafting the bill no such requirement is put into it, and no such conditions, as it seems to me.

Mr. HALL. Well, on page 20 there is the only one that I see, and that is not explicit and distinct enough so that minds can agree in its construction, and that is what I am asking to have brought about. I am very much obliged to you for your attention.

The CHAIRMAN. We are glad to have heard you, Mr. Hall.

STATEMENT OF ARTHUR C. HASTINGS.

Mr. HASTINGS. Mr. Chairman and gentlemen, I would like to make some corrections in regard to the questions asked in yesterday's hearing by Mr. Hill as to the exportation of paper into Canada from the United States, as it appeared in this reciprocity agreement. On page 19, Mr. Hill, you seemed to have somewhat misunderstood in regard to the amount of paper which had been imported into Canada from the United States. It gives there 3,600,000 pounds. The value of that paper, by their own statement, was 6½ cents a pound, showing that it was not print paper. The amount of print paper, which is noted in the same column, was 2,300 pounds; and although they call the next section "print paper," it is not print paper, but is printing paper, which is an entirely different thing, because anything that is to be printed upon could be called printing paper.

On page 63 we have, of printing paper, 9,000,000 pounds, to which you called our attention as the quantity which had been imported into Canada during the year 1910. You will find that that figures in the valuation at 4½ cents a pound.

Mr. McCALL. That is on page 63?

Mr. HASTINGS. That is on page 63. Mr. Hill was wondering how it was that we could send paper into Canada.

Mr. HILL. Yes.

Mr. HASTINGS. It is paper that Canada, at the present moment, does not manufacture; it is the finer grades of paper.

I desire to appear before this committee representing the manufacturers of paper of the United States, of all grades of paper, and all grades of pulp. We view this proposed or so-called reciprocity with great alarm, as manufacturers. While it is true we do not believe that for a few—possibly two or three—years it will make very much difference, with certain grades of paper, because Canada will not manufacture those grades, yet every ton of paper that Canada does bring or send in here, of any grade, will displace some paper of some quality, because the country absorbs just so many tons in a year, or so much from Canada, and there will be a change of manufacturing going on in this country which will be ruinous to many mills which are now running.

Mr. RANDELL. Would that reduce the price?

Mr. HASTINGS. Would it reduce the price?

Mr. RANDELL. Yes.

Mr. HASTINGS. Well, the probabilities are that it would, and very seriously.

Mr. RANDELL. Then the shipping of paper to England at about cost price, at a much less price than it is sold for here, does not that raise the price of paper?

Mr. HASTINGS. Shipping paper to England?

Mr. RANDELL. Yes.

Mr. HASTINGS. I made some inquiries, after the statement I made yesterday, from a gentleman who does the exporting and he says up to this time they have secured really a better price for paper they have exported, on the average, than they have for the same paper in this country, due possibly to good quality and due to the fact that a great deal of that exportation has gone to southern countries, where they have had the trade. Gradually Canada is getting that trade.

Mr. RANDELL. If you can compete in those markets, why can you not hold your own in this country without keeping the price up on these people?

Mr. HASTINGS. We can compete in this country often by reason of location.

Mr. RANDELL. In England is your trade increasing or not?

Mr. HASTINGS. No, not as a whole.

Mr. RANDELL. What do you mean by "not as a whole"?

Mr. HASTINGS. It is decreasing now.

Mr. RANDELL. Do the statistics show that the amount of exportation has been increasing constantly for 10 or 12 years?

Mr. HASTINGS. It will go down rapidly from now on, in England.

Mr. RANDELL. Why?

Mr. HASTINGS. Because Canada is making a very much better paper than she ever did before, and much of our trade there has been because of the excellence of our paper as compared with that from Norway and Sweden.

Mr. RANDELL. Then your fear of the taking down of this tariff wall is a fear of what is going to take place instead of a fear of what has been in the past?

Mr. HASTINGS. Yes.

Mr. RANDELL. That is, it has been unnecessary in the past and has had a tendency to put up the price in this country under normal conditions?

Mr. HASTINGS. No, sir. Under the $6 tariff under the McKinley bill paper was sold cheaper than ever before.

Mr. RANDELL. Then reducing the tariff did not reduce the price?

Mr. HASTINGS. Not necessarily.

Mr. RANDELL. Is not that purely and simply for the reason that both tariffs, both the $6 tariff and the one that averages, as you say, $4.75, are prohibitive?

Mr. HASTINGS. Not at all. They are not, because you are getting into this country to-day every pound of paper that Canada has over and above her own use, so that it is not prohibitive.

Mr. RANDELL. The exportation from Canada all comes to this country, then?

Mr. HASTINGS. Practically all; it is her market. They are coming in.

Mr. RANDELL. Does that paper go to England?

Mr. HASTINGS. Very little. Some of it does, and has been going there.

Mr. RANDELL. Does not that show that Canada is competing with you simply in places where it is more convenient, and that she really cannot compete with you in England and other countries?

Mr. HASTINGS. They have competed with us there, and are doing so. But you must remember, Mr. Randell, that paper, like any other commodity, seeks the market in which it can be sold best, and that the supply and demand of the world is what affects the markets and the market conditions.

Mr. RANDELL. And proximity cuts some figure?

Mr. HASTINGS. And proximity.

Mr. RANDELL. And transportation?

Mr. HASTINGS. Yes, certainly.

Mr. RANDELL. And all the paper that Canada can export comes into the United States because the amount is so small that it can be absorbed in the places that are most convenient; and therefore Canada can not compete in England, either.

Mr. HASTINGS. No; you do not understand the conditions of the business. Very often the contracts are made for a year or 18 months, and she might compete and sell all to this market, and then be out of the market entirely.

Mr. RANDELL. If you can not compete under general market conditions with Canada, you certainly could not in England; I think I understand that.

Mr. HASTINGS. I do not think that, at all.

Mr. RANDELL. I can understand how there would be certain places in the United States that might absorb, say, 2,000,000 tons; I believe that is about the amount that is shipped?

Mr. HASTINGS. No; you are mistaken as to your figures. There is not 2,000,000 tons made in both the United States and Canada.

Mr. RANDELL. Two million tons?

Mr. HASTINGS. I do not know to what you are referring.

Mr. RANDELL. Mr. Hill gave the figures.

Mr. HASTINGS. Canada exported about 60,000 tons last year, at that ratio.

Mr. RANDELL. That is, into this country?

Mr. HASTINGS. Into this country. Now, she exports, altogether——

Mr. RANDELL. Canada exported 2,000,000 tons, or is that the manufacture in Canada, altogether?

Mr. HASTINGS. I do not know what that is. That is not paper.

Mr. RANDELL. What is the total manufactured in this country?

Mr. HASTINGS. In this country, of all kinds of paper, the total is about 5,000,000 tons, and of news paper the total is about 1,300,000 pounds. Canada makes, altogether, about 150,000 tons, of which she exports to this country, or to some country, about 90,000 tons. Speaking as to what the price would be, I wish to state that I have what purports to be a copy mailed January 24 from the office of the American Newspaper Publishers' Association, to all members of that association, marked "Confidential," which reads as follows:

For your confidential information, I take pleasure in advising you that the negotiations of the United States Government with Canada provide for the admission of print paper and wood pulp free of duty when made from wood cut on private lands or free from restrictions of exportation.

If ratified by Congress, this arrangement will immediately and automatically insure a full supply of print paper free of duty, and will exert pressure upon provincial authorities, which will ultimately force them to remove their restrictions on exportation of pulp wood. The advance thus far made is a matter for mutual congratulation among members of the association.

Yours, faithfully,   [HERMAN RIDDER, *President.*

You will note the date of that is January 24, while no manufacturer of news paper or any kind of paper that I know of was in any way consulted as to what the effect would be of a bill that was entered on the 26th. Now, as I understand it, we are all manufacturers and we are interested in this bill as such, and yet the people to whom the benefits are to accrue have inside information.

I do not care to extend my remarks here in a general way, except to say that in my estimation this bill as proposed is the greatest blow that was ever aimed at an industry in the United States, and it is not fair and it is not proper. If we are going on to a free-trade basis for everything, all right; we will take our chances, as we have to, and as we may have to in the next year; but to pick this one industry out of the thousands in this country and treat us differently from what you do other industries is not a fair deal, under any circumstances, and I want to go on record to that effect. As I say, I do not care to take the time of the committee. There are other gentlemen here who want to be heard. If there are any questions to be asked, I shall be glad to answer them, but as to the effect of this, I want to be on record.

Mr. FORDNEY. I did not know until just now that the Province of Quebec had put an embargo on wood.

Mr. HASTINGS. That is within one or two months.

Mr. FORDNEY. I did not know until now that Quebec had put on an embargo, but that is true, too?

Mr. HASTINGS. Yes.

Mr. FORDNEY. So that there is from no Province in Canada to-day any freedom of transportation of wood from Canada into this country for the making of pulp, is there, except from the deeded lands?

Mr. HASTINGS. New Brunswick is open, unless there has been some change very recently. It always has been.

Mr. FORDNEY. Oh, yes; I was speaking of the Dominion.

Mr. LONGWORTH. You and the other members of your association approve this bill as Mr. Hall has suggested that it be amended?

Mr. HASTINGS. I did not follow Mr. Hall as closely as I might have, and his was a legal opinion; but we do fear it, because of the fact that on the 24th of January it was satisfactory to the men who desire to get free paper. From that fact alone I am afraid of it, and I do not care what the wording is.

Mr. FORDNEY. Have you any idea of the relative proportions of land in Canada on which there is timber—that is deeded land—as compared with the Crown land?

Mr. HASTINGS. It is proportionately small. I could not tell you that.

Mr. FORDNEY. I used to deal in lands in Canada, and I operated in Canada, and it is my opinion that there is none at all except a few scattering pieces, besides those in Indian reservations, which have all been picked up since the embargo was put upon logs at the time the Dingley bill became a law; so that there is no possibility of getting any wood to amount to anything from Canada, from those lands.

Mr. HASTINGS. I do not agree with you there, because from the Government reports from Quebec, out of a possible exportation of 800,000 to 900,000 cords, they claim that only 140,000 cords came from Crown lands.

Mr. FORDNEY. Yes; but what I mean is, in proportion to the great forests there.

Mr. HASTINGS. I think that is so.

Mr. FORDNEY. The amount of deeded lands is very small indeed?

Mr. HASTINGS. Yes.

Mr. HILL. Is Mr. Hall still here? He seems to have left. It makes no difference. Unless there is objection from the committee, I ask that the Canadian bill be printed in the record as a supplement to Mr. Hall's statement, and also that Treasury Decision 30591 shall be printed following the Canadian bill. I suppose Mr. Hall would have no objection to that.

Mr. HASTINGS. I think not, from what he said.

Mr. HILL. Does any other gentleman desire to be heard?

Mr. HASTINGS. Mr. Sensenbrenner, because of sickness in his family, was obliged to return, and he asked Mr. Barrett to represent him this morning.

STATEMENT OF EDGAR G. BARRETT, OF NEW YORK CITY, N. Y.

Mr. BARRETT. Mr. Sensenbrenner began his remarks and expected to return to the subject this morning, but found it was impossible, as he had to return home. He prepared some memoranda, and I think possibly that matter had better go right in here about as he prepared it.

The agitation of the past four years for the reduction in or the removal of the duty on news print paper and mechanically ground wood and chemical pulp has been founded pretty much altogether on the argument that in order to preserve and prolong the life of the paper industry in this country it is essential that the pulp-wood forests of Canada be made available to our manufacturers, and that that was impossible unless we conceded a reduction of our duties on news print paper and pulp or made the importation entirely free. As you gentlemen of the committee undoubtedly know, Quebec issued an order in council nearly a year ago prohibiting the exportation of wood cut from Crown lands, thus following the example set by Ontario something over 11 years ago, and the bill now under consideration gives us no relief from the prohibition. Undoubtedly also you know that on all pulp wood cut from Canadian privately owned lands there is not now, nor has there ever been, any restriction of any kind or character upon the exportation to this country.

Congressman Mann in a recent interview said that if the bill under consideration becomes a law Canadian paper and pulp made from wood cut from privately owned lands will immediately be admitted into this country free.

Mr. Herman Ridder, president of the American News Publishers' Association, in a confidential letter, dated January 24, addressed to members of his association two days before the trade agreement was submitted to the Congress by the President, and in a confidential letter of January 27, expresses the same opinion.

If the construction put upon the proposed bill by Messrs. Mann and Ridder is correct and the bill becomes a law, not only will we not increase the Canadian pulp wood supply available to us but we will further restrict it. For surely, to secure admission of their paper and pulp products into this country free of duty, the Canadian manufacturers may be trusted to make all of such products out of wood cut from privately owned lands, and competition with us for such wood will undoubtedly deprive us of that source of supply to the extent of their requirements, which in a comparatively short time will undoubtedly absorb the entire supply.

During the last year our manufacturers received from Canada of wood cut from privately owned lands between 700,000 and 800,000 cords, to which extent our available supply will undoubtedly be curtailed very promptly, thus forcing us to have recourse to our own forests for our entire requirements, and the natural result is a quicker devastation of them and the gradual transference of the industry to Canada.

Ours is the only industry the manufacture of whose product furnishes employment to a great deal of labor (and the like of whose product is manufactured extensively in Canada) singled out for the free and unrestricted competition of Canada.

When the present law was under consideration two years ago the paper manufacturers proved conclusively, not only by reason of the materially greater cost of wood and labor but because of the admission into Canada free of duty of a number of articles American manufacturers are obliged to use and import upon which they pay a considerable duty, as per schedule hereto appended; that the difference in cost of manufacture in this country and in Canada of the several grades affected by the bill under consideration was and is higher than the present rates of duty. In spite of such duties, during the fiscal year ended June 30, 1910, there was an increase in the importation of Canadian paper into this country of over 240 per cent.

My conclusion is, first, that our industry is entitled to protection to the extent of the difference in cost of manufacture here and in Canada, and the present rates of duty are, in fact, not high enough to afford us that; and, secondly, the present bill contains no element of reciprocity. It proposes to admit Canadian paper and pulp free without giving us in return Canadian pulp wood, which unquestionably would result, as heretofore stated, in the gradual transference of the industry from this country to Canada.

(The following table submitted by Mr. Barrett is here printed in full as follows:)

Articles.	Canadian tariff item No.	Amount of duty into Canada.	United States tariff item No.	Amount of duty into United States.
China clay...................	295	Free.....................	90	$2.50 per ton.
Chloride of lime.............	208	.....do.....................	8	$4 per ton; ¼ cent per pound.
Feltings.....................	567	Great Britain, 30 per cent; others, 35 per cent.	....	
Alum........................	212	Great Britain, free; others, 10 per cent.	4	1.4 cents per pound.
Copper-wire cloth............	418	Great Britain, 17½ per cent; France, 22½ per cent; others, 25 per cent.	199	45 per cent.
Aniline dyes.................	203	Free.....................	15	30 per cent.
Ultramarine.................	240	.....do.....................	50	3 cents per pound.

In this schedule there are a few things to be noted. One company, for instance, in this country manufacturing book paper uses at least $50,000 worth a year of china clay. The duty on that is $2.50 a ton into the United States. It goes into Canada free. The duty on chloride of lime, used in bleaching, is $4 a ton into the United States, and it goes into Canada free, and so on.

Mr. Sensenbrenner wished me to express his regrets that he could not address the committee further to-day and answer questions that might be asked.

It seems to me that in this discussion I have heard practically only the words "print paper." I am not a print-paper manufacturer. We manufacture the higher grades of paper, manila paper; we manufacture sulphite; we manufacture other grades; and the book paper men, who could be better represented, of course, by Mr. Sensenbrenner, as he is a manufacturer of that quality of paper, have something of an interest in this bill. Wrapping paper and book paper have heretofore had a duty of 35 per cent from all countries. That amounts to $17.50 to $28 per ton. As we read this bill, without any discussion, without any reference to previous arguments made a year or so ago, and the data collected, that duty is absolutely wiped off. During the last two or three years the manufacture of the so-called craft paper, which is a peculiarly strong paper made by a rather difficult process, has sprung up in Norway and Sweden. That paper has come into this market and has superseded the ordinary wrapping paper to quite an extent. Attempts are being made to manufacture it in this country. It is a difficult thing to get at, and requires a plant different from what anybody has, but slowly we will get into operation and manufacture that paper. To-day mills are being built in Canada to manufacture that paper, which will come in competition, as it has no duty on it.

Mr. Fordney asked the question——

Mr. UNDERWOOD. Let me ask you a question, there. Do you say that this particular kind of paper is made in Sweden?

Mr. BARRETT. In Norway and Sweden.

Mr. UNDERWOOD. It has no duty coming into this country?

Mr. BARRETT. Yes; I say that it has. It has a duty of practically $28 a ton; but it is a light, thin paper, and the area of the paper is so much greater than that of any paper of the same weight manufactured in this country of equivalent strength, that when a man buys a ton of it and pays the price for it, he has a great deal more paper to wrap up his articles in.

Mr. UNDERWOOD. How many of those mills are they building in Canada to make that paper?

Mr. BARRETT. There are two of them in Canada—one at Latouche, and another is being constructed at Three Rivers.

Mr. UNDERWOOD. Is there any reason why the American manufacturer can not build mills here on the same basis as they are being built on in Canada?

Mr. BARRETT. So far as I know there is only one being built in Wisconsin and another in Michigan. Heretofore, up to date, there has been no way of taking care of the very intensely disagreeable odor from those mills. In Michigan they claim that they have gotten rid of that pretty well. Up there in Canada, take it at Latouche, you do not need to worry about odors. It is too much in the wilderness. You probably could not build a mill that is operated as the Norwegian and Scandinavian mills are operated in our northern country. That will be taken care of in time. But why should we build any mill that is going to use wood when we can not get wood from Canada and we are threatened with free paper?

Mr. UNDERWOOD. I was merely asking you about your argument so far as this Norwegian and Swedish paper is concerned, and this new process. There is no reason why anyone should expect that the American manufacturer should not keep abreast of the times, and when modern improvements are made, take advantage of them as anyone else does.

Mr. BARRETT. He should. He is trying to take advantage of this now and construct new plants.

Mr. RANDELL. Do they use a different sort of wood in making this new kind of paper?

Mr. BARRETT. They use various kinds of wood; the same as you use in making ordinary sulphite paper.

Mr. UNDERWOOD. Would the raw material be the same for either mill?

Mr. BARRETT. Practically.

Mr. UNDERWOOD. Then this new mill is merely an advance in the process of manufacture?

Mr. BARRETT. Merely an advance in the process of manufacture, slowly being adopted in this country. But there has been absolutely no encouragement to an American manufacturer to manufacture that pulp and that paper, when in the face of this duty, even, that paper can be brought over here, and he can not make his own paper out of his own product with his present machinery to compete with it. In other words, even that $28 a ton duty is not a protection against that Norwegian paper.

Mr. UNDERWOOD. Then the only way the manufacturers of this country could compete would be to adopt the new methods themselves?

Mr. BARRETT. That would not help them to compete at all. You can not make the stuff in this country. The sulphite proposition is practically the same as that. In three years the importations of sulphite into this country from foreign countries increased from 50,000 to over 220,000 tons per annum; that is, for 1908 and 1909 and 1910. The duty on that is $3.33 a ton. The American manufacturers are running from 65 to 80 per cent of their normal capacity, and we were being undersold by Germans and Scandinavians right straight along, in the face of that duty, and also being undersold by the Canadian mills, which export that same material here.

Mr. UNDERWOOD. That argument of course leads to the conclusion that the reason our mills can not compete is because our natural conditions are not such that we are in a position to manufacture paper as cheaply as countries which are better supplied with wood, and therefore we are maintaining an industry that the natural conditions of our country do not justify.

Mr. BARRETT. It seems to me rather—have you ever been in Maine?

Mr. UNDERWOOD. No.

Mr. BARRETT. Or in West Virginia?

Mr. UNDERWOOD. Yes.

Mr. BARRETT. There are trees left, are there not? There is wood left; but we can not get that wood as cheap as they can get it abroad; we can not get our labor as cheap as they can get it abroad; we can not get our sulphur as cheap as they can get it abroad; we get not one single thing that goes into the process of manufacture, except possibly here and there some little items, where they are close by, like lime and marble, as cheap as it can be gotten abroad.

Mr. UNDERWOOD. I want to understand that proposition. You contend that even a duty of $28 a ton does not protect you from paper made under this new process?

Mr. BARRETT. It has not done it.

Mr. UNDERWOOD. How much wood goes into a ton of paper? What does the wood cost?

Mr. BARRETT. What kind of paper?

Mr. UNDERWOOD. The class of paper we are speaking of, this Norwegian paper.

Mr. BARRETT. It is all sulphite, and it would take, perhaps, approximately 2 cords of wood per ton of paper.

Mr. UNDERWOOD. What is the cost of the 2 cords of wood in this country?

Mr. BARRETT. At mills in northern New York about $10.25 per cord.

Mr. UNDERWOOD. That would be $22.50 for the wood?

Mr. BARRETT. Yes.

Mr. UNDERWOOD. What is the cost of that wood in Canada?

Mr. BARRETT. Six dollars per cord.

Mr. UNDERWOOD. That would be $12?

Mr. BARRETT. And less than that at some mills.

Mr. UNDERWOOD. Say there is a difference in the cost of wood, in view of your claim, of $10 in the amount of wood that goes into a ton of paper. Now, what is the difference of labor cost? You say the labor cost there is less.

Mr. BARRETT. The average wages paid to a man in the mills, in most of the mills in New York State and in Maine, for common labor is $1.75 for nine hours' work.

Mr. UNDERWOOD. Of course, I can not follow you on that. If you have the figures will you give me the amount of labor per unit of value that goes into a ton of paper? Have you those figures?

Mr. BARRETT. No; I have not those figures; I have not got them here. But right in our office, for pretty nearly one month, was sitting the Tariff Commission. We turned our office inside out and sent our accountant up to our mills with those men, and I am informed that not a single report has come out from that Tariff Commission in connection with this proposed bill as to the facts of the manufacturer. Not the facts that the manufacturers may state, but the actual facts as shown by their operations for a term of years, are unknown to this committee or to Congress. They are apparently unknown to anybody, yet.

Mr. UNDERWOOD. As I understand, in the Mann report, which you are familiar with, they state that difference in the cost of wages in this country and in Canada in the production of paper to be merely nominal; they say that the cost is practically the same.

Mr. BARRETT. I do not remember. Mr. Hastings suggests that it is about $2.

Mr. HASTINGS. About $2, the report says.

Mr. UNDERWOOD. Then the labor cost, added to the wood cost, if that Mann report is correct, would make only $12.50 difference between the cost of production here and in Canada on labor and raw material, and you claim that you can not compete with a $28 tariff. Where does that come in?

Mr. BARRETT. The figures Mr. Hastings spoke of here were for labor on news papers. They are not craft papers or high-grade wrapping papers. Is that correct?

Mr. HASTINGS. Yes; that is correct.

Mr. BARRETT. News paper can be run on machines that will give 50 tons a day, and the same quantity of craft paper on that same machine would not be more than 27 to 30 tons of the same size.

Mr. HASTINGS. It would not be that.

Mr. BARRETT. It would not be that. Some of these Watertown people have tried that, so that they know.

Mr. HILL. Mr. Underwood, do you want to inquire further?

Mr. UNDERWOOD. No, sir.

Mr. HILL. Does any other gentleman want to be heard? If not, there will be no hearing this afternoon on this or any other subject. Do you wish to proceed further, Mr. Barrett.

Mr. BARRETT. Just to answer one question which I think Mr. Fordney asked. There was a statement made at the recent conservation congress at Quebec which indicated that there were about 4,000,000 acres of freehold and seigniory lands. Three paper companies in Canada own more than that in Crown land. I think Mr. Hastings's statement of, I think it was, one one-hundredth, or 1 per cent, would probably cover the amount, as compared with the forest area of Quebec.

Mr. HARRISON. I understand that these gentlemen do not want to be heard further, and in connection with the hearing to-morrow morning, I understand that the New York malsters were to be heard, and I received from a representative of those interests a brief which is directed to the chairman of the committee, and I would ask unanimous consent that this brief be printed in the record, and these gentlemen would then waive their request for a hearing.

Mr. HILL. If there is no objection, the brief will be printed in the record. Does anyone know of anybody who desires to be heard to-morrow morning on any subject? I understand that other gentlemen do desire to be heard on other subjects to-morrow morning, so that the committee will stand adjourned until to-morrow morning at 10.30.

(At 12 o'clock noon the committee adjourned until to-morrow, Wednesday, February 8, at 10.30 a. m.)

The Canadian bill is here printed in full from the copy presented by Mr. Hall, as follows:

[House of Commons. January 26, 1911.]

Mr. Fielding—In Committee of Ways and Means—

Resolved, That it is expedient to amend the customs tariff, 1907, and to provide as follows:

1. That the articles the growth, product, or manufacture of the United States specified in schedule A shall be admitted into Canada free of duty when imported from the United States.

2. That the articles the growth, product, or manufacture of the United States specified in schedules B and D shall be admitted into Canada upon payment of the rates of duty specified in the said schedules when imported from the United States.

That the advantages hereby granted to the United States shall extend to any and every other foreign power which may be entitled thereto, under the provisions of any treaty or convention with His Majesty.

That the advantages hereby granted to the United States shall extend to the United Kingdom and the several British colonies and possessions with respect to their commerce with Canada. Provided, however, that nothing herein contained shall be held to increase any rate of duty now provided for in the British preferential tariff.

That it is expedient to provide that the act proposed to be founded on the foregoing resolutions shall not come into operation until a date to be named by the governor in council in a proclamation to be published in the Canada Gazette, and that such proclamation may be issued whenever it appears to the satisfaction of the governor in council that the United States Congress has enacted or will forthwith enact such legislation as will grant to Canada the reciprocal advantages provided for in certain correspondence dated Washington, January 21, 1911, between the Hon. P. C. Knox, Secretary of State for the United States, and the Hon. W. S. Fielding, minister of finance of Canada, and the Hon. William Patterson, minister of customs of Canada.

SCHEDULE A.—ARTICLES FREE OF DUTY.

Live animals, viz, cattle, horses and mules, swine, sheep, lambs, and all other live animals.

Poultry, dead or alive.

Wheat, rye, oats, barley, and buckwheat; dried peas and beans, edible.

Corn, sweet corn, or maize (except for distillation).

Hay, straw, and cowpeas.

Fresh vegetables, viz, potatoes, sweet potatoes, yams, turnips, onions, cabbages, and all other vegetables in their natural state.

Fresh fruits, viz, apples, pears, peaches, grapes, berries, and all other edible fruits in their natural state.

Dried fruits, viz, apples, peaches, pears, and apricots, dried, desiccated, or evaporated.

Dairy products, viz, butter, cheese, and fresh milk and cream. Provided that cans actually used in the transportation of milk or cream may be passed back and forth between the two countries free of duty, under such regulations as the respective Governments may prescribe.

Eggs of barnyard fowl, in the shell.

Honey.

Cotton-seed oil.

Seeds, viz, flaxseed or linseed, cotton-seed, and other oil seeds; grass seed, including timothy and clover seed; garden, field, and other seed not herein otherwise provided for, when in packages weighing over one pound each (not including flower seeds).

Fish of all kinds, fresh, frozen, packed in ice, salted or preserved in any form, except sardines and other fish preserved in oil; and shell fish of all kinds, including oysters, lobsters and clams in any state, fresh or packed, and coverings of the foregoing.

Seal, herring, whale, and other fish oil, including cod oil.

Salt.

Mineral waters, natural, not in bottles or jugs.

Timber, hewn, sided or squared otherwise than by sawing, and round timber used for spars or in building wharves.

Sawed boards, planks, deals and other lumber, not further manufactured than sawed.

Paving posts, railroad ties, and telephone, trolley, electric light and telegraph poles of cedar or other woods.

Wooden staves of all kinds, not further manufactured than listed or jointed, and stave bolts.

Pickets and palings.

Plaster rock or gypsum, crude, not ground.

Mica, unmanufactured or rough trimmed only, and mica ground or bolted.

Feldspar, crude, powdered or ground.

Asbestos not further manufactured than ground.

Flourspar, crude, not ground.

Glycerine, crude, not purified.

Talc, ground, bolted or precipitated, naturally or artificially, not for toilet use.

Sulphate of soda, or salt cake; and soda ash.

Extracts of hemlock bark.

Carbon electrodes.

Brass in bars and rods, in coil or otherwise, not less than 6 feet in length, or brass in strips, sheets or plates, not polished, planished or coated.

Cream separators of every description, and parts thereof imported for repair of the foregoing.

Rolled iron or steel sheets, or plates No. 14 gauge or thinner, galvanized or coated with zinc, tin, or other metal, or not.

Crucible cast steel wire, valued at not less than 6 cents per pound.

Galvanized iron or steel wire, curved or not, Nos. 9, 12, and 13 wire gauge.

Typecasting and typesetting machines and parts thereof, adapted for use in printing offices.

Barbed fencing wire of iron or steel, galvanized or not.

Coke.

Round rolled wire rods in the coil, of iron or steel; not over three-eights of an inch in diameter, and not smaller than No. 6 wire gauge.

Pulp of wood mechanically ground; pulp of wood, chemical, bleached, or unbleached; news prin paper, and other paper, and paper board, manufactured from mechanical wood pulp or from chemical wood pulp, or of which such pulp is the component material of chief value, colored in the pulp, or not colored, and valued at not more than 4 cents per pound, not including printed or decorated wall paper.

Provided, That such wood pulp, paper, or board, being the products of the United States, shall only be admitted free of duty into Canada from the United States when such wood pulp, paper, or board, being the products of Canada, are admitted from all parts of Canada free of duty into the United States.

NOTE.—Fish oil, whale oil, seal oil, and fish of all kinds, being the products of fisheries carried on by the fishermen of the United States shall be admitted into Canada as the product of the United States.

SCHEDULE B.—ARTICLES SUBJECT TO THE UNDER-MENTIONED RATES OF DUTY.

Articles.	Rates of duties.
Fresh meats, viz: Beef, veal, mutton, lamb, pork, and all other fresh or refrigerated meats excepting game.	1¼ cents per pound.
Bacon and hams, not in tins or jars	Do.
Meats of all kinds, dried, smoked, salted, in brine, or prepared or preserved in any manner not otherwise herein provided for.	Do.
Canned meats and canned poultry	20 per cent ad valorem.
Extract of meat, fluid or not	Do.
Lard, and compounds thereof, cottolene and cotton stearine, and animal stearine.	1¼ cents per pound.
Tallow	40 cents per 100 pounds.
Egg yolk, egg albumen, and blood albumen	7½ per cent ad valorem.
Fish (except shellfish) by whatever name known, packed in oil, in tin boxes or cans, including the weight of the package:	
(a) When weighing over 20 ounces and not over 36 ounces each	5 cents per package.
(b) When weighing over 12 ounces and not over 20 ounces each	4 cents per package.
(c) When weighing 12 ounces each or less	2 cents per package.
(d) When weighing 36 ounces each or more, or when packed in oil, in bottles, jars, or kegs.	36 per cent ad valorem.
Tomatoes and other vegetables, including corn, in cans or other air-tight packages, and including the weight of the package.	1¼ cents per pound.
Wheat flour and semolina; and rye flour	50 cents per barrel of 196 pounds.
Oatmeal and rolled oats, including the weight of paper covering	50 cents per 100 pounds.
Corn meal	12½ cents per 100 pounds.
Barley malt	45 cents per 100 pounds.
Barley, pot, pearled, and patent	½ cent per pound.
Buckwheat flour or meal	Do.
Split peas, dried	7½ cents per bushel of 60 pounds.
Prepared cereal foods, not otherwise provided for herein	17½ per cent ad valorem.
Bran, middlings, and other offals of grain used for animal food	12½ cents per 100 pounds.
Macaroni and vermicelli	1 cent per pound.
Biscuits, wafers, and cakes, when sweetened with sugar, honey, molasses, or other material.	25 per cent ad valorem.
Biscuits, wafers, cakes, and other baked articles composed in whole or in part of eggs or any kind of flour or meal when combined with chocolate, nuts, fruits, or confectionery; also candied peel, candied pop corn, candied nuts, candied fruits, sugar candy, and confectionery of all kinds.	32½ per cent ad valorem.
Maple sugar and maple sirup	1 cent per pound.
Pickles, including pickled nuts; sauces of all kinds, and fish paste or sauce	32½ per cent ad valorem.
Cherry juice and prune juice, or prune wine, and other fruit juices, and fruit sirup, nonalcoholic.	17½ per cent ad valorem.
Mineral waters and imitations of natural mineral waters, in bottles or jugs	Do.
Essential oils	7½ per cent ad valorem.
Grape vines; gooseberry, raspberry, and currant bushes	17½ per cent ad valorem.
Farm wagons, and finished parets thereof	22½ per cent ad valorem.
Plows, tooth and disk harrows, harvesters, reapers, agricultural drills and planters, mowers, horserakes, cultivators; thrashing machines, including wind stackers, baggers, weighers, and self-feeders therefor; and finished parts thereof imported for repairs of the foregoing.	15 per cent ad valorem.
Portable engines with boilers, in combination, horsepowers and traction engines for farm purposes; hay loaders, potato diggers, fodder or food cutters, grain crushers, fanning mills, hay tedders, farm or field rollers, manure spreaders, weeders, and windmills; and finished parts thereof imported for repair of the foregoing, except shafting.	20 per cent ad valorem.
Grindstones of sandstones, not mounted, finished or not	5 cents per 100 pounds.
Freestone, granite, sandstone, limestone, and all other monumental or building stone, except marble, breccia, and onyx, unmanufactured, or not dressed, hewn, or polished	12½ per cent ad valorem.
Roofing slates	50 cents per 100 square feet.
Vitrified paving blocks, not ornamented or decorated in any manner, and paving blocks of stone.	17½ per cent ad valorem.
Oxide of iron, as a color	22½ per cent ad valorem.
Asbestos further manufactured than ground; manufactures of asbestos, or articles of which asbestos is the component material of chief value, including woven fabrics wholly or in chief value of asbestos.	Do.
Printing ink	17½ per cent ad valorem.
Cutlery, plated or not, viz, pocketknives, penknives, scissors and shears, knives and forks for household purposes, and table steels.	27½ per cent ad valorem.
Bells and gongs; brass corners and rules for printers	Do.
Basins, urinals, and other plumbing fixtures for bathroom and lavatories; bathtubs, sinks, and laundry tubs, of earthenware, stone, cement, or clay, or of other material.	32½ per cent ad valorem.
Brass band instruments	22½ per cent ad valorem.
Clocks, watches, time recorders, clock and watch keys, clock cases, and clock movements.	27½ per cent ad valorem.
Printers' wooden cases and cabinets for holding type	Do.
Wood flour	22½ per cent ad valorem.
Canoes and small boats of wood, not power boats	Do.
Feathers, crude, not dressed, colored, or otherwise manufactured	12½ per cent ad valorem.
Antiseptic surgical dressings, such as absorbent cotton, cotton wool, lint, lamb's wool, tow, jute, gauzes, and oakum, prepared for use as surgical dressings, plain or medicated; surgical trusses, pessaries, and suspensory bandages of all kinds.	17½ per cent ad valorem.

SCHEDULE B.—ARTICLES SUBJECT TO THE UNDER-MENTIONED RATES OF DUTY—Continued.

Articles.	Rates of duties.
Plate glass, not beveled, in sheets or panes exceeding 7 square feet each, and not exceeding 25 square feet each.	25 per cent ad valorem.
Motor vehicles, other than for railways and tramways, and automobiles, and parts thereof, not including rubber tires.	30 per cent ad valorem.
Iron or steel digesters for the manufacture of wood pulp......................	27½ per cent ad valorem.
Musical instrument cases, fancy cases or boxes, portfolios, satchels, reticules, card cases, purses, pocketbooks, fly books for artificial flies, all the foregoing composed wholly or in chief value of leather.	30 per cent ad valorem.

SCHEDULE D.—ARTICLES SUBJECT TO THE UNDERMENTIONED RATES OF DUTY.

Articles.	Rates of duty.
Cement, Portland, and hydraulic or water lime in barrels, bags, or casks, the weight of the package to be included in the weight for duty.	11 cents per 100 pounds.
Trees, viz, apple, cherry, peach, pear, plum, and quince, of all kinds, and small peach trees known as June buds.	2½ cents each.
Condensed milk, the weight of the package to be included in the weight for duty.	2 cents per pound.
Biscuits without added sweetening..	20 per cent ad valorem.
Fruits in air-tight cans or other air-tight packages, the weight of the cans or other packages to be included in the weight for duty.	2 cents per pound.
Peanuts, shelled..	1 cent per pound.
Peanuts, unshelled..	½ cent per pound.
Coal, bituminous, round and run of mine, including bituminous coal such as will not pass through a ¾-inch screen.	45 cents per ton.

(T. D. 30591.)

Wood pulp—Printing paper.

Instructions as to the assessments of duty on wood pulp and printing paper under paragraphs 406 and 409, tariff act of 1909.

TREASURY DEPARTMENT, *May 5, 1910.*

SIR: The Secretary of State has forwarded to the department from the American consul at Sherbrooke, Canada, a copy of certain new regulations in the Province of Quebec, from which I quote the following:

"(A) All timber cut on Crown lands after the 1st of May, 1910, must be manufactured in Canada—that is to say, converted into pulp or paper, into deals or boards, or into any other article of commerce or merchandise as distinguished from such timber in its raw or unmanufactured state. There shall not be considered as manufactured, within the meaning of the present regulations, timber merely cut into lengths or logs piled up, barked or otherwise worked preliminary to the fabrication of pulp or paper, of deals or boards or of any other articles of commerce, nor waney timber nor poles; but actual square timber and railway ties are considered as manufactured."

As the foregoing regulation in effect forbids the exportation for use in the manufacture of wood pulp of wood cut on Crown lands, duties will be assessed on wood pulp and printing paper produced from pulp wood cut on such lands after May 1, 1910, as follows:

On mechanically ground wood pulp, the regular duty, under paragraph 406 of the tariff act of August 5, 1909, at the rate of one-twelfth of 1 cent per pound, dry weight.

On chemical wood pulp, the regular duties, under paragraph 406 of said act, at the following rates: Unbleached, one-sixth of 1 cent per pound, dry weight; bleached, one-fourth of 1 cent per pound, dry weight.

On printing paper, the regular rates of duty and in addition thereto the additional duty of one-tenth of 1 cent per pound when valued at 3 cents per pound or less, under paragraph 409 of said tariff act.

T. D. 29968 and 30045 of August 26 and October 16, 1909, are hereby amended accordingly.

Respectfully,

(67747.)

JAMES F. CURTIS,
Assistant Secretary.

COLLECTOR OF CUSTOMS, *Plattsburg, N. Y.*

RECIPROCITY WITH CANADA.

COMMITTEE ON WAYS AND MEANS,
HOUSE OF REPRESENTATIVES,
Washington, D. C., Wednesday, February 8, 1911.

The committee met at 10.30 o'clock a. m.

Present: Representatives McCall (acting chairman), Hill, Boutell, Needham, Calderhead, Fordney, Gaines, Longworth, Dwight, Ellis, Underwood, Pou, Randell, Broussard, and Harrison.

The ACTING CHAIRMAN (Mr. McCALL). Mr. Bradley, of New York, submits a statement on the pending bill, relating to pen and pocket cutlery. Without objection, that will be printed in the record as a part of our proceedings.

Then there is a communication from the American Society of Equity, from Evanston, Ill., in which a gentleman who appeared before the committee makes an extension in writing of his remarks. Without objection, that will be printed in the record.

(The papers mentioned above are as follows:)

COMMITTEE ON MILITARY AFFAIRS,
HOUSE OF REPRESENTATIVES,
Washington, D. C., February 7, 1911.

Hon. SERENO E. PAYNE,
Chairman Committee on Ways and Means, House of Representatives.

DEAR SIR: Notwithstanding the seeming impossibility of amending H. R. 32216, a proposed reciprocity agreement with Canada, I have the honor to submit for the printed hearings the attached statement in support of my earnest protest against that which I know will prove a serious injury to American manufacturers of pocket cutlery, should the proposed agreement be confirmed.

Respectfully,

THOS. W. BRADLEY.

RECIPROCITY AGREEMENT WITH CANADA—PEN AND POCKET CUTLERY.

So far as pocket cutlery is concerned. American manufacturers can have no opportunity of enlarging their market in the Canadian field. Canadian official reports show that for the year ending March 31, 1910, the total importations of pocketknives from Great Britain amounted to $67,542; from Germany, $5,703; and from the United States, $1,202, the latter being imports of patent self-opening novelty knives only. It is unreasonable to suppose that a decrease from 30 to 27½ per cent in the Canadian duty will in any way benefit our American manufacturers or workmen while the English goods pay only 20 per cent.

Should the Canadian reciprocity treaty be enacted into law, it would mean, in the case of pocketknives, a reduction of 65 per cent from the existing Payne tariff rates. While it is true that no pocket cutlery is at the present time manufactured in Canada, the first consideration is whether American manufacturers can compete in the markets of Canada under 27½ per cent duty as against a preferential duty of 20 per cent on English cutlery; and a later consideration is sure to be whether American manufacturers can compete in the markets of the United States with the product of Canadian manufacture after cutlery works shall have been established in Canada. Under the cheaper cost of living there, should Sheffield manufacturers install plants in Canada, man them with mixed English and Canadian labor, and pay the average of foreign wages, a duty of 27½ per cent ad valorem would measure little more than one-third the difference between cost of production in Canada and the United States. In this connection, it may be noted that English steel, dutiable at 20 per cent, is used in the manufacture of American pocket cutlery. Against this, Canadian manufacturers may import forged steel knife blades at 5 per cent, the British preferential rate of duty.

Reciprocity, in this instance, to American manufacturers of pocket cutlery, simply puts in jeopardy their home market, worth $4,497,575, in exchange for a vain attempt to secure a larger portion of the Canadian market, the total value of which for the year ending March 31, 1910, was less than $75,000.

It is also absolutely unjust to this American industry to lump mother-of-pearl handled, highly finished articles in the same class with iron-handled knives, forks, and shears.

In simple justice to the manufacturers of American pocket cutlery, now struggling in their home market against the keen competition of British and German production, the words, "penknives, pocketknives," in line 3, page 6, and the same words in line 10, page 13, of H. R. 32216, should be stricken out.

EVANSTON, ILL., *February 6, 1911.*

Representative PAYNE,
     Chairman Ways and Means Committee, Washington, D. C.

HONORABLE SIR: Your acting chairman, at the hearing on February 4, granted us permission to file a supplementary brief protesting in the name of the American Society of Equity against the ratification of the reciprocity agreement with the Dominion of Canada. We will do this as briefly as possible. The President has said, "If we can enlarge our supply of natural resources, and especially food products and the necessities of life, without substantial injury to any of our producing and manufacturing classes we should take steps to do it now."

We have endeavored to prove that this can not be done without serious financial injury to that great army engaged in sowing and reaping the products of the soil.

Not only will the introduction of free grain from that vast Dominion of Canada, upon the quantity of which there is no limitation, reduce the value of the cereals raised by our farmers (as is the purpose of our President), but is now having the effect of reducing the value of the crops of 1910 even in advance of any positive assurance of its ratification.

What the detrimental effect will be in case of ratification is incalculable.

Much of the crops of 1910 is still in the farmers' granaries. Just how much we will know exactly when the crop bulletin of March 1 is issued by the Department of Agriculture. Taking, however, the amounts shown by this same authority on March 1, 1910, we will have some idea of the magnitude of what is involved in this issue.

Cereals.	Amount.	Price per bushel, Chicago.	Value.
	Bushels.		
Wheat	173,000,000	$1.18	$204,000,000
Corn	1,000,000,000	.64¾	680,000,000
Oats	363,000,000	.47	170,600,000

The probabilities are that the figures will show on March 1 fully as much on hand of these cereals, especially the corn and oats, because both of these crops are very much larger than the crops of 1909 above calculated on.

We will therefore ask you to seriously consider what effect the ratification of the proposed agreement will have on the value of these vast amounts of wheat, corn, and oats, still the property of the farmers and yet to find a market.

Already the loss, as compared with a year ago, is stupendous. The wheat is worth 95 cents in Chicago, or $40,000,000 less than on March 1, 1910. The corn $186,000,000 less, being worth in Chicago to-day only 47 cents. The oats $54,000,000 less, being worth in Chicago to-day only 32 cents. The total of this is $280,000,000, and the farmers have on hand a total of over 1,500,000,000 bushels, and every decline of 1 cent per bushel on this amount is the equivalent of $15,360,000.

This is another serious matter for the life insurance companies and financial institutions who have their millions invested in farm mortgages.

In the course of his remarks the honorable Representative from Missouri, Mr. Champ Clark, said that we had better prepare for the annexation of the Dominion of Canada.

This we do not fear, because when the at present aliens become citizens of the United States they no longer enjoy the advantage over the farmers of the United States given by the free trade relations between the Dominion of Canada and England, in buying their necessities of life. They no longer contribute the mite to the purchasing power in the United States, but they contribute their all and the equilibrium is thus maintained.

Another honorable Representative also asked what would be the result if the present undeveloped vast areas of northwest Canada were located within the borders of our own country.

The above answer to a situation arising from the annexation of the Dominion of Canada also answers this question.

The proposed reciprocity agreement does, however, mean an entirely different situation and an opposite result to our own farmers. The Canadian farmer would be within the United States only so far as his selling power was concerned, while he would be within the Dominion of Canada enjoying free trade with England so far as his buying power was concerned, buying his necessities at home at greatly reduced prices, to the disadvantage of our farmers with the yoke of a high protective tariff on manufactured products around their necks.

The honorable acting chairman found that his figures did not agree with those of our representative on the increase in the barley crop in the Dominion of Canada between the years 1903 and 1909, the amount given by us being 55,000,000 bushels for the latter year. We promised to furnish our authority and it is the Crop Bulletin, published under the authority of the Department of Agriculture.

It is true that the Canada barley crop for 1910 was less than this, but close investigation will show that barley crops of Manitoba, Saskatchewan, and Alberta were almost entirely destroyed last summer by the unusual drought and it is not a fair criterion for production, because a normal crop was grown in 1909 and amounted to 55,000,000 bushels.

So far as the barley crop itself is concerned, this society desires to make and record a vigorous protest against the destruction of this barley-growing industry by the removal of the protection that has been in part instrumental in building up this industry in the great barley-producing States of Minnesota, Wisconsin, Iowa, and the Dakotas.

We do not include the States of Nebraska and Missouri and Kansas, because the barley grown in those States is mostly only fit for and used for feeding purposes. The honorable Representative from Missouri asked why Missouri did not or could not raise as good barley for brewing purposes as the great States farther north. We can assure him that Mr. Adolphus Busch, of St. Louis, who has seen the brewing barley line of production advance northward with great regret, can inform him as to the wherefores and whys, but so far as Nebraska and Kansas are concerned we are in a position to say that the introduction of the Bay Brewing seed of the Pacific coast was responsible for the deterioration of the quality. This seed has not an affinity in the soil of these States and produces a mongrel barley. Even if the barley grown from this seed in these two States thrashed out equal in quality to that on the Pacific coast it would still be unsatisfactory to the brewers. We can furnish authorities that clearly explain why such is the case. This barley has not high diastatic properties. It can not, therefore, be used with a large proportion of raw grain or the products of raw grain that require the diastase for their conversion into sugar and alcohol.

Although not generally known nor labeled nor advertised our brewers are all using as much of the substitutes for barely malt above mentioned as they can without absolutely destroying the quality of the beers. These same substitutes are disguised for selling purposes and the expression "barley malt" is the fig leaf used to cover up the nakedness of the act.

Bass & Co., the large brewers of England, keep a representative in the barley-growing districts of California to buy this particular barley for their purposes, because they do not use substitutes, and this barley is especially valuable to brewers who desire to obtain their starch and sugar and alcohol from the barley itself.

Another honorable Representative asked why, if the barley grown in western Canada just over the invisible boundary line from North Dakota was not suitable for brewing purposes, why it was that the barley on this side of the invisible boundary line was adaptable simply because it happened to be grown in territory that is within the United States. The answer to this is that the barley grown in the northern part of North Dakota, because of the alkali in the soil, is not desirable malting barley or brewing barley and is used more for feeding than any other purpose.

The brewing industry of the United States is responsible for the present great quantity grown, and so far as the majority of the barley growers is concerned they realize that they are growing it for brewing purposes. At the annual meeting of the

United States Brewers' Association in June, 1908, the advisory committee said: "It is now seven years since the Department of Agriculture first gave its attention to the work of improving the barley crop." The following annual meeting in June, 1909, brought up the same subject and the advisory committee reported as follows: "The United States Department of Agriculture issued on April 24, 1909, Bulletin No. 124, which contains the preliminary results of investigations authorized by Congress in the agricultural appropriation bill for the fiscal years 1903 to 1907, to study the barleys grown in different sections of the United States with a view of improving their quality." The evidence all shows that about the year 1900, the United States Brewers' Association solicited the United States Department of Agriculture to use its efforts (and later on for four years money appropriated) toward improving and enlarging the barley crop. They also solicited the aid of the State agricultural colleges and to such an extent were they successful, this coming only a few years after the imposition of the protective duty, that the farmers within the ten years trebled their crop.

In October next in the city of Chicago an international barley exposition is to be held by the brewers and prizes offered the barley growers to still further enlarge and improve the growing of barley. And it is because barley is grown for but one purpose, except to a very small extent, and because the industry has been nourished by the United States Brewers' Association and the Department of Agriculture that we believe the barley growers have special claims for a continuation of the protection that has been in part instrumental in adding many millions of acres to the growing of this particular cereal.

We can not see where the imposition of this protective duty was in any way responsible for the deterioration of the barley-growing industry in the State of New York, because they still have the acres and the seed is available, but we are inclined to believe that the elements necessary to the soil for the production of barley are now lacking. In any event we would be glad to hold out the helping hand to the farmers in any of our own States who desire to engage in the growing of barley and to furnish them with the seed at cost. We do, however, protest strongly against competition from a foreign country of vast areas and conveniently situated to our home markets, and we beg careful consideration for all of the reasons given for your better guidance and understanding.

AMERICAN SOCIETY OF EQUITY,
By JOHN R. MAUFF.

STATEMENT OF HON. WILLIAM E. HUMPHREY, REPRESENTATIVE FROM THE STATE OF WASHINGTON.

Mr. HUMPHREY. I hardly think it will be necessary for me to state to the committee that I have not prepared myself to present my case as I should. You will soon discover that. But I do want to submit a few thoughts to the committee as affecting the industries of the State of Washington.

First, I want to call your attention to the fish industry. It may be a surprise to the gentlemen upon the committee to know that the fish industry of the State of Washington is our largest industry. It now exceeds our lumber industry, and is the largest of any State in the Union. This treaty—if I may term it a treaty—proposes to place fish on the free list. I have not yet been able to decide in my own mind what it is. If it is a treaty, I do not know why it is over here. If it is an act to regulate commerce, I do not understand why Congress did not do it. If it is for the purpose of revising the tariff, I am unable to understand why it did not originate in the House. But whatever it may be termed, it proposes to place fish upon the free list.

Upon our coast we have, as I have said, a great fishing industry. The Canadian Government, just across the line, subsidizes its fisheries by giving them special rates of transportation over its railways. When the new Government line is completed and reaches Prince Rupert, the Canadian Government is going to establish there a great cold-storage plant, costing a good many millions of dollars (I have seen it stated at all the way from ten to twenty millions of dollars), where the fishermen may take their catch and keep it in perfect condition until the Government railroad can carry it at special rates into the markets of this country. The question that is agitating the fisher-men upon our coast is, how does Congress expect a private industry to compete with the Canadian Government in this respect if you are going to take off all protection in the way of a tariff?

Mr. GAINES. Mr. Humphrey, what are those special rates on the Government railroads? Can you elaborate on that point?

Mr. HUMPHREY. No: I can not, because I have been unable to get definite information in regard to them.

Mr. HARRISON. What is the total value of the fishing industry of your State?

Mr. HUMPHREY. I can not tell you that, either. I do not know.

Mr. HARRISON. Is it a fish-packing industry or a fish-catching industry?

Mr. HUMPHREY. It is both.

Mr. HARRISON. In about what proportions?

Mr. HUMPHREY. I am not able to tell you. As I said at the beginning, I have not been able to get definite information. It is a long way out to my country, and the mails have been held up. Such statements as I have received have been principally by telegram, and what I happen to know, just in a general way.

Mr. HARRISON. Do you happen to know the comparative price of fish on the Canadian side of the border and in your State?

Mr. HUMPHREY. No; I do not know that.

Mr. HARRISON. Fresh fish, in the market?

Mr. HUMPHREY. I do not know that either.

The ACTING CHAIRMAN. Mr. Humphrey, is your fishing industry chiefly a salmon industry?

Mr. HUMPHREY. No. The salmon is first.

The ACTING CHAIRMAN. That is the largest?

Mr. HUMPHREY. That is the largest.

The ACTING CHAIRMAN. Is that a river industry?

Mr. HUMPHREY. No; it is not confined to the rivers. It is on both rivers and sound, and a great portion of it is in Alaska, where they do their fishing in what are not exactly inland waters, but sounds and bays.

The ACTING CHAIRMAN. I was not including the Alaska fisheries.

Mr. HUMPHREY. The Alaska fisheries would all be affected by this bill in the same way.

The ACTING CHAIRMAN. But you are including those in the fishing industries that you are speaking of?

Mr. HUMPHREY. Yes; I am including that fishing industry, although I am speaking of the State of Washington. I have a letter that I received this morning—I think probably it is here—in which the statement is made, somewhat to my surprise, that during the last year the value of our fish was greater than the value of our lumber. I presume when this treaty was being negotiated those who were representing our Government were not aware of the fact that Canada subsidized her fisheries. This, to my mind, illustrates one of the dangers of revising the tariff in secret, with no opportunity to be heard.

Mr. HARRISON. Mr. Humphrey, if it should turn out (as I believe to be the case) that the principal part of the fishing industry of your State is canning or packing, would it not be a benefit to the State to have the raw material come in free from Canada?

Mr. HUMPHREY. No; we do not need to get the raw material from Canada. We have our own raw material. We no not have to fish in Canadian waters. We have all of our own raw material so far as fish is concerned. And while I think it is probably true that the packing industry is the largest, yet we send a great deal of fish to the eastern coast, as far as Boston, now. We send a great many halibut.

Mr. POU. I am not sure whether you were asked this question or not; but if you were, I will repeat it: Did you say that you did or did not know the extent to which Canada subsidizes its fishing industry?

Mr. HUMPHREY. No; I have not the figures definitely. This is what I know they do: They give special rates over the railroads. The roads in Canada are largely owned by the Government. They give special rates to fisheries. Then they propose to establish a great cold-storage plant at Prince Rupert, so as to assist the fishing in that way. Whether there are any additional advantages or not, I am not prepared to say.

The next item that I want to call your attention to briefly is lumber. You have heard a great deal of discussion of the lumber question, and no doubt the members of the committee know more about the details of the lumber business in our State than I do. But I want to call your attention to the fact that the persons who framed this agreement overlooked the attitude of Canada—especially British Colombia—and its policy in regard to putting an export duty upon logs. Sometimes they not only have a duty, but the exportation is absolutely prohibited. If the lumbermen in my State could have absolute free trade in all forest products between this country and Canada, there would be very little objection so far as the lumbermen are concerned. But if we change the law and provide for free lumber, and at the same time permit British Colombia to put an export duty upon logs or to absolutely prohibit their being brought into this country, it seems to me we are giving something for nothing.

Mr. BROUSSARD. Right there, let me ask this question: You say that some of the provinces absolutely prohibit the exportation of timber?

Mr. HUMPHREY. At times.

Mr. BROUSSARD. Can you refer us to the law under which the Provinces exercise that right?

Mr. HUMPHREY. No. Perhaps Brother Fordney knows.

Mr. BROUSSARD. I have looked up the law, and I find only the act of 1897, which permits the Provinces to impose an export tax of not exceeding $3 a thousand. It makes that tax operative by the governor and the council passing such a law and publishing it in the Canada Gazette. Many witnesses have come here and said that some Provinces absolutely prohibit the exportation of logs. I am unable to find that law, and I wanted to get a reference to it from some of the gentlemen who have looked up the matter.

Mr. FORDNEY. If the gentlemen will permit me to say so, all the Provinces of Canada now have an embargo placed upon their logs by the governors of the various Provinces; and the governor has the right, by making publication of it in the Gazette, to remove that embargo at any time he chooses.

Mr. BROUSSARD. Under what authority is the governor acting when he prohibits the exportation?

Mr. FORDNEY. I can not cite you to the law, but it is a provincial law. All the forests of Canada are absolutely under the control of the various Provinces. The Dominion Government of Canada has no forests at all. The lands in the various Provinces belong to the Provinces, and they are absolutely under their control.

Mr. GAINES. Mr. Fordney, if you will permit me just a minute, let us see if that is necessarily correct. As I understand Mr. Broussard, his point is this: He has seen an act of the Dominion Government which authorizes the provincial governments to put on an export tax of not exceeding $3 a thousand. But it has been generally stated here, as you have just stated, that some of the Provinces have an embargo. Now, under what authority is that? And if the power of the Provinces comes from an act of the Dominion Government, may not the Dominion Government pass another law at any time revoking that power, or exercise it themselves, even if we pass this bill or this treaty? (We are as much at sea as you are about the proper language to use in designating it.) And even if the Provinces took off their export tax, or their embargo, or whatever it is, as long as the Dominion Government permits the power to remain in their hands to do it, might they not instantly at any time put it on again?

I am trying to get at two propositions: The first is, Would the passage of this act, even if we got the anticipated reductions in export duties, or their removal, insure any permanency? The second proposition is that it is a strange thing to me that the proponents of this bill leave us here to fish out for ourselves all these difficult problems. None of them comes forward and states the legal conditions under which we are expected to act, so far as they are affected by the law of Canada and the various Provinces.

I think, Mr. Chairman, that the proponents of this bill, the man who drafted the bill, ought to be here to explain its provisions and furnish us the information in the light of which he proceeded when he drafted the bill.

Mr. BROUSSARD. I want to say that a reading of the act of 1897 shows that the governor and council not only can reduce or repeal all export taxes, but at any time may reimpose them to the extent that their judgment may dictate.

So that even if all of the Provinces were to revoke the export tax now being imposed, and bring about free paper between this country and Canada, subsequently, under that act, by simply advertising the fact, these Provinces might reinstate the tax upon either the wood, the pulp, or the paper.

The ACTING CHAIRMAN. Mr. Broussard, do you think that in an agreement of this kind between nations, where one nation makes a provision in its laws on condition that the other nation shall make a similar provision in its laws, there is any danger of the consideration being withdrawn by the other nation after it gets what it desires?

Mr. BROUSSARD. I certainly do, Mr. McCall.

The ACTING CHAIRMAN. Can there be anything practical in that suggestion?

Mr. BROUSSARD. I certainly think so; because it occurs to me that if the commissioners of the Canadian Government had intended to bring about free paper between our country and theirs, they should have proceeded first by either having the Provinces revoke the tax or securing the assurance that they would do so in case this treaty was adopted by both countries. The fact that they came here and dealt with this entire subject, and, after it had been dealt with, notified the Secretary of State on the 21st of January that they could not be held to represent the Provinces, and that the Provinces must act on their own individual motion subsequently to the ratification of the treaty, indicates to me that the Provinces may or may not repeal this tax, or may repeal it and subsequently reimpose it.

In other words, it does not appear to me that the commissioners, in acting with this Government in framing this agreement, undertook to bind the Provinces, either because they knew the Provinces would not be bound, or else because they knew the party would not revoke the law by which the entire jurisdiction of the Provinces which enables them to impose the export tax was to be taken away from them. So I believe, in answer to your question, that they would——

Mr. POU. There is this consideration, also: The Government has 50 majority—so I saw in the papers. Nobody knows how long that 50 majority is going to remain. They may have an experience over there like we had in the last election here.

Mr. GAINES. This matter seems to me of considerable importance, in view of the information, or partial information, which we now possess. The letter from the Canadian authorities accompanying the President's message calls our attention, apparently with great frankness, to the fact that the Dominion Government can not control the action of the Provinces. Yet it would appear from the statement made this morning that the power of the Provinces in this respect is due to a voluntary (and therefore, I take it, a revocable) grant of power on the part of the Dominion to the Provinces. In that case the Dominion might have resumed the power, and then it would be in the position to control the situation.

Mr. BROUSSARD. If you will read the wording of a part of this letter of Mr. Fielding and Mr. Paterson (the Canadian commissioners) to the Secretary of State, written after this agreement had been drafted, you will find this language:

The restrictions at present existing in Canada are of a provincial character. They have been adopted by several of the Provinces with regard to what are believed to be provincial interests. We have neither the right nor the desire to interfere with the provincial authorities in the free exercise of their constitutional powers in the administration of their public lands.

In other words, the commissioners recite that the power to impose this tax is a constitutional power in the Provinces; that the lands belong to the Provinces; and that they have neither the desire nor the power to exercise any influence at all with the Provinces. This letter was not written until after there had been entered into this agreement in which appears this provision with regard to wood pulp, pulp wood, and print paper. So that, judging from the language of this letter, if this treaty is ratified, we need not expect any influence to be exercised hereafter by the Government of Canada over the governments of the various Provinces with regard to the removal of the restrictions that may be imposed.

Mr. CALDERHEAD. I think you are right on that point, because on the 1st of May the Province of Quebec absolutely prohibited the exportation of timber from any crown lands.

Mr. BROUSSARD. That is the point I wanted to bring out in asking the question I did of Mr. Humphreys—to ascertain under what authority they do that.

Mr. FORDNEY. Mr. Chairman, let me tell you this: I started a while ago to explain to you (and if you permit me, I will do so) what I know to be a fact, because I have held those licenses myself.

The commissioners of Crown lands in the various Provinces have absolute control over the lands in the Provinces. They have a commissioner of Crown lands as we have a Commissioner of the General Land Office here. A purchaser of timber on those Crown lands buys only the timber, not the lands. The lands are not for sale. They are for homestead after the timber has been removed or disposed of. If to-day you or any other person should purchase the timber on any portion of the Crown lands in the Province of Quebec, or the Province of Ontario, or any other Province—by the way, on the Pacific coast they have another law, which I will explain, in addition to the one I am now explaining—you would get a license to go and remove that timber on or before the 1st day of next May, no matter what time of the year you might buy that right. But when you cut and remove it, there is a condition in the license itself that you must pay to the Crown land department of that Province a certain rate per thousand feet of stumpage for your logs, or so much per cord for your wood. They reserve the right in the license to change the rate that you are to pay—either to lower it or to raise it. It is set forth in the license that the timber must be manufactured in Canada. That is all there is to it. You have no authority in your license to remove it from the Province in which you cut it, or from Canada.

Mr. GAINES. Let me ask you a question right there.

Mr. FORDNEY. All right; go ahead.

Mr. GAINES. Is the commissioner of Crown lands an officer of the Province or is he an officer of the Dominion Government?

Mr. FORDNEY. The commissioner of Crown lands is an officer of the Province.

Mr. GAINES. And is that power on the part of the Provinces a constitutional power in the sense in which we understand the term "constitutional," or does it originate in Dominion statutes which may be repealed at any time?

Mr. FORDNEY. I have never seen the act myself, Mr. Gaines; but it is my understanding that the commissioner of Crown lands is absolutely under the control and authority of the Province itself, the same as a State officer in the United States would be under our State laws.

Mr. GAINES. We are trying to reach the source of the power.

Mr. FORDNEY. Now, let me go further. There is no export tax on logs coming from Canada into this country. I have never known of any, although I have heard that there was at one time, many years ago, an export tax on logs. There is an embargo upon logs—that is to say, a prohibition against their coming into this country when cut from Crown lands. The Provinces have no control over the timber on lands that have passed out of the possession of the Province and have been deeded either to Indian reservations or to individuals who obtained title to the lands under some of their land laws. The right to remove that embargo is in the governor, by publishing, as you mentioned, Mr. Broussard. But in British Columbia the practice has been that whenever the log market became flooded with logs, and a large amount was on hand, and the price of logs was likely to go down, and the market for logs was good in the State of Washington, just across the line, he would immediately remove that embargo, and they would dump their surplus logs upon our market, and immediately put back the embargo. That has been the custom. That has been often done, and it was done this last year and the year before; and it is the practice every time they have a surplus of logs on hand.

Mr. HILL. Mr. Chairman, I think I can relieve the situation a little in regard to the log question. At the time of the tariff hearings, copies of the contracts under which logs were sold were sent from Canada. I have over in my office a copy of such a contract. My understanding of the situation is that the logs on the Crown lands are owned by the respective Provinces; they are their property, just as I might own them if they were private lands. In the specifications for bidding at the auction sales there is a clause which provides that whatever purchases are made shall be made with the understanding that the logs shall be manufactured in Canada. It applies to Canadian citizens, British citizens, French citizens, and American citizens alike. There is no restriction that they shall not be taken into the United States, any more than there is that they shall not be taken to England. It is simply a provision that when a man starts to make a bid, whoever he is, he makes it with the distinct understanding that he shall manufacture that timber in the Dominion of Canada. That is my understanding of the matter.

Mr. FORDNEY. That is absolutely correct. There is no discrimination against any one country, or against the United States, in favor of any other country. All persons obtaining licenses to cut timber in those Provinces are compelled to manufacture it in Canada.

The ACTING CHAIRMAN. Now, Mr. Humphrey, will you proceed?

Mr. JOHN NORRIS. Mr. Chairman, I am Mr. John Norris, the chairman of the committee on paper of the American Newspaper Publishers' Association. Later on I expect to ask the committee for an opportunity to make a statement upon paper and pulp, which I think will entirely clarify the situation, which is evidently confused in the minds of the members, and give them accurate information as to the restrictions and as to the questions which relate to the duty and the reasons which affect the present text of the treaty arrangement so far as it relates to paper and pulp.

The ACTING CHAIRMAN. The committee will be very glad to hear you. At what time would it be convenient? It is now half past 11 o'clock.

Mr. NORRIS. I did not expect to make any statement to-day. I have sent to New York for my tables, in order that when I answer your questions as to prices and other things respecting paper and pulp I may give you accurate, detailed information, and not mislead you in any respect.

The ACTING CHAIRMAN. You could go on to-morrow, could you?

Mr. NORRIS. Surely.

Mr. FORDNEY. To-morrow was set aside for the lumber people, and the committee decided that the meetings are to close at 5 o'clock to-morrow.

The ACTING CHAIRMAN. We understood that you were willing to divide the time to-morrow with some gentlemen from New York or some other State that were notified to come to-day. Do you think you will occupy all the time, so that Mr. Norris could not be heard before 5 o'clock?

Mr. FORDNEY. No; I think time ought to be given to everybody, but I will ask Mr. Norris this question: Have you a copy of the Canadian laws that you are going to speak of, that you are proposing to present to the committee?

Mr. NORRIS. A copy of the location ticket?

Mr. FORDNEY. No, no; have you a copy of their land laws under which lumber is cut? If not, your information is not any better than that of any other witness, is it?

Mr. NORRIS. No.

The ACTING CHAIRMAN. Mr. Norris can be heard, of course.

Mr. FORDNEY. Yes; we shall be glad to hear him.

The ACTING CHAIRMAN. I understand that it will not be convenient for you to go on this afternoon?

Mr. NORRIS. I have not the tables of the accurate information which I think you will want.

Mr. POU. I did not understand whether Mr. Norris answered Mr. Fordney's question as to whether he had a copy of the land laws of Canada relating to the cutting and removal of timber.

Mr. NORRIS. I am not clear as to that. I shall have to look over my papers. I rather think not, however, except with regard to the Dominion regulations.

Mr. HILL. Mr. Norris, can you not get the laws and other papers that you want over at the Congressional Library?

The ACTING CHAIRMAN. I was just going to say that if any member of the committee will indicate what laws of Canada he wants produced I think they can be obtained by the clerk at the Congressional Library.

Mr. GAINES. I want to know what the Canadian situation is as to the relation between the Provinces and the Dominion Government, and then I want the Dominion land laws.

The ACTING CHAIRMAN. I will ask the clerk to secure them from the Library, so as to have them here this afternoon.

Mr. GAINES. Mr. Chairman, these hearings are very interesting, and there are a whole lot of things we ought to know. We have been told that we prepare legislation and report it from this committee without sufficient and proper information. I was not present the other day when the committee voted to conclude the hearings on Thursday. I was in the chair in the Committee of the Whole on the agricultural appropriation bill. I propose to move to reconsider the action by which the hearings were closed at that time. I am not ready to vote on this bill.

The ACTING CHAIRMAN. Of course each member must be his own judge.

Mr. GAINES. Certainly; but I thought I ought to give this notice. I did not know until yesterday that such action had been taken when I was elsewhere; necessarily detained in the House itself from attendance upon the committee.

The ACTING CHAIRMAN. I will ask the clerk to secure those laws, and so forth, from the Library.

Mr. GAINES. I think we shall have time to hear you, Mr. Norris.

Mr. FORDNEY. We want to hear everybody who wants to be heard.

Mr. GAINES. I want to give everybody a full hearing.

Mr. HUMPHREY. Mr. Chairman, shall I proceed?

Mr. HILL. Just one moment. I have here the figures which you said you did not have a moment ago. If you like, I will give them to you.

Mr. HUMPHREY. All right.

Mr. HILL. The entire fishery industry of British Columbia in 1908 aggregated $6,465,038. A statement of the entire fishery industry of the United States for the Pacific Coast States, showing the various forms and kinds of fish, will be found in Table No. 90 in the Statistical Abstract; and it aggregates about $17,000,000, including Alaska.

Mr. HUMPHREY. Oh, that is not right. I know it is more than that.

Mr. HILL. It was $680,000 for the Pacific Coast States in 1904.

Mr. HUMPHREY. I do not know what it was in 1904; but I know it was over $12,000,000 for Alaska alone last year.

Mr. HILL. For Alaska, in 1908, it was $11,536,926.

Mr. HUMPHREY. Last year it was something over $12,000,000.

Mr. HILL. I presume very likely it is growing. So far as the subsidies paid by Canada are concerned, there is the document giving them. You can look them all over. You will find there pig iron, steel, wire, rods, manila fiber, lead, and crude petroleum; but I see nothing in regard to fisheries. This contains the entire statement of all moneys paid by Canada for subsidies and subventions.

Mr. UNDERWOOD. I should like to ask unanimous consent to have that document printed in the hearings.

Mr. HILL. It is rather an extensive document.

Mr. UNDERWOOD. I mean the portion that you refer to, if you will indicate that part.

The ACTING CHAIRMAN. Without objection, then, those parts will go in.

(The matter referred to will appear at a later point in the hearings.)

Mr. HUMPHREY. The part about the fisheries to which I was calling especial attention was in regard to the Canadians having special rates over their Government railroads, and in regard to the assistance coming from the Government in the way of the great cold-storage plants. You may not call that a subsidy, but that is what it is. It is the same thing in the end.

In regard to lumber and logs: It is true, as has been stated by Mr. Fordney, as I understand, that there is no discrimination made against the United States; but as a matter of fact the State of Washington is the principal sufferer. There is where the surplus of logs comes. I know that this has occurred frequently: I remember very distinctly having met one of our leading lumbermen one morning, and he was very much disconcerted, for this reason: He had made a contract for a large number of cedar logs in British Columbia, and was running his mill and operating upon logs brought from there. He had made his contracts and his arrangements to run for a certain period of time upon logs that he was to get from British

Columbia, and he received notice that morning that no more could be brought out.

What we complain about is this: When the commissioners were making this reciprocity treaty, why were not these facts gone into, and why were not the interests of our industries out there taken care of? It seems, as a matter of fact, that those who were negotiating this treaty on behalf of the United States knew nothing about these conditions, so far as I am able to ascertain. They apparently did not know that any such conditions existed, in regard to either lumber or logs or fisheries.

Just a word more in regard to lumber. When we were revising the tariff we heard a great deal of talk about taking the tariff off of lumber and revising it for the benefit of the consumer and of the poor man who is going to construct his house. I do not know what the result was all over the country, but I do know that in the State of Washington, instead of lumber being reduced in price, it went up. It went up immediately after the tariff on it was lowered, and it has been up ever since.

Mr. DWIGHT. Was that the producer's price or the consumer's price—the retail or the wholesale price?

Mr. HUMPHREY. It was the price of the manufacturer—at which he sold it. The mills of the State of Washington increased the price of lumber within 30 days after the tariff on it was reduced. The only difference out there was that the Government lost the revenue and the timberlands over in British Columbia increased in price, and the consumer paid more for his lumber. I am not going to stop to reason it out, but those are the facts.

Mr. HARRISON. Was that the wholesale or the retail price?

Mr. HUMPHREY. That was the price of the mills that sold the lumber. I did not trace it any further than that. I do not know what happened from that point on.

Mr. RANDELL. How did the business get hurt, then? It looks as if the Treasury is the only thing that got a lick there.

Mr. HUMPHREY. As far as I am able to discover, the Government Treasury got licked and the man who owned timberlands over in British Columbia got the advantage of it.

Mr. RANDELL. And the man here was not interfered with, because the manufacturer here sold lumber still higher than he did before?

Mr. HUMPHREY. Yes.

Mr. RANDELL. And yet he comes here and swears by all that is holy that it will ruin him if you remove the tax. It seems to me he has a cinch on it in some way.

Mr. UNDERWOOD. Did the mills in Canada advance the price on lumber at the mill as soon as we made the change?

Mr. HUMPHREY. I am not sufficiently informed to speak by the card; but they must have done so.

Mr. RANDELL. Then, on that point, the present condition does not injure the lumber industry in your section of the country, although it prevents the lumber from the northern section of Canada from reaching down toward the southwest prairies?

Mr. HUMPHREY. Oh, I do not think the tariff upon the lumber has the slightest effect whatever anywhere east of the Rocky Mountains.

Mr. RANDELL. Or west of them?

Mr. HUMPHREY. It does, probably, at some points; but when the freight rates—when you get into the Mississippi Valley—are from $10 to $15 a thousand, it is absurd to talk about the tariff of a dollar a thousand affecting the price of the lumber to the consumer, especially when you retail it.

An instance was given to me the other day of where a lumber dealer—that is, a man who manufactured the lumber—had sold to a certain retail dealer here in the city of Washington. I may not quote the figures exactly, but I am giving it to you approximately correctly. He had sold that lumber for $28 a thousand, and he went down here and saw his identical lumber in the lumber yard, and the price of it was $68 a thousand. What is the use of talking about $1 in the way of tariff making a difference to the retailer when there is such a tremendous difference as that after it reaches the market?

Then I want to call your attention to the matter of shingles. I have been unable to ascertain just what the effect of this treaty would be upon shingles; but according to a statement I have received from the president of the Lumbermen's Association of our State, he thinks it reduces it from 50 to 30 cents a thousand, and puts it back where it was before we increased the tariff upon shingles.

Now, I want to give you gentlemen another illustration. Immediately after you increased the tariff upon shingles, the price of shingles went down, and it has been down ever since. It is the only product in our State that did decrease in price after the tariff was changed. In addition to that fact, last year was the first time in 12 or 15 years that our shingle mills have run full time and were not compelled to shut down half of their time; and we are reaching out into new markets to-day. We are now over in these eastern markets, as far east as Boston. We have gotten into a great portion of the American markets that we never reached before; and instead of the consumer being outraged by the tariff upon shingles, he has bought his shingles cheaper than he ever did before, and our mills have been running 12 months of the year instead of 6.

The ACTING CHAIRMAN. Just how do you explain that, Mr. Humphrey?

Mr. HUMPHREY. I have an explanation for it, if you wish to hear it.

The ACTING CHAIRMAN. How has the tariff had that effect?

Mr. HUMPHREY. If the committee wants to hear me, I shall be glad to give my explanation of it.

The ACTING CHAIRMAN. I did not know but that you might like to give it to the committee.

Mr. HUMPHREY. It is not very long. My explanation of that is this—and I may say that that is one time when I prophesied correctly. I made the statement on the floor of the House that that would be the result in regard to shingles.

In the first place it gave to our people in the State of Washington a confidence that they were going to have new markets. There were additional mills established in my State. The increasing of the tariff on shingles did shut out the Canadian shingle very largely—not entirely, but very largely—and it did give the American producer additional markets. By having the additional markets and by being able to run his mill 12 months in the year instead of 6 he was able to produce shingles for a less price, and did do it. That is the whole story, so far as shingles are concerned. I can not see what advantage you are going to have by putting it back again where it was and letting the Canadians supply the market and closing our mills 6 months of the year.

Mr. BOUTELL. It shows that there is a very powerful psychological factor in the tariff, as well as an economical one?

Mr. HUMPHREY. Yes. The very fact that they thought they were going to have new markets made a difference at once.

Mr. BOUTELL. The explanation of it would seem to be all in the one word "confidence;" and the lowering of the rate, creating apprehension, gives the explanation in one word of why disaster has so often followed a reduction.

Mr. HUMPHREY. Of course it is not necessary for me to point out to you again the condition as to oriental labor. Although it was strenuously denied upon the floor of the House at the time, no one who has investigated the question denies now that 75 per cent of the labor engaged in the shingle mills of British Columbia is oriental labor. There is no question about it. It was disputed at the time; but since they have had an opportunity to investigate it no one disputes it.

Now, take the item of coal: You reduced the tariff upon coal——

Mr. HILL. In this bill?

Mr. HUMPHREY. No; before. You propose to do it now.

Mr. HILL. No; this bill increases it.

The ACTING CHAIRMAN. No; it does not increase it.

Mr. HILL. It increases it 4½ cents.

The ACTING CHAIRMAN. No; you are mistaken.

Mr. GAINES. You are mistaken. It simply brings the Canadian tariff on coal down to the 45 cents in America.

Mr. HILL. It reduces the ton to 2,000 pounds.

The ACTING CHAIRMAN. No; it does not, Mr. Hill. By carefully going through the bill you will see that it does not.

Mr. HUMPHREY. Of course, if it does not affect coal, that is another matter. The impression I had was that it did reduce it.

Mr. RANDELL. Mr. Chairman, is it not this way: Does it not leave it at 45 cents, and reduce the ton from 2,240 pounds to 2,000 pounds?

Mr. HILL. That is the way I understand it.

The ACTING CHAIRMAN. No; if you go through all the papers you will see that it does not do that. Canada has a short ton and we have a long ton. There is a mistake in that respect. They tried to give one joint figure for Canada in the tables, by an error. But there is nothing in the agreement, there is nothing in the bill that reduces our ton from 2,240 to 2,000 pounds.

Mr. RANDELL. It gives the ton as a ton of 2,240 pounds in many cases, but in the case of coal it simply says "a ton," and does not say "2,240 pounds."

The ACTING CHAIRMAN. There is no question that the present law makes a ton 2,240 pounds, and the bill makes no change in that.

Mr. RANDELL. Then why does it describe some things as "a ton of 2,240 pounds" and others as "a ton"?

The ACTING CHAIRMAN. Ours is a 2,240-pound ton, and Canada's is a 2,000-pound ton.

Mr. HUMPHREY. Mr. Chairman, I will not discuss the question of coal, then, except to make this observation, that they employ oriental labor quite largely in the coal mines of British Columbia. They are situated at tidewater, and it is easier mining in British Columbia than it is in Washington. It is not so costly. You reduced the tariff upon coal, and the only difference was that the company bringing coal into the city of Seattle—which they do to a very large extent—put the difference in their pockets, and immediately put up the price of their coal; and coal has been higher every day since the tariff was reduced than it was before.

The ACTING CHAIRMAN. There is no proposition in this bill to reduce the duty on coal.

Mr. HUMPHREY. I have nothing to say on that point, then.

The next point I want to call the committee's attention to is in regard to the paper industry. I want to read just a paragraph from a letter that I have received from the Everett Paper & Pulp Co., and then, with the consent of the committee, I should like to leave it to be published—the whole of it. This is written by the president of the company:

It has been drawn to the writer's attention by one of our employees, who was connected with the British Columbia Pulp & Paper Co., that in the operation of that plant Japanese labor was employed, and whilst it may be said that Japanese labor may be available in the State of Washington, still it is our policy not to employ oriental labor as against the American workman.

The British Columbia Government some years ago offered subsidies and concessions by which anyone erecting a paper mill and operating the same was given a selection of large bodies of timber at a very low nominal stumpage, and at this time three of the concessions have been taken up by large plants, and there are at this time two large plants, one in operation at Swanson Bay and another under construction at Powell Lake, the products of which, upon the taking off of the tariff, will place the paper industry on the Pacific coast at a disadvantage.

(The above letter will be found printed in full at the end of Mr. Humphrey's statement.)

The same thing is true here as in the case of the fisheries. Those who were negotiating this treaty seemed to lose sight of the fact that the Canadian Government looks after its own industries in various ways, in the way of subsidies and protections, which this Government does not do; and there is the same question here as in the case of the fisheries. Do you expect private industry in America, with just an imaginary line located a few miles away, to compete with those industries in Canada, backed by the Canadian Government and given these various advantages?

I want to say just a word in regard to oriental labor. While it is not prohibited by the laws of Washington, yet, as a matter of fact, take it in the shingle industry, which employs a good many thousand men: There are very, very few orientals, as shown at the time the matter was under discussion—something less than a thousand, I think—in all the shingle mills of Washington. We do not employ oriental labor in our State. It is not the policy of our people to do it.

Mr. HILL. I should like to ask you a question. Perhaps Mr. Fordney can answer it if you can not. Is there not also a provision in these auction-sale agreements that oriental labor shall not be employed in the manufacture of the timber?

Mr. FORDNEY. Not in any that I ever had or ever saw.

Mr. HILL. I have an indistinct recollection of something of the kind.

Mr. FORDNEY. There is nothing at all in regard to the labor employed in the manufacturing.

Mr. HUMPHREY. I understood that there was a provision in some of the Canadian provinces prohibiting the employment of oriental labor in logging.

Mr. HILL. That is what I understand.

Mr. HUMPHREY. But not in the mills.

Mr. HILL. I thought there was some.

Mr. HUMPHREY. There is a provision prohibiting the employment of oriental labor, as I understand, in logging, but not in the mills.

Mr. FORDNEY. There may be in British Columbia. I am not so familiar with their laws.

Mr. HUMPHREY. I understand that there is a provision of that kind.

Mr. FORDNEY. But that is not so in Ontario and Quebec.

Mr. BOUTELL. How does the oriental labor compare, man for man, with the Caucasian race?

Mr. HUMPHREY. In what respect?

Mr. BOUTELL. In efficiency.

Mr. HUMPHREY. It is not as efficient; but while that is true, it costs less to produce a thousand shingles by oriental labor than it does by white labor, and it costs less to produce a thousand feet of lumber by oriental labor than by white labor.

Mr. BOUTELL. What are these orientals, mostly?

Mr. HUMPHREY. In British Columbia? Chinamen, Japanese, and Hindus. There are more Chinamen than any other race employed in the mills.

The next industry I wish to call the attention of the committee to is the dairying industry. The dairying industry of western Washington is one of our greatest industries. As far as area is concerned, I presume Puget Sound is as great a dairying country as we have in the United States. Under this proposed agreement, we let Canada right down to our markets. They have no markets for dairying products—practically none. I do not see what we receive in return.

The next is the general farming of our Puget Sound country, which is very great, especially in oats and hay. The farmers of my district have furnished the oats for the Government to send to the Philippines, very largely—in fact, almost entirely. But last year the contractor bought his oats in Canada, and paid the duty, and then got them for less than he could buy them for in the State of Washington.

Mr. HARRISON. What is the price of oats in Washington?

Mr. HUMPHREY. I can not tell you that.

Mr. HARRISON. Do you know what the price of hay is?

Mr. HUMPHREY. No; I never bought a ton in my life.

Mr. HARRISON. Or the price on the Canadian side of the border?

Mr. HUMPHREY. No; I do not know that; but I know that the duty is 15 cents a bushel on oats and $4 a ton on hay. They have not been seriously disturbed in the case of hay, but they have been so far as oats are concerned. It will directly affect that industry; and taking all of the products that I have mentioned, I am unable to see where we will get a market for a single one of them in Canada. So far as this bill is concerned, as it affects the State of Washington, we give everything and get nothing.

The ACTING CHAIRMAN. I have been informed that there is a delegation of Canadian farmers at Ottawa protesting against the treaty because of the provisions relating to fruit, claiming that it will admit our fruit into Canada free.

Mr. HUMPHREY. There may be something in that. I think that is probably true.

Mr. DWIGHT. If they are there protesting, let me have this message read in regard to our farmers.

The ACTING CHAIRMAN. You may have it read; but let Mr. Humphrey conclude.

Mr. HUMPHREY. Yes; I will only take a moment more.

In regard to fruit, I want to make an explanation, so that you may not be misled as to that. I think it would be an advantage to some of the fruit raisers of my State—those in the irrigated district, where they raise a fruit that is finer than can possibly be produced anywhere else. They might get an additional market in Canada, not because fruit is not raised in Canada, but because of the higher quality of their fruit, which would perhaps give them a market. I think that is true; and so far as the fruit industry is concerned, it might be of some advantage to the irrigated districts in eastern Washington. However, that does not apply to the western section.

Mr. RANDELL. With reference to oats, you have rather a scarcity of land for the production of oats, have you not?

Mr. HUMPHREY. No. I will say to the gentleman that the greatest oat-producing region in the United States (and I think the greatest in the world) is just south of the Canadian border.

Mr. RANDELL. Do you mean in extent or in quality?

Mr. HUMPHREY. No; not in extent, although it is not very small, either.

Mr. RANDELL. But it is the extent I am talking about. In other words, agricultural land is not abundant in your State, is it? Do you not need all your agricultural land?

Mr. HUMPHREY. We raise more wheat than any State of the Union. We have the greatest wheat country, and our oats——

Mr. FORDNEY. If you will permit me, I will state that the States of California, Washington, and Oregon now use for feed for horses more barley than they do oats, and they always have done so on the Pacific coast. The barley is of such a character on the Pacific coast that it makes extraordinarily good food in the place of oats, and you are very extensive raisers of barley on that coast.

Mr. HUMPHREY. Yes; but that is principally on the eastern side of the State. I am speaking more particularly of the western side. I am speaking more particularly of my own district naturally, because I know more about it, and because it is the one that is the nearest to Canada. We are there where we have no protection in the way of distance, in the way of freight rates. We are right at the border; we have the highway of Puget Sound running up into British Columbia, and we have no protection at all. If you take off the tariff, there will be absolutely open competition. That is the only thing we have to protect us.

Mr. FORDNEY. You speak of the Canadian farmer. Will you please let that telegram be read at this point?

Mr. HUMPHREY. Yes. Just let me make one more statement, and then I am through.

Mr. FORDNEY. I want to ask you some questions.

The ACTING CHAIRMAN. I should like to have Mr. Humphrey conclude. Then we will have the telegram read. There is another gentleman here from New York who wants to be heard.

Mr. HUMPHREY. I have just one more statement to make. I want to call the committee's attention to this fact—and it applies to all products in British Columbia that can be shipped economically for long distances—as soon as the Panama Canal is completed what will happen? Take lumber as an illustration, if you remove the tariff upon lumber the foreign tramp vessel can go into British Columbia and get its cargo and come around into the eastern markets into New York City and the markets upon the Atlantic coast. The American lumberman can not take advantage of that cheap tonnage. If you take off the tariff and place yourselves absolutely upon the same basis, the American manufacturer will be greatly handicapped by that one thing alone. And that is not going to be an inconsiderable item as soon as the Panama Canal is finished.

Mr. LONGWORTH. What would be the freight on 1,000 feet of lumber around the Horn?

Mr. HUMPHREY. I have not any idea, but I do know this, I was talking yesterday with a gentlemen who told me that he was contemplating putting on a line of steamers between the Atlantic and the Pacific coasts as soon as the canal was open. He said he was now thinking of building them, to be ready for that trade; and he told me that he would put the freight rates so low that no railroad could compete with them. So they are going to be very much lower.

Mr. FORDNEY. I will answer the gentleman's question by saying that the freight rate at the present time is from $12 to $15 per 1,000 feet from the Pacific coast to New York.

Mr. HUMPHREY. I might say that by sailing ships, Mr. Longworth, they bring freight to-day from Europe into Seattle for $1.25 a ton. That is by sailing ships.

Mr. HILL. Mr. Humphrey, we shipped 150,000,000 feet of lumber into Canada in 1909. That is about the average. Sometimes it is a good deal more. In 1905 we shipped something over 200,000,000 feet. Do you know where that went from?

Mr. HUMPHREY. No; I have not the slightest idea. I am not a lumberman.

Mr. HILL. Did you hear that two years ago the Canadian Parliament were discussing the question of putting a protective tariff on lumber to protect British America?

Mr. HUMPHREY. Did I hear that?

Mr. HILL. Do you not know that that was a fact? Do they not fear your competition from Washington and Oregon more than you fear their competition from British America?

Mr. HUMPHREY. I do not see why they should. I do not know of any market over there for lumber. There are 90,000,000 people down here.

Mr. HILL. But you know there is a good deal shipped now from Puget Sound into Canada, do you not—into British America?

Mr. HUMPHREY. I did not know there was very much. I do not see why there should be.

Mr. FORDNEY. It is special big building timber and such stuff that they can not get over there.

Mr. HUMPHREY. Exactly.

Mr. FORDNEY. They can not get it to Ontario and Quebec from any other country than from the south or the Pacific coast.

Mr. HUMPHREY. Who is going to buy lumber over in British Columbia?

Mr. LONGWORTH. How much did you say we shipped over there?

Mr. HILL. Two hundred million feet in 1905, and last year about 160,000,000 feet.

Mr. HUMPHREY. Where did that go?

Mr. HILL. That is what I ask you—if you know where it went.

Mr. HUMPHREY. It certainly could not go into British Columbia, because they have over there about how many people? About 500,000 people, and half of those are Orientals. You want to open up the market here all along the northern border, including probably 40,000,000 people, to get into a market over there of a few thousand as far as British Columbia is concerned, and half of those are Orientals.

As far as we are concerned, we are not getting anything out of this bill. There is no market for American products from our part of the country over in Canada. What market they have they raise their own supplies for, with the single exception of this high-class fruit. I am unable to see where there is a market in Canada for any of the products I have mentioned. It is probably true that the manufacturers of Seattle can get over there with some of their logging engines and some of their machinery; and they do that anyway. But so far as farm products are concerned, or lumber, or fish, or shingles, there is no market over there; and if there were, they would supply it themselves right at their door.

Mr. FORDNEY. I can answer the question put by Mr. Hill. The heft of the lumber that goes into Canada is bridge timbers, 9 by 16 bridge sills, and all sorts of timber for construction which they can not produce in Canada unless they cut it out of white pine, which is too high priced to go into that class of timber; so it comes from the South, long-leaf pine from Georgia and Mississippi and other Southern States. It goes into that country for that purpose, and it can be obtained nowhere else in the whole United States unless it comes from the Pacific coast, and there the freight is anywhere from $15 to $35 or $40 per 1,000 feet.

Mr. HUMPHREY. May I submit a little later on, probably to-day or in the morning, some letters that I have received upon this subject?

The ACTING CHAIRMAN. You may. If you will hand them to the stenographer to-day they will be printed to-morrow.

(Mr. Humphrey subsequently handed to the stenographer the letters referred to, which are as follows:)

EVERETT PULP & PAPER CO.,
Everett, Wash., January 30, 1911.

W. E. HUMPHREY,
Representative State of Washington, Washington, D. C.

DEAR SIR: Herein you will please find confirmation of telegram which was sent to you in regard to the President's message to Congress advising the ratification of the reciprocal treaty with Canada.

At the time of the investigation of the pulp and paper industry in 1908, the facts were reported upon to Congress, and you will find, on pages 1862, 1863, 1864, 1865, and 1866 the report of this company, and to which we would most respectfully refer you, for the reason that on page 1865 you will find our argument in regard to the effect upon our plant, and the paper industries of the Pacific coast, in the event of the tariff being taken off paper entirely.

It has been drawn to the writer's attention by one of our employees, who was connected with the British Columbia Pulp & Paper Co., that in the operation of that plant Japanese labor was employed, and while it may be said that Japanese labor may be available in the State of Washington, still it is our policy not to employ oriental labor as against the American workman.

The British Columbia Government some years ago offered subsidies and concessions by which anyone erecting a paper mill and operating the same, was given a selection of large bodies of timber at a very low nominal stumpage, and at this time three of the concessions have been taken up by large plants, and there are at this time two large plants, one in operation at Swanson Bay and another under construction at Powell Lake, the products of which, upon the taking off of the tariff, will place the paper industry on the Pacific Coast at a disadvantage.

The principles of protection, as outlined both by Presidents Roosevelt and Taft, have been that protection should only be given to the extent of the difference in the cost of labor, but it certainly should include also any subsidies or concessions which may be given to manufacturing industries; otherwise the advantages of those subsidies and concessions may mean the annihilation of the plant which has no such subsidies or concessions.

The Pacific coast is still in its development period, and at the present time the very life of our paper industries is dependent upon the protection as against cheaper labor and subsidies of other countries.

We therefore submit the foregoing for your kind consideration, hoping that the paper industries will not be subjected to such a serious blow as the abolishing of the tariff at this time would result in.

Respectfully submitted.
Yours very truly,

W. HOWARTH, *President.*

[Night telegram.]

EVERETT PULP & PAPER CO.,
Everett, Wash., January 28, 1911.

W. E. HUMPHREY,
Representative of State of Washington,
House of Representatives.

Referring President's message to Congress regarding reciprocal treaty with Canada recommending putting printing paper valued under 4 cents upon the free list means practically the annihilation of our plant at this point or any other point in the State of Washington. The subsidies granted by British Columbia Government in the form of valuable timber rights and concessions in consideration of erecting paper and pulp mills in British Columbia and the competitive available cheap labor of Japanese and Chinese, which we have always declined to employ in competition with American labor, places the paper industry of Pacific coast at great disadvantage and against which the tariff passed at last session of Congress gave protection, but which now it is proposed to abolish. We respectfully ask your consideration.

EVERETT PULP & PAPER CO.

OCCIDENTAL FISH CO. (INC.),
Seattle, Wash., January 28, 1911.

The Hon. WILLIAM E. HUMPHREY,
House of Representatives, Washington, D. C.

DEAR SIR: This is to confirm our night letter to you to-day, as follows:

"We urge you to prevent proposed action on reciprocity treaty with Canada so far as it abolishes duty on Canadian fish. Seattle is growing to be headquarters of the fish industry, which amounts to over a half a million dollars monthly. Proposed act would permit at least half of this business passing through Canadian ports instead of Seattle. We also understand Canadian Government rebates one-third of transportation charges to Canadian shippers, which in addition to free entry of their products would injure our business greatly.

"OCCIDENTAL FISH CO. (INC.)."

This matter is one of very great interest to Seattle and the Northwest in general and it would affect all branches of the business. We hope that you will use every effort to prevent anything of this nature being passed as large interests operating in Canada.

would be in a position, with the Government subsidy that they are now receiving, to materially damage us in the conduct of our business, as they could lay these goods down on this side of the line and dispose of them cheaper than we could.

We are sending you under separate cover one of our 1911 calendars, which will, we hope, be of interest—showing the manner in which these fish are taken. The steamer *Weiding Bros.*, mentioned thereon, landed last year about 4,000,000 pounds at Seattle, and this coming season we expect to greatly increase our output.

The fishing industry is the largest in the State of Washington and greatly exceeds in volume the lumber which until recently was the greatest product of our Northwest.

Yours, very truly,

OCCIDENTAL FISH CO. (INC.),
By EDWIN RIPLEY, *Secretary.*

WESTERN CODFISH CO.,
Seattle, January 31, 1911.

Hon. WM. E. HUMPHREY,
   House of Representatives, Washington, D. C.

MY DEAR MR. HUMPHREY: With the approval of all the parties in interest we wired you on January 25 as follows:

"Strong effort now making by importers for reciprocity with Canadian provinces involving free entry green and salted fish. Their cheaper labor and nearness fishing grounds would destroy entirely United States codfisheries, transferring entire business from States to provinces, including British Columbia. On this coast codfishing alone involves permanent investment nearly $1,000,000. Annual outfitting expenditure, $150,000. Annual pay roll, $250,000. Employes 400 fishermen, all sailors. We ask you to join with Massachusetts protective Congressmen in vigorously opposing this fatal blow to this industry of coast."

And last night we again wired you as follows, all of which we now beg to confirm:

"We request and trust that you may make it convenient to appear before the congressional committee to-morrow protesting against Canadian reciprocity measure detrimental to our industry in accordance with our telegram to you January 25."

There is little to be said in addition to the foregoing, except as supplemental, as our first wire conveys to you in brief all that might be said in protest against this proposed Canadian reciprocity measure. The codfish industry of this coast, particularly in regard to Puget Sound, is one of the unproductive industries that has been exploited with the view to putting it on an income-producing basis, the result of which has been a series of financial wrecks brought about largely by reason of lack of proper transportation facilities, lack of population to consume the product, and high cost of production. To those of us who have invested in the business it means the life or death of the industry on this coast, as we could not under any circumstances compete with the Canadian product. As an industry there has never been a cent of dividends paid by the numerous concerns that have attempted to build it up on Puget Sound.

As to the Canadian markets being opened up under this reciprocity arrangement, beg to say that we are practically unable to do business in Victoria and Vancouver, as fish is brought into those markets from Halifax, laid down at prices with which we are unable to compete at a profit. Our sales, therefore, in that market are very small and only occasional, and in such quantities as to meet their immediate requirements when their stock is low. In view of these prevailing conditions we again urge you to join with the Massachusetts Congressmen in vigorously opposing this measure, which will not only work a hardship on the vested interests, but will cause a loss to this country of an industry that bids fair in time to be productive of good results.

We sincerely hope for your consideration and energetic cooperation.

Yours, very truly,

WESTERN CODFISH CO.,
Per D. DAUN EGAN.

PORT BLAKELY MILL CO.,
Port Blakely, Wash., January 30, 1911.

Hon. W. E. HUMPHREY,
   House of Representatives, Washington, D. C

MY DEAR MR. HUMPHREY: I wish to sincerely compliment you on the serious and effective efforts you are making in behalf of the vital question involved in the protection of our shores against foreign invasion. Your speech at Detroit, which I have had the pleasure of reading, is most opportune and convincing.

I also beg to acknowledge receipt of your prompt and very favorable reply Saturday to my night letter wire requesting you to suggest to those who may favor the administration's Canadian reciprocity measure, that in all fairness we are entitled to the same consideration from Canada as we grant her, and especially equivalent to the President's demand in favor of other wood products, viz, pulp and print paper.

We have much territory, including the northern part of Washington and that lying along the shores of the Great Lakes where milling operations are and have been conducted. The latter necessarily removed to Canada when Ontario absolutely prohibited the exportation of logs.

The laws of British Columbia provide that all timber purchased from the province must be manufactured within the province. This would deprive us in the future, and possibly soon, of the privilege of utilizing our plants and labor in the manufacture of this raw material.

Until such time as the Canadian provinces are willing to reciprocate in kind and withdraw all taxes and restrictions of any nature whatever from the exportation of logs of all kinds to be manufactured in our mills, we are certainly not bound to open our markets to their manufactured products.

We will necessarily have to strenuously oppose this reciprocity measure, as the most serious competition we would expect in the removal of the duty would be from Canada and later from Mexico.

I can not understand why the President is so set upon this sacrifice of our industry. It appears to me that he is influenced by the vicious and untrue claims that lumber interests are organized and exacting undue profits on their commodity.

You are well advised that this is not true, and that our industry has been so depressed for several years that more recently many of the larger mills were absolutely compelled to close because of the showing of loss of money in their operations last year.

This is practically true at present, as the majority of the large mills are now idle on the Columbia River and some have gone into receivers' hands and others of minor importance closed on and adjacent to the Sound.

There is no need of our rehearsing the many arguments in our behalf in favor of a reasonable duty on our commodity, but the menace of this reciprocity measure brings sharply to mind the absolute necessity of the enactment of some measure refunding the Panama Canal tolls to American vessels, especially plying between the two coasts.

If we remove the duty and the canal tolls are not refunded, our interests will be vitally demoralized until years from now when the timber in British Columbia and Mexico may be sufficiently exhausted to enable us to successfully compete with them, if in the meantime no vessels will be constructed to carry our commodities between American ports on each coast.

Either the unfavorable and last resort permitting the use of foreign vessels between the two coasts must be resorted to or the Panama tolls refunded, and moderate duties such as exist at present be maintained to furnish a sufficient offset between the cost of operating American and foreign vessels to enable us to secure any means of transportation by water through the canal, and earn enough interest on the investment in the vessels to pay for their continued operation and increased construction.

This measure is vitally menacing to this coast, and I am still more astonished at the serious efforts of the newspaper interests to have the duty removed on wood pulp and print paper, since I know that the entire duties collected on these commodities amount to only about $500,000 last year as shown by the report of the Treasury Department, while the very moderate duty on lumber brought two and half times as much revenue on a minimum ad valorem basis. Surely the moderate amount of duty collected on the material employed in print paper does not merit such a strenuous and vital fight as the entire press of the United States have made against this duty for several years.

I am presuming to send a copy of this letter to Senator Piles and Mr. Fordney.

Yours, very truly,

D. E. SKINNER, *President.*

LARSON LUMBER CO.,
Bellingham, Wash., February 2, 1911.

Hon. W. E. HUMPHREY,
House of Representatives, Washington, D. C.

MY DEAR CONGRESSMAN: Am pleased to note your telegram of February 1 stating that you do not think it will be necessary for any representative from the lumber industry to come on at present and that you will keep us posted, for which I thank you.

I have a copy of the treaty agreement as reported to Congress, sent me by Senator Piles. I note that shingles are reduced from 50 cents to 30 cents, rough lumber from $1.25 to the free list, surfaced lumber protected from 50 cents to $1.50. The average price of lumber imported from Canada figures about $15, hence the protection on surfaced lumber, one and two sides, would be about 5 per cent ad valorem and not to exceed 10 per cent ad valorem on surfaced four sides. The Canadian tariff remains, as I understand it, rough lumber on the free list, shingles on the free list (these two items have never been dutiable in Canada), and lumber surfaced more than one side, matched, tongued and grooved, or otherwise worked, 25 per cent ad valorem. Shiplap, worth $9 at the mill, is the lowest grade of lumber shipped into Canada that is dutiable and on this the Canadian tariff demands $2.25 per 1,000 duty. Flooring, which is the highest grade shipped, is worth about $25 ad valorem and on this the Canadian tariff demands $6.25 duty. If we must have reciprocity on lumber, then the Canadian tariff should be no higher than the American tariff. Eighty-five per cent to 90 per cent of the lumber shipped from the United States into Canada is surfaced, matched, or tongued and grooved.

Of course you understand that conditions at present are very much depressed in the lumber business on the American side, whereas they are very much inflated on the Canadian side on account of their abnormal prosperity. Two years ago, when we sought the protection of the present Payne-Aldrich bill, conditions were just the reverse, and the fact is that any time when Canada's prosperity is checked and our own conditions recovered somewhat, she is the exporter of lumber and not the importer.

Another feature of the reciprocity agreement is that it grants free lumber without asking Canada to withdraw her restrictions on the exportation of saw logs. The result of the present reciprocity agreement will be that many mills will move from the American side to the Canadian side and manufacture there, exporting the rough lumber into the United States. Again, if reciprocity must come, we should have an equal opportunity with British Columbia in manufacturing the raw material. I am giving you these facts in order to place them before you for use in case you may require them.

I want to congratulate you on your very able speech before the National Association of Manufacturers in Washington and again in Detroit on the question of the merchant marine and its relation to the commerce and naval protection of this country. You are rapidly making a name for yourself along the line of this subject, and as one of your friends and well-wishers I want to see you push the ship-subsidy matter to a successful conclusion.

Yours, very truly,   J. H. BLOEDEL.

Mr. FORDNEY. I wish you would have that telegram read now for the benefit of the gentlemen who have been asking these questions.

(The clerk thereupon read aloud the following telegram:)

TROY, N. Y., *February 7, 1911—5 p. m.*
Hon. JOHN W. DWIGHT, M. C.,
          Washington, D. C.:

The Tompkins County State Grange delegation oppose pending Canadian reciprocity as unjust discrimination against the farmer in favor of the manufacturer.

E. T. WALLENBECK, *Chairman.*

The ACTING CHAIRMAN. Mr. Grant, do you wish to be heard?
Mr. GRANT. Yes, sir.

STATEMENT OF MR. R. P. GRANT, OF CLAYTON, N. Y.

Mr. GRANT. Mr. Chairman and gentlemen of the committee, I come here as the representative of the Watertown Produce Exchange and the northern farmers.

The ACTING CHAIRMAN. Watertown, N. Y.?

Mr. GRANT. Yes, sir; along the Canadian frontier.

The Watertown Produce Exchange is the largest inland cheese board that there is on the American continent. In fact, it is the largest cheese board in the world. Our output of cheese there this last season was approximately 200,000 boxes. The total receipts from the sale of those 200,000 boxes was $1,600,000. We have several milk trains running out of Jefferson County to the eastern markets; and we also manufacture butter. The dairy output of our cheese parish is approximately $4,000,000 per annum. Our county is a dairy and hay and manufacturing county. According to the census of 1900, Jefferson County was the tenth greatest county in the United States in the total amount of her products. So you will see from that that we stand at the head of the New York counties as a dairy and cheese county.

We are producers of a large amount of hay for our county. We sell at least $1,000,000 worth of hay to the eastern markets. During this last season, our farmers received for their hay from eleven to fourteen dollars per ton, according to the quality. You can buy Canada hay to-day, and the best of it, at $7 a ton. You will see that if you allow this Canada hay to come into the United States in competition with our American hay, it will reduce the market price of that hay from one to two dollars per ton.

Mr. HILL. What is the price of your hay, on the average?

Mr. GRANT. This season it is from eleven to fourteen dollars, according to the quality.

Mr. HILL. Where do you get your authority for the statement that the price of Canada hay is $7 a ton?

Mr. GRANT. I get it from a hay buyer.

Mr. HILL. That is an individual instance?

Mr. GRANT. No; I understand that is the ordinary price for the best of hay.

Mr. HILL. The average price of all hay in Canada, according to the Canadian Government reports, in 1909 was $11.14 on the farm, and in 1910 it was $9.66. So that it is higher in Canada than it is in Watertown, on your own statement.

Mr. GRANT. I do not so understand; pardon me.

Mr. HILL. I am giving you the Government statistics.

Mr. ELLIS. That would include British Columbia, where the price is very much higher than it is in the statistics given by the gentleman.

Mr. FORDNEY. Mr. Chairman, if you will permit me, I will have here in three minutes a letter from the Hay Dealers' Association in New York, dated December 10, that will bear out the gentleman's statement that in Quebec hay is selling for from $7 to $8 a ton.

Mr. GAINES. Is it not notorious that hay is considerably higher in America than it is in Canada?

Mr. FORDNEY. Why, certainly.

Mr. GAINES. We have had so much evidence of the fact that I do not think it is worth while questioning it.

Mr. GRANT. I am a banker as well as a cheese manufacturer, and we are furnishing money to-day for American hay buyers to go into Canada and buy hay at $7 per ton. They tell me that they go and buy the best of the hay in Canada for $7 per ton, just opposite the New York State line. I am also credibly informed that a New York City buyer went into Canada two weeks ago and picked up all the hay he could get, and all he paid was $7 per ton. I know the buyer very well. He is an eastern buyer.

Mr. RANDELL. Is there a scarcity on this side that causes you to go over there and get that hay?

Mr. GRANT. No, sir; we had a big crop this season. Northern New York had more than double the amount of hay this year that it had last year.

Mr. RANDELL. Is it not the plan to keep up the price so high that they have to go and scour all over the country to get hay?

Mr. GRANT. If the hay buyers can buy it for $7 it is cheaper to buy it there and pay duty on it than to pay the Americans from $11 to $14.

Mr. RANDELL. But when you have a great big crop do you not hold your price up?

Mr. GRANT. We have to take the market price.

Mr. RANDELL. Do you not make the market price?

Mr. GRANT. No, sir; we do not make it.

Mr. RANDELL. Who makes it?

Mr. GRANT. The eastern hay market makes the price of our hay.

Mr. BOUTELL. I suppose you try to do the same with hay that they do farther south with cotton, do you not—get all you can for it?

Mr. GRANT. I am not familiar with cotton. It costs our farmers about $10 a ton to make their hay. You understand that American labor is very high and very scarce, so far as farm labor is concerned.

Mr. RANDELL. That is because the cost of living is so high that they have got to charge higher wages, is it not?

Mr. GRANT. I do not understand it so.

Mr. RANDELL. You do not understand that?

Mr. GRANT. No.

Mr. RANDELL. In reference to the cotton of the South, I will say that neither there nor any were else is the price enhanced by the brutal power of law over the tariff. You understand that cotton is free; do you not? I suppose the gentlemen of the committee understand that, Mr. Boutell. Whatever price cotton brings is the natural price of the market. Now, why could you not prosper in that way in New York in reference to hay?

Mr. GRANT. As I understand, the cotton market is controlled by speculators and operators. There is no one that controls hay. It simply goes into the market and is sold on the market for what it is worth.

The ACTING CHAIRMAN. Mr. Grant, with regard to hay, I find that we export to Canada about twice as much hay as we import from Canada.

Mr. GRANT. I was not aware of that.

The ACTING CHAIRMAN. The movement is not large in either direction; but we export about twice as much to Canada, I find by the figures, as we import from Canada, taking the year 1909 as the basis.

Mr. GRANT. The year 1909 is not a fair basis of comparison, Mr. Chairman.

The ACTING CHAIRMAN. That is the only year for which I happen to have the figures.

Mr. GRANT. I will tell you why.

Mr. RANDELL. Before we leave that question, Mr. Grant, you said that cotton is controlled by speculators and manipulators. You are talking about the New York Cotton Exchange, are you?

Mr. GRANT. All I know is what I read.

Mr. RANDELL. I say, is that what you are talking about?

Mr. GRANT. Yes.

Mr. RANDELL. There is some legislation on foot to knock that out; and there is also legislation on foot to knock out this tariff and to keep us from bringing it into Canada.

Mr. GRANT. Your statement, Mr. Chairman, is undoubtedly correct, for this reason: Northern New York had a drought last season a year ago, and the fact was that many of our farmers had to buy hay and grain to carry their stock through.

Mr. HARRISON. What was hay worth last year, Mr. Grant?

Mr. GRANT. We could get from $15 up to $20 for hay.

Mr. HARRISON. Yes.

The ACTING CHAIRMAN. Mr. Grant, is not there pretty often a shortage of hay in northern New York and northern New Hampshire and northern Vermont, and do not the farmers who are in the dairy business there sometimes find it difficult to carry their cows through the winter, and would it not be worth something to them to be able to buy hay without having this duty upon it, if they could get it?

Mr. GRANT. I am not familiar with the States of Vermont and New Hampshire, but I am living on the frontier. I live at the Thousand Islands, on the St. Lawrence River. The same drought conditions that would affect northern New York would affect southern Canada, and the southern Province of Ontario is quite a hay and dairy Province. They would have the same conditions from a drought that we would have. But we do occasionally have a drought, although not very often.

Now, speaking of cheese: Ten or 15 years ago the United States only took about one-third of our output that was made in the United States. Two-thirds of our cheese had to go to England to be sold; and when it went to England to be sold it had to be sold at the Englishman's price—not the American's price. That cheese sold for from 6 to 10 cents a pound. That paid the farmer that furnished the milk from 60 to 80 cents a hundred for his milk. Now that condition has changed. For the last two or three years the United States has taken virtually our whole output of cheese. We have a home market in the United States which virtually takes all our cheese, and takes it at good prices.

To illustrate: Along in the summer, when cheese was the highest, we got 14, 14½, and 15 cents a pound for cheese. The Canadian farmer was selling his best Ontario cheese at the same time for 10 cents, 10⅜, or 10¼ cents.

Mr. HARRISON. What is the amount of the duty?

Mr. GRANT. Six cents a pound. If our cheese had gone up three-quarters of a cent higher, the Canadian cheese could have come into our market as a competitor and could have paid the 6 cents a pound duty.

Mr. RANDELL. How much would that reduce the price of cheese to the laboring man who wanted to eat it?

Mr. GRANT. I think it would reduce the price of cheese to the farmer that produces it.

Mr. RANDELL. I am talking about the laboring man that eats it.

Mr. GRANT. I will tell you about the laboring man that eats it: The minute you get cheese up so high that it becomes a luxury, the laboring man does not buy it.

Mr. RANDELL. Did it get that high last year?

Mr. GRANT. Our grocery men there sold it for about 18 cents a pound, when cheese was——

Mr. RANDELL. It got to be a luxury, then?

Mr. GRANT. No. They will buy it up to 16 or 17 or 18.

Mr. GAINES. When the grocery man sold it for 18 cents a pound, cheese was what? What were you about to say?

Mr. GRANT. The average price that the farmers received for the cheese in 1909 was 13.7 cents. In 1910 the average price was 13.9 cents a pound. Our grocery men are perfectly willing to sell cheese at 2 cents a pound profit, and our laboring men are perfectly willing to buy cheese if they can buy it at 16, 17, and 18 cents. But if you get cheese up to 20 or 21 cents or upward, it becomes a luxury, and they cut it out. Still, at the same time, cheese is a very economical food even at 20 cents, for this reason: There is no bone, there is no gristle; it is a pound of solid food. It is not like a pound of beef or mutton, where two-thirds of it or one-third of it is waste.

Mr. RANDELL. Without any tariff on cheese would not the laboring people in New York get cheese much cheaper and use it a great deal more for food?

Mr. GRANT. I do not think the laboring man would buy any more as long as he could buy it up to 18 cents; but the farmer that produced it would get less if you let this Canada cheese come in. If this duty of 6 cents a pound is taken off it will reduce the price to the farmer at least 2 cents a pound.

Mr. RANDELL. And that would not make it cheaper for the laboring man?

Mr. GRANT. Yes; it naturally would make it a little cheaper for the laboring man. That is true.

Mr. HARRISON. Mr. Grant, where do the most of your farm hands come from?

Mr. GRANT. They come from Canada.

The ACTING CHAIRMAN. Do you know where the Canadian cheese goes?

Mr. GRANT. Yes, sir. The Canadians have no home market.

The ACTING CHAIRMAN. It goes to England, does it not?

Mr. GRANT. It all goes to England. It goes at the Englishman's prices. That is the reason why they could only get 10 cents for their best cheese when we were getting, in the height of the season, for about four weeks, 14, 14½, and occasionally as high as 15 cents, for a few factories.

The ACTING CHAIRMAN. Do you think England, where the Canadian market is now, would stop consuming Canadian cheeses if we took off the duty, and that they would entirely change the market and send all the surplus here? Or would not they keep on sending to England and supplying their trade there?

Mr. GRANT. They would sell it wherever they could get the most money for it; and they could get more money in the United States than they could in England for the cheese to-day if you would throw off this 6 cents a pound duty.

Mr. LONGWORTH. You say your laboring men, your farm hands, come from Canada. Do you mean that they come during the busy season and then go back?

Mr. GRANT. Yes; many of them do.

Mr. LONGWORTH. It is imported labor, then?

Mr. GRANT. It is not imported labor, because they come over there and ask for work. Nobody sends for them.

Mr. LONGWORTH. Yes; but having gotten their wages, then they return to Canada?

Mr. GRANT. They return. The farmers have to pay them $50 a month through the haying and harvesting. The farmers of northern New York are short of help.

Mr. RANDELL. Would it not be better for them to lose their cheese business than it would for the laboring people that live in this country to have to pay more for their food?

Mr. GRANT. Well, we are an agricultural county. I can not answer your question. I am looking at it from the farmer's standpoint. I am interested in and managing owner of six cheese factories, and help sell for and control five more; so that I have quite an interest in the cheese industry.

Mr. RANDELL. Do you export any cheese?

Mr. GRANT. Not now. We used to export cheese. I used to export cheese 10 or 12 years ago.

Mr. RANDELL. Did you do it profitably?

Mr. GRANT. No, sir; it was not profitable.

(Thereupon, at 12.20 o'clock p. m., the committee took a recess until 2.30 o'clock p. m. of the same day.)

AFTERNOON SESSION.

COMMITTEE ON WAYS AND MEANS,
HOUSE OF REPRESENTATIVES,
Wednesday, February 8, 1911.

The committee met, pursuant to the taking of recess, at 2.30 o'clock p. m., Hon. Samuel W. McCall presiding.

Mr. FORDNEY. If you are willing, Mr. Chairman, I will complete this letter. As I stated before, it is dated December 16, 1910, written by the American Hay Co., 24–26 Stone Street, New York, directed to Mr. E. C. Forrest, secretary-treasurer Michigan Hay Association, Saginaw, Mich., and is as follows:

THE AMERICAN HAY CO.,
24-26 Stone Street, New York, December 16, 1910.
Mr. E. C. FORREST,
Secretary-Treasurer Michigan Hay Association, Saginaw, Mich.

DEAR SIR: Replying to yours of December 14, the Canadian hay situation is as follows:

Ontario: Crop very similar to Michigan. Very little western Ontario hay shipped to the United States; some going to the Canadian far west, with the exception of a limited section. In the eastern section Ontario hay cuts no figure in our supplies.

New Brunswick: Crop immense; mostly clover grades; considerable No. 2; some of the best timothy finding its way into New England. Mixed grades will be mostly fed where raised. Some will go out of St. John, New Brunswick, for the United Kingdom and continental ports. During the winter months a few thousand tons of timothy will go to the West Indies and the United Kingdom.

Prices: Around $8 to $8.50 f. o. b. on No. 2; $7 to $7.50 f. o. b. on clover grades. Rate to Boston, around $4.50 to $5 per ton. Rate to St. John, New Brunswick, around $2 per ton.

Quebec is practically the "main tent" as far as our Michigan and Ohio friends are concerned.

First. Quantity inexhaustible.

Second. Grades, a limited amount of No. 1, plenty of No. 3; a good proportion of No 2, and a large surplus of extra nice bright clover and clover mixed.

Third. Outlet, a limited amount of the best timothy going to Scotland and a somewhat large quantity of clover grades to other United Kingdom and continental ports; but with a large crop generally on the other side, hay must be bought very low in Quebec to place it there at a profit.

The situation is such that a very large quantity of hay, such as we can get in Quebec, must find its way into New York and New England; and the quicker the Michigan and Ohio shippers realize what they are up against, they will quit paying exhorbitant prices, with the expectation of placing the hay East.

Prices in Quebec at present: Good No. 2 timothy, $8.50 to $10.50, according to size of bales and location; some No. 1 large bales, $12, and No. 1 small, $11; No. 1 light mixed, $8 to $10, according to location and size of bales; No. 1 clover and heavy mixed, $6.50 and $7. Freight and duty combined runs about $7.50 per ton both to New York and New England points.

If there is to be any improvement in our markets on hay similar to the Quebec grades, it should be with us about May, as the roads in Quebec are then very bad. Unless the next growing crop shows unusually bad in Quebec there will be heavy canal-boat receipts to arrive in New York from the middle of June. The hay is there to come all right. There are thousands and thousands of tons all pressed in many sections at present.

Very truly, yours,   THE AMERICAN HAY CO.

STATEMENT OF MR. R. P. GRANT, OF CLAYTON, N. Y.

Mr. GRANT. I do not want to try to answer the gentleman, for I can not do it from an intelligent standpoint, when he speaks about Nova Scotia and New Brunswick and the West. I can only talk from a local standpoint—for northern New York. When I say you can buy the best hay in Canada on the frontier, opposite the State of New York, for $7, I am telling you what is being done day after day. And you want to remember that the man who buys this hay has to press it. That makes an additional tax on the hay of $1, so that the best Canada hay, when he buys it and presses it, stands him in $8 per ton. That is all I have to say on the hay business. I am familiar with it, because we have five hay buyers in the town where I live, four of them doing their business through our bank. We are sending bills of lading day after day with the shipments of hay, and our American farmers are getting from $11 to $14 per ton for their hay, according to quality. The less clover, the higher the price; the more clover, the lower the price, and so on.

Speaking about milk, when the McKinley tariff was established we had a tariff of 2 cents a gallon on milk. At that time the American farmer was getting from 60 to 80 cents per hundred pounds for his milk. That condition has changed in the last two years. In the last year, say, 1910, the farmers of northern New York have been getting about $1.25 a hundred, net, for their milk. Instead of reducing this tariff of 2 cents a gallon on the raw milk, it should be increased to 3 cents. Two cents a gallon on raw milk would be to make a duty of about 24 cents on a hundred pounds of milk, when the American farmer was only getting 60 to 80 cents a hundred for his milk. If the duty were 3 cents on a gallon, as it should be, that would make on or about 36 cents.

Mr. McCALL. Then the higher the price of a necessary of life the higher you would make it still by raising the tariff accordingly?

Mr. GRANT. Yes.

Mr. McCALL. Do you not think it should operate the other way, that when a necessary gets up very high you should not use the law to make it still higher, but you should use the law to pull it down, if you can?

Mr. GRANT. I will tell you why I make that statement: I claim to protect the American farmer; there should be a duty of 3 cents a gallon, or 36 cents a hundred, on milk, for this reason: To-day there is an overproduction of milk in the State of New York, and what is the result? The farmers get on or about 3 cents a quart for their milk. The men in New York peddle it out at 9 cents a quart. If you can tell me why the high cost of living does not rest with the middle man I would like to hear you. The honest farmer gets 3 cents a quart for his milk, and the man who sells it gets 9 cents. There is a profit of 6 cents a quart for the middle man.

Mr. HILL. Would that be relieved any by stopping the importation? Is not the trouble what you are now specifying?

Mr. GRANT. The overproduction?

Mr. HILL. Not at all; but the excessive cost of distribution. You say you get 3 cents a quart. Do we have any importations of milk from Canada?

Mr. GRANT. I do not think so; not that I know of, not in our locality.

Mr. HILL. Then why would you want to raise the duty if we do not have any importations?

Mr. GRANT. The minute you let that Canadian milk come in free of duty it will only go into our eastern markets and make a still larger surplus than we have at the present time.

Mr. HILL. Is there any surplus to come from Canada now?

Mr. GRANT. The southeast frontier of Canada, joining the northern frontier of the State of New York, is a dairy province, all along the frontier.

Mr. HILL. Then why do we not import now with a lower duty? You say it ought to be increased. Why do we not import now?

Mr. GRANT. I made the statement that we ought to protect the American farmer. When you come to cream I will agree with you. At the time the McKinley bill made the duty 2 cents a gallon on milk the duty on cream was made 5 cents a gallon. I have been told by two different importers who have been importing Canada cream into the States during the last year that the intention of the original bill was to have it 5 cents per quart on cream instead of 5 cents a gallon.

Mr. HILL. Do we import much cream?

Mr. GRANT. A lot of it.

Mr. HILL. But no milk?

Mr. GRANT. But no milk.

Mr. HARRISON. Has there not been a reclassification of the customs duty levied on cream under the last tariff law?

Mr. GRANT. No, sir; it is still 5 cents a gallon, when it should be 5 cents a quart. You take raw milk at 3 cents a quart and raw cream at 5 cents a gallon, and there is a ratio of $2\frac{1}{2}$ where the ratio ought to be 10 to 1.

Mr. McCALL. Is there not such a growing demand for cream and such an increased consumption of it in cities by reason of methods they have of preserving it, putting it in sealed bottles and things of that sort, that we can not get all the cream now we need, and that it commands an artificially high price when it goes into the market?

Mr. GRANT. The importers of cream I am familiar with make it into butter; it is not sold as cream.

Mr. McCALL. Is not butter practically as high as it ever has been?

Mr. GRANT. Yes.

Mr. McCALL. It has not affected, then, the price of butter, although we get cream for 5 cents a gallon?

Mr. GRANT. The market on butter has been affected very much.

Mr. HARRISON. Is there not a reclassification of cream under the present tariff act, by assessing it at the amount of butter fat in it?

Mr. GRANT. I am not aware of it.

Mr. HARRISON. I think the witness is not fully informed on that. I know that is a fact. Just one more question. Will you tell me how, when you have stated the profits the farmers are making are twice as much on milk as they were a couple of years ago, you think they need more protection or any protection at all?

Mr. GRANT. You misunderstood me. It was 10 or 15 years ago when they were getting 60 to 80 cents net for their cream.

Mr. HARRISON. Are they not getting twice as much as they were?

Mr. GRANT. At that time they were struggling for existence.

Mr. HARRISON. It is a pretty big margin when you double it.

Mr. GRANT. Not when you take everything else into consideration— the cost of living, the cost of labor, and everything they have to buy. When the farmers were selling their raw milk for from 60 to 80 cents a hundred, they could not pay their mortgages; they could not pay the interest on their mortgages.

Mr. HARRISON. I can assure you that there is no evidence of any overproduction of milk in New York City.

Mr. GRANT. I have been told so within a week.

Mr. HARRISON. Not from the consumer's point of view.

Mr. GRANT. I have been told so by reputable men in my own county. I am only quoting them; I can not say, except what I get from headquarters in New York City. But I got it from a milkman.

Mr. BOUTELL. What kind of cheese do you make in your neighborhood?

Mr. GRANT. We make mostly a cheddar cheese.

Mr. BOUTELL. Is that one of the orange-colored cheeses?

Mr. GRANT. Either all plain white or colored. The southern trade demands a colored cheese; the eastern trade demands a white cheese.

Mr. BOUTELL. Then it is the same cheese, except with a different color?

Mr. GRANT. The same cheese, only colored.

Mr. BOUTELL. With what is it colored?

Mr. GRANT. It is a vegetable color. I do not know that I can tell you the chemical analysis of it. It is a vegetable compound.

Mr. BOUTELL. And how is it with butter?

Mr. GRANT. Butter is colored also, in the winter time. You take fodder-hay milk and make it into butter, and you have a light, white butter, and you have to use cheese color to give it a natural grass color.

Mr. BOUTELL. And is butter colored to meet the tastes of the different markets, too, the same as cheese?

Mr. GRANT. No; just to get the natural straw color of what would be made from grass.

Mr. BOUTELL. The reason why I ask is that I have often noticed in certain sections of the country, in the hotels, where a stranger goes, they are apt to have a very, very white butter.

Mr. GRANT. Yes.

Mr. BOUTELL. That is, in the northern hotels, in New York, or Boston.

Mr. GRANT. Yes.

Mr. BOUTELL. I have noticed also in the West, in the hotels of the same grade, that they have a highly colored butter.

Mr. GRANT. That is the butter color, as we call it, used in coloring it.

Mr. BOUTELL. I was wondering whether you colored butter for different markets.

Mr. GRANT. No; we do not in our locality.

Mr. McCALL. That is the oleomargarine color, is it not; that was invented first by the oleomargarine people?

Mr. GRANT. The natural grass color would be a nice straw color for butter, and the coloring matter is used to try to imitate, to get a natural grass color to butter.

Mr. BOUTELL. And they get it a good deal more vivid sometimes, do they not; a good deal brighter color than the natural grass color?

Mr. GRANT. They may overcolor it, possibly, sometimes. Some churnings might be overcolored; that is true.

Mr. HILL. Mr. Grant, have you examined the statistics at all in connection with the reciprocity message?

Mr. GRANT. No, sir.

Mr. HILL. I wish you would do it before you leave town. I think it would modify your views very considerably. I find this statement, and I would like to know whether it is correct or not: On page 32, amongst the articles imported into the United States from the Dominion of Canada in 1910, $1,779 worth of milk and $577,698 worth of cream.

Mr. CALDERHEAD. That seems to corroborate what he has been saying.

Mr. HILL. And I find in the statistics that Canada exports, to all countries, milk and cream, condensed, in 1909, $90,520 worth all told, and exported to the United State of condensed milk and cream, $8,256 worth. So that it would seem to be, so far as milk is concerned, absolutely of no consideration; but of cream, there seems to have been a large quantity, $577,000 worth.

Mr. GRANT. The 5 cents duty on the gallon of cream would let it in, and it has broken up, or shut up, a good many cheese factories in the Province of Ontario, shipping their cream into the States. But in our locality there is no cream shipped.

Mr. McCALL. Do you think that would reduce the price of cream materially in the United States?

Mr. GRANT. Shipping that in?

Mr. McCALL. Yes.

Mr. GRANT. It made so much more butter in the United States.

Mr. McCALL. Yes; but does it meet the consumption? I understand, on the basis of 25 cents a pound, we use something like $350,-000,000 or $400,000,000, in value, of butter every year. What is a little item of about a half a million dollars for cream? Would that be a drop in the bucket?

Mr. GRANT. It would affect our northern New York farmers a good deal, because they come right in there in direct competition with them.

Mr. McCALL. Such an infinitesimal amount as that? How could it affect the price of butter?

Mr. GRANT. It would affect us locally. The Canadian farmers want this free trade. They had a mass meeting at Ottawa three or four weeks ago, and they were bound and determined that Sir Wilfred Laurier, the prime minister there, should give them free trade with the United States, so they could get their dairy products in here—their hay, butter, cheese, eggs, poultry, and things of that kind. But our local grangers are opposed to letting that stuff come in, and I understand our State grangers are also opposed to letting it in.

Mr. HARRISON. Do you know it is estimated that there are about 12 American farmers to 1 Canadian farmer, and yet you would have us people believe that the 1 Canadian farmer could terrorize the 12 American farmers?

Mr. GRANT. The most of those Canadian farmers are right north of us on the border, there, in the Province of Ontario. They are not strung out in the far West.

Mr. FORDNEY. Mr. Grant, one genuine burglar can terrorize the whole people of New York. [Laughter.]

Mr. HARRISON. You do not know our town. [Renewed laughter.]

Mr. GRANT. Two or three did in London, anyway.

Mr. FORDNEY. Mr. Grant, the chairman asked you a little while ago, if the importation of milk and cream at the present time did injure or jeopardize your industry, why have it? Is there any condition existing to-day that did not exist when the Dingley law and the Payne law were effected in which there was a duty put on those articles?

Mr. GRANT. There were no shipments of milk or cream into the States.

Mr. FORDNEY. If it was wise to put a duty on cream at that time, is there any good reason why it would not be wise to hang on to it now?

Mr. GRANT. I think it would be wise to hang on to it now.

Mr. FORDNEY. That is my opinion, unless there are some conditions that the friends of this measure can point out that change conditions to-day from what they were before; this duty should be retained, do you not think so?

Mr. GRANT. Yes.

Mr. HARRISON. And meanwhile the price that the farmer gets for his cream has increased from 60 cents to $1.25.

Mr. GRANT. That was the exception. A year ago they got from $1 to $1.05, and the year before that they got from 90 cents to $1.

Mr. FORDNEY. I want to ask Mr. Harrison if he is in favor of lowering the price of milk or any other American products to the farmer?

Mr. HARRISON. To the consumer. I do not think the farmer gets more than his fair share for any agricultural product to-day.

Mr. FORDNEY. Do you think it is possible to lower the price to the consumer without also lowering it to the farmer?

Mr. HARRISON. I do.

Mr. FORDNEY. I would like to know how you could do that.

Mr. HARRISON. I think the retailers, the middlemen, are responsible for holding up these prices. If we have a larger supply from which to buy our food products, we are going to get cheaper food in the cities without hurting the American farmer, in my judgment. I think the so-called protection to the American farmer is a fake.

Mr. FORDNEY. I do not know anything about the price of cream, because I have not dealt in it; but I do know that when prices were lower on wheat, wheat sold in my home city for 48 cents a bushel that is now bringing 90 cents. The farmer gets that. I would like to know how we are going to lower the price of flour without also lowering the price of wheat to the farmer, the man who produces it.

Mr. GRANT. Mr. Chairman, on the heels of what has been said, I wish to read just a short article, what the minister of agriculture in Canada says. There was a dairymen's convention at Cowansville, Canada, Monday—that is, a week ago last Monday—and the question of reciprocity was discussed from the Canadian viewpoint. Hon. Sydney Fisher, minister of agriculture in Canada, said:

We have made an arrangement with the United States for the free entry into their markets of our butter and cheese, milk and cream. That at one blow gives you not only the markets of Montreal, Sherbrooke. St. Hyacinthe, and such towns, but the markets of New York, Boston, Worcester, Lowell, and the New England States.

You see how the minister of agriculture there is crowing over this proposed treaty.

Mr. McCALL. He was talking to his constituents, was he not?

Mr. GRANT. No; he was talking facts. You take the duty off the agricultural products, and the American farms along the northern frontier will depreciate in value at least 20 per cent or more; and as the American farms go down, the Canadian farms, across the river, will go up. Our farms along our northern frontier are worth from $40 to $60 an acre for agricultural purposes; the farms along the Canadian frontier are worth from $25 to $30 an acre for agricultural purposes, with this duty left as it is at the present time. To remove this duty on agricultural implements would make the Canadian farms go up and the American farms go down. Now, Mr. Chairman and gentlemen, as the representative of the farmers of northern New York, I am very much obliged to you for having given me the privilege of appearing and stating our side of the case.

Mr. BROUSSARD. Before you go away, may I ask you a question?

Mr. GRANT. Yes, sir.

Mr. BROUSSARD. If what you gentlemen who are protesting against the removal of duties on farm products say is true, will it not result in a good many people engaged in agriculture on the farms abandoning that vocation and moving to the cities and towns?

Mr. GRANT. The poor farmers will have to do it.

Mr. BROUSSARD. That is your conclusion?

Mr. GRANT. And the good farmers, instead of sending their sons and daughters to school to be educated, will have to keep them home, or they will have to flood the villages and cities looking for employment.

Mr. BROUSSARD. Will not this result, that if the farmers move from the farms to the towns and villages the consequent lesser production on the farms will tend to increase the prices to the consumer of the products of the farms, instead of lowering them?

Mr. GRANT. That might be.

Mr. BROUSSARD. What is your opinion about that?

Mr. GRANT. If they vacate the farms and go to the villages, of course that will make a less supply to be furnished.

Mr. BROUSSARD. What would the effect be upon labor in the towns and cities where this population would go?

Mr. GRANT. That depends upon the prosperity of the country, whether the machine shops can run, and the like of that, and give employment to them.

Mr. BROUSSARD. Is it not a fact that there is a complaint in this country now that too many people move from the farms to towns and cities?

Mr. GRANT. Yes, sir.

Mr. BROUSSARD. And that is one of the things charged by the people as one of the reasons why the cost of living is so high?

Mr. GRANT. Yes, sir. But, gentlemen, you want to reach the middleman. He is one of the main factors in the high cost of living. Take the milk question, for instance. I saw an article the other day where a man put $350,000 in butter. He paid 31 and 32 cents a pound for the butter; he could not sell that butter in the American markets, and he was forced to ship it to European ports and got only 23 cents a pound for his butter.

Mr. HILL. Have you any idea how much butter Canada produces?

Mr. GRANT. I have not.

Mr. HILL. Have you any idea how much she exports?

Mr. GRANT. I have not.

Mr. HILL. Have you any idea how much she imports?

Mr. GRANT. I have not.

Mr. HILL. Then what grounds have you, without knowing those facts, for expressing an opinion as to the effect of Canadian reciprocity with the United States on butter? As a matter of fact, Canada exported last year enough butter to give the American people two-thirds of 1 ounce in a year, not enough for a single breakfast for the American people. They exported that to every country in the world, taking it altogether. Now, the export is insignificant, trivial. It is the same with milk. It is the same with all of those butter products; they have not got any surplus to amount to anything. If all the eggs that were exported from Canada to the United States were sent to the city of New York alone, each citizen of New York could have one egg in two years and a half. How can it hurt us?

Mr. GRANT. I am not very well posted on eggs.

Mr. HILL. My suggestion is that while we personally appreciate the information, I would like to have it based on facts and not surmises.

Mr. FORDNEY. Mr. Grant, if all the eggs that the gentleman has mentioned came into the State of New York, or into practically one port of entry, it would amount to a great deal, would it not?

Mr. GRANT. As I understand it, yes, sir.

Mr. FORDNEY. And again, when he speaks about the eggs, some gentleman made a statement here the other day that there were not enough eggs coming into this country from Canada to make one egg omelet for the American people. When he began to figure out how long that egg omelet would be if it were stretched out in a natural way, put upon a dish at the Waldorf-Astoria, it would go seven times around the earth. But let me tell the gentleman this, that at the present time there is a 5-cent duty on cream; there is a 25-cent duty per bushel on potatoes, and the statistics show that we imported only 96,000 bushels of potatoes from Canada last year. When potatoes were on the free list in 1896 there were more than a thousand carloads of potatoes coming from Canada to the ports of entry of Port Huron and Detroit, in the State of Michigan, over 600,000 bushels through those two ports into the State of Michigan. There is protection now to those industries, to the American farmer. But put them on the free list and they will make things blue.

Mr. GRANT. It will certainly make the farmers blue.

Mr. HILL. I will ask the clerk to give you a copy of the reciprocity message and the statistics. You will find that we imported last year from Canada 39,000 dozen eggs, and we sent to Canada 750,000 dozen.

Mr. CALDERHEAD. I want to suggest to you that the statistics will bear investigating.

Mr. FORDNEY. Those statistics were made by the friends of the measure.

Mr. GRANT. Gentlemen, I am very much obliged to you.

(Thereupon, at 3.15 o'clock p. m., the committee adjourned until to-morrow, Thursday, February 9, 1911, at 10 o'clock a. m.)

[Telegram.]

COLUMBUS, OHIO, *February 7, 1911.*

Hon. RALPH D. COLE,
  Member of Congress, Washington, D. C.:

The Ohio State Grange stands opposed to any reciprocal relations that fail to protect the agricultural equal with other interests. Therefore we are opposed to the Canadian reciprocity treaty as now proposed.

L. G. SPENCER, *Chairman,*
EUGENE F. CRANZ, *Secretary,*
Executive Committee Ohio State Grange.

RECIPROCITY WITH CANADA.

COMMITTEE ON WAYS AND MEANS,
HOUSE OF REPRESENTATIVES,
February 9, 1911.

The committee met at 10.30 o'clock a. m., Hon. Samuel W. McCall (acting chairman) presiding.

Present: The acting chairman and Messrs. Hill, Boutell, Needham, Calderhead, Fordney, Gaines, Longworth, Dwight, Ellis, Underwood, Randell, Broussard, Harrison, and Brantley.

Mr. McCALL. Mr. Norris, there is a gentleman here who wishes to make a brief statement. The full membership of the committee is not present, and would you object to his making that statement now, before you begin?

Mr. NORRIS. I will suit the pleasure of the committee.

STATEMENT OF AARON JONES, OF SOUTH BEND, IND., REPRESENTING THE NATIONAL GRANGE.

Mr. JONES. Mr. Chairman, I represent the National Grange and will present this argument on its behalf. We feel that we would be very seriously damaged and wronged by the enactment of this bill.

Mr. McCALL. Proceed.

Mr. JONES. I do not care to take much of your time, but just a little, so as to get what we want before you. Our organization is composed of the National Grange, with subordinate branches in 30 States. We wish to enter our emphatic protest against the proposed reciprocity agreement with Canada.

I have been a working farmer all my life; have been actively identified with the Grange, or Patrons of Husbandry, for more than 20 years, and was for eight years master of the National Grange. I have gone among the farmers in every State of the Union, and have met thousands of them at various State and national grange meetings. I am thoroughly familiar with their views on this and other public questions, and I am here to declare that the farmers of the country are unalterably opposed to the reciprocity bill which you are now considering, and that they believe it would inflict a serious and permanent injury to their industry.

The principle on which the protective policy has been defended during the past 20 years is that all classes and interests of the country should receive equal protection against the competition of foreign products. It was to carry out this principle that the duties on farm products were imposed by the McKinley law and reimposed by the Dingley and Payne tariff acts. Had it not been for the tariff on farm products the protective system would long ago have been abolished.

237

I understand that your committee does not wish to hear a repetition of arguments on the general question of protection, but to learn of facts bearing on the pending bill. I will therefore endeavor to set before you briefly the essential features of this measure and their relation to the welfare of the great agricultural interests of the country.

I wish first to call your attention to the fact that the rate of protection given by our present tariff laws to farm products is much lower than the duties on manufactured articles which the farmer buys. An analysis of Schedule G of the tariff act of 1909 shows that on the staple products of the soil the average rate of duty is about 25 per cent. The average rate on imported manufactures is about 45 per cent, and on many articles largely consumed by the farmers the rates are still higher. It is therefore clear that the farmers are not receiving the same measure of protection as is given the manufacturers.

In view of these undeniable facts the farmers have learned with amazement and indignation the proposition to abolish the comparatively slight protection now given them and to establish free trade in practically everything that they produce. Let there be no mistake about the effect of this reciprocity bill. The only country from which any considerable quantity of farm products can be imported into the United States is Canada. We do not fear the competition of other countries. The purpose of the tariff on farm products has been to exclude those of Canada from our markets, and if this bill becomes law it means the end of protection, so far as the farmers are concerned.

The next fact on which we base our protest against this bill is that it will subject us to the unfair competition of products which can be more cheaply produced in Canada than in this country. The Canadian farmer pays much lower duties on his machinery, implements, and manufactured goods, and under preferential trade agreements the majority of these duties are greatly lower than the schedule rates. The cost of farm labor is materially less in Canada than in this country, thus putting our farmers at a disadvantage in this respect. It is notorious that the prices of farm lands are far lower in Canada than in the United States, and the Canadian farmer is therefore under less fixed charges on his investment. The principal farming sections of Canada are largely virgin soil, requiring no fertilizers, while the farms in this country have long been cultivated, and large amounts of fertilizers are necessary. For these reasons it is self-evident that the cost of production must be greater in the United States than in Canada.

Perhaps the most important fact for your consideration is that there are in the Canadian Northwest enormous areas of unoccupied fertile prairie lands, probably 100,000,000 acres, selling for a few dollars per acre. Large tracts of this land have been taken up by speculators on both sides of the boundary line, and it was these speculators who started the agitation for the free admission of Canadian farm products into this country, with the avowed purpose of raising the value of their lands. If, as the Canadian advocates of reciprocity contend, the effect of this measure will be to greatly increase the value of Canadian farm lands, it is clear that it can only do so by decreasing the value of our farms.

In view of these facts, which can not be denied, the manifest result of this bill, if it becomes law, will be to abolish all the protection now given the farmers, and leave them open to the free competition of products which under existing conditions can be more cheaply grown in Canada than in this country. The advocates of reciprocity do not deny that Canadian farm products will to a large extent displace the produce of our farms; on the contrary, they try to justify the measure by claiming that it will reduce the cost of those products to the consumer. As against this claim I wish to submit certain facts set forth in the Annual Report of the Secretary of Agriculture for 1910, pages 19–26. As the result of a careful investigation of the increase of prices of farm products in their transfer to the consumer, Secretary Wilson shows that the difference between the price paid the farmer, and the cost to the consumer is in many cases from 40 to 50 per cent. For instance, it was found that the poultry grower received only 55.1 per cent of the price paid by the consumer; that the dairyman receives a scant 50 per cent of the price paid for milk; the apple grower, 55.6 per cent; that beef cost the consumer 38 per cent more than the price paid the great slaughtering houses; and other farm produce from 41 to 50 per cent over the original cost. The conclusion of this section of Secretary Wilson's report is:

From the details that have been presented with regard to the increase of the prices of farm products between farmer and consumer, the conclusion is inevitable that the consumer has no well-grounded complaint against the farmer for the prices that he pays.

After consideration of the elements of the matter, it is plain that the farmer is not getting an exorbitant price for his products and that the cost of distribution from the time of delivery at destination by the railroad to delivery to the consumer is the feature of the problem of high prices which must present itself to the consumer for treatment.

Mr. BOUTELL. Right there, Mr. Witness, I would like to ask you a question.

Mr. McCALL. Will you not let him finish before you ask questions?

Mr. BOUTELL. I think my question would come in a little more logically in this connection, if there is no objection.

Mr. McCALL. Very well.

Mr. BOUTELL. Right on that matter of the cost of distribution, we had a witness here yesterday, representing the farmers of northern New York, and he gave these figures: Price of milk to the farmer, 3 cents, in his county.

Mr. JONES. Yes.

Mr. BOUTELL. Price paid by the consumer in New York, 9 cents, or an advance of 200 per cent; a much greater advance than any of those figures pointed out by the Secretary of Agriculture.

Mr. JONES. Yes; much larger.

Mr. BOUTELL. Now, can you tell what those figures are for milk to the farmer in Indiana, and the amount paid by the consumer, say, in Indianapolis and Chicago?

Mr. JONES. Well, in Chicago it is a little more than 50 per cent on the milk on the milk trains that run from Indiana to Chicago. Now, I understand that this is a generalization of the entire problem. It differs in different sections of the country, as in your New York instance; as in New England.

Mr. BOUTELL. Well, in that New York instance, is that difference of 200 per cent caused by the small price that the farmer gets, or by the relatively larger price paid by the consumer?

Mr. JONES. It arises from two causes; first, the price to the farmer is too low; that is, less than the cost of production.

Mr. BOUTELL. What does the Indiana farmer get for milk?

Mr. JONES. He gets about the same price, about 3 cents.

Mr. BOUTELL. What does the consumer pay now in Chicago?

Mr. JONES. The consumer pays 8 cents in Chicago.

Mr. BOUTELL. It is very nearly, then, the same thing?

Mr. JONES. Yes; very nearly. The milk producers in our State, in the smaller towns, get about 3 cents for their milk, and it retails for 6 and 7 cents, usually 6 cents; an increase of from 50 to 100 per cent. Then I maintain that there are other problems; the problem of transportation, commissions, and exchanges, all enter into this problem of the high cost of farm living, and when it is charged to the farmer it is erroneous and wrong, and places the farmer at a serious disadvantage before the public; and it raises the question before the consumers in the small towns, the men who are working in the factories, and they charge this home to the farmer when it should belong to the other fellows, and it is a serious wrong.

Mr. DWIGHT. Is it not true that the Borden company, with over $30,000,000 of capital, has to have its percentage?

Mr. JONES. What is that?

Mr. DWIGHT. Is it not true that the Borden company has to make a percentage off of it?

Mr. JONES. That is all right.

Mr. DWIGHT. The farmer has no objection to that?

Mr. JONES. We are willing to receive anything that makes a fair, reasonable profit for us.

Mr. DWIGHT. You are not objecting to that, then.

Mr. JONES. Certainly not. No; it is not the tariff on farm products that is responsible for the high cost of food, but the excessive freight charges of the railways, and the exorbitant profits of the commission houses, wholesale dealers, and retailers, through whose hands farm products must pass to reach the consumer.

I have submitted these facts for the purpose of showing the serious injury to the farming interests that would follow the enactment of this bill. What compensation does this measure offer the farmers for the loss of the very moderate protection now given them? Does it materially reduce the burden of high protective duties which the farmer is compelled to pay on all the manufactured goods he uses? Not at all. The pretended reduction of duties on Canadian manufactured goods is a fraud and a sham. No duty is removed or reduced on Canadian manufactures that wil permit of their general importation for use by our farmers.

An attempt has been made to fool the farmer by removing the duty from steel wire and wire fencing. But Canada makes practically no wire and only sold to this country last year about 150,000 pounds, while we exported to Canada more than 9,000,000 pounds. The removal of this duty will not reduce the cost of fence wire in the slightest degree, and the same is true of the other manufactured articles in the reciprocity schedule. Canada is not a manufacturing country in the same sense that the United States, Great Britain, and

Germany are, and the few manufactures affected by this bill will not be made cheaper to our people.

And I want to say right here that I have been a lifelong Republican and have supported, from Lincoln down, the policies of that party, believing in protection, and I am wholly unable to comprehend the amazing action of those higher in authority who have been responsible for this reciprocal agreement. Is it possible that they believe that 6,000,000 farmers will tamely submit to free trade in farm products and high tariff for manufactures?

If so, I wish to state here and now that we have come to the parting of the ways. The farmers believe in real reciprocity, that is, for an equal reduction in the tariff on manufactures, and at the same time that the duties on farm products are reduced. They favor an honest revision of the tariff, but they do not believe in revising the tariff on farm products out of existence, while leaving the exorbitant taxes on manufactures untouched.

Years ago, when this matter was up, and the high commission met in Quebec, Gov. Bachelder and myself were upon the legislative committee of the National Grange, and we went before that commission and presented the argument of the farmers on this side at that time in Quebec. You know that that reciprocity did not prevail, and I am just as sure to-day, if the American people had time to consider, digest, and properly understand this treatment, nobody on earth, or no set of men, could ever pass this act as it is presented to-day. If this bill is intended as an honest measure to reduce the cost of living in the interest of the consumer, why does it impose a tax of 50 cents per barrel on flour, while putting wheat on the free list? Why are cattle, sheep, and swine on the free list, while meats, fresh and cured, are taxed 1¼ cents per pound? Are not the farmers as much entitled to protection as the millers or the great meat packers of Chicago?

Mr. RANDELL. Is not that in favor of the meat packers, to have cattle on the free list, and meats not on the free list?

Mr. JONES. It has been in their favor.

Mr. RANDELL. Is not that in their favor?

Mr. JONES. Certainly; and that is why it is put in here.

Mr. RANDELL. I understood you to say that the legislation was not in their favor.

Mr. JONES. Certainly; why should a beef on the hoof come in free, and if it slaughtered in Canada come in at an expense of $10 or $12? You and I know that the cost of slaughtering is less than 10 per cent of the duties imposed, and it is discriminating against people in this country; and if those who are responsible for the enactment of this measure suppose that the farmers have not discovered all this, they will be finding themselves woefully mistaken. This is not a party measure; it is a business measure, and individuals will be held responsible. The consumers do not eat wheat, or cattle, or sheep; they consume flour and meat. But this bill puts the farmer's products on the free list, and taxes the articles in the form in which they reach the consumer. Do you suppose for one single instant, gentlemen, that the farmers of this country, who have furnished the money, and are to-day furnishing the money for the best market of our manufacturing interests in this country, do not understand this argument? Do you believe that they will tamely submit? No; never.

Mr. UNDERWOOD. Will you let me ask you a question there?

Mr. JONES. Yes.

Mr. UNDERWOOD. If they are not going to submit, are they going to help the Democratic party pull down the tariff?

Mr. JONES. They would help the devil, before they would allow themselves to be abused by their friends.

Mr. UNDERWOOD. They propose to reduce the duties on manufactured products, then?

Mr. JONES. Certainly, they will do it; and just as sure as this bill becomes law, you cut from under your tariff protection all its support.

Mr. UNDERWOOD. That is good.

Mr. JONES. And the men who make the law—the men who vote upon this law—will be held responsible for it, more than parties.

Now, gentlemen, I trust that there will be no misunderstanding as to the position of the farmers in this matter. They believe that they are entitled to exactly the same measure of protection as the manufacturers. We can not get it on what we export, but we can keep the other fellows out. They are not now receiving equal protection, and the pending measure proposes to make the discrimination against them still more unjust by establishing, to all intents and purposes, free trade in farm products, while making no reduction of duties on manufactures that will decrease the cost to the farmer.

Mr. RANDELL. Your idea is to keep the farmer's products out, so that they will not compete with you?

Mr. JONES. How is that?

Mr. RANDELL. It is your idea to keep the farm products from Canada from coming in here so that they will not compete with you?

Mr. JONES. No, sir; let them pay for our market. They live in a country where they have cheaper lands, cheaper taxes, and less cost for labor. We are supporting an entirely different condition of things, and let them pay for our market. That is what they ought to do; the same as every foreigner; if he wants to come in, let him throw out the Stars and Stripes, and let them float over that country, and then he can come in, and we are perfectly willing to let him.

Against this proposition we earnestly protest, and we insist that there shall be no free trade for the farmers and high tariff for the manufacturers, but that if farm products go on the free list, manufactured articles must also be made free, and they will, inside of a very short time.

STATEMENT OF MR. JOHN NORRIS.

Mr. McCALL. Mr. Norris, the committee will hear you now. Will you give the committee some idea of how much time you will require?

Mr. NORRIS. For my statement, of course excluding interruptions, which I can not measure, I can finish inside of 25 minutes.

Mr. McCALL. Go ahead.

Mr. NORRIS. Mr. Chairman, I regard the Canadian reciprocity agreement now before you as the greatest economic advance that has been made by the United States in the present generation. It broadens our market; it permits interchanges that will immediately and directly benefit 90 per cent of the population.

I appear as the representative of newspapers which pay more than $55,000,000 per annum for news print paper. They are deeply concerned in the paper-and-pulp clause of the treaty, and they ask you to approve that clause exactly as it appears in the agreement.

The tangle of the American Government with Canadian Provinces and the tariff burdens imposed upon print paper have added more than $6,000,000 per annum to the price which newspapers would pay for raw material under normal conditions. The complication with Canada and the excessive duty have enabled American paper makers to combine for advance in print-paper prices. They have an organization that is more oppressive and more elusive than the General Paper Co. which the Government suppressed in 1906. The paper makers are systematically starving the market. The entire stock of paper on hand at the beginning of this year was less than an 8-day supply for the newspapers of the country. In December, 1910, they exported more print paper than Canada shipped to us.

The president of the Union Bag & Paper Co., Mr. Edgar G. Barrett, in an interview printed last August, a copy of which I now submit, gave details of the methods by which the larger paper companies reduced their production to 35 per cent of their normal output to allow weaker mills to get a market. The president of the American Paper & Pulp Association on July 11, 1910, issued a letter to the paper makers urging curtailment of production; a copy of that letter I now furnish to the committee. The Wrapping Paper Pool advanced prices to the extent of $5,000,000 per annum, pleaded guilty in the United States court, and paid a fine. The Box Board Pool also pleaded guilty and paid a fine. Both these interests are affected by this paper clause. The West Virginia Pulp & Paper Co., according to a recent announcement, increased its capital stock to $20,000,000. Paper salesmen report that when that company changes its prices the other book paper mills follow within 24 hours. The paper makers established a statistical bureau, ostensibly to ascertain the condition of the market. We welcome the information gathered by that bureau, but we object to the use which the paper makers have been making of it to regulate prices. A simultaneous reduction recently of $3 per ton by the sulphite-pulp makers was evidence of concerted action by them in price fixing.

All but 2 of the 50 print-paper makers of the country are violating the Sherman law by restricting the use to which the paper they sell can be put. No print paper can be bought f. o. b. mill unless the name of the buyer, the destination of the paper, and the use to which it is to be put are disclosed, as well as the assurance that the buyer has no contract with any other mill. Here are all the essentials of a gentleman's agreement. I have been unable to buy paper from the paper mills, although I offered spot cash for delivery f. o. b. mill. During the past summer the largest paper companies refused to quote paper for 1911 at any price. To-day it is impossible for the larger newspapers to obtain quotations from more than one mill at any price. The largest buyer in the country, who uses 100,000 tons per annum, will probably pay an increase of $600,000 per annum for his paper because of the methods of the paper makers.

Since the passage of the Payne-Aldrich law, though the duty on print paper had been reduced $2.25 per ton, that is from $6 to $3.75 per ton, the paper combination has advanced prices $2.50 per ton and threatens further advances. Publishers whose contracts are expiring find that they can not get any terms except from the mill which had supplied them. A uniform price of $45 per ton has been established by the paper makers. It makes no difference what the freight rate is within a given zone.

Mr. Barrett, in an interview in London, had urged the British manufacturers to adopt a similar price of $45 per ton. Paper has been sold abroad by the paper makers at less than the domestic price.

The president of the American Pulp and Paper Association disclosed to your committee in November, 1908, that his paper mill at Niagara Falls, on an investment of $100,000, had paid dividends regularly and had accumulated a surplus of $400,000. That mill is an antique. The International Paper Co. acquired 111 paper machines 13 years ago; it has sold or diverted many of them, and has less than 67 machines now making print paper. In 13 years it has added only 2 machines to its equipment. The average capacity of its machines is 21 tons per day per machine, whereas modern machines turn out 56 tons per day.

Foreign pulp has displaced American pulp in American paper mills because of the primitive conditions which prevail in American mills. Only 67 per cent of the wood which reaches an American paper mill is converted into print paper. An American print paper mill requires 110 pounds of raw material to make 100 pounds of paper, whereas English and German mills require 103 pounds of raw material to make 100 pounds of print paper. The waste of wood and of material and the bad workmanship, due to lack of technical equipment, add over $20,000,000 per annum to the cost of print paper which publishers must pay. This waste is attributable to the fact that the paper combinations and the paper tariff have enervated the American paper maker. Nevertheless the modern paper mills in the United States make print paper cheaper than the Canadian mills. The price of print paper has been advanced nearly 50 per cent, that is from $32 to $45 per ton, since the combination of 32 mills into the International Paper Co. occurred in January, 1898.

The increase of $2.50 per ton in price of print paper made by the paper makers since the reduction in duty under the Payne-Aldrich law has been maintained in face of a temporary glut in the pulpwood market, with a recent drop in price of pulp wood of $3 per cord, or $4.20 per ton of paper. I refer you to the statement made by Mr. James R. Mann to the House of Representatives June 3, 1910, for the information respecting the restrictions on pulp-wood exportation imposed by each of the provinces of Canada.

At the instigation of the print-paper makers the American Congress attempted to impose coercive measures upon the Province of Quebec. The disastrous results of that policy are now seen in the withdrawal by Quebec of 95 per cent of all the available pulp-wood supply of that Province. It has been trying to starve the American mills and to force their transfer to Quebec. The paper clause of the pending reciprocity agreement overcomes all the difficulties of that situation.

The snarl with the Provinces of Canada has been completely avoided by an entirely new turn to the stipulations, which now follow the wood—not the Province. If wood is free from restriction, such as wood from private lands, the products of that wood will come into the United States free of duty.

The distinction between wood free from restriction of exportation and wood that is not free will show itself in various ways. Print paper made from wood cut on lands subject to restriction will be liable to a duty of $5.75 per ton of paper. That duty will be prohibitory in competition with paper made from wood cut on private lands. The Provinces of Quebec and Ontario have been offering premiums and inducements for the transfer of American paper industries to Canada. Brown Bros., of Berlin Mills, N. H., recently installed a plant at La Tuque, Quebec, and propose to expand it materially. That plant depends on Crown lands for its timber supply. The International Paper Co. has been flirting with the Quebec Government for similar concessions. The reciprocity clause will give no encouragement to such diversion of industry from the United States to Canada. A barrier of $5.75 per ton on print paper will confront such products until the Quebec Government removes the prohibition. The revenues which the Province now obtains on wood cut from its Crown lands and shipped in manufactured form to the United States will be diverted from the Quebec treasury to the owners of private lands. The pressure from holders of Crown lands limits upon the provincial authorities for an opportunity to reach the greatest market in the world, that of the United States, will be irresistible and a diplomatic victory in the removal of restrictions will have been achieved without harshness or coercion or ill feeling of any sort. Each side will obtain an advantage and that is the element of a good trade.

Our complete dependence on outside sources for wood is shown in the fact that we bought last year pulp wood and pulps to the extent of 1.716,000 cords in order that we might make paper in American paper mills, as follows:

	Cords.
Pulp wood	931,000
Mechanical pulp, in cords	228,000
Chemical pulp, unbleached	404,000
Chemical pulp, bleached	153,000
Total	1,716,000

The supply of pulp wood was so inadequate that we paid over $150,000 in penalties to get wood from Canadian Crown lands. We paid $19,406,074 to foreigners for pulp wood and pulps to keep American mills going. The figures of recent years show that the sales of paper by the United States to Canada were three times as great as the sales of paper by Canada to the United States. This excess in our favor is due to the fact that Canada makes no high-grade papers but draws on the United States for much of its supply.

Prior to the passage of the Payne law, Canada had shipped print paper to the United States to the extent of 46 tons per day during the fiscal year 1908, and 56 tons per day in 1909, though Mr. Hastings said it was nothing.

Subsequent to the passage of the Payne law the shipment was 143 tons per day toward our consumption of 4.200 tons of print paper per day, or 3½ per cent. American paper companies have engaged in woodland speculations in Canada. The International Paper Co., instead of pursuing its legitimate business of paper making, has acquired about 4,000 square miles of timber rights in Canada. Its representative told the congressional committee in 1908 that he had figured out a profit of $10,000,000 on its timber holdings. It concealed the low cost of its paper making by wash entries of the price it paid to its subsidiary companies. The figures submitted by it to the United States Senate in June, 1909, when compared with the figures furnished by it to the Mann committee, will disclose that deception.

The amendment to the paper section proposed by the paper makers is intended to nullify, and will, if adopted, nullify every effort to straighten the pulp-wood tangle with Canada.

Mr. LONGWORTH. What amendment do you refer to?

Mr. NORRIS. The amendment proposed by Mr. Hall.

Mr. LONGWORTH. Here, the other day?

Mr. NORRIS. Here, the other day; that is right. The paper makers would pass along the additional cost of their wood and would thrust upon the ultimate consumer the burden of the immense increases in the cost of pulp wood. If the paper-makers' figures respecting the quantity of available private land in Canada are correct, that is 1 per cent of the total area, then this treaty clause which permits free paper only when made from free wood can not be injurious to them.

Gentlemen, I thank you for this opportunity to make a statement.

Mr. FORDNEY. Did I understand your figures right? Did you say 39,000 cords of wood had been imported? You mentioned a minute ago the number of cords imported from deeded lands, did you not?

Mr. NORRIS. The number of cords from what?

Mr. FORDNEY. The pulp wood and pulp. You gave the figures a minute ago. Was it 39,000 cords that have been imported?

Mr. NORRIS. Nine hundred and thirty-one thousand cords of pulp wood; and with the mechanical pulp and chemical pulp, it made a total of 1,716,000 cords.

Mr. FORDNEY. Nine hundred and thirty-one thousand cords?

Mr. NORRIS. Of pulp wood.

Mr. FORDNEY. Of wood. Now, how did your figures agree with those given by Mr. Hugo the other day as to the amount of wood necessary for the production of a ton of paper?

Mr. NORRIS. He says 1½ tons. The Treasury Department and all of the authorities agree that 1.4 cords of wood make 1 ton of paper.

Mr. FORDNEY. He said 1½?

Mr. NORRIS. He said 1½. One and four-tenths is accurate, and that is the figure that controls the Treasury Department.

Mr. FORDNEY. Then the paper made from the 931,000 cords would be just two-thirds that in tons of paper produced, would it not?

Mr. NORRIS. Substantially.

Mr. FORDNEY. That is, according to him?

Mr. NORRIS. In paper of some kind; not necessarily print paper.

Mr. FORDNEY. Yes; whatever it was. It does not take any more wood to make a ton of other kinds of paper?

Mr. NORRIS. If it was converted into print paper, of course it would be that, upon the assumption of 1½ tons, slightly more than upon the 1.4.

Mr. FORDNEY. Well, it would not be very much. Now, you suggested that the International Paper Co. had a profit on its lands of how much?

Mr. NORRIS. $10,000,000.

Mr. FORDNEY. That has been estimated; has it not?

Mr. NORRIS. That was their estimate, made by Mr. Lyman. I think it was before the Ways and Means Committee, on November 21. 1906, when he furnished that information.

Mr. FORDNEY. How many acres of woodland did you say those people owned in Canada?

Mr. NORRIS. Approximately 4,000 square miles.

Mr. FORDNEY. Four thousand square miles?

Mr. NORRIS. They control, altogether, in the United States and Canada, between 6,000 and 7,000 square miles of timber. They have three times the quantity necessary for the supply of their present output in perpetuity.

Mr. FORDNEY. Four thousand square miles; that would be 2,560,000 acres?

Mr. NORRIS. Yes.

Mr. FORDNEY. In other words, about $4 per acre profit, that would be?

Mr. NORRIS. What do you mean?

Mr. FORDNEY. $10,000,000 profit?

Mr. NORRIS. Well, no; you are confounding two things. In addition to this land in Canada, these timber rights, they have immense tracts in the United States which they own in fee.

Mr. FORDNEY. I am speaking of what they own in Canada.

Mr. NORRIS. The statement which he made was that their timber holdings altogether——

Mr. FORDNEY. In this country and in Canada?

Mr. NORRIS. In this country and in Canada; in Maine, New Hampshire, Vermont, and New York——

Mr. FORDNEY. What they own in this country cuts no figure in this argument. We are talking about in Canada.

Mr. NORRIS. I am talking about speculations in woodlands, and about the fact that, instead of applying the money they have in legitimate business development, and giving us the benefit of the profit, they have been spending money on investments in Canadian lands and have not added but two machines in 10 years, and are now running on 21 tons capacity, when the modern machines are making 56 tons per day.

Mr. FORDNEY. Have you any right to criticize any man for his investments in this country or anywhere else?

Mr. NORRIS. I have a right to criticise the International Paper Co. and the paper makers of this country, because of the fact that they are tariff beneficiaries. The Government has undertaken to protect and nurse and coddle them.

Mr. FORDNEY. Are you not a beneficiary?

Mr. NORRIS. They are under an obligation——

Mr. FORDNEY. I asked you a question.

Mr. NORRIS. They are under an obligation to see that at least the needs of the market and of the consumer are assured, and that the market is not starved, and that they do not participate in the agreements by which prices are maintained at the expense of the consumer.

Mr. FORDNEY. In other words, you are of opinion that they ought to furnish a nurse and bottle for you and take care of you?

Mr. NORRIS. No; we need no caretakers. They are the ones that have been taken care of.

Mr. FORDNEY. If you do not want to be taken care of. what are you kicking about?

Mr. NORRIS. Because they are stopping our supply, and they are coming in here and asking this committee of Congress to stop the supply of pulp wood and stop the further development of American paper industry.

Mr. HILL. Can you not put in these improved machines?

Mr. NORRIS. We are going to.

Mr. HILL. You could put in 200 of them if you wanted to?

Mr. NORRIS. We are going to put them in and be absolutely independent of these people.

Mr. FORDNEY. Who has advocated the stopping of the importation of pulp wood and paper into this country?

Mr. NORRIS. Who has what?

Mr. FORDNEY. Who has advocated stopping its coming in? Who has advocated the stopping of the shipping from Canada into this country of pulp wood? You made that statement a minute ago. that these people were here asking for it. Who are they?

Mr. NORRIS. Mr. Hall, representing ostensibly the International Paper Co., but actually representing the combination of paper makers.

Mr. FORDNEY. Mr. Norris, do you know that no living soul ever appeared before this committee who asked that a prohibition be put upon Canadian pulp wood coming into this country?

Mr. NORRIS. Directly; no.

Mr. FORDNEY. Either directly or indirectly.

Mr. NORRIS. But the practical application of the amendment which they proposed would simply check and stop the whole thing.

Mr. FORDNEY. Oh, Mr. Norris!

Mr. NORRIS. I do not mean from private lands; no.

Mr. FORDNEY. There are no private lands to amount to anything in Canada, and you know it, if you know anything about it.

Mr. NORRIS. I know that you do not know, for the reason that while you are talking of Ontario, you are not talking with knowledge of the Province of Quebec.

Mr. FORDNEY. I will submit my case to this committee, as to who knows more about the matter, you or I. Do not let us argue about that.

Mr. NORRIS. No.

Mr. FORDNEY. I have been in the business there, and you do not claim to have been, do you?

Mr. NORRIS. I have been buying paper, and I have been traveling through Quebec and Ontario and New Brunswick, and studying this particular subject, for 12 years altogether. but three years recently, with deep concern and keen interest.

Mr. FORDNEY. Mr. Norris, you were here two years ago advocating free print paper, were you not?

Mr. NORRIS. I was; and proud of it.

Mr. FORDNEY. Why did you want it?

Mr. NORRIS. Sir?

Mr. FORDNEY. Why did you want it? I suppose for the benefit of the American people and your own business?

Mr. NORRIS. I wanted it, as I want it to-day, because the paper makers were in a combination and abusing their opportunity, and because they were not giving to the consumer that freedom and that supply which was his right.

Mr. FORDNEY. As a paper consumer, a consumer of print paper, can you not go abroad and buy paper just as well as anybody else, if you have the money to pay for it?

Mr. NORRIS. No, sir; I can not do it, for various reasons. I have a trial shipment of 20 tons of paper from Sweden now on the way here, but the Scandinavian paper is not as good as the American paper or the Canadian paper, for the reason that the fiber in the spruce wood is more slivery, and it does not make as feathery a mat as that of the Canadian or American spruce, and therefore we can not get the same service from it; and American paper in the English market in competition with Swedish paper will command an additional price of 5 per cent.

Mr. FORDNEY. Do you mean to say that the Canadian paper is a more valuable and high-priced paper than the Swedish paper?

Mr. NORRIS. I think so. I think so.

Mr. FORDNEY. That is the reason why you pay the price for it, is it not?

Mr. NORRIS. No, sir—pay the price for what?

Mr. FORDNEY. For paper; what you are talking about.

Mr. NORRIS. For what paper, Canadian or Swedish?

Mr. FORDNEY. The better paper. That is why you pay the higher price, because it is better paper, is it not? And you pay more for it?

Mr. NORRIS. No; with all the difficulties there we can only get it for a price which is practically the market here.

Mr. FORDNEY. Tell me, Mr. Norris, why you or any other citizen of the United States has not a right to go into Canada and buy print paper?

Mr. NORRIS. We have.

Mr. FORDNEY. You just said a minute ago that you could not do it. I asked you that question.

Mr. NORRIS. There are in Canada to-day print paper mills which have a total capacity of substantially 450 tons per day.

Mr. FORDNEY. Yes.

Mr. NORRIS. As against our consumption of 4,200 tons per day.

Mr. FORDNEY. What prevents you from going over there and getting it?

Mr. NORRIS. Let me finish answering that question.

Mr. FORDNEY. Well, let me ask you a question. You have answered that question.

Mr. NORRIS. No; I have not.

Mr. FORDNEY. Very well; go ahead.

Mr. NORRIS. And 90 tons of that 450 tons are used in Canada for domestic purposes, and 180 tons come to the United States, and the rest goes abroad to the British market, to Australia, and to South America.

Mr. FORDNEY. Why do they not make more and ship it to the United States?

Mr. Norris. I think they will as soon as they can get the opportunity.

Mr. Fordney. Why do they not do it now?

Mr. Norris. Sir?

Mr. Fordney. Why do they not do it now?

Mr. Norris. Because they can not get in the market.

Mr. Fordney. Why, the difference in cost of wood you have got will more than offset the duty.

Mr. Norris. Sir?

Mr. Fordney. The difference in the cost of wood, enough wood to make a ton of print paper in Canada, on any of this wood in this country to-day, in a paper mill, will offset the difference in duty.

Mr. Norris. Excuse me; it will not.

Mr. Fordney. That is what you said a minute ago; or about that.

Mr. Norris. I said that up-to-date American mills will make paper more cheaply than the Canadians.

Mr. Fordney. But you said——

Mr. Norris. But offsetting this item of wood are supplies, advantages in labor, more efficient labor in the United States, and difference in the cost of transportation, which enable the American mills, like the Great Northern and the St. Croix and the Berlin mills to make paper at approximately $25 a ton, which is much less than any Canadian mill can make it for, notwithstanding their advantage on the wood.

Mr. Fordney. Do you mean to say that labor is cheaper in the United States than it is in the mills of Canada?

Mr. Norris. I mean to say that the skilled labor in the Canadian mills has been paid more than that in the United States mills, by reason of the fact that the skilled labor must come from the United States; it is here, and they must offer inducements to those men to leave home and country and go there to make paper.

Mr. Fordney. They are intelligent people in Canada, are they not?

Mr. Norris. The paper makers, the skilled workers in the Canadian mills, come from the United States.

Mr. Fordney. How long does it take a man to become skilled in the manufacture of paper, especially at ordinary labor—common labor? Is common labor over there as high priced as it is here or is it not?

Mr. Norris. I think it is no more efficient. I think that the figures of the labor cost per ton of paper, as gathered by the Mann Committee, established that the——

Mr. Fordney. Have you employed labor over there, and yet you do not know?

Mr. Norris (continuing). Established that the cost was no greater here than there, and in many mills was less.

Mr. Gaines. Mr. Norris, that is a conclusion. I would like to have an answer——

Mr. Norris. No. That is facts furnished by the Mann committee.

Mr. Gaines. Give us a little chance.

Mr. Norris. Certainly.

Mr. Gaines. If you please. There is no occasion for excitement, Mr. Norris. Be perfectly cool. Mr. Fordney's question was whether the wages were larger or smaller in Canada. You have answered about your conclusion as to the unit of cost. Please give us the facts about the labor, and let us draw our conclusions.

Mr. NORRIS. You are asking me about cost. You were asking me about the cost, and then about the unit of labor.

Mr. GAINES. I am not asking you about the unit of labor. As I say again, do not be excited. Please answer the question. Are wages greater or less in Canada? Please answer that, and do not give us your conclusions.

Mr. NORRIS. I think on skilled labor they have been higher, in a number of the mills. The last time I took that up was at the time when the Payne-Aldrich bill was under discussion, and in many of the mills the Canadian pay was higher than the average in the American mills; and let me add——

Mr. GAINES. Let me ask you a question there.

Mr. NORRIS. Let me answer this first.

Mr. GAINES. No; you have said what you have to say—just what you know.

Mr. McCALL. Do not repeat your answer.

Mr. NORRIS. I am not going to repeat the answer.

Mr. FORDNEY. That is all right.

Mr. NORRIS. I said at that time in the State of New York, where the greatest quantity of paper is made, according to the statistics of the State bureau, the labor employed in the paper mills was paid less than any other class of organized labor in the State.

Mr. GAINES. Let me put this question. Now, will you answer the question: Is common labor in Canada paid more or less than in America?

Mr. NORRIS. I do not know. I assume it is paid less, and is less efficient.

Mr. FORDNEY. Then you do not know anything about it? You are merely giving your opinion?

Mr. NORRIS. I gathered the data from each paper mill in Canada at the time of that Payne-Aldrich discussion, and submitted it in print, and have here ready for the committee a compilation showing the pay of each class of labor in each mill, Canadian and American.

Mr. UNDERWOOD. Will you file that with your remarks?

Mr. NORRIS. Yes.

Mr. FORDNEY. I want the stenographer to note, please, that I asked the gentleman what he knew about it. He is here to give information to the committee. He states that he thinks, but does not know.

Mr. GAINES. He assumes.

Mr. FORDNEY. He assumes, but does not know. I want that to go in the record.

Mr. Norris, have you had any experience in the manufacturing of print paper as a manufacturer or superintendent of an institution?

Mr. NORRIS. As a consumer of paper, and at one time the largest buyer in the United States, I have had occasion for 12 years to closely study the costs of paper making.

Mr. FORDNEY. Have you been a receiver or in some way connected with the handling or managing of a paper company since you were here two years ago?

Mr. NORRIS. I am glad that you referred to that.

Mr. FORDNEY. I am glad to please you some way. [Laughter.]

Mr. NORRIS. I am glad you did. On July 7, 1910, I was appointed receiver of the Boston Herald, a newspaper which had involved itself in financial difficulties. In the discussion in June, 1909, at the suggestion of a United States Senator, the International Paper Co. arranged to set up scenery that would justify its action in raising the rate above that recommended by the Mann committee and passed by the House. It obtained from that Boston newspaper a letter prepared by the International Paper Co., and transmitted it to the Senate committee, as the protest of a newspaper against any disturbance of, or interference with, the paper-making interests of New England. The sequel you have. That letter also referred to my statements as being utterly valueless. It is a sad fatality that the man who was attacked by that newspaper was appointed to take hold of it and readjust its finances and save the wreck that had been made of it.

Mr. FORDNEY. Did he save it?

Mr. NORRIS. Sure.

Mr. BOUTELL. I did not understand you. Was it the International Paper Co. that put the Boston Herald into bankruptcy?

Mr. NORRIS. It did. It had been carrying the paper along for more than five months on its paper bills.

Mr. BOUTELL. And you were appointed receiver of that paper?

Mr. NORRIS. I was appointed, not because the International Paper Co. loved me more than any other newspaper man, but because I was available at that time for the purpose of the receivership; and I am proud to say that I think I justified the appointment.

Mr. BOUTELL. But you were appointed on the recommendation of the International Paper Co.?

Mr. NORRIS. I was appointed on the application of the International Paper Co.

Mr. FORDNEY. You were on a representative of the International Paper Co. for some time?

Mr. NORRIS. I was not. I was the representative of all the creditors.

Mr. FORDNEY. Are you a representative of the International Paper Co. now? [Laughter.]

Mr. NORRIS. I am afraid that you are a joker.

Mr. FORDNEY. Well, that is what my wife says when she is provoked. [Laughter.] But let me ask you this: Since the Payne-Aldrich tariff bill became a law, in which the duty on print paper has been lowered, have the newspapers of this country lowered their advertising rates to the people, to the merchants of the country?

Mr. NORRIS. That would be very difficult to answer.

Mr. FORDNEY. As a paper man, as well versed in the business as you seem to be, and claim you are, you ought to know that.

Mr. NORRIS. That would mean to keep track of from 1,100 to 1,200 newspapers as to just what they are doing. Wherever they can get it on equal classification, where their circulation justifies it, they will do it, and where it is necessary to meet competition they will meet competition.

Mr. FORDNEY. As you have been giving opinions only, have you any objections to giving an opinion on that?

Mr. NORRIS. No; I have been giving just a few facts.

Mr. DWIGHT. Where there is no competition, they take all they can get?

Mr. NORRIS. Surely; but they are forced, as a result of competition, to reduce their prices, the price to the public, the price of the paper to the public. We have had that in Washington, here, recently, with the Washington Star and the Washington Herald. We had it in Chicago recently with the Chicago Tribune and the Chicago Record-Herald and other Chicago papers, and it is one of the tendencies of the times.

Mr. DWIGHT. But they are not patriots unless there is competition?

Mr. NORRIS. No; no more than some Congressmen.

Mr. FORDNEY. Mr. Norris, have you figures to give to this committee as to the cost of the production of a ton of print paper in this country and in Canada?

Mr. NORRIS. Well, my figures are more or less approximate and they are supplemented or supplanted by the recent investigations of the Tariff Board. I know approximately what it is costing some of the news paper mills, and I know that with the International Paper Co. there is a difference of $10 a ton in the cost of print paper in one mill as compared with another mill.

Mr. FORDNEY. Well, now, if you do not know what the average difference in cost of producing a ton of paper in Canada and in the United States——

Mr. NORRIS. I do not know.

Mr. FORDNEY. Mr. Norris, you have talked all morning. Let me finish this. If you do not know the average cost of production of print paper in Canada and in this country, you are not very competent to enlighten this committee, are you?

Mr. NORRIS. Oh, I think I am.

Mr. FORDNEY. Just tell us what that cost is. If you do not know——

Mr. NORRIS. It will depend upon the age of the mill, and it will depend upon the location of the mill with respect to its supply of wood, and it will depend upon the river upon which it is located, as to whether they can make pulp all of the year or only part of the year—whether they are under water or whether they are out of water. It will depend on so many conditions that even the statement of an average will be misleading; but the up-to-date modern mills can make paper at from $25 to $27 per ton f. o. b. the mills. The Minnesota & Ontario Paper Co., which started in June last, issued a prospectus wherein it printed figures to show that it could make paper at $23 per ton f. o. b. the mills.

Mr. FORDNEY. I give you up as a hopeless case.

Mr. McCALL. With reference to the suggested amendment, to insert, after the word "imposed," that no export duty or tax shall have been imposed——

Mr. NORRIS. By Canada or any of its Provinces.

Mr. McCALL. It was proposed to add there, "by Canada or any Province thereof."

Mr. NORRIS. That is not the most material——

Mr. McCALL. I have not asked you about that.

Mr. NORRIS. Yes.

Mr. McCall. In connection with that, I would call your attention to a bill that was introduced and is now pending before this committee, introduced by Mr. Mann on the 6th of December, 1909, wherein he says that printing paper, and so forth, "shall be admitted into the United States free of duty when imported from the Dominion of Canada, being the product thereof, on the condition precedent that neither the Dominion of Canada nor a Province or other subdivision of government thereof"—that is, this bill was drawn on the theory of that amendment.

Mr. Norris. No. There is this distinction which you make. That dealt with each Province. You are dealing with all the Provinces in that amendment. That is one point.

Mr. McCall. I will read the words of the bill: "On the condition precedent that neither the Dominion of Canada nor the Province or other subdivision of government thereof where the same is in whole or in part produced or manufactured, and from which it is imported into the United States, forbids or restricts," and so forth.

That means applying to the political subdivision from which it is imported.

Mr. Boutell. I would like to ask a few questions, Mr. Chairman.

Mr. McCall. I am through.

Mr. Norris. May I, before finishing, Mr. McCall, refer to the second amendment, wherein the draft of the treaty refers to the wood used in the manufacture. The amendment is "or any wood used in the United States in the manufacture." It is the difference between free wood and all wood in Canada. Under Mr. Hall's amendment it must mean that no reduction can be made, that no step can be taken, until every Province of Canada shall have removed its restrictions.

Mr. Underwood. I do not know whether I understand you correctly. Do you approve of the suggestions made by Mr. Hall, or do you disapprove of them?

Mr. Norris. I absolutely disapprove, and say that it would not only nullify but destroy every prospect of everything of the kind, and would precipitate more aggression. The proud and mighty United States Government has already bent its knee to the Province of Quebec.

Mr. Underwood. Do you contend, Mr. Norris, that the bill introduced by Mr. McCall to carry out the treaty will carry it out in toto, as it stands, or should it be amended?

Mr. Norris. It will carry it out absolutely as it stands, with this qualification, that in the last paragraph on the last page there is a classification which is a part of the proviso; in other words, that no commodity can be made free under this proviso until President Taft will proclaim that Canada has made free every article enumerated, including wood pulp and print paper from the United States, and that can not be done by Canada until all of her provinces have removed their restrictions. But as that is not possible, therefore the President will never be able to proclaim that Canada has complied with the agreement.

Mr. McCall. May I just state to you that it is rather clear, in reading the last two or three pages of the bill, that none of those duties, none of the other reciprocal duties provided for there, would go into effect until Canada had proclaimed the removal of practically these restrictions on wood pulp, pulp of wood mechanically ground and so forth, appearing on page 24. That is involved with the other articles in that part of the bill.

Mr. UNDERWOOD. Then you agree with the contention that the bill should be amended to carry it out.

Mr. McCALL. I agree that that part of the bill should be amended, and furthermore, I have been informed by the State Department that there is no provision in the treaty that is pending upon this, or with regard to wood pulp, and I have no question but that entire subject is open to the committee.

But I wish further, because it is an important point, to ask Mr. Norris this: There were two parts to the amendment proposed by Mr. Hall on page 20, one inserting the words "the Dominion of Canada or any Province thereof," and the other applying to wood. Do you object to both those amendments particularly, or only to the last one?

Mr. NORRIS. Well, I would not like, offhand, without even seeing the text, to answer that question. My impression is that both of them are hostile; that they are intended to stop the operation of and the intent of the treaty, and that therefore the committee should not adopt them.

Mr. McCALL. Now, Mr. Norris, I just want to get at your idea and clear this up. With regard to the first amendment, inserting the words "Dominion of Canada or any Province thereof," I may have been misinformed, but I had the idea that that was your idea until not very long ago. Am I correct about that? Now, the committee wish to get the exact facts about it.

Mr. NORRIS. There are phases of that proposition which I am afraid I am not at liberty to discuss publicly; but I can say that after that proposition had been made, the situation with respect to the Provinces of Canada entirely changed, and we are now menaced with a very serious situation, which the newspapers must bear the burden of, and not the paper makers, because the paper maker will simply pass along the increased cost of his pulp wood to the consumer.

Mr. BOUTELL. Mr. Norris, I would like to have these five items put into the hearing, partly to appear in what you have already said, and the rest you undoubtedly have in your paper, given orally or answered them. First, for the year 1910, calendar or fiscal, which-ever we have the figures for——

Mr. NORRIS. I have both.

Mr. BOUTELL (continuing). The total amount in tons of print paper consumed by the newspapers of the country? You gave the figures——

Mr. NORRIS. It is approximately 1,250,000. One million two hundred thousand is what we talk of.

Mr. BOUTELL. If you care to modify this in the hearing you may do so.

Mr. NORRIS. No; 1,200,000 I would say, safely. I get those figures from the paper makers' reports of production.

Mr. BOUTELL. Second, the price paid for the same. I think you gave that.

Mr. NORRIS. The uniform price which they are now asking is $45 per ton.

Mr. BOUTELL. I meant the total amount paid.

Mr. NORRIS. $55,000,000.

Mr. BOUTELL. For 1910?

Mr. NORRIS. For 1910.

Mr. BOUTELL. $55,000,000. The net profit to the seller on those sales?

Mr. NORRIS. The paper maker and the Lord only know, and the Lord will not tell.

Mr. BOUTELL. Well, fourth, the total net profits of all the newspapers purchasing that paper?

Mr. NORRIS. The total net profits? You mean the earnings of the newspapers?

Mr. BOUTELL. Yes; the total net profit as it would be returned to the Internal Revenue Commissioner. Those figures are all available there.

Mr. NORRIS. I do not know that.

Mr. BOUTELL. You could not give that?

Mr. NORRIS. No; I have not the least idea. I know some of them are not making a cent. I know that at the Mann committee hearings Gen. Agnus, of the Baltimore American, came before that committee and said: "Gentlemen, for the year 1907 my paper price was $1.90, or $38 per ton, and when I went to these folks for a supply for the year 1908 they told me that the price on me would be raised to $50 per ton, an increase of $12 per ton."

Mr. BOUTELL. We are wandering afield. I am asking for the figures on the profits.

Mr. NORRIS. I was going to say that they wiped out all of his profits with that increase. That was my point.

Mr. BOUTELL. He may have done better in 1910.

Mr. NORRIS. I think he did.

Mr. BOUTELL. I want the figures of the profits.

Mr. NORRIS. I think the price was approximately $45 per ton.

Mr. BOUTELL. You can not give the total profits of the papers consuming that paper?

Mr. NORRIS. No, sir.

Mr. BOUTELL. The fifth question I ask is, the net profit of each of the five most profitable papers in the country?

Mr. NORRIS. I do not know but one, and that I will not tell.

Mr. BOUTELL. Yes; so that you can not, or do not wish to, give it?

Mr. NORRIS. I have no means. I do not know that anyone has the means for ascertaining the total profits of a newspaper.

Mr. BOUTELL. They all ought to be on file in the Internal Revenue Commissioner's office. I did not know but what you had them. We can send for them.

Mr. NORRIS. No, sir; I have not got them.

Mr. GAINES. How many newspapers are in the association which you represent?

Mr. NORRIS. Three hundred and one.

Mr. GAINES. Three hundred and one?

Mr. NORRIS. Representing substantially all of the important newspapers in the United States.

Mr. GAINES. Representing substantially all of the important newspapers in the United States; and by that you mean the large dailies, I take it?

Mr. NORRIS. The large dailies. I am talking only of daily newspapers.

Mr. GAINES. You are representing only the large daily newspapers and no others in the country. There are about 301 of them. What is the total capital invested in their business?

Mr. NORRIS. I do not know. I do not know.

Mr. GAINES. But you know about the business of the other people. Let us know something about yours. You can give us that, can you not, Mr. Norris?

Mr. NORRIS. I can not. I can refer you only to the census, to which I would go.

Mr. GAINES. Well, can you not give me an approximation of the value of those plants?

Mr. NORRIS. I would not attempt it.

Mr. GAINES. You say you would not attempt it. My question is, can you do it?

Mr. NORRIS. I can not, without reference to the books.

Mr. GAINES. Will you refer to the books and put it in your hearing?

Mr. NORRIS. It will give me pleasure to do so.

Mr. GAINES. Thank you. Will you file a copy of the articles of association?

Mr. NORRIS. Of what?

Mr. GAINES. Of this association?

Mr. NORRIS. The American Newspaper Publishers' Association?

Mr. GAINES. Yes.

Mr. NORRIS. Surely; it is a voluntary organization——

Mr. GAINES. I have no doubt of it. I simply want the facts. You speak of the price to the consumer; you mean the price to the large newspaper consumer, do you not?

Mr. NORRIS. Certainly; that is the consumer, and that is what I mean.

Mr. GAINES. That is what you mean. The reduction in the price of paper would not result in a reduction of the price of newspapers to the final buyer out of whom the newspapers make their profit, would it?

Mr. NORRIS. Yes. Not a reduction in the retail price, but in the enhanced value which the buyer obtains.

Mr. GAINES. He would still pay the price for the newspaper?

Mr. NORRIS. The price of a newspaper is like the price of a postage stamp; you can not reduce it, neither can you increase it, especially when the paper makers get together and add $12 a ton to the cost of the paper.

Mr. GAINES. In the cost of print paper to the newspapers, the effect of that operation on the cost is so slight that it can not be manifest in the final retailer's price, as you have just stated. That is all, Mr. Chairman.

Mr. BRANTLEY. You state that a ton of print paper costs $45?

Mr. NORRIS. Not in Georgia. It costs more than that there, because of the increased freight. That is outside of the $45 zone.

Mr. BRANTLEY. Well, but you stated that the average price of paper was $45 a ton.

Mr. NORRIS. The International Paper Co., for instance, broadly makes the statement that for the year 1910 every customer on its books was paying $2.25 except four—namely, the Hearst papers, the Chicago Tribune, the Chicago News, and the Chicago Record-Herald. The announcement was that for the year 1911 they would make all pay $45 per ton.

Mr. BRANTLEY. What I was going to ask you was this: Cutting a ton of print paper up into newspaper form and selling the paper at a cent a copy, what would that amount to for a ton of paper? How much would a ton of paper yield in price, selling the papers at a cent each?

Mr. NORRIS. It would depend, of course, on the size of the paper.

Mr. BRANTLEY. Well, the average paper.

Mr. NORRIS. I will give you the units which we have in the newspaper business. We always measure paper by the weight of one thousand 8-page sheets. The New York papers vary in size, whether they are 7 or 8-column papers in width. But, as I have thought with respect to some of the papers that I have been connected with, it was substantially 64 pages to a pound, or eight 8-page sheets to a pound, and therefore there would be sixteen thousand 8-page sheets in a ton of news print paper of 2,000 pounds. Sixteen 8-page papers, upon the basis of 64 pages to the pound, or eight 8-page sheets to the pound.

Mr. BRANTLEY. How much would a pound of paper yield, then, at a cent a paper?

Mr. NORRIS. Well, I am not a prodigy. I can not carry this mental arithmetic to the extent, offhand, without a pencil, of going into that. I will be pleased to send that information to you, but I do not want, offhand here, to engage in mental arithmetic.

Mr. BRANTLEY. Will you put it in the record?

Mr. NORRIS. Surely.

Mr. LONGWORTH. I want to ask you a question in regard to your construction of this proposition. Have you read the Canadian bill?

Mr. NORRIS. Yes.

Mr. LONGWORTH. Do you approve of that bill in regard to print paper?

Mr. NORRIS. It is in accordance with their understanding.

Mr. LONGWORTH. I read you the proviso:

Provided, That such wood pulp, paper, or board, being the products of the United States, shall only be admitted free of duty into Canada from the United States when such wood pulp, paper, or board, being the products of Canada, are admitted from all parts of Canada free of duty into the United States.

Mr. NORRIS. That is incorporated in the agreement, and the reason for it is obvious, as you will see when I make the explanation. As I gather, the Canadian commissioners were unable to bind the provincial authorities. The demand was first made by the American Government—I do not know whether I ought to talk about that. Anyhow, the suggestion was made that if the United States should reduce the duty on paper and pulp, Canada ought to make corresponding reductions in paper and pulp; and when this draft was made it left in the law a tax of $5.75 per ton on all print paper from Crown lands, or restricted lands in Canada.

Mr. LONGWORTH. That is the duty of $3.75 plus——

Mr. NORRIS. Plus the retaliatory duty of $2?

Mr. LONGWORTH. Yes.

Mr. Norris. And that when the situation had reached a point where the Provinces, by reason of the operation of this paper clause, should remove their restrictions, and the United States would then be imposing no duty upon print paper from Canada, then Canada would pull down its bars on American paper shipped into Canada.

Mr. Longworth. Now, I am not perfectly sure that I understand your position. I understand that you suggest that our bill as it is written be adopted, except that the last paragraph on page 24 be stricken out?

Mr. Norris. Is that the last page of the bill?

Mr. Longworth. Yes.

Mr. Norris. Yes. That may be entirely independent of the paper proposition, because your treaty is not workable unless that is stricken out.

Mr. Longworth. Now, suppose that was stricken out; I would like to know your understanding of just what the bill would provide with relation to the admission of print paper into this country and in relation to the admission of our print paper into Canada?

Mr. Norris. It would provide that where the wood comes from private lands, that is, where the wood is free, the paper from those lands would be free.

Mr. Longworth. Into this country?

Mr. Norris. Yes; into this country.

Mr. Longworth. Yes.

Mr. Norris. And that where the paper came from the Crown lands it would be subject to a duty of $5.75 per ton.

Mr. Longworth. Now, how about print paper going from this country into Canada?

Mr. Norris. It would continue to pay the duty of 15 per cent now imposed by Canada, until the United States had removed its duty on all Canadian paper.

Mr. Longworth. Which it would not do until the last Canadian Province had freedom of export.

Mr. Norris. Yes.

Mr. Longworth. Now, I want to know just how you understand it. In other words, what you favor is that all print paper coming from any Province in Canada which does not impose a restriction of some kind on wood should at once come into this country free of duty?

Mr. Norris. Surely.

Mr. Longworth. From those Provinces?

Mr. Norris. Yes; that is right.

Mr. Longworth. But, on the contrary, that the full Canadian duty should remain against American print paper until every Province of Canada had removed its restriction on wood. Is that your idea?

Mr. Norris. That is accurate. That is an accurate statement.

Mr. Longworth. That is what I wanted to know.

Mr. Calderhead. How is it that the price of news print paper was $45 a ton this year?

Mr. Norris. Sir?

Mr. Calderhead. How is it that the price of news print paper was $45 a ton this year?

Mr. Norris. That is the uniform agreed price. There have been exceptions; there are exceptions because of various conditions, such as credit and time of payment.

Mr. CALDERHEAD. Exactly. Here are some Canadian papers, one from Montreal and one from Toronto. What is the price of print paper in those cities?

Mr. NORRIS. I am not clear. I think it is about $2.10 or $2.15; but that is not public information. I mean, I have had no opportunity, no facility, for getting that information, and I do not know.

Mr. CALDERHEAD. $2.10 to $2.15 in Canada and $2.25 in the United States would be about your idea of it?

Mr. NORRIS. Well, the Canadian paper makers are selling in the United States, paying the duty, and the price of that Canadian paper is very close to the price of the American paper mill. Of course the difference in their receipts is the difference in the duty, which is substantially 19 cents a hundred, or $3.75 per ton.

Mr. CALDERHEAD. There is not much to prevent the Canadian from selling his paper in the United States now?

Mr. NORRIS. Oh, they are selling 183,000 tons here now.

Mr. CALDERHEAD. That is all.

Mr. McCALL. Mr. Norris, I am interested very much in the form of this bill. Now, this objection has been made to the bill. This is a reciprocity measure, but on this question of paper there is no reciprocity at all; that is, Canada does not do a thing. We do not provide in this bill that she shall do a thing. We simply provide that she shall have free entrance into our markets for her print paper and wood, and things of that sort, from Provinces that impose no export duty; and we do not even require of her that when she shall see fit to remove all of the export duties that she shall then take our paper free of duty.

Mr. NORRIS. She can not do that any more than you could control the State of Minnesota, which owns swamp lands.

Mr. McCALL. You do not understand my question. Canada does not even agree—if we strike out the last provision of this bill there is no requirement that Canada shall agree—even to admit print paper free from the United States.

Mr. NORRIS. Oh, there is every element of good faith. That is in their bill; that is in the memoranda between them; it is in the writings; and if nations can not in those matters rely upon the faithful carrying out of the arrangement, then you may as well tear up this treaty.

Mr. McCALL. Well, then, this would follow, at any rate: That Canada would have print paper from these several Provinces which impose this export tax, or whatever it is called——

Mr. HILL. Mr. Chairman, the Canadian bill provides that paper shall be admitted from the United States free of duty when the duty from the Crown lands comes off.

Mr. McCALL. Yes. Then it follows that when the export duty has been removed from all parts of Canada, from all the Provinces, and not until then, paper can go into Canada from the United States free of duty. That is, it can go into any part of Canada free of duty. I want to get your exact understanding, Mr. Norris, because you have studied it. It can not go into any part of Canada free of duty until all parts of Canada are without restrictions upon exports?

Mr. NORRIS. Let me state it in another light. That is substantially correct, but let me put it in this way: That when the United States shall have made paper and pulp free from all parts of Canada, then

Canada will admit paper and pulp from the United States free into Canada; and I tell you if that is brought about we will swamp their markets, that we will sell them, and that we will show them that the American paper mills can, under competitive conditions, beat the world, and beat the Canadian paper maker in his own market.

Mr. McCall. Yes; but my understanding is that this condition is to be brought about by Canada itself. Until Canada itself sees proper in all of its Provinces to remove this export duty, then the United States can not send any paper into Canada free of duty.

Mr. Norris. Canada is powerless, as a dominion government.

Mr. McCall. Yes; and is not the United States put in a condition, by reason of her powerlessness, so that we can never have the benefit of her market until every part of Canada stands in an attitude, as to these restrictions, to remove them?

Mr. Norris. Yes.

Mr. McCall. You understand that?

Mr. Norris. Yes.

Mr. McCall. Then would it not be possible that these two great Provinces should build up a paper industry there, a powerful industry, and then this powerful industry could secure action subsequently in any Province imposing a restriction upon the export of wood to the United States, and the United States mills would be entirely excluded from the whole Canadian market without paying the 15 per cent duty?

Mr. Norris. That is, if restrictions were imposed upon export wood.

Mr. McCall. If these two Provinces should remove their restrictions upon export wood, and then a powerful paper industry should build up there, they could then secure a restriction in one Province, and would not that serve to bar the mills of the United States from free entrance into any part of the Canadian market?

Mr. Norris. But you lose sight of the fact that those powerful mill interests in Canada would confront a situation of this character, that the powerful mill interests must rely ultimately upon the Crown lands for their supply, and relying upon those Crown lands they would confront a prohibitory duty of $5.75 per ton.

Mr. McCall. No; but they would come in free, because the Provinces in which they happened to be built, the wooded Provinces, would not put on this export duty, and they could send their paper free. But if the Province of Manitoba or some far western Province had a nominal restriction imposed, they would have the Canadian market absolutely protected to them, which might mean for all time, and they could come into our market.

Mr. Norris. In two words I will tell you why Manitoba and Alberta and Saskatchewan will not do that.

The Chairman. I simply wished to get clearly in my mind exactly the provisions of this bill.

Mr. Gaines. I do not think that Mr. Norris has exactly grasped your construction, based as it is on the construction of the language, for his replies are not responsive. I think if you would put that again, and Mr. Norris would withhold his answer until you had fully put your question, you could get an answer. I do not think he has grasped your question.

Mr. NORRIS. I think I did grasp it. I understood you had asked me whether if these mills in some Province which had removed the restriction should set up some minor Province with a restriction by which the Canadian wall should be kept against us, while our wall against their paper had been removed—would that be possible?

Mr. McCALL. Would not that be the effect of putting on a restriction in any part of Canada; not necessarily the two Provinces that now have it?

Mr. GAINES. Restrictions of what kind?

Mr. McCALL. The imposition of some export restriction, as we call it, an export tax, in any part of Canada—this is Canadian action, and not ours—would not that serve to keep paper from going from the United States free into any part of Canada?

Mr. NORRIS. It certainly would prevent the application of the free-paper clause of the Canadian statute until every Province had removed all kinds of restrictions upon exportation.

Mr. McCALL. I think we understand each other. Perhaps I did not ask the question clearly, but that was my understanding.

Mr. NORRIS. Yes.

Mr. CALDERHEAD. Do you mean the restriction to include the ground tax or the stumpage?

Mr. McCALL. I used that word "restriction" to escape repeating half a dozen lines.

Mr. NORRIS. Yes; certainly.

Mr. McCALL. This export restriction, or whatever it is called, which you will find on page 19.

Mr. CALDERHEAD. Of course an export tax would be a restriction.

Mr. McCALL. It would be making it free, as I understand.

Mr. CALDERHEAD. A ground tax levied on the timber cut would not be.

Mr. McCALL. You will find it very clear on page 20.

Mr. GAINES. Do I understand that it is agreed that a proper construction of this bill is——

Mr. LONGWORTH. Cutting out the last provision on page 24 is what the chairman asked Mr. Norris. If you cut out that, premise your question with that.

Mr. GAINES. If you cut out the last paragraph on page 24, the last provision on page 24, is it then your construction of this treaty that we would not, under it, get our print paper free into Canada——

Mr. LONGWORTH. Into any part of it.

Mr. GAINES (continuing). Into any part of Canada until every part of Canada had removed all of her restrictions against the importation of wood and pulp into this country?

Mr. McCALL. Exportation of wood.

Mr. GAINES. Exportation into this country?

Mr. NORRIS. There are no restrictions except on pulp wood.

Mr. RANDELL. That is not an answer to the question.

Mr. NORRIS. Yes; until all restrictions had been removed.

Mr. GAINES. That does not even pretend to be responsive to the question I asked you. You say there are no restrictions——

Mr. NORRIS. I answered "yes."

Mr. GAINES. Well, you did not. You now do.

Mr. NORRIS. I answered three times.

Mr. BROUSSARD. The Canadian Government will not permit the free importation of paper from this country into the Dominion of Canada until the United States shall have removed its restrictions against paper manufactured in the Dominion of Canada imported into the United States; is that a correct statement?

Mr. NORRIS. That is one way of stating it; yes.

Mr. BROUSSARD. Well, it is a correct statement?

Mr. NORRIS. May I restate that?

Mr. BROUSSARD. Yes; you may restate it. I want to keep the sequence of my question.

Mr. NORRIS. That when the United States shall admit all Canadian print paper and pulp free, that then Canada will admit all American print paper and pulp free.

Mr. BROUSSARD. All right. Now, then, the United States can not, under this agreement, admit Canadian paper and pulp free until the Provinces of Canada shall have removed any tax which they now impose under the law upon the same article in Canada or upon the wood; is that a correct statement?

Mr. NORRIS. That is right.

Mr. BROUSSARD. So that in order to carry this agreement out and bring about free traffic in paper between the two countries the duty devolves upon the United States to secure from the provincial government the repeal of all taxes now existing, whatever they may be?

Mr. NORRIS. That is true, and this paper clause does automatically work that result, and does it without bulldozing.

Mr. BROUSSARD. How?

Mr. NORRIS. By setting up the private land ownership and production free, as against a duty of $5.75 upon the product of Crown lands.

Mr. BROUSSARD. I understand you to have said here that there were paper factories being constructed in Canada, and I also understand you to have said——

Mr. NORRIS. Yes; there is one by Mr. Barret's company, the American paper makers going there, being driven there.

Mr. BROUSSARD. It does not make a particle of difference who is doing it. I understand that to be your statement. I also understand that you have deduced from the articles of that treaty, when carried out, that the American paper manufacturer will, in the United States, manufacture paper, place it on the market in Canada, and drive the Canadian manufacturer out of that market.

Mr. NORRIS. As a loyal American, that is my belief.

Mr. BROUSSARD. That is your belief?

Mr. NORRIS. And I am absolutely confident that upon even terms he will do it; but the Canadian has a different view, and he is entirely welcome to it.

Mr. BROUSSARD. Now, then, Mr. Norris, do you believe that?

Mr. NORRIS. Absolutely.

Mr. BROUSSARD. Pardon me; you believe, then, if that is the logical deduction from the operation of this treaty, that with that condition regarding wood pulp and paper framed in that way in the agreement it will work itself automatically, as you have said; in other words, that we will not have to use any other influence to repeal the internal taxes now being imposed on pulp wood by the Provinces?

Mr. NORRIS. I believe that, absolutely.

Mr. BROUSSARD. You believe that the provincial governments would of their own volition do a thing by which they would put out of business the paper manufacturers of Canada?

Mr. NORRIS. Put out of business the paper manufacturers of Canada?

Mr. BROUSSARD. Yes.

Mr. NORRIS. It would give them the great American market.

Mr. BROUSSARD. But you said the American manufacturer would drive them out from his market.

Mr. NORRIS. But, as Canada uses 90 tons a day in comparison with 4,200 tons a day used in the United States, is not the consideration of getting access to this market irresistible?

Mr. BROUSSARD. But, Mr. Norris, you said that under the conditions of this agreement the American manufacturer of paper would drive the Canadian manufacturer of paper out of his own market. Now, how can you now argue that the Canadian manufacturer of paper will drive the American manufacturer of paper out of his own market?

Mr. NORRIS. That the Canadian manufacturer——

Mr. BROUSSARD. You have stated that if this agreement is carried out the American manufacturer of paper will enter the Canadian market and drive the Canadian manufacturer of paper out of his own Canadian market.

Mr. NORRIS. I was referring to the——

Mr. BROUSSARD. You now say that the Canadian manufacturer of paper will come into this country and give you cheaper paper than the American manufacturer is giving you now or will give you under that treaty.

Mr. NORRIS. You misapprehended my statement. When I referred to the American manufacturer going into the Canadian market I referred to the high-grade papers.

Mr. BROUSSARD. We are talking about print paper.

Mr. NORRIS. No; I said that the United States had been selling and is to-day selling more paper to Canada, in value, than Canada is selling to the United States.

Mr. BROUSSARD. I thought you were speaking about the matter in which you are interested, in which your association is interested—print paper.

Mr. NORRIS. In that particular aspect I would prefer—there is a gentleman here who represents the New York World and who is a member of the committee on paper, who came to appear here as a witness in connection with this paper matter. Mr. Seitz, and I would like to have him testify for a minute or so, if you have the time.

Mr. McCALL. Mr. Seitz, we will hear you in just a minute.

Mr. LONGWORTH. I just want you, Mr. Norris, to answer one more question. The bill as it stands, including the paragraph on page 24, would do what?

Mr. NORRIS. It would be absolutely unworkable.

Mr. LONGWORTH. Would it do this—as it stands, would this be the effect of it—that no Canadian print paper would be admitted free into this country until the last Province of Canada had removed any restrictions?

Mr. NORRIS. Its effect would be that.

Mr. Longworth. That is what I mean.

Mr. Norris. But, as a matter of fact, you never would have any reciprocity, because so long as that remains in there Canada will never proclaim this treaty.

Mr. Longworth. I am only asking your construction of the bill as it stands.

Mr. Norris. Because it couples up with the other articles to go free into Canada this stipulation, that none of these are made possible until the Provinces of Canada, all of them, have removed all of their restrictions on wood.

Mr. Longworth. I am not arguing as to what it ought to be.

Mr. Norris. I understand that.

Mr. Longworth. I am simply asking you your construction of this bill as it stands.

Mr. McCall. Let me call your attention to one matter that shows the difficulty of that clause on page 24. If you will look on page 20 of your bill, at the proviso on page 20, it reads:

Provided, That the articles above enumerated—

set forth in the previous pages, several pages back—

the growth, product, or manufacture of the Dominion of Canada, shall be exempt from duty when the President of the United States shall have satisfactory evidence and shall make proclamation that the following articles, the growth, product, or manufacture of the United States or any of its possessions (except the Philippine Islands and the islands of Guam and Tutuila), are admitted into the Dominion of Canada free of duty.

And then after a long list of articles follows print paper.

Mr. Longworth. That is true.

Mr. McCall. If you make an allowance that print paper is admitted free of duty, the duty on live animals and poultry, etc., then would go into effect.

Mr. Longworth. Is that your understanding?

Mr. Norris. That is my understanding.

Mr. Longworth. I was not asking that question. I was simply asking about the effect on print paper alone, and not on anything else.

Mr. McCall. Did you get Mr. Norris's answer?

Mr. Longworth. Yes.

Mr. McCall. I thought I would just point out the exact effect of it.

STATEMENT OF DON C. SEITZ.

Mr. Seitz. I will not take but a moment of your time, Mr. Chairman. I thought perhaps I might enlighten the committee a little on the question of profit on the daily newspapers that some of the gentlemen were interested in. On the basis of $40 a ton for white paper, which is the average cost to us now in the World office—we are under an old contract that has another year yet to run—a 16-page paper exactly pays for itself in the amount we receive from the wholesaler, who delivers it to the trade. In other words, we receive $5 a thousand copies for this morning newspaper of ours, and it is delivered by the news company, which in turn charges the newsdealer 10 cents a hundred copies for delivering it, and the newsdealer in turn sells it to the customer at 1 cent per copy. Now, you will readily see that it is difficult for us to reduce our price satisfactorily, even if we benefited by the tariff, because you gentlemen have no smaller coin than a cent. I assume that if there was a one-half cent coin there would be found newspapers immediately that would cut down their price. We sell our wares at a fixed price. That is one disadvantage that a newspaper is under in meeting this cost of material. I think you will perceive that. We can not raise in fractions, as the man who is selling our supplies to us can.

Mr. Broussard. Where do you make your profit, then?

Mr. Seitz. I will come to that in a moment.

Mr. Broussard. All right.

Mr. Seitz. The average cost of a 16-page paper is $5 a thousand, which is just the amount we receive. Our average size last year was 17$\frac{1}{3}$ pages, so that we lost, as near as I can recollect it, something like 35 to 40 cents on every $5 worth of paper we put out. Of course when I say we lost that, I mean above the bare cost of the white paper. The circulation revenue is computed on the basis of the cost of ink and paper, and no other charge is made against it in the average newspaper office. So you will see that the circulation itself is carried at a loss on the average paper if it exceeds 16 pages in size, and if its price is 1 cent to the customer and one-half cent to the trade; and that is the rule all over the country, that we charge a half a cent to the trade and the trade deliver it for 10 cents a hundred, and the retailer sells it for 1 cent, or $1 a hundred. Some years ago we made a computation in our office as to the amount of money we would have to charge against each line of advertising in order to overcome the other expenses incidental to getting out this publication, and we found this: that 18 cents had to be taken away from every line of advertising printed in the paper to overcome the additional cost of getting out the publication.

Mr. Broussard. How much?

Mr. Seitz. Eighteen cents on every line.

Mr. McCall. That is, to pay the expense of editing and so forth?

Mr. Seitz. To pay for editors, telegraph, rent, fuel, printers, and all minutiæ that go to make up an office. There is no margin of profit at all on white paper except on some Sunday editions. There, of course, we receive from the wholesaler in the city $3.25 a hundred. There is a margin of profit on the Sunday edition, which shrinks, of course, with size. But these are the figures that I have given you for the daily, they are for six days a week as against one day in the week. We have no way out except to secure some form of competition in getting our supplies. I have noticed that the paper makers make a statement that seems as inconsistent as any statement can be. They point out that we should not reduce the tariff on one product, that that could not be reciprocity, because it will injure their business, and in the next breath they tell you gentlemen that the reduction made under the Aldrich-Payne bill has not reduced the cost of paper to the consumer, but, on the contrary, the price of paper has gone up; that they are now charging us more for white paper than they did before the reduction in the duty.

Now, that is true; but in what way it can be used as an argument against this measure I am unable to understand. If a reduction in the tariff of nearly one-half has the effect of increasing their ability to charge us, then it would be readily assumed, following the arguments out consistently, that if you took the tariff altogether off, they could raise the price $3 more a ton, and they ought to be encouraging you gentlemen to reduce the tariff instead of hampering you and asking you not to make this great change. There is that inconsistency in their point of view to which I want to invite the attention of the committee. They tell you that this is adverse to their interests in one breath, and in the next they show you conclusively, if their figures are accurate, that they have increased the cost of paper to us since that tariff was substantially reduced. Now, that actually represents the truth.

Mr. RANDELL. Do you think one reason why they could do that was that each tariff, the higher and the lower tariff, is prohibitive?

Mr. SEITZ. Frankly, I think this is the situation. They have an association that is absolutely ironclad, the business is in the hands of comparatively few interests now, and they are closely allied. It is, perfectly impossible to buy paper in the market—I know about this because I buy 60,000 tons in a year—it is impossible to secure any bid from any person except your own mill, and you can not always do that. Our chief competitor in New York sent its ablest representative all over the United States last fall seeking for bids on a magnificent order for white paper, and he was absolutely unable to get a single pound anywhere, or to get any paper manufacturing concern that would bid for it. That is not due to the tariff, essentially; it is due to combination. Now, we broke two combinations. We came to Washington and appeared before the Judiciary Committee and made our statement and we took our statement to the Attorney General of the United States, and we broke the Western Paper Co. in Wisconsin, showing that the combination had been a leading factor in the matter.

The reason I come here to advocate this reciprocal agreement is that the reason why they are able to effect this combination and maintain their prices is that they control all of the available water supplies and timber lands that exist on this side of the border. Our establishment, which is not poor, but has ample capital, can go out and invest its money, as some of the members of the committee have suggested, if we could go across the border, and save our industry. You must know that the newspaper industry is the seventh largest industry in the United States, and we feel that we are benefited in this paricular. If I may be allowed to diverge from the subject for just a moment, I want to call attention to the fact that nearly all the oppressions under the existing tariff come from the control of what might be called semimanufactured raw material. This sheet of paper that I hold in my hand is nothing until we take it and print it and make it alive. An ingot of steel is nothing until it is rolled and changed into some useful form, and the numerous manufacturers with whom I have come in contact in the last two years, since the agitation has come on, have said we are victims of competition with each other, and are being held up in the rear by the suppliers of our semimanufactured raw materials. And that is where our difficulties come in. The individual manufacturer feels strongly oppressed.

I was at a meeting in the rock-bound Republican town of Portland, Me., the other night, where there were 120 business representatives, and when the chairman asked them to express their views on this reciprocity agreement by a rising vote every single man in that hall stood up. They have found out there is behind them a combination of those large interests from which there is no escape on the primary raw material. Now, all we ask is a chance to take our money and go somewhere else with it and see if we can not preserve what we have without oppression to our public.

A line of questions was asked by Mr. Fordney that indicated a thought on his part that we had some public-oppressive combination. Certainly you can not oppress the public very much when you sell your product to them for the lowest coin we make at our mints.

As to the advertising, that is borne by comparatively a few people. You will be surprised when I tell you that less than 30 mercantile establishments pay for the bulk of advertising in the city of New York, and they tax their customers only $3\frac{1}{2}$ per cent, on an average, for advertising to the public to afford them cheap and prompt access to bargains and utilities. So that here we start on this extraordinarily low basis of a newspaper that sells itself to the merchant for a half a cent, and is sold to the public for a cent, that puts before the public this business knowledge for $3\frac{1}{2}$ per cent upon the article. an infinitesimal sum.

Now, we have got away off of our business. When the typesetting machine came along it represented a change in the cost of newspapers. The average of the New York World then was 12 pages. Now, as I have told you, it is $17\frac{1}{2}$ pages. The average rate for our advertising was then $12 a column more than it is now. Through competition and one thing and another those benefits have vanished, until finally we have got down to the position of making our profits only by extraordinary skill, mechanical efficiency, and close economic study of our conditions.

We have cut off every bit of the waste and have endeavored to withstand the constant pressure of other forms of organization against us—organizations of manufacturers, of the labor unions, of the advertisers, all of these things we have to constantly contend against— and I might say that newspapers pay the highest wages of any trade in the world. There is not among our 1,100 trades-union employees in the World office a single man who receives less than $1,200 a year. The ordinary compositor, limited by his union to working six days in the week and seven and one-half hours a day, earns $1,600. The average stereotyper in the World office earns $41 a week with his overtime, and his regular day time is only seven and one-half hours, with six hours for night work. You will readily see that we are paying enormous wages, supplying a great public need, in the New York newspapers, and I say this with knowledge, that these newspapers do not earn a net percentage of more than 5 per cent on their gross annual business.

Mr. BROUSSARD. That is very interesting testimony to me, but I have not gotten away from the proposition—my mind has not wandered from the proposition which you stated—that the price of paper as it is to-day is not altogether due to the duty on the print paper, but to the combination that the manufacturers in this country have formed. What is to prevent your going into Canada now and reducing the price in this country to what the price should be, plus the tariff, and doing away with the abnormal profits which this combination of newspaper manufacturers bring about?

Mr. SEITZ. Primarily, I have not said that they were abnormal profits on their existing capitalization, but I will call your attention to an abnormal fact in their business. The International Paper Co., for instance, has a capital account of $69,000,000, and has never yet done a gross annual business in excess of $22,000,000.

Mr. McCALL. Right there, I have heard it said about the paper industry that it takes an enormous capital compared to the value of the product.

Mr. SEITZ. That is quite true. I was coming to that.

Mr. McCALL. That it takes $3 of capital to produce $1 of output.

Mr. SEITZ. The Great Northern Co., which supplies our supply, and which, I think, is properly capitalized—the others I do not think are properly capitalized—does a gross annual business of about $7,000,000 a year, and it has a $10,000,000 investment; and then it has, I think, about $4,000,000 in its town, which is quite outside of the mill proposition, so that it has $14,000,000 altogether. Of course they created the town, but the town is an incidental profit and ought not to be charged to it. But what I wanted to say was that we do not go to Canada because of unsettled tariff conditions. If I was to start in to supply the World and the Post-Dispatch I would have to invest $7,000,000 to supply the 250 to 300 tons of paper per day, perpetually, and we could not do it for less than that. But no one wants to go across the border and invest a large sum of money when he is at the mercy of legislation. We might say our paper bill this next year would be increased a very large sum, as our competitors' was; but that might only last a year, possibly. But a tariff war might come on and destroy your investment of $7,000,000 a year; and we say, in the interest of this seventh greatest industry in the United States, and the tendency of the times, that precautions should be taken to perpetuate our business.

Mr. BROUSSARD. But you are not safe with this tariff agreement in effect; you are not safe in your investments from the standpoint you are talking on, because the Canadian Parliament has granted the power to the Provinces to take off and put on duties at any time they please.

Mr. SEITZ. But only on Crown lands.

Mr. BROUSSARD. Only on Crown lands; that is true.

Mr. SEITZ. Yes.

Mr. BROUSSARD. But that, I understand, is the bulk of the timber land.

Mr. SEITZ. No; there are very large areas of private land, still.

Mr. BROUSSARD. It has been stated the proportion of private lands is as low as 2 per cent.

Mr. SEITZ. I have, perhaps, a dozen offers in my desk at home from owners of very large timber tracts. I have one over above Duluth, where I can get a perpetual supply on absolutely free lands.

Mr. BROUSSARD. Can you get us figures as to what proportion of the pulp wood in Canada is on the Crown lands and what proportion is on privately owned lands?

Mr. SEITZ. I think I can, and I will do so, and send it to the chairman.

Mr. Broussard. I understood one of the witnesses here to say that it was something like 2 per cent.

Mr. Seitz. Two per cent in a country as large as Canada might be a very large factor.

Mr. Broussard. I am talking about the amount of timber.

Mr. Seitz. Well, it might be a very large tract of timber.

Mr. Broussard. Under this treaty you are still at the mercy of the Provinces, because the Canadian commissioners have notified us that these rights are constitutional with the Provinces, and that they can not presume to bind the Provinces, but we must go to the Provinces and have them revoke their taxes before they will receive our paper, and we can not receive theirs free under this agreement until they receive ours free, and yet the act of 1897, the act of the Parliament which conveys the authority to the Provinces to impose taxation on the Crown lands, gives that power, fixing merely the maximum tax that may be imposed, and gives the power to impose at will, increase, or take off, the tax. Now, if the Provinces were all to comply with this agreement for the ratification of this treaty by both Governments, after this paper had begun crossing the line from this country they could reimpose this tax there, and there is no power in the Canadian Government, and there is no power in the American Government, to go there and compel the Provinces to reinstate the conditions under which this treaty has been made effective. So that it is absolutely in the power of a third and independent power to cause this treaty at any time to be suspended so far as this article in which you are interested is concerned.

Mr. Seitz. That is true; we would have to take that risk.

Mr. Broussard. So that your investment would not be any safer than it is now.

Mr. Seitz. But the answer to that is that if we are willing to take this risk, you ought not to complain.

Mr. Broussard. But you are asking other interests to make concessions. You are not any safer. You say you will take the chances; the fact of it is, you are taking no chances. The other industries are taking chances to give you an opportunity.

Mr. Seitz. But they have been able to raise the price on this paper in the face of a reduction of the tariff.

Mr. Broussard. I do not understand you.

Mr. Seitz. I say the testimony shows that in the teeth of the reduction in the Payne-Aldrich bill they have been able to raise the price of print paper.

Mr. Broussard. That is true.

Mr. Seitz. They have raised it fully 5½ to 6 per cent.

Mr. Broussard. Still, that does not apply to the matter I am speaking of.

Mr. Longworth. That happens in a good many cases; for instance, in the case of hides, where the placing of hides on the free list was followed by an increase in price.

Mr. Seitz. Frankly, I am not here asking for privileges. I am asking for a chance. Other gentlemen are coming here asking to have their privileges retained, and iron clad. I am asking to have an open door, and we will take our chances. You are constantly assailed by gentlemen who are coming here asking for individual favors. We are not here asking for individual favors, we are asking to have an open door, and let us come in if we can. It is possible that in other lines of industry where they have to use this semimanufactured raw material they can compete constantly, although they have no competition in the basis on which they do their business. We compete all the time with other newspapers springing up around us, and we have no competition on the raw material which we must buy.

Mr. LONGWORTH. Do you not suppose that the increased demand for news paper all over the world is largely responsible for that?

Mr. SEITZ. I am perfectly willing to admit it.

Mr. LONGWORTH. There is a world-wide movement?

Mr. SEITZ. There is a world-wide movement; there is no question about that.

Mr. LONGWORTH. The tariff had very little to do with it?

Mr. SEITZ. The tariff may or may not have very little to do with the existing conditions, but it has this effect upon us, ourselves.

I will be glad to answer any questions about profits or prices, or anything else.

The CHAIRMAN. Mr. Longworth, do you wish to ask anything more?

Mr. LONGWORTH. No, sir.

Mr. MCCALL. Then, that is all.

Mr. SEITZ. I am very much obliged to you.

(At 12.30 p. m. the committee took a recess until 2 o'clock.)

The following letters were submitted for printing in the record:

NEW YORK, *January 31, 1911.*

DEAR SIR: The paper and pulp manufacturers of the United States are deeply interested in the proposed reciprocity with Canada, and we wish to protest most vigorously against its adoption by the Congress of the United States.

I will briefly state our position as American manufacturers:

A careful investigation made by this association absolutely disproves the statement made by the American Publishers' Association, and others, that unless the Province of Quebec withdraws its restrictions upon the exportation of Crown-land pulp wood the United States print-paper mills will be unable to obtain their supply of pulp wood at reasonable prices.

The only material change in the pulp-wood situation which has occurred in recent years, or which is likely to occur for many years to come, is due to an order in council of the provincial government of Quebec, promulgated April 26 last, which provides that pulp wood cut from Crown lands of Quebec after May 1, 1910, shall be manufactured into pulp or paper in Canada. The Ontario Government has had such a restriction for 11 years, but our mills have long since adjusted themselves to that restriction. The Province of New Brunswick, according to legal opinion of both Canada and the United States, can not, before 8 years, restrict the export of its pulp wood without gross violation of contract, and then only Crown-land wood. Therefore the worst has already happened, and yet our manufacturers are not at all disturbed as to the immediate future or eventual outcome.

The action of Quebec applies to only the Crown lands of that Province. It is not a matter of any immediate concern as to how large a territory is thus affected. The point is simply how much pulp wood have we been getting from that particular source and how can we make up for the deficiency?

According to the records of the Crown land department of Quebec, there were exported during the fiscal year, from 1905 to 1909, an average of 133,000 cords annually of pulp wood cut on Crown lands of that Province. The present demand may be considered 140,000 cords per year. Much of this was used for making other kinds of paper than newspaper, and to this extent the requirements of our news mills are therefore decreased. At least 20 per cent of this wood is fir, which can be obtained in unlimited quantities from innumerable sources. The essential part of the exportations is the spruce wood, and of the spruce that portion which is used for making sulphite or chemical pulp; it is perfectly feasible to replace with hemlock, fir, tamarac, and other kinds of wood to a very large extent. That portion which is used for making ground wood or mechanical pulp for news paper is alone indispensable. This quantity can not—probably does not—exceed 75,000 cords annually. Practically, therefore, the problem is merely how can the 75,000 cords of pulp wood from Quebec Crown lands annually imported, which is used for making ground wood pulp for use in news paper, be secured from other sources?

The paper mills in the United States use altogether about 4,000,000 cords of pulp wood a year. It is thus obvious that Quebec's action affects an almost negligible part of our consumption.

There are made in the United States about 4,000 tons of news paper a day, or 1,200,000 tons per annum. Thus 75,000 cords of Quebec Crown-land spruce wood, used by news mills, would furnish ground wood pulp for about 100,000 tons of news paper, or only one-fifth of the total production.

This imported Quebec Crown-land wood, as a matter of fact, has been used by only 10 or 12 print-paper concerns out of 51 in the United States. Again, therefore, the problem is seen to be one not affecting the industry generally, but simply one confronting these dozen mills. It would be extremely unjust and unreasonable to jeopardize the large majority of mills by tariff concessions for the relief of so small a number of mills, assuming that, which is not the case, viz, that they need relief. These mills are located in New Hampshire, Vermont, Massachusetts, and New York State; no other section of the country is in any way affected. With possibly one or two exceptions, the owners of all these mills have expressed themselves as in no wise concerned as to their ability to get all the pulp wood they require as far into the future as they can see.

By contrasting the vast forest domain of Quebec Crown lands with the amount of private lands, the American Publishers' Association makes it appear that the latter is insignificant; whereas the practical question is not how large a territory are we shut out from, but is the territory, to which we still have access, ample? We are convinced that it is, at least for a good many years to come, and that during this period, which we can regard as protected with certainty, there can and will be a readjustment of the industry which will not occasion the shock of disastrous results that would be sure to follow any further reduction in the tariff on paper. We can surely get all the wood we require at reasonable figures for 10 years, and if Quebec persists in its policy of restriction during that period, naturally all mills, both old and new, will take that restriction into consideration in their plant.

The island of Anticosta, at the mouth of the St. Lawrence River, comprises about 3,000,000 acres mostly of virgin spruce timberland. This island is 150 miles long; about three times the area of our Long Island. It is owned in fee by Mr. Menier, of France, and preparations for cutting pulp wood on a large scale are now being made. It is the expectation that 40,000 cords will be cut this year, and that the annual output can be and will be increased as fast as the market demands, up to 100,000 cords a year. Thus from this new source alone almost the equivalent of Crown-land wood now used by us may be obtained. The island is estimated to contain 30,000,000 cords of pulp wood. This is not subject to the Quebec restriction, nor is this area a part of the 5,000,000 acres of private lands already referred to. On the south shore of the St. Lawrence are extensive tracts of timberland owned in fee which have never been operated for pulp wood. There is not the slightest question but that the withdrawal of Crown-land wood will stimulate the production of pulp wood on many areas of private lands not yet operated for pulp wood. At present the market is glutted and almost every day offers of wood from new sources are received by our mills.

Canada can offer us no concession with pulp wood to compensate for a reduction in the tariff, which will wipe our mills out of existence and make the United States hereafter dependent upon Canada for practically its whole supply of news paper.

I venture to say that the ultimate result of the conditions confronting us, as manufacturers, in case this reciprocity committee report should be enacted, will be as follows:

Canada will produce from private-land wood all the paper and pulp that she can, which will be exported into the United States free of duty, and until such time as all her provinces take off the prohibition from Crown-land wood, we, as United States manufacturers, have no access to the Canadian market excepting at a higher rate of duty than under the last Payne tariff law.

If, for instance, the Province of Quebec should conclude to take off her restriction, then all the paper and pulp made in Quebec could come into the United States free of duty and we would still be prohibited from any trade in Canada, and the ultimate result to us as manufacturers would be that we would be forced out of the manufacture of the so-called wood papers, and mills which are financially in condition to make radical changes will endeavor to manufacture other grades of paper, and this in time would lead to a disorganization through unintelligent overproduction in certain grades, and we protest against any such unfair treatment of an industry of the magnitude of ours in the United States.

There is hardly an article that goes into the manufacture of paper upon which there is not a duty, and we do not object to this if we in turn have a similar protection, but to throw open our market to our largest competitor, on any such basis as is proposed, is most unfair and unjust.

Yours, very truly,

ARTHUR C. HASTINGS, *President.*

NEW YORK & PENNSYLVANIA CO.,
New York, February 8, 1911.

The manufacture of high-grade book papers, which, next to news paper, is the most important in this country, and in which great sums of money have been invested under the protective system, find a clause in the proposed treaty in the McCall bill " provided such paper and board valued at 4 cents per pound or less." Notwithstanding that those of us who have been engaged for the past 30 years in the production of chemical fibers and their conversion into high-grade book and other papers have reduced their price from 20 cents per pound to 4 cents per pound, and some grades even at a lower figure than that, it is proposed to admit up to 4 cents per pound everything free.

The figures I give you herewith are correct and taken from the records of one of our largest mills for the past year.

	Duty into Canada.	Duty into United States.	Increased cost to us.
English china clay	Free	$2.50 per ton	$75,000
Bleaching powder	do	⅛ cent per pound	70,000
Alum	do	¼ cent per pound	21,000
Copper-wire cloth	17½ per cent	45 per cent	18,000
Aniline dyes	} Free	{ 30 per cent	} 5,000
Ultramarine		{ 3 cents per pound	
Colors			
Paper-makers' feltings and jacketings	30 per cent	44 cents per pound and 55 per cent.	[1] 35,000
			224,000

[1] About.

Leaving out the question of labor altogether and the lower cost of water powers and wood in Canada, please note what an advantage the Canadians will have in addition. Last year, owing to the duties on the items specified, the additional cost to one manufacturer, everything else being equal, amounted to $224,000. This does not take into account a considerable number of small items which are not of sufficient importance to be considered in this statement, which I am prepared to verify by oath, if necessary.

How this question could be overlooked is startling to those of us who understand the business of making paper.

If we are to have free trade in paper with Canada, we must have the duties to the United States correspond to those in Canada, or our industry can not be sustained.

Will you kindly call the attention of Mr. McCall and Mr. Payne to these figures, which are authentic. If the influence of the press is too strong to get a fair deal as regards news paper, then the McCall bill should be amended, on page 19, line 22, to read: "*Provided,* such paper and board valued at 2¾ cents per pound or less," instead of 4 cents, as in the McCall bill. This would help us materialy to maintain our position, or take off the duty on all the chemicals and articles we are compelled to import, and give us the same free trade that Canada has with England.

Can I be assured that these figures will reach Mr. McCall and Mr. Payne in time to save us from the possible passage of a bill containing the original figures?

Faithfully, yours, AUGUSTUS G. PAINE.

COMMITTEE ON WAYS AND MEANS,
HOUSE OF REPRESENTATIVES,
Thursday, February 9, 1911.

AFTERNOON SESSION.

The committee reconvened at 2.15 p. m., Hon. Samuel W. McCall presiding.

Mr. HUMPHREY of Washington. I have a telegram here that I would like to have printed in the record.

Mr. McCALL. Just hand it to the stenographer.

(The telegram referred to is as follows:)

OLYMPIA, WASH., *February 8, 1911.*

Hon. WILLIAM E. HUMPHREY, *Washington, D. C.:*

Following passed Washington Legislature to-day:

House joint memorial 15.

To the honorable Senate and House of Representatives of the United States in Congress assembled:

Your memorialists, the Senate and House of Representatives of the State of Washington, in legislative session assembled, would most respectively represent:

Whereas congressional action with reference to the revision of the tariff seems more or less probable; and

Whereas contemplated congressional action with reference to the tariff involves and concerns certain industries of the Pacific coast and the State of Washington; and

Whereas the continued prosperity and well-being of the State of Washington is to a large extent involved by the contemplated tariff revision: Now, therefore,

Your memorialists, in the name of the people of the State of Washington, and speaking in behalf of the State and the entire Pacific slope we earnestly and respectfully petition and urge that no congressional action be taken with reference to the revision of the tariff without careful consideration of the industries of the western portion of the United States, and particularly of the northwestern portion. Your memorialists further urgently and earnestly petition and urge that the interests so vital to the welfare of the State of Washington and the Pacific northwest are entitled to the same full consideration and thorough review by a nonpartisan, unbiased tariff board as are all other industries of the Nation, and for that reason and in that behalf your memorialists urge congressional action accordingly, and that no action be taken without such consideration and review.

LOREN GRINSTEAD,
Chief Clerk of the House.

STATEMENT OF MR. EDWARD S. HINES, OF CHICAGO, ILL, PRESI. DENT OF THE NATIONAL LUMBER MANUFACTURERS' ASSO. CIATION.

Mr. HINES. Mr. Chairman and gentlemen, in viewing the proposed reciprocity agreement with Canada, as president of the National Lumber Manufacturers' Association I am called upon to voice in the strongest terms possible a protest from 48,000 lumber manufacturers of the United States. Of this large number of lumber manufacturers, not to exceed one-half, and, conservatively speaking, probably only one-quarter, own any standing timber, but purchase their raw ma. terial practically from year to year in the open market.

The summary of the total values of imported articles affected by this arrangement amounts to $47,333,155. Of this value $23,626,010, 49.9 per cent of the total, is for boards, deals, and planks, laths and shingles, poles, and other dutiable lumber items. The lumber indus. try, therefore, has to carry the greater portion of the load, The ex. ports involved amount to $47,827,959. The only lumber items in. volved are stave and shingle bolts, etc., valued at $73,536. The lum. ber industry, therefore, carries practically the entire burden of the reciprocity.

In addition, of course, we have the benefit of the assurance that Canada will not place a duty upon rough lumber, etc., now imported free into the Dominion. The entire value of timber, lumber, posts, ties, poles, and staves admitted into Canada from the United States during the last fiscal year free of duty amounted to $4,653,682. Therefore, our industry is giving up its protection on over $23,000,000 worth of its product in order that less than $5,000,000 worth of its product exported to Canada may not possibly in the future be charged a duty when it enters that country. In addition, we are ex. porting to Canada dressed lumber which has been and will be dutia. ble and is not affected.

In the first place, within the past 18 months, under the so-called Payne-Aldrich tariff bill, lumber suffered a cut of 37½ per cent ad valorem, being the greatest cut suffered by any of the important commodities. Under the workings of the present tariff law the im. portations from Canada increased enormously, 1909 showing 836,795,000 feet, while during 1910 there was imported 1,043,823,000 feet, this being the first fiscal year experienced after its adoption.

Before the hearings of your body, prior to the adoption of the recent tariff bill, the lumbermen from various parts of the country showed by most intelligent and indisputable facts and argument that the former duty on lumber of $2 per thousand was really not a pro. tective duty, but simply revenue; that owing to the advantageous position of the Canadian operators, located in most cases right across the line for several thousand miles along our northern border, di. rectly contiguous to the greatest consuming lumber markets of the United States, commencing at Portland, Me., and taking in Boston and the various large New England cities, New York, Brooklyn, Oswego, Buffalo, and the Tonawandas, and through the Erie Canal at comparatively low water transportation, reaching the heart of New York State, and traversing west on the Great Lakes, Cleveland, Toledo, Detroit, Bay City, Saginaw, Chicago, and Milwaukee, and then going farther west, reaching the Northern States of Minnesota, the Dakotas, Idaho, Montana, and Washington, at comparatively and generally low water rates. The Canadian manufacturers have a great advantage over the American manufacturer, which is in itself sufficient, in place of reducing the duty from the old Dingley rate of $2, to have justified an advance. A direct, strong illustration is the comparatively low transportation charge from any point on Georgian Bay, where a large part of the Ontario lumber is manufactured, to the greatest consuming markets of the United States like Chicago, Milwaukee, Toledo, Cleveland, Erie, Buffalo, as well as the greatest gateways to the great consuming States, which can be reached at an average cost of transportation of not to exceed $1.75 per thousand feet by water; next, the comparatively cheap transportation from the Ottawa district and from Nova Scotia and New Brunswick to our New England coast.

Compare such low water transportation costs with the rates via rail to these points from the greatest manufacturing district of the United States at the present time, namely, the South, the States of Alabama, Georgia, Mississippi, Louisiana, Texas, and Arkansas, which points take a rate of from 24 cents per hundred pounds to 32 cents per hundred pounds, which, on rough lumber, averages from $7 to $11 per thousand feet, an average of at least 400 per cent more than the cost of transporting lumber from the Canadian districts to the same territory where most of the lumber is used.

In the extreme West, as will be more particularly explained in detail by representatives from the Pacific coast, practically the entire common help of the mills in the Canadian west is composed of Hindus, Japanese, Chinese, etc., and who work on a very much lower wage scale than the American labor can be hired for right across the border, which constitutes almost entirely the class of help in the American sawmill. (See testimony taken one and one-half years ago.)

Another most important fact, as was illustrated in detail before the former hearings of the Ways and Means Committee, the timber in the United States is bought outright at a fixed price, subject to immediate interest and taxes upon taking possession, and the amount of taxes levied is based on the value of the timber from year to year, constituting a steady fixed charge upon the timber. The American timber owner must also consider the danger and risk attendant by fire, cyclone, etc., which was most forcibly illustrated last year in the forest fires which raged in the States of Minnesota, Wisconsin, and the far West. Compare this with the conditions existing across the border in Canada, the Government owning the timber, carrying the entire risk of fire, and practically carrying the entire risk attendant upon holding the timber and licensing the timber to the manufacturer at practically no taxes, making hardly any risk for the Canadian operator and tying up no excessive sums in stumpage. This in itself would amount, at a reasonable basis, to a difference of 10 per cent per annum. Consider how soon an article at 10 per cent per annum doubles itself. Consider, therefore, the relative positions of the Canadian and American manufacturer.

Is it not fair, therefore, to draw your particular attention to the fact that, taking the entire duty off of lumber, you are placing the

American operator, as compared with the Canadian operator, at a very great disadvantage? The American manufacturers, having gone ahead and purchased their timber outright on a basis of conditions existing at the time of the purchase, have built their sawmills, have made heavy investments, all contingent upon a supposed reasonable protective theory, and at least based upon reasonable and equitable treatment, and based upon the assumption of a reasonable permanency of the situation.

The direct difference in the transportation charge alone would more than warrant an increase over the old tariff rate in place of reducing it, and, as now contemplated, eliminating the duty entirely, if any degree of fairness is to be shown this great industry, which in rank, considering the amount of capital invested, number of employees, and value of the product, ranges from third to fourth among the largest interests of this country.

We particularly call to the Members' attention the most intelligent and conservative statements of facts, which you have on file, in the previous tariff hearings, which we feel unnecessary, considering the intervening short period, to again enumerate. We then showed that if the tariff were reduced great suffering would occur to this industry, and the results have more than borne out our statements at that time. Lumber at manufacturing points, commencing on the Pacific coast, has reached the lowest point since 1902, wages and cost of supplies considered, prices ranging from $6 to $8 per thousand at mill points for common building material, netting the manufacturer practically nothing for stumpage; such figures proving that lumber is down to practically the cost of production, and in many cases showing a loss on the stumpage. A very few of the most modern and best equipped plants show a small return on the stumpage, but the majority, under the present basis of prices for the finished product, show practically nothing for the stumpage. What, then, can the manufacturer do? Labor, the chief item in the cost of manufacturing, refuses a reduction, and challenges any such attempt. The next item is supplies—almost all articles used in the construction of a sawmill, in tools, saws, machinery, and other accessories, are fully protected by duty, and the American manufacturer must pay the full price. Transportation lines, bringing their product to the consumers, as you well know, are clamoring and insisting upon advances in rates. What, then, can be reduced to make the cost less? And we are now confronted with the probability of taking down the bars entirely and admitting Canadian lumber entirely free into the United States. Such action will absolutely force many manufacturers into bankruptcy, compelling, in certain sections of our country, skilled American workmen, used to the highest standard of living, to compete directly with Hindus, Japs, Chinese, and other foreign labor used to the foreign manner of living, and further giving Canada, in addition to the many great advantages above mentioned, the additional advantage of the present duty.

Let us leave for a moment the direct interest of the lumber industry in this matter and consider the interest of conservation; in the President's special message to Congress of January 26, Senate Document No. 787, on page 7, he says:

Free lumber we ought to have. By giving our people access to Canadian forests we shall reduce the consumption of our own, which, in the hands of comparatively few owners, now have a value that requires the enlargement of our available timber resources.

It is true that we might have access to the Canadian resources, but only by way of a large benefit to the Canadian sawmill as against our own. But granting that we should increase our importation of Canadian lumber under this measure, and therefore decrease the price of our own low-grade lumber, we would but accentuate the effect caused by lowering the duty under the Payne-Aldrich bill. I do not ascribe the low prices of lumber during the past three years entirely to that measure, for it was in part brought about by the panic of 1907, but while other industries revived quickly, lumber did not. We were just beginning to feel a recovery from the business depression when the tariff bill was passed, and at once we had a further reduction in the price of low-grade lumber, the upper grades being little, if at all, affected.

The important fact, as shown by investigations conducted by the National Lumber Manufacturers' Association, as to the conditions existing in the various producing centers of the country was that, following the cry for conservation, the lumbermen had been using up very closely the timber found on the ground, going most conscientiously into the utilization of defective trees, and endeavoring to use up all that was available in the trees; but it has been found necessary, owing to the decline in values, to limit the amount cut in the woods, to make a better selection of timber, and to leave a large amount of material that would not stand transportation and cost of manufacturing. The extent of this change and methods is a little difficult to determine definitely, but we can safely say that 5 to 10 per cent more material is now being left in the woods than in 1906. This material is not in shape to reproduce itself, to grow or become available in the future, but simply wastes itself by rot and fire, and is a menace to the young timber. Taking the lowest percentage named, namely, 5 per cent, on the total product of lumber, we are showing a waste of 2,000,000,000 feet more than in 1906, a tremendous waste, in order that a few hundred thousand feet more of lumber may be imported from Canada, which is not needed in our markets, and which does not in any way benefit the ultimate consumer, the reduction in the duty being more than 50 per cent absorbed by the Canadian manufacturer, who, prior to this, was in position to market practically all the low-grade lumber he wished to in this country. The balance was largely absorbed by the box manufacturers and the wholesale dealers, and part of it absorbed by some recent advances of the railroads. The retail dealers, as a whole, have made no change whatsoever in the price to the consumer since the change of duty, and we contend that if the duty is removed entirely it will practically make no difference in the price to the consumer.

Again quoting the President:

Free lumber we ought to have. By giving our people access to Canadian forests we shall reduce the consumption of our own, which, in the hands of comparatively few owners, now have a value that requires the enlargement of our available timber resources.

We challenge this assertion by the President, and offer as an offset the statement on testimony of the Hon. Gifford Pinchot before your body during the tariff hearings, now on file, in substance, that lowering the duty or removing the duty, would not serve the ends of conservation, but, on the contrary, would force a great deal of loss on our own resources, and we attach hereto copy of his testimony justifying such contention.

We directly challenge the statement of the President in which he says that our American forests are in the hands of comparatively few owners. The lumber manufacturers of the United States, under a resolution of the Senate, known as the Kittridge resolution, adopted in December, 1906, have been under direct investigation during the past four years by the Department of Commerce and Labor under the jurisdiction of Herbert Knox Smith. For several years the lumbermen have heartily cooperated by giving ready access to their books and records of all kinds, both through association work and as individuals.

Up to the present time, although we have made repeated demands and requests upon Mr. Smith, as well as the Chief Executive, for a report, no report has been forthcoming, and this great industry, by being morally indicted, so to speak, for the past five years, as voiced by the public press from day to day, as being under investigation, has been convicted in the minds of the American people as being a great trust and subject to daily attack. If such a report has been made, in justice to the great lumber industry, a copy of it should be made public. In place of the timber being in the hands of comparatively few owners, there is no class of raw material in this country in the hands of so many diversified and small owners.

In the President's annual message to Congress he virtually states that 30 per cent of the standing timber of the United States is in the hands of about 200 corporations and individuals. This statement is in error, but accepting it as being true for the sake of argument, it shows a more diversified ownership than any other great natural resource of this country. The President says: * * * "We shall have direct access to her (Canada's) great supply of natural products." In taking the duty off manufactured lumber, this in no way gives direct access to Canada's natural products, but to her manufactured products. We contend that if the spirit of the reciprocity idea is carried out, as is directly done in the case of pulp and pulp wood, if such a rule is equitable as to the one, then the same features should surround the raw product of standing timber as surround pulp wood, namely, that not alone the manufactured article be admitted free, but in return for this benefit Canada should also permit the free exportation of logs to this country.

Quoting from page 8, the President says:

That the broadening of the sources of food supplies, that the opening of the timber resources of the Dominion to our needs, that the addition to the supply of raw materials, will be limited to no particular section does not require demonstration.

While he argues for the free importation of raw materials, so far as the free importation of raw timber is concerned no provision is made, while such provision is made in the case of wood pulp.

Again, on page 9, he says:

Reciprocity with Canada must necessarily be chiefly confined in its effect on the cost of living to food and forest products.

There seems to have been an entire oversight, as surely it can not be intentional, in using an argument for the free importation of forest products, so far as wood pulp is concerned, while no provision is made to carry out this same plan so far as timber is concerned, coming from the same land in Canada as that which grows the wood pulp, and even on the same acre or portion of the acre. If pulp wood under the provisions of the Canadian reciprocity agreement is to be admitted to this country free, what argument can be used to debar raw timber likewise to be imported without restraint. In most cases both are logged at the same time, in the same manner, and floated down the same streams. Why stop one to be manufactured in Canada by Canadian workmen, fed by Canadian supplies and manufactured with Canadian tools, as compared with wood pulp being floated down the same stream to the American paper mills to be manufactured by American labor, American machinery, and American supplies? If such argument is good for pulp wood, why not use this same argument for the free and unrestricted importation of timber of all kinds?

The President states, on page 10:

Since becoming a nation, Canada has been our good neighbor, immediately contiguous across a wide continent without artificial or natural barrier except navigable waters used in common.

This stretches over an extent of several thousand miles. In most cases, or at least a great many cases, such navigable waters flow from the Canadian forests, down to navigable streams entering our own country, nature, so to speak, aiding in helping to transport raw material or logs, as well as pulp wood, to our own country, so as to enable us to manufacture not alone pulp wood into wood pulp, but likewise to manufacture saw logs into lumber in the United States, and by so doing, create new towns in this country or, at least, support towns now in existence entirely dependent upon sawmills for the support of their several thousand inhabitants. Such timber should be manufactured in this country, because the entire product will be sold and marketed in this country. What is more broad or fair or equitable than. if Canada is to have the added advantage of marketing her products in the great markets of this country at a higher price on account of the entire removal of the duty, which particularly means an advance in the price of her products, that she should also agree to the free and unrestricted exportation of her saw logs to our country, where they can be manufactured into lumber by American labor, American machinery, American farm products to be consumed and manufactured in American factories?

A further fact and argument, if it is your wish to have the lumber reach the American consumer at the lowest possible cost. is that the timber can be floated down to the American mills for manufacturing at about one-tenth of the cost of transporting the same amount of the manufactured product; therefore a further decrease in the cost can be made by allowing saw timber to be imported free and manufactured on this side, as against the present arrangement by which, even though the duty is eliminated on lumber, it must be manufactured in Canada. Such conditions extend over practically the entire border between the United States and Canada. Prior to Ontario enacting a law forbidding the exportation of logs there were sawmills located at all of our Great Lake ports, commencing at Sault Ste. Marie and extending several hundred miles, including Saginaw, Cheboygan, Alpena, Bay City, Port Huron, and other minor ports, all sawing Canadian logs at comparatively a very small cost of transportation, an average of about 25 cents per thousand, as compared with $1.75 per thousand on the manufactured product.

Further, in the transporting of logs the entire product comes into the United States at a comparatively small cost of transportation, in addition to the offal coming here, which at the present time can not stand the cost of transportation, in the way of slabs, sawdust, firewood, short box lumber; in fact, practically 30 per cent of the entire log, which at the present time will not bear the cost of transporting to the United States in its finished state, and this would all reach the United States free of any extra charges, to the advantage of the consumer, if the logs were imported free in place of the manufactured product.

Also consider that if only the manufactured product is to be admitted into this country free Canada will immediately commence increasing her manufacture, which will mean that a great many of our Americans will go to Canada to seek employment, and this will mean the loss to our American farmers of sustaining such employment. If a provision is made that Canada shall permit the free exportation of pulp wood in consideration for the removal of our duty on wood pulp and print paper imported from Canada into this country, we fail to see why the same provisions should not be enacted so far as the importation of saw logs and timber is concerned if we are to admit her lumber free.

After a very careful diagnosis of the situation we fail to see where the great American lumber-manufacturing industry participates in any way in this proposed reciprocal agreement. As previously explained, many of the manufacturers of this country have no supply of raw material, therefore it would be only justice to give them an opportunity to obtain from Canada a supply of raw material in compensation for taking off the present duty on their finished product. Canada, having the opportunity of reaching our great markets free, surely could not complain of such an arrangement.

On page 5 the President says:

A farsighted policy requires that if we can enlarge our supplies of natural resources, and especially of food products and the necessities of life, without substantial injury to any of our producing and manufacturing classes, we should take steps to do so now.

This is exactly what we are contending for, namely, to increase our natural resources in the form of raw material or logs, in order to keep employed our producing and manufacturing classes located on this side of the border. It is just as important that the employees and manufacturing classes employing labor in these 48,000 sawmills of the United States be considered and furnished employment as it is the employees of manufacturing interests which are clamoring for enlarged territory in western Canada to supply an increased amount of goods.

If therefore, in your judgment, we have not sustained our position that the present duty on lumber should be retained in its present form, there surely can be no reason why you should not agree with us that the same provision embodied in the pulp and paper clauses should also be incorporated in connection with the clauses that put sawed lumber and other such products on the free list. We therefore respectfully offer, as an amendment to the reciprocity agreement, the attached proposed amendment.

PROPOSED AMENDMENT TO RECIPROCITY AGREEMENT BETWEEN UNITED STATES AND CANADA.

On page 18, H. R. 32216, after line 7, insert:

Provided, That such timber, sawed lumber, posts, ties, poles, staves, stave bolts, pickets, and palings, being the products of Canada, when imported therefrom directly into the United States, shall be admitted free of duty on the condition precedent that no refund of royalties, dues, or charges of any nature, export duty, export-license fee, or other export charge of any kind whatsoever (whether in the form of additional charge or license fee, or otherwise), or any prohibition or restriction in any way of the exportation (whether by law, order, regulation, contractual relation, or otherwise, directly or indirectly) shall have been imposed by Canada or any Province or part thereof upon such timber, lumber, posts, and so forth, or the woods (in whatever form, whether saw logs, shingle bolts, or other form) used in the manufacture of such timber, sawed lumber, posts, ties, poles, staves, stave bolts, pickets, and palings: *And provided further,* That Canada shall not impose a higher duty on dressed lumber the product of the United States when imported into Canada from the United States than the duty imposed by the United States upon dressed lumber the product of Canada when imported into the United States from Canada.

Mr. HINES. There is just one point further to which I wish to call your attention in this reciprocal agreement—the question of dressed lumber. Lumber going from this side to Canada, if finished more than one side, pays a duty of 25 per cent ad valorem because it is dressed; lumber coming from Canada to the United States, when dressed, pays from 3 to 5 per cent duty. In other words, there is a difference of about 500 per cent in favor of the Canadian manufacturer as compared with the American manufacturer. As a direct illustration, in shipping lumber, for instance, from Louisiana, timber dressed or sized, to Montreal or Toronto, the duty would be 25 per cent ad valorem. Shipping the same lumber from Canada to the United States, the duty would be about 3 per cent. So that there is an important provision to be considered. I thank you, gentlemen, for your kind consideration. I have an exceptionally good map showing the territory of the United States and Canada, and I would like to pass it around for the gentlemen to look at.

Mr. LONGWORTH. I understand, now, that you deny the truth of the assertion made in the President's message as follows: "By giving our people access to Canadian forests, we shall reduce the consumption of our own," and that you cite Mr. Pinchot in support of the proposition that a $2 duty on lumber is more in the interest of conservation than the present duty of $1.25. On that point—and I am asking you these questions not in any spirit of controversy, but to get the benefit of your judgment—why, if that is true, would not a duty of $3 on lumber be more in the interest of conservation than a duty of $2?

Mr. HINES. I would answer that this way: I think I can satisfy you that Mr. Pinchot's reasoning was correct. In a tree there are all kinds of lumber. For instance, the first and second logs might sell at an average of $30 a thousand. The top log might sell at an average of $10 a thousand; that is, in good, sound tree. Right alongside of it is a different tree that produces a lot of low-grade lumber. Anything in the way of reducing the duty helps Canada to put into this country, not her good lumber, but her low-grade lumber. The good lumber is practically all exported to Europe, the low-grade lumber comes over here. In our sawmills when the price of low grade gets to a certain point we can not afford to manufacture; therefore that low grade will be left in the forests; a quarter or a fifth of the entire tree will be left to rot and decay. It is not used at all. So, in the interest of conservation it would become an absolute waste on a certain proportion.

Another thing, on your real small timber you can not afford to do it. If your sawmill is sawing 200,000 a day, in order to keep it employed you have to go over a greater acreage than if you took the entire land clean. When you leave a fourth in the woods to decay, you are not conserving the timber; you are wasting it.

Mr. LONGWORTH. Because when the price of lumber is low that waste occurs?

Mr. HINES. Yes.

Mr. LONGWORTH. The higher it goes the less waste there is. If it is true that the tariff adds to the cost of lumber, that the higher the price of lumber, the less tendency there is to waste, why is it not also true that it would be advisable to raise the tariff so as to raise the price of lumber?

Mr. HINES. We contend, and we think we showed by the cleanest argument possible, that a duty of $3 a thousand would not stop in any way the importation of the same quantity of lumber that has been imported for a period of five years. But it would have stopped, probably, that increased amount of low-grade lumber. In other words, Canada's position, her cost of transportation, being located so close to our large consuming cities, her position is so advantageous that if the duty were $3 a thousand she could then compete with the same advantage the American manufacturer has to-day, except on the low-grade lumber. For instance, as a direct illustration, when the cost of transportation on an average is not to exceed $2 a thousand from 50 of the leading Canadian manufacturing points to the greatest consuming cities of the United States, the great gateways to our great consuming States, as compared with the Southern States, as compared with Western States, it is not one-fifth of the cost of rail transportation to the same markets. You see the position she is in.

Mr. LONGWORTH. I think you are getting a little bit away from my question. Your answer is now devoted somewhat to the question of transportation as affecting the cost. I am simply trying to get at the point where you stop in your proposition that high-priced lumber is in favor of conservation. How much higher would that have to be to be in the best interests of conservation?

Mr. HINES. You take high-priced lumber; it is not only in the interest of conservation, but also in the interest of tree growing. If lumber is at a point where the manufactured article does not pay the cost of transportation it becomes of no value; it is wasted; it is left in the woods to rot. We not only lose that lumber, but labor loses its proportion of the product, the transportation lines lose their proportion, and so it is a waste. That stuff may be worth only a dollar a thousand in the woods, but if manufactured and shipped to Detroit or Cleveland it would pay some one from $6 to $8; it would be the labor cost and the transportation cost. If lumber comes from Canada and that lumber in Kentucky or Mississippi is left to waste or rot that is a loss to the American people. You are not conserving that amount of money, you are losing it.

Mr. LONGWORTH. Then you and Mr. Pinchot, I presume, take this position, That in the interests of forest conservation it would be wise to force the price of lumber so high that it would not be used for purposes that it is now being used for?

Mr. HINES. No; I do not take that radical position, and I do not think Mr. Pinchot does for a minute.

Mr. LONGWORTH. How can you help it?

Mr. HINES. That would be, I think, a very unreasonable position. You could not sustain that position for a minute.

Mr. LONGWORTH. How can you help being forced to that position? We will start with the assumption that it is not wise to destroy all the American forests; everybody will admit that. But if we continue using lumber for the purposes for which we are now using it, eventually those forests will be destroyed, will they not; our forests will be destroyed eventually?

Mr. HINES. Yes.

Mr. LONGWORTH. If we continue to use lumber for the purposes for which we are now using it, that is true, is it not?

Mr. HINES. No; you could not put that rule down. You have to take what has occurred in the past. If you go back 5, 10, 15 or 20 years, the great purposes for which lumber was used are no longer filled with lumber. Conditions have changed, and lumber is not used for those purposes. Cement has come to take its place. Look at the thousands of miles of walks in the villages where cement has taken the place of wood. Look at the houses that used to be built with wood which are now constructed of reinforced concrete. These conditions have taken care of themselves. When lumber gets to a certain point in price some other substance will take its place.

Mr. LONGWORTH. Then you do not think that if lumber stays at its present price, and the destruction of our forests keeps on at the same rate it is going on now, they will eventually be destroyed?

Mr. HINES. I do not; no, sir.

Mr. LONGWORTH. I understood you to say before that you did.

Mr. HINES. You meant on the same proportion, but conditions there change every day. Take the last 10 years as an illustration. Billions of feet of lumber used for certain purposes are not being used at all any more. Look at the railroad cars. It is entirely a steel proposition now. Three years ago it was entirely a wood proposition. Look at bolts. You can mention hundreds of articles of that kind.

Mr. LONGWORTH. I can understand perfectly why, if lumber got to such a high price that people would not use it for the purposes for which they are now using it, building sheds, fences, and so forth, just as it is, I understand, in Germany, it will be much easier to conserve the forests. But so long as it remains at its present price, substantially, and is used for those purposes, at the present rate of destruction, the forests will be wiped out in a not great number of years.

Mr. HINES. My position is this: The actual practice has shown a certain amount of lumber coming from Canada for the past 10 years under the present conditions—a very large amount. Even at an advance of 50 per cent in the tariff the same quantity will come to this country, but it will give the operators of this country a certain protection on the low-grade lumber. On the high-priced lumber we do not need any protection.

Mr. LONGWORTH. Suppose there was a duty of $10 on lumber; what would be the effect of the destruction of the forests?

Mr. HINES. I think the effect would be as bad as taking the duty off entirely. It would make prices here largely prohibitive. I am not in favor of any such excessive duty at all. Human nature is the same all over the world, and the operators here would take advantage of such a condition as that. We are only contending for a reasonable duty. We are contending that the present duty is not a revenue duty in itself.

Mr. LONGWORTH. In other words, if, in this country, the duty was so high that no lumber could, under any circumstances, be imported, would not the result be a more rapid destruction of the forests?

Mr. HINES. No; on the contrary, in my judgment, the very fact of some operators advancing the price, and the excessive prices, would more quickly bring in substitutes, absolutely.

Mr. LONGWORTH. How could they advance those prices?

Mr. HINES. Every time you advance an article, then you invite substitution, absolutely. The higher you advance an article in price the greater the substitution that comes into competition.

Mr. LONGWORTH. Yes; but does not your proposition involve a combination to raise prices?

Mr. HINES. How do mean a combination?

Mr. LONGWORTH. A combination of those engaged in the business.

Mr. HINES. That is perfectly ridiculous when you reflect that there are 48,000 manufacturers located in the United States, in five different groups, different interests, so to speak—the New England operators, the southern operators, the operators down South, the operators in Wisconsin and Michigan, and the operators on the extreme coast—all competing for the same territory. Take, for instance, Springfield, Ill.; a man wants to buy 12-inch boards. He can buy those from five distinct groups.

Mr. LONGWORTH. I am not saying there is or is not a combination. But you say if the duty were $10 the prices would be raised.

Mr. HINES. Naturally, I believe they would.

Mr. LONGWORTH. Then I ask you how?

Mr. HINES. Human nature would assert itself. We are alike in that particular. You would see an advantage there right for the moment; you would like to take advantage of the situation.

Mr. GAINES. Mr. Longworth wants to know how you could take advantage of it.

Mr. HINES. Mark your lumber up.

Mr. LONGWORTH. Would there be any difference in that respect in a duty of $10 and a duty of $100?

Mr. HINES. Oh, yes. The higher the duty the higher prices people would try to get. But supply and demand would govern that.

Mr. Longworth. Do you think it makes any difference, after you have a duty that is considered prohibitive, how much higher it is?

Mr. Hines. That is a different thing.

Mr. Longworth. $10 would be prohibitive?

Mr. Hines. On certain kinds of lumber; on certain kinds it would not be. You see, lumber is in grades.

Mr. Longworth. What would be a prohibitive duty?

Mr. Hines. You take, for instance, a perfectly clear lumber; it might take an even higher duty to keep that out of this market. There is only about 1 per cent of that in the log, and the larger portion of the log is a low-grade lumber. That is what we want to conserve in this country and utilize. We do not use it; it is left in the woods to rot.

Mr. Longworth. I do not know whether you caught my question or not, or understood it. I assumed, when I said $10, that that would be a prohibitive duty on lumber. Given a duty of $10 on lumber, how could you increase the price when you say it is an absolutely competitive article all over the country; how could you increase the price correspondingly without a combination?

Mr. Hines. You could not.

Mr. Longworth. I thought you said you could?

Mr. Hines. You could not arbitrarily increase it all over the country at the same time. One section might advance it $2, one three, another four, and different prices. One man might want to rush ahead and put up four or five sawmills and cut all the timber off in a year or two, and that means a decrease in price. Supply and demand would govern that proposition, as it always has. Lumber fluctuates, depending on supply and demand, irrespective of the duty.

Mr. Fordney. When the price of low-grade lumber is very low the amount of low grade in the logs in the tree left in the woods is far greater than the amount of low grade imported, is it not?

Mr. Hines. Yes, sir.

Mr. Fordney. At the present time, Mr. Hines, I believe you will agree with me, in Louisiana, Mississippi, Florida, Georgia, and all the Southern States, the price of the average product of the log at the mill is somewhere from $12.50 to $14 per 1,000, depending on the average quality of the log and the location of the mill?

Mr. Hines. That is within 5 or 10 per cent.

Mr. Fordney. That price to-day is five or six or seven dollars per 1,000 feet lower than it was in 1906?

Mr. Hines. I would say from four to six dollars.

Mr. Fordney. So, consequently, when the price was $18 for this lumber at the mill, in 1906 and the fore part of 1907, much more low-grade timber was taken out of the woods, converted into finished products, and marketed than is being taken out of those forests to-day?

Mr. Hines Yes, sir; the land was practically logged clear four years ago, and to-day there is about 25 per cent left in the woods to rot.

Mr. Fordney. In any lumbering operation in the South, in order to get the good grade out of the tree, the low grade is now fallen on the ground and left lying there on account of the low prices?

Mr. Hines. Generally speaking, that is true.

Mr. FORDNEY. Now, put your tariff high enough and it would furnish a market for this low-grade lumber. You speak of conserving our forests. Instead of leaving all this lumber to rot we would be stripping the lands clean.

Mr. HINES. Yes, sir; a reasonable tariff would enable that low-grade lumber to be transported to the consuming markets and used, where now it will not bear the cost of transportation.

Mr. FORDNEY. In the President's message to Congress, in the fore part of December, 1910, as I remember now on page 36, the President made the statement that the Bureau of Corporations, in the Department of Commerce and Labor, had investigated the question as to whether or not there was a combination or a trust among the manufacturers of lumber, and that that bureau reported that there was no combination or trust among the manufacturers of lumber; is not that correct?

Mr. HINES. That is absolutely a fact.

Mr. FORDNEY. The press reports went out, reporting the President's message, and they were just the reverse, were they not?

Mr. HINES. They were.

Mr. FORDNEY. It was certainly intentional; it could not have been a mistake, because the word sent out in the press reports was that the matter was being further investigated and had not been determined. Is not that correct?

Mr. HINES. Yes, sir; absolutely.

Mr. FORDNEY. So that a wrong impression was sent out by some press reporter, who sent that dispatch from Washington?

Mr. HINES. All over the United States.

Mr. FORDNEY. For the purpose, undoubtedly, of discrediting men in their business, was it not?

Mr. HINES. That is the conclusion we drew from it.

Mr. FORDNEY. No other conclusion could be arrived at, could it?

Mr. HINES. Not within reason, I do not think.

Mr. FORDNEY. I wanted that to be known, and I want it to go in the record that that is a fact. I want it further stated that, whoever that press reporter might be, I would like to see him excluded from the House of Representatives, because he misstated facts.

Mr. HILL. For whom do you appear to-day?

Mr. HINES. I appear as president of the National Lumber Manufacturers' Association.

Mr. HILL. You are president of it, are you not?

Mr. HINES. Yes, sir; this year.

Mr. HILL. For whom did you appear the other day? For yourself, did you not?

Mr. HINES. In both ways—in a dual position.

Mr. HILL. Then you spoke for them the other day and you speak for them again to-day?

Mr. HINES. Yes, sir.

Mr. HILL. Who were the 48,000 people; did you refer to manufacturers?

Mr. HINES. Manufacturers.

Mr. HILL. As manufacturers only?

Mr. HINES. Only.

Mr. HILL. Not for dealers, or consumers?

Mr. HINES. No; principally manufacturers.

Mr. HILL. And you have no desire or intention of contradicting to-day anything you said the other day?

Mr. HINES. If I made any mistake I want to correct it.

Mr. HILL. That is your privilege. But you have no intention of contradicting to-day what you said the other day, and had no intention the other day of contradicting anything you have said to-day?

Mr. HINES. Not intentionally; no, sir.

Mr. HILL. All right; that is all.

Mr. HINES. I thank you.

STATEMENT OF MR. HERBERT W. BLANCHARD, OF BOSTON, MASS., PRESIDENT OF THE BLANCHARD LUMBER CO., OF BOSTON; PRESIDENT OF THE PORTAGE LAKE MILL CO., OF PORTAGE LAKE, ME., REPRESENTING THE MANUFACTURERS OF THE STATE OF MAINE.

Mr. BLANCHARD. Mr. Chairman and gentlemen, I have been asked to appear before you as the representative of the following companies, who manufacture lumber in the State of Maine: St. John Lumber Co., Van Buren, Me., manufacturing 55,000,000 feet a year; the South Gardner Lumber Co., South Gardner, Me., manufacturing 12,000,000 feet; the Portage Lake Mill Co., of Portage, Me., manufacturing 12,000,000 feet; Augusta Lumber Co., of Augusta, Me., manufacturing 15,000,000 feet; Lawrence Bros., of South Gardner, Me., manufacturing 12,000,000 feet; Sterm Lumber Co., of Bangor, Me., manufacturing 12,000,000 feet; Lowell & Elgel, of Bangor, Me., manufacturing 15,000,000 feet. These concerns have a capital invested of more than a million and a half, and they employ upward of a thousand men.

In order that your committee may understand the reason for this protest which I am making, I think it proper to give you something of the conditions that exist in the spruce manufacturing business, both in Maine and in Canada. Ten years ago stumpage in Maine was $3 per thousand; it then advanced to $4, then $5, and now to $6 per thousand. The cost of stumpage has doubled in the past 15 years. There are very few manufacturers in Maine who own their own timber land. They are obliged in nearly every instance to buy their stumpage of individuals. This applies to nearly every mill on the Kennebec, Penobscot, St. John River, and mills in northern Maine. They can not get their logs less than $6 per thousand on the stump, to which must be added expenses of logging and driving. Across the line conditions are different. Most of the Canadian mills acquired their land in large blocks years ago when prices were low and when the Government wished to sell. In Canada the Government first owns the land, then deeds it to individuals, and in many cases these individuals in turn have sold it to the present owners. Fifteen years ago prices were very cheap, and most mills do not figure that their stumpage costs them over a dollar to $1.50 per thousand. To this must be added the Crown dues of $1.25 per thousand. Probably $2.50 is the cost of Canadian stumpage to-day, as against $6 for American stumpage.

Freight rates on the line of the Bangor & Aroostook Railroad, where my Portage Lake mill is located, are 15 cents per hundred on long lumber.

Mr. GAINES. Repeat that about those freight rates; 15 cents from where?

Mr. BLANCHARD. Fifteen cents from Portage Lake, Me. This place is located on the Bangor & Aroostook Railroad, which runs north to the line. Some rates from that country are 14 cents, but almost all the large shippers are paying 15 cents from there to Boston.

Mr. HARRISON. There is no competition among any of the Maine railroads, is there?

Mr. BLANCHARD. Practically none.

Mr. HARRISON. It is practically all one big railroad?

Mr. BLANCHARD. The Boston & Maine controls the Maine Central, and the C. P. R. Road joint onto that.

Mr. HILL. But neither of them controls the Aroostook Road?

Mr. BLANCHARD. No, sir.

Mr. HILL. It is used largely by lumbermen, and is owned and controlled by them?

Mr. BLANCHARD. No, sir; it is not owned by the lumbermen.

Mr. McCALL. Does the Bangor & Aroostook extend to the ocean?

Mr. BLANCHARD. It has recently, within two years, built a spur down to tidewater from Northern Maine Junction, in the hope of getting into New York by way of their terminal at Stockton Springs.

Mr. FORDNEY. Is that road owned by the lumbermen?

Mr. BLANCHARD. It is not.

Mr. HILL. Does not Mr. Sam Sterns own a good deal of the stock and did he not help build it?

Mr. BLANCHARD. I do not know. But I do know now that the rates have recently advanced on the Bangor & Aroostook Road 1 cent per hundred all over the line. The rate is now 15 cents, where it was 14.

Mr. FORDNEY. If there is one lumberman interested in that road, Mr. Hill thinks the entire lumber industry should be held up for it.

Mr. HILL. Is it not a fact that the Bangor & Aroostook Road was built by lumbermen, just as the Michigan lumbermen have done, to take out lumber, largely for that purpose?

Mr. BLANCHARD. It may have been built to take out lumber.

Mr. HILL. Certainly, and the lumbermen owned it in the beginning; whether they own it now or not I do not know. How long is the Bangor & Aroostook Railroad?

Mr. BLANCHARD. The main line, I think, was 250 miles long.

Mr. FORDNEY. There is not a lumberman in the country wealthy enough to build such a road. [Laughter.]

Mr. BLANCHARD. This is a little bit diverting from the question, but I can tell you that road is to-day the most arbitrary road in Maine I have any business with. That is absolutely a fact. The Bangor & Aroostook Road has issued a lot of bonds for that new extension that we were just talking about, down to the seaboard, and the New York capitalists who have put up that money have to be paid for the extension. The railroad has put up the rate 1 cent a hundred, and the only reason for doing it is to pay for these extra bonds. The last spur they built was not a success. They have a great many million dollars invested in this spur, which runs to the seaboard, and the advance in the rates was due to that cause, and not because there was any real reason for it, because we were paying enough before.

Mr. HARRISON. As a matter of fact, that road runs through the richest agricultural region in New England.

Mr. BLANCHARD. It is a great potato country. They ship out a great many potatoes on that road.

The rate of freight from many points in Canada is 13 and 14 cents to Boston and Boston points, where the haul is considerably longer. In other words, the Canadian railroads have made no rates of freight, so as to assist the Canadians to market their lumber.

The manufacturers of this side of the line for the past three years have not made any profit whatever. The last year proved an actual loss to nearly every mill in the State of Maine manufacturing lumber. Across the line mills are prosperous. A Canadian friend of mine in my office two or three days ago informed me that they almost always netted $3 per thousand profit, and the last year showed them a profit of $4 per thousand. You will see from these figures that the Canadians are physically able to put their lumber into the States at $2 or $3 per thousand less than we possibly can manufacture it in the State of Maine.

Almost all the Maine mills cut their logs full length, from 40 to 50 feet long, and endeavor to saw this stock as much as possible into frames and long random suitable for the American market. Almost all of the Canadian mills—and by Canada I mean Nova Scotia, Province of Quebec, and eastern Canada—cut their logs 16 feet long. They have been accustomed to sell 80 per cent of their product in England, South America, Cuba, and the West Indies. We have been getting during this period the stock that is unsuitable for these markets, namely, the narrow random plank and boards and all the laths that the mills produce. As soon as the duty was reduced from $2 to $1.25 per thousand many of these mills began to turn their eyes toward the States, and they have been shipping in during the last year a very much larger amount than hitherto.

Of this added competition the result has been that on everything that the Canadians could produce the market has gone down. Several mills that have been shipping entirely abroad under the reduced duty have been taking orders for our market, and this competition has been felt a lot during this last year with the duty at $1.25. If the foreign markets continue strong it is probable that we shall not feel this Canadian competition very much, except on the narrow sizes which the people abroad do not want. During the past year a lot of this narrow stuff has been put into the New York market at $3 per thousand less than the stock can be produced on this side of the line. New York was simply a dumping ground for their by-product, and I can assure you that this hurt tremendously. Now, let us suppose that the English market, which takes a very large amount of lumber, gets down. Immediately our Canadian friends will commence to ship their lumber onto our market, and the competition will be fatal. They can undersell us if they want to, and the State of Maine manufacturers could look forward to several disastrous years. We all of us had a theory that when the duty was reduced from $2 to $1.25 that we would have little to fear from Canada, provided this foreign market held good, but even with the duty at $1.25 we have been bothered a lot by this low-priced Canadian lumber.

The present reciprocity treaty proposes to reduce the duty from 20 cents to 10 cents on laths. The strength or the weakness of the New

York market makes the price high or low. Laths are a by-product of all Nova Scotia and Canadian mills, and can not be shipped abroad. They must be shipped to the States any way, and I fail to see where the duty would have any effect one way or the other in the price of this commodity. It seems entirely foolish for the United States Government to take off the duty on laths, as it is simply giving this duty to the Canadians and will not put one penny into the pockets of the American consumer.

Mr. HILL. What do you sell laths for in Maine, at Bangor shipping points?

Mr. BLANCHARD. I was speaking at that moment of the laths that were shipped by cargo.

Mr. HILL. I mean laths shipped by cargo.

Mr. BLANCHARD. Most of the laths that are shipped by cargo come from over the line.

Mr. HILL. What are laths worth? What did they close at last fall?

Mr. BLANCHARD. I should have to figure that out. Laths closed in New York last fall at about $3.35 to $3.40. That would net the shipper about $2.55.

Mr. FORDNEY. Five thousand laths, Mr. Blanchard, represent about 1,000 feet of lumber, do they not?

Mr. BLANCHARD. Yes, sir; 5 to 1.

Now, going back to lumber, it is against this Canadian competition that we ask this very small protection of $1.25 per thousand. Given a depressed market on the other side of the water the low cost of Canadian lumber makes it entirely possible for American manufacturers to do their business at a heavy loss. The American mills in Maine have considerable sums invested in them. I can count up 25 mills that have several million dollars invested in them, to say nothing of the smaller mills which would bring up the total to a very large figure. We ask to have the tariff left as it is. It is about as near free trade as anything can be. It would be a shame for the American Congress to subject the American manufacturers of the State of Maine to this Canadian competition. It is a pretty serious thing, gentlemen, to own any manufacturing enterprise, I care not of what kind, and to feel that you are losing money every day you operate. The last year was a disastrous year for the Maine manufacturers. I know that many did business at an actual loss. The strength of any Nation is in the prosperity of its individuals. If the Maine mills were forced out of business it would bring widespread hardship. First, to the mill owners, and next to the men who have built little homes, and whose children are dependent on their father's labor for their necessities of life and for their education. If the mills in the State of Maine were forced to shut down for one or two years to meet new conditions I shudder to think of the hardship that would result to the whole State. With duty at $1.25 per thousand, we in the State of Maine have had a pretty hard time this year. We don't want a worse time with free trade. I thank you.

Mr. HILL. You are not allowed to take logs out of Canada into the United States to manufacture them, into Maine?

Mr. BLANCHARD. No, sir.

Mr. HILL. Suppose that restriction were removed, would your objections to the reciprocity treaty be removed?

Mr. BLANCHARD. I do not agree with Mr. Hines in that respect. There are only certain mills in the State of Maine that would be benefited by that duty being taken off. There are mills located on the St. John River which logs that come down from Canada would unquestionably help very much.

Mr. HILL. It would not help any other part of the State of Maine?

Mr. BLANCHARD. It would not help any mills except those located on the St. John watershed. There are certain branches of the St. John River that run up into Canada, the Little Black and other rivers in that locality, that bring down a lot of timber, and those mills would undoubtedly be helped. But, on the other hand, the number of those mills are very small compared with the mills that are obliged to get timber from the other rivers of the States, the Penobscot, the Kennebec, the Fish River country, and other places farther down in the State that are away from the St. John River.

Mr. LONGWORTH. Is the lumber interest of Maine a very large one?

Mr. BLANCHARD. It is not large compared with the industry in the West. I quoted the capital invested in a few mills. I was talking with a gentleman from the West and he told me that one of the mills on the Pacific coast gets out 500,000 feet a day. That is as much as five of our mills produce.

Mr. LONGWORTH. I meant large as compared with other industries.

Mr. BLANCHARD. It is the principal industry of the State of Maine.

Mr. LONGWORTH. Do you interpret the last election in Maine to be a protest against reducing the duty on lumber from $2 to $1.25?

Mr. BLANCHARD. I think the last election in the State of Maine was due to a very different cause. It seems to me that it is popular to jump on the Republican Party.

Mr. LONGWORTH. Why?

Mr. BLANCHARD. Because living is high and all sorts of things, and then there was a liquor trouble down there. They tell me that liquor trouble was the real reason for the Republicans losing the State of Maine in the last election.

Mr. LONGWORTH. Mr. Harrison, on our committee, knows all about that.

Mr. HARRISON. Not about the liquor question. [Laughter.]

Mr. BLANCHARD. I may be wrong in stating that, but I have been given to understand that that was the reason for it.

Mr. LONGWORTH. You think it was the liquor question?

Mr. BLANCHARD. I have been told so by men who pretended to know a lot about it. I do not believe the State of Maine would have gone back on the Republican Party anyway, except for special cause for that local reason.

STATEMENT OF MR. D. E. SKINNER, OF SEATTLE, WASH., REPRESENTING THE PORT BLAKELEY MILL COMPANY.

Mr. FORDNEY. How many sawmills are you interested in on the Pacific coast, in California, Washington, and Oregon, or all three of those States?

Mr. SKINNER. Two; one manufacturing redwood, in California, and one manufacturing Douglas fir, in Washington.

Mr. FORDNEY. What is the capacity of your mill at Port Blakeley, on Puget Sound?

Mr. SKINNER. The capacity, previous to the recent conflagration, was 120,000,000 feet for a number of years.

Mr. FORDNEY. What is the capacity of your California mill?

Mr. SKINNER. About 30,000,000. In addition to that we had to buy about twenty-five or thirty million; so that we were handling about 175,000,000 feet.

Mr. FORDNEY. You do a very large business, as compared with other mills on the coast, in foreign trade. Will you state to the committee something about that during your remarks?

Mr. SKINNER. About 60 per cent of our trade is of that character. We established our first mill in 1857, and practically have been continually in the business, with the exception of the time that our plant has been idle because of destruction by fire, twice in its existence. We have been practically 53 years in continuous operation, and during that time probably 60 per cent of our output has been exported. I think it averages within 1 per cent of 60 per cent.

Mr. HILL. To what countries?

Mr. SKINNER. All over the world.

Mr. HILL. To China and Japan?

Mr. SKINNER. Yes; China, Japan, Australasia, the west coast of South America, sometimes Buenos Aires, when they take cattle fittings there; the coast of South Africa—everywhere lumber can go and meet the competition in lumber from elsewhere.

Mr. LONGWORTH. That is shipped in the form of rough lumber?

Mr. SKINNER. Yes, sir; sometimes dressed, however, although a very small proportion of it.

Mr. HILL. You come in direct competition with British Columbia in that trade?

Mr. SKINNER. We do. The reason why we can come in direct competition with British Columbia is because of the fact that we ordinarily have a market for all of the commodity of the tree. You must appreciate that on the Pacific coast we have a different-sized tree to handle than you have in the East or the South. Our trees grow to such size that we have some poor lumber on the inside of the tree, but we also have the sap, and on that account we can not ship very far off shore; in other words, you can not confine the lumber in a vessel for a long period of time without it deteriorating, so that you could not send it to far countries. Therefore we have a greater proportion of low-grade lumber to contend with on the coast.

Mr. ELLIS. Give these gentlemen some information as to how large an output you have known a single tree to yield.

Mr. SKINNER. The other day we had a discussion at the mill as to the largest log we had ever cut. It came from the woods 36 by 36, 150 long, a tree which we shipped to the World's Fair. Finally, on account of trouble in getting it out of the woods, accidents, etc., it was reduced to 126 feet.

Mr. FORDNEY. That is to say, it was a stick of square timber——

Mr. SKINNER. We left one side in the rough.

Mr. FORDNEY. One hundred and thirty-six feet long.

Mr. SKINNER. One hundred and twenty-six feet long. I think it was reduced to that. It originally came out of the woods 150 feet long.

Mr. FORDNEY. How many feet of wood, board measure, would that tree have made if you sawed it into lumber?

Mr. SKINNER. I am afraid I would have to ask you to answer that.

Mr. FORDNEY. I will answer it, as I happen to know. I have frequently seen trees in the State of Washington that would cut 50,000 feet.

Mr. SKINNER. I should think 40,000 to 50,000 feet. It seems rather a difficult proposition for Mr. Longworth and others to realize that it costs just as much to manufacture a grade of lumber that sells for $7 a thousand on the Pacific coast as it does for a grade of lumber that sells for $20. There is absolutely no difference in the cost until you add the extra cost of planing and work. The mere cost of logging it, of hauling it to your train, putting it on the cars, and towing it to the mills, and putting it through your mills, is just as much to manufacture a No. 2 log or a low grade as it is a high-grade log; and until you commence to surface the material, which you do not do with the low-grade material, the cost is just as much. We are rather philanthropic, but I am frank to say that our philanthropy ceases when we have to sell stuff at $7 that costs us $10 right along. As long as we can get $10, $11, or $15 we can continue to manufacture it, even if we only get cost, because we must operate our plants at normal capacity at least. If we can get cost we can operate. However, we can not continue to sell lumber at $7 a thousand that costs us $10; and the result is that the amount we are compelled to leave in the woods is such that the proportion is larger, and will be larger on the Pacific coast alone, where the greatest supply of timber in the United States still remains standing, than you will ever import from Canada, it does not make any difference if you pay them a bounty.

Mr. LONGWORTH. When you sell in this country, where do you sell?

Mr. SKINNER. In this country, which is our natural territory.

Mr. LONGWORTH. Yes.

Mr. SKINNER. The Northern States, principally; North and South Dakota, Minnesota; California takes a billion and a half feet a year from us alone.

Mr. LONGWORTH. Would you say what that lumber that you sell for $10 retails for to the consumer?

Mr. SKINNER. I should say through our own yards it retails for about $9, because we have lost money on every retail yard we have had for years.

Mr. LONGWORTH. You have retail yards?

Mr. SKINNER. What I mean to say, f. o. b. the plant. We have some wholesale yards and some retail yards. We have had one for years in Manila, and all over California, and also in Seattle, and in every instance I should be very glad, indeed, if anybody could compute the bare cost to us and pay us back for it. In other words, if you go to the consuming centers, like New York, London, and San Francisco, you will find that 9 chances out of 10, at retail, lumber is sold at less price than anywhere else in the world; but you go into the consuming territory where you find a small community, where the people who handle it sit around the same stove and put their feet up and spit tobacco juice, and you will usually get a fair price. We have found that this discussion, which has created so much attention throughout the United States because of the maintenance of the high price on lumber, is due not to the maintenance of the price by the manufacturers in the last few years but from the fact that the prices that they secure in these small retail centers in the Central West have been maintained regardless of the fact that our prices have been cut in two. In other words, I saw our price, in 1905 and 1906, advance from $9 to $18 per thousand export, and the inferior lumber followed to a certain extent in proportion. Our coast trade went from about $9 a thousand to $15 f. o. b. at the mills.

Mr. LONGWORTH. You say in cases where your price has been cut in two, but the retail price——

Mr. SKINNER. Has not been reduced anywhere nearly in proportion.

Mr. LONGWORTH. Not at all?

Mr. SKINNER. I did not say not at all. I say possibly a dollar or two, where our price has receded $6 or $7.

. Mr. LONGWORTH. At least, not correspondingly?

Mr. SKINNER. Not in proportion. That is the conclusion we have made right along, that we would be very glad to have this investigation made by Mr. Herbert Knox Smith, and either hang us or cut the rope that we are tied with—the statement of the newspapers that we are in a trust. I can absolutely prove to you, without any question, that conditions are worse on the Pacific coast to-day, in Mr. Ellis's territory and our territory, than they have been in 20 years. Lumber is selling at less prices to-day than it has in 20 years in proportion to the cost.

Mr. LONGWORTH. The statement has been made that since the passage of the Payne law the price of lumber has gone up. That, I assume, is the retail price of lumber.

Mr. SKINNER. No, sir; I did not know anybody had made the statement that the price of lumber had advanced. I think there is never any time when the price of lumber remains absolutely stationary for 30 days. It may advance or decline 50 cents or $1 a thousand in every six months' period. The general tendency and the absolute fact is that the price of lumber for the past three years has receded, and to-day it is lower, as Mr. Hines said, from $6 to $7 a thousand at the mill for the ordinary building material.

Mr. LONGWORTH. You and Mr. Hines, I understand, are speaking of the producer's price?

Mr. SKINNER. Yes.

Mr. LONGWORTH. I am speaking of the retail price.

Mr. SKINNER. The retail price, of course, we have no control over, unfortunately. We are not quite as well prepared to take care of the retailer as they are in Canada. In Canada they consider that a product of the soil which should be conserved. I never heard any discussion at all in reference to a violation of the Sherman Act when the farmers got together to raise their prices on cereals or anything else. But when we get together to arrange a price on a product of the soil there is immediately a hue and cry of combination and monopoly. Over there when they tried this same trick in the retail yards the manufacturers simply went to them from the Pacific coast and told them that if they did not reduce their price they would put yards right alongside of them and sell at a reasonable price, or at less than cost if necessary.

Mr. LONGWORTH. Generally speaking, it is true, is it not, that the retail price of lumber has gone up in the last year?

Mr. SKINNER. I could not say so. I should say it has gone down in all points I have any knowledge of. I should say that in the last year the price did advance the fore part of the year, say, a dollar a thousand, and then it has receded since then a dollar a thousand. It has fluctuated somewhat during the past year.

Mr. LONGWORTH. I myself have seen copies of circulars sent out by lumber dealers, shortly after the passage of the Payne law, to this effect:

We regret to inform our customers that owing to the passage of the Payne law we have been compelled to increase the price of lumber.

Mr. SKINNER. I have seen some other circulars myself that I should like to disavow. Why in the world anybody should make such a statement I do not know. There are some insane asylums yet.

Mr. LONGWORTH. But they are not in them.

Mr. SKINNER. They are not there. You see, the difficulty we meet is this: In the foundation of the President's statement he says plainly and simply:

A farsighted policy requires that if we can enlarge our supply of natural resources, and especially of food products and necessities of life, without substantial injury to any of our producing and manufacturing classes, we should take steps to do so now.

In order to answer that proposition you say you will not hear anything along that line at all. I do not blame you for not wanting to hear anything about it, and I did not want to come here and say anything along that line. Still, he says if it is not going to interfere with the manufacturing interests, we should adopt it; conversely, if it is, we should not. I say to you now that you will prostrate the manufacturing interests on the Pacific coast and the shipping interests, and those dependent on them, which are probably 60 or 70 per cent of the interests on the Pacific coast, for years and years, until I doubt very much whether the present manufacturer will be able to stand the strain. We are paying at least 60 or 70 cents per acre a year taxes in the State of Washington.

Mr. FORDNEY. Would you permit me to interrupt you just at this point? What is the price of logs, No. 1 and No. 2, on Puget Sound that you are paying at your mill now?

Mr. SKINNER. The price of logs is supposed to range from $6 to $9.

Mr. FORDNEY. $6 for No. 2——

Mr. SKINNER. And $9 for the other.

Mr. FORDNEY. What is a normal price for those logs?

Mr. SKINNER. What do you mean?

Mr. FORDNEY. When the market is at such a point that some profit is made out of the manufacture for that grade of log.

Mr. SKINNER. Do you mean to say what price should we receive for the logs, and add the cost of manufacture to it and a bare profit?

Mr. FORDNEY. The point I am trying to make is this: For instance, in 1906 the price of lumber was very satisfactory to the mill men. What did you pay for such logs at that time?

Mr. SKINNER. $9 and $12.

Mr. FORDNEY. So the value of the logs to-day is $6 to $9, as against $9 to $12 at that time, or a difference of $3 per 1,000 feet?

Mr. SKINNER. About.

Mr. FORDNEY. That is greater than the value of the stumpage as it stands in the tree to-day for any group of timber in the State of Washington, is it not?

Mr. Skinner. Yes; except the Government's. They are asking a fancy price for theirs. I want to say that I learned on my way East that the Government has been endeavoring to sell 3,000,000 feet burned over in Idaho, Montana, and eastern Washington, and their prices, prior to the time of the conflagration last year, were $4 for white pine and $3 for mixed timber. Since then, in order to move this, they very generously advertise that they will offer the stumpage at $2. Since this reciprocity agreement has been proposed you can buy the stumpage at from $2 to 50 cents per thousand, according to the kind of timber and its location. That is the Government's position in reference to it to-day. So I want to assure you that this is not a personal proposition with us. The Government, the people, have as much at stake in the conservation of natural resources as we have.

Mr. Fordney. What I wanted the committee to understand and know, was that it has been stated here, and I know it to be correct, that a few of the mills on the Pacific coast own their timber; that a great many of them do not; perhaps a large majority purchase their logs from men who make it their business to cut and put logs on the market, dispose of logs, but who are not manufacturers. I want them to know that to the logger to-day the price is enough lower to amount to more than what their entire stumpage cost them.

Mr. Skinner. You have not got the exact price of logs, because the price oftentimes is cut in order to induce the sale of a quantity of logs. The actual price is like the price of lumber. A man may be driven sometimes to do things he would not want to do.

Mr. Fordney. His bank account forces him to do a great many things; sometimes to cut the price below what he ought to sell for.

Mr. Randell. When they sell stumpage, how do they sell it, by the thousand feet?

Mr. Skinner. They cruise it; estimate the amount of timber on the land, and then sell it outright at the amount of the cruise, so much per thousand. For instance, if you own a tract of land and desire to sell it to me, you submit it to me at a price which you have estimated in your own mind from your cruising reports at so much per thousand. I will look at that land and have another cruise made.

Mr. Fordney. Suppose there are two manufacturers; one uses up all the timber there is in the tree, manufactures the common part of it as well as the superior; another one does not do that, he manufactures the best lumber and leaves inferior lumber to rot in the forest. Does not each save the same for stumpage?

Mr. Skinner. But they lose it.

Mr. Fordney. So, as a matter of fact, when they leave the common stuff, inferior grade, they leave what they could not manufacture without extra cost of stumpage, do they not?

Mr. Skinner. They leave what they could not manufacture.

Mr. Fordney. That is capable of manufacture.

Mr. Ellis. In the first instance, each buys the same, pays for the stumpage, and if he leaves it it is his loss.

Mr. Skinner. You want to remember this, that the value of stumpage is about one-tenth the value of lumber delivered to the consumer.

Mr. Randell. Is not stumpage a very serious matter to-day in the lumber business?

Mr. Skinner. Do you mean to obtain it?

Mr. RANDELL. In reference to the supply of timber.

Mr. SKINNER. No; there is plenty of timber to last until your generation and mine will be gone, as far as I can see.

Mr. RANDELL. That is not the estimate of all the people who have given it study.

Mr. SKINNER. I do not have to agree with them.

Mr. RANDELL. Can you explain to me why it is that ordinary timber, just ordinary material for building farmhouses, sheds, and barns, is twice as high in the Middle West to-day as it was 12 years ago to the man who wants to build? Do you know of any reason why that should be, or any reason why it is?

Mr. SKINNER. I tried to explain a while ago that we had nothing to do with the retail price; could not have anything to do with it. I do not think the price of material is twice as high as it was, because if it was twice as high as it was 12 or 15 years ago, it would not then have paid the freight rate. It is cheaper to-day, I think.

Mr. RANDELL. Was the freight rate lower than now?

Mr. SKINNER. It was established in 1893 at 40 cents. They endeavored to advance it to 50 cents. That has been one of the pleasant propositions we have had to meet.

Mr. RANDELL. The freight rates are not higher than they were before?

Mr. SKINNER. The freight rates are not higher in the last 12 years, except points east of the western line of Minnesota. There they range from 1 to 5 cents a hundred higher.

Mr. RANDELL. The methods of manufacturing lumber are more efficient and economical than they were before?

Mr. SKINNER. I doubt very much if they have reduced the cost a great deal, because we have constructed a new mill since the destruction of our old one, and we have tried to use all the ability we could, but we have not found the cost of manufacturing with the new mill is much less than that of the old one, if any.

Mr. RANDELL. Then there has been no improvement in the business, so far as methods are concerned?

Mr. SKINNER. You are handling a crude product, and it is hard to decrease the cost very materially. Besides that, you must take into consideration that the cost to us to-day, as compared with years ago, has advanced materially.

Mr. RANDELL. The labor is one of the main items, is it not?

Mr. SKINNER. Yes; always.

Mr. RANDELL. And the high cost of living, of course, has something to do with it?

Mr. SKINNER. Yes; the prices we must pay the laborers in order to enable them to exist.

Mr. RANDELL. Of course, each industry that gets a favor that affords an opportunity to make its products higher contributes its part toward increasing the cost of living and the cost of business, necessarily.

Mr. SKINNER. Possibly. Following that to a natural conclusion, instead of taking the duty off lumber, take it off everything; put us all on the free list, and give us all a fair chance.

Mr. RANDELL. That might be very much better than the present system.

Mr. SKINNER. That might be better than your proposal.

Mr. RANDELL. I am not making a proposal; I am asking you.

Mr. SKINNER. Then I make the proposal; if this act is going to be consistent, wipe the whole slate clean; if we will prosper better under free trade, let us try it.

Mr. RANDELL. I want to get back to my proposition. Has the method of manufacturing lumber been improved and made more efficient and economical in the last 12 years, or not?

Mr. SKINNER. We had the experience of building a new mill——

Mr. RANDELL. I am not asking you whether it cost more to build a mill.

Mr. SKINNER. We are saving the loss, because we are manufacturing now, with a band saw instead of a broad circular saw, like we used to. We are saving the waste and also using electricity.

Mr. RANDELL. The methods of manufacturing lumber have been improved, have they not?

Mr. SKINNER. Yes, they have; but they have not reduced the cost of manufacturing materially, as compared with the past 12 years.

Mr. RANDELL. The independent mill that operates on a small scale, that does not own it own timber, is really handicapped at present by the question of obtaining stumpage more than by any other one thing, is it not?

Mr. SKINNER. I do not know of anybody who is denied the privilege of obtaining stumpage.

Mr. RANDELL. Do you manufacture the rough lumber you speak of?

Mr. SKINNER. We own our own timber and have a railroad of our own which transports a good deal of it. Some of it we buy in the open market. We manufacture the lumber.

Mr. RANDELL. You manufacture the rough lumber?

Mr. SKINNER. Yes; and surface lumber as well, and we have for a great many years bought a great deal of lumber.

Mr. RANDELL. Do you sell any of that in the Middle West?

Mr. SKINNER. Yes; we are located on the west side of Puget Sound, and we are principally a water-shipping firm. Practically 90 per cent of our trade is water-shipping trade.

Mr. RANDELL. Do you sell any in Minnesota, Iowa, Michigan, and through there?

Mr. SKINNER. We do not sell any in Michigan now.

Mr. RANDELL. At what price do you lay down this rough lumber in Iowa?

Mr. SKINNER. The freight rate to the principal Iowa points is 50 cents, and the weight on rough lumber is from 3,000 to 3,300 pounds. The f. o. b. price now is about $7 a thousand for dimension stuff, ordinary building material. I should say that the average rate of freight from our territory is about $12 per thousand. I say that is all labor, except 10 per cent that the railroad gets in the way of dividends.

Mr. RANDELL. Do you not think it would be a great saving to the people of Iowa, Kansas, Nebraska, Oklahoma, Texas, and all that great Middle West, if they were free to get their lumber from Canada, Mexico, anywhere, as against buying it at a price like that?

Mr. SKINNER. At $7 a thousand f. o. b. the mill?

Mr. RANDELL. F. o. b. the mill over there on the coast next to Japan.

Mr. SKINNER. You will not find the freight much less from the Canadian territory than it is there unless they want to buy it from Michigan or Ontario, shipped through Chicago.

Mr. RANDELL. If you were trying to build up a prairie home out there, with your knowledge of the lumber business, would you not think you had a better opportunity if there were no restriction on this lumber, so as to give you a fair show in the markets of the world, to build your house?

Mr. SKINNER. I do not think the housebuilders have very much to complain of in the price of lumber.

Mr. RANDELL. You did not answer my question.

Mr. SKINNER. I will answer in my own way. You asked it in your way. The investment in a home, usually, constructed of wood, is about 15 per cent in lumber. That is, the rough lumber.

Mr. RANDELL. I beg your pardon. I live in that section of the country where the lumber is about four-fifths of the price of the whole thing.

Mr. SKINNER. Of the house?

Mr. RANDELL. Yes; just a frame house.

Mr. SKINNER. You mean the labor involved or just the rough lumber?

Mr. RANDELL. Not the labor alone. On a house that cost $447.50 there were two hundred and fifty-odd dollars of it lumber.

Mr. SKINNER. Just the rough lumber?

Mr. ELLIS. It costs a man more to put in the heating plant and build the chimneys than the rough lumber.

Mr. SKINNER. I want to answer your questions courteously. The difference between us of a dollar a thousand f. o. b. at the mill will depend on whether we will take out the low-grade lumber. If it all cost $10 a thousand, and we have to sell it for $9, we will eventually leave that that we must sell for $9. But the difference to the builder of the home, if lumber enters into his home, is only 15 per cent—I mean the rough lumber, without the manufacturing—all but the labor, the putting it in. That only makes 1 per cent of the whole construction. I think we are all aiming toward a reasonable conservation problem and trying to save a factor in our living that is worth while, that is worth saving. I think the way to save it is exactly as we have determined, exactly as this report determines from the forestry commission of Canada, and I would like to be permitted to read a paragraph of it. It says:

Your commissioners have had their attention drawn to the fact that the duty on imported shingles was increased by the United States Government upon representations made by the lumbermen of Washington, with the hearty indorsement of various forestry associations and of prominent members of the Forest Service. It was held by those familiar with conditions in the West that an increased levy on foreign shingles would enable the people of Washington and other States to utilize much timber that was being wasted in left tops, high stumps, and low-grade logs; a view of the matter that has proven correct.

Your commissioners recommend that the Government of British Columbia should take such steps as may be within its power to secure similar legislation.

This is of vital importance with us, and one reason why we want to get right directly at this point. I have offered a map to Mr. Fordney that I think is a little bit plainer than the one offered before, because it shows the timber limits of western Canada, and especially those that lie adjacent to our territory on Vancouver

Island, that reach right down into our territory. This report further says:

Since the care of our forests will be rewarded by great results, and since in any case this work is absolutely essential to the prosperity of the Province, we see plainly that it must be undertaken with the utmost thoroughness. The natural advantages of our country must remain unimpaired, the public revenue and the lumbering industry must both be protected; in other words, a sound policy of conservation must be established.

In doing this a difficulty arises from the changes that are inevitable in political life—changes in the governments and legislatures in which supreme control of these matters is vested. One administration may have a wise and intelligent appreciation of the benefits of conservation; the next may be careless of such considerations. Yet so great is the time required to produce, or even to foresee, results in forest administration, that sustained efforts over long periods of time, is essential; and a policy that vacillates, not because fresh knowledge of forests has been obtained but simply because changes have taken place in politics, can have no value.

Mr. HILL. How much lumber did you sell in British Columbia last year?

Mr. SKINNER. None; not because we could not, but because we did not care to. We had inquiries for it, but did not care to.

Mr. HILL. But you do compete with them in other countries?

Mr. SKINNER. We do compete with them in other countries, simply because we can utilize all of the tree and because they are manufacturing their portion of their product. There are only two or three mills that can export. They can just as well get our price.

Mr. HILL. Is the lumber that is sold from Washington in British Columbia run in by rail or by water?

Mr. SKINNER. By rail, mostly.

Mr. HILL. Does that go east or west of the mountains?

Mr. SKINNER. East.

Mr. HILL. Into the Edmonton country?

Mr. SKINNER. Yes, sir; Winnipeg and that territory.

Mr. HILL. Can they not get that at just as low rates from Washington as they can from over the mountains?

Mr. SKINNER. If the rates are regulated the same.

Mr. HILL. I mean the rates are regulated so they do it.

Mr. SKINNER. They possibly do and possibly can. As I said, my business is nearly all done, of course, by water, and 10 per cent of my business comes within the purview of those I employ, and I am not as well posted as those who make a specialty of the rail business.

Mr. HILL. Do you employ orientals of any kind in your mills?

Mr. SKINNER. Yes, we do; a small number—about 30 out of 264. We have had all kinds. We pay the same rate we do to white men, and at the same time we are competing with oriental labor right across an imaginary line at 80 cents a day, when we pay $1.75.

Mr. GAINES. Is that the lowest you pay?

Mr. SKINNER. We have paid $1.50. We paid $1.75 all last year. I want to say that it is absolutely inconsistent to restrict us from the use of the labor and yet at the same time compel us to meet the results of that labor in the same locations exactly.

Mr. HILL. That is another question, a very burning question.

Mr. SKINNER. It is a very serious question with us. There seems to be a question in the minds of the committee as to whether the point we have raised as to the freedom of the use of timber is of particular value to the majority of the mills in the United States. Perhaps that point is well taken; but at the same time if there is any justice or any right in this reciprocity act, then, I say if you are going to have reciprocity let us have reciprocity; let us have reciprocal treatment upon every part wherever we can secure any benefit, no matter whether it is 10 per cent or anything else.

Mr. HILL. You are on the shore of Puget Sound?

Mr. SKINNER. Yes, sir.

Mr. HILL. Do you use any Canadian logs?

Mr. SKINNER. No, sir; but there are plenty of mills in Washington that are using them when they can get them.

Mr. HILL. They are sold by the Government, are they not?

Mr. SKINNER. No. sir; they are sold by the private owners.

Mr. HILL. From private lands?

Mr. SKINNER. Yes, sir; Crown-grant lands. And there are only about 8 per cent of the Crown-grant lands in the hands of private owners in fee simple taken prior to 1888.

Mr. HILL. The restriction clause does not apply to that 8 per cent?

Mr. SKINNER. The Dominion has some restriction over those.

Mr. HILL. What is this case we heard of here yesterday or the day before of Canadian logs being dumped on the American manufacturers from Victoria?

Mr. SKINNER. They use a good deal of freedom in Canada, evidently because this law, which covers all the land, allows a good deal of discretion in the lieutenant governor, and sometimes, when the logs have been in the water long enough so that they are fearful they will be eaten up by torredos, they will be released for 24 hours. They do that a great deal upon cedar logs, because there is not such a demand for cedar logs.

Mr. FORDNEY. There is no importation of logs from British Columbia to Puget Sound except where those restrictions have been removed, and there has not been for years?

Mr. SKINNER. No.

Mr. FORDNEY. There is none imported from private or deeded land except where that restriction is removed?

Mr. SKINNER. Not to my knowledge, because I do not believe any of that private deeded land is being operated so that the logs can be obtained from it.

Mr. FORDNEY. I will say to you that under their regulations it can not be done now.

Mr. GAINES. As a matter of fact, Mr. Skinner, do these restrictive measures of the Provinces there apply only to the Crown lands, or do they apply also to lands privately owned in the same Province?

Mr. SKINNER. The only lands that can be privately owned are those taken prior to 1887, and they were so small and the percentage is so small that they are not to be taken into consideration at all, even though they may not come within this act. It is unquestionable that they do come within this act. I think the Dominion does retain control over them. Here is a short clause that covers practically all of it:

All timber cut under lease, special license, or general license from provincial lands lying west of the Cascade Range of mountains must be manufactured within the confines of the Province of British Columbia, otherwise the lease or special license or general license shall be canceled.

Mr. HILL. That does not refer to private lands?

Mr. SKINNER. There are no private lands.

Mr. HILL. You said 8 per cent.

Mr. SKINNER. You can find further in this law that it does apply to Crown grants.

Mr. HILL. Mr. Gaines asked you if the restriction applied to private lands. That law which you have read does not apply to private lands.

Mr. SKINNER. The private lands which they are selling that were taken prior to the time this law took effect.

Mr. FORDNEY. Merril & Ring own lands in Vancouver that were purchased at cash entry from the Canadian Government in 1882. They began operations five or six years ago to lumber that timber and bring it over to the American side, and were stopped by regulations.

Mr. SKINNER. Here is another provision that covers the Crown lands, under leaseholds, some of them licensed, some Crown lands and some leaseholds, and it seems to me this provision would make us blush with modesty. The substance of it is:

> There shall be due and payable to His Majesty, his heirs, and successors, a tax upon all timber cut within the Province of British Columbia, save and except that upon which a royalty is reserved by this section or that upon which any royalty or tax is payable to the Government of the Dominion of Canada, which fact shall be in accordance with the following schedule:
> The following rebates on tax shall be allowed when the timber upon which it is due or payable is manufactured for use in the Province of British Columbia rate per thousand feet, board measure, on grade.

It starts in with logs 40 feet long and 24 inches in diameter, No. 1, $2 per thousand; No. 2, $2.50 per thousand; No. 3, $1. It runs down to 80-feet logs, which, on No. 1, are $4 a thousand. We do not have any No. 3 logs; we do not know what they are. For logs of larger diameter, from 24 inches to 48 inches, it runs from $2.20 to $5.50 for No. 1, and from $1.70 to $4.50 per thousand for No. 2.

Mr. GAINES. What are you reading from now?

Mr. SKINNER. This is the tax that is exacted if you do not manufacture the timber in British Columbia.

Mr. GAINES. Can you give the act?

Mr. SKINNER. I will submit this to you (see p. 307).

Mr. GAINES. I think maybe I have it here.

Mr. SKINNER. Chapter 30 of "An act to amend and consolidate the laws affecting Crown lands, consolidated for convenience only March 21, 1910."

Mr. GAINES. I have the 1910 copy, I think. Let me see if I follow that. Am I to understand that that is a tax which the Dominion imposes upon timberlands unless the timber is manufactured over there?

Mr. SKINNER. That is right. If manufactured there it is reduced to 1 cent a thousand.

Mr. GAINES. Is that a Dominion law?

Mr. SKINNER. That is a provincial law.

Mr. GAINES. So that the provincial law does prevent, as a matter of fact, the free exportation of logs cut from private lands?

Mr. SKINNER. It does. It takes in the Crown grants and all.

Mr. GAINES. That has been denied here.

Mr. SKINNER. As I say, I was hurried away from the Pacific coast, from matters of vital importance to me there, to protest against this action. and to show, if I could, why we were entitled to reciprocal consideration with other wood products. Mr. Roosevelt was at least consistent, even if we did not agree with him, when he said he wanted to take the duty off all wood products. Mr. Pinchot afterwards agreed with us; he would not segregate the wood products and give the news paper and print paper people the benefit of the differential.

Mr. RANDELL. Does that affect your business in any way?

Mr. SKINNER. It would affect our business to this extent, if the price of lumber got so low, as it is at present, and we wanted to manufacture lumber—as we have to with our plant—we could buy the logs from British Columbia, and we are entitled to the same consideration whether we buy print paper or whether the provision is applied to wood pulp and to print paper.

Mr. RANDELL. Whatever the conditions in reference to wood pulp and paper, would that have anything to do with the lumber business?

Mr. SKINNER. I do not know that it would have anything to do with the lumber business, but I should like to have the act consistent and applied to all commodities. If it is reasonable to apply it to pulp wood, it ought to be to wood of all kinds.

Mr. RANDELL. It really does not affect your lumber interests any more than it does sugar interests?

Mr. SKINNER. I do not think it does. But we would like to have the same privilege as they recognize by providing for the print paper and pulp people. I can not see why they should exclude a commodity that is used a thousandfold more than that.

Mr. RANDELL. You think if anything is taxed lumber ought to be?

Mr. SKINNER. I think if anything should be allowed to be imported it would be logs for lumber. I will tell you why I believe that, because I do not believe if you reduce the price of print paper from $45 to $42 a ton that you would buy your paper at seven-eighths of a cent each; in other words, that you would reach the ultimate consumer. On the coast we pay 5 cents a piece for papers. I do not believe if they would reduce the price of paper to the newspapers I would get any newspaper on Sunday at 4½ or 4 cents. But I will tell you that I might get 10 pounds of paper full of slander and slush.

Mr. HILL. Do I understand that you would favor the policy of a bill that would seek to get free importation?

Mr. SKINNER. I frankly say to you that we are opposed to it.

Mr. HILL. I mean that particular feature. Do we understand that you are opposed to that feature of the bill seeking to get unrestricted exportation of pulp wood?

Mr. SKINNER. I say we think we are entitled to the same consideration they get. There is no consistency in our not getting it. I say to you that it is of vital importance to us. If we want to buy our timber from Canada, we can tow rafts of logs a hundred miles just as well as you can a mile; from the terminus of our own railroads we tow them 60 miles. If you want to truly conserve the timber—if that is what you are after—let us use theirs; let us have the privilege of using it, and if our lumber reaches such a price that it is too low for us to cut our own timber we will save ours and cut theirs.

Mr. RANDELL. Then you are in favor of having free trade in timber and lumber between Canada and the United States?

Mr. SKINNER. I say, if you take the duty off, you get your competition very severe. I do not agree with Mr. Hines that the increase in duty would increase the price proportionately. If there ever was a commodity that proved the tariff protection theory, that internal competition will regulate the price, we have proven it on lumber. The internal competition, our own competition, is enough to regulate the price as it is to-day. And when we do get down to a cost price, and when we do have to compete with the oriental labor which you will not allow us to import, and when we have to compete with the cost of labor as it is we will suffer a great loss. I saw an article by one authority who said that the average cost in some of the building trades for labor in San Francisco was 77 cents an hour; in Los Angeles it is 57 cents, and in Montreal 35 cents. That only carries out the contention that they do live cheaper. Their racial instincts may be the same, but, at the same time, you can live cheaper in British Columbia than we can. You would have to pay more and the American manufacturers are entitled to more. We are entitled to compensation, and I say, to be consistent with this thing, we ought to follow out the regulation and the recommendation of the protective tariff and the last Republican platform, which said we should ascertain the difference between the cost here and abroad.

Mr. RANDELL. And a reasonable profit.

Mr. SKINNER. Yes; a reasonable profit on the cost of building the plant in my place and building a plant 100 miles across an imaginary line. If it is consistent to absolutely remove the duty without any consideration of the difference between the cost of manufacture here and abroad, I do not know what we meant when we voted that way.

Mr. BROUSSARD. Can you give us the quantity of timber lands owned by the Crown in the various Provinces and the timber lands that are in private ownership? Is there any way in which we can get at that?

Mr. SKINNER. Yes; I think I can give you that. They have variously estimated the standing timber in the United States and in Canada a good many times. I think they know less about it in Canada than they do here.

Mr. BROUSSARD. I do not care about that as applying to the United States. I want the Canadian timber.

Mr. SKINNER. I think they have it down now to where they estimate about 240,000,000,000 feet lies in the Province of British Columbia and that intermountain territory, and about forty or fifty billion feet of it is under concession to the railroads. There is 192,-000,000,000 feet, and 16,650,000,000 feet in Crown grants timber, constituting 8¾ per cent of the total.

Mr. BROUSSARD. The railroads owns timber land under the Dominion control or provincial control?

Mr. SKINNER. I would like to verify some of these figures I am giving, as I am handing them out promiscuously. I do not want to stand sponsor for something, and then, if I have to appear again, have you ask me about it, without verifying it.

Mr. FORDNEY. You have spoken offhand, and it would be proper for you to look over the minutes and correct any error in figures you may have made.

Mr. SKINNER. One thing that we would get a benefit from in this tariff commission investigation would be the fact that they would have to take into consideration all of the collateral issues, as to what it really cost us to manufacture lumber compared with what it cost across the line, what the timber cost, and things of that kind. That seems to be thrown out of the equation here entirely. That seems to have been settled by the mere statement that we must have their lumber. There is also the collateral issue of the cost of transportation to the principal markets. We are looking with considerable interest to the opportunity of shipping to the east coast of the United States through the canal.

In taking the statistics for your tariff debates it is unfortunate that 1907 was taken as that happened to be the highest year in the known history of the lumber industry, as compared with one of the lowest years in the lumber industry, that is, 1897. They should have taken the comparison for the past 10 years. They would have found the comparison was much more advantageous for lumber. It did not show such an apparently abnormal advance.

In 1906, I exhausted every vessel on the Pacific coast that was obtainable for shipment to New York, and to our concern there, and I advanced my own freight rate, by means of bids to secure tonnage, from $12.50 on the first vessel to $16.50 on the last vessel I got. I was informed at that time that the average rate of freight from British Columbia was $8 to $12 a thousand, and it has since been confirmed.

Now it is a serious question what is going to happen on the Pacific coast when the Panama Canal is opened. I consider it the most serious menace we have ever met.

I was considerably amused the other day at hearing that some one telegraphed the President that we on the Pacific coast ought to celebrate the opening of the Panama Canal as a great event, because it will open the trade of the Orient to us. Now, if anybody can tell me what we should celebrate for on the Pacific coast when the Panama Canal is opened I wish they would do so. I have been unable to find it, and the oriental trade will pass right by our doors from the canal instead of passing through our ports. What we have got to have is more means of transportation, and we want to encourage means of water transportation in American vessels. Now, if you take the lumber and compel them to manufacture it in British Columbia and ship it over the Canadian Pacific line, we Americans are not only going to lose the $10 a thousand involved in the cost of logging the tree and the manufacturing of the lumber, but also an average, say, of $12 a thousand for hauling and in labor in the transportation.

We are also going to be deprived of any possibility of utilizing the canal in competition with foreign vessels from British Columbia to the eastern coast because of our coastwise shipping laws. Now, you have got to do one thing or the other. If you are going to be so radical as to put us out of business, then you have got to be radical enough to put us back into business by giving us the use of foreign ships between the two coasts, or by allowing us to buy foreign-built ships and put them under the American flag, and so change our navigation laws so that we can use them in competition with vessels of other flags.

Mr. FORDNEY. Or rebate the tolls going through the canal.

Mr. SKINNER. I was quite confident, when we asked for a rebate going through the canal, that we would have this moderate duty as well as that rebate. Of course the shorter you make your haul in a foreign ship the more you approximate the cost of operating the American vessel. I can produce, if the committee wishes it, an offer within the last year to construct a vessel abroad at $196,000, and the lowest bid here was $400,000 for a common freight carrier, carrying lumber on the Pacific coast. That bid was to build it in England for $196,000, and the lowest bid here was $400,000, which makes a difference of 100 per cent. Now they can operate at half the cost. We can not live in competition with them, and we know that there is no dispute over it. I have also wanted, if possible, to have this duty maintained in addition to the rebate on canal tolls, so that we would have that additional advantage, because it takes 65 days around the Horn, and the difference in cost of labor and the difference in cost of interest and taxes and insurance and everything involved in the case is a great deal more than if it takes 25 days to pass through the canal from Puget Sound to New York; consequently your difference is larger in favor of a foreign vessel on a two month's passage than on a passage of 25 or 30 days.

Mr. HILL. If the people on Puget Sound can send their ships to Australia in competition, do you think that you ought to lie awake nights worrying about competing?

Mr. SKINNER. We have got the same ships he has to send from Puget Sound to Sidney, but not a ship to send from Puget Sound to New York, because of the coastwise laws. The coastwise laws prevent us. Give us the same facilities for transportation, and we can meet him on his own ground, but take it the other way and we can not meet him at all, because the coastwise laws prevent us from using foreign vessels, and we hope they will prevent it. That is offset by the waiving of the tolls in the Panama Canal, and this moderate duty.

Mr. McCALL. Is there anything that you want to put in your remarks, to supplement what you have said in the record? If so, you might hand it to the stenographer sometime this afternoon or evening.

Mr. SKINNER. Thank you, Mr. McCall, for your courtesy.

CHAPTER 30.—An act to amend and consolidate the laws affecting Crown lands.

[Consolidated for convenience only, Mar. 21, 1910.]

His Majesty, by and with the advice and consent of the Legislative Assembly of the Province of British Columbia, enacts as follows:

SHORT TITLE.

1. This act may be cited as the "land act." (C. A. 1888, c. 66, s. 1.)

INTERPRETATION.

2. *Meaning of certain terms.*—In the construction and for the purposes of this act (if not inconsistent with the context or subject matter), the following terms shall have the respective meanings hereinafter assigned to them:

Crown lands.—" Crown lands " shall mean and include such ungranted Crown or public lands or Crown domain as are within and belong to His Majesty in right of the Province of British Columbia, and whether or not any waters flow over or cover the same. (1906, c. 24, s. 2.)

Patented lands.—" Patented lands" shall mean lands granted by the Crown during the period commencing on the 7th day of April, A. D. 1887, and ending on the 28th day of April, A. D. 1888.

Timber leasehold.—" Timber leasehold" shall mean lands included in timber leases granted after the 31st day of December, 1879, and lands included in any timber lease hereafter granted.

Timber limits.—" Timber limits" shall mean lands specified and comprised in any timber license. (C. A. 1888, c. 66, s. 2 and 62; 1906, c. 24, s. 2; 1907, c. 25, s. 2.)

PREEMPTION OF CROWN LANDS.

31. *Land that may be preempted—Cancellation of records—Timberlands not to be preempted.*—No preemption record shall be granted except for land taken up for agricultural purposes, and the chief commissioner may cancel any such record when it shall be shown to his satisfaction that the same has been obtained for other than agricultural purposes. Timberlands, as specified in subsection (5) of section 34 of this act, shall not be open for preemption (1907, c. 25, s. 8).

SALE OF CROWN LANDS.

(5) *First-class lands—Second-class lands—Timberlands not to be sold.*— Lands which are suitable for agricultural purposes or which are capable of being brought under cultivation profitably, or which are wild hay meadow lands, shall rank and be classified as first-class lands. All other lands, other than timberlands, shall rank and be classified as second-class lands. Timberlands (that is lands which contain milling timber to the average extent of eight thousand feet to the acre west of the Cascades, and five thousand feet per acre east of the Cascades, to each one hundred and sixty acres), shall not be open for sale.

CROWN GRANTS OF SUBSIDY LANDS.

38. All grants of Crown lands made, or to be made, to any person or corporation to aid the construction of a railway or other work shall be subject to the land laws of the province, except to the extent that such laws are expressly varied by the terms of such subsidy act. The provisions of this section shall apply to all grants of Crown lands heretofore made (1908, c. 30, s. 38).

LEASES.

48. *Saving clause re existing pulp leases.*—Notwithstanding anything contained in chapter 30 of the Statutes of 1903–4, the powers and discretion of the Crown and the just rights and privileges of those persons who in good faith have complied with the provisions of the sections of the "land act" relating to pulp leases shall be preserved. (1903–4, c. 30, s. 18.)

TIMBER LANDS.

49. *Renewal of leases.*—All leases of unsurveyed and unpreempted Crown timber lands, which have been granted for a period of twenty-one years, may be renewed for consecutive and successive periods of twenty-one years, subject to such terms, conditions, royalties, and ground rents as may be in force by Statute at the time of the expiration of such respective leases: Provided, that such renewal is applied for within one year previous to the expiration of the then-existing lease; and provided, that all arrears of royalties, ground rents, and other charges are first fully paid.

All existing leases of Crown timber limits which have been granted previous to the passage of this section of the "land act" and now in force may be renewed for consecutive and successive periods of twenty-one years: Provided, that such existing leases shall be surrendered within one year from the date of the enactment of this section.

And it is further enacted that such leases may be renewed for the unexpired portion of the term mentioned in the leases to be surrendered on the same, terms, conditions, rents, and royalties as so specified in the said leases to be surrendered, the remainder of the term of twenty-one years for which the said leases shall be renewed on surrender shall be subject to such terms, conditions, royalties, and ground rents as may be in force by statute at the time the existing leases, surrendered under the conditions of this section, would expire.

Conditions as to manufacture of timber.—All timber cut under lease, special license, or general license from provincial lands lying west of the Cascade Range of Mountains must be manufactured within the confines of the Province of British Columbia, otherwise the lease, special license, or general license shall be canceled. (1901, c. 30, s. 7; 1906, c. 24, s. 10.)

50. *Leases for purpose of stripping hemlock trees of bark.*—It shall be lawful for the lieutenant governor in council to grant leases of unpreempted Crown lands for a term not to exceed thirty years for the purpose of stripping hemlock trees of bark, subject to such rent and conditions as the lieutenant governor in council may see fit to impose. (1891, c. 15, s. 13; 1892, c. 25, s. 8.)

52. *License required to cut timber on Crown lands.*—It shall be unlawful for any person, without a license in that behalf, to be granted as hereinafter mentioned, to cut, fell, or carry away any trees or timber upon or from any of the Crown lands of this Province. (C. A. 1888, c. 66, s. 63; 1903-4, c. 30, s. 4.)

53. *Penalty for cutting timber without license.*—Every person who shall violate the provisions of the preceding section shall for each offense be liable, upon summary conviction before any two justices of the peace or any stipendiary or police magistrate, to a penalty of not less than five dollars nor more than five hundred dollars. (C. A. 1888, c. 66, s. 64.)

54. *Chief commissioner of lands and works may grant special licenses to cut timber.*—The chief commissioner of lands and works may grant licenses, to be called special licenses, to cut timber on Crown lands at the rates by this act imposed, and subject to such conditions, regulations, and restrictions as may from time to time be established by the lieutenant governor in council, and of which notice may be given in the British Columbia Gazette. (C. A. 1888, c. 66, s. 65; 1903-4, c. 30, s. 5.)

55. *Special timber licenses.*—Any person desirous of obtaining such special license shall comply with the following provisions:

57. *Special timber licenses for logging purposes.*—(1) A special timber license for logging purposes shall not be granted for a larger area than six hundred and forty acres of land, which shall be in one block bounded by straight lines drawn to the cardinal points, none of which lines shall be less than forty (40) chains in length, except in cases where such a length can not be obtained; nor shall the license be granted for a longer period than one year, and the fees payable for such special license shall be as follows:

Fees.—For each license: West of the Cascade Range, one hundred and forty dollars; east of the Cascade Range and in the electoral district of Atlin, one hundred and fifteen dollars.

Royalty tax—Chief commissioner may offer limits to public competition.—Such license may be granted at the discretion of the chief commissioner, and shall be subject to such tax and royalty as may be by this act, or from time to time by any act of the legislature of the Province of British Columbia, imposed or reserved: Provided that the chief commissioner of lands and works may, before granting any special license, offer the limits to public competition, when he has reason to believe that the public interests will be served by so doing.

Transfer and renewal of special timber licenses now in force.—(2) All special timber licenses which are now in force or any which may have been applied for, or notice of which application has appeared in the British Columbia Gazette on or before the fifteenth day of April, 1905, shall be transferable and may be renewed each year for sixteen successive years, and the fees for each renewal of any such license shall be paid in advance, and shall be of the same amount as is now paid for such license: Provided, That the right of such annual renewal shall not be acquired by the holder of any license unless he shall, at the time of applying for the first renewal of his license, have given notice in writing to the chief commissioner of lands and works of his intention to avail himself of the privileges of this clause. In addition to the royalty which is now reserved by section 66 of this act, there shall be paid to His Majesty ten cents per thousand feet, board measure, upon and in respect to all timber suitable for spars, piles, saw logs, railroad ties and props for mining purposes, cut and removed from lands comprised within any special license heretofore issued or coming within the scope of this subsection.

Transfer and renewal of special timber licenses hereafter issued—Renewal of special timber licenses.—(3.) All special timber licenses which may hereafter be issued shall be transferable and shall be renewable each year for twenty-one successive years. When any such license shall be granted in respect of land situated within ten miles of an incorporated town or city, or in respect of land situate in the vicinity of any registered town site, the same may be renewed only at the discretion of the chief commissioner. (1906, c. 24, s. 12.)

Transfer and renewal of special timber licenses.—(3a.) Every special timber license shall be transferable and shall be renewable from year to year while there is on the land included in such license merchantable timber in sufficient quantity to make it commercially valuable (proof whereof must be furnished to the satisfaction of the chief commissioner), if the terms and conditions of the license and the provisions of the land act and of any regulations passed by order in council respecting or affecting the same have been complied with: Provided, however, that the holder of any license who wishes to renew under the provisions of this subsection shall surrender his old license and all privileges appertaining thereto within two years from the first day of April, 1910, and shall at such time apply for the renewal thereof under the provisions of this subsection, and shall, in addition to all other payments to be made hereunder, pay a fee of twenty dollars: Provided, that such renewal shall be subject to the payment of such rental or license fee and such tax or royalty and to such terms and conditions, regulations and restricions as are fixed or imposed by any statute or order in council in force at the time renewal is made, or at any time thereafter. When any such license shall be granted in respect of land situated within ten miles of an incorporated town or city, or in respect of land situate in the vicinity of any registered town site, the same may be renewed only at the discretion of the chief commissioner: Provided, that whenever the land included within any such license shall, after an inspection has been made by the chief commissioner, be ascertained to be fit for settlement and to be required for that purpose, the chief commissioner may require the licensee to carry on and complete the cutting and removal of the timber thereon within such reasonable time as the chief commissioner may fix and prescribe, and on the expiration of such time, or any extension thereof, the license shall be cancelled and the land included therein shall be opened for settlement on such terms and conditions as the lieutenant governor may think fit. (1910, c. 28, s. 6.)

Fees for renewal of special timber license.—(4.) The fee for such renewal of special timber license shall be paid before the expiration of such license: Provided, however, that if it shall appear that the holder of any such license has failed or neglected to pay the renewal fee before the expiration of the license he shall, upon payment of such fee and an additional sum of twenty-five dollars within three months after such expiration, be entitled to a renewal of the license: Provided also, that the holder of any special timber license who has failed or neglected to pay the renewal fee for any license which expired on or since the first day of November, 1907, shall have the privilege of obtaining a renewal of such license, provided the land covered thereby is still vacant crown land, upon payment of such fees as would have been payable had such license been kept in good standing and an additional sum of fifty dollars for each license if application for the same be made within sixty days from the passing of this act.

Survey.—(5.) No licensee who elects to renew his license under the provisions of subsection (2) of this section, and no person who takes out a license after the fifteenth day of April, 1905, shall be allowed to cut or carry away any timber from off any such timber limit unless the said license has, at his own expense, had the land surveyed by a duly qualified provincial land surveyor. The chief commissioner of lands and works may, however, at any time notify the holder of any special timber license to have the land covered by such license surveyed by a duly qualified provincial land surveyor within a time to be mentioned in such notice, and if such land shall not be surveyed within such time, or within such further time as may be granted by the chief commissioner of lands and works therefor, the holder of such license shall forfeit all his rights to the timber on said land, and such license shall become null and void. (1905, c. 33, s. 3; 1909, c. 28, s. 5.)

58. *Right of way across lands for timber chutes, etc.*—Any holder of a timber leasehold, timber land in fee simple, or of a special timber license who may desire to secure a right of way across any lands for the purpose of constructing chutes, flumes, roads, or other works, for use in getting out timber from the limit covered by his lease or license, shall give thirty days' notice of his inten-

tion to apply to the chief commissioner of lands for authority to construct such chutes, flumes, roads, or other works by an advertisement published one month in the British Columbia Gazette and in a newspaper published or circulated in the district in which the land is situated. The applicant shall also give thirty days' notice to the owner of the land over, through, or upon which such chutes, flumes, roads, or other works are to be constructed. Such notice may be given personally or in such manner as may be directed by the chief commissioner. The chief commissioner is hereby empowered to grant or refuse such applica. tion upon such terms and conditions as the circumstances may warrant. The applicant shall be granted only a right of way forty feet wide, and all works shall be confined to said area, and the title obtained by the applicant shall be only an easement: Provided, that compensation for said right of way shall be paid for before an entry is made on said land, and if the parties can not agree on the amount of said compensation, then the same shall be submitted to arbi. tration and settled in accordance with the terms and under the provisions of the "arbitration act." Such chutes, flumes, roads, or other works shall not be located or constructed on any lands on which buildings have been erected or which may be in use as gardens or orchards. The benefits and burdens herein. before mentioned shall insure to the heirs, executors, administrators, successors, and assigns of the persons affected. (1906, c. 24, s. 19; 1907, c. 25, s. 20; 1910, c. 28, s. 7.)

59. *Rights and powers of licensee under a special license.*—The special license shall vest in the holder thereof all rights of property whatsoever in all trees, timber, and lumber cut within the limits of the license during the term thereof, whether the trees, timber, and lumber are cut by authority of the licensee or by any other person with or without his consent, and such license shall entitle the holder thereof to seize, in revindication or otherwise, such trees, timber, or lumber where the same are found in the possession of any unauthorized person, and also to institute any action against any wrongful possessor or tres. passer, and to prosecute all trespassers and other offenders to punishment, and to recover damages, if any; and all proceedings pending at the expiration of any license may be continued to final termination as if the license had not expired.

Quarrying leases may be issued in respect of lands held under special timber license or timber lease.—Notwithstanding anything in this act contained, it shall be lawful for the lieutenant governor in council to grant leases for quarry. ing purposes of any lands held under special timber license or timber lease, or any part thereof. upon such terms and conditions as may be deemed advisable. (C. A. 1888, c. 66, s. 69; 1909, c. 28, s. 6.)

60. *Hand logger's license.*—(1.) In addition to the special licenses authorized by section 54 of this act. and notwithstanding the reserve placed upon timber by order in council, dated 24th December, 1907. the chief commissioner may. upon payment of the sum of twenty-five dollars therefor. grant a general license to cut timber from Crown lands, not being timber limits or leases; and within such area as may be specified or designated in such license or lease; but such license shall be personal, and shall only grant authority to the person named therein to cut timber as a hand logger, and such license shall be in force for one year from the date thereof, and no longer.

Licensees, except in case of Indians, must be Provincial voters.—(2.) No license under this section shall be granted to any person who is not on the list of voters for the legislature of the Province of British Columbia, except persons of the Indian race.

Determination of area to be included in license.—(3.) The area to be specified or designated in each license granted under this section shall, before the grant. ing of the license, be inspected by the forest ranger or one of the assistant timber inspectors, or such other person as may be authorized by the chief commissioner for that purpose.

Steam power, etc., not to be used by licensee.—(4.) The holder of a license granted under this section shall not use steam power, or machinery operated by steam power, in carrying on lumber operations under such license.

Penalty.—(5.) Any person being the holder of a license granted under this section, who shall violate the provisions of the preceding subsections hereof, shall be liable, on summary conviction before a stipendiary magistrate, to a pen. alty of not less than twenty-five dollars and not exceeding one hundred dollars for each offense. (1909, c. 28, s. 7.)

61. *Assignments of timber leases and special timber licenses.*—Every assign. ment of a timber lease or special timber license shall be filed in the department

of lands, and a fee of five dollars shall be payable in respect of each lease or license assigned. (1906, c. 24, s. 13; 1907, c. 25. s. 17; 1910. c. 28. s. 8.)

62. *Validation of special timber licenses heretofore issued.*—All special timber licenses and all renewals thereof heretofore granted shall be deemed to have been legally granted, but nothing in this section contained shall affect any legal proceeding now pending respecting any such license or renewal thereof. (1906, c. 24, s. 14.)

63. *Validation of certain leases heretofore granted.*—The leases hereinafter set out and which have already been granted are hereby validated and confirmed, and shall have the same force and effect as if granted after the passing of this act:

Lease dated September 12th, 1909, issued to Andrew Richards.

Lease dated October 15th, 1901, issued to Ross Mahon.

Lease dated February 26th, 1904, issued to W. E. Norris and P. A. Hovelaque.

Lease dated July 28th, 1904, issued to the Crescent Oyster Company. Limited.

Lease dated June 27th, 1905, issued to Crescent Oyster Company, Limited.

And lease dated June 27th, 1905, issued to Crescent Oyster Company, Limited.

Provided that with respect to any applications for leases of Crown lands within the meaning of this act, made before the passage of this act, if the applicants therefor have bona fide complied with the provisions of subsections (2) and (3) of section 41 of said chapter 113 to the satisfaction of the chief commissioner of lands and works, the chief commissioner of lands and works may, notwithstanding that the said applications were made and the provisions of the said subsections (2) and (3) were complied with before the passage of this act, grant leases of such Crown lands under the provisions of this act. (1906, c. 24, s. 16.)

64. *Licenses not to be granted over Indian reserves, etc.*—No timber license shall be granted in respect of lands forming the site of an Indian settlement or reserve, and the chief commissioner may refuse to grant a license in respect of any particular land if, in the opinion of the lieutenant governor in council, it is deemed expedient in the public interest so to do. (C. A. 1888. c. 66, s. 71.)

65. *Ground rent, five cents per acre.*—In addition to the royalty hereinafter reserved on all timber cut on timber leaseholds, there shall be paid annually, as ground rent, the sum of five cents per acre for each acre included in any timber lease which has been granted since the 31st day of December, 1879, and prior to the 28th day of April. 1888. (C. A. 1888, c. 66, s. 72.)

66. *Royalty reserved to the Crown on all timber and wood cut upon Crown lands, patented lands, or timber leaseholds.*—(1.) There is reserved to and for the use of His Majesty. his heirs and successors, a royalty of fifty cents for every thousand feet. board measure, upon and in respect of all timber suitable for spars. piles, saw logs, or railroad ties, props for mining purposes, shingle or other bolts of cedar, fir, or spruce. and a royalty of twenty-five cents for every cord of other wood cut upon Crown lands, patented lands. timber leaseholds, or timber limits, and upon any lands hereafter granted. Piles shall be measured by the running foot, and railway ties and props shall be measured by the cord; and for the purposes of this act two hundred running feet of piles. or one cord of ties or props, shall be taken respectively as equal to one thousand feet board measure. (1896, c. 28, s. 2.)

Tax upon all timber except that upon which royalty reserved by preceding subsection.—(2.) There shall be due and payable to His Majesty. his heirs and successors, a tax upon all timber cut within the Province of British Columbia, save and except that upon which a royalty is reserved by this section or that upon which any royalty or tax is payable to the Government of the Dominion of Canada. which tax shall be in accordance with the following schedules:

SCHEDULE No. 1.

Timber.	Lengths, not over—	Diameters, not over—	Rate per M feet B. M. on grade.			Additional rate to be added for increased sizes.					The following rebate on tax shall be allowed when the timber upon which it is due or payable is manufactured or used in the Province of British Columbia—
						Diameters.		Grade.			
			No. 1.	No. 2.	No. 3.	Not under—	Not over—	No. 1.	No. 2.	No. 3.	
	Feet.	*In.*				*In.*	*In.*				
Spars and saw logs, and saw bolts, of all kinds.	40	24	$2.00	$1.50	$1.00	25	31	$0.20	$0.15	$0.10	
Do............	50	24	2.25	1.75	1.25	32	36	.40	.30	.20	All the tax over and above 1 cent per M feet B. M.
Do............	60	24	2.50	2.00	1.50	37	41	.60	.45	.30	
Do............	70	24	2.75	2.25	1.75	42	45	.80	.60	.40	
Do............	80	24	3.00	2.50	2.00	46	48	1.00	.75	.50	
Do............	(1)	24	4.00	3.00	2.50	(2)	......	1.50	1.00	.75	

¹ Over 80 feet.　　　　　　² Over 48 feet.

SCHEDULE No. 2.

Timber.	Lengths, not over—	Diameters, not over—	Rate per linear foot.	All piles or poles over 12 inches, in diameter shall be scaled, graded No. 1, and taxed at rates as under—		The following rebate on tax shall be allowed when the timber upon which it is due or payable is manufactured or used in the Province of British Columbia—
				Length.	Per 1,000 feet B. M.	
	Feet.	*Inches.*		*Feet.*		
Piles, poles, and crib timbers.	40	11	$0.01	40	$2.00	
Do..................	50	11	.01¼	50	2.25	All the tax over and above one two-hundredths of 1 cent per linear foot.
Do..................	60	11	.01½	60	2.50	
Do..................	70	11	.01¾	70	2.75	
Do..................	80	11	.02	80	3.00	
Do..................	(1)	11	.02½	(1)	4.00	

¹ Over 80 feet.

Provided always, that the lieutenant governor in council may allow such rebate on piles, telegraph poles, and crib timber not manufactured or used in the Province as may be deemed advisable.

SCHEDULE No. 3.

Mining props and lagging, (50c.) fifty cents per cord.
Railway ties, (50c.) fifty cents per cord.
Cord wood, (25c.) twenty-five cents per cord.
A rebate will be allowed of all the tax over and above one cent per cord on all railway ties and mine props and lagging and cord wood used in the Province.

SCHEDULE No. 4.

Shingle or other bolts of cedar, fir, or spruce, one dollar per cord. The rebate to be allowed when manufactured or used in the Province of British Columbia shall be all over and above one cent per cord.
Scaling.—(3) All timber upon which any royalty or tax is payable to the Crown shall be scaled and graded by an official scaler in accordance with the provisions of the "timber measurement act, 1906."
Exemption from payment of royalty on cord wood.—(4) Actual settlers who are preemptors of Crown lands, who have occupied their preemption claim for two years, who have had the said claim surveyed, and who have taken out certifi-

314 RECIPROCITY WITH CANADA.

cates of improvement, shall be exempt from payment of royalty or tax upon cord wood cut upon their preemption claims for sale: Provided that such exemption shall cease when a Crown grant is issued for the land. (1903–4, c. 30, s. 9; 1907, c. 25, s. 18.)

67. *Lien for royalty, tax, and rent.*—All timber or wood upon which a royalty or tax is reserved, or which has been cut upon timber leaseholds, shall be liable for the payment of the royalty or tax (and in the case of leaseholds, for the rent) by this act imposed, so long and wheresoever the timber, or any part of it, may be found in British Columbia, whether in the original logs or manufactured into deal boards or other stuffs; and in case such timber or wood has been made up with other timber or wood into a crib, dam or raft, or in any other manner has been so mixed up as to render it impossible or difficult to distinguish the timber liable to the payment of royalty, tax, or rent from timber or wood not so liable, such other timber or wood shall also be liable for all royalty, tax, and rent imposed by this act; and all officers or agents entrusted with the collection of the royalty, tax, or rent may follow all such timber or wood and seize and detain the same wherever it is found until such royalties, tax, and rent, and the reasonable costs and expenses of seizure and detention, are paid or secured. (1903–4, c. 30, s. 10.)

68. *Lien upon steamships, etc.*—The Crown shall have a lien upon all sawmills or other factories, steamships, railway and stationary engines, smelters, concentrators, and all furnaces or machinery in or for which any timber or wood upon which a royalty or tax is reserved or payable in any way or manner, or for any purpose, has been or is being manufactured, used, or consumed, also upon all steamships, towboats, scows, or other vessels, upon all engines, logging plant or material, and upon all railway trains, teams, and wagons in any way engaged in taking out or in transporting such timber; such lien to confer the same rights, and to be enforceable in the same manner as the lien and rights of recovery of royalties conferred by the provisions in that behalf of this act. (1903–4, c. 30, s. 11.)

69. *Accounts and returns.*—Every lessee or licensee of timber lands, and every person operating a mill or other industry which may cut or use timber or cord wood upon or in respect of which any royalty or tax is by this act reserved or imposed, shall keep correct books of account of all timber or cord wood cut or received by or for them, and shall render monthly statements thereof, or if demanded shall furnish a true copy of the tallyman's or scaler's daily work, duly sworn to, which shall contain all such particulars as the chief commissioner may require; and such books of account shall be open at all reasonable hours for the inspection of any person appointed for carrying out the provisions of this act, and such lessee or licensee, or person operating a mill or other industry, shall pay monthly all sums of money, as are so shown to be due, to the chief commissioner of lands:

(a) Provided that, if, after said inspection of such books of account, it shall be found that in any previous statement there is still an amount of timber not reported, and which is subject to royalty or tax, then the said lessee, or licensee, of timber lands, and every person operating a mill or other industry, who is in arrear of such royalty, shall forthwith pay such arrears, and shall be subject to all the provisions of this act for nonpayment of same. (1908, c. 30, s. 69; 1910, c. 28, s. 9.)

70. *Millowners may collect royalties due—Crown lien on mill and timber thereat.*—It shall be lawful for any person owning or operating any mill to collect the royalties due to the Crown upon any logs which may be brought to his mill, and to give receipts therefor. All moneys so received shall be accounted for and paid over to the Crown. The Crown shall have a lien upon the mill and all timber thereat, or on any lands or waters appurtenant thereto, for all royalties collected under this section; such lien to confer the same rights and to be enforceable in the same manner as the lien held under section 66 of this act may from time to time be. (1903–4, c. 30, s. 13.)

71. *Timber that may be cut without license.*—This act shall not be construed to inflict penalties upon free miners (within the meaning of the term "free miner," as described in the "mineral act"), engaged in prospecting or in preliminary development work of any mineral or placer claim, who shall give satisfactory proof to the gold commissioner or government agent of the district in which such mineral or placer claim is situate that the said mineral or placer claim is not being operated so that any income or profit is derived therefrom, nor upon travellers, nor upon persons engaged in merely scientific pursuits or exploring, nor upon farmers cutting timber in connection with their farms, nor

upon persons cutting cord wood for personal use for fuel for domestic purposes and not for sale, or cutting cord wood for school purposes, nor shall such person be required to pay any loyalty or tax thereon. (1900, c. 17, s. 1; 1903–4, c. 30, s. 14.)

72. *Title can not be acquired to timber cut on Crown, etc., lands without license—Seizure of same by the Crown.*—If any person, without authority or otherwise than is permitted by this act, cuts or employs, or induces any other person to cut, or assist in cutting, any timber of any kind on any of the Crown lands, patented lands, timber leaseholds, or timber limits, or removes or carries away any merchantable timber of any kind so cut, from any such Crown or patented lands, or timber leaseholds, or limits, he shall not acquire any right to the timber so cut, or any claim to any remuneration for cutting, preparing the same for market, or conveying the same to or towards market. Any such timber may be seized by the chief commissioner, or any government agent, or by any agent or person appointed under this act, or any person acting under the authority or by direction of either of them, and shall be sold for the benefit of the Crown:

(*a*) When the timber or saw logs made has or have been removed by any such person out of the reach of the chief commissioner or assistant commissioner, or any agent appointed for the purpose of carrying out the provisions of this act such first-mentioned person shall, in addition to the loss of his labour and disbursements, forfeit a sum of ten dollars for each tree (rafting stuff excepted) which he is proved to have cut, or caused to be cut or carried away.

(*b*) Such sum shall be recovered with costs in the name of the chief commissioner, or any government agent, in any court having jurisdiction in civil matters to the amount of the penalty.

(*c*) In such cases it shall be incumbent upon the party charged to prove his authority to cut, and the averment only of the party seizing or prosecuting that he is employed under the authority of this act shall be sufficient proof thereof, unless the defendant proves the contrary. (C. A. 1888, c. 66, s. 78; 1903–4, c. 30, s. 15.)

73. *When timber so cut is mixed up with other timber, the whole to be forfeited unless separated by the holder thereof.*—Where timber has been cut without authority on Crown lands, patented lands, timber leaseholds, or timber limits, and has been made up with other timber into a crib, dam, or raft, or in any other manner has been so mixed up as to render it impossible or difficult to distinguish the timber so unlawfully cut on Crown lands, patented lands, timber leaseholds, or timber limits, from other timber with which it is mixed up, the whole of the timber so mixed up shall be held to have been cut without authority, and shall be liable to seizure and forfeiture until separated by the holder satisfactorily to the officer making the seizure. (C. A. 1888, c. 66, s. 79.)

74. *Power of officer making the seizure.*—The officer making any seizure under this act may call in any assistance necessary for securing and protecting the timber seized. (1896, c. 28, s. 6.)

75. *Sale of seized timber.*—All timber seized under this act shall be deemed to be condemned unless the amounts due for rent, royalty, or tax, and the costs and expenses of seizure and detention, be paid within ten days from the day of seizure, or unless the person from whom it was seized, or the owner thereof, within ten days from the day of seizure, give notice to the seizing officer or nearest government agent that he disputes the seizure; failing such payment or notice the chief commissioner may order the sale of said timber, or of so much thereof as may be sufficient to pay all rents or royalties due, and all the costs and expenses of seizure, detention, and sale. (1903–4, c. 30, s. 16.)

76. *Determination of validity of seizures.*—Any judge of the supreme or of a county court may, upon petition in a summary way, try and determine such seizures, and may order the delivery of the timber to the alleged owner, upon his complying with the following requirements:

(*a*) He shall first pay the full amount of the rent, royalty, or tax claimed, together with a sum equal to the costs and expenses to that time incurred in respect of such seizure, and shall give sufficient and acceptable security for such amount to meet further costs and expenses as the judge trying the case may consider requisite for that purpose.

(*b*) Such security shall be taken in the name of the chief commissioner to His Majesty's use, and shall be delivered up to and kept by the chief commissioner.

(*c*) If such seized timber is condemned, the value thereof, or the amount due for royalty, tax, rent, and costs or expenses, shall be forthwith paid to the chief commissioner, otherwise the penalty shall be enforced and recovered.   (1903-4. c. 30, s. 17.)

77. *Penalty for making false statements to evade payment of royalties, etc.*— Every person availing himself of any false statement or oath to evade the payment of any moneys payable under this act in respect to timber, or endeavouring to convey out of British Columbia any timber in respect of which the royalties by this act imposed are payable, without first paying such royalties, shall forfeit the timber in respect of which payment of such moneys is attempted to be evaded, and shall, upon summary conviction before any two justices of the peace, or any stipendiary or police magistrate, be liable to a penalty not exceeding five hundred dollars.   (C. A. 1888, c. 66, s. 83.)

78. *Drawback on exported timber, etc.*—The lieutenant governor in council may allow, on the exportation beyond the limits of the Province of any piles and spars, or of any timber manufactured at any mill in British Columbia upon which the royalty by this act imposed has been paid, a drawback or rebate equal to one-half of the royalty paid upon such timber.   (C. A. 1888, c. 66, s. 84.)

79. *Rules and regulations may be made.*—The chief commissioner of lands and works may, with the approval of the lieutenant governor in council, appoint such persons and make all such rules and regulations as he may deem proper for carrying out the provisions of this act.   (C. A. 1888, c. 66, s. 85.)

RESERVATION OF COAL AND PETROLEUM.

96. No Crown grant issued under the land act for land, the title to which has been acquired after the twenty-seventh day of February, A. D. 1899, shall convey any right to coal or petroleum which may be found on such land, and Crown grants issued for such land shall contain an express reservation to the Crown of all the coal and petroleum found therein.   (1899, c. 38, s. 18.)

REMOVAL OF TRESPASSERS.

99. When any person is wrongfully or without lawful authority in possession of any public land and refuses to vacate or abandon possession of the same, the chief commissioner of lands and works, or any officer or agent of the department of lands and works authorized by the chief commissioner for that purpose, may, upon affidavit of the facts, apply to the county judge of the county, or any stipendiary magistrate of the district, in which the land lies, for a summons directed to such person calling upon him forthwith to vacate or abandon possession of the said land, or within ten days after service of said summons to show cause why an order for his removal should not be made, and if upon return of the summons it shall appear that he has not vacated or abandoned possession, or he shall not show good cause to the contrary, the judge or stipendiary magistrate shall make an order for the summary removal of such person from such land, and such order shall be executed by the sheriff, or any bailiff, or constable, or other person to whom it shall be delivered.   (1897. c. 21. s. 2.)

CROWN GRANTS OF LAND PURCHASED BEFORE 1870.

110. In any case in which the chief commissioner of lands and works, or other the officer for the time being charged with the duty of issuing Crown grants to persons claiming grants of land purchased previous to the thirteenth day of April, 1870, either directly or derivatively from the Crown, shall not be satisfied with the evidence of the validity of the claim of any applicant for such Crown grant, such chief commissioner or officer aforesaid is hereby authorized and empowered to, and shall, if required by the applicant so to do, refer such claim, and all other matters in anywise relating thereto, to the registrar general of titles, who shall examine into the claim, title, or matter so referred, and proceed therein in the manner hereinafter provided.   (C. A. 1888, c. 66, s. 106.)

MISCELLANEOUS PROVISIONS.

127. *Chinese not to record or acquire Crown lands—Such record or grant to be void.*—It shall not be lawful for a commissioner or any other person to issue a preemption record of any Crown land, or sell any portion thereof, to any Chinese, nor grant authority under the said act to any Chinese to record or divert any water from the natural channel of any stream, lake, or river in this Province. Any record or grant made contrary to the provisions of this section shall be void and of no effect.   (C. A. 1888, c. 66, s. 122.)

132. *Saving clause.*—Notwithstanding anything in chapter 25 of the Statutes of 1907 contained, all persons who, before the twenty-fifth day of April, A. D. 1907, staked lands for the purpose of applying for permission to purchase or lease the same, or to acquire a special timber license over the same, and who shall have commenced to publish in the British Columbia Gazette notice of their intention to apply for such permission, or for such special timber license, before the first day of June, 1907, and all persons who, before the said twenty-fifth day of April, A. D. 1907, applied to purchase surveyed lands, shall be entitled to complete their applications as under the provisions of the act in force at the time of such staking, or at the time of making such application for surveyed lands. (1907, c. 25, s. 21.)

133. *Repeal clause.*—Chapter 113 of the Revised Statutes, 1897, chapter 38 of the Statutes of 1899, chapters 16 and 17 of the Statutes of 1900, chapter 30 of the Statutes of 1901, chapter 15 of the Statutes of 1903, chapter 30 of the Statutes of 1903–4, chapters 33 and 34 of the Statutes of 1905, chapter 24 of the Statutes of 1906, and chapter 25 of the Statutes of 1907, are hereby repealed.

The following telegrams were submitted by Mr. Skinner:

PORTLAND, OREG., *February 9.*

RUSSELL HAWKINS,
  Care Ways and Means Committee, House of Representatives,
                      Washington, D. C.

Resolution Canadian reciprocity passed House of Oregon Legislature this morning to come up under suspension rules in Senate this afternoon. Prospects favorable.

L. J. WENTWORTH.

PORTLAND, OREG., *February 7–8, 1911.*

RUSSEL HAWKINS,
  New Willard, Washington, D. C.

This association, representing about 100 mills, with annual output worth $80,000,000, protests against proposed Canadian reciprocal measure for following reasons:

Owing to the low prices for lumber which have prevailed for past 18 months, especially the lower grades, excessive freight rates, and overproduction we have been forced to leave considerable percentage of the lower grades in the woods. To allow influx Canadian lumber, especially common, will materially increase waste in logging, and instead of conserving our timber as claimed will work for further loss in our natural resources. Owing to more favorable shipping laws, by which Canadian mills can ship in foreign bottoms into States while we are restricted to American bottoms, the California market already demoralized, and our largest consumer of common lumber will buy freely from Canada. This association represents only 50 per cent of Oregon mills to which these arguments apply with equal force. Which lumber does Canada accept under proposed agreement? Refer to Department Agriculture Forest Service for data, capital, and labor employed. Following resolution submitted to Oregon Legislature to-day:

Whereas the Canadian reciprocal agreement, proposing the removal of duties upon farm and timber products, is now under consideration by Congress; and

Whereas the removal of these existing tariffs upon its products will work inestimable damage to the welfare of the State; and

Whereas by reason of the shipping laws of the United States foreign vessels can not be used between domestic ports, while vessels under any flag can be used between Canadian ports and those of the United States, thereby securing very much lower rates and making the competition more difficult to meet; and

Whereas tariff commission has been appointed by the President of the United States to examine into and report on the necessity of changes in our present tariffs on all commodities, both raw and manufactured: Now, therefore, be it

Resolved, That the Legislature of the State of Oregon requests its Senators and Representatives in Congress to oppose the ratification, or consent of, or to said Canadian reciprocal agreement at this time and until said tariff commission has reported, and the country is more fully advised as to the effect such agreement will have upon the industries and development of the United States.

OREGON & WASHINGTON LUMBER
MANUFACTURERS' ASSOCIATION.
L. J. WENTWORTH, *President.*

PORTLAND, OREG., *February* 7-8, *1911.*

RUSSEL HAWKINS,
New Willard Hotel, Washington, D. C.:

Any reduction in the present tariff on cedar shingles will result in disaster to the industry of the Pacific Northwest, and we wish to lay before you this matter, earnestly requesting that you oppose any change being made. The industry now is in a bad way due to the business depression in all forest products. More than 50 per cent of the shingle mills being now closed down and the commodity selling during entire term of present tariff from 15 to 25 cents per thousand below prices prevailing prior thereto. To change present tariff schedule will result in additional loss and depression to the industry. As a committee representing the mills of the Columbia River district we authorize you to place this protest against any change before he proper commitees.

THE HOWELL SHINGLE CO.
UNIVERSITY LUMBER & SHINGLE CO.
ALLEN SHINGLE CO.

The following extracts were submitted by Mr. Norris:

THE LABOR COST OF PRODUCTION.

The select committee caused investigations to be made in 15 eastern paper mills, 17 eastern ground wood mills, 3 western paper mills, and several Canadian mills, covering a period of 13 years, that is from 1895 to 1907. The result of that investigation is stated by Mr. Mann (p. 819 of Congressional Record) as follows:

"The daily wage paid in the Canadian mills is about the same as in the American mills." "Many of the skilled workmen in the paper mills of Canada are brought from the United States."

TOTAL LABOR COST FROM ROUGH WOOD TO PAPER.

[Page 820 of Congressional Record.]

	Per ton.
15 eastern mills	$8.52
3 western mills	7.52
18 United States mills	8.43
St. Regis mill	6.89
International Paper Co.'s mills	8.33
Booth mill (Canadian)	9.05

If the inquiry into the cost of labor in news print paper be approached from the basis of the living wage we find that Canada is on the same level as the United States, as is shown by testimony of David S. Cowles (p. 908), George Chahoon, jr. (p. 805), Carl Riordan (p. 805), F. B. Lynch, of Minneapolis (p. 2400), and J. R. Booth (p. 3361).

Mr. J. T. Carey (p. 1376), president of the International Brotherhood of Paper Makers, testified that his union controlled 5 or 6 mills in Canada, that the wages in the Laurentide mill, the Belgo-Canadian mill, the Windsor Locks mill, were practically the same as in the United States.

The United States consul at Three Rivers said the wages were higher in Canada because all the skilled labor came from the United States and inducements were offered those men to leave home and country.

Mr. Cowles had declared that the pay was, if anything, higher in Canada than in the United States, and that this applied to unskilled as well as skilled labor. The figures which I attach in comparative tables of pay of positions give the relative pay for each position so far as received and establish absolutely and without qualification that the living wage in the Canadian mill is the same if not more than the average of all the American news print mills.

Mr. Carl Riordan, of Montreal (p. 806), summarized the entire situation in a dispatch submitted to the committee that common labor was paid an average of $1.75 in Michigan and New York, $1.50 in Maine, $2 in northern Ontario, $1.50 to $1.60 in Southern Ontario, and $1.25 in Quebec and New Brunswick.

The amounts paid by various companies for labor on paper machines, that is for machine tenders, back tender, third hand, and fourth hand, may be stated as follows:

Page.	Hours.	Mill.	Comparisons of pay of positions.					
			Machine tenders.	Back tenders.	Third hand.	Fourth hand.	Beater Eng.	Beaters.
807	12	Bureau of Labor (p. 807), 1906	$2.88	$2.06	....	....	....	$2.07
	8	International (average)	3.16	2.08	$1.70	$1.68	$2.30	1.68
1592	8	Cliff	3.32	2.34	1.82	1.50	2.31	1.82
1091	12	Gould	3.25	2.00	1.50	....	1.87½	1.50
1410	12	Gilbert	3.40	1.87	1.50	....	2.62	1.80
			3.15	1.77	1.37	....	....	....
937	8	St. Regis	4.00	2.75	2.00	....	3.00	1.50
			3.75	2.50	1.90	1.65	....	....
			3.50	....	....	....	....	....
	8	Pejepscot	4.00	....	....	....	....	....
			3.50	....	....	....	....	....
1693	12	John Edwards	3.75	2.40	....	....	2.75	1.80
1676	12	Cloquet	3.85	2.76	2.16	1.92	2.76	1.92
1784	12	Flambeau	3.84	2.40	1.92	1.80	2.76	1.92
1712	12	Consolidated	4.00	2.64	....	....	3.00	1.92
1871	12	Niagara (Wisconsin)	4.35	2.50	1.92	1.65	3.00	1.80
1861	12	Wisconsin Paper & Pulp Co	3.84	2.52	1.80	1.35	2.76	1.80
1866	12	Everett	4.45	2.50	2.00	....	3.00	2.25
805	8	Laurentide	4.00	2.50	1.80	1.50	....	....
			3.75	....	....	....	....	....
	8	Canada Paper Co	4.00	2.50	1.75	1.25	....	....
883	12	Booth	4.25	3.00	2.00	1.75	3.00	1.75
1400	8	Berlin Mills	4.00	3.00	2.00	1.80	3.50	2.00

Page.	Hours.	Mill.	Comparisons of pay of positions.				
			Grinders.	Finishers.	Screen men.	Laborers.	Firemen.
807	12	Bureau of Labor (p. 807), 1906	$1.77	$1.78	....	$1.56	....
	8	International (average)	1.65	1.75	$1.65	1.65	$2.00
1592	8	Cliff	1.82	2.00	1.82	1.50	2.25
1091	12	Gould	....	2.00	1.50	1.80	{ 1.75 / 2.00
1410	12	Gilbert	....	1.62	....	1.80	2.57
937	8	St. Regis	1.50	....	....	....	1.65
	8	Pejepscot	....	....	....	....	....
1693	12	John Edwards	1.80	....	....	1.70	2.25
1676	12	Cloquet	1.92	....	....	....	2.04
1784	12	Flambeau	1.85	1.75	1.60	1.75	1.92
1712	12	Consolidated	2.00	2.00	....	....	1.75
1871	12	Niagara (Wisconsin)	1.80	....	....	1.65	....
1861	12	Wisconsin Paper & Pulp Co	1.80	1.75	....	....	1.92
1866	12	Everett	....	2.50	....	2.25	2.35
805	8	Laurentide	....	....	....	....	....
	8	Canada Paper Co	....	....	....	....	....
883	12	Booth	1.70-2.50	1.50-1.75	....	....	1.75
1400	8	Berlin Mills	1.80	1.64	1.80	1.52	1.85

Mill.	Hourly rate, in cents.				Total per hour.
	Machine tender.	Back tender.	Third hand.	Fourth hand.	
Berlin	$0.50	$0.37½	$0.25	$0.22¾	$1.35¼
St. Regis	.47	.32	.24	.20	1.24
Laurentine (Canadian)	.48	.31	.22	.19	1.21
Canada Paper Co. (Canadian)	.50	.31	.21	.15	1.18
Cliff	.41	.29	.25	.19	1.15
International	.42	.26	.21	.21	1.10
Booth (Canadian)	.35	.25	.17½	.14	.92½
Everett	.37	.21	.16	.16	.90
Cloquet	.32	.23	.18	.16	.89
Consolidated	.33½	.22	.16	.13¾	.85¼
Flambeau	.32	.20	.16	.15	.83
Wisconsin	.32	.21	.15	.11	.79
Gould	.27	.16	.12	.12	.68
Gilbert	.27	.15	.12	.12	.66

Earnings of organized wageworkers (males) in New York State for first
quarter, 1906.

(See page 234 of New York State Bureau of Labor for 1906.)

Building and stoneworking, etc		$220. 19
(a) Stoneworking	$247. 27	
(b) Building and paving trades	245. 98	
(c) Building and street labor	155. 41	
Transportation		209. 94
(a) Railways	234. 05	
(b) Navigation	254. 24	
(c) Teaming and cab driving	174. 23	
(d) Freight handling	155. 16	
(e) Telegraphs	162. 51	
Clothing and textiles		161. 86
(a) Garments	159. 41	
(b) Shirts, collars, and laundry	190. 36	
(c) Hats, caps, and furs	160. 66	
(d) Boots, shoes, and gloves	171. 81	
(e) Textiles	173. 51	
Metals, machinery, and shipbuilding		212. 36
(a) Iron and steel	210. 82	
(b) Metals, other than iron and steel	225. 27	
(c) Shipbuilding	213. 65	
Printing, binding, etc		251. 58
Compositors	255. 89	
Electrotypers and stereotypers	234. 43	
Mailers	225. 89	
Photo-engravers	306. 08	
Pressmen	273. 96	
Woodworking and furniture		194. 00
Food and liquors		184. 32
(a) Food products	177. 76	
(b) Beverages	190. 36	
Theaters and music		367. 26
Tobacco		146. 96
Restaurant and retail trade		175. 66
(a) Hotels and restaurants	186. 11	
(b) Retail trade	151. 56	
Public employment		223. 74
Stationary enginemen		229. 16
Miscellaneous:		
Glass and glassware	311. 78	
Other distinct trades	243. 53	
Cement and clay products	200. 41	
Leather and leather goods	170. 58	
Barbering	153. 83	
Paper and paper goods	143. 06	

MR. HASTINGS'S SUGGESTION FOR CURTAILMENT.

The full text of Mr. Hastings's letter to paper makers under date
of July 11, 1910, is as follows:

GENTLEMEN: The dull season is again here, and there is apparently less demand for all grades of paper, and yet as a matter of fact there is a better demand
than there has been for a number of years at this season. Annual vacations
are being taken; buyers are listless. In spite of the concerted action of some
buyers to reduce prices through misinformation as to quotations made, and
through refusal to buy, except that which is absolutely needed, deliveries in
one grade of paper, for instance, May showed more delivered than was manufactured, and yet prices were demoralized in that particular grade. In another
grade of paper 98 per cent was shipped of all produced. Still another grade
99 per cent shipped of production, and in that particular division one of the

grades manufactured has been sold at less than it cost to produce. The consumer knowing this, contracted where he could for a long period ahead. Where he could not contract he purchased all he could carry. The result will be that when prices st'ffen in the fall, the manufacturers in this particular grade will have to face some of their own paper put on the market at less than the cost to produce. The buyer has done what the mill should do.

Why is it that the manufacturer does not hesitate to go to his banker to borrow money to buy his pulp, or to carry on his wood operations, yet seems to think that he could not afford to hold his manufactured goods when he positively knows that by so doing he would earn much more than the legal rate of interest?

You have noticed that all the great commodities are in a healthy condition as to manufacturing, supply and demand, still at this time of the year their demand falls off, the result being that furnaces have gone out of blast, cotton mills have restricted production by a week or more shut down, and by curtail to five days a week work. Has not the experience of the cotton manufacturers, for instance, shown them that it is better to fill the demand and keep a uniform price for their product than it is to endeavor to do the impossible, by forcing upon the market something that the market can not possibly absorb? Have we not, as paper manufacturers, a good deal to learn from some of the other large industries?

Have we ever heard in late years of the steel industry in all its branches, through low prices, expecting to increase the demand? The same is true of cotton and woolen goods.

The paper manufacturers used to think that if a man would not buy a certain article for 5 cents a pound, he would at 4½, but such is not the case. He will buy just as much at 5 cents, because he will not buy at 4½ unless he needs it.

It is against the law to curtail production through any concerted action. It should be up to each individual manufacturer to judge of the market conditions, and to operate his plant according to the demand, and when the manufacturers have gotten in that frame of mind, then will they get the best results from their business, and not until then. A contract made at the time of low demand means a low price for 12 months, but you have sold no more tons, and have a contract that you will be held to. I talk with manufacturers from all sections of the United States, and the exception is the one who does not admit that they are in better condition as to orders than is usual at this season of the year. Nearly all buyers prefer uniform fair prices rather than a low price now and a higher price later on.

Think it over.

Yours, very truly,

ARTHUR C. HASTINGS,
President American Paper and Pulp Association.

[Paper Mill, Aug. 27, 1910, pp. 4 and 38.]

EDGAR G. BARRATT—TALKS OF PAPER MATTERS WITH A LONDON TRADE PAPER—WHAT HE IS REPORTED TO HAVE SAID.

We were agreeably surprised on July 28 to receive a wire from Edgar G. Barratt, president of the Union Bag and Paper Co. of the United States, informing us that he had landed safely from the *Royal Edward* at Bristol and hoped to spend that evening with us in London, says the British Paper Maker. It was our privilege to introduce Mr. Barratt to a few congenial spirits, who, we hope, spent an enjoyable evening, and the following day the writer spent an hour with Mr. Barratt at a West End club, and found this most interesting and well-informed gentleman in a communicative mood. Mr. Edgar G. Barratt is a very good type of the progressive, strenuous, keen, invariably civil and successful American, who controls with conspicuous abilities an undertaking which claims a capital of £6,000,000, and runs 19 mills for the production of chemical pulp, ground wood, and paper.

It is a somewhat refreshing experience to interview a wide-awake American business organizer who is brimful of facts and figures, and able and willing to impart the same with avidity and intelligence. Such a man is Edgar G. Barratt, and although he very adroitly "closed down" on one or two questions which perhaps one had no right to expect an answer to, his opinions were well worth having, and we have no doubt that our readers will be greatly interested in what Mr. Barratt had to impart.

In answer to our question, he observed: "Our business is, of course, a big one, even for America, and we have a big capital of which $4,000,000 is, I think, well invested in Canada. We cut about 35,000,000 feet of lumber per annum, and we make a large quantity of high-grade sulphite which we chiefly use for our own consumption, on the bag side, which is, as you know, a considerable business with us; but we make no 'news,' although at times the making of 'news' has been a tempting proposition, owing to conditions with which you are probably familiar. In my opinion," said Mr. Barratt, "trade in America generally has improved very much and is improving, and, inferentially, this means a good thing for England. There are many reasons why this should be so, and, if experience counts for anything, it will be so. As regards prices for paper, I consider they are fairly good, excepting perhaps as regards wrappings. The makers of book papers and 'news' papers are in for a good time, and they are very busy. At a dinner I was at last night," remarked Mr. Barratt, "I said something which perhaps was not quite understood, but I am quite sure of my facts and figures, because all the paper men of any position in the States to-day do not take much for granted. They prefer to get the absolute rock-bottom facts, and it is now realized that it is not such a difficult matter to get exact information on matters of supply and demand as some people once imagined and others, if what I hear is true, still seem to think.

" I do not think that makers in Great Britain need have very great concern as regards damaging competition from the States, so far as one can see ahead. The facts have been published regarding various strikes and lockouts, and on the second day of the great railway strike on the Grand Trunk Booth's Mill shut down because they were forced to, and the result is, of course, so much less output. I would like to reiterate what I said at the complimentary dinner to Mr. Powers, that to me it was a most pleasurable surprise to meet such a crowd of good fellows, all in the very best of spirits, and with such a splendid feeling of good-fellowship prevailing among competitors. It was also an even greater pleasure to me to observe how kind your people were to 'Billy' Powers. and it was a splendid testimony to your business men to observe what kindness they showed to an American who had, of course, come over to do business up against them in their own markets, and I repeat what I said at the Powers dinner, that so far as I am personally concerned—and I am also speaking for my friends—we appreciate such a kindly feeling, and I hope they will not fail to let us be of any assistance to them should they visit our country at any time, either individually or collectively.

"These little touches of human kindness," said Mr. Barratt, "make one's heart beat faster, and when I was at the Powers dinner I felt that I was at a very extraordinary gathering, an occasion when Britishers were giving an enthusiastic farewell to an intruding American, who had come over here to do business in their markets, and, as I have already said. I think that such a gathering is well calculated to cultivate a spirit of international friendship which, in my judgment, might with advantage be extended to all concerned."

Conversation then turned on to Mr. Barratt's well-known views on the spirit of cooperation among competitors in the paper trade.

Mr. Barratt had something very interesting to say on this point, and he observed: "Three or four years ago some of the best men in the paper trade in the States appreciated the fact that a better knowledge of the conditions of the paper business in the States and in the countries doing business with us was really necessary, and an effort was made to collect and compile more exact information. We had many difficulties at first, as those who were in a position to give us the information were in many cases afraid to do so, and there was a spirit of mistrust, which militated against the success of the efforts of Arthur C. Hastings and his association. However, I am pleased to know that at the present time that spirit of hostility and suspicion has very largely passed away, and we are now in a position to obtain first-hand fairly detailed information which prevents a lot of reckless competition, and also serves the general interests of the trade in various ways. We have come to realize that there can be no danger in knowing exact facts, and this spirit of trustfulness and good-fellowship has extended to such an extent that we have now no difficulty in the States in approaching a competitor and asking him facts regarding a transaction which may be of interest and importance to the trade as a whole. We have also found that during periods of depression the possession of precise information has been most useful, and we have got so far as to be in the position of the stronger mills assisting the weaker ones and, when the demand has been down, certain concerns have reduced their output as low as 35 per cent of their normal production; and another concern I know was working on 60 per cent of their output; and we are beginning to get inside a lot of general facts which help to strengthen the trade as a trade, and some of the big undertakings, which 'hold the bag,' as we say in America, are helping the weaker concerns when they are tempted to rush in and do business on unsound lines."

Mr. Barratt gave the writer some extraordinary figures, showing how both Scandinavia and Germany have poured thousands of tons of chemical pulp into the States at ridiculous prices, very considerably below what might be considered a fair market figure, and certainly at a price which no American maker could entertain. Mr. Barratt added with emphasis: "They are doing it to-day to some extent, but not to the extent of a short time ago, and our country is buying unbleached sulphite, sulphate, Kraft pulp, and a little soda pulp, and the organization we have enables us to see at a glance exactly what is being done. Mr. Barratt mentioned the sum of $41 as the quotable market price of domestic sulphite to-day, and he expressed the opinion that there was now no reason why the chemical-pulp market should not be in a satisfactory condition.

On the subject of ground wood Mr. Barratt gave us some very interesting information. He said that in the western streams and New York State the water supply had fallen off very rapidly, and early in July a number of the mills had to shut down owing to the scarcity of water. The effect of this would be obvious, and he did not see how it would be possible to replenish the supplies of wood pulp which would be depleted, and he was very anxious to see what would happen as the result. "You are quite aware, of course," added Mr. Barratt, "that as regards the States the demand for wood pulp far exceeds the supply, and America is buying nearly 200,000 tons of ground wood per annum from Canada. I am myself building a new mechanical pulp mill near Three Rivers, in Canada. It is not a very great mill, but it will produce 40 tons of air-dry mechanical pulp in 24 hours. You may guess that I should not build this mill unless I was fairly satisfied in my own mind that there is not much danger of any restriction being put on the exportation of ground wood from Canada at present."

Mr. Barratt then referred to another element which may have an important influence on wood-pulp manufacture, and he mentioned the fact that in some of the undertakings he controlled it paid them much better to generate electricity from the water power and supply light and current rather than turn the power to wood-pulp production.

"We make about 66,000 tons of paper a year, chiefly high grade sulphite papers for our bags," Mr. Barratt added, and went on to give some very interesting comparisons on American methods in regard to the bag trade as compared with the methods in England. He observed: "In the bag trade we work on a carload as a unit, and our bags are all standardized. I admit quite frankly that your prices and your methods of dealing in England are not attractive to us. Your prices are too low for us, and the quantities ordered are too small. About 80 per cent of our business is done in orders of carloads, and in the States, when we deal with a carload, the shipper loads the car and the receiver unloads, and this means that we get a very favorable rate.

"If we send less than a carload the rate is considerably higher, and we do not encourage that business. The railroad companies have a minimum car-load, which represents about 2,000,000 bags per car generally, and I am pleased to say that the general outlook in regard to our bag departments is very healthy, and trade is improving."

Mr. Barratt incidentally mentioned the fact that the consumption of paper in the States seemed to be increasing at about the proportion of 10 per cent per annum, and "news" at the proportion of 8 per cent. Personally he had had no difficulties with his workpeople, and was pleased to say that he got on very well with them in a general way. His own mills were worked on the mixed principle, no difference being made between union and nonunion men, and he remarked: "I have some Englishmen—very good men, too—under me. I have one man named Marriott, who came along quite on his own account one day. He formerly worked for Messrs. Bibby & Baron, and he has stayed with me."

On the subject of wages, Mr. Barratt said that the wages of a head machine man varied from $3.50 to $5.50 for eight hours, and he added: "The cost of living and the amount of wages paid have been undoubtedly going up of late, not only in America but in other parts of the world." Mr. Barratt gave his views on this subject, and said that in America there seemed to be a spirit of

common sense among the workpeople as a whole, and in his mills they did
not object to overtime or working the week ends at certain periods when it
meant finding employment, say, for the paper mills when they were in danger
of running scarce of pulp. Mr. Barratt, in conclusion, spoke very generously
of British methods, and the kindly people he had met on this side, and he
also said that the policy of Great Britain investing English money in Canada
was a most sagacious one and was producing wonderful results. "Canada,"
he added, "is going ahead by leaps and bounds, and I imagine that few people
in this country have any idea to what extent that marvelous progress is being
made in that great country of illimitable possibilities."

STATEMENT OF Z. W. WHITEHEAD, OF WILMINGTON, N. C.

Mr. WHITEHEAD. Mr. Chairman and gentlemen of the committee,
I feel that the gentlemen who have preceded me have so thoroughly
covered this question that it is hardly necessary for me to add much
to what they have already said. I am here, however, representing
over 18,000 saw and planing mills and certainly more than 500,000
employees in the South Atlantic and Gulf States. I am commis-
sioned here to register their most emphatic protest against the ratification of this proposed reciprocity treaty with Canada or that of any
other measure which carries with it any repeal or reduction of the
present duty on lumber. I know of no section of the country, Mr.
Chairman and gentlemen, that would be more disastrously affected
by such a reciprocal measure as has been advanced than the section
of the country that I represent here more especially. In the South,
during the past few years, we have enjoyed a rather phenomenal
development in the lumber industry. That development of the lumber industry has contributed a wonderful part to the development of
the allied and other industries throughout the South, until to-day the
development of the South is the pride and boast of every man within
our borders, and I can truthfully say, and I could bring forth the
figures to show, if it was necesary to show to you, that no other industry in all the whole southern country has contributed more to this
general development than our lumber industry. We have extended
the right hand of fellowship to our brethren in other parts of the
country, showing and telling them what we have in the way of stumpage, and they have come into our midst and invested their money.

A great deal of the timber lands in the South has been sold and
bought up during the past decade. They were bought and sold upon
the basis of that measure of protection and that guaranty of good
faith on the part of the United States, that the duty of $2 per thou-
sand against the importation of Canadian lumber vouchsafed to them.
I am keenly alive that the fact, Mr. Chairman, that I hail from a
section of the country where protectionists are not very numerous;
but I want to say to you, gentlemen, that our sympathies and our
demands—or rather our requests—with reference to this duty on
Canadian lumber are not based upon any political theories or any
political vagaries or any moon chasing, but they are based upon our
experiences that we endured and went through with during that
period known as the period of the existence of the Wilson-Gorman
tariff bill, when Canada sold lumber as far south and shipped her
box boards as far south as the city of Baltimore, which is recognized
as the northern line of the southern territory. By reason of our
geographical location we naturally find in the South Atlantic and
Gulf States our chief markets for the lumber in that territory in

what is known as the Eastern and and Middle Western States. We had a large business in the coastwise trade. We reach the Northern States both by rail and by water, and we are only able to compete with our Canadian cousins by reason of our ability to reach the northern and eastern markets by way of the water as the lesser freight-rate route.

Mr. HILL. Let me ask you a question; would it be beneficial to your interests, or detrimental, to let Canadian logs come free into the United States and be manufactured here?

Mr. WHITEHEAD. Why, so far as the interests, per se, that I represent are concerned I do not know that it would make any material difference; but the lumber people in the South Atlantic and Gulf States feel that there is a common interest among manufacturers of lumber in all the United States, and if the free importation of logs from the Provinces of Canada would benefit our friends in another part of the country we would most gladly acquiesce in that move.]

Mr. RANDELL. Would you be willing to let lumber come in free so that these people that want to build homes out West would have a better chance to do it, out of charity to them?

Mr. WHITEHEAD. Our friends out West, it seems to me, are clamoring for that measure of protection on their wheat and barley and food products in that country that we are asking for our people down in the South Atlantic and Gulf States.

Mr. RANDELL. Then you are asking for a tariff on this because you think that the proper thing is to have a tariff on everything, and have protection all around, as far as it can go?

Mr. WHITEHEAD. No, sir; I do not say that. I mean this, that the present rate of duty, the present basis of operation, is predicated upon the original duty upon foreign importations of lumber, and if you are going to give those people the benefit of free lumber, then give us the benefit of free machinery and free sawmill supplies.

Mr. RANDELL. Would you not be in favor of it?

Mr. WHITEHEAD. Of free logs?

Mr. RANDELL. Would you not be in favor of that?

Mr. WHITEHEAD. I can not say that I would.

Mr. RANDELL. Then what is the use of making that argument to me, if you are not in favor of it?

Mr. WHITEHEAD. I would oppose that, not upon the ground that you suggest, but upon the broad principle that on every occasion, that in every era that I can recollect and that history furnishes an account of, the periods when we have had the lowest tariffs and the lowest rates of duty in this country have been the most oppressed periods in our history; and when we have had the highest rate of duty and the highest rate of tariff there has been the highest degree of prosperity in this country.

Mr. RANDELL. We differ very materially on that.

Mr. WHITEHEAD. Yes, sir; that is a matter upon which a great many people differ.

Mr. FORDNEY. You have had only one such period in your life and mine, and that was between 1894 and 1906, and that rings loud in your ears and mine.

Mr. WHITEHEAD. Yes; it rings loud in my ears and the ears of those whom I represent to-day.

Mr. RANDELL. You think if we had had a different bill from the Wilson-Gorman bill then it might have been better?

Mr. WHITEHEAD. Well——

Mr. RANDELL. Did it ever occur to you that Cleveland would not sign that bill because it was not, he said, a Democratic measure? And yet the Republicans claim that that is a great blot on the Democratic record, when the Republicans in the Senate made that bill? Did you ever think about that?

Mr. WHITEHEAD. I do not know that I ever thought about that, but if they had made it any worse than that, I am glad that nobody signed it.

Mr. RANDELL. They made 600 changes in it, and Cleveland would not sign it because it was no longer a Democratic measure and there were only five Democratic Senators who voted for those changes, but the Republicans took advantage of it and called it a Democratic measure. I am asking if you remember those things?

Mr. WHITEHEAD. I do not remember those things.

Mr. RANDELL. Then do you charge against the Democratic Party what the Republicans did in a Democratic administration?

Mr. FORDNEY. The Republicans were not in control. The Populists were in control in the Senate and dictated what should go in that bill.

Mr. RANDELL. It was the Republicans who voted for the changes.

Mr. FORDNEY. No, indeed.

Mr. RANDELL. Well, I withdraw the question, as you have no chance to answer it anyway, and it seems that the committee are divided on the proposition.

Mr. McCALL. Have you anything further to say about this bill?

Mr. WHITEHEAD. Mr. Chairman, I want to add this much to that. You understand that the lumber business is of such tremendous proportions, such ramifications, that it involves a vast amount of money to conduct it. I suppose it is safe to say that the lumber people are the largest borrowers of money of any class of people in the South, or possibly are larger borrowers of money than any other class of people in the country. To-day, with the possibility of the duty being removed on lumber, you are all well aware of the fact that the banks have at their heads some of their wisest and ablest men, who must necessarily keep their fingers on the pulse of trade, and who must necessarily look ahead. If this duty should be repealed, and the banks, knowing that there are these large investments in standing timber, large investments in mills and equipment, based upon this one idea, or rather at least in particular upon this one idea, that we would be shielded to some extent, at least, from free lumber from Canada where they make lumber infinitely cheaper than we can make it in this country—as I know, because I have been over there and seen—is it not reasonably understood that it will be only a question of time when the banks will necessarily be compelled to withdraw from the lumber people that measure of credit which they have accorded them during all these years of development; and could you picture in your mind a greater degree of demoralization and disaster than that which would overtake not only the people of the South Atlantic and Gulf States, but the people of every other part of the country where money is borrowed? Has it ever appealed to you where that disaster would stop?

Mr. Fordney. The banks would withdraw their support if the prices were lowered on lumber; and unless a reduction of the duty will lower the price of lumber, it is not a wise proposition to put into the law?

Mr. Whitehead. That is right. You are correct on that.

Mr. Fordney. And the consumer is the man that the friends of this measure are aiming to aid?

Mr. Whitehead. Yes; I think so.

Mr. Fordney. Then, if it does not lower the price of lumber, we would have nothing to fear in regard to the banks; but if it does lower the price of lumber, the lumbermen would fear the restrictions put upon them in the money market?

Mr. Whitehead. Naturally, sir.

Mr. McCall. Is there anything more?

Mr. Whitehead. Now, Mr. Chairman, I can say for my section of the country, and I can speak for the South in that particular. that there is not a cotton mill, there is not a bank, there is not a manufacturing enterprise of any character, I do not care what you take, but what some lumberman—but what more often more than one lumberman— has an interest in, is a prime factor in; there is not a trust company, and I know of nothing, absolutely. in the whole of the Southern States, but what the lumberman of to-day is contributing his full share to it, and, if measured by the standards of others. is contributing double his share to its progress and development.

Mr. Fordney. From a financial standpoint you speak advisedly, because you are a banker?

Mr. Whitehead. I am connected with a bank, and I do speak advisedly. I know when this trouble commences these banks. as a matter of necessity. will have to withdraw their credit. Now. Mr. Chairman and gentlemen, it was contended here before and during the discussion of the Payne-Aldrich tariff bill that if you made a reduction of 25 per cent, or $37\frac{1}{2}$ per cent, or even, some one assumed to say. if you had cut the duty 50 per cent on lumber, it would make no difference. You reduced the duty on lumber $37\frac{1}{2}$ per cent. Now, what is the concrete result? I refer you to the largely increased receipts of Canadian lumber in New York City, in Boston. and Maine ports, and in the lake ports. With what result? Is there a consumer before you to-day. or has a consumer appeared before you during any of these hearings. or do you hear of any consumer who says he has gotten lumber any cheaper?

Mr. Fordney. None at all.

Mr. Whitehead. Now, what is the result? The result is simply this: The Canadian manufacturer has supplanted to that extent the American manufacturer; the Canadian employee in Canada has supplanted the American employee to the same extent. In the meantime Canadian capital, Canadian industries, are boosted at the expense of American industries. And I do not believe that any member of this Ways and Means Committee would intentionally do anything or commit this Government to any policy that would build up and profit the industries of Canada or any other country upon the ruins of the industries of the United States.

Now. Mr. Chairman, I am frank to tell you that I know of no uglier feature to this entire proposition. carrying with it the repeal of the duty on lumber. than that to which I have just referred. The gentlemen who have preceded me have covered the field so thoroughly that I hardly think it is necessary for me to dwell upon any other feature, nor do I care to emphasize any other feature quite so much as that to which I have referred.

It has been well said that we do not live unto ourselves. Although it may be charged that there is a vast difference between the interests of the South and the interests of the West, or between the interests of the East and the interests of the West, yet our interests are so interlocked one with the other, either directly or indirectly, that you can not legislate against one industry in one part of the country without doing some measure of damage to the allied industries in various other parts of the country; and when you think possibly that you may be legislating in behalf of one section of the country and in behalf of one class of people against another, it has been usually a well-known fact that you were undermining some part of the fabric of this great Government and doing violence when you little dreamed of it.

I am here to say that from our standpoint, we regard this proposed reciprocity treaty as placing a burden upon the products of the forests, the waters, and farms. Those articles that are placed on the free list are the articles produced by the farmer, which become dutiable just as as soon as they leave the farmer, and are responsible more for the high prices of living than any other agency that is known.

Mr. Chairman, as I said, the gentlemen who have preceded me have covered this field so thoroughly that I hardly think it is necessary for me to refer to more than that feature which I have just talked on; and yet it is one that is fraught with more danger, and is well calculated to do more harm to ourselves, and bring greater disaster to this country, than any other, and you can only point to the past as a justification for what I have said, without anticipating anything else. and in view of what the other gentlemen have told you. I think we have given ample arguments to convince you that there is nothing to be gained for the United States as a whole by giving Canada an opportunity to monopolize our markets and rob American labor and American manufacturers of that which we pay our taxes to have and to enjoy, and the privilege of carrying on. I thank you.

Mr. HINES. Mr. Chairman, I want the privilege of just answering one question. I think it is very important.

Mr. McCALL. I think you had better let these other gentlemen address the committee, Mr. Hines.

Mr. HINES. This will take only a second.

Mr. WHITEHEAD. Mr. Chairman, I yield a part of my time to Mr. Hines.

Mr. HINES. You asked the question, Mr. Randell, why our people in the Middle West and in the States of Texas and Oklahoma. if the duty was taken off of lumber, could not import lumber from Canada and have it delivered in that territory cheaper than they are getting it at present. I do not think they quite understand your question. In the first place, the great State of Texas is one of the largest manufacturing lumber States in the United States. The average price of lumber all over the State of Texas to-day is less than the average price of lumber in Canada, absolutely.

Next, the cost of transportation of lumber to any point in Oklahoma or Texas from Canada would be prohibitive against shipping in lumber from Canada to that territory, while that territory can procure its lumber from Texas for a great deal less price.

Mr. RANDELL. Will you answer one question that has troubled my comprehension very much? Why is it that our lumbermen are just wild to keep a tariff on lumber between this country and Canada? They could not possibly be touched.

Mr. HINES. I have tried to show that the particular territory to be directly affected was from New York to St. Paul, bordering on the Great Lakes. And that indirectly affected us clean along the line.

Mr. RANDELL. Then their market is not affected in the rest of the country. If that market would not be affected there, why do they claim the same thing that you do? It would not affect them at all, and yet they are wild to keep the duty on lumber.

Mr. HINES. It would affect the market slightly.

STATEMENT OF A. J. WILSON, OF SPOKANE, WASH.

Mr. WILSON. Mr. Chairman and gentlemen, this has been gone into so thoroughly by the other gentlemen here that there is nothing new to offer. I wish to protest for the manufacturers of northern Idaho and eastern Washington, where the lumber industry is the great industry. The mills that I represent, about 15 mills, with $25,000,000 invested there, wish to file their protest against this reciprocity agreement, especially on the lumber schedule.

One thing that seems to be in the minds of some of the members of the committee is that you get the price, the retail lumber price, confounded with the wholesale price; that is, with the manufacturer's price. The price of lumber throughout Iowa, North Dakota, and South Dakota is not established by the manufacturer. The manufacturer who sells in that district can not control the price that the retailer asks for his lumber, and that seems to be one of the reasons why the President and a good many members of this committee wish to take the small tariff off of rough lumber that is on it at present. I have nothing new to offer to this committee.

Mr. GAINES. Before you conclude, just on what you are talking about: I have been trying to impress some of my associates with the idea that while the tariff may affect manufacturers' prices, it does not, in my opinion, in many cases, at least, affect retail prices, and you have now mentioned the same thing. Are you able to give us any comparison of manufacturers' prices and the retail prices finally charged the ultimate consumer for the same lumber?

Mr. WILSON. Yes, sir; I can: in prices in Iowa and Dakota, and Nebraska. I am familiar with the retail prices and also familiar with the prices received by the manufacturer.

Mr. GAINES. Now, give us those prices.

Mr. WILSON. You take a No. 2, or 2-inch, board, No. 2 western pine board, delivered at Aberdeen, S. Dak. That would cost a retailer approximately $24. $9 of that is freight.

Mr. GAINES. What does the manufacturer sell it for in Washington?

Mr. WILSON. The manufacturer gets $15 for that board.

Mr. GAINES. The manufacturer gets $15?

Mr. WILSON. Yes.

Mr. GAINES. It carries a $9 freight rate to Aberdeen?

Mr. WILSON. To Aberdeen, S. Dak.

Mr. GAINES. To Aberdeen, S. Dak.?

Mr. WILSON. Yes.

Mr. GAINES. What is the retail price?

Mr. WILSON. The retail price of that board in Aberdeen, S. Dak., is $32.

Mr. FORDNEY. $8, or 25 per cent of the total sale price, is added there?

Mr. WILSON. Yes.

Mr. FORDNEY. Thirty-three and one-half per cent of this cost, then, is added, approximately?

Mr. WILSON. Approximately, yes; the usual way of figuring line-yard prices is to add 10 per cent for operation and 25 per cent profit.

Mr. FORDNEY. Mr. Wilson, what does $15 a thousand give the manufacturer in profit, at Spokane, about?

Mr. WILSON. On Western pine boards?

Mr. FORDNEY. Yes; I mean the board you mentioned?

Mr. WILSON. It costs him about $2.15.

Mr. FORDNEY. $2.15?

Mr. WILSON. Yes.

Mr. FORDNEY. So that his profit with an investment of $12.85 is $2.15, where the retailer in Aberdeen, S. Dak., puts in $24 and takes out $32?

Mr. WILSON. Yes; that is about it.

Mr. HILL. Are you conducting a retail business?

Mr. WILSON. I am not conducting retail yards at the present time. We sold our retail yards in July.

Mr. HILL. Did you add 25 per cent and 10 per cent to your manufacturer's prices?

Mr. WILSON. No, sir.

Mr. HILL. Why did you do any differently?

Mr. WILSON. It was impossible for us to do any differently from that, where we were located. We were located in the city of Spokane.

Mr. HILL. Why was it not possible in Spokane?

Mr. WILSON. There are a good many yards, and the competition forced us down.

Mr. HILL. Then, wherever there is more than one yard, or wherever there are several yards, this statement is not correct.

Mr. WILSON. No; that is not true, Mr. Hill. In certain sections there seems to be a better understanding among retailers.

Mr. HILL. Yes.

Mr. WILSON. And they get a very good profit on retailing lumber. In the cities or open markets lumber is sold very cheap.

Mr. HILL. Is there any understanding among manufacturers that they will not sell to retailers unless they hold up the price?

Mr. WILSON. No, sir.

Mr. HILL. You are sure of that?

Mr. WILSON. Yes, sir.

Mr. HILL. How far does your sureness extend?

Mr. WILSON. As far as knowledge.

Mr. HILL. No restriction whatever?

Mr. WILSON. No restriction at all.

Mr. FORDNEY. You never heard of such a thing?

Mr. WILSON. No, sir.

Mr. HILL. I have.

Mr. WILSON. And I hape been in the lumber business all my life.

Mr. FORDNEY. I have been in the lumber business since I was a boy, and I never heard of it until before this committee.

Mr. GAINES. Is it not true that the retail price generally carries less profit in the neighborhood where the article is produced in large quantities, because people there know how cheaply the manufacturer sells it?

Mr. WILSON. I think that is true.

Mr. GAINES. So that the retail conditions existing in Spokane and those existing in Aberdeen, S. D., would be in that respect quite different?

Mr. WILSON. I think so.

Mr. GAINES. Now, the manufacturer of an article gets all he can for it, does he not?

Mr. WILSON. Yes; invariably.

Mr. GAINES. The retail dealer gets all he can for it when he sells it, of course?

Mr. WILSON. Yes, sir.

Mr. GAINES. Is it not a fact that the retail price generally through-out the country to the final retail consumer, the price to the ultimate consumer, or the retail price, does not vary, as a rule, when there may be slight variations in the manufacture of the products? Does it not happen with lumber that very frequently the manufacturers' price goes down $3, and even $4; and in the Middle West, far away from the production of any lumber, from any sawmills, the retail price remains precisely the same?

Mr. WILSON. That would depend upon the district. Now, in some places where there is very severe competition, why, it might change; but it usually does not. It usually remains about the same.

Mr. GAINES. As a general rule there is not much competition in towns between the lumber yards and the various coal yards there, is there?

Mr. WILSON. As a usual thing.

Mr. GAINES. For instance, the price of lumber in this city of Washington bears very little relation to the price of lumber at the lumber mills in West Virginia. That is true. By what gentleman's agreement or otherwise they do it, I do not know, but I do know that the combinations which put up the price are not those which are called trusts, generally, or are subject to the jurisdiction of the Federal Government. They are the small local combinations in the communities, patronized by the retail purchasers.

Mr. WILSON. It is just the same as the farmers holding their hogs for the same price, or their horses.

Mr. GAINES. Yes; but a million farmers can not hold their hogs like three lumber yards, for instance, can hold lumber; neither can 48,000 lumbermen do what three retail dealers can do.

Mr. WILSON. No, sir.

Mr. FORDNEY. Is there not such a thing known in the West through the trade as line yards?

Mr. WILSON. Yes.

Mr. FORDNEY. They are in a combination, are they not? It is understood that way, is it not?

Mr. WILSON. It is so understood, that they are in combination.

Mr. GAINES. What are line yards?

Mr. FORDNEY. For instance, we had a gentleman here a year and a half ago named Brooks, from Minneapolis, I think.

Mr. WILSON. Mr. Rogers.

Mr. FORDNEY. Mr. Rogers?

Mr. WILSON. Yes.

Mr. FORDNEY. And upon investigation it was shown that he was interested in 99 yards in North Dakota and that he absolutely controlled the prices of lumber all over North Dakota. Mr. Rogers fixed the price to the consumer of lumber in North Dakota.

Mr. GAINES. Is he the gentleman who claimed that $2 a thousand was too much on lumber and enhanced the price of lumber to the consumer, and it turned out that he had received his lumber $2 a thousand cheaper and had never modified his price at all?

Mr. FORDNEY. Yes: and he had purchased a large tract of timberland in Canada at 25 cents a thousand and was selling bonds on the basis of $4 a thousand. [Laughter.]

Mr. WILSON. Eighty-two per cent of the yards in North and South Dakota are in the hands of the line yard concerns. About seven line yard concerns, with headquarters in St. Paul and Minneapolis, control the retail business in lumber in North and South Dakota.

Mr. FORDNEY. That was the point I wanted to bring out.

Mr. WILSON. Yes.

Mr. FORDNEY. The manufacturers are in no way connected with any of those line yards?

Mr. WILSON. To my knowledge, they are not.

Mr. FORDNEY. Do the proprietors of those line yards have the whole territory of the United States to buy from?

Mr. WILSON. Yes.

Mr. FORDNEY. Without competition; without any combination?

Mr. WILSON. Yes, sir. Mr. Rogers testified to that before this committee a year and a half ago. He testified that it would not make any difference to the consumer how much they reduced the tariff on lumber. it would not make any difference to the buyer.

Mr. FORDNEY. We had a man here, a secretary of a forest association.

Mr. HILL. Yes, sir; I remember him very well—Mr. Knappen.

Mr. FORDNEY. And he admitted that he was the only one that belonged to that association. It was a big association, however. [Laughter.]

Mr. WILSON. Yes, sir.

Mr. HILL. Are these Minneapolis and St. Paul people who control these yards any of them manufacturers, or are they wholesale dealers?

Mr. WILSON. They are manufacturers, some of them, in a small way. There are some in Canada. The Rogers Lumber Co. operates a mill in Canada.

Mr. HILL. Yes; but you said that these line yards were controlled by seven or eight firms in Minneapolis and St. Paul.

Mr. WILSON. Yes.

Mr. HILL. What I wanted to know was whether any of them are manufacturers?

Mr. WILSON. The Imperial Elevator Co. have a mill in western Canada, and the Atlas Elevator Co. have a small mill in northern Montana. The Rogers Co. have a very large mill in Canada.

Mr. McCALL. Is there anything more? Are there any other questions? If not, these hearings are closed.

Mr. GAINES. I would like to read a telegram here and ask Mr. Skinner to explain it to me if he can. It reads as follows:

SAN FRANCISCO, *February 8.*

HARRISON G. FOSTER,
   New Willard Hotel, Washington, D. C.:

Shipowners of Pacific coast most emphatically opposed to section of reciprocity treaty which admits lumber free and enables foreign ships to carry such lumber from British Columbia ports to American ports. This feature of treaty positively inimical to American shipping. Will deprive American vessels of whatever benefit and protection they are now afforded by our coastwise shipping laws. As our vessels can not successfully compete with foreign vessels in the coastwise trade, the effecting of this measure will inevitably ruin American shipping.

SHIPOWNERS' ASSOCIATION OF THE PACIFIC COAST.

Mr. McCALL. I think Mr. Skinner amplified that point quite clearly.

Mr. SKINNER. Through the canal I did, but not a thing on the coast.

Mr. McCALL. But the point was that they having operated through a foreign port and domestic ports had an advantage over our shippers who had to take the coastwise ships.

Mr. SKINNER. They will come in and absolutely wipe us out, as our foreign vessels have been wiped out by our inability to compete with foreign vessels. As it is, with a short haul from Puget Sound to San Francisco, we can remain within the coastwise laws.

Mr. McCALL. If you get a long haul you can not afford it?

Mr. SKINNER. No, sir; and if this duty is removed we absolutely can not live, and the ships will be destroyed.

Mr. FORDNEY. I have here a telegram which was handed to me by a gentleman from Portland, Oreg., which I wish to have go in the record.

Mr. McCALL. Very well, put that in the record. The committee will meet at 10.30 to-morrow morning in executive session.

Mr. FORDNEY. If any of these gentlemen have telegrams or any arguments that they have not presented here may they not present them and have them go in our record?

Mr. McCALL. Yes. Let them hand them to you, and those you think should go in the record give them to the stenographer and they will be put in the record.

(At 5 o'clock p. m. the committee adjourned.)

[H. R. 32216, Sixty-first Congress, third session.]

A BILL

TO PROMOTE RECIPROCAL TRADE RELATIONS WITH THE DOMINION OF CANADA, AND FOR OTHER PURPOSES.

Be it enacted by the Senate and House of Representatives of the United States of America in Congress assembled, That there shall be levied, collected, and paid upon the articles hereinafter enumerated, the growth, product, or manufacture of the Dominion of Canada, when imported therefrom into the United States or any of its possessions (except the Philippine Islands and the islands of Guam and Tutuila), in lieu of the duties now levied, collected, and paid, the following duties, namely:

Fresh meats: Beef, veal, mutton, lamb, pork, and all other fresh or refrigerated meats excepting game, one and one-fourth cents per pound.

Bacon or hams, not in tins or jars, one and one-fourth cents per pound.

Meats of all kinds, dried, smoked, salted, in brine, or prepared or preserved in any manner, not otherwise herein provided for, one and one-fourth cents per pound.

Canned meats and canned poultry, twenty per centum ad valorem.

Extract of meat, fluid or not, twenty per centum ad valorem.

Lard and compounds thereof, cottolene and cotton stearine, and animal stearine one and one-fourth cents per pound.

Tallow, forty cents per one hundred pounds.

Egg yolk, egg albumen, and blood albumen, seven and one-half per centum ad valorem.

Fish (except shellfish) by whatever name known, packed in oil, in tin boxes or cans, including the weight of the package: (a) When weighing over twenty ounces and not over thirty-six ounces each, five cents per package; (b) when weighing over twelve ounces and not over twenty ounces each, four cents per package; (c) when weighing twelve ounces each or less, two cents per package; (d) when weighing thirty-six ounces each or more, or when packed in oil, in bottles, jars, or kegs, thirty per centum ad valorem.

Tomatoes and other vegetables, including corn, in cans or other air-tight packages, and including the weight of the package, one and one-fourth cents per pound.

Wheat flour and semolina, and rye flour, fifty cents per barrel of one hundred and ninety-six pounds.

Oatmeal and rolled oats, including the weight of paper covering, fifty cents per one hundred pounds.

Corn meal, twelve and one-half cents per one hundred pounds.

Barley malt, forty-five cents per one hundred pounds.

Barley, pot, pearled, or patent, one-half cent per pound.

Buckwheat flour or meal, one-half cent per pound.

Split peas, dried, seven and one-half cents per bushel of sixty pounds.

Prepared cereal foods, not otherwise provided for herein, seventeen and one-half per centum ad valorem.

Bran, middlings, and other offals of grain used for animal food, twelve and one-half cents per one hundred pounds.

Macaroni and vermicelli, one cent per pound.

Biscuits, wafers, and cakes, when sweetened with sugar, honey, molasses, or other material, twenty-five per centum ad valorem.

Biscuits, wafers, cakes, and other baked articles, composed in whole or in part of eggs or any kind of flour or meal, when combined with chocolate, nuts, fruits, or confectionery; also candied peel, candied popcorn, candied nuts, candied fruits, sugar candy, and confectionery of all kinds, thirty-two and one-half per centum ad valorem.

Maple sugar and maple sirup, one cent per pound.

Pickles, including pickled nuts, sauces of all kinds, and fish paste or sauce, thirty-two and one-half per centum ad valorem.

Cherry juice and prune juice, or prune wine, and other fruit juices and fruit sirup, nonalcoholic, seventeen and one-half per centum ad valorem.

334

Mineral waters and imitations of natural mineral waters, in bottles or jugs, seventeen and one-half per centum ad valorem.

Essential oils, seven and one-half per centum ad valorem.

Grapevines, gooseberry, raspberry, and currant bushes, seventeen and one-half per centum ad valorem.

Farm wagons and finished parts thereof, twenty-two and one-half per centum ad valorem.

Plows, tooth and disk harrows, harvesters, reapers, agricultural drills and planters, mowers, horserakes, cultivators; thrashing machines, including windstackers, baggers, weighers, and self-feeders therefor and finished parts thereof imported for repair of the foregoing, fifteen per centum ad valorem.

Portable engines with boilers, in combination, horsepowers and traction engines for farm purposes; hay loaders, potato diggers, fodder or feed cutters, grain crushers, fanning mills, hay tedders, farm or field rollers, manure spreaders, weeders, and windmills, and finished parts thereof imported for repair of the foregoing, except shafting, twenty per centum ad valorem.

Grindstones of sandstone, not mounted, finished or not, five cents per one hundred pounds.

Freestone, granite, sandstone, limestone, and all other monumental or building stone, except marble, breccia, and onyx, unmanufactured or not dressed, hewn, or polished, twelve and one-half per centum ad valorem.

Roofing slates, fifty-five cents per one hundred square feet.

Vitrified paving blocks, not ornamented or decorated in any manner, and paving blocks of stone, seventeen and one-half per centum ad valorem.

Oxide of iron, as a color, twenty-two and one-half per centum ad valorem.

Asbestos, further manufactured than ground; manufactures of asbestos or articles of which asbestos is the component material of chief value, including woven fabrics, wholly or in chief value of asbestos, twenty-two and one-half per centum ad valorem.

Printing ink, seventeen and one-half per centum ad valorem.

Cutlery, plated or not—pocketknives, penknives, scissors and shears, knives and forks r household purposes, and table steels, twenty-seven and one-half per centum ad valorem.

Bells and gongs, brass corners and rules for printers, twenty-seven and one-half per centum ad valorem.

Basins, urinals, and other plumbing fixtures for bathrooms and lavatories; bathtubs, sinks, and laundry tubs of earthenware, stone, cement, or clay, or of other material, thirty-two and one-half per centum ad valorem.

Brass band instruments, twenty-two and one-half per centum ad valorem.

Clocks, watches, time recorders, clock and watch keys, clock cases, and clock movements, twenty-seven and one-half per centum ad valorem.

Printers' wooden cases and cabinets for holding type, twenty-seven and one-half per centum ad valorem.

Wood flour, twenty-two and one-half per centum ad valorem.

Canoes and small boats of wood, not power boats, twenty-two and one-half per centum ad valorem.

Feathers, crude, not dressed, colored, or otherwise manufactured, twelve and one-half per centum ad valorem.

Antiseptic surgical dressings, such as absorbent cotton, cotton wool, lint, lamb's wool, tow, jute, gauzes, and oakum, prepared for use as surgical dressings, plain or medicated; surgical trusses, pessaries, and suspensory bandages of all kinds, seventeen and one-half per centum ad valorem.

Plate glass, not beveled, in sheets or panes exceeding seven square feet each and not exceeding twenty-five square feet each, twenty-five per centum ad valorem.

Motor vehicles, other than for railways and tramways, and automobiles and parts thereof, not including rubber tires, thirty per centum ad valorem.

Iron or steel digesters for the manufacture of wood pulp, twenty-seven and one-half per centum ad valorem.

Musical instrument cases, fancy cases or boxes, portfolios, satchels, reticules, card cases, purses, pocketbooks, fly books for artificial flies, all the foregoing composed wholly or in chief value of leather, thirty per centum ad valorem.

Aluminum in crude form, five cents per pound.

Aluminum in plates, sheets, bars, and rods, eight cents per pound.

Laths, ten cents per one thousand pieces.

Shingles, thirty cents per thousand.

Sawed boards, planks, deals, and other lumber, planed or finished on one side, fifty cents per thousand feet, board measure; planed or finished on one side and tongued and grooved, or planed or finished on two sides, seventy-five cents per thousand feet, board measure, planed or finished on three sides, or planed and finished on two sides and tongued and grooved, one dollar and twelve and one-half cents per thousand feet, board measure, planed and finished on four sides, one dollar and fifty cents per thousand feet, board measure; and in estimating board measure under this schedule no deduction shall be made on board measure on account of planing, tonguing, and grooving.

Iron ore, including manganiferous iron ore, and the dross or residuum from burnt pyrites, ten cents per ton: *Provided*, That in levying and collecting the duty on iron ore no deduction shall be made from the weight of the ore on account of moisture which may be chemically or physically combined therewith.

Coal slack or culm of all kinds, such as will pass through a half-inch screen, fifteen cents per ton.

Provided, That the duties above enumerated shall take effect whenever the President of the United States shall have satisfactory evidence and shall make proclamation that on the articles hereinafter enumerated, the growth, product, or manufacture of the United States, or any of its possessions (except the Philippine Islands and the islands of Guam and Tutuila), when imported therefrom into the Dominion of Canada, duties not in excess of the following are imposed, namely:

Fresh meats: Beef, veal, mutton, lamb, pork, and all other fresh or refrigerated meats excepting game, one and one-fourth cents per pound.

Bacon and hams, not in tins or jars, one and one-fourth cents per pound.

Meats of all kinds, dried, smoked, salted, in brine, or prepared or preserved in any manner, not otherwise herein provided for, one and one-fourth cents per pound.

Canned meats and canned poultry, twenty per centum ad valorem.

Extract of meat, fluid or not, twenty per centum ad valorem.

Lard, and compounds thereof, cottolene and cotton stearin, and animal stearin, one and one-fourth cents per pound.

Tallow, forty cents per one hundred pounds.

Egg yolk, egg albumen, and blood albumen, seven and one-half per centum ad valorem.

Fish (except shellfish), by whatever name known, packed in oil, in tin boxes or cans, including the weight of the package: (a) when weighing over twenty ounces and not over thirty-six ounces each, five cents per package; (b) when weighing over twelve ounces and not over twenty ounces each, four cents per package; (c) when weighing twelve ounces each or less, two cents per package; (d) when weighing thirty-six ounces each or more, or when packed in oil, in bottles, jars, or kegs, thirty per centum ad valorem.

Tomatoes and other vegetables, including corn, in cans or other air-tight packages, and including the weight of the package, one and one-fourth cents per pound.

Wheat flour and semolina; and rye flour, fifty cents per barrel of one hundred and ninety-six pounds.

Oatmeal and rolled oats, including the weight of paper covering, fifty cents per one hundred pounds.

Corn meal, twelve and one-half cents per one hundred pounds.

Barley malt, forty-five cents per one hundred pounds.

Barley, pot, pearled, or patent, one-half cent per pound.

Buckwheat flour or meal, one-half cent per pound.

Split peas, dried, seven and one-half cents per bushel of sixty pounds.

Prepared cereal foods, not otherwise provided for herein, seventeen and one-half per centum ad valorem.

Bran, middlings, and other offals of grain used for animal food, twelve and one-half cents per one hundred pounds.

Macaroni and vermicelli, one cent per pound.

Biscuits, wafers, and cakes, when sweetened with sugar, honey, molasses, or other material, twenty-five per centum ad valorem.

Biscuits, wafers, cakes, and other baked articles, composed in whole or in part of eggs or any kind of flour or meal, when combined with chocolate, nuts, fruits, or confectionery; also candied peel, candied popcorn, candied nuts, candied fruits, sugar candy, and confectionery of all kinds, thirty-two and one-half per centum ad valorem.

Maple sugar and maple sirup, one cent per pound.

Pickles, including pickled nuts; sauces of all kinds, and fish paste or sauce, thirty-two and one-half per centum ad valorem.

Cherry juice and prune juice, or prune wine, and other fruit juices, and fruit sirup, nonalcoholic, seventeen and one-half per centum ad valorem.

Mineral waters and imitations of natural mineral waters, in bottles or jugs, seventeen and one-half per centum ad valorem.

Essential oils, seven and one-half per centum ad valorem.

Grapevines; gooseberry, raspberry, and currant bushes, seventeen and one-half per centum ad valorem.

Farm wagons, and finished parts thereof, twenty-two and one-half per centum ad valorem.

Plows, tooth and disk harrows, harvesters, reapers, agricultural drills and planters, mowers, horserakes, cultivators; thrashing machines, including windstackers, baggers, weighers, and self-feeders therefor, and finished parts thereof imported for repair of the foregoing, fifteen per centum ad valorem.

Portable engines with boilers, in combination, horsepower and traction engines, for farm purposes; hay loaders, potato diggers, fodder or feed cutters, grain crushers, fanning mills, hay tedders, farm or field rollers, manure spreaders, weeders, and windmills, and finished parts thereof imported for repair of the foregoing, except shafting, twenty per centum ad valorem.

Grindstones of sandstone, not mounted, finished or not, five cents per one hundred pounds.

Freestone, granite, sandstone, limestone, and all other monumental or building stone, except marble, breccia, and onyx, unmanufactured or not dressed, hewn or polished, twelve and one-half per centum ad valorem.

Roofing slates, fifty-five cents per one hundred square feet.

Vitrified paving blocks, not ornamented or decorated in any manner, and paving blocks of stone, seventeen and one-half per centum ad valorem.

Oxide of iron, as a color, twenty-two and one-half per centum ad valorem.

Asbestos further manufactured than ground: Manufactures of asbestos, or articles of which asbestos is the component material of chief value, including woven fabrics wholly or in chief value of asbestos, twenty-two and one-half per centum ad valorem.

Printing ink, seventeen and one-half per centum ad valorem.

Cutlery, plated or not: Pocketknives, penknives, scissors and shears, knives and forks for household purposes, and table steels, twenty-seven and one-half per centum ad valorem.

Bells and gongs, brass corners and rules for printers, twenty-seven and one-half per centum ad valorem.

Basins, urinals, and other plumbing fixtures for bathrooms and lavatories; bathtubs, sinks, and laundry tubs, of earthenware, stone, cement, or clay, or of other material, thirty-two and one-half per centum ad valorem.

Brass band instruments, twenty-two and one-half per centum ad valorem.

Clocks, watches, time recorders, clock and watch keys, clock cases, and clock movements, twenty-seven and one-half per centum ad valorem.

Printers' wooden cases and cabinets for holding type, twenty-seven and one-half per centum ad valorem.

Wood flour, twenty-two and one-half per centum ad valorem.

Canoes and small boats of wood, not power boats, twenty-two and one-half per centum ad valorem.

Feathers, crude, not dressed, colored or otherwise manufactured, twelve and one-half per centum ad valorem.

Antiseptic surgical dressings, such as absorbent cotton, cotton wool, lint, lamb's wool, tow, jute, gauzes, and oakum, prepared for use as surgical dressings, plain or medicated; surgical trusses, pessaries, and suspensory bandages of all kinds, seventeen and one-half per centum ad valorem.

Plate glass, not beveled, in sheets or panes exceeding seven square feet each, and not exceeding twenty-five square feet each, twenty-five per centum ad valorem.

Motor vehicles, other than for railways and tramways, and automobiles, and parts thereof, not including rubber tires, thirty per centum ad valorem.

Iron or steel digesters for the manufacture of wood pulp, twenty-seven and one-half per centum ad valorem.

Musical instrument cases, fancy cases or boxes, portfolios, satchels, reticules, card cases, purses, pocketbooks, fly books for artificial flies; all the foregoing composed wholly or in chief value of leather, thirty per centum ad valorem.

Cement, Portland, and hydraulic or water lime in barrels, bags, or casks, the weight of the package to be included in the weight for duty, eleven cents per one hundred pounds.

Trees: Apple, cherry, peach, pear, plum, and quince, of all kinds, and small peach trees known as June buds, two and one-half cents each.

Condensed milk, the weight of the package to be included in the weight for duty, two cents per pound.

Biscuits without added sweetening, twenty per centum ad valorem.

Fruits in air-tight cans or other air-tight packages, the weight of the cans or other packages to be included in the weight for duty, two cents per pound.

Peanuts, shelled, one cent per pound.

Peanuts, unshelled, one-half cent per pound.

Coal, bituminous, round and run of mine, including bituminous coal such as will not pass through a three-quarter inch screen, forty-five cents per ton.

That the articles mentioned in the following paragraphs, the growth, product, or manufacture of the Dominion of Canada, when imported therefrom into the United States or any of its possessions (except the Philippine Islands and the islands of Guam and Tutuila), shall be exempt from duty, namely:

Live animals: Cattle, horses and mules, swine, sheep, lambs, and all other live animals.

Poultry, dead or alive.

Wheat, rye, oats, barley, and buckwheat, dried peas and beans, edible.

Corn, sweet corn, or maize.

Hay, straw, and cowpease.

Fresh vegetables: Potatoes, sweet potatoes, yams, turnips, onions, cabbages, and all other vegetables in their natural state.

Fresh fruits: Apples, pears, peaches, grapes, berries, and all other edible fruits in their natural state, except lemons, oranges, limes, grape fruit, shaddocks, pomelos, and pineapples.

Dried fruits: Apples, peaches, pears, and apricots, dried, desiccated, or evaporated.

Dairy products: Butter, cheese, and fresh milk and cream: *Provided*, That cans actually used in the transportation of milk or cream may be passed back and forth between the two countries free of duty, under such regulations as the respective Governments may prescribe.

Eggs of barnyard fowl, in the shell.

Honey.

Cottonseed oil.

Seeds: Flaxseed or linseed, cottonseed, and other oil seeds; grass seed including timothy and clover seed; garden, field, and other seed not herein otherwise provided for, when in packages weighing over one pound each (not including flower seeds).

Fish of all kinds, fresh, frozen, packed in ice, salted, or preserved in any form, except sardines and other fish preserved in oil; and shellfish of all kinds, including oysters, lobsters, and clams in any state, fresh or packed, and coverings of the foregoing.

Seal, herring, whale, and other fish oil, including sod oil· *Provided*, That fish oil, whale oil, seal oil, and fish of all kinds, being the product of fisheries carried on by the fishermen of the United States, shall be admitted into Canada as the product of the United States, and, similarly, that fish oil, whale oil, seal oil, and fish of all kinds, being the product of fisheries carried on by the fishermen of Canada, shall be admitted into he United States as the product of Canada.

Salt.

Mineral waters, natural, not in bottles or jugs.

Timber, hewn, sided or squared otherwise than by sawing, and round timber used for spars or in building wharves.

Sawed boards, planks, deals, and other lumber, not further manufactured than sawed.

Paving posts, railroad ties, and telephone, trolley, electric-light, and telegraph poles of cedar or other woods.

Wooden staves of all kinds, not further manufactured than listed or jointed. and stave bolts.

Pickets and palings.

Plaster rock, or gypsum, crude, not ground.

Mica, unmanufactured or rough trimmed only, and mica, ground or bolted.

Feldspar, crude, powdered or ground.

Asbestos, not further manufactured than ground.

Fluorspar, crude, not ground.

Glycerine, crude, not purified.

Talc, ground, bolted, or precipitated, naturally or artificially, not for toilet use.

Sulphate of soda, or salt cake, and soda ash.

Extracts of hemlock bark.

Carbon electrodes.

Brass in bars and rods, in coil or otherwise, not less than six feet in length, or brass in strips, sheets, or plates, not polished, planished, or coated.

Cream separators of every description, and parts thereof imported for repair of the foregoing.

Rolled iron or steel sheets, or plates, number fourteen gauge or thinner, galvanized or coated with zinc, tin, or other metal, or not.

Crucible cast-steel wire, valued at not less than six cents per pound.

Galvanized iron or steel wire, curved or not, numbers nine, twelve, and thirteen wire gauge.

Typecasting and typesetting machines and parts thereof, adapted for use in printing offices.

Barbed fencing wire of iron or steel, galvanized or not.

Coke.

Rolled round wire rods in the coil, of iron or steel, not over three-eighths of an inch in diameter, and not smaller than number six wire gauge.

Pulp of wood mechanically ground; pulp of wood, chemical, bleached, or unbleached; news print paper, and other paper, and paper board, manufactured from mechanical wood pulp or from chemical wood pulp, or of which such pulp is the component material of chief value, colored in the pulp, or not colored, and valued at not more than four cents per pound, not including printed or decorated wall paper: *Provided*, That such paper and board, valued at four cents per pound or less, and wood pulp, being the products of Canada, when imported therefrom directly into the United States, shall be admitted free of duty, on the condition precedent that no export duty, export license fee, or other export charge of any kind whatsoever (whether in the form of additional charge or license fee or otherwise), or any prohibition or restriction in any way of the exportation (whether by law, order, regulation, contractual relation, or otherwise, directly or indirectly), shall have been imposed upon such paper, board, or wood pulp, or the wood used in the manufacture of such paper, board, or wood pulp, or the wood pulp used in the manufacture of such paper or board.

Provided, That the articles above enumerated, the growth, product, or manufacture of the Dominion of Canada, shall be exempt from duty when the President of the United States shall have satisfactory evidence and shall make proclamation that the following articles, the growth, product, or manufacture of the United States or any of its possessions (except the Philippine Islands and the islands of Guam and Tutuila), are admitted into the Dominion of Canada free of duty, namely:

Live animals: Cattle, horses and mules, swine, sheep, lambs, and all other live animals.

Poultry, dead or alive.

Wheat, rye, oats, barley, and buckwheat; dried peas and beans, edible.

Corn, sweet corn, or maize (except into Canada for distillation).

Hay, straw, and cow peas.

Fresh vegetables: Potatoes, sweet potatoes, yams, turnips, onions, cabbages, and all other vegetables in their natural state.

Fresh fruits: Apples, pears, peaches, grapes, berries, and all other edible fruits in their natural state.

Dried fruits: Apples, peaches, pears, and apricots, dried, desiccated, or evaporated.

Dairy products: Butter, cheese, and fresh milk and cream: *Provided*, That cans actually used in the transportation of milk or cream may be passed back and forth between the two countries free of duty, under such regulations as the respective Governments may prescribe.

Eggs of barnyard fowl in the shell.

Honey.

Cotton-seed oil.

Seeds: Flaxseed or linseed, cotton seed, and other oil seeds; grass seed, including timothy and clover seed; garden, field, and other seed not herein otherwise provided for, when in packages weighing over one pound each (not including flower seeds).

Fish of all kinds, fresh, frozen, packed in ice, salted or preserved in any form, except sardines and other fish preserved in oil; and shellfish of all kinds, including oysters, lobsters, and clams in any state, fresh or packed, and coverings of the foregoing.

Seal, herring, whale, and other fish oil, including sod oil: *Provided*, That fish oil, whale oil, seal oil, and fish of all kinds, being the product of fisheries carried on by the fishermen of the United States, shall be admitted into Canada as the product of the United States, and similarly that fish oil, whale oil, seal oil, and fish of all kinds, being the product of fisheries carried on by the fishermen of Canada, shall be admitted into the United States as the product of Canada.

Salt.

Mineral waters, natural, not in bottles or jugs.

Timber, hewn, sided or squared otherwise than by sawing, and round timber used for spars or in building wharves.

Sawed boards, planks, deals, and other lumber, not further manufactured than sawed.

Paving posts, railroad ties, and telephone, trolley, electric light, and telegraph poles of cedar or other woods.

Wooden staves of all kinds, not further manufactured than listed or jointed, and stave bolts.

Pickets and palings.

Plaster rock or gypsum, crude, not ground.

Mica, unmanufactured or rough trimmed only, and mica, ground or bolted.

Feldspar, crude, powdered, or ground.

Asbestos not further manufactured than ground.

Fluorspar, crude, not ground.

Glycerine, crude, not purified.

Talc, ground, bolted or precipitated, naturally or artificially, not for toilet use.

Sulphate of soda, or salt cake, and soda ash.

Extracts of hemlock bark.

Carbon electrodes.

Brass in bars and rods, in coil or otherwise, not less than six feet in length, or brass in strips, sheets, or plates, not polished, planished, or coated.

Cream separators of every description, and parts thereof imported for repair of the foregoing.

Rolled iron or steel sheets or plates, number fourteen gauge or thinner, galvanized or coated with zinc, tin, or other metal, or not.

Crucible cast-steel wire, valued at not less than six cents per pound.

Galvanized iron or steel wire, curved or not, numbers nine, twelve, and thirteen wire gauge.

Typecasting and typesetting machines and parts thereof, adapted for use in printing offices.

Barbed fencing wire of iron or steel, galvanized or not.

Coke.

Rolled round wire rods in the coil, of iron or steel, not over three-eighths of an inch in diameter, and not smaller than number six wire gauge.

Pulp of wood mechanically ground; pulp of wood, chemical, bleached or unbleached; news print paper and other paper, and paper board, manufactured from mechanical wood pulp or from chemical wood pulp, or of which such pulp is the component material of chief value, colored in the pulp or not colored, and valued at not more than four cents per pound, not including printed or decorated wall paper.

INDEX.

O

Lightning Source UK Ltd.
Milton Keynes UK
UKHW021958190219
337571UK00011B/1867/P